Study Guide

Thomas M. Beveridge
North Carolina State University

Farrokh R. Zandi
York University

PRINCIPLES OF microeconomics

SECOND CANADIAN EDITION

KARL E. CASE

RAY C. FAIR

J. FRANK STRAIN

MICHAEL R. VEALL

Prentice Hall

Toronto

Original edition published by Prentice Hall, Inc., a division of Pearson Education, Upper Saddle River, New Jersey. © 1999 Prentice Hall, Inc. This edition is authorized for sale in Canada only.

ISBN 0-13-042242-8

Acquisitions Editor: Dave Ward
Developmental Editor: Maurice Esses
Production Editor: Julia Hubble
Production Coordinator: Janette Lush

3 4 5 06 05 04 03 02

Printed and bound in Canada.

Contents

Preface

This Study Guide accompanies the second Canadian edition of *Principles of Microeconomics* by Karl Case, Ray Fair, J. Frank Strain, and Michael Veall. It draws on the Study Guide to the American edition by Thomas M. Beveridge and its graphing tutorial by Steven C. Pitts, and takes chapters 21 and 22 from the corresponding chapters by Deborah Fretz, Michael Veall, and Lonnie Magee in the companion Study Guide for *Principles of Microeconomics*. We thank the team at Pearson Education Canada: Maurice Esses, Developmental Editor, Deanne Walle, EMM Coordinator, Julia Hubble, Production Editor, and Dave Ward, Acquisitions Editor. This Guide has been devised to help you as you learn the concepts that are presented in the text. Most economics instructors stress the need to develop competence in three major areas—the application of economic concepts to real-world situations, the interpretation of graphs, and the analysis of numerical problems. This Guide gives you practice in developing these skills.

We believe that learning how to apply concepts creates a better and more long-lasting understanding of the material than mere memorization does. A reasonable goal for a non-economics major is to have absorbed enough insight to understand the economic content of an article in a publication like *The Globe & Mail* or *The National Post.*

Study Guide Contents

The Study Guide contains one chapter for each chapter in the text. Each chapter has three main sections.

- The *Objectives: Point by Point* section summarizes what you should be able to accomplish after you've studied the material. These objectives match those given in the text. Each point is followed by some multiple choice questions to enable you to monitor how well you're understanding the concepts. You'll find some applications and examples, along with specific learning tips, graphing pointers, and "helpful hints." Many of these "tricks" have been suggested by students.

- The *Practice Test* section contains *Multiple Choice Questions* and *Application Questions*. These questions provide opportunities to practise the skills—graphing, numerical analysis, application of concepts—presented in the text. Think of each multiple choice question as four true/false statements. Don't just decide on the one "right" answer; determine why the other three options are wrong.

- The *Answers and Solutions* section contains the answers to the *Practice Test*. If you need more practice questions with answers, the answers to the even-numbered problems in the text are provided at the back of the text.

A conscientious and consistent use of this Guide, along with reading the text and regular class attendance (in mind as well as in body!), will improve your ability to use and apply economics.

Best wishes to you in your study of economics.

Farrokh Zandi
York University

Acknowledgements

I am grateful to Mike Veall for pointing out some errors in the previous edition of this Study Guide. At Pearson Education Canada I thank Dave Ward and Maurice Esses for their support. Please send any comments or suggestions about this Study Guide directly to Pearson Education Canada (Dave Ward, Acquisitions Editor, Economics, Pearson Education Canada, 26 Prince Andrew Place, Don Mills ON M3C 2T8) and to me, Farrokh Zandi (Schulich School of Business, York University, 4700 Keele St., Toronto, ON M3J IP3; email: fzandi@schulich.yorku.ca).

1 The Scope and Method of Economics

OBJECTIVES: POINT BY POINT

After completing this chapter, you should be able to accomplish the objectives listed below.

General Comment

Much of this chapter is devoted to setting out the framework of economics. Don't be overwhelmed and don't try to remember it all. Chapter 1 is simply a good place to gather together this information, which will be dealt with more fully as the chapters go by.

OBJECTIVE 1: State the importance of studying economics.

Summarize the importance of studying economic issues and describe how an economic way of thinking enables us to understand society and international affairs and thus become more informed voters. (page 2)

Other important concepts are marginalism and efficiency.

Practice

1. Which one of the following best describes the study of economics? Economics studies
   - A. how businesses can make profits.
   - B. how the government controls the economy and how people earn a living.
   - C. how society uses its scarce resources to satisfy its unlimited desires.
   - D. the allocation of income among different sectors of the economy.

   ANSWER: C. All of the options represent aspects of the study of economics. However, the most general statement is given in C—economics is the study of choice.

"Marginal" is a frequently used term in economics and it's important to understand it right away. "Marginal" means "additional" or "extra." "Marginal cost," then, means "additional cost."

Suppose you've bought a non-returnable, non-transferable ticket to the zoo for $10. This is a *sunk cost*. You've paid whether or not you visit the zoo.

Let's change the example a little. Suppose you win a free admission to the zoo and decide to go this Saturday. The trip is not entirely free, however. You still have to bear some costs—travel, for example. There is certainly an additional cost (caused by the trip to the zoo). It is a *marginal cost*. Suppose you always buy lunch on Saturdays. The cost of lunch is not a marginal cost since you'd have had lunch whether or not you went to the zoo. In this sense, the cost of lunch is not contingent on the trip to the zoo—it's not an extra cost.

You choose to visit the zoo this Saturday. The *opportunity cost* is the value of the activity you would have undertaken instead—that is, the next most-preferred activity. Perhaps it might be playing a round of golf or studying for a big economics test. The opportunity cost of the trip to the zoo is the value you attach to that *one* activity you would otherwise have chosen. (page 2)

Opportunity Cost and Marginalism: The "big concept" in this chapter is *opportunity cost*, with *marginalism* and *efficiency* a close second and third. You'll see all three repeatedly throughout the textbook. For practice on the concept of opportunity cost, try Application question 5 below. For practice on marginal thinking, look at Application question 8.

> **TIP:** Any time you make a choice, remember that an opportunity cost is involved.

Practice

2. Your opportunity cost of attending university includes
   A. the money you spend on meals while at university.
   B. your tuition and the money you spend on travelling between home and university.
   C. the income you could have earned if you'd been employed full-time.
   D. Both B and C.

   ANSWER: A. You would have bought food whether or not you were at university. All the other expenses occur solely because of attending university.

3. ___________ may be defined as the extra cost associated with an action.
   A. Marginal cost.
   B. Sunk cost.
   C. Opportunity cost.
   D. Action cost.

   ANSWER: A. See p. 3.

4. Jean owns a French restaurant—*La Crème*. Simply to operate this week, he must pay rent, taxes, wages, food costs, and so on. This amounts to $1000 per week. This evening, a diner arrives and orders some Chambolle-Musigny 1995 wine to go with her meal. Jean has none and sends out to the nearest liquor store for a bottle. It costs $40, and Jean charges his guest $60. Which of the following is true for Jean?
   A. The marginal cost of the wine is $40.
   B. The marginal cost of the wine is $60.
   C. The sunk cost of the meal is $1040.
   D. The sunk cost of the meal is $1060.

   ANSWER: A. The sunk cost is the up-front expense of $1000. The extra cost that Jean bears for buying the wine is $40.

OBJECTIVE 2: Distinguish between the two main branches of economics.

Economics is split into two broad parts. *Microeconomics* focuses on the operation of individual markets and the choices of individual economic units (firms and households, for example). *Macroeconomics* deals with the broad economic variables such as national production, total consumer spending, and overall price movements. Economics also contains a number of subfields, such as international economics, labour economics, and industrial organization. (page 7)

Practice

5. **Macroeconomics** approaches the study of economics from the viewpoint of
   A. individual consumers.
   B. the government.
   C. the entire economy.
   D. the operation of specific markets.

   ANSWER: C. Macroeconomics looks at the big picture—the entire economy.

6. **Microeconomics** approaches the study of economics from the viewpoint of
   A. the entire economy.
   B. the government.
   C. the operation of specific markets.
   D. the stock market.

   ANSWER: C. Microeconomics examines what is happening with individual economic units (households and firms) and how they interact in specific markets.

7. Which of the following is most appropriately a microeconomic issue?
   A. The study of the relationship between the unemployment rate and the inflation rate.
   B. The forces determining the price in an individual market.
   C. The determination of total output in the economy.
   D. The aggregate behaviour of all decision-making units in the economy.

   ANSWER: B. Microeconomics examines what is happening with individual economic units (households and firms) and how they interact in specific markets.

OBJECTIVE 3: Identify the roles played by theories, models, and empirical evidence in economics.

Economic theory is a statement (or a set of statements) about cause and effect. It attempts to generalize and explain what is observed. An economic model is a formal statement of an economic theory. A theory is accepted (or rejected) when it succeeds (fails) to explain what is observed. The observations that are based on the collection and use of data are empirical results. (page 14)

OBJECTIVE 4: Describe the roles played by positive and normative economics in economic policy analysis.

Economists classify issues as either positive or normative. Positive questions explore the behaviour of the economy and its participants without judging whether the behaviour is good or bad. *Positive economics* collects data that describe economic phenomena (descriptive economics) and constructs testable—cause-and-effect—theories to explain the phenomena (economic theory). *Normative economic questions* evaluate the results of behaviour and explore whether the outcomes might be improved. (page 8)

Practice

8. A difference between positive statements and normative statements is that
   A. positive statements are true by definition.
   B. only positive statements are subject to empirical verification.
   C. economists use positive statements and politicians use normative statements when discussing economic matters.
   D. positive statements require value judgments.

ANSWER: B. A positive statement is not necessarily true by definition and can be disproved by empirical verification.

OTHER RELATED POINTS.

POINT 1: Explain the value of the *ceteris paribus* assumption within the context of economic modelling.

Economists (and other scientists) construct models—formal statements of relationships between variables of interest—that simplify and abstract from reality. Graphs, words, or equations can be used to express a model. In testing the relationships between variables within a model, it is convenient to assume *ceteris paribus*, that all other variables have been held constant. (page 12)

Practice

9. "An increase in the price of shampoo will cause less shampoo to be demanded, *ceteris paribus*." *Ceteris paribus* means that
   A. there is a negative relationship between the price and quantity demanded of shampoo.
   B. the price of shampoo is the only factor that can affect the amount of shampoo demanded.
   C. other factors may affect the amount of shampoo demanded; these are assumed not to change in this analysis.
   D. the price of shampoo is equal for all buyers.

   ANSWER: C. The price of shampoo is equal for all buyers, and there may be a negative relationship between the price and quantity of shampoo demanded, but *ceteris paribus* means that any other factors that may affect the amount of shampoo demanded are assumed to be constant.

POINT 2: State the fallacies discussed in the text, give examples, and explain *why* such statements are fallacious.

Beware of false logic! The *fallacy of composition* involves the claim that what is good for one individual remains good when it happens for many. The fact that one farmer gains by having a bumper harvest *doesn't* mean that all farmers will gain if each has a bumper crop. The *post hoc, ergo propter hoc* fallacy occurs when we assume that an event that happens after another is caused by it. (page 13)

Two examples of the fallacy of composition: One person who stands up to see a good play at a game derives a benefit—therefore all will benefit similarly if the entire crowd stands up. Running to the exit when there is a fire in a theatre will increase your chances of survival—therefore, in a fire, we should all run for the exit.

Practice

10. Which of the following is an example of the fallacy of composition?
   A. Jane leaves work at 3:00 each day and avoids the rush-hour traffic. Therefore, if businesses regularly closed at 3:00, all commuters would avoid the rush-hour traffic.

B. John stands up so that he can see an exciting football play. Therefore, if the entire crowd stands up when there is an exciting play, all spectators will get a better view.
C. Since society benefits from the operation of efficient markets, IBM will benefit if markets become more efficient.
D. Both A and B.

ANSWER: D. The example in C is arguing from the general to the specific. The fallacy of composition argues from the specific to the general. Therefore, D is correct.

POINT 3: State and explain the four criteria used to assess the outcomes of economic policy.

Economists construct and test models as an aid to policy making. Policy makers generally judge proposals in terms of efficiency, equity (fairness), growth, and stability. (page 15)

Practice

11. The nation of Arboc claims to have achieved an equitable distribution of income among its citizens. On visiting Arboc, we would expect to find that
    A. each citizen receives the same amount of income.
    B. Arbocali residents believe that the distribution of income is fair.
    C. Arbocali residents believe that the distribution of income is equal.
    D. each citizen receives the amount of income justified by the value of his or her contribution to production.

    ANSWER: B. Whether or not the distribution of income is equitable depends on what Arbocali citizens believe to be fair.

Use the following information to answer the next two questions.

Nicola and Alexander each have some dollars and some apples. Nicola values a kilo of apples at $3, while Alexander values a kilo of apples at $1.

12. In which of the following cases has an economically efficient trade taken place?
    A. The market price of apples is $3 per kilo. Nicola sells apples to Alexander.
    B. The market price of apples is $1 per kilo. Nicola sells apples to Alexander.
    C. The market price of apples is $2 per kilo. Nicola sells apples to Alexander.
    D. The market price of apples is $2 per kilo. Alexander sells apples to Nicola.

    ANSWER: D. When the market price of apples is $2 per kilo and Alexander is the seller, he gains $1. Nicola also gains because she receives goods she values at $3 for a payment of only $2.

13. In which of the following cases has an economically efficient trade not taken place?
    A. The market price of apples is $3 per kilo. Alexander sells apples to Nicola.
    B. The market price of apples is $1 per kilo. Nicola buys apples from Alexander.
    C. The market price of apples is $4 per kilo. Alexander sells apples to Nicola.
    D. The market price of apples is $2 per kilo. Nicola buys apples from Alexander.

    ANSWER: C. An efficient trade can occur only when some participant is better off and no participant is worse off. In Option A, Alexander gains and Nicola does not lose. In Option B, Nicola gains and Alexander does not lose. In Option D, Alexander and Nicola both gain. In Option C, Alexander gains but Nicola loses.

OBJECTIVE 5: Appendix 1A, read and interpret graphs and linear equations.

Economic graphs depict the relationship between variables. A curve with a "rising" (positive) slope indicates that as one variable increases, so does the other. A curve with a "falling" (negative) slope indicates that as one variable increases in value, the other decreases in value. Slope is easily measured by "rise over run"—the extent of vertical change divided by the extent of horizontal change. (page 19)

> **TIP:** Economists almost automatically begin to scribble diagrams when asked to explain ideas, and you'll need to learn how to use some of the tools of the trade. In economics, graphs often feature financial variables like "price," "the interest rate," or "income." Usually the dependent variable is placed on the vertical axis and the independent variable on the horizontal axis. In graphing economic variables, however, it's a pretty safe bet that the financial variable will go on the vertical axis every time. Application questions 9 and 10 and the Tutorial offer some graphing Practice.

> **TIP:** Make a point of examining the graphs you see accompanying economics-based articles in the daily newspaper or news magazines. It's quite common to find examples of deceptive graphs, especially when variables are being compared over time. A graph comparing, say, the difference between government spending and tax revenues can be quite misleading if the vertical axis does not start at zero.

> **Graphing Pointer:** It is a natural tendency to shy away from graphs—they may seem threatening—but this is a mistake. To work with economic concepts, you must master all the tools in the economist's tool kit. Trying to avoid graphs is as unwise as trying to cut a piece of wood without a saw. See the Graphing Tutorial if you are uneasy.

Practice

Use the diagram below to answer the next four questions.

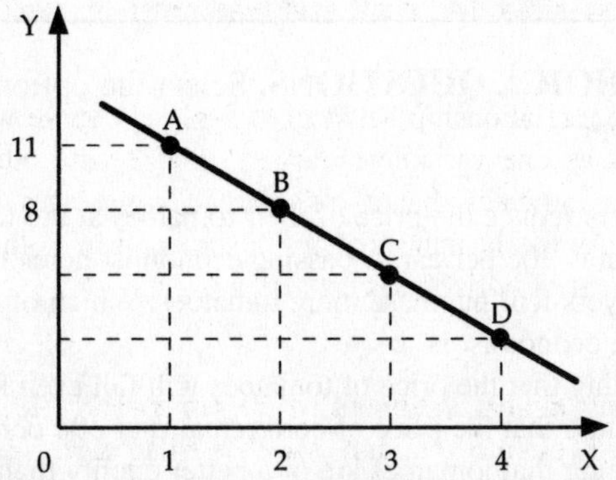

14. In the diagram above, the slope of the line is
    A. positive and variable.
    B. positive and constant.
    C. negative and variable.
    D. negative and constant.

    ANSWER: D. The diagram shows a straight line—straight lines have a constant slope. Visually, or by using the "rise over run" formula, the relationship is negative because, as one variable increases in value, the other decreases in value.

15. The slope of line between Point A and Point B is
    A. 3.
    B. 1/3.
    C. –3.
    D. –1/3.

    ANSWER: C. Use the "rise over run" formula. The rise is -3 (from 11 to 8), and the run is +1 (from 1 to 2).

16. At Point D, the value of Y is
    A. –3.
    B. 3.
    C. 5.
    D. 2.

    ANSWER: D. As X "steps up" in value by 1, Y "steps down" in value by 3. At Point B, X has a value of 2 and Y has a value of 8. Moving to Point D, X increases by 2 and Y decreases by 6, from 8 to 2.

17. In the diagram above, when the line reaches the vertical (Y) axis, the value of Y will be
    A. 3.
    B. 8.
    C. 11.
    D. 14.

    ANSWER: D. As X "steps down" in value by 1, Y "steps up" in value by 3. At Point A, X has a value of 1 and Y has a value of 11. X decreases by 1 and Y increases by 3, from 11 to 14.

PRACTICE TEST

I. MULTIPLE CHOICE QUESTIONS. Select the option that provides the single best answer.

____ 1. Local farmers reduce the price of their tomatoes at the farmers' market. The price of corn is 30¢ per ear. A passing economist notes that, *ceteris paribus*, buyers will purchase more tomatoes. Which of the following is TRUE? The economist is
- A. implying that the price of tomatoes will fall even further.
- B. assuming that the price of corn remains at 30¢ per ear.
- C. assuming that tomatoes are of a better quality than before.
- D. implying that corn is of a poorer quality than before.

____ 2. Which of the following is **not** given in the textbook as a criterion for judging the results of economic policy?
- A. economic stability.
- B. energy conservation.
- C. efficiency and equity.
- D. both A and C.

____ 3. Economic growth may occur if
- A. more machines become available.
- B. more workers become available.
- C. workers become more efficient.
- D. all of the above.

____ 4. Economics is the study of how
- A. scarce resources are used to satisfy unlimited wants.
- B. we choose to use unlimited resources.
- C. limitless resources are used to satisfy scarce wants.
- D. society has no choices.

____ 5. The opportunity cost of Choice X can be defined as
- A. the cheapest alternative to Choice X.
- B. the most highly-valued alternative to Choice X.
- C. the price paid to obtain X.
- D. the most highly-priced alternative to Choice X.

____ 6. In economics, efficiency means that
- A. income is distributed equally among all citizens.
- B. there is a low level of inflation and full unemployment of economic resources.
- C. total productivity is increasing at a constant and equal rate within each sector of the economy.
- D. the economy is producing those goods and services that citizens desire and is doing so at the least possible cost.

____ 7. Which of the following statements is true?
- A. Microeconomics studies consumer behaviour, while macroeconomics studies producer behaviour.
- B. Microeconomics studies producer behaviour, while macroeconomics studies consumer behaviour.
- C. Microeconomics studies behaviour of individual households and firms, while macroeconomics studies national aggregates.
- D. Microeconomics studies inflation and opportunity costs, while macroeconomics studies unemployment and sunk costs.

_____ 8. Which of the following statements is true?

A. There is a positive relationship between the price of a product and the quantity demanded.

B. There is a positive relationship between the number of umbrellas bought and the amount of rainfall.

C. There is a negative relationship between height and weight.

D. There is a negative relationship between sales of ice cream and noon temperature.

_____ 9. Oliver Sudden discovers that if he cuts the price of his tomatoes at the farmers' market, his sales revenue increases. Expecting similar results, all the other tomato sellers follow his example. They are guilty of committing

A. the fallacy of composition.

B. the fallacy of *post hoc, ergo propter hoc*.

C. the fallacy of correlation.

D. *ceteris paribus*.

_____ 10. The quantity of six-packs of Labatt Blue beer demanded per week (Qd) in Hometown is described by the following equation:

$$Qd = 400 - 100P,$$

where P (in dollars) is the price of a six-pack. This equation predicts that

A. 300 six-packs will be bought this week.

B. a $1 rise in price will cause 100 more six-packs to be bought this week.

C. 300 six-packs will be bought per $100 this week.

D. a 50¢ rise in price will cause 50 fewer six-packs to be bought this week.

_____ 11. The *ceteris paribus* assumption is used

A. to make economic theory more realistic.

B. to make economic analysis more realistic.

C. to avoid the fallacy of composition.

D. to focus the analysis on the effect of a single factor.

Use the diagram (not drawn to scale) below to answer the next four questions.

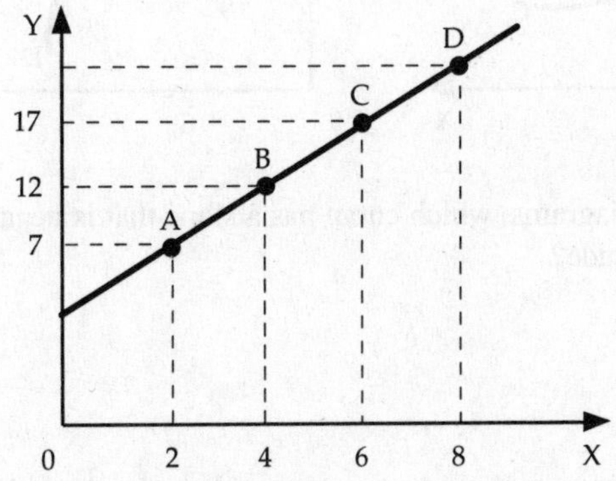

_____ 12. In the diagram above, the slope of the line is

A. positive and variable.

B. positive and constant.

C. negative and variable.

D. negative and constant.

_____ 13. The slope of the line between Point A and Point B is
A. 5/2.
B. 2/5
C. -2/5.
D. –5/2.

_____ 14. At Point D, the value of Y is
A. 5.
B. 8.
C. 19.5.
D. 22.

_____ 15. In the diagram above, when the line reaches the vertical (Y) axis the value of Y will be
A. 2.
B. 5/2.
C. 7.
D. 12.

Use the diagrams below (not drawn to scale) to answer the next four questions.

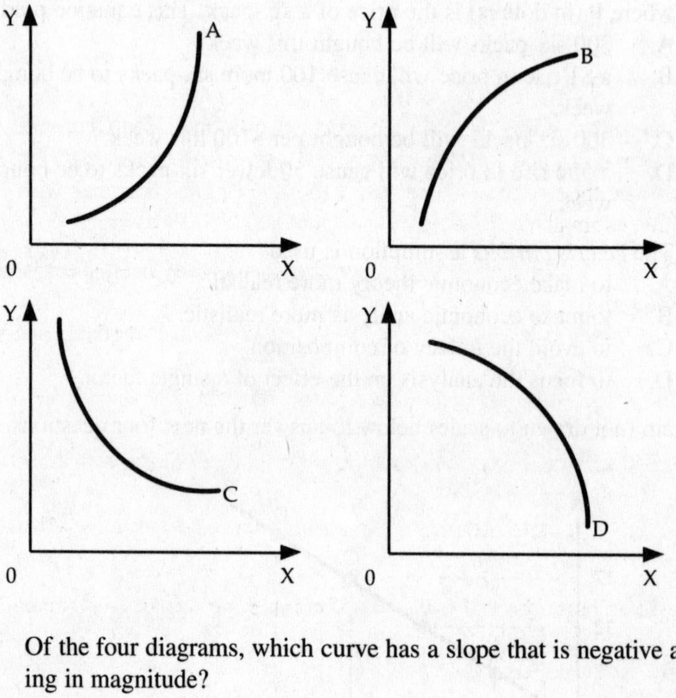

_____ 16. Of the four diagrams, which curve has a slope that is negative and decreasing in magnitude?
A. A.
B. B.
C. C.
D. D.

_____ 17. Of the four diagrams, which curve has a slope that is positive and increasing?
A. A.
B. B.
C. C.
D. D.

_____ 18. Of the four diagrams, which curve has a slope that is positive and decreasing?
- A. A.
- B. B.
- C. C.
- D. D.

_____ 19. Of the four diagrams, which curve appears to be described by the equation $y = x^2$?
- A. A.
- B. B.
- C. C.
- D. D.

_____ 20. During the debate about balancing the federal government budget, it has been proposed that transfer payments to provinces be reduced. This proposal has been criticized because it would force provinces to cut their respective social services, which would hurt the low-income families the most. This argument is based on concerns about
- A economic growth.
- B efficiency stability.
- C economic stability.
- D equity.

Use the following information to answer the next two questions. The Channel Tunnel, linking the United Kingdom and France, was originally planned to cost $100 million. After work had begun and the two excavators were under the English Channel, with $70 million already spent, the estimate of the total bill was revised to $150 million.

_____ 21. To an economist, the $70 million that had already been spent is best thought of as a
- A. sunk cost that was important in determining whether to complete the project.
- B. sunk cost that was not important in determining whether to complete the project.
- C. marginal cost that was important in determining whether to complete the project.
- D. marginal cost that was not important in determining whether to complete the project.

_____ 22. At this point the marginal cost of completion was best estimated as
- A. $30 million.
- B. $50 million.
- C. $70 million.
- D. $80 million.

II. APPLICATION QUESTIONS.

1. The small nation of Smogland is unhappily situated in a valley surrounded by mountains. Smogland's Minister of the Environment has determined that there are 4000 cars, each of which pollutes the air. In fact, Smogland's air is so unhealthy that it is rated as "hazardous." If emission controls, costing $50 per car, are introduced, the air quality will improve to a rating of "fair." A survey has revealed that, of the 40 000 inhabitants, 10 000 would value the air quality improvement at $5 each, and the other 30 000 would value it at $7 each. The Minister of the Environment has asked you to analyze the issue and make a recommendation.

2. Refer to the following diagram.

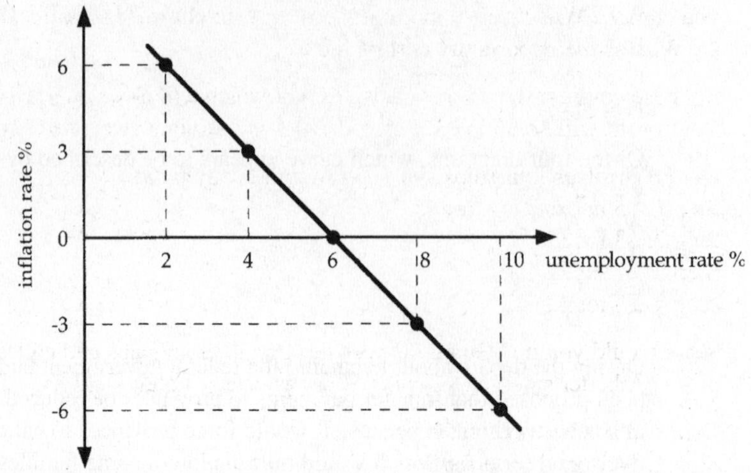

a. Construct a table from the data presented in the diagram.
b. Calculate the slope of the line.
c. Calculate the inflation rate when the unemployment rate is 9%.
d. Calculate the inflation rate when the unemployment rate is 5%.

3. What are some elements of the opportunity cost of "clean" air? In total, the "cost" of cleaner air increases as we remove more and more pollution. Do you think, however, that the extra (marginal) cost of cleaner air increases as we progressively remove pollution? Graph the behaviour of "extra cost" (vertical axis) and "cleanness of air" (horizontal axis).

4. Suppose that the opportunity cost of attending today's economics class is study time for a math test. By not studying you will lose fifteen points on your test. Attending the econ. class will increase your future econ. test score by no more than three points. Was your choice—to attend the econ. class—rational?

5. Suppose you had a summer internship in a bank just before your final year. You are "noticed" and are offered a full-time position in the bank, with a salary of $30 000 a year. A rival bank, also keen to attract you, offers you $32,000 for a similar position. After much thought, you decide to return to university to complete your economics degree. Based on the information given, what was the opportunity cost of your decision?

If you had chosen one of the banking jobs instead of resuming your studies, how could you have explained your decision to your parents, who would have pointed out that you would have "wasted" three years of university? How might "sunk costs" figure into your explanation?

6. Choose a local natural resource with which you are familiar, e.g., a hectare of farm land or a nearby lake.

a. List three alternative uses for your chosen raw material.
b. Choose one of the three uses. What is the opportunity cost of this use? Should you include the cost of clean-up (if this is appropriate) following use?
c. Is the resource renewable or not? If not, should this be factored into your calculations?
d. Describe how [illegible] community has chosen to use the resource so far, if at all. Wh[illegible] ave determined that choice?

7. Suppose you're asked to choose one job out of three. Job A pays $30 000; Job B, $20 000; and Job C, $15 000. In all other respects, they are identical. Which would you choose? What is the opportunity cost of your choice? Is it rational to choose Job C? What is the opportunity cost of Job C?

8. Suppose you're offered three deals, each of which will give you $11 in return for $8. Your profit will be $3 in each case. *Deal A* is a straight swap—$11 for $8.

   Deal B involves four steps and you can quit at any point.
   Step 1. $5 in exchange for $2
   Step 2. $3 for $2
   Step 3. $2 for $2
   Step 4. $1 for $2

   What would you do? Go all the way through the four steps and collect a total of $3 profit? A better solution, stopping after two steps, would yield $4.

   Deal C also involves four steps.
   Step 1. $4 in exchange for $1
   Step 2. $4 for $2
   Step 3. $2 for $2
   Step 4. $1 for $3

   Would you collect your $3 profit or stop after two steps and gain $5?

   Moral: If the effects of extra (marginal) steps are assessed, you can raise your profits above $3. Without examining each step, the chance of greater profits would have been missed.

9. Using your own intuition, graph each of the following relationships in the space below.
   a. height and weight of males.
   b. (on the same graph) height and weight of females.

   c. Do these lines have a positive slope or negative slope?
   d. Have you drawn the relationships differently? If so, why? By referring to your own observations, you have constructed a model.
   e. Which factors have you "held constant"?
   f. i. Again using your own intuition, sketch in the space on the following page the relationship between the price of Ontario wine and the consumption of Ontario wine.
      ii. According to your theory and your diagram, is there any point, even if wine is free, at which consumers will not wish to buy any more wine?

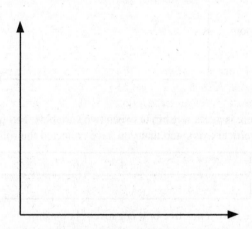

iii. Will the total number of dollars spent on wine remain the same at every price level?

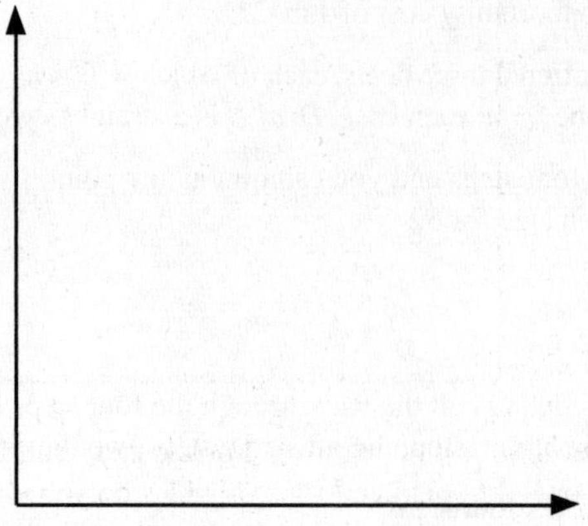

g. i. Using your own intuition, sketch in the space below the relationship between the interest rate and house purchases.

ii. According to your theory and your graph, is there any interest rate that will completely deter house purchases?

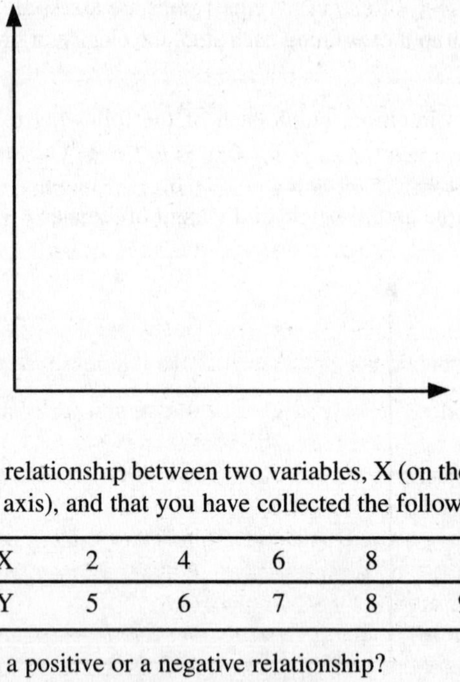

10. Suppose there is a relationship between two variables, X (on the horizontal axis) and Y (on the vertical axis), and that you have collected the following data.

X	2	4	6	8	10
Y	5	6	7	8	9

a. Do we have a positive or a negative relationship?
b. Describe (in words) what these data would look like graphically.
c. Calculate the slope (rise over run) of the line.
d. Graph the relationship below.

11. Suppose that you have a new brand of low-alcohol, calorie-reduced beer, "Coors Light," that you intend to market. What variables do you think will be important in determining the amount of Coors Light that people will want to buy? You should be able to develop a fairly long list of variables. You have begun to construct an economic model of consumption behaviour. Now prune down your list to include, say, the five most important variables.

    Now work out in which way each variable will impact the consumption of Coors Light. You should be able to work out a specific cause-and-effect pattern in each case. A higher price for Coors Light should cause less to be bought. A price hike for competing beers should increase the demand for Coors Light. Note that not all variables have been included in the model; an all-inclusive list would (1) be cumbersome and (2) distract from the major elements in the model.

    The variables that you have compiled in your list will be continually changing their values. To isolate the effect of any one on the consumption of Coors Light you must invoke the *ceteris paribus* assumption. You might think of this as being the economic equivalent of the "standard temperature and pressure" conditions applied in the natural sciences.

    Use the model that you developed for Coors Light beer. Putting "quantity demanded" on the horizontal axis, graph each of the relationships in the model.

12. Which of the following statements are positive and which are normative?
    a. The moon is made of green cheese.
    b. Provinces to the east of Quebec have lower provincial income tax rates than those to the west of Quebec.
    c. The federal government should be made to balance its budget.
    d. The most serious economic problem confronting the nation is unemployment.
    e. We should abolish the minimum wage.
    f. We should index-link the minimum wage to the rate of price inflation.
    g. If the federal budget deficit is reduced, then interest rates will decrease.

ANSWERS AND SOLUTIONS

PRACTICE TEST

I. SOLUTIONS TO MULTIPLE CHOICE QUESTIONS

1. B. If the price of corn fell, perhaps very sharply, buyers might buy more corn and fewer tomatoes. Therefore, the economist is assuming that the price of corn is not going to change. That's what *ceteris paribus* implies.
2. D. Energy conservation might be part of economic efficiency, but it is not one of the criteria for evaluating the results of economic policy. See p. 15.
3. D. Growth will occur if resources become more plentiful or more productive.
4. A. Economics is about choice—how we ration scarce resources to meet limitless wants.
5. B. Price is not necessarily a reliable guide to value for a particular individual. Opportunity cost is the measure of the value placed on the next most-preferred item forgone as a result of Choice X.
6. D. Efficiency means that producers are using the least costly method of production to supply those goods that are desired by consumers.
7. C. To review the micro/macro distinction, see p. 7.
8. B. There is a *negative* relationship between price and quantity demanded, so A is incorrect. The greater the rainfall, the larger the number of umbrellas bought.
9. A. Just because an action done by one individual produces a given outcome, the same action done by many need not.
10. D. Put in numbers. If P = $2, then Qd will equal 400 – 100(2), or 200. If the price rises by 50¢, then Qd will equal 400 – 100(2.5), or 150—a fall of 50.
11. D. The *ceteris paribus* assumption freezes the effect of all but one change so that the effects of that change may be examined.
12. B. The diagram shows a straight line—straight lines have a constant slope. Visually, or by using the "rise over run" formula, the relationship is positive because, as one variable increases in value, the other also increases in value.
13. A. Use the "rise over run" formula. The rise is +5 (Y goes from 7 to 12) and the run is +2 (X goes from 2 to 4).
14. D. As X "steps up" in value by 2, Y "steps up" in value by 5. At Point C, X has a value of 6 and Y has a value of 17. Moving to Point D, X rises by 2 and Y rises by 5, from 17 to 22.
15. A. As X "steps down" in value by 2, Y "steps down" in value by 5. At Point A, X has a value of 2 and Y has a value of 7. X decreases by 2 and Y decreases by 5, from 7 to 2.
16. C. As the X variable increases in value, the Y variable decreases in value—a negative relationship. The slope is decreasing in magnitude because, as X increases in value, the decrease in the value of Y becomes smaller and smaller.
17. A. The relationship shows that as the X variable increases in value, the Y variable also increases in value—a positive relationship. The slope is increasing because, as X increases in value, the increase in the value of Y becomes larger and larger.
18. B. The relationship shows that as the X variable increases in value, the Y variable also increases in value—a positive relationship. The slope is decreasing because, as X increases in value, the increase in the value of Y becomes smaller and smaller.
19. A. As x assumes higher values, the values of y will increase more rapidly.
20. D. For equity, read "fairness." Critics of this proposal argue that a cut in transfer payments, and thereby social spending, creates an unequitable redistribution of income against low-income families.

21. B. The $70 million had already been spent and was unrecoverable—a sunk cost. Sunk costs should have no impact on the decision to continue the project. See p. 3.
22. D. To complete the project would cost $80 million more than had already been spent.

II. SOLUTIONS TO APPLICATION QUESTIONS

1. The (marginal) cost of the air quality improvement is valued at $50 x 4000, or $200 000. The benefit derived from the improvement is valued at ($5 x 10 000) + ($7 x 30 000), or $260 000. Smogland should proceed with the implementation of emission controls.
2. a.

Unemployment Rate (%)	Inflation Rate (%)
2.0	6.0
4.0	3.0
6.0	0.0
8.0	-3.0
10.0	-6.0

   b. Slope is –1.5.
   c. –4.5%.
   d. 1.5%.
3. In order to have cleaner (if not clean) air, we might wish to reduce emissions of cars, homes, and factories. The next most preferred use of the resources used to achieve this would be included in the opportunity cost. An initial 5% improvement in the quality of the air might be accomplished quite simply—perhaps by requiring more frequent car tune ups—but, progressively, the "cost" of achieving more stringent air cleanliness standards will rise. The marginal cost will increase. This will graph as an upward-sloping line that rises progressively more steeply.
4. The answer cannot be determined given the information. This choice may well have been rational. Perhaps the three extra points save you from flunking the course while, in the math class, you are confident of making an easy "A."
5. The opportunity cost is the salary forgone—$32 000 if you had chosen the rival bank. Presumably, the offer of the job at the bank was based on your abilities—some of which would have been developed while at university. That time, then, was not wasted. You could have taken the bank job and explained that the three years of university got you the internship and sufficient skills to be noticed in the first place. Also, the three university years cannot be relived—decisions should be based on the future, not the past.
6. This is an open question. The natural resource might be a river, a seam of coal, deer, a piece of wasteland used as a dump, prime agricultural land, or downtown lots. The main point is that using the resource one way means that it is not available for other uses. The final part of the question may lead you into a consideration of private property rights, social pressure, and the role of the government.
7. Choose Job A. The opportunity cost is $20 000 (the value of the next best alternative forgone—Job B). The opportunity cost of both Job B and Job C is $30 000—the value of the surrendered Job A. Choosing either B or C is not rational since the reward is less than the cost.
8. No answer necessary.
9. a. and b. See the diagram below.

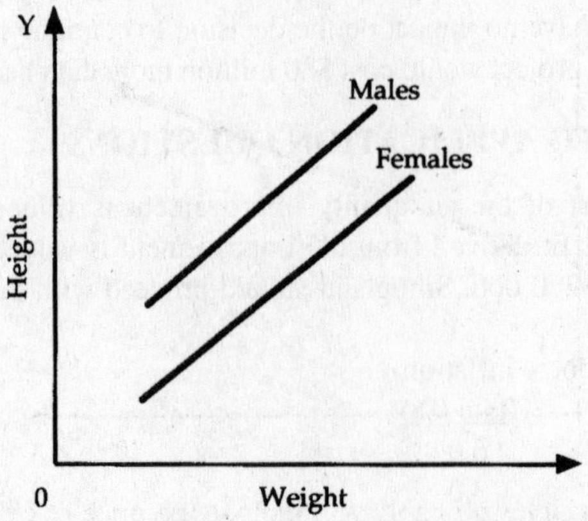

c. Both positive—as height increases, so does weight.
d. Probably the lines will be different. Perhaps, at any given height, males may weigh more than females, for example.
e. Race, geographical location, and age are factors that have been ignored.
f. i. See the diagram below.
   ii. Even if wine is free, consumers are likely to reach a point of satiation. This is shown on the diagram as the quantity at which the line reaches the horizontal axis.
   iii. It depends on your demand for wine, of course, but probably not. We take up this issue in Chapter 5, when we consider elasticity of demand. In general, we'll find that total spending declines at high prices.

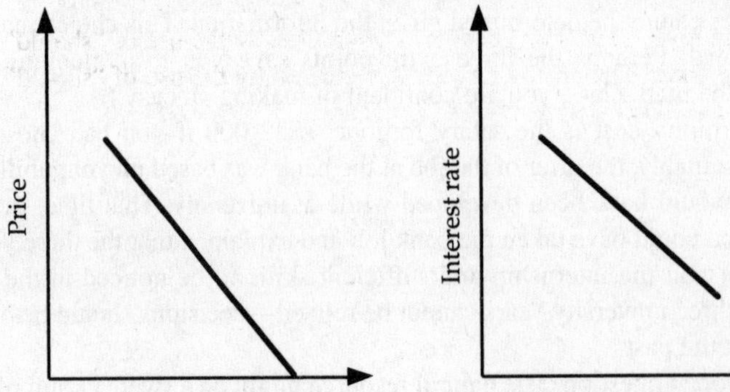

g. i. See the diagram above.
   ii. It depends on the demand for houses, of course, and is shown as the point at which the line reaches the vertical axis.
10. a. It's a positive relationship.
    b. The line would be "rising" to the right.
    c. Rise over run: Y rises by one unit every time X rises by two units, so the slope is +1/2.
    d. See the diagram below.

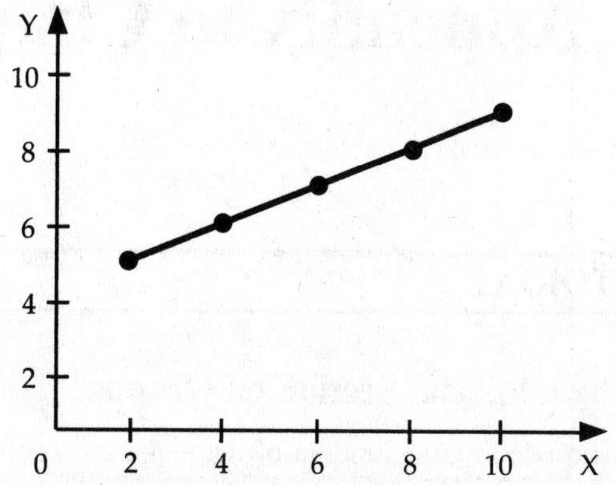

11. Your shortlist of variables probably will include the price of Coors Light, the prices of its competitors, advertising, the time of year, health attitudes, the income of potential buyers (launching a new product during an economic downturn might be difficult, for instance), and so on.
The negative relationship you will have modelled (if not, why not?) between price and quantity demanded is called the demand curve. A movement along this curve indicates that price has changed causing a change in the amount of beer demanded, with all other variables held constant (*ceteris paribus*). (Keep this conclusion in mind when you read Chapter 4.)
12. Positive statements are testable; normative statements are opinions.
    a. Positive. A statement need not be correct to be positive.
    b. Positive. Data can be gathered and analysis undertaken.
    c. Normative, as signalled by the use of "should".
    d. Normative. This is an opinion, even during the Great Depression.
    e. Normative. This is an opinion, as signalled by the use of "should".
    f. Normative. This is an opinion, as signalled by the use of "should".
    g. Positive. This statement can be tested.

1A Appendix to Chapter 1

GRAPHING TUTORIAL

Introduction: Why a Special Section on Graphs?

Many of you will be surprised by the amount of mathematics—geometry in particular—that you encounter in economics. Professors introduce a new concept and quickly draw a graph on the blackboard to illustrate the idea. Once past the initial chapter, the textbook reinforces the notion that economic theory and graphs are inseparable. This unexpected union of a social science course and mathematical methodology baffles some students. Often, you struggle so much with the techniques that you miss the powerful insights that economics has to offer. This section is designed to help you gain a working understanding of graphing techniques and to help you apply this knowledge to economics.

Why Are Graphs Important?

Graphs are important for several reasons. First, graphs represent a compact way to convey a large amount of information. An old adage says that "one picture is worth one thousand words." This is particularly true in economics as the movement of an economic variable over time or the relationships between two economic variables can be quickly grasped through the use of graphs. Second, as this textbook mentions in the appendix to Chapter 1, economics uses quantitative (mathematical) techniques more than any other social science. Every academic discipline possesses its own "tool kit" that must be mastered in order to truly appreciate the content of the course. In an economic principles class, the primary "tool" is graphs. Third, there is a clear correlation between student success in economics and graphing skills. Research on student performance indicates that of the skills that lead to success (verbal, quantitative reasoning, graphing), graphing ability is vital. Fourth, an important component of a vibrant democratic society is *economic literacy*: a basic understanding of certain central economic concepts. Citizens who follow current events will constantly encounter graphs as prints and television journalists use the visual medium to communicate with their audience.

Why Graphs Trouble Many Students

There are several factors that may cause you to have difficulty with graphs. Several years may have elapsed since you completed a high-school geometry course. Consequently, many graphing skills that were developed have been forgotten. More fundamentally, you read every day; however, you do not practise math every day. Therefore, most students will enter an economic principles class with a stronger reading ability than a mathematical ability. Because of this, you must remember that the graphs in this textbook are not photographs worthy of only a glance; *graphs must be studied.*

General Tips for Studying Graphs

Here are some general tips that should assist you in developing your graphing skills:

1. *Relax*! Remember that math is simply another language; therefore, graphs are just a specific form of communication;

2. When studying a graph, first identify the labels that are on the graph axes and curves. These labels are like road signs that inform the reader;

3. Once the labels are recognized, try to understand what economic intuition lies behind the curve (e.g., the demand curve indicates that as the product price falls, the amount that consumers wish to buy increases);

4. Get into the habit of tracing the graphs that are in the text and copying the graphs as reading notes are taken; and

5. *Draw, draw, draw*!!! The process of learning economics must be an active process. Graphing skills can be enhanced only by repeated attempts to graph economic concepts.

What Are Graphs?

Graphs are a visual expression of quantitative information. Economic theory attempts to establish relationships between important concepts. If the value of a concept changes, the concept is considered a *variable*. Graphs illustrate the relationship between two variables. If two variables have a *direct* (positive) relationships, the value of one variable increases as the value of the other variable increases. If two variables have an *inverse* (negative) relationship, the value of one variable decreases as the value of the other variable increases.

Example 1: As children get older, they grow taller. Thus, there exists a direct relationship between a child's age and his or her height.

AGE	6	7	8	9	10
HEIGHT (cm)	120	125	130	135	140

This relationship can be graphed:

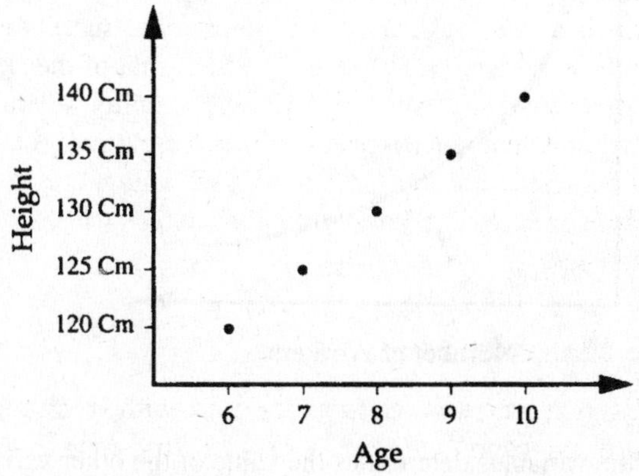

Example 2: After attending class, sleeping, eating, and working at a part-time job, a student has seven hours that can be used for studying or socializing. There exists an inverse relationship between time spent studying and time spent socializing.

STUDYING	7	5	3	1	0
SOCIALIZING	0	2	4	6	7

A graph of this relationship is shown below:

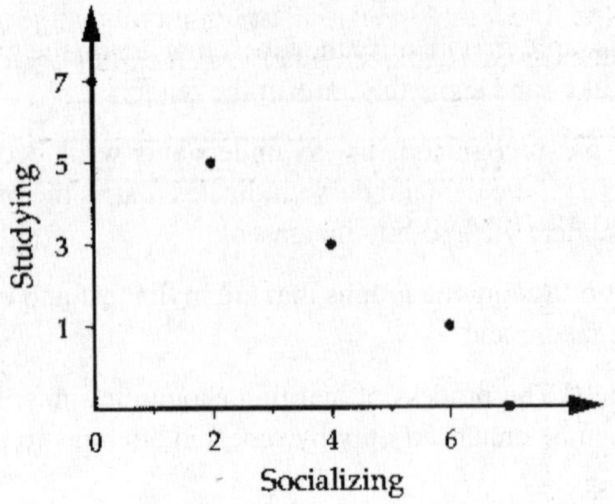

Types of Graphs

There are two types of graphs. *Descriptive* graphs relate the observed association of two variables. The graphs in Examples 1 and 2 are descriptive graphs. Newspapers often express monthly unemployment data in descriptive graphs. *Analytical* graphs convey the hypothetical relationship, or association, between two variables. The existence of association is derived from economic theory, and its accuracy is the object of economic research.

Example 3: An understanding of a firm's goals and its constraints leads to the development of a hypothesis which states that as wages rise, a firm will hire fewer workers. Graphically, this relationship is expressed as:

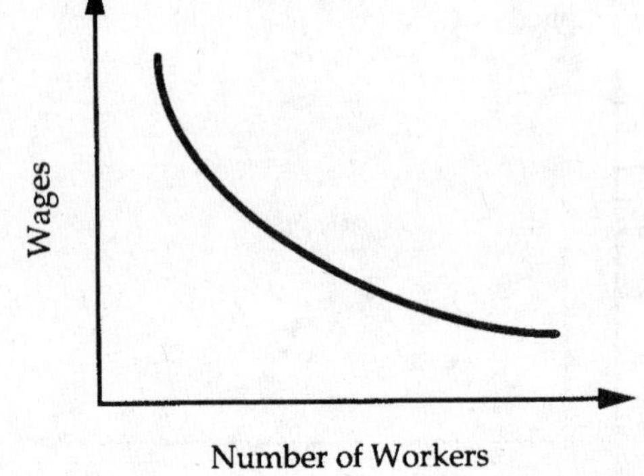

Often, the value of one of the variables determines the value of the other variable. In these cases, the former variable is called the *independent* variable; the latter variable is called the *dependent* variable. Normally (but not always), the independent variable is placed on the horizontal axis and the dependent variable is placed on the vertical axis.

Drawing Graphs

Earlier, we examined the direct relationship between a child's age and his or her height. One would expect another direct relationship between a child's age and his or her weight.

AGE	6	7	8	9	10
WEIGHT	35 kg	37.5 kg	40 kg	42.5 kg	45 kg

Example 4: Graph this relationship below:

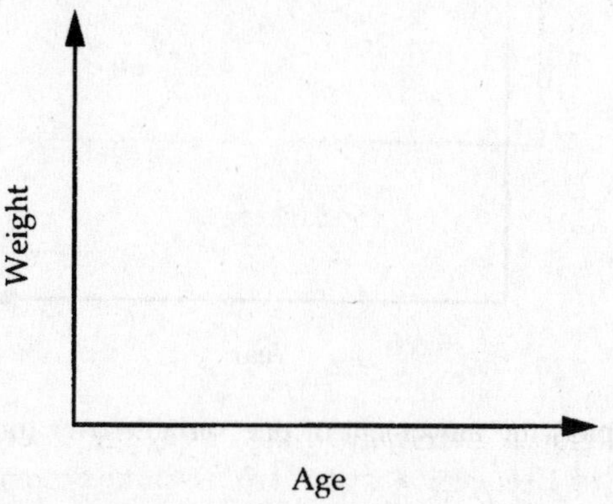

Combining the two series of data yields the table below:

AGE	6	7	8	9	10
HEIGHT (cm)	120	125	130	135	140
WEIGHT (kgs)	35	37.5	40	42.5	45

Example 5: Graph the height–weight combination for each age.

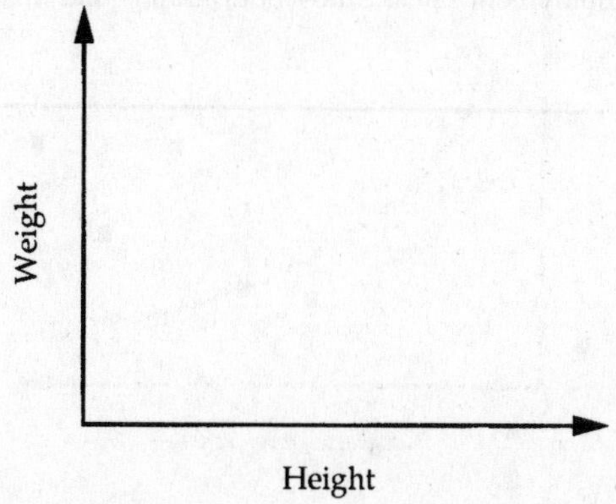

Is the relationship between height and weight direct or inverse? ____________

Because the graph depicts the changes in two variables over time, it is called a *scatter diagram.*

Example 6: Graph the relationship between the annual Canadian unemployment rate (U%) and the years 1987–1996.

YEAR	87	88	89	90	91	92	93	94	95	96
U(%)	8.9	7.8	7.5	8.1	10.4	11.3	11.2	10.4	9.5	9.7

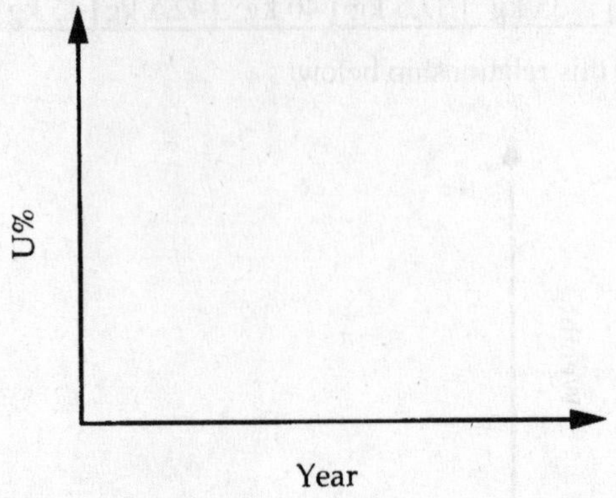

Because this graph depicts the movement of one variable over time, it is called a *time-series graph.*
Between what years is there a direct relationship? ________________
Between what years is there an inverse relationship? ________________

Reading Graphs

In addition to graphing economic relationships, students must develop the skill of reading graphs. Below are a time-series graph of the movement of the poverty rates for Canadian families between 1987 and 1995 and a scatter diagram indicating the association between poverty rates and unemployment rates. Study both graphs and answer the questions that follow.

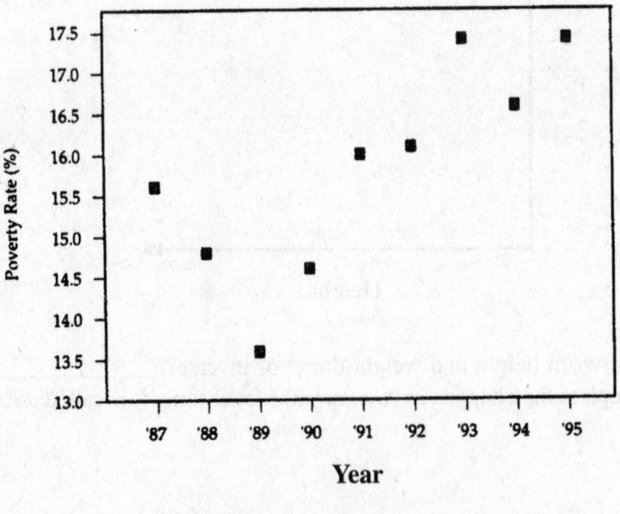

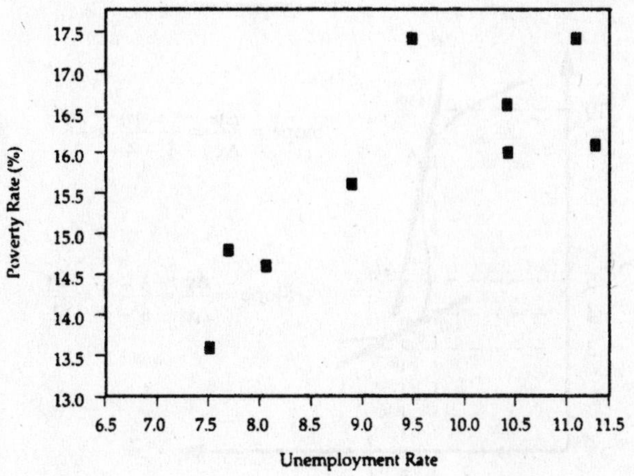

Example 7:

1. What are the poverty rates in:
   a. 1988 ________
   b. 1992 ________
   c. 1995 ________
2. What are the poverty rate/unemployment rate combinations in:
   a. 1990 ________ ________
   b. 1993 ________ ________
   c. 1995 ________ ________
3. When is there a direct relationship between poverty rates and time?
4. Is there ever an inverse relationship between poverty rates and unemployment rates?

Understanding and Calculating Slopes

The *slope* of a curve is one measure of the relationship between two variables. It indicates both the type of relationship (direct or inverse) and the rate of change of one variable as the other variable changes. For a straight line, the slope is constant. For a curve, the slope changes from one point along the curve to another. At any particular point, the slope of the curve is identical to the slope of the straight line that is tangent to that point. The slope of a line is calculated by identifying two points on the line and computing the ratio of the change in the variable on the vertical axis and the change in the variable on the horizontal axis. (In high school geometry, this was referred to as "the 'rise'; over the 'run'"; more formally, the slope was the "change in Y (ΔY) divided by the change in X (ΔX)".)

Example 8:

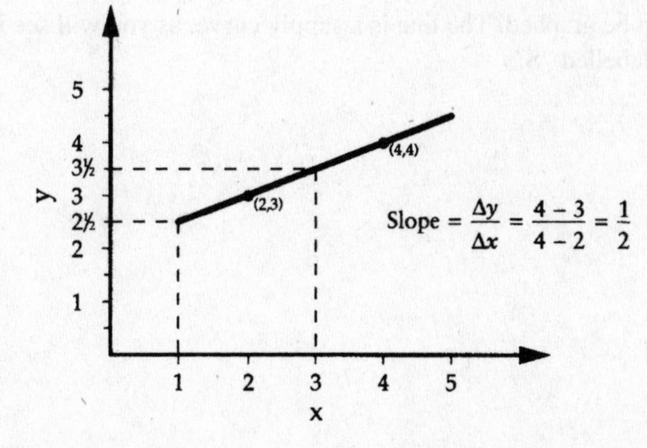

Example 9:

Slope $= \dfrac{\Delta y}{\Delta x} = \dfrac{5 - 10}{5 - 4} = \dfrac{-5}{1}$

Slope $= \dfrac{\Delta y}{\Delta x} = \dfrac{3 - 4}{6 - 4} = \dfrac{-1}{2}$

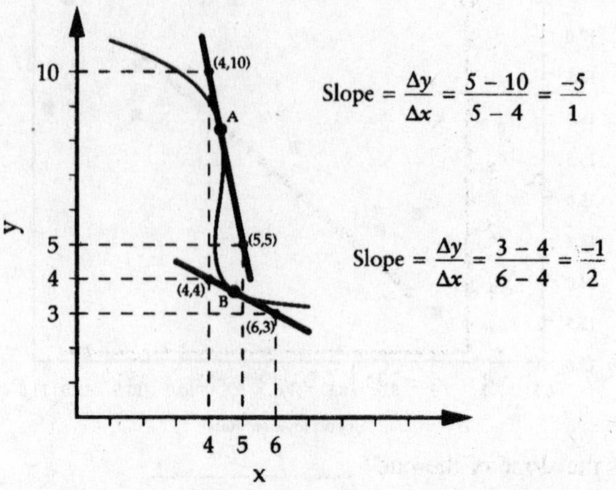

In Example 8, any two points along the line will show a slope of 1/2. In Example 9, the slope varies: at point A, the slope is –5; at point B the slope is –1/2. These slope numbers can be interpreted as indicating the unit change in the value of Y in response to a one unit change in X. For Example 8, Y will increase by 1/2 unit in response to a one unit change in X. At point A in Example 9, Y decreases by 5 units and, at point B, Y decreases by 1/2 unit in response to a one unit change in X. The fact that the slope is positive in Example 8 means that there is a direct relationship between X and Y (as X increases, Y increases). The negative slope in Example 9 illustrates an inverse relationship between X and Y (as X increases, Y decreases).

Solving Equations

Often, the economic relationship between two concepts can be expressed algebraically with an equation. The advantage of this approach is that we can calculate the specific impact that a change in one variable has upon another variable.

Example 10: It is a reasonable assumption that as the price of a good rises, more of that good will be supplied. This positive relationship can be expressed with an equation. Let P represent price and Qs represent quantity supplied. For our purposes, let Qs = –10 + 80P. Thus, if P = 1, then Qs = 70. The table below captures this relationship:

PRICE	1	2	3	4	5
QUANTITY SUPPLIED (Qs)	70	150	230	310	390

1. What is Qs if P = 7? _____

2. What is Qs if P = 10? _____

The table can be graphed. The line is a supply curve, as you will see in Chapter 4—it is usually labelled "S,"

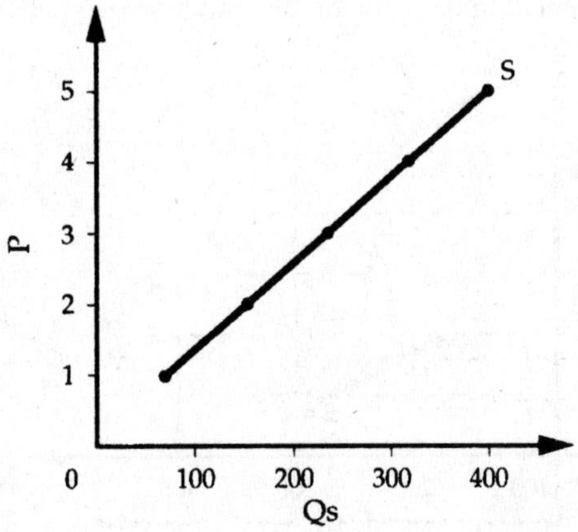

3. What is the slope of the line? ____________

If the equation is Qs = –10 + 50P, the slope of the line will change. Below is a new table:

PRICE	1	2	3	4	5
QUANTITY SUPPLIED (Qs)	40	90	140	190	240

4. Draw this new line on the graph below. Label it S1.

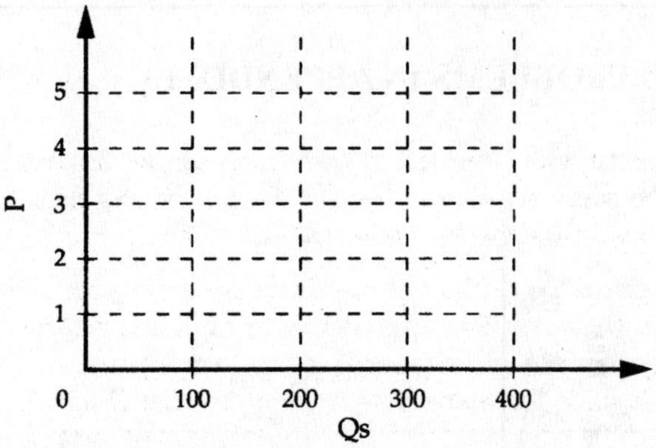

5. What is the shope of this line? ____________

If the equation for the supply curve is Qs = –20 + 75P, answer the questions below.

6. Complete the following table:

PRICE	1	2	3	4	5
QUANTITY SUPPLIED (Qs)					

7. Graph the line represented in the table on the graph below. Label it S2.

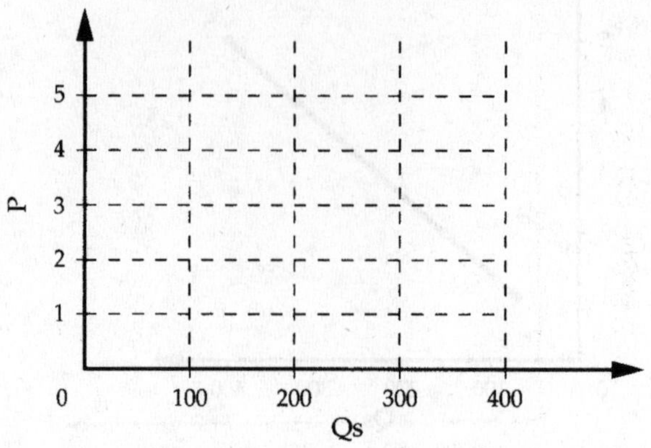

8. What is the slope of the line? ____________

9. What is Qs if P = 8? ____________

10. What is Qs if P = 20? ____________

ANSWERS AND SOLUTIONS

SOLUTIONS TO PROBLEMS IN APPENDIX 1A

Example 4:

See the diagram below:

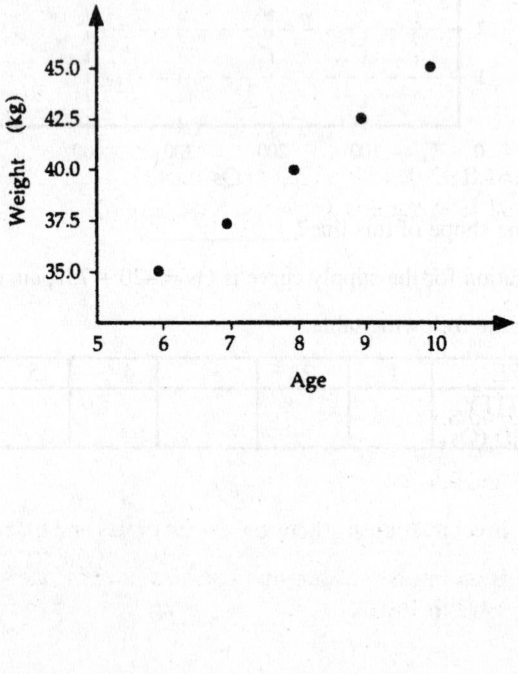

Example 5:

See the diagram below:

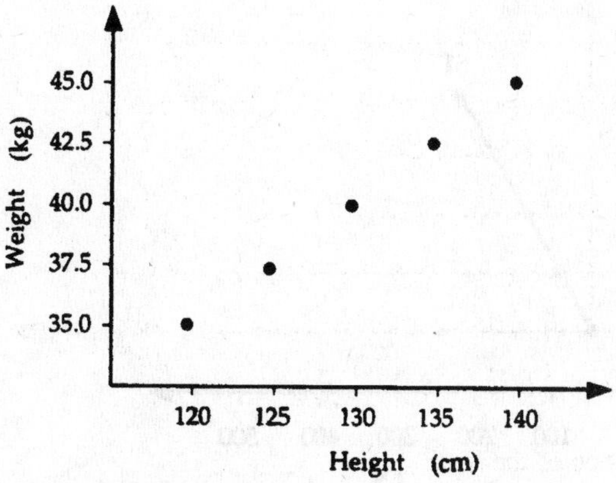

The relationship between height and weight is direct.

Example 6:

See the diagram below:

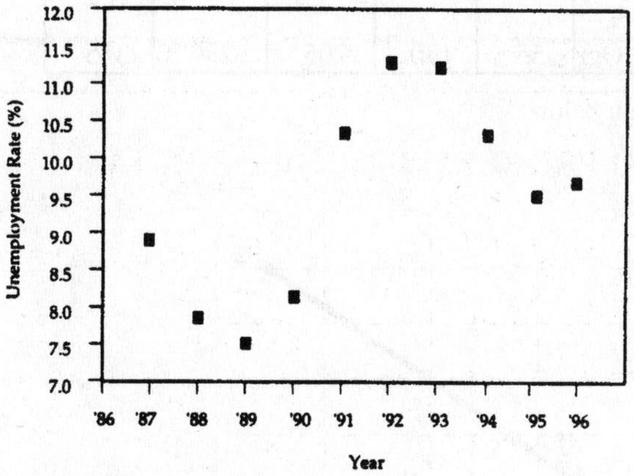

Between 1989 and 1992 there is a direct relationship.
Between 1992 and 1995 there is an inverse relationship.

Example 7:

1. a. 14.8
   b. 16.1
   c. 17.4

2. a. 14.6 and 8.1
   b. 17.4 and 11.2
   c. 17.4 and 9.5

3. There is a direct relationship between poverty rates and time from 1989 to 1995.

4. Yes, there is an inverse relationship between poverty rates and unemployment rates from 1992 to 1993.

Example 10:

1. Qs = –10 + 80P = –10 + 80(7) = 550.

2. Qs = –10 + 80P = –10 + 80(10) = 790.

3. Slope = rise/run = 1/80. A 1 unit increase in P leads to an 80 unit increase in Qs.

4. See the diagram below.

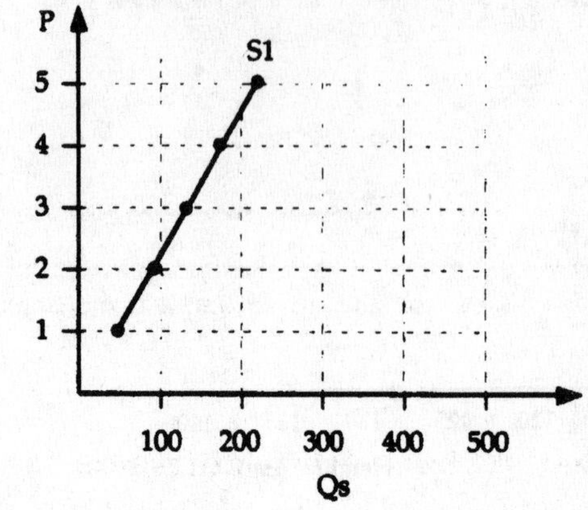

5. Slope = rise/run = 1/50. A 1 unit increase in P leads to a 50 unit increase in Qs.

6.

PRICE	1	2	3	4	5
QUANTITY SUPPLIED (Qs)	55	130	205	280	355

7. See the diagram below:

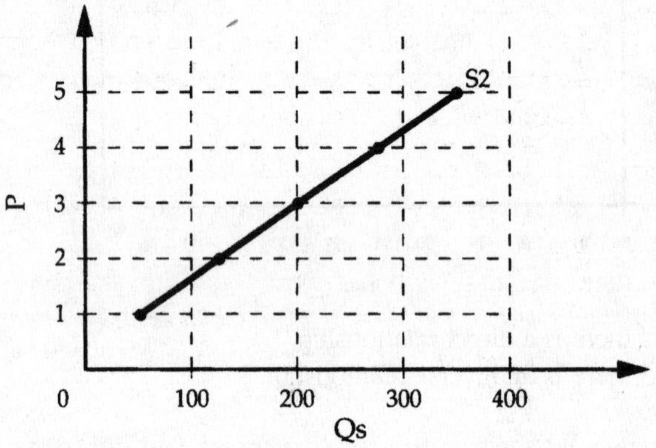

8. Slope = rise/run = 1/75. A 1 unit increase in P leads to a 75 unit increase in Qs.

9. Qs = –20 + 75P = –20 + 75(8) = 580.

10. Qs = –20 + 75P = –20 + 75(20) = 1480.

2 The Economic Problem: Scarcity and Choice

OBJECTIVES: POINT BY POINT

After completing this chapter, you should be able to accomplish the objectives listed below.

OBJECTIVE 1: Define the three basic economic questions.

Economics studies the production and consumption choices that are made by society and the outcomes that occur. Solutions must be found to three "basic questions": *what* goods should be produced?; *how* should the goods be produced?; and *for whom* should the goods be produced?

OBJECTIVE 2: State the significance of scarcity, choice, and opportunity cost.

Every economy (consisting of firms, households, and the government sector) must transform its scarce natural, capital, and human resources into usable production. In a complex society, the opportunity to cooperate and specialize offers great scope for increased production—but decisions must be made regarding the extent of cooperation, who specializes in what, and how goods are distributed. (page 27)

Opportunity Cost: Economics has to do with making choices when constraints (scarcity) are present. Constrained choice occurs, for example, when you go to the grocery store with only a $5 bill in your pocket—you have to make choices based on this limitation. Unconstrained choice would be if you were allowed to take as many groceries home as you wanted, free of charge. Sadly, though, we know there's "no such thing as a free lunch."

Practical examples of the consequences of choice and the costs of such choices include: present vs. future benefits (for example, do you study hard now so that, at exam time, reviewing is easier, or do you take it easy now and sweat it before the exam?), and capital vs. consumer production (for example, should we produce taxicabs or sports cars?).

> **TIP:** Everyone has been confronted with some version of the following scene: A favourite grandmother gives you a free choice from two or more items (ice cream sundaes, for example). From your viewpoint, is your chosen ice cream sundae free? Or is there an opportunity cost? If you have a range of sundaes from which to choose, what is the cost? The dollar amount of the chosen sundae? All the other sundaes you could have had? The opportunity cost is the next most favourite sundae.

Practice

1. Which of the following statements about the operation of an economy is true? Each economy has a mechanism to determine
   A. what is produced and how much is produced.
   B. how to satisfy all of the desires of its citizens.
   C. how goods and services are distributed among its citizens.
   D. both A and C.

   ANSWER: D. Because resources are limited, the economy cannot satisfy all the desires of its citizens. Therefore, B is incorrect. A and C are correct.

LEARNING OBJECTIVE 3: Distinguish between absolute and comparative advantage and explain why comparative advantage is critical in the theory of specialization and exchange.

A producer has an absolute advantage over another producer if she can produce each and every product that both can make more efficiently (less costly).

A producer has a *comparative advantage* in the production of Good A if, compared with another producer, she can produce Good A at a lower opportunity cost.

The *theory of comparative advantage* provides the rationale for free trade. Given a two-country, two-good world, Ricardo showed that trading partners can benefit from specialization in the production of the good in which they have the comparative advantage. The increased production could be traded. In terms of the *production possibility frontier* (ppf) diagram, trade will be advantageous if the ppfs have differing slopes because differing slopes indicate differing costs. (page 29)

> **TIP:** If you're like most individuals, you'll need several numerical examples to strengthen your grasp of comparative advantage. The Applications take you through all the steps included in the text.

Comparative advantage hinges on the concept of opportunity cost. The producer (person, firm, or country) with the lowest opportunity cost will hold the comparative advantage in that product. Don't be misled—it is irrelevant whether or not the producer can produce *more* of the good. The issue revolves around the relative opportunity costs.

Practice

Use the following information to answer the next five questions. Arboc and Arbez are two economies that produce computer chips and VCRs. In Arboc, a one-unit increase in computer chips requires a four-unit decrease in VCR production. In Arbez, a one-unit increase in computer chips requires a three-unit decrease in VCR production. In each economy, costs remain constant.

2. Which of the following statements is false?
   A. in Arboc, the opportunity cost of 1 computer chip is 4 VCRs.
   B. in Arbez, the opportunity cost of 1 computer chip is 3 VCRs.
   C. the opportunity cost of 1 computer chip is greater in Arboc than in Arbez.
   D. an increase in the Arbocali production of computer chips requires a decrease in the Arbezani production of VCRs.

ANSWER: D. An increase in the Arbocali production of computer chips requires a decrease in the Arbezani production of VCRs. In fact, both independent economies might choose to increase computer-chip production.

3. Which of the following statements is true?
   A. In Arboc, the opportunity cost of 1 VCR is 4 computer chips.
   B. In Arbez, the opportunity cost of 1 VCR is 3 computer chips.
   C. The opportunity cost of 1 VCR is greater in Arbez than in Arboc.
   D. Arbez can produce more VCRs than Arboc can produce.

   ANSWER: C. We don't know whether Arbez has an absolute advantage in VCRs (Option D). The information tells us only about relative performance. Arbez, in fact, may be a very small country capable of producing only a few VCRs. In Arboc, the opportunity cost of a VCR is 1/4 of a computer chip, and in Arbez, the opportunity cost of a VCR is 1/3 of a computer chip.

4. In ________, the opportunity cost of 1 computer chip is ______ VCRs, which is less than the opportunity cost of 1 computer chip in ______.
   A. Arboc, 1/4, Arbez.
   B. Arboc, 4, Arbez.
   C. Arbez, 3, Arboc.
   D. Arbez, 1/3, Arboc.

   ANSWER: C. In Arboc, each computer chip "costs" 4 VCRs. In Arbez, each computer chip "costs" 3 VCRs. Computer chips cost less in Arbez.

5. In ________, the opportunity cost of 1 VCR is ______ computer chips, which is less than the opportunity cost of 1 VCR in ______.
   A. Arboc, 1/4, Arbez.
   B. Arboc, 4, Arbez.
   C. Arbez, 3, Arboc.
   D. Arbez, 1/3, Arboc.

   ANSWER: A. In Arboc, each VCR "costs" 1/4 of a computer chip. In Arbez, each VCR "costs" 1/3 of a computer chip. VCRs cost less in Arboc.

6. According to the information above,
   A. Arboc has a comparative advantage in the production of both goods.
   B. Arboc has a comparative advantage in producing computer chips, and Arbez has a comparative advantage in producing VCRs.
   C. Arboc has a comparative advantage in producing VCRs, and Arbez has a comparative advantage in producing computer chips.
   D. Arbez has a comparative advantage in the production of both goods.

   ANSWER: C. Arboc has a comparative advantage in the production of VCRs (1 VCR costs 1/4 of a computer chip), and Arbez has a comparative advantage in the production of computer chips (1 computer chip costs 3 VCRs). Note: No country can be relatively better at producing both goods.

OBJECTIVE 4: Define and use the production possibility frontier.

The ppf shows all the combinations of Good A and Good B that can be produced when all resources are employed efficiently. Points inside the ppf represent unemployment and/or inefficiency, while points outside are currently unattainable. An outward movement of the ppf represents growth. Growth occurs if more resources become available or if existing resources become more productive (e.g., through better education, more efficient techniques of production, or technological innovations). (page 32)

Production and Economic Efficiency: The thought of a great volume of production, with all resources employed, is an attractive one. For this reason, it's often difficult to understand that, in serving the needs of consumers, producing the right goods is more important than mere quantity. This distinction lies at the heart of most confusion about productive and economic efficiency. Having the Inuit economy fully employed and producing refrigerators may help you see the point. It would be "better" (more efficient) for the Inuit to have some unemployment but be producing warm clothing. Turning out the refrigerators is productively efficient, while making the warm clothing is economically efficient. Ideally, you'd want to be on the ppf (being productively efficient) and producing the economically efficient mix of output.

TIP: Think of the ppf as a way to depict opportunity cost and constrained choice. In general, you want to be somewhere on the curve because any production combination inside the curve means that you're losing production, which is inefficient. Production on the curve means that resources are being used to the maximum (no unemployment). The inefficiency of a mismatch between an "efficient" production mix and society's needs is easily explained—just because we're producing "on the line" doesn't mean we're meeting society's needs as effectively as possible. Employing all our resources to produce taxicabs, for example, is unlikely to be desirable!

Graphing Pointer: Suppose we are on the ppf and, at one point, can produce 16 cars and 5 pickups while, at another point, we can produce 12 cars and 7 pickups. Note that the opportunity cost is calculated by looking at the change in production levels—2 extra trucks cost 4 cars.

Graphing Pointer: Reducing unemployment does not shift the ppf. Remember the underlying assumptions. The ppf is drawn *given* a set of resources (whether or not the resources are being used). Unemployment represents a situation where the resources are not fully utilized. If unemployment is reduced, the economy moves closer to the ppf.

Practice

7. Which of the following is an assumption underlying the ppf?
   A. technological knowledge is fixed.
   B. resources are not fully employed.
   C. resources are efficiently employed.
   D. both A and C.

   ANSWER: D. When drawing a ppf, all resources are assumed to be fully employed.

8. The production possibility frontier represents
   A. the maximum amount of goods and services that can be produced with a given quantity of resources and technology.
   B. those combinations of goods and services that will be demanded as price changes.
   C. the maximum amount of resources that are available as the wage level changes.
   D. those combinations of goods and services that will be produced as the price level changes.

   ANSWER: A. The production possibility frontier represents what it is "possible to produce" given the available resources and technology.

9. The Arbezani economy is operating at a point inside its ppf. This may be because
   A. the economy has very poor technological know-how.
   B. Arbez is a very small nation and can't produce much.
   C. poor management practices have led to an inefficient use of resources.
   D. Arbez has only a small resource base.

   ANSWER: C. Very poor technological know-how or a small resource base will result in a ppf that is close to the origin. Fully and efficiently employed resources would still be on the ppf.

Choosing to employ resources for one use prevents them from being employed for other uses—there is an *opportunity cost* involved in the choice. The *production possibility frontier* portrays graphically the opportunity cost of transferring resources from one activity to another in a two-good environment. Assuming that all resources are fully employed, as more of Good A is produced, fewer resources are available to produce Good B. (page 33)

> **Why Does the ppf Slope Downward?:** The production possibility frontier is the key piece of economic analysis in this chapter. It's always presented as having only two goods or bundles of goods. It slopes downward because "the more you get of one thing, the less you get of the other." The more you study economics, the less time you have for other activities. The opportunity cost of an extra hour of studying economics is the value of an hour of other activities.

> **Graphing Pointer:** When drawing a ppf, remember that the frontier extends from the vertical axis to the horizontal axis. It is a mistake to leave the frontier unconnected to the axes. If the frontier is not connected, it implies that an infinitely large quantity of either good could be produced, which is exactly the opposite message that the ppf is intended to give.

> **Graphing Pointer:** Don't be concerned with which goods should be placed on the vertical axis and which goods should be placed on the horizontal axis. This is a case (one of many) where the geometry (a negative slope) is directly linked to economic theory (scarce resources). Recognizing these linkages helps graphical understanding.

Graphing Pointer: The slope of the ppf is the geometric representation of the opportunity costs of transferring resources from one activity to another activity. Due to scarcity, additional time spent studying results in less time for other activities. If you place study time on the horizontal (X) axis and "all other activities" time on the vertical (Y) axis, the graphical analysis of the cost of one hour of studying (the loss of other activities due to extra studying) is the change in Y divided by the change in X. The slope of a curve can be measured by the "rise" over the "run."

Practice

10. Along the production possibility frontier, trade-offs exist because
    - A. buyers will want to buy less when price goes up, but producers will want to sell more.
    - B. not all production levels are efficient.
    - C. at some levels, unemployment or inefficiency exists.
    - D. the economy has only a limited quantity of resources to allocate between competing uses.

    ANSWER: D. Along the ppf, resources are fully and efficiently employed. However, since resources are scarce, an increase in the production of Good A requires that resources be taken from the production of Good B.

OTHER RELATED POINTS:

POINT 1: Explain why increasing opportunity costs occur and how this relates to the production possibility frontier diagram.

Increasing opportunity costs are present when the production possibility frontier bulges outward from the origin. Increasing costs occur if resources are not equally well suited to the production of Good A and Good B. (page 34)

TIP: Why is the ppf bowed out? The geometry of the ppf flows from its economics. A bowed-out production possibility frontier indicates that the opportunity cost is increasing as resources become more heavily allocated to the production of one good. The ppf has that bowed-out shape because of the lack of adaptability of resources to different uses. A farmer wishing to produce dairy products, for example, will select the most suited resources first, and production will increase sharply. Further increases will be less easy to achieve and more expensive in terms of lost production of other goods as resources more suited to other endeavours are pressed into dairy service.

Graphing Pointer: Productive resources have different abilities, so the opportunity cost of reallocating the resources are different, and the ppf is bowed outward (concave with respect to the origin). If resources are identical in their productive abilities, the opportunity cost of reallocation would be constant, and the ppf would be a straight line (a constant slope).

Practice

11. There are increasing costs in the economy of Arbez. To portray this fact in a production possibility diagram, we should
    A. move the ppf outward (up and to the right).
    B. draw the ppf bulging outward.
    C. shift the ppf's end point on the horizontal axis to the right.
    D. shift the ppf's end point on the vertical axis upward.

    ANSWER: B. The slope of the ppf represents the behaviour of opportunity cost as production level changes. A straight ppf represents constant costs. To show increasing costs the ppf is bowed outward from the origin.

POINT 2: Identify ways in which economic growth may occur.

Economic growth may occur if an economy increases the quantity or quality of its resources—the production possibility frontier shifts outward. Additionally, technological change and innovation can increase productivity. (page 35)

> **Investment and Capital:** "Investment" and "capital" are two terms that have very specific meanings in economics. Beware! Investing doesn't just mean buying something. To an economist, investing means only the creation of capital. What, then, is capital? Capital refers to man-made resources usable in production. A hammer is capital; a share of Bell Canada stock is not. A nail is capital; a dollar is not. Buying a hammer or nail is capital investment; buying Bell Canada stock is not.
>
> If this capital/non–capital distinction is giving you problems, ask yourself if the purchase of the item in question increases the economy's ability to produce. If it does, it's an investment in capital.

OBJECTIVE 5: Identify the two main types of economic systems and describe the strengths and weaknesses of each.

The two "pure" types of economic systems are the command economy and the *laissez-faire* economy. A *command (planned) economy* has a central agency that coordinates production and finds answers for the three basic questions. In a *laissez-faire (market) economy*, the three basic questions are answered through the operation of individual buyers and sellers following their own self-interest in markets.

All economies, in fact, are driven by a mixture of market forces and government intervention and regulation. Government intervention is felt to be necessary to correct *laissez-faire* "mistakes" such as an excessive inequality in the distribution of income, inadequate provision of public goods, and periodic spells of unemployment or inflation. (page 38)

Practice

12. Advocates comparing the performance of a pure *laissez-faire* system with that of a command economy would claim that a pure *laissez-faire* system would do all of the following except
    A. promote efficiency.
    B. stimulate innovation.
    C. achieve an equal income distribution.
    D. be directed by the decisions of individual buyers and sellers.

ANSWER: C. A pure *laissez-faire* system, which rewards those who contribute most, would have an unequal income distribution.

PRACTICE TEST

I. MULTIPLE CHOICE QUESTIONS. Select the option that provides the single best answer.

_____ 1. Since the nation of Arboc is operating at a point inside its ppf, it
- A. has full employment.
- B. has unemployed or inefficiently employed resources.
- C. must cut output of one good to increase production of another.
- D. will be unable to experience economic growth.

_____ 2. Arboc commits more of its resources to capital production than does Arbez. _______ should experience a(n) _______ rapid rate of economic growth.
- A. Arboc, more.
- B. Arbez, more.
- C. Arboc, less.
- D. Both, equally.

_____ 3. Which of the following does not count as a productive resource?
- A. Capital resources, such as a tractor.
- B. Natural resources, such as a piece of farmland.
- C. Financial resources, such as a twenty-dollar bill.
- D. Human resources, such as a hairdresser.

Use the following diagram to answer the next four questions.

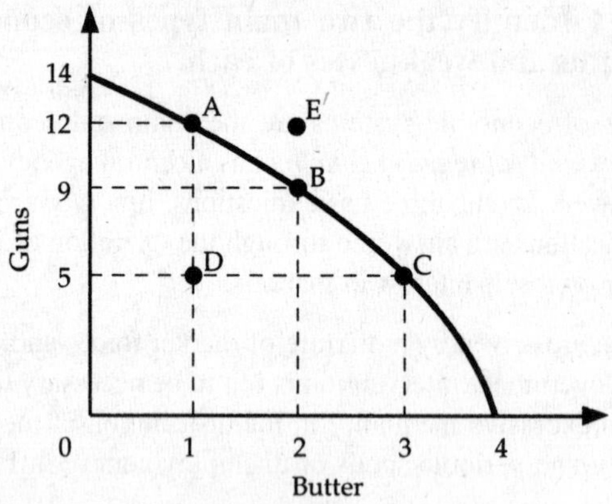

_____ 4. Point E might become attainable if this economy
- A. becomes more efficient.
- B. reduces wages.
- C. improves the quality of its workforce.
- D. encourages emigration.

_____ 5. A movement from A to B and then to C indicates that
A. the cost of additional butter is decreasing.
B. the cost of additional guns is increasing.
C. the economy is becoming more efficient.
D. the cost of additional butter is increasing.

_____ 6. To move from D to A indicates that
A. the opportunity cost would be zero.
B. some butter would have to be given up.
C. there would have to be an increase in the quantity of resources.
D. the opportunity cost would be 7.

_____ 7. The opportunity cost of producing another unit of butter is
A. higher at B than at C.
B. lower at D than at C.
C. higher at A than at B.
D. equal at D and at C.

_____ 8. A production possibility frontier illustrates the following concepts
A. scarcity.
B. unlimited wants.
C. opportunity cost as well as scarcity.
D. both A and C.

_____ 9. Of the following, the least serious problem for *laissez-faire* economies is
A. unemployment.
B. income inequality.
C. provision of public goods.
D. satisfaction of consumer sovereignty.

Use the following production possibility table to answer the next three questions. Suppose that wheat is on the Y-axis.

Alternative	A	B	C	D	E	F
Wheat	0	1	2	3	4	5
Tobacco	15	14	12	9	5	0

_____ 10. The opportunity cost of a unit of wheat as the economy moves from C to D is
A. –3 units of tobacco.
B. 3 units of tobacco.
C. –1/3 unit of tobacco.
D. 1/3 unit of tobacco.

_____ 11. The opportunity cost of a unit of tobacco as the economy moves from C to B is
A. 2 units of wheat.
B. –2 units of wheat.
C. 1/2 unit of wheat.
D. –1/2 unit of wheat.

_____ 12. An output of 3 units of wheat and 7 units of tobacco indicates that
A. this economy has poor technology.
B. resources are being used inefficiently.
C. tobacco is preferred to wheat.
D. it is not possible for this economy to produce at a point on the production possibility frontier.

_____ 13. Which of the following is most likely to shift the production possibility frontier outward?
A. A sudden expansion in the labour force.
B. An increase in stock prices.
C. A shift of productive resources from capital goods to consumer goods.
D. A general increase in the public's demand for goods.

_____ 14. Which of the following is *least* likely to be a public good?
A. Medical treatment for cancer patients.
B. The National Park system.
C. The police force.
D. National defence.

_____ 15. Private markets work best when
A. they are competitive.
B. they are regulated by a government agency.
C. a monopolist is present.
D. public goods are demanded.

_____ 16. The opportunity cost along an increasing-cost ppf must be
A. positive and increasing.
B. positive and decreasing.
C. negative and increasing.
D. negative and decreasing.

_____ 17. For Jill to have a comparative advantage in the production of pins means that, relative to Jack, with the same resources
A. Jill is relatively better at producing pins than at producing needles.
B. Jill is relatively better at producing both pins and needles.
C. Jill can produce fewer needles than Jack can produce.
D. Jill can produce more pins than Jack can produce.

_____ 18. Each of the following is a basic concern of any economic system except
A. the allocation of scarce resources among producers.
B. the mix of different types of output.
C. the distribution of output among consumers.
D. all of the above.

The table below shows the maximum output of each good in each country, e.g., maximum Arbezani production of goat milk is 3 units.

	Arbez	*Arboc*
Goat Milk	3	6
Bananas	5	2

_____ 19. According to the table above,
A. Arbez has a comparative advantage in producing both goods.
B. Arbez has a comparative advantage in the production of bananas, and Arboc has a comparative advantage in the production of goat milk.
C. Arbez has a comparative advantage in the production of goat milk, and Arboc has a comparative advantage in the production of bananas.
D. Arboc has a comparative advantage in the production of both goods.

_____ 20. The nation of Regit has a bowed-out production possibility frontier with potatoes on the vertical axis and steel on the horizontal axis. A movement down along the ppf will incur _______________ costs; a movement up along the ppf will incur _______________ costs.

A. increasing, increasing.
B. increasing, decreasing.
C. decreasing, increasing.
D. decreasing, decreasing.

II. APPLICATION QUESTIONS.

1. Farmer Brown has four fields that can produce corn or tobacco. Assume that the trade-off between corn and tobacco within each field is constant. The maximum yields are given in this table:

Field	**A**	**B**	**C**	**D**
Corn	40	30	20	10
Tobacco	10	20	30	40

a. Draw Farmer Brown's ppf.
b. To be on the ppf, what conditions must hold true?
c. Brown is currently producing only corn. If he wants to produce some tobacco, in what order would he switch his fields from corn to tobacco production?
d. Explain your answer to c.

2. Two countries, Arboc and Arbez, produce wine and cheese, and each has constant costs of production. The maximum amounts of the two goods for each country are given in the table below.

Arboc	*Arbez*	*Goods*
40	120	wine
20	30	cheese

a. Draw the production possibility frontier for each country.

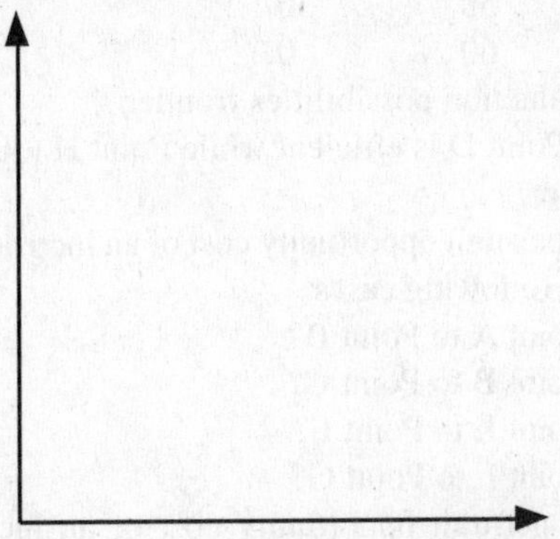

b. Calculate the opportunity cost of wine in Arboc and in Arbez.
c. In which country, then, is wine production cheaper?
d. Answer questions b. and c. for cheese production—remember that the opportunity costs are reciprocals of one another.

Note that Arbez has an advantage in both goods in terms of total production, but a comparative advantage only in wine production.

Now assume that Arboc becomes more efficient and can double its output of both wine and cheese.

e. Graph the new ppf on the diagram above.
f. Which good should Arboc now produce?

Suppose, instead, that Arbez has a specific technological advance that permits it to increase cheese production to a maximum of 90.

g. Now which nation should produce wine?

3. In a national contest, the first prize is a town. The winner receives a furnished house, a general store and gasoline station, a pick-up truck, and 100 hectares of land. The store comes fully stocked with everything you might find in a country general store. The town is located 100 kilometres from a small city. It is the shopping centre for about a thousand families who live in the countryside. In addition, the road through the town is fairly well travelled. Suppose you win the contest and decide to try running the town as a business for at least a year.
   a. Describe the resources available to the economy of your town. What is the potential labour force? What are the natural resources?
   b. Describe the capital stock of your town.
   c. List some of the factors that are beyond your control that will affect your income.
   d. List some of the decisions you must make that could affect your income, and explain what their effects might be.
   e. At the end of the year, you must decide whether to stay or go back to university. How will you decide? What factors will you weigh in making your decision? What role do your expectations play?

4. The following data give the production possibilities of an economy that produces two types of goods, cloth (horizontal axis) and wheat (vertical axis).

Production Possibilities	Cloth	Wheat
A	0	105
B	10	100
C	20	90
D	30	75
E	40	55
F	50	30
G	60	0

   a. Graph the production possibilities frontier.
   b. Explain why Point D is efficient while Point H (30 units of cloth and 45 units of wheat) is not.
   c. Calculate the per-unit opportunity cost of an increase in the production of cloth in each of the following cases.
      i. From Point A to Point B?
      ii. From Point B to Point C?
      iii. From Point E to Point F?
      iv. From Point F to Point G?
   d. Calculate the per-unit opportunity cost of an increase in the production of wheat in each of the following cases.
      i. From Point G to Point F?
      ii. From Point D to Point C?
      iii. From Point C to Point B?
      iv. From Point B to Point A?

5. Draw a production possibilities frontier with farm goods (x-axis) and manufacturing goods (y-axis) on the axes. In each of the following cases, explain what will happen to the production possibilities frontier.

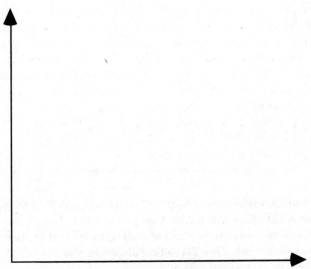

a. There is an increase in the unemployment rate.
b. There is an improvement in farming techniques.
c. There is a decrease in quantity of physical capital.
d. The productivity of workers doubles.
e. The government requires farmers to slaughter a portion of their dairy herds.

6. Consider the following ppf diagram.

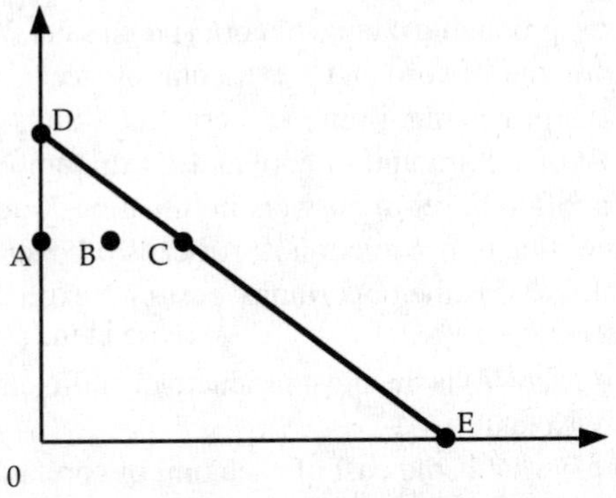

a. Which point is "best" and which is "worst"?
b. Now suppose that you're told that the axes measure food (horizontal) and moonshine whisky (vertical). Would your answer be different?
c. Point B may be preferable to Point D, although Point B is productively less efficient. Why might it be preferable?

7. The nation of Arbez can produce two goods, corn and steel. The table shows some points on the Arbezani ppf.

Alternative	A	B	C	D	E	F
Corn	0	1	2	3	4	5
Steel	20	16	12	8	4	0

a. Draw the ppf in the space below.

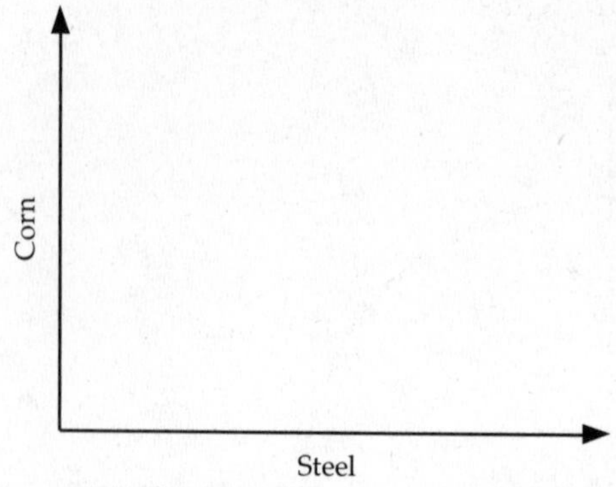

b. Moving from Alternative A to B, B to C, and so on, calculate the opportunity cost of each additional unit of corn. Going from F to E, E to D, and so on, calculate the opportunity cost *per unit* of steel. Confirm that the pairs of values are reciprocals of each other. (This must always be true.)

Opportunity Cost of 1 Unit of:

Alternative	*Corn*	*Steel*
A – B		
B – C		
C – D		
D – E		
E – F		

c. Consider each of the following situations.
Situation X: Arbez is producing 4 units of corn and no steel. What is the opportunity cost of 1 extra unit of corn and 1 extra unit of steel?
Situation Y: Arbez is producing 4 units of corn and 4 units of steel. What is the opportunity cost of 1 extra unit of corn and 1 extra unit of steel?

d. Why do you find a different set of answers in Situation X and Situation Y?

e. Now consider a new situation, Situation Z: Arbez is producing 3 units of corn and 5 units of steel. What is the opportunity cost of 1 extra unit of corn and 1 extra unit of steel?

f. Which Situation (X, Y, or Z) is the most productively efficient and which is the least productively efficient?

g. On the Arbezani ppf, what is the cost of each unit of corn and what is the cost of each unit of steel?

The nation of Arboc also produces corn and steel. The following table shows some points on the Arbocali ppf.

Alternative	**A**	**B**	**C**	**D**	**E**	**F**
Corn	0	1	2	3	4	5
Steel	20	16	12	8	4	0

h. On the Arbocali ppf, what is the cost of each unit of corn and what is the cost of each unit of steel?

i. Point to ponder: Because steel is relatively cheaper to produce in Arboc/Arbez and corn is relatively cheaper to produce in Arboc/Arbez, might mutually beneficial trade be possible?

8. Refer to the following diagram.

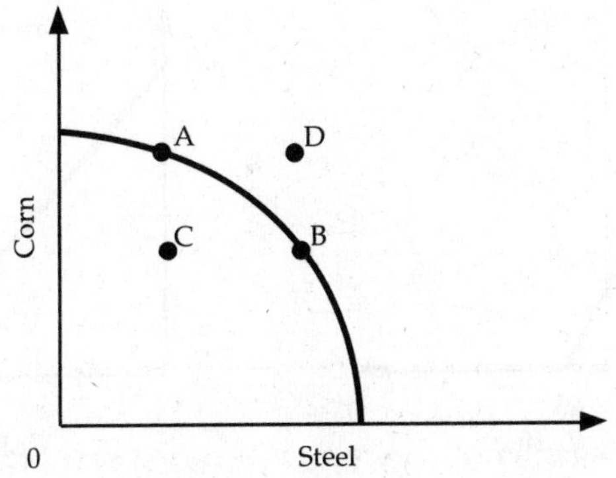

a. Which point is unattainable?
b. To achieve this currently unattainable production combination, what must happen (two possible answers)?
c. Which point represents unemployment or inefficiency?
d. Will a movement from B to A increase corn production or steel production?
e. What is the opportunity cost of moving from C to B?

9. Draw the axes of a ppf. Use corn (on the vertical axis) and steel (on the horizontal axis) as the two goods.

Choose a point, A, that represents some corn and some steel production. Suppose that this point is on the ppf—it's a maximum point. Split the diagram up into quarters, with Point A in the centre.

a. Is a production mix to the south-west possible?
b. Would such a mix be productively efficient?
c. Would such a mix be economically efficient?
d. Is a move to the north-east quadrant possible? What do you know about it?

Only the north-west and south-east quadrants are possible locations in which productively efficient output alternatives can occur.

e. What would happen if the present level of corn production (at Point A) was reduced?

If steel production does not change, unemployment occurs. The unemployed resources can be absorbed by the steel industry and more steel can be produced. A parallel case can be made given cutbacks in steel production. Can you see how the ppf must have a negative slope and that it portrays the concept of opportunity cost?

10. Use the diagrams below to answer this question.

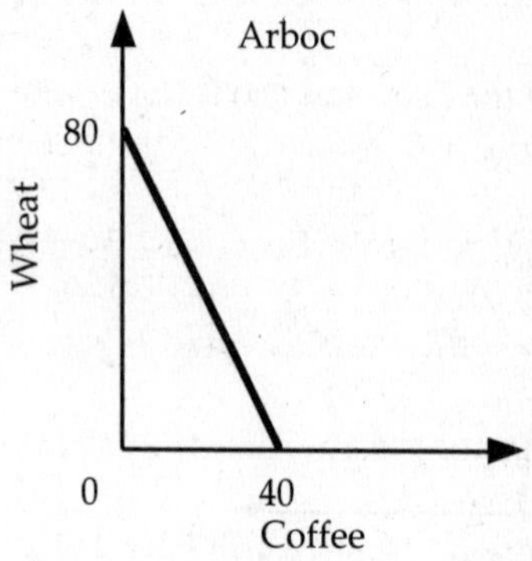

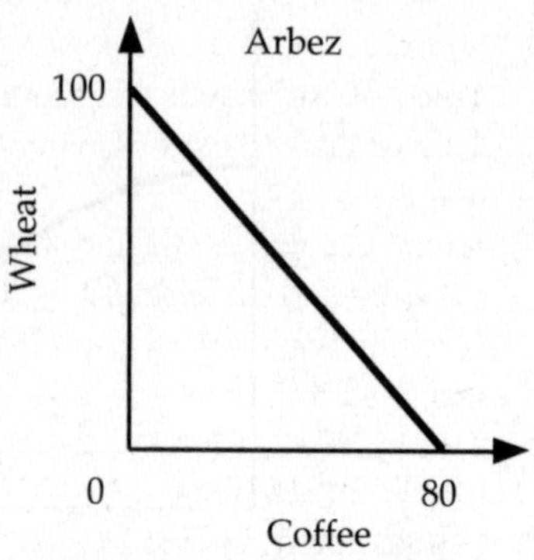

a. What is the opportunity cost of one unit of coffee in Arboc?
b. What is the opportunity cost of one unit of coffee in Arbez?
c. Which country has a comparative advantage in the production of coffee?
d. What is the opportunity cost of one unit of wheat in Arboc?
e. What is the opportunity cost of one unit of wheat in Arbez?
f. Which country has a comparative advantage in the production of wheat?
g. *Ceteris paribus*, ignoring other issues, which good should Arboc produce and which good should Arbez produce?

11. Draw a production possibility curve. Put cloth on the vertical axis and wheat on the horizontal axis. Suppose that the technology for producing wheat improves but the technology for producing cloth does not. Describe how your diagram would change. In general, how will this technological advance affect the opportunity cost of producing cloth?

12. Jennie has set 10 hours this weekend to study for an Economics test and a Physics test. She believes that, with no studying at all, she would score 40 points on each test. Suppose that for each hour studying Economics, she can raise her Economics score by 10 points, and that for each hour studying Physics, she can raise her Physics score by five points.
    a. Draw a production possibility frontier graph and show all the points that are feasible if Jennie has 10 hours to divide between Economics and Physics. Put "hours of study for Economics" on the vertical axis and "hours of study for Physics" on the horizontal axis.

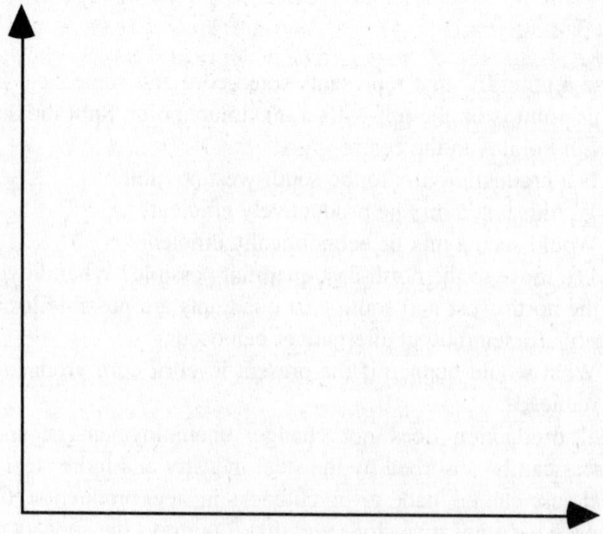

b. Show Point A, where Jennie studies Econ. for 5 hours and Physics for 5 hours.
c. Show Point B, where Jennie studies Econ. for 0 hours and Physics for 10 hours.
d. True or false? Jennie can score 60 on the Econ. test and 80 on the Physics test.
e. True or false? Jennie is lying when she tells us that, in fact, she scored 80 on both tests.
f. Jennie decides to spend 4 hours studying for the Econ. test. What's the highest score she can expect to get on the Physics test?
g. If Jennie was satisfied with 60 on both tests, how many hours would she have had to study?
h. True or false? If Jennie scored 70 on both tests, we know that she did not study for the full 10 hours.
i. Draw a line (labelled EE) showing all the points which have exactly 2 hours of study time for the Econ. test.

ANSWERS AND SOLUTIONS

PRACTICE TEST

I. SOLUTIONS TO MULTIPLE CHOICE QUESTIONS

1. B. To be on the ppf, Arboc must have all of its resources fully and efficiently employed. Since it is operating inside the ppf, at least one of these conditions must have been violated.
2. A. If Arboc produces relatively more capital, then it is expanding its resource base more rapidly and, *ceteris paribus*, it will grow more rapidly.
3. C. Financial resources may be used to purchase real productive resources but are not themselves productive. Note that, to an economist, "investment" is the creation of real productive capacity, not merely the purchase of stock in a company.
4. C. To reach Point E the economy must grow, shifting out its ppf. This could occur if the labour force became more efficient.
5. D. This is an increasing cost ppf. As we increase the production of one good (butter), the cost in terms of the other good increases. In this case, a one-unit increase in butter (A to B) costs three guns; the move from B to C costs more (four guns).
6. A. Opportunity cost is defined (loosely) as the quantity of Good B given up to increase production of Good A. The quantity of butter remains at one unit while gun production is increased.
7. B. See the answer to Question 6. Opportunity cost of one unit of butter is zero at Point D. The opportunity cost of one unit of butter at Point C is five guns.
8. D. The ppf depicts what it is possible to produce but nothing about what is wanted. Therefore B is the odd one.
9. D. *Laissez-faire* economies respond well to the needs of private consumers, in general. One exception worth noting is the provision of public goods.
10. B. The opportunity cost is positive. A one-unit increase in wheat results in a three-unit decrease in tobacco production.
11. C. A two-unit increase in tobacco results in a one-unit decrease in wheat.
12. B. This point is inside the ppf. (We could be producing two more units of tobacco with the same amount of wheat production, for example.) This indicates that our resources are unemployed and/or inefficiently employed.

13. A. The labour-force expansion represents an increase in productive resources. Note that the ppf depicts what can be supplied—demand is not reflected in the diagram.
14. A. Parks, police, and defence, which become available to all once they become available, do not lend themselves to private sale and purchase as readily as cancer treatment. The benefits of treatment can be retained exclusively by the purchaser.
15. A. A general theme in economics is that private competition is highly efficient in providing most goods.
16. A. Opportunity cost is *always* positive. With a curving ppf, the cost of producing one good in terms of the other accelerates as production level increases.
17. A. Comparative advantage is a relative concept. If, relative to Jack, Jill is better at producing pins, then she has a comparative advantage in this.
18. D. The first three answers are statements of the three "basic" questions. They are all correct.
19. B. The cost of one unit of goat milk in Arbez is 1 and 2/3 unit of bananas while the cost of one unit of goat milk in Arboc is 1/3 unit of bananas. Arboc has the advantage here. One unit of bananas in Arbez costs 3/5 unit of goat milk while one unit of bananas in Arboc costs 3 units of goat milk. Arbez has the advantage in bananas.
20. A. A bowed-out ppf indicates increasing costs; the costs increase whether the movement is down along the ppf or up along the ppf.

II. SOLUTIONS TO APPLICATION QUESTIONS

1. a. Your ppf should include the following points:

Corn	100	90	70	40	0
Tobacco	0	40	70	90	100

There will be a straight line between each of the points.

b. Resources must be fully employed, and employed in the more efficient activity. For example, Field A may be producing its maximum output of tobacco, but (since the opportunity cost of tobacco production in that field is high) it should be used to produce tobacco only after the other fields have been switched over to tobacco production. If it is switched before Field B, for instance, Brown will be producing inefficiently and inside his ppf.

c. D, C, B, A.

d. See the explanation for b.

2. a, e. See the diagrams below.

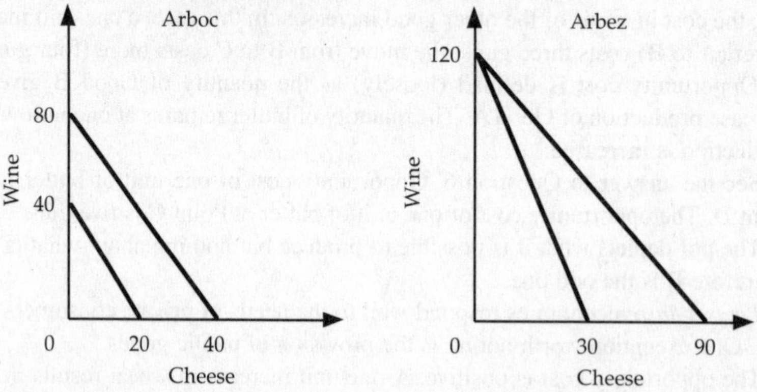

b. 1 wine = 1/2 cheese, 1 wine = 1/4 cheese.

c. Arbez.

d. 1 cheese = 2 wine (Arboc), 1 cheese = 4 wine (Arbez). Arboc can produce cheese more cheaply than Arbez can.

f. Arboc should still produce cheese since the comparative costs have not changed.

g. Arboc. Recompute the opportunity costs. Note that the relative steepness of the ppfs has changed.

3. a-b. This question is intended to get you to think about all of the decisions that must be made in an economic system. The owner has land, labour, and capital at his/her disposal. The capital stock includes the store, the gas station, inventories, trucks, the house, and so forth. The road is also capital even though it was produced by the government. We are not told much about the natural resources of the town. These would include the fertility of the land. The potential labour force includes some fraction of those who live nearby.

c. The people who travel the road, the general economic circumstances of the people who live nearby, the weather, gasoline prices, the potential for competition from other stores, and so forth.

d. What to sell, whether to advertise, what prices to change, whether to fix up the town, how many people to hire, and so forth.

e. I will add up all the future income I will earn, net of costs. I must consider all the alternatives and my expectations about them. How much will I earn here? How much will university cost? What am I likely to earn when I have graduated from university? I also need to consider carefully the personal pleasure I will derive from the two situations.

4. a. See the diagram below.

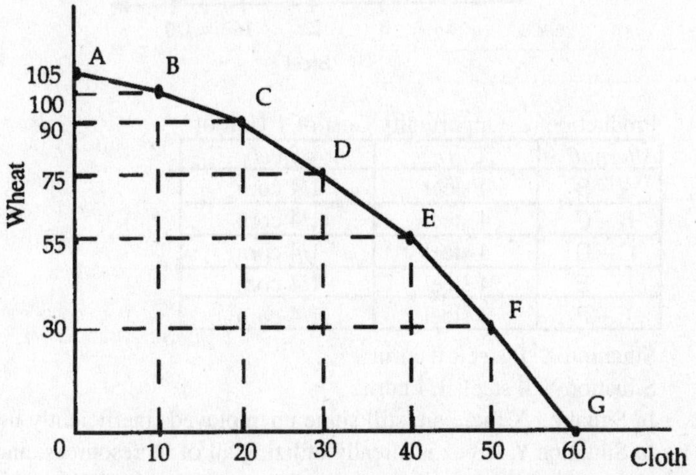

b. Point D is on the ppf, indicating full employment of resources, while Point H is inside the curve, indicating underproduction and an underutilization of scarce resources.

c. i. 1/2 unit of wheat.
ii. 1 unit of wheat.
iii. 21/2 units of wheat.
iv. 3 units of wheat.

d. i. 1/3 units of cloth.
ii. 2/3 units of cloth.
iii. 1 unit of cloth.
iv. 2 units of cloth.

5. a. No change in the position of the ppf.

b. The end of the ppf on the x-axis will shift out. The end on the y-axis will not move.

c. The ppf would shift inward.

d. The ppf would shift outward.

e. The end of the ppf on the x-axis will shift in. The end on the y-axis will not move.

6. a. You might think C and A are "best" and "worst," respectively—but the question is a trap. What do we mean by "best"? Perhaps a particular point inside the ppf is better than a particular point on it. There's not enough information to give a complete answer.
   b. Clearly, all points on the ppf are not created equal, and Point E might be the "best" choice of those depicted.
   c. The "best" output mix depends on what best meets society's wants. If you think about it, what society *wants* isn't shown on a ppf diagram—only what can be *produced*.
7. a. See the diagram below.

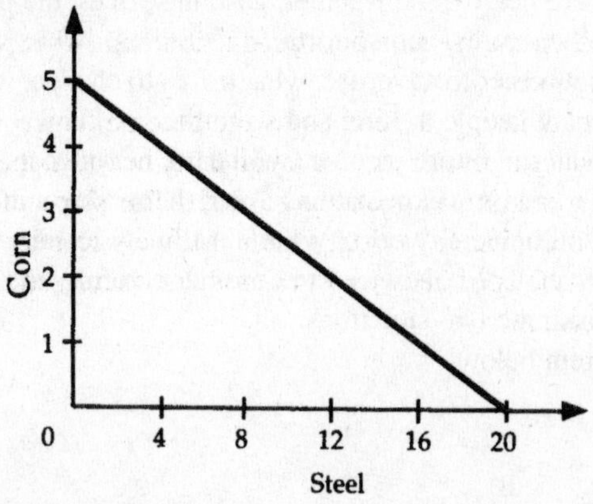

   b.

Production Alternative	Opportunity Cost of 1 Unit of: Corn	Steel
A – B	4 steel	1/4 corn
B – C	4 steel	1/4 corn
C – D	4 steel	1/4 corn
D – E	4 steel	1/4 corn
E – F	4 steel	1/4 corn

   c. Situation X: 0 steel; 0 corn.
   Situation Y: 4 steel; 1/4 corn.
   d. In Situation X there are still some unemployed (inefficiently used) resources. In Situation Y, Arbez is already utilizing all of its resources, and a trade-off is necessary. (Plot the points on the diagram to see the difference.)
   e. Situation Z: 1 steel; 0 corn.
   f. Situation Y is the most productively efficient. Either X or Z is the least productively efficient—we don't have enough information.
   g. Each unit of corn costs 4 units of steel; each unit of steel costs 1/4 unit of corn.
   h. Each unit of corn costs 2 units of steel. Each unit of steel costs 1/2 unit of corn.
   i. Arbez; Arboc. Yes, trade can be mutually beneficial.
8. a. D.
   b. The economy must either grow (more resources) or experience a technological improvement.
   c. C.
   d. Corn.
   e. There is no opportunity cost; more steel is produced without any reduction in corn production. Note that there are "free lunches" if the economy is operating at an inefficient point.
9. a. Yes.
   b. No, because it is possible to produce more of each good. Also some resources are unemployed.

c. No, not relative to Point A, where consumers would have more of each good available to them.

d. It is beyond the maximum level of production, given current resources and technology.

e. Resources would be released and transferred to steel production.

10. a. 2 units of wheat.

b. 1 1/4 units of wheat.

c. Arbez.

d. 1/2 unit of coffee.

e. 8/10 unit of coffee.

f. Arboc.

g. Arboc should specialize in wheat production and Arbez should specialize in coffee production.

11. The ppf would pivot at its "cloth" end point and become flatter, which indicates that it is possible to produce a greater maximum quantity of wheat than before, while still producing the same maximum quantity of cloth. The slope of the ppf represents opportunity cost. Producing only cloth means that we surrender a larger quantity of wheat than before—the opportunity cost of cloth has increased (and the opportunity cost of wheat has decreased).

12. a. See the diagram below.

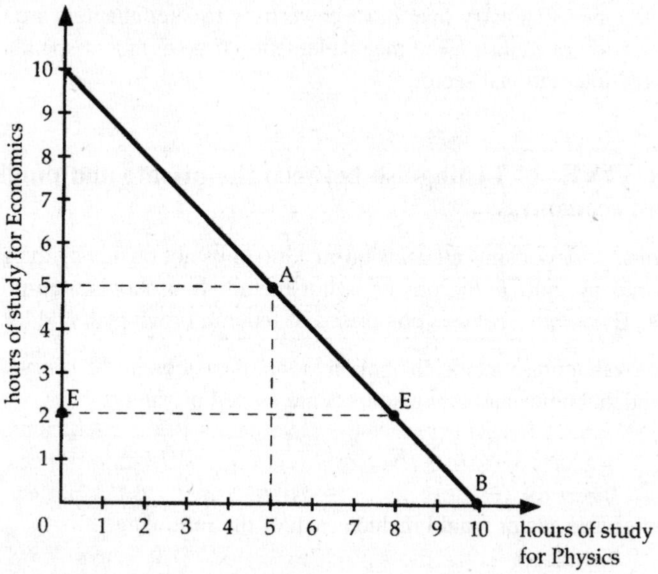

b. See the diagram above.

c. See the diagram above.

d. True. Economics: 40 + (10 x 2) = 60. Physics: 40 + (5 x 8) = 80.

e. True. Economics: 40 + (10 x 2) = 60. Physics: 40 + (5 x 8) = 80. If she gets 80 on the Physics test, 60 is the maximum she can get on the Economics test.

f. She has 6 hours for Physics. Physics: 40 + (5 x 6) = 70.

g. Economics: 40 + (10 x 2) = 60. Physics: 40 + (5 x 4) = 60. This totals 6 hours.

h. True. Economics: 40 + (10 x 3) = 70. Physics: 40 + (5 x 6) = 70. This totals 9 hours.

i. See the diagram above.

3 The Structure of the Canadian Economy: The Private, Public, and International Sectors

OBJECTIVES: POINT BY POINT

After completing this chapter, you should be able to accomplish the objectives listed below.

General Comment

This chapter contains a lot of facts and numbers. Try to look past these to the broader issues. The topics that carry over most powerfully to later chapters are those dealing with the organization of industry, the major elements of government spending and tax collection, and the international sector.

OBJECTIVE 1: Distinguish between the private and public sectors of the Canadian economy.

The *private sector* contains all decision-making units not owned by the government. These decision-making units in the private sector include households, non-profit organizations, and firms. The *public sector* is comprised of federal, provincial, and local governments.

The key private/public sector distinction is that decisions in the private sector are subject to independent choice and that resources are owned privately. (page 49)

Practice

1. The private sector would include each of the following
   A. Nortel.
   B. Noranda.
   C. Canada Post.
   D. both A and B.

   ANSWER: C. Canada Post is a Crown corporation. Although a Crown corporation is different from a government department, it is still accountable to its respective federal or provincial government, and therefore not part of the private sector.

2. The public sector would include each of the following organizations except
   A. the United Way, a charitable organization.
   B. the Federal Department of Finance.
   C. the office staff of your local MP.
   D. both B and C.

   ANSWER: D. The United Way is a private non-profit organization, and not part of the public sector. Both B and C are.

OBJECTIVE 2: Describe the diversity of consumption and production activities engaged in by Canadian households.

As consumers, Canadian households purchase a wide variety of goods and services dictated by their diverse tastes, preferences, and income. There are thousands of occupations in Canada. Some are high-paying jobs and some low-paying jobs. Furthermore, many Canadians earn income because of their ownership of real and financial assets, which are not evenly distributed.

When we look at the productive activities of Canadian households we notice even more dramatic diversity. There are as many specialized jobs requiring specialized tools or intellectual powers, as there are workers. (page 49)

Practice

3. The most popular category of occupation of Canadians, in 1996 was
   A. arts, culture, recreation and sport.
   B. business, finance, and administrative occupations.
   C. sales and service occupations.
   D. health occupation.

   ANSWER: C. There are over 3.7 million working in this sector, more than any other sector in this country, in 1996.

4. The highest income earners in Canada, in 1999 are
   A. lawyers.
   B. investment Dealers.
   C. plumbers.
   D. physicians.

   ANSWER: D. The average income of physicians in that year was more than $107,000—more than other income groups.

OBJECTIVE 3: Describe the three main legal forms taken by Canadian business firms.

Sole proprietors have the disadvantage of unlimited liability—their personal assets, outside the firm, might be taken if their company runs up sufficiently high debts. Advantage: The sole proprietors are their own boss and are free to follow their business instincts. Also, they keep all of the profits they make. Usually, *partnerships* have the same unlimited liability drawback. Indeed, perhaps it's worse—partners may be held responsible not only for their own debts, but also for those of their partners. Advantage: greater expertise and financial resources. *Corporations* have the advantage of limited liability because they exist as separate legal entities—XYZ, Inc. can be taken to court. If the firm runs up debts, the owners' maximum liability is the value of their stock investment. After-tax profits may be distributed as dividends or held by the company as retained earnings. A major disadvantage is that the corporation's management structure may become cumbersome. Also, owners of corporations are subject to double taxation. (page 52)

Practice

5. The most common form of business organization is
   A. the proprietorship.
   B. the partnership.
   C. perfect competition.
   D. the corporation.

   ANSWER: A. See page 52.

6. In terms of total economic activity, the most important form of business organization is
   A. the proprietorship.
   B. the partnership.
   C. monopoly.
   D. the corporation.

   ANSWER: D. See page 53.

7. The Cumfy Chair Corporation has a net income of $300 000 in 1998. Of this income, $160 000 is paid in taxes and $40 000 is retained to buy capital. The Cumfy Chair Corporation will pay dividends of
   A. $140 000.
   B. $120 000.
   C. $100 000.
   D. more than $100 000 but less than $140 000.

   ANSWER: C. Net income—the profits of a corporation—may be split up into corporate income tax payments, dividends, and retained earnings.

OBJECTIVE 4: State the main characteristics of the Canadian public sector.

The Canadian public sector is organized on a federal basis. The Canadian federal system has two levels of government, federal and provincial, enjoying a special constitutional status. The federal government has jurisdiction over national defence and an integrated economy and is responsible for employment insurance, old age security, and the Canadian Pension Plan. Provincial governments are responsible for medical care, social welfare and education.

There is a third level of government—municipal governments. Municipal governments do not have constitutional power and are subordinate to provincial governments. (page 56)

OBJECTIVE 5: Outline the sources of government revenue and the main areas of government expenditure.

The government is a major employer of resources and purchaser of goods. The federal government is the largest branch of government. Today, the largest components of federal spending are the interest payment on the national debt and transfers to persons and other levels of government; however, spending on goods and services—education, health and hospitals, and highways—is the main expenditure category for provincial and local governments.

The main sources of federal revenue, in order of importance, are personal income tax, general sales taxes, health and insurance levies, and corporate income tax. At the provincial and local levels, property taxes are immediately behind personal income tax. See Table 3.9. (page 59)

> **TIP:** Note the important distinction between government purchases and transfer payments—the former is a payment for goods and services received by the government; the latter is not. A welfare cheque is given precisely because the recipient is *not* providing a service.

Practice

8. The salary of your local MP is classified as
   A. a government transfer payment.
   B. a government interest payment.
   C. government spending.
   D. a government subsidy payment.

   ANSWER: C. Your local MP's salary (which he or she has earned for work performed) is government spending. A transfer payment is a payment that requires no good or service in return. Your member of Parliament would strongly resent the implication if you answered Option A.

9. The largest single source of federal revenue is
   A. sales taxes.
   B. property taxes.
   C. health and insurance levies.
   D. personal income tax.

   ANSWER: D. See Table 3.9 and p. 60.

10. The largest single source of provincial and local revenue is
   A. sales taxes.
   B. property taxes.
   C. corporate taxes.
   D. personal income taxes.

   ANSWER: D. See Table 3.9 and p. 60.

OTHER RELATED POINTS:

POINT 1: Describe and give reasons for the changing expenditure patterns within the three levels of government over the past decade.

A study of the structure of the Canadian public sector brings out three important features. First, the provincial/local/hospital sector is a much more important provider of goods and services than the federal government. The provincial governments have primary responsibility for health, social services, and roads. Second, the federal government is more active in directly transferring income than other levels of government combined. Finally, debt charges are most significant at the federal level. (page 57)

OBJECTIVE 6: Discuss the importance of international trade to Canada.

International trade has always played an important role in the growth of the Canadian economy. This role has become more significant in recent years. Canada's trade pact with Mexico and the United States, NAFTA, has contributed to the growth of our trade. (page 61)

Practice

11. In 1995 exports were ______ of GDP and imports were ______ of GDP.
   A. 25%, 18%.
   B. 28%, 20%.
   C. 30%, 15%.
   D. 43%, 40%.

   ANSWER: D. See p. 61.

PRACTICE TEST

I. MULTIPLE CHOICE QUESTIONS. Select the option that provides the single best answer.

_____ 1. Which of the following would not be included in the private sector?
A. The bookstore chain "Chapters."
B. Alcan Aluminum Ltd.
C. University of Victoria.
D. The local charity organization "Meals on Wheels."

_____ 2. The type of business organization with limited liability from debt for its owner(s) is a
A. proprietorship.
B. partnership.
C. corporation.
D. company.

_____ 3. Statement 1: "After all the corporation's expenses have been paid, the retained earnings are distributed to the stockholders."
Statement 2: "Welfare cheques are a part of transfer payments."
Statement 1 is ______; Statement 2 is _____________.
A. false, false.
B. true, true.
C. false, true.
D. true, false.

_____ 4. Government expenditures are made up of
A. government purchases, transfer payments, and interest payments.
B. government purchases, welfare payments, and national defence.
C. transfer payments, national defence, and employment benefits (EI).
D. transfer payments, tax payments, and interest payments.

_____ 5. The biggest single revenue earner for the federal government is the
A. personal income tax.
B. corporate income tax.
C. sales tax.
D. payroll tax.

_____ 6. As a percentage of GDP, the federal interest payment on the public debt _________ between 1970 and 1995.
A. has increased.
B. has decreased.
C. has remained unchanged.
D. has not been considered as a government outlay.

_____ 7. Which of the following is not a government transfer payment?
A. Old Age Security payments.
B. Employment insurance payments (EI).
C. Payments to the widow of a war veteran.
D. Payroll taxes payment by an employee.

II. APPLICATION QUESTIONS.

1. Are your local radio broadcasts a public good? Are Céline Dion's concerts a public good? Of the two goods, why is the market system more likely to underproduce radio broadcasts? In practice, how has radio reduced the problem of non-payers?

2. Suppose that you are a senior advisor to Federal Minister of Finance, Paul Martin. The government has committed to balancing the budget before the next election, and Mr. Martin asks you how this can be achieved. (Remember, if the current government is not returned to office, you lose your job!)

   Come up with three distinct policy recommendations. If the government cuts expenditures, where should the cuts fall? Be specific. Who would be hurt by such a proposal? Would it affect particular social or regional groups? Does the political power of a province, such as Ontario or Quebec, have any bearing on the political decision process? If taxes are to be raised, which ones? Again, who might be hurt by a specific tax hike? Should producers be taxed, or should consumers? Wage earners or investors? Are there any parts of the budget that are "not negotiable" (education or health care, for example)?

3. Give the advantages and disadvantages of organizing a firm as a
   a. proprietorship.
   b. partnership.
   c. corporation.
   d. Give an example of each form of business organization.

4. You are considering setting up a small business. Which factors would you take into account when deciding whether to establish a single proprietorship or a partnership?

5. Think up a simple business enterprise—such as doing yard work, typing term papers, opening a hot dog stand, or selling vitamins—and decide which would be the most appropriate form of legal organization for your firm. Why is this form of organization the best choice? List the drawbacks that might occur. How might you solve the problems? What advantages do the other forms of organization offer, for example? If you have a proprietorship, how would you feel about giving up control/ownership of "your" business to a group of unknown shareholders and about making decisions by committee?

   Major point: No single legal organization is always "best"—it depends upon the particular circumstances of the business and the objectives of the owner(s).

6. In a sense, the three levels of government specialize. For the federal government, Revenue Canada and Foreign Affairs and International Trade are major sources of employment. Why? Because there's a need for a "national" organization. At the provincial level, education, health, and highways are the main sources of employment. At the local level, fire, police, and sanitation (all "local" issues) are prominent.

   Now do a thought experiment: Try to imagine what would happen if Ottawa tried to control fire, police, and sanitation, while turning national defence over to local government. Not very efficient! Also, observe that the public sector can *complement* private endeavours through the provision of public goods (roads and education, for example) and through the enforcement of compliance with a legal system designed to protect the rights of private consumers and firms.

7. What are the three kinds of legal organization for the firm? List them and give your own example of the sort of firm you'd expect to find in each category.

8. List the four factors used in defining market organization. Into which market structure is entry easiest?

9. Which form of legal organization is most likely for each of the following businesses?
   a. Coca-Cola ____________
   b. an accounting firm ____________
   c. a legal firm ____________
   d. a plumbing firm ____________
   e. a car manufacturer ____________
   f. a small corn grower ____________
   g. a small convenience store ____________
   h. the Music Channel ____________
   i. a law firm ____________
   j. McDonald's ____________

   In each case, which factors led you to your answer, and what do you think is the main advantage that each firm derives from this form of organization?

ANSWERS AND SOLUTIONS

PRACTICE TEST

I. SOLUTIONS TO MULTIPLE CHOICE QUESTIONS

1. C. Universities in Canada are financed by the government.
2. C. Corporations have limited liability. See p. 52. Note that a partnership may have limited liability, but only in some cases.
3. C. Retained earnings are just that—retained (by the corporation). Welfare cheques are payments that do not require a service in return—i.e., transfers.
4. A. National defence is an element in government purchases, and welfare payments as well as EI are included in the more general category of "transfer payments."
5. A. Personal income taxes are now the largest component of federal revenues. See Table 3.9.
6. A. See Table 3.7.
7. D. This is a tax payment by an individual to the government.

II. SOLUTIONS TO APPLICATION QUESTIONS

1. Local radio broadcasts are a public good—my consumption does not diminish your consumption. A public concert is not a public good—if I buy a seat, fewer seats are available for others. The market system is likely to underproduce local radio because it is impossible to exclude non-payers. In practice, commercial radio does not sell programming to listeners; it sells listeners to advertisers who pay for advertising time.
2. The answer to this question is open to opinion. Most economists would claim that, to cut the deficit, the government must increase taxes or reduce transfer payments and expenditures.
3. a. proprietorship: advantages—the proprietor is his own boss, keeps all the profits, the firm is flexible, possible tax breaks
   disadvantages—unlimited liability, no pool of specialized experience at the top

b. partnership: advantages—pool of expertise
disadvantages—unlimited liability, less flexibility, greater need for consultation between partners

c. corporation: advantages—limited liability, market power, political power
disadvantages—possible lack of communication and coordination

d. proprietorship—corner grocery store; partnership—law firm; corporation—Petro-Canada.

4. The most important consideration is likely to be financial—can the business be started without outside help. Additionally, can the business be run effectively with only one individual in control—can a manager be hired?

5-6. The answer to each question is open to opinion.

7. Proprietorship, a family grocery store; partnership, a legal firm; corporation, a manufacturing firm.

8. Market organization (the way an industry is structured) is defined by how many firms there are in the industry, whether products are differentiated or are virtually the same, whether or not firms in the industry can control prices or wages, and whether or not competing firms can enter and leave the industry freely.

9. a. corporation.
b. partnership.
c. partnership.
d. proprietorship.
e. corporation.
f. proprietorship.
g. proprietorship.
h. corporation.
i. partnership.
j. corporation.

4 Demand, Supply, and Market Equilibrium

OBJECTIVES: POINT BY POINT

After completing this chapter, you should be able to accomplish the objectives listed below.

General Comment

The single best piece of advice, particularly for this essential chapter, is "practise, practise, practise." A second piece of advice must be "draw, draw, draw." Don't be put off by the graphs—try to develop a solid intuitive feel for demand and supply by talking your way through how the market should behave.

In most of the multiple choice questions in this chapter, the *first* thing to do is to start to sketch a demand and supply picture.

Get into the habit of asking "What should happen to demand?" and "Will this make supply increase or decrease?" Predict whether price should rise or fall in a given circumstance (common sense should carry you a long way here). Don't try to avoid graphs—they'll make your course a lot easier *and* more rewarding. If you have some initial problems, check the Appendix to Chapter 1 and the "Graphing Pointers" sections in this Guide.

OBJECTIVE 1: Describe the relationship between input and output markets in a simple market economy.

To produce goods and services, firms buy resources or inputs. The markets in which the resources (inputs) used to produce products (output) are exchanged are called input or factor markets. The markets in which goods and resources are exchanged are called product or output markets. (page 66)

OBJECTIVE 2: Explain the role of price and other factors in the basic theory of demand.

The willingness and ability of a household to buy units of a good (quantity demanded) are likely to depend principally on the price of the good itself. Other factors—including the household's income and wealth, the prices of other products, tastes and preferences, and expectations about price, income, and wealth—will influence demand.

> **Comment:** This section of the textbook will probably be your most frustrating section. Be patient—time spent understanding demand/supply analysis will serve you well in future chapters.

Quantity demanded is the amount of a product that a household would buy, in a given period, if it could buy all it wanted at the current price. The *law of demand* states that there is a negative relationship between the price and the quantity demanded of a product. When the price of McDonald's fries increases, we buy less.

A *demand schedule* is a table showing how much of a given product households would be willing and able to buy at different prices in a given time period; a *demand curve* shows this relationship graphically. Demand curves slope downward. (page 69)

> **Graphing Pointer:** These graphs *always* have price on the vertical axis and quantity (demanded or supplied, as appropriate) on the horizontal axis. It is a bad, though common, mistake to reverse the variables.

> **Graphing Pointer:** Learn to draw the demand and supply graphs quickly. A demand curve slopes down; a supply curve slopes up. Practise to increase your speed. Label each curve as you go. In diagrams where there are several curves, clear, consistent labelling is critical.

Practice

1.

Price per apple	Quantity demanded
60¢	30
50¢	35
40¢	50
30¢	55
20¢	70
10¢	80

Suppose the above is your demand schedule for apples. In the blank space to the right of the demand schedule, draw vertical (price) and horizontal (quantity) axes. Plot your monthly demand curve for apples. Label the curve D_1.

ANSWER: This line is unlikely to be smooth like those in the textbook, but it should have a general downward slope—the lower the price, the more you're likely to buy. You should have the horizontal axis labelled "quantity demanded" and the vertical axis labelled "price."

When you constructed your demand schedule and demand curve with varying price levels in Practice Question 1, you made assumptions about your income level, wealth, prices of other goods, and so on. Change the assumptions and you will change the diagram. The curve shifts position—*a change in demand.*

Factors that can cause a change in demand are:

a. income.
b. wealth.
c. prices of related products.
d. tastes or preferences of the household.
e. expectations.

Increases in income and wealth, improved preferences, or expectations of a higher price, income, or wealth will increase demand for normal goods. An increase in the price of a substitute product or a decrease in the price of a complementary product will also increase demand, i.e., the entire demand curve shifts to the right. Graphically, an increase in demand (D_1 to D_2) appears as shown below:

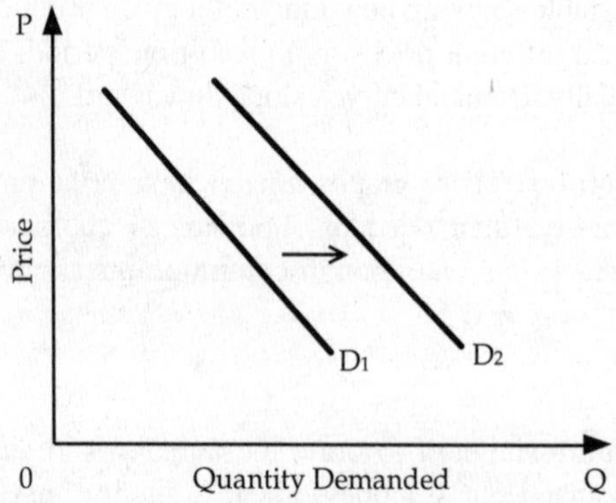

Tip: When shifting the demand or supply curve, think in terms of the curve sliding *left* for a decrease (demand less or supply less) and *right* for an increase (demand more or supply more), *not* up and down.

Graphing Pointer: You might naturally associate "rise" and "fall" with a vertical shift. This causes no problems in the case of demand, and you'd expect to be correct in using the same approach in the case of supply—but you'd be wrong.

OBJECTIVE 3: Distinguish between changes in quantity demanded (movements along the demand curve) and changes in demand (shifts in the demand curve).

When important factors other than the price of the product change, such as tastes or income, the entire demand curve shifts position. This is called a *change in demand* to distinguish it from a movement along the demand curve, which represents a *change in quantity demanded* and which can be caused *only* by a change in the price of the commodity. (page 73)

Graphing Pointer: Changes in Quantity Demanded (Supplied) vs. Changes in Demand (Supply). Some students experience confusion regarding the distinction between a "change in quantity demanded" and a "change in demand." Perhaps the distinction is rather artificial; the six factors (listed on page 75) that affect demand do include price of the product. However, we regard the price–quantity demanded relationship as the most important and draw the demand curve with these two variables on the axes, assuming that all other factors are fixed at a "given" level. This is the *ceteris paribus* assumption.

Look at a demand curve; price and quantity demanded can have a range of values while all other variables (income, other prices, etc.) are fixed at a particular level. If price changes, we move along the curve; if another factor changes, our *ceteris paribus* assumption is broken and we must redraw the price–quantity demanded relationship.

The *only* thing that can cause a "change in the quantity demanded" of Pepsi is a change in the price of Pepsi—a movement from one point on the demand curve to another point on the same demand curve.

Pointer, continued: If any other factor on the list changes, we will have to redraw the entire diagram—a "change in demand"—because the "all else being equal" assumption has been broken.

Similarly, a "change in the quantity supplied" of chicken can only be caused by a change in the price of chicken. A change in any other factor on the list on page 88 of the text causes a "change in supply."

Graphing Pointer: Remember—if you would do more of the activity (buying more, producing more) because of the change in a factor (demand, supply), draw a new curve to the right of the original curve. If you reduce the activity, draw the new curve to the left of the original curve.

TIP: Here is an example that points out the difference between a "change in quantity demanded" and a "change in demand." In the diagram below, we have a demand curve for Ford Rangers on the left and a demand curve for Dodge Rams on the right.

Initially, the price of the Ranger is $17 000 and 2000 are demanded per week. The Ram sells for $16 000 and has 2500 demanders at that price. (Note: It's irrelevant whether the Ram's price is above, below, or equal to that of the Ranger—at any realistic price, each truck will have some enthusiasts.)

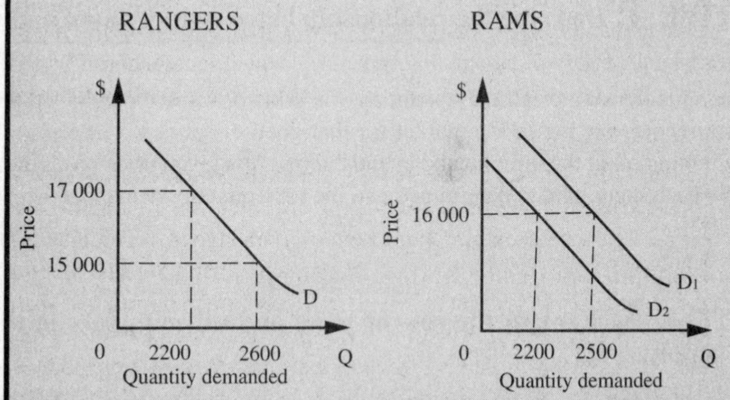

Suppose that the price of Rangers decreases to $15 000. More truck buyers will order Rangers—an increase in quantity demanded as there is a movement along the demand curve from *A* to *B*. Some of those new Ford customers would have bought the Dodge Ram but now will not. At the same price ($16 000) as before, demand for Rams has decreased, perhaps to 2200. The entire demand curve for Rams has shifted.

Practice

2. Return to Practice Question 1. Suppose that the prices of other fruits you might buy increase. What would happen to the number of apples you demand per month? Sketch this change on your diagram. Label the demand curve D_2. What is likely to happen to the price of apples?

   ANSWER: See your diagram for Practice Question 1. Presumably, you'd demand more apples at each price. The demand curve shifts right, to D_2. Because apples are more popular now, the price of apples will likely rise.

3. A "change in demand" means
   A. the quantity demanded changes as price changes.
   B. a movement along a given demand curve or schedule.
   C. a shift in the position of the demand curve.
   D. a change in the shape of a demand curve.

   ANSWER: C. A "change in demand" means that, at every price level, more or less is being demanded. This is represented as a shift in the position of the demand curve. See p. 73.

4. Which of the following will cause a decrease in the demand for tennis rackets?
   A. a rise in the price of squash rackets.
   B. a rise in the price of tennis rackets.
   C. a rise in the price of tennis balls.
   D. a fall in the price of tennis shoes.

   ANSWER: C. A decrease in the demand for tennis rackets will occur if a complement (tennis balls) increases in price because fewer tennis balls will be bought. See p. 72.

OBJECTIVE 4: Describe the relationship between individual and market demand.

Market demand is the sum of all the quantities of a good or service demanded per period by all the households buying in the market for that good or service. The *market demand curve* is a summing of all the individual demand curves. At a given price level, the quantity demanded by each household is determined and the total quantity demanded is calculated. (page 75)

OBJECTIVE 5: Explain the role of price and other factors in the basic theory of supply.

The decision to supply is affected by the ability to earn profits (that is, the difference between revenues and costs). The willingness and ability of a firm to offer units of a good for sale (quantity supplied) are likely to depend principally on the price of the good itself. If other factors important to producers change, then the supply curve diagram will change. The supply curve shifts position—a *change in supply.*

The quantity supplied is the amount of a product that a firm would be willing and able to offer for sale at a particular price during a given period of time. The law of supply states that there is a positive relationship between the price and the quantity supplied of a product. When McDonald's raises its hourly wage, we want to work more hours there.

A supply *schedule* is a table listing how much of a product a firm will supply at alternative prices in a given period; a supply curve shows this relationship graphically. A *supply curve* slopes upward. (page 78)

Factors that can cause a change in supply are:

a. changes in costs of production (input prices)
b. new costs and market opportunities
c. changes in prices of related products. (page 78)

Improvements in technology, decreases in the costs of inputs and other costs of production, or increases in the price of complementary products will increase supply. Decreases in the price of substitute products will also increase supply, i.e., the entire supply curve will shift to the right. Graphically, an increase in supply (S_1 to S_2) appears as shown below:

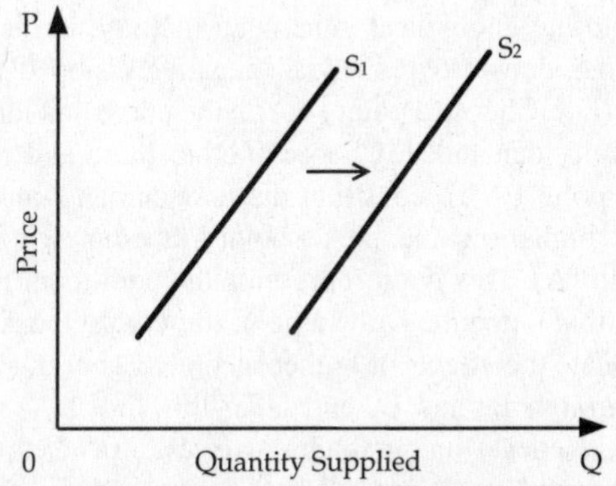

Graphing Pointer: At first glance, a leftward shift of a supply curve looks like the supply curve has moved up, but it's still a *decrease* in supply—at each price level, less is being supplied. Second, when considering if a given factor will cause supply to increase or decrease, ask "Will this change increase or decrease profits?" Producers will want to supply more if their profits are rising—so, if the answer to the question is "increase profits," you should predict an increase (rightward shift) in supply.

TIP: These lists of factors that can change demand or supply should be kept in a place very close to your heart. Write them on an index card and review them frequently.

Demand: Pick a good that you buy frequently (preferably a name brand), such as Petro-Canada gasoline. Do "thought experiments." What would your demand do if Petro-Canada hiked the price of its gas? If your income fell? If the price of engine oil (a complement) increased? If the price of Esso gas (a substitute) decreased?

Supply: Perhaps you have a part-time job—that is, you supply labour. Think of factors that would affect how many hours you would work per week. The wage (price) you earn would affect the quantity of labour you supply. What other factors would make you more or less willing and able to work?

TIP, continued: Note the reference to the *short run* and the *long run* on page 78. These are important economic concepts that you'll meet later on. Essentially, suppliers will be more responsive to demand-side changes in a longer time period than they will be in a shorter time period.

Graphing Pointer: The "change in demand" and "change in supply" concepts are tough; ask yourself, what would you do if the price of a good (say, steak) remains constant and your income rises substantially? If you would buy more steak, this is an increase in demand. To graph this change, draw a hypothetical (negatively sloped!) demand curve for steak (D_1). Choose a point (A_1) on the curve and identify the associated quantity demanded. Choose another price and repeat the operation with point B_1. To construct the new demand curve which results from the higher income, pick a point immediately to the right of A_1 and label it A_2. This point represents the additional purchases due to the additional income. Draw a point directly to the right of B_1 which will indicate the effects of higher income. Label this point B_2. Draw a line through B_1 and B_2 and label this line D_2—your new demand curve. Repeat this graphing exercise for each of your "thought experiments" mentioned above. As you practise this for all of the factors which change demand and supply, your mastery of graphical analysis will develop.

(These "thought experiments" will be easier for demand factors than for supply factors because you buy things every day while most of you are not producers. Once again, be patient and ask yourself: if you were a business owner committed to maximizing profits, how would you respond if your product's price remained the same but one of the supply factors changed?)

Graphing Pointer: Many students feel that a "curve" must be curved. Our demand and supply curves are models, however. Keep it simple—draw straight lines.

TIP: When you are told to imagine that income or some other variable has changed, imagine an *enormous* change—this will help you work out the effects. If a can of Pepsi has risen in price, suppose that it has tripled in price—it's easier to see what will happen to the quantity demanded or supplied of Pepsi and to the demand for Coke.

Practice

5. In the diagrams below, match each of the numbers with the appropriate term below to produce a correct demand or supply diagram for apples.
   A. Price of apples demanded.
   B. Price of apples supplied.
   C. Quantity of apples supplied.
   D. Quantity of apples demanded.
   E. Demand curve.
   F. Supply curve.

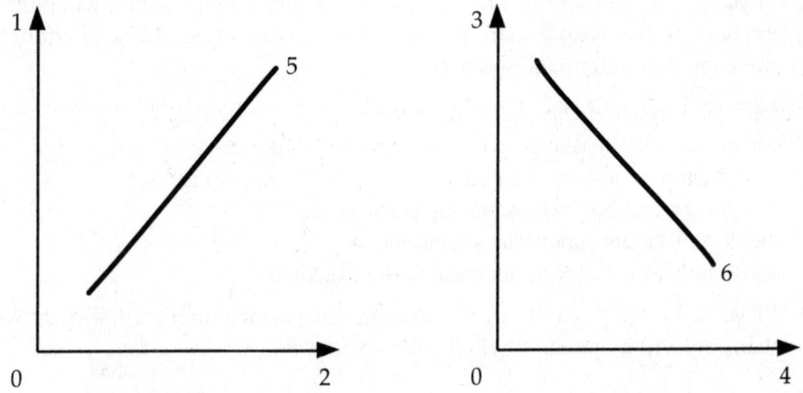

ANSWER: 1. B 4. D
2. C 5. F
3. A 6. E

6. A decrease in the supply of domestic cars might be caused by
   A. an increase in the price of imported Japanese cars.
   B. an increase in the wages of Canadian car workers.
   C. an increase in demand that causes car prices to rise.
   D. a reduction in the cost of steel.

   ANSWER: B. The supply of domestic cars will decrease if input prices, such as the wages of Canadian car workers, increase. See p. 79.

7. Energizer and Duracell's Coppertop batteries are substitutes. The Energizer Bunny increases the price of its batteries. Equilibrium price will ________ and quantity exchanged will _________ in the market for Duracell.
   A. rise, rise.
   B. fall, rise.
   C. fall, fall.
   D. rise, fall.

   ANSWER: A. If Energizer increases the price of its batteries, consumers will switch over to substitutes such as Duracell, increasing the demand for Duracell. This will raise both equilibrium price and quantity. See p. 85.

8. Bicycles and bicycle helmets are complements. The producers of helmets notice a decrease in the quantity of their products demanded (a movement along their demand curve). This could have been caused by
   A. a decrease in the income of helmet producers' customers.
   B. an increase in the price of these helmets.
   C. an increase in the price of bicycles.
   D. an increased expectation that manufacturers of bicycles will reduce the price of their bicycles in the near future.

   ANSWER: B. This is a change in quantity demanded, not a change in demand. The only thing that can cause a change in quantity demanded is a change in price. See p. 73.

9. As the price of oranges increases, orange growers will
   A. use more expensive methods of growing oranges.
   B. use less expensive methods of growing oranges.
   C. increase the supply of oranges.
   D. decrease the supply of oranges.

ANSWER: C. An increase in price results in an increase in quantity supplied. Suppliers are able to produce more because, at the higher price, they can afford to hire more expensive resources. See p. 80.

10. The supply of 4-cylinder cars will shift to the right if
    A. consumers switched over to 6 (and higher)-cylinder cars.
    B. manufacturers of 4-cylinder cars see the price of larger cars (6-cylinder and higher) decreasing permanently.
    C. the cost of labour inputs stays constant.
    D. consumers experience an increase in their income.

    ANSWER: B. As the price of larger cars drop, car manufacturers will switch over to another production option: 4-cylinder cars. See p. 86.

OBJECTIVE 6: Distinguish between changes in quantity supplied (movements along the curve) and changes in supply (shifts in the supply curve).

When important factors other than price change for a producer, the amount of a given product offered for sale will change even if the price level is unchanged. This is a *change in supply*. If *only* the price of the product itself changes, there will be a movement along the original supply curve—a *change in quantity supplied.* (page 80)

Practice

11. If the firms producing fuzzy dice for cars must obtain a higher price than they did previously to produce the same level of output as before, then we can say that there has been
    A. an increase in quantity supplied.
    B. an increase in supply.
    C. a decrease in supply.
    D. a decrease in quantity supplied.

    ANSWER: C. Draw the supply curve. At the same output level and at a higher price, the supply curve has shifted to the left—a decrease in supply. See p. 80.

12. The market supply curve for wheat depends on each of the following except
    A. the price of wheat-producing land.
    B. the price of production alternatives for wheat.
    C. the tastes and preferences of wheat consumers.
    D. the number of wheat farmers in the market.

    ANSWER: C. Tastes and preferences are determinants of demand, not supply. See p. 78.

OTHER IMPORTANT POINTS.

POINT 1: Provide explanations for the slope of a typical demand curve.

Demand curves slope down—as price rises, quantity demanded falls. We know this intuitively, but economists have explored this important relationship ("social law") more analytically. The higher the price of a good, low-fat milk, for instance, the higher the opportunity cost of buying it, (i.e., the more of other goods we will give up, and the less willing we will be to buy low-fat milk).

Utility is a conceptual measure of satisfaction. Successive units of a good bestow satisfaction, but typically at a decreasing rate—the second cup of coffee may be less enjoyable than the first. Accordingly, the price we will be willing to pay will decrease.

As the price of steak rises, you become poorer because your food dollar can't stretch as far as it did before (this is called the *income effect*), and you seek cheaper substitutes such as chicken (this is called the *substitution effect*). Both effects result in a decrease in the quantity demanded of steak as its price increases. (page 69/70)

Practice

13. The demand curve has
    A. "price" on the vertical axis, "quantity demanded per time period" on the horizontal axis, and an upward sloping demand curve.
    B. "price" on the horizontal axis, "quantity demanded per time period" on the vertical axis, and an upward sloping demand curve.
    C. "price" on the vertical axis, "quantity demanded per time period" on the horizontal axis, and a downward-sloping demand curve.
    D. "price" on the horizontal axis, "quantity demanded per time period" on the vertical axis, and a downward-sloping demand curve.

    ANSWER: C. See p. 70.

14. We are trying to explain the law of demand. When the price of pretzels rises,
    A. the opportunity cost of pretzels increases along the demand curve.
    B. sellers switch production and increase the quantity supplied of pretzels.
    C. income rises for producers of pretzels.
    D. the opportunity cost of other goods increases.

    ANSWER: A. See p. 69.

POINT 2: Distinguish the relationship that exists between two goods that are substitutes and the relationship that exists between two goods that are complements.

If, when the price of Good A rises, the demand for Good B also rises, then A and B are *substitutes*; however, if the demand for B falls when the price of A rises, then A and B are *complements*. (page 72)

> **TIP:** Think of several ready-made examples of substitute goods and complementary goods from own life. Working with your own examples (e.g., during an exam) makes it easier to work through the analysis correctly. Here are a few examples:
>
> **Substitutes:** Coke and Pepsi, pre-recorded audiotapes and CDs.
>
> **Complements:** peanut butter and jelly, CDs and CD players, cars and gasoline, cameras and film, left and right shoes.

Practice

15. The demand for Kraft peanut butter will decrease if there is
    A. an increase in the price of Kraft peanut butter.
    B. an increase in the price of Equality, the Dominon Store brand of peanut butter.
    C. a decrease in the demand for jelly.
    D. an increase in the price of bread.

    ANSWER: D. Bread and peanut butter are complements. An increase in the price of bread will result in less bread being bought and a lower demand for Kraft to spread on it. See p. 72.

16. Good A and Good B are substitutes for one another. An increase in the price of A will
    A. increase the demand for B.
    B. reduce the quantity demanded of B.
    C. increase the quantity demanded of B.
    D. reduce the demand for B.

    ANSWER: A. Suppose A is Coke and B is Pepsi. If Coke rises in price, we would buy less Coke (a fall in quantity demanded of Coke) and more of Pepsi (an increase in the demand for Pepsi). See p. 71-72.

POINT 3: Distinguish between a good that is normal and a good that is inferior.

When income increases, demand increases for *normal* goods. If demand for a good decreases when income increases, then the good is *inferior*. (pages 71-72)

> **TIP:** Think of several ready-made examples of both normal goods and inferior goods from your own life. Working with your own examples (during an exam, for instance) makes it easier to work through the analysis correctly. Here are a few examples:
>
> **Normal goods:** movie tickets, steak, and more expensive imported beers.
>
> **Inferior goods:** second-hand clothes, store-brand (versus name-brand) foods, generic medicines, rice, beans, bus rides.

Practice

17. You expect your income to rise. For a normal good, this would result in
    A. an increase in quantity demanded and a fall in price.
    B. an increase in demand and a fall in price.
    C. an increase in quantity demanded and a rise in price.
    D. an increase in demand and a rise in price.

    ANSWER: D. If you expect your income to rise, you will demand more of a normal good. This will cause the price to increase. See p. 71.

18. The demand for Good A has been increasing over the past year. Having examined the following facts, you conclude that Good A is an inferior good. Which fact led you to that conclusion?
    A. The price of Good A has been increasing over the past year.

B. An economic slowdown has reduced the income of the traditional buyers of Good A.
C. Good B, a substitute for Good A, has cut its price over the past twelve months.
D. Household wealth has increased among the traditional buyers of Good A.

ANSWER: B. Inferior goods experience increasing popularity as income levels fall. See p. 72.

19. Turnips are available in both Canada and in Mexico. During the past year, incomes have grown by 10% in each country. The demand for turnips has grown by 12% in Canada and 3% in Mexico. We can conclude that turnips are
A. normal goods in Canada and normal goods in Mexico.
B. normal goods in Canada and inferior goods in Mexico.
C. inferior goods in Canada and normal goods in Mexico.
D. inferior goods in Canada and inferior goods in Mexico.

ANSWER: A. In each case, demand has increased as income has increased. See p. 72.

OBJECTIVE 7: Describe the relationship between individual and market supply.

The market supply is a horizontal summing of all the supply curves for a given product. (page 83)

OBJECTIVE 8: Describe the three market outcomes: excess demand, excess supply, and equilibrium.

If the quantity demanded is greater than the quantity supplied of a good, there is *excess demand*, and we would expect the price of that good to rise. If quantity supplied is greater than the quantity demanded of a good, there is an *excess supply*, and we would expect the price of that good to fall. (pages 81–86)

Practice

20. When there is an excess supply, quantity supplied _________ quantity demanded. Price will _____________.
A. exceeds, rise.
B. is less than, fall.
C. is less than, rise.
D. exceeds, fall.

ANSWER: D. An excess supply occurs when quantity supplied exceeds quantity demanded. This excess supply will force price down. See p. 84.

21. The equilibrium price of a litre of unleaded gas is 50¢. At a price of 45¢
A. quantity supplied will be less than quantity demanded, causing an excess demand for unleaded gas.
B. quantity supplied will be greater than quantity demanded, causing an excess supply of unleaded gas.
C. quantity supplied will be greater than quantity demanded, causing an excess demand for unleaded gas.
D. quantity supplied will be less than quantity demanded, causing an excess supply of unleaded gas.

ANSWER: A. If the current price is less than the equilibrium price, an excess demand will occur (quantity supplied will be less than quantity demanded). This excess demand will force price to increase.

OBJECTIVE 9: Use the demand/supply market equlibrium model to analyze the impact of market changes on market prices, sales, and expenditures.

In the market for a particular good or service, quantity demanded may be greater than, less than, or equal to quantity supplied. *Equilibrium* occurs when quantity demanded equals quantity supplied. There is no tendency for the price to change because, at that price, there is a perfect match between the quantity of the good demanded and the quantity supplied. (page 81)

TIP: Equilibrium. The notion of equilibrium is important throughout the remainder of the course. The simple, less analytical, way to think about this concept is as "the point where the lines cross." It will help your understanding if you remember that equilibrium is the "balance" situation in which there is no tendency for change—unless some outside factor intervenes.

Graphing Pointer: Sometimes demand and supply will change position simultaneously. If the magnitudes of the shifts are unknown, then either the effect on equilibrium price or on equilibrium quantity *must* be uncertain. It's easy to forget this important fact, particularly when demand and supply are still new concepts to you. See the following Tip for assistance.

TIP: Changes in Equilibrium Price and Quantity. If demand and supply change position simultaneously, break down each situation into two separate graphs, one for the "demand shift" and the other for the "supply shift." In each case, decide the direction of change in price and quantity, and then add them together.

Example: Demand decreases and supply increases.

	Price Change	Quantity Change
Demand-side effect	decrease	decrease
Supply-side effect	decrease	increase
Total effect	decrease	uncertain

In this case, where demand decreases and supply increases, we predict a certain decrease in price and an uncertain change in equilibrium quantity.

Graphing Pointer: A change in price does not cause the demand curve or the supply curve to shift position. Analyze the following sequence of events for errors. "Demand goes up. That makes price go up, which encourages sellers to supply more. But, when more is supplied, price goes down. When price goes down, demand goes up again, and so on."

ANSWER: A demand increase from D_1 to D_2 will make price rise from P_1 to P_2. Sellers will supply more from Q_1 to Q_2 —an increase in *quantity supplied*, not an increase in supply, as the statement claims. Price, therefore, will *not* go back down. The remainder of the statement is incorrect. Draw this example.

Practice

22. Equilibrium quantity will certainly decrease if
    A. demand and supply both increase.
    B. demand and supply both decrease.
    C. demand decreases and supply increases.
    D. demand increases and supply decreases.

    ANSWER: B. A decrease in demand will decrease equilibrium quantity. Similarly, a decrease in supply will decrease equilibrium quantity.

23. The market for canned dog food is in equilibrium when
    A. the quantity demanded is less than the quantity supplied.
    B. the demand curve is downsloping and the supply curve is upsloping.
    C. the quantity demanded and the quantity supplied are equal.
    D. all inputs producing canned dog food are employed.

    ANSWER: C. A market is in equilibrium when price has adjusted to make the quantity demanded and the quantity supplied equal. See p. 81.

24. Equilibrium price will certainly increase if
    A. demand and supply both increase.
    B. demand and supply both decrease.
    C. demand decreases and supply increases.
    D. demand increases and supply decreases.

    ANSWER: D. An increase in demand will increase equilibrium price. Similarly, a decrease in supply will increase equilibrium price.

25. In the market for mushrooms, the price of mushrooms will certainly increase if
    A. the supply curve shifts right and the demand curve shifts right.
    B. the supply curve shifts right and the demand curve shifts left.
    C. the supply curve shifts left and the demand curve shifts right.
    D. the supply curve shifts left and the demand curve shifts left.

    ANSWER: C. When demand increases and supply decreases, both shifts are prompting a price increase.

OBJECTIVE 10 (APPENDIX 4A): Use simple algebra to represent demand, supply, and market equilibrium.

As the Appendix shows, supply and demand can be analyzed using algebra. Application Question 5 below is an example.

PRACTICE TEST

I. MULTIPLE CHOICE QUESTIONS. Select the option that provides the single best answer.

_____ 1. Households are
A. suppliers in the input market.
B. demanders in the labour market.
C. suppliers in the product market.
D. demanders in the input market.

_____ 2. Good C increases its price. The demand for Good D increases. The goods are
A. complements.
B. substitutes.
C. normal.
D. inferior.

_____ 3. The demand for CDs is down-sloping. Suddenly the price of CDs rises from $8 to $10. This will cause
A. demand to shift to the left.
B. demand to shift to the right.
C. quantity demanded to increase.
D. quantity demanded to decrease.

_____ 4. Which of the following will cause a movement along the supply curve of Frisbees?
A. an increase in price of Frisbees.
B. an improvement in the production processes used to manufacture Frisbees.
C. a reduction in the price of plastic from which Frisbees are made.
D. an improvement in storage resulting in fewer defective Frisbees.

_____ 5. Along a given supply curve for eggs
A. supply increases as price increases.
B. supply increases as technology improves.
C. quantity supplied increases as price increases.
D. quantity supplied increases as technology improves.

_____ 6. Price is currently below equilibrium. There is a situation of excess __________. We would expect price to __________.
A. demand, rise.
B. demand, fall.
C. supply, rise.
D. supply, fall.

_____ 7. You expect income to rise. For a normal good, this would result in
A. an increase in quantity demanded and a fall in price.
B. an increase in demand and a fall in price.
C. an increase in quantity demanded and a rise in price.
D. an increase in demand and a rise in price.

_____ 8. The price of Frisbees (a normal good) will definitely increase if
A. there is an improvement in the technology of making Frisbees and Frisbees become more popular.
B. the cost of plastic used to produce Frisbees increases and people have more leisure time to throw Frisbees.
C. Frisbee workers negotiate a wage increase and boomerangs (a Frisbee substitute) decrease in price.
D. a sales tax is imposed on Frisbees and (because of widespread unemployment) incomes fall.

_____ 9. A rightward shift in the supply of domestic cars might be due to
A. an increase in the price of steel.
B. a reduction in foreign competition.
C. the introduction of cost-saving robots.
D. increased popularity of foreign cars.

_____ 10. If the market is initially in equilibrium, a technological improvement will cause price to _________ and quantity demanded to ________.
A. fall, fall.
B. rise, rise.
C. fall, rise.
D. rise, fall.

_____ 11. The price of beans rises sharply. Which of the following cannot be true?
A. The supply of beans may have decreased with no change in the demand for beans.
B. The demand for beans may have increased with no change in the supply of beans.
C. The demand for beans may have increased with an increase in the quantity supplied of beans.
D. The supply of beans may have increased with an increase in the quantity demanded of beans.

_____ 12. The market for peas is experiencing an excess supply. You should predict that
A. price will increase, quantity demanded will fall, and the quantity supplied will rise.
B. price will increase, quantity demanded will rise, and the quantity supplied will fall.
C. price will decrease, quantity demanded will rise, and the quantity supplied will fall.
D. price will decrease, quantity demanded will fall, and the quantity supplied will rise.

_____ 13. Equilibrium price will certainly decrease if
A. demand and supply both increase.
B. demand and supply both decrease.
C. demand decreases and supply increases.
D. demand increases and supply decreases.

_____ 14. If a demander demands less of a product at each possible price, there has been
A. a decrease in the quantity demanded.
B. a decrease in demand.
C. an increase in demand.
D. an increase in the quantity demanded.

_____ 15. Frito Lay Chips and Knorr's Dip are complements. Costs of chip production fall. At the same time, a government health report alleges that dip consumption causes bone cancer. For Knorr's Dip, the equilibrium price will __________, and the equilibrium quantity will __________.
A. fall, be indeterminate.
B. be indeterminate, rise.
C. be indeterminate, fall.
D. be indeterminate, be indeterminate.

_____ 16. Suppose there is a simultaneous increase in the demand for legal secretaries and a decrease in the supply of legal secretaries. If there is no change in the wage paid to legal secretaries
A. there will be an excess demand for legal secretaries.
B. there will be an excess supply of legal secretaries.
C. law firms will have no difficulty in hiring the desired number of legal secretaries at the current wage.
D. the supply of legal secretaries will decrease even more.

Use the diagram below to answer the next six questions. The diagram refers to the demand for and supply of hot dogs. The hot dog market is initially in equilibrium at Point A. Assume that hot dogs are a normal good.

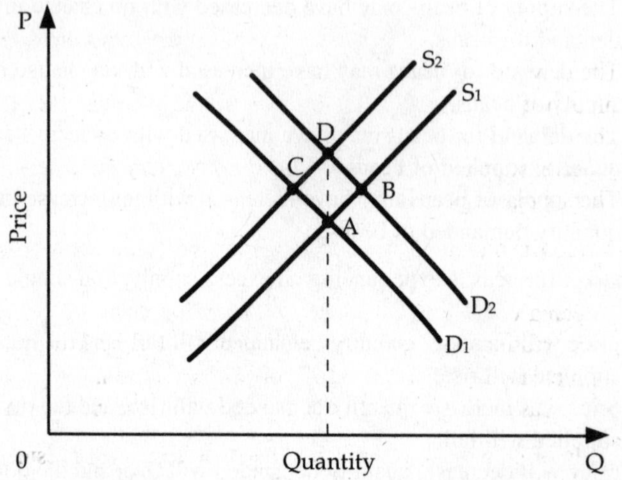

_____ 17. The hot dog market moves from Point A to a new equilibrium at Point B. There has been
A. an increase in demand and an increase in supply.
B. an increase in demand and an increase in quantity supplied.
C. an increase in quantity demanded and an increase in quantity supplied.
D. an increase in quantity demanded and an increase in supply.

_____ 18. The movement from Point A to Point B might have been caused by
 A. an increase in the price of hamburgers (a substitute for hot dogs). $P_H \uparrow Q_{D_H} \downarrow \quad Q_{D_D} \uparrow$
 B. an increase in the price of fries (a complement for hot dogs).
 C. a new widespread belief that meat products are bad for the heart. $Q_{D_D} \downarrow$
 D. a decrease in the price of ketchup (an ingredient used in making hot dogs). $\downarrow P_D \uparrow Q_{D_D}$

_____ 19. The hot dog market moves from Point A to a new equilibrium at Point C. There has been
 A. a decrease in demand and a decrease in supply.
 B. a decrease in demand and a decrease in quantity supplied.
 C. a decrease in quantity demanded and a decrease in quantity supplied.
 D. a decrease in quantity demanded and a decrease in supply.

_____ 20. The movement from Point A to Point C might have been caused by a
 A. decrease in the price of hamburgers (a substitute for hot dogs). $P_H \downarrow Q_{D_H} \uparrow \quad Q_{D_D} \downarrow$
 B. tightening of sanitary regulations required for the preparation of hot dogs. $costs \uparrow \quad S \downarrow$
 C. decrease in the wages of workers in the hot dog industry.
 D. decrease in the price of hot dog buns.

_____ 21. The hot dog market moves from Point A to a new equilibrium at Point D. There has been
 A. an increase in demand and an increase in supply.
 B. an increase in demand and a decrease in supply.
 C. a decrease in demand and an increase in supply.
 D. a decrease in demand and a decrease in supply.

_____ 22. The movement from Point A to Point D might have been caused by
 A. an increase in the price of hot dogs and no change in the equilibrium quantity of hot dogs.
 B. an expected increase in the income of hot dog consumers and a hike in the wages of hot dog preparers.
 C. an expected decrease in the price of hot dogs and an increase in the cost of making hot dogs.
 D. a decrease in the income of hot dog consumers and a reduction in the cost of making hot dogs.

_____ 23. Generic aspirin is an inferior good. As Pierre's income decreases, we would expect
 A. a decrease in Pierre's demand for generic aspirin.
 B. an increase in Pierre's quantity demanded of generic aspirin.
 C. an increase in Pierre's demand for generic aspirin.
 D. a decrease in Pierre's quantity demanded of generic aspirin.

_____ 24. The supply of computer software packages increases. As a result, the demand for personal computers rises. These two goods are _____. The price of microchips, used to produce personal computers, will _____.
 A. substitutes, increase.
 B. substitutes, decrease.
 C. complements, increase.
 D. complements, decrease.

_____ 25. Along a given demand curve for corn, which of the following is not held constant?
A. The price of corn.
B. The income of corn farmers.
C. The income of corn demanders.
D. The price of wheat.

_____ 26. The law of demand is best illustrated by
A. the price of Pepsi rising, leading consumers to buy more Coke.
B. increased purchases of Coke as the price of Coke decreases.
C. an increase in income which results in reduced purchases of store-brand soft drinks.
D. an increase in income which results in increased purchases of Coke.

Use the table below to answer the next three questions. The table refers to the demand for and supply of tuna.

Price of Tuna	Quantity Demanded	Quantity Supplied
90¢	30	80
80¢	45	70
70¢	60	60
60¢	75	50
50¢	90	40
40¢	105	30

_____ 27. The equilibrium price is ______ and the equilibrium quantity is _______.
A. 70¢, 60.
B. 60¢, 75.
C. 60¢, 50.
D. 70¢, 70.

_____ 28. There would be an excess demand for tuna if the price were at
A. 90¢.
B. 80¢.
C. 70¢.
D. 60¢.

_____ 29. If the price were 80¢, there would be
A. an excess demand of 70.
B. an excess demand of 25.
C. an excess supply of 25.
D. an excess supply of 70.

_____ 30. New costly regulations to protect workers are introduced in the production of tuna. We would expect the equilibrium price of tuna to ________ and the equilibrium quantity of tuna to ________.
A. increase, increase.
B. increase, decrease.
C. decrease, increase.
D. decrease, decrease.

II. APPLICATION QUESTIONS

1. Consider the following information regarding the quantity of cardboard demanded and supplied per month at a number of prices.

Price per square metre	Quantity demanded	Quantity supplied
40¢	39 000	83 000
35¢	48 000	78 000
30¢	58 000	74 000
25¢	67 000	67 000
20¢	75 000	62 000
15¢	81 000	59 000

a. What is the equilibrium price? What is the equilibrium quantity?
b. Describe the situation when the price is at 40¢ per square metre and predict what will happen.
c. Describe the situation when the price is at 15¢ per square metre and predict what will happen.
d. Explain what would happen if a serious transport strike reduced cardboard quantity supplied (at each price) by 30 000 square metres.

2. Pita bread is a normal good. What will happen to the equilibrium price and quantity of pita bread in each of the following situations?
a. Due to a recession, households which buy pita bread experience a decrease in income.
b. The cost of wheat used in pita bread increases significantly.
c. Bakeries buy improved ovens that reduce the costs of pita bread.
d. The prices of other types of bread fall.
e. Consumers become health conscious and switch to low-calorie breads.

3. How will each of the following changes affect the supply of hamburgers?
a. There is an increase in the price of hamburger buns (used in the production of burgers).
b. There is an increase in the price of hamburgers.
c. Producers discover that the price of cheeseburgers is increasing.

4. Pietro Cavalini sells ice cream at the beach. He is in competition with numerous other vendors. How will each of the following changes affect the demand for Pietro's ice cream?
a. Hot dog vendors reduce the price of hot dogs. Hot dogs are substitutes for ice cream.
b. The cost of refrigeration decreases.
c. Fine weather attracts record crowds to the beach.

5. The market for video cassettes has supply and demand curves given by $Qs = 3P$ and $Qd = 60 - 2P$, respectively.
a. Complete the following table.

Price	Quantity Demanded	Quantity Supplied
$30	______	______
$25	______	______
$20	______	______
$15	______	______
$10	______	______
$ 5	______	______
$ 0	______	______

b. Calculate the equilibrium price and quantity. You can do this either by graphing the curves or algebraically.
c. Suppose that the current market price is $20. Calculate the number of units that will be traded.

d. Suppose that the demand equation changed to Qd = 80 − 2P. Is this an increase or a decrease in demand? Suggest what might have caused such a change.

e. Calculate the new equilibrium price and quantity.

6. Here is a demand and supply schedule for bread in Lethbridge, Alberta.

Price ($)	Quantity Demanded	Quantity Supplied
5.00	1000	6000
4.50	1300	4500
4.00	1600	4000
3.50	2000	3500
3.00	3000	3000
2.50	3200	2700
2.00	4000	2200
1.50	4500	1800
1.00	5400	1400
.50	7000	1200

a. Find equilibrium price and equilibrium quantity.

b. Graph the demand (D_1) and supply (S_1) schedules in the space below and confirm the equilibrium values.

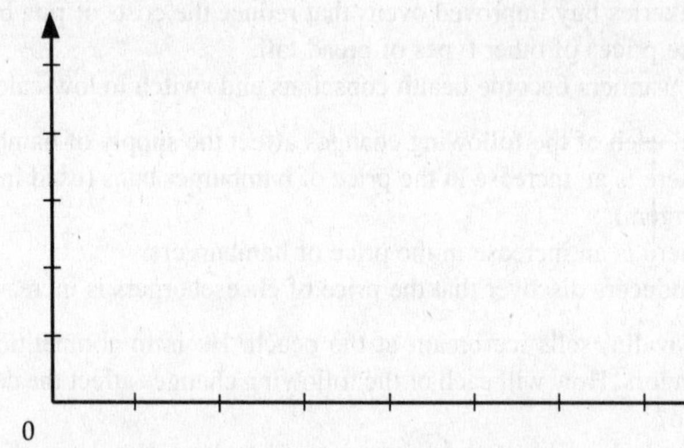

c. At a price of $1, is there an excess demand or supply? How great is the excess?

Suppose supply increases by 1800 units at each price level.

d. Draw the new supply curve (S_2) on the graph in b. above.

e. At the original equilibrium price level, is there an excess demand or an excess supply?

f. What will now happen to price, quantity demanded, and quantity supplied?

7. The diagram below shows the labour market. D is the demand for labour and S is the supply. The minimum wage is $6.85, and unemployment is 150 workers.

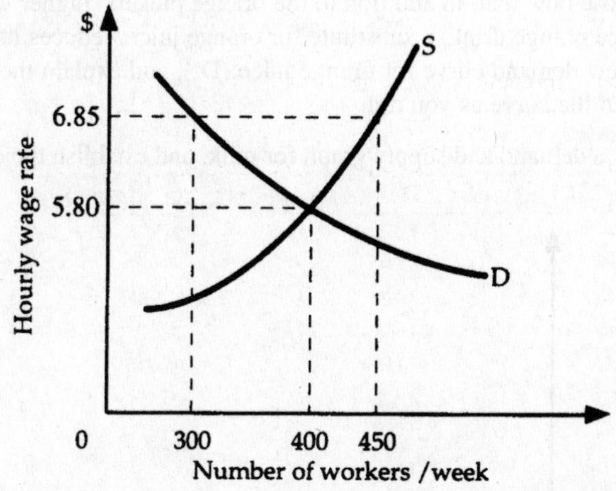

If the minimum wage law was revoked, the wage would fall to an equilibrium level of \$5.80, and there would be no unemployment because quantity demanded would be equal to quantity supplied. However, the number of workers demanded would rise by only 100, not 150. Reconcile this apparent contradiction.

8. Here are the demand schedules for orange juice for 3 buyers in the orange juice market and the supply schedules for 3 sellers in the orange juice market.

Price/ litre	Quantity demanded by: Brown	Black	White	Quantity supplied by: Gray	Green	Scarlett
\$5.00	1	0	0	5	10	14
\$4.00	3	2	0	4	7	9
\$3.00	7	5	4	3	6	7
\$2.00	9	9	5	0	4	5
\$1.00	11	12	7	0	0	1

a. Graph market demand (D_1) and market supply (S_1).

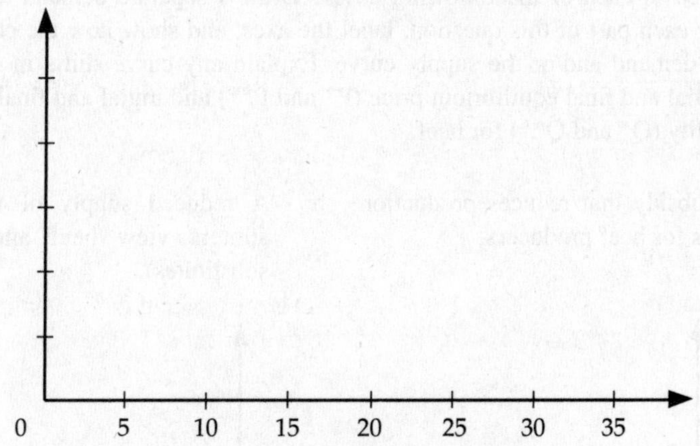

b. Show equilibrium price (P*) and quantity (Q*).

c. Now suppose the farm workers who pick oranges are given a higher wage rate. Show on your graph the changes that will occur in the orange juice market. Label any new demand curve D_2 and supply curve S_2. Discuss why curves shift, why price changes, and the significance of excess demand or excess supply. Note that you don't have the data to draw precise curves.

d. Suppose now that, in addition to the orange pickers' higher wage rate, Master Choice orange drink, a substitute for orange juice, reduces its price. Sketch in the new demand curve for orange juice (D_3), and explain the reason why you moved the curve as you did.

9. a. Draw a demand and supply graph for milk, and establish the equilibrium price (P*).

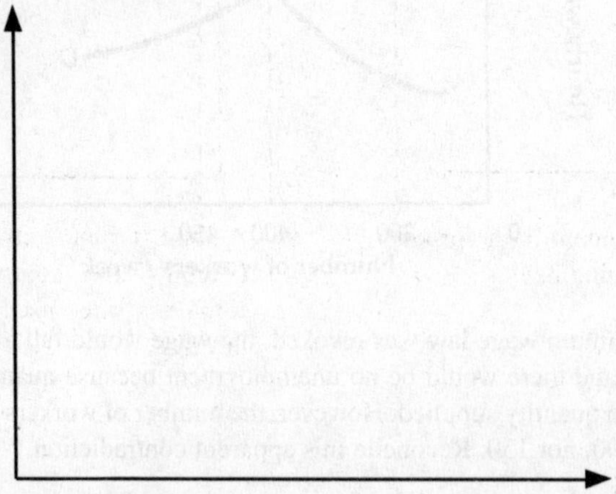

b. There is an increase in demand for milk (from D_1 to D_2). How will this change affect the equilibrium price?

c. In terms of the diagram you just sketched, what is the only way that the equilibrium price can increase, if the supply curve doesn't shift?

d. Draw in the new demand curve. Now trace through the process by which a new equilibrium is established.

On one diagram, you can display the distinction between a change in demand and a change in quantity demanded.

10. Assume that beef is a normal good. What happens to the amount of beef demanded or supplied in each of the following cases? Draw a separate demand and supply graph for each part of this question, label the axes, and show how the change will shift the demand and/or the supply curve. Explain any curve shifts in each case. Show initial and final equilibrium price (P* and P**) and initial and final equilibrium quantity (Q* and Q**) for beef.

a. A subsidy that reduces production costs for beef producers.

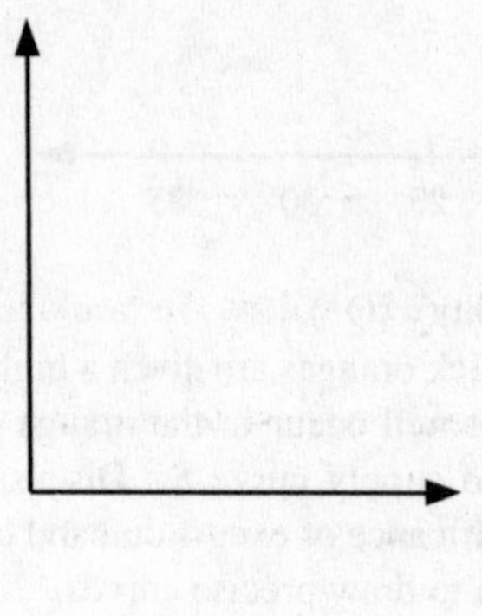

b. A reduced supply of fish (consumers view beef and fish as substitutes).

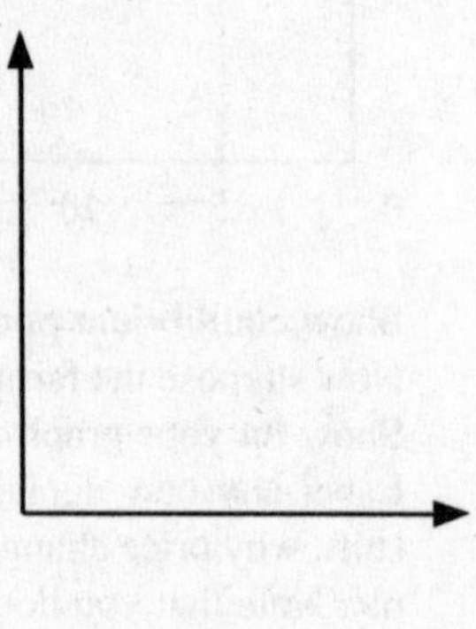

c. A rise in the wage rate in the beef industry.

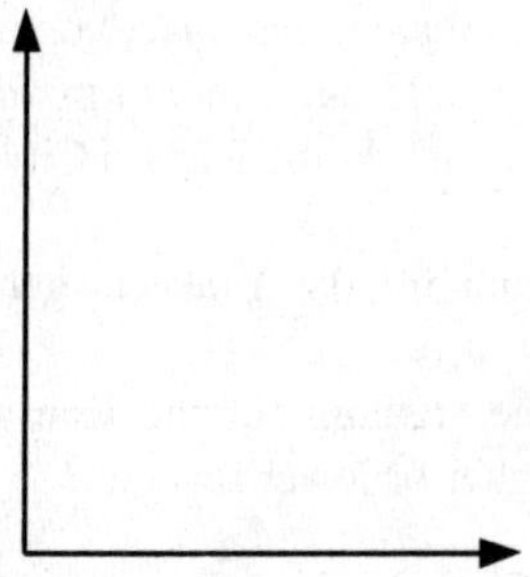

d. A rise in income.

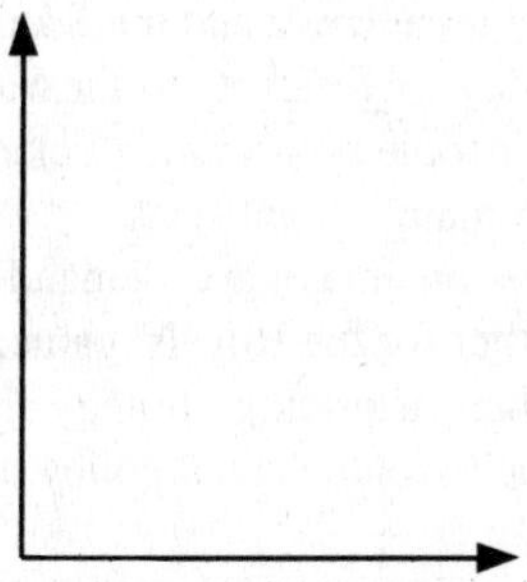

e. An improvement in the productivity of producing beef.

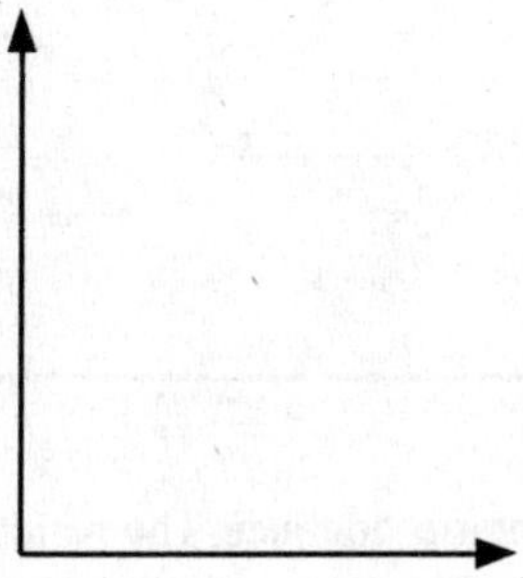

f. A bad tomato crop (beef and ketchup are complements and tomatoes are used to produce ketchup).

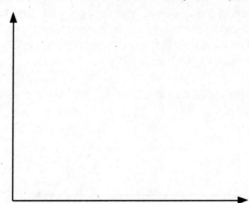

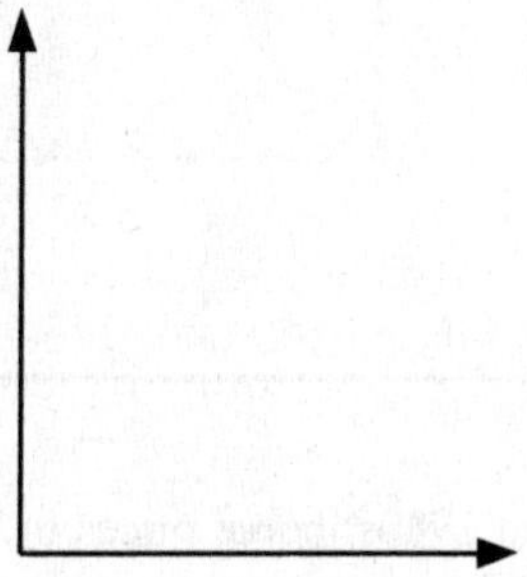

11. Think of some commodity that you like. Try to avoid "lumpy" things, like cars or houses, and pick something like coffee, movies, CDs, or long-distance phone calls.
    a. Roughly sketch your demand curve for this good. Does it intersect the price axis? Where? How much of this commodity would you buy at a zero price?

    b. Are there substitutes for this commodity? How does the availability of substitutes affect the shape of your curve?
    c. How would your demand curve change in response to an increase in the price of a substitute?
    d. How would your demand curve change if you won the lottery and were to receive $2 million?

12. Assume that the Toronto Blue Jays baseball team charges $15 per ticket for all seats at all regular season games. Assume also that the capacity of their stadium, SkyDome, is 50 000. In August, the Jays played games against the New York Yankees (a great rival) and the Kansas City Royals (a team in last place) on consecutive Sundays. All tickets to the Yankees game were sold out a month in advance, and many people who wanted tickets could not get them. At the Kansas City game, there were many vacant seats.
    a. Draw an imaginary demand and supply graph for the Yankees' game and another for the Royals' game.
    b. Is there a pricing strategy that would fill the stadium for the Kansas City game? Would such a policy bring the Jays higher or lower revenue?

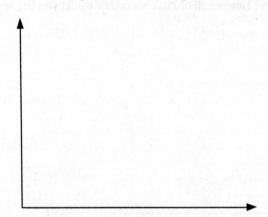

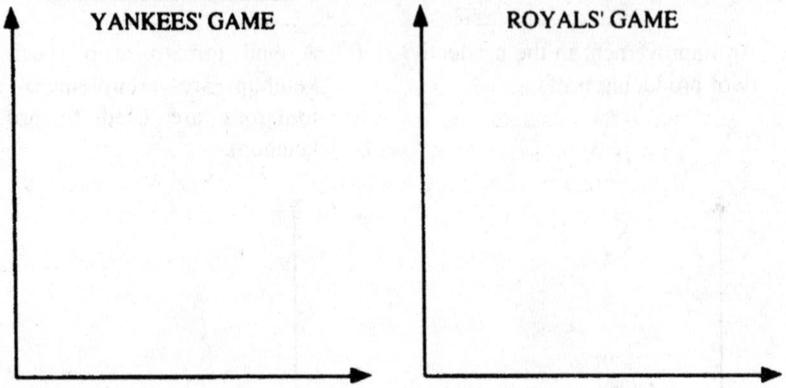

13. During the 1980s, home prices in the Southern Ontario doubled. The result was a significant increase in new home construction and a large increase in the demand for labour in the region. At the same time, though, high home prices caused a drop in the supply of labour as people found it too expensive to live in the region. Draw a diagram of the labour market and discuss the impact of these events on wages and thus on the costs of doing business in this region.

14. In London, England, cabbies must be able to demonstrate a knowledge of at least 400 streets in order to obtain a licence. This is quite difficult, so the number of cabbies is rather limited.
    a. Draw a demand and supply diagram for taxi service in London. How has this diagram been affected by the presence of the test?

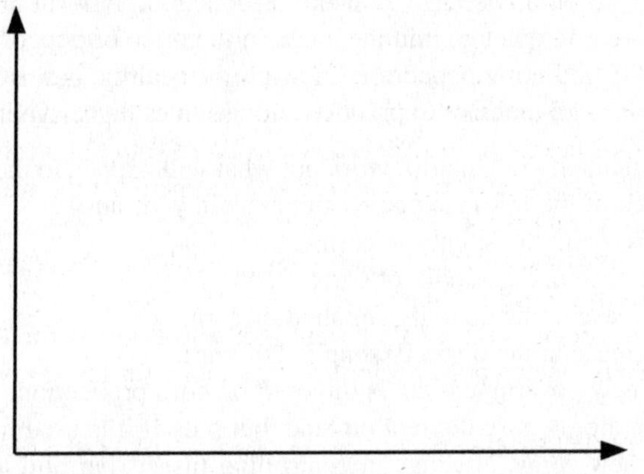

b. How has the presence of the test affected usage of other forms of public transport—for example, the red double-decker buses and the "tube" (subway)? How have these prices responded?

c. If the effect of restricting the numbers of cabbies is to reduce the number of customers, why might cab drivers favour the restriction?

15. Indicate in each case whether demand for steak (a normal good) will increase (I), decrease (D), or remain unchanged (U) in the following cases.

a. ____ Pork, a substitute for steak, decreases in price.
b. ____ High levels of unemployment sweep the nation.
c. ____ The price of steak falls.
d. ____ The price of steak sauce increases dramatically.
e. ____ A government report establishes a conclusive link between the consumption of steak and cancer.
f. ____ New refrigeration techniques reduce spoilage of steaks before they reach the market.
g. ____ It is expected that the price of steak will skyrocket within two months.

16. Indicate in each case whether the supply of beer will increase (I), decrease (D), or remain unchanged (U) in the following cases.

a. ____ Wine coolers become more popular with consumers.
b. ____ Beer decreases in price.
c. ____ Provinces impose a new tax on beer producers.
d. ____ Beer workers' wages increase.
e. ____ The price of hops, an important ingredient in brewing, decreases.
f. ____ Costs of transportation decrease.
g. ____ Improved technology results in less waste of beer.
h. ____ The economy enters a downturn, and many beer drinkers become unemployed.
i. ____ Fuel costs rise at the brewery.

17. Indicate in each case whether the market price and quantity of popcorn will increase (I), decrease (D), or be uncertain (U) in the following cases. Assume that popcorn and lemonade are normal goods.

	Price	*Quantity*	
a.	____	____	The price of lemonade, a complement of popcorn, rises while the harvest of popping corn is unusually poor this year.
b.	____	____	Consumers' income falls; lower farm wages this year cause the cost of popping corn to decline.

c. ____ ____ Oil, used in popcorn production, falls in price; consumers expect an imminent rise in the price of popcorn.

d. ____ ____ Eating popcorn is shown to be healthy; new hybrid corn is less expensive to produce and provides higher yields.

18. Chatham is a small city in Ontario. Work out what will happen to the amount of corn supplied in each of the following cases and explain your answer.
Result A = increase in the supply of corn.
Result B = decrease in the supply of corn.
Result C = increase in the quantity supplied of corn.
Result D = decrease in the quantity supplied of corn.

a. ____ A new government tax is imposed on corn production.

b. ____ Landlords raise the rent on land, but only if it is used for growing corn.

c. ____ A new spray, effective in controlling insects harmful to corn plants, is made available.

d. ____ The local MP campaigns effectively for an increase in the price of corn, which can be grown in Chatham.

e. ____ The local MP campaigns effectively for a rise in the price of beets, which are grown in Chatham.

f. ____ Many corn-growing farmers suffer bankruptcy.

g. ____ The cost of diesel fuel, used in farm machinery, falls.

h. ____ The wages of agricultural workers increase.

i. ____ Cornflakes (which are made from corn) become much more popular. (Careful!)

ANSWERS AND SOLUTIONS

PRACTICE TEST

I. SOLUTIONS TO MULTIPLE CHOICE QUESTIONS

1. A. In the input market, firms demand inputs and household supply inputs.
2. B. To check your answer, put in a pair of substitutes, such as Pepsi and Coke. If Pepsi increases in price, we will buy less Pepsi, and the demand for Coke will increase.
3. D. A change in price leads to a movement along the demand curve. This is a "change in quantity demanded." An increase in price causes a decrease in quantity demanded.
4. A. A change in price leads to a movement along the supply curve. See p. 80.
5. C. A movement along a supply curve (a change in quantity supplied) can only be caused by a change in the price of the good itself. See p. 80.
6. A. Draw the demand and supply diagram. In equilibrium, quantity demanded equals quantity supplied. At lower prices, quantity demanded exceeds quantity supplied.
7. D. For a normal good, higher income will stimulate additional demand. Higher demand will cause the equilibrium price to rise. See p. 79.
8. B. If the cost of plastic increases, supply will decrease. If buyers have more leisure time, demand for leisure goods (like Frisbees) will increase. A decrease in supply, coupled with an increase in demand, will push up the price.
9. C. A rightward shift—an increase in supply—will occur if costs are reduced.
10. C. A technological improvement will increase supply. This will drive down the equilibrium price. As the price decreases, quantity demanded will increase.
11. D. If the price of beans rises, then it cannot have been caused by an increase in the supply of beans.

12. C. An excess supply means that quantity supplied is greater than the quantity demanded. To reduce the excess supply, sellers will accept lower prices. As price falls, quantity demanded will increase and quantity supplied will decrease.
13. C. A decrease in demand will drive down price; an increase in supply will drive down the price. Draw the diagram to confirm the result.
14. B. Try drawing this. At each price level, the demand curve will be further to the left.
15. D. Frito Lay's supply increases because costs have fallen. This will increase chip (and dip) demand. The health report will reduce demand for dip. Because we don't know which has the stronger effect on the demand for dip, the change in both equilibrium price and quantity is indeterminate.
16. A. Higher demand and less supply will lead to an excess demand if the wage level doesn't increase.
17. B. The demand curve has shifted right from D_1 to D_2. As the price increased, quantity supplied increased.
18. A. There has been an increase in demand. This could have been due to an increase in the price of hamburgers because consumers would wish to buy fewer hamburgers and would switch over to demanding hot dogs.
19. D. The supply curve has shifted left, from S_1 to S_2. As the price increased, quantity demanded decreased.
20. B. There has been a decrease in supply. This could have been due to a tightening of the sanitary regulations required for the preparation of hot dogs (which would have increased costs and/or reduced the number of sellers).
21. B. The demand curve has shifted right, from D_1 to D_2, and the supply curve has shifted left, from S_1 to S_2.
22. B. An expected increase in the income of hot dog consumers will increase demand for a normal good, and a hike in the wages of hot dog preparers will increase costs and reduce supply. Option A is incorrect—it describes the effect rather than the cause.
23. C. As income changes, it changes the *demand* for a good. A decrease in income results in a decrease in the demand for a normal good. A decrease in income results in an increase in the demand for an inferior good. See p. 71.
24. C. If the supply of software increases, the price will fall. As one might expect, software and computers are complements—the evidence in the question bears this out. As the quantity of computers traded increases, the demand for microchips will increase, which pushes up their price. See Figure 4.12, graph 6.
25. A. A movement along a demand curve is a change in quantity demanded. The only factor that can cause such a change is a change in the price of the good. See p. 68.
26. B. The law of demand relates the relationship between the price of a good and the quantity demanded. See p. 69.
27. A. Equilibrium occurs where quantity demanded equals quantity supplied. See p. 81.
28. D. At 60¢, quantity demanded is 25 units greater than quantity supplied.
29. C. At 80¢, quantity supplied is 25 units greater than quantity demanded.
30. B. The new regulations will decrease the supply of tuna which, in turn, will increase the equilibrium price and decrease the equilibrium quantity.

II. SOLUTIONS TO APPLICATION QUESTIONS

1. a. 25¢. 67 000 square metres.
   b. There is an excess supply of 44 000 square metres at a price of 40¢ per square metre. Pressure is present to force price down.
   c. There is an excess demand of 22 000 square metres at a price of 15¢ per square metre Pressure is present to force price up.
   d. Supply would shift to the left by 30 000 square metres. Equilibrium price would increase to 35¢ per square metre and the equilibrium quantity would be 48 000 square metres.

2. a. A decrease in income will reduce demand. Equilibrium price will fall and equilibrium quantity will fall.

b. An increase in the cost of wheat will decrease supply. Equilibrium price will rise and equilibrium quantity will fall.

c. A decrease in the cost of wheat will increase supply. Equilibrium price will fall and equilibrium quantity will rise.

d. A fall in the price of a substitute will reduce the demand for pita. Equilibrium price will fall and equilibrium quantity will fall.

e. There will be a decrease in demand. Equilibrium price will fall and equilibrium quantity will fall.

3. a. Supply will decrease—cost of inputs has increased.

b. Supply will not change. A change in the price of a good results in a change in quantity supplied.

c. Supply of hamburgers will decrease—producers will switch resources to cheeseburger production.

4. a. Hot dogs are substitutes for ice cream. Demand for ice cream will decrease.

b. No effect on demand. Changes in the cost of refrigeration will affect supply.

c. Demand will increase as the number of buyers increases.

5. a.

Quantity Price	Quantity Demanded	Quantity Supplied
$30	0	90
$25	10	75
$20	20	60
$15	30	45
$10	40	30
$ 5	50	15
$ 0	60	0

b. Equilibrium price is $12 and equilibrium quantity is 36.
In equilibrium, Qd = Qs, therefore,

$$60 - 2P = 3P$$
$$60 = 5P \text{ and } P = 12.$$

If P = 12, then Q = 60 – 2(12) = 36.

c. At $20, there is an excess supply of 40 units. It's a buyers' market—only 20 units will be traded.

d. This is an increase in demand. Tastes might have changed, consumer incomes may have risen (if video cassettes are a normal good), and so on.

e. Equilibrium price is $16 and equilibrium quantity is 48.
In equilibrium, Qd = Qs, therefore,

$$80 - 2P = 3P$$
$$80 = 5P \text{ and } P = 16.$$

If P = 16, then Q = 80 – 2(16) = 48.

6. a. $3; 3000.

b. See the diagram below.

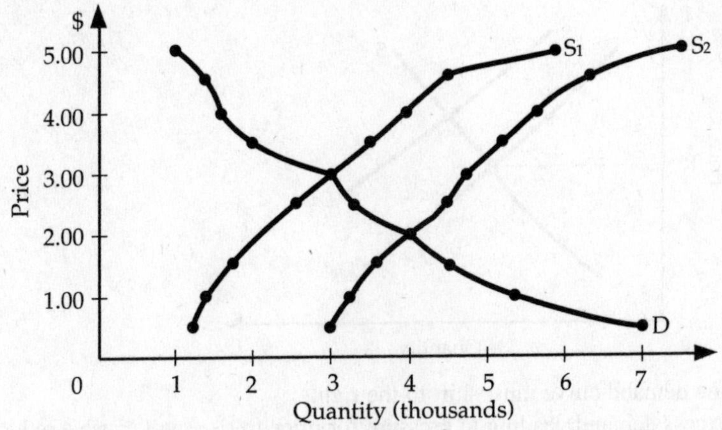

c. There is an excess demand equal to 4000 units (5400 – 1400).
d. See the diagram above ($2, 4000).
e. There will be an excess supply of 1800 units.
f. Price will fall to $2; quantity demanded and supplied will move to 4000 units.

7. The unemployment was removed because 100 extra jobs were created (increase in quantity demanded) and, because the wage had become too low, 50 workers decided to cease offering themselves for employment (decrease in quantity supplied).

8. a. See the diagram below.
b. P* = $3; Q* = 16.

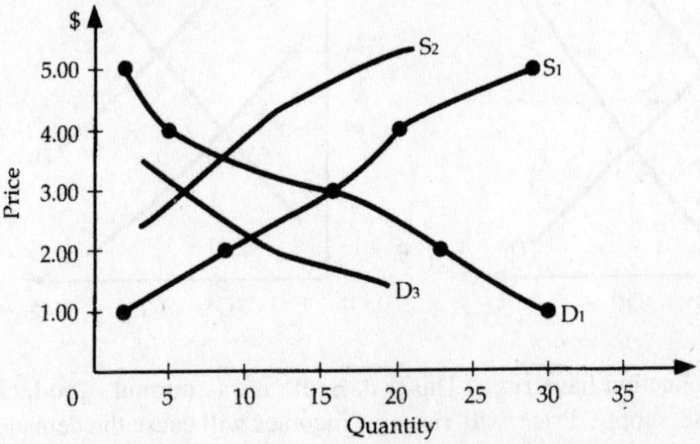

c. See the diagram above. There will be no change in demand. Costs have risen, reducing profits, so supply will shift to the left (although we can't say how far). At $3, an excess demand now exists, which will push prices higher.
d. See the diagram above. Demand for orange juice will fall (although we can't say by how much). Consumption of Master Choice orange drink will rise, and some consumers of orange juice will substitute the relatively cheap Master Choice orange drink.

9. a. See the diagram below.
b. Increase.

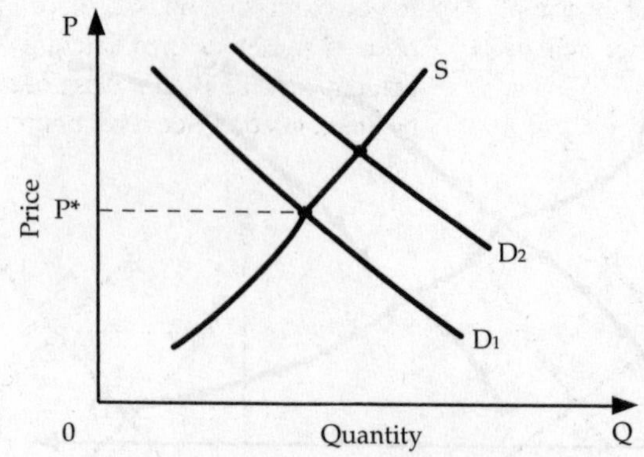

c. The demand curve must shift to the right.
d. Excess demand, leading to pressure for price to rise, will cause a reduction in the quantity demanded and an increase in the quantity supplied. This will continue until a new equilibrium is established.

10.

a. The subsidy will increase supply. Price will fall and output will rise.

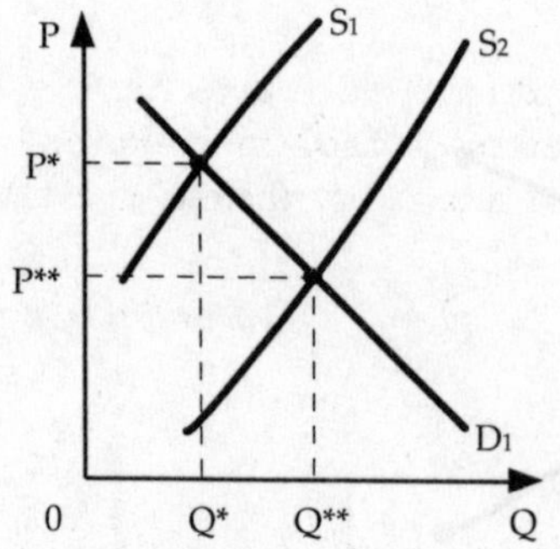

b. The price of fish will increase and consumers will switch to beef. The demand for beef will increase. Price will rise and output will rise.

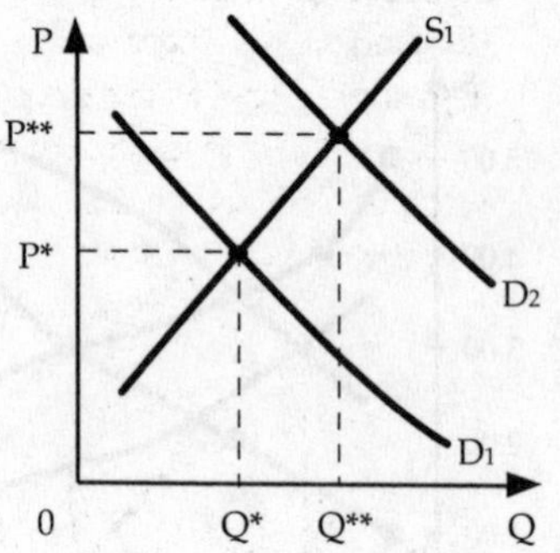

c. Costs of production have risen. This will decrease supply. Price will rise and output will fall.

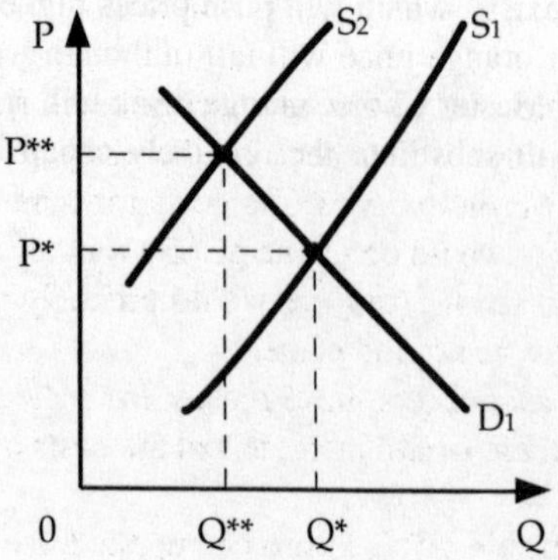

d. Beef is a normal good. Higher incomes will cause the demand curve to shift right. Price will rise and output will rise.

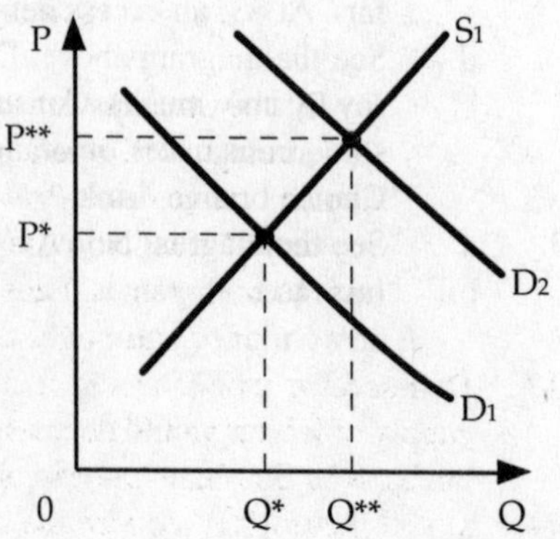

e. Costs of production will fall. Supply will shift to the right. Price will fall and output will rise.

f. A poor tomato crop will drive up the price of tomatoes (and ketchup). Less ketchup will be used so less beef will be demanded. Price and output will fall.

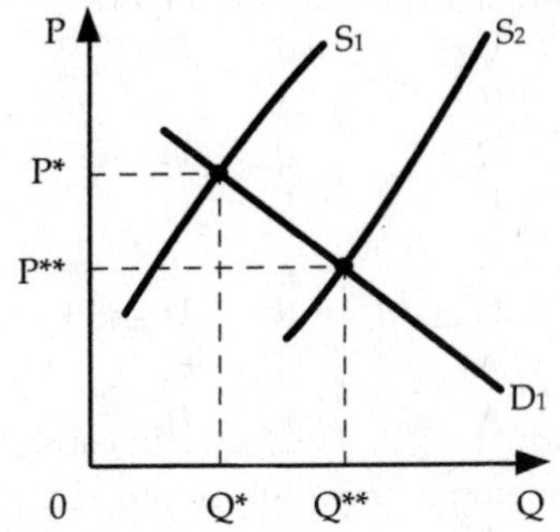

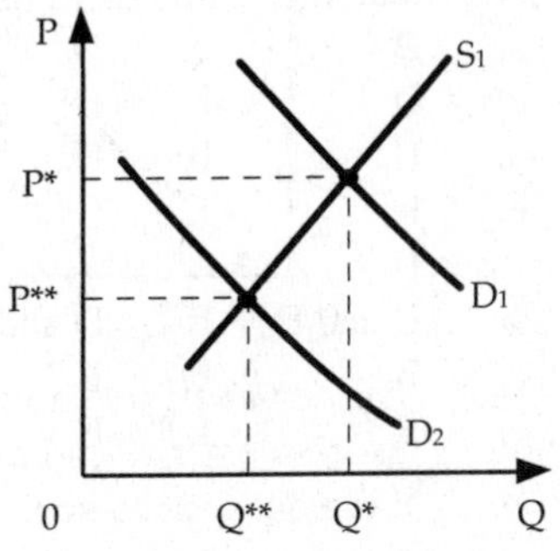

11. a. Presumably, your demand curve is downsloping and intersects the price axis at some point.
   b. With a greater number of substitutes, you will be more sensitive to changes in the price of your good. The curve will tend to be flatter.
   c. Presumably, the demand curve would shift to the right.
   d. If this is a normal good, demand would increase. If it is an inferior good, demand would decrease.

12. a. The supply curves are the same (vertical at 50 000). In the Yankees' case, at a price of $15 per ticket, there is an excess demand. In the Royals' case, at a price of $15 per ticket, because demand is so low, there is an excess supply. See the diagram below.

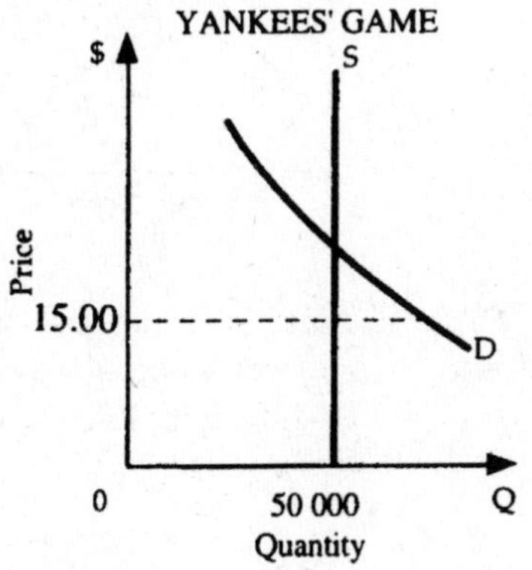

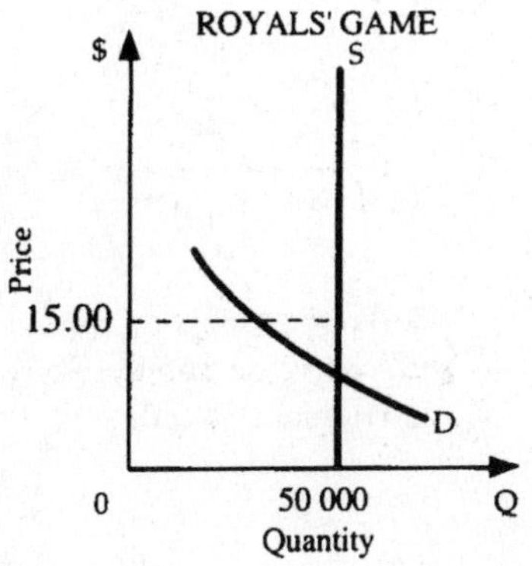

   b. To fill the stadium, let the ticket price fall to the equilibrium level. Whether this strategy will bring in more revenue will depend on the elasticity of the demand curve—see *Principles of Microeconomics* Chapter 5 for more on the concept of elasticity. Another strategy would be to charge $30 for a combined pass to both games. Fans wanting to see the Yankees would probably pay out more money and might also come to the second game.

13. Demand for labour would increase and, as workers moved away from the region, supply of labour would decrease. Wages, then, would increase and the costs of doing business in Southern Ontario would rise.

14. a. The test has reduced the supply of cabbies. This has forced up the price of taxi rides in London.

b. Given the raised price of cab rides, the demand for substitutes will have increased. Other forms of public transportation will have been able to increase their prices.

c. Cabbies who have passed the test and earned their licence like the scheme because it reduces competition. This is especially true if the degree of substitutability with other types of public transportation is slight.

15.	a. D		b. D		c. U		d. D	
	e. D		f. U		g. I			
16.	a. U		b. U		c. D		d. D	
	e. I		f. I		g. I		h. U	
	i. D							
17.	a. U and D		b. D and U		c. U and I		d. U and I	
18.	a. B		b. B		c. A		d. C	
	e. B		f. B		g. A		h. B	
	i. C							

5 The Price System, Supply and Demand, and Elasticity

OBJECTIVES: POINT BY POINT

After completing this chapter, you should be able to accomplish the objectives listed below.

OBJECTIVE 1: Explain and demonstrate how the market uses the price-rationing mechanism to allocate resources and distribute output.

The price system has two important functions—it rations scarce output and determines how productive resources are allocated. Because of scarcity, rationing always occurs. Price rationing operates to distinguish those who are "willing and able" to buy from those who are only able but no longer willing, i.e., it allocates according to the willingness and ability of consumers to pay—those who are willing and able to pay as the price increases will get the good. Demand is constrained by income and wealth but, within those limits, individual preferences will prevail. If demand increases, price rises, signalling producers that profits may be made. More of the good will be produced with resources being switched from other lines of production. (page 97)

> **TIP:** Note the lobster example in the textbook, which describes the rationing and allocative roles that prices play in the market place.
>
> Note, too, that the profit motive is highly durable. Limitations (such as price ceilings or rationing) placed on the operation of the market can lead to black markets so that demand can be serviced.

Practice

1. In a free market, non-price rationing must occur when ___________ exists.
   A. an excess demand.
   B. an excess supply.
   C. a perfectly elastic demand.
   D. a perfectly inelastic demand.

   ANSWER: A. Given an excess demand, either price will increase (price rationing) or non-price rationing must be enforced.

2. In a free market, the rationing mechanism is
   A. price.
   B. quantity.
   C. demand.
   D. supply.

ANSWER: A. Given an imbalance between quantity demanded and quantity supplied, a free market will adjust price to achieve equilibrium.

OBJECTIVE 2: Describe the alternative rationing mechanisms.

Price rationing may be considered "unfair"—poor people might be priced out of the market for some essentials—so other non-price-rationing methods, including queuing, ration coupons, favoured customers, and lotteries, are applied. Such schemes usually involve hidden costs (queuing costs time, for example) that may make them inefficient. Note that different types of rationing benefit different groups of people. (page 105)

At many universities, basketball tickets are distributed on a first come first served basis—meaning that students must queue, perhaps for days, to get tickets to the big game. Not-so-hidden costs include the inconvenience, loss of study time, and possible health effects. As an example of a lottery, universities may allocate dorm rooms, not by price or need, but by random number selection.

> **TIP:** Remember that a price ceiling stops the price going higher (just like a ceiling in a room), while a price floor is a lower limit. To have an effect on equilibrium price, a ceiling must be set below the equilibrium price and a floor above the equilibrium price.
>
> **Comment:** The conceptual companion of a price ceiling is a price floor. A price ceiling sets a maximum price; a price floor sets a minimum price. The minimum wage is a price floor. An effective price ceiling creates an excess demand; an effective price floor creates an excess supply. This may seem confusing—to have a ceiling below the equilibrium price.

> **Graphing Pointer:** It is not true that a price ceiling must be established below the equilibrium price, although a ceiling set above the equilibrium has no effect. If demand and/or supply conditions change however, the ceiling could become effective. For instance, in the U.S., the adjustable rate mortgages have "caps" on how high the interest rate can move in response to market conditions—this is a price ceiling.

Practice

3. A price ceiling is established below the equilibrium price. We can predict that
   A. quantity demanded will decrease.
   B. quantity supplied will be greater than quantity demanded.
   C. demand will be less than supply.
   D. quantity supplied will decrease.

   ANSWER: D. Price will be reduced by the price ceiling. A decrease in price causes quantity supplied to decrease (not a shift in the supply curve).

4. A price ceiling is established below the equilibrium price. We can predict that
   A. there will be a leftward shift in the demand curve.
   B. there will be a leftward shift in the supply curve.

C. quantity demanded will be greater than quantity supplied.
D. quantity supplied will be reduced to equal quantity demanded.

ANSWER: C. A change in price does not cause the demand and/or supply curve to shift position. If price is "too low," an excess demand (quantity demanded greater than quantity supplied) will occur.

5. Ticket scalping will be successful if
A. demand is elastic.
B. demand is inelastic.
C. the official price is below the equilibrium price.
D. the official price is above the equilibrium price.

ANSWER: C. Elasticity is irrelevant in this case. The important issue is that an excess demand for tickets exists because the official price has been set too low.

OBJECTIVE 3: Apply the demand and supply model in a variety of situations.

The text offers the gasoline market and the developments since February of 1999 that caused a dramatic surge in the price of gasoline as an example of the usefulness of demand and supply analysis. The analysis shows that the agreement by OPEC and two non-OPEC (Mexico and Norway) nations to lower crude oil production caused the supply of crude oil to drop. This in turn resulted in a drastic jump in the price of crude oil and a decline in the quantity demanded. Furthermore, the subsequent surge in the world demand for oil caused the demand to rise resulting in a further jump in the price.

The higher price of oil, however, tends to generate further developments. While such increases offer significant gains for oil-producing countries in the short term, by encouraging the development of alternative sources of energy and possibly causing a worldwide recession, theytend to breed their own downfall. (page 105)

Practice

Refer to the following world oil markets in 2001, diagram for the next three questions:

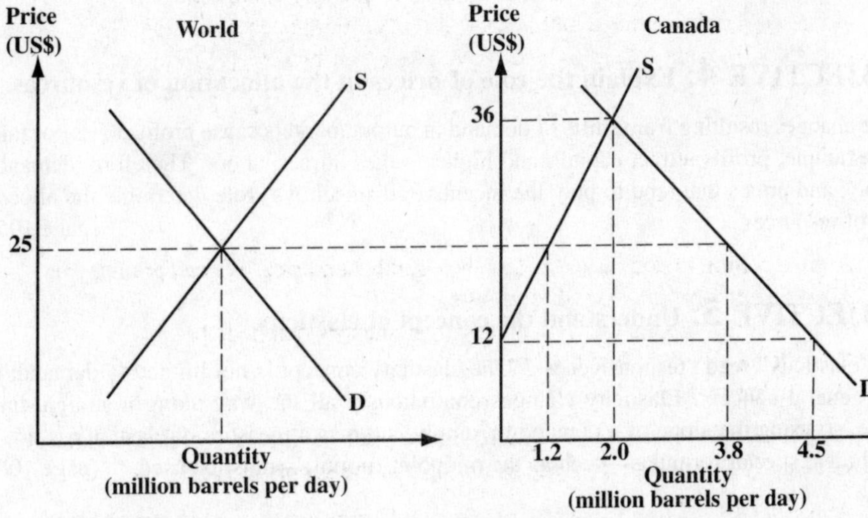

6. If the world price, $25 per barrel, is the market price in Canada, then there will be an_________of ________ million barrels per day.

A. excess supply, 1.2.
B. excess supply, 2.6.
C. excess demand, 3.8.
D. excess demand, 2.6.

ANSWER: D. At $25 per barrel, quantity supplied is 1.2 million and quantity demanded is 3.8 million.

7. If the world price, $25 per barrel, is the market price in Canada, then Canada's domestic production will be_______ and Canada's imports of oil will be _______ million barrels per day.
A. 3.8, 3.8.
B. 3.8,1.2.
C. 1.2, 2.6.
D. 3.8, 2.6.

ANSWER: C. At $25 per barrel, quantity supplied is 1.2, whereas quantity demanded is 3.8, leaving an excess demand of 1.6 to be imported.

8. At the price of $12 per barrel, domestic (Canadian) production of oil would have been_______ and Canada's imports__________ million barrels per day.
A. zero, 4.5.
B. zero, 2.0.
C. 2.0, 2.0.
D. 1.2, 3.8.

ANSWER: A. At the price of $12 per barrel, Canada's production level (quantity supplied) will be zero (where the supply curve crosses the vertical axis) and the quantity demanded is 4.5.

9. Suppose that Canada wishes to be self sufficient in oil. This could be done by
A. establishing a price ceiling (maximum price) of $13 per barrel of oil.
B. establishing a price ceiling (maximum price) of $24 per barrel of oil.
C. imposing a fee of $36 per barrel on imported oil.
D. imposing a fee of $24 per barrel on imported oil.

ANSWER: D. A fee of $24 per barrel on foreign oil will result in equilibrium in the Canadian market.

OBJECTIVE 4: Explain the role of prices in the allocation of resources.

Price changes resulting from shifts of demand in output markets cause profits to rise or fall. For example, profits attract capital, and higher wages attract labour. Therefore, demand, supply, and prices that tend to play the incentive (disincentive) role determine the allocation of resources. (page 105)

OBJECTIVE 5: Understand the concept of elasticity.

For "elasticity" read "responsiveness." The elasticity concept is not limited to demand; it is a general concept. Elasticity changes continuously all the way along a straight-line curve, so using the slope of a demand or supply curve as a measure of elasticity is not a good idea; special formulas—such as the midpoint formula—must be used. (page 108)

TIP: The best way to understand "elasticity" is to equate the term with "responsiveness." The responsiveness of one's clients to price changes can be valuable information to the business person. The responsiveness of clients to changes in their income can be valuable information during a downturn in the economy. Firms often hire consultants to estimate elasticities so that they can fine-tune their marketing strategies.

Graphing Pointer: Elasticity ≠ Slope. It's difficult to resist associating the slope of the demand curve with elasticity—after all, since a perfectly inelastic curve is vertical and a perfectly elastic curve is horizontal, it seems like a safe bet. A couple of simple diagrams will show you the danger. Draw two parallel demand curves (D_1 and D_2, as in the diagram below).

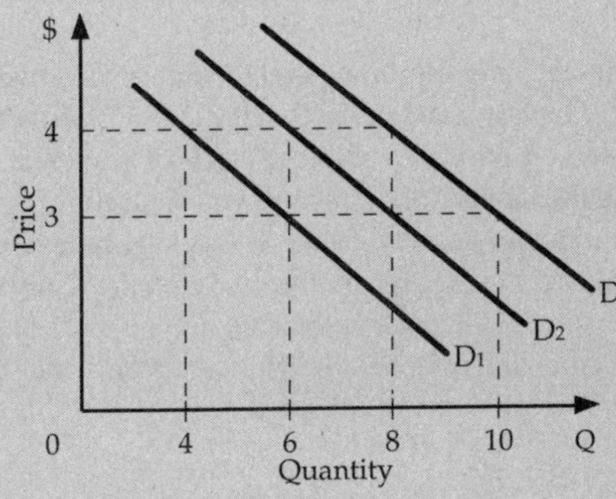

Do they have the same elasticity? (No—the elasticity between \$3 and \$4 is greater for D_2 than for D_1. Calculate this for confirmation and practice.) Now draw demand curve D_3. In one diagram, with demand curves having equal slopes, you have displayed inelasticity, unitary elasticity, and elasticity. Clearly, slope is not a good guide to elasticity. The textbook even shows you that a straight-line demand curve can be inelastic in one area and elastic in another.

Why doesn't elasticity remain constant along a straight-line demand curve? Simply, the formula we use calculates the *relative* change in quantity and price. A one-unit increase in quantity demanded is a relatively large change when quantity is low, but quite insignificant when quantity demanded is substantial. Similarly, a \$1 decrease in price is a relatively small change when price is high, but a large change when price is already low. In the first case, the numerator (quantity) value is large and the denominator (price) value is small (E_D is large). In the second case, the numerator (quantity) value is smaller and the denominator (price) value is larger (making E_D relatively small).

TIP: Here is a simple memory aid for elasticity graphs. The demand curve is vertical (|) for perfectly (**I**)nelastic demand, but horizontal (—) for perfectly (**E**)lastic demand.

OBJECTIVE 6: Distinguish between the different types of elasticity.

Demand responsiveness may be classified in *absolute* terms as:

a. perfectly elastic $E_D = \infty$ (infinity),
b. elastic $E_D > 1$,
c. unitarily elastic $E_D = 1$,
d. inelastic $E_D < 1$, or
e. perfectly inelastic $E_D = 0$. (page 110)

Recall that elasticity measures responsiveness. The more responsive a buyer is to a price change, the more elastic is demand and, in absolute terms, the larger is the price elasticity of demand.

Graphing Pointer: Initially, you might confuse the two extreme cases—perfectly inelastic and perfectly elastic. For "perfectly," think "completely." If you have a "complete" lack of response to higher prices, what would happen to the amount you buy? Higher prices will not change the amount you buy. Demand is totally unresponsive and is drawn as a vertical curve. If you have a "complete" response to a higher price what would happen to the amount you buy? The demand is perfectly elastic and graphically, you are "off" the horizontal demand curve. You buy none of the good.

OBJECTIVE 7: Learn to calculate elasticities.

Price elasticity of demand is the most frequently used measurement and sets a pattern for all the formulas: it is the percentage change in quantity demanded divided by the percentage change in price. (page 111)

TIP: By cancelling the 2s in the textbook formula, the midpoint elasticity formula can be simplified to:

$$\frac{\dfrac{Q_1 - Q_2}{Q_1 + Q_2}}{\dfrac{P_1 - P_2}{P_1 + P_2}}$$

Make sure you have the "quantity" term in the numerator and the "price" term in the denominator—we're measuring how much *quantity* (top) responds to a change in the *dollar* amount (bottom).

Practice

Use the following information to answer the next three questions: Three for One Pizzeria has been experimenting with the price of its Extra Thick Pan Pizza. At a price of $12, quantity demanded is 100. At $10, quantity demanded increases to 120 pizzas. When the price is $8, quantity demanded increases to 140 pizzas.

10. Using the midpoint formula, the price elasticity of demand between $12 and $10 is
    A. elastic with a coefficient of –2.
    B. unitarily elastic with a coefficient of –1.
    C. elastic with a coefficient of –10.
    D. inelastic with a coefficient of –.1.

    ANSWER: B. P_1 is 12; P_2 is 10; Q_1 is 100; Q_2 is 120. Plug the values into the formula. Note: Confirm your result using the total revenue test.

11. Using the midpoint formula, the price elasticity of demand between $10 and $8 is
    A. elastic with a coefficient of –13/9.
    B. elastic with a coefficient of –9/13.
    C. inelastic with a coefficient of –13/9.
    D. inelastic with a coefficient of –9/13.

    ANSWER: D. P_1 is 10; P_2 is 8; Q_1 is 120; Q_2 is 140. Options B and C must be incorrect—an elastic demand cannot have a coefficient of –9/13. Note: Confirm your "inelastic" result using the total revenue test.

12. Using the midpoint formula, the price elasticity of demand between $12 and $8 is
    A. elastic with a coefficient of –6/5.
    B. elastic with a coefficient of –5/6.
    C. inelastic with a coefficient of –6/5.
    D. inelastic with a coefficient of –5/6.

    ANSWER: D. P_1 is 12; P_2 is 8; Q_1 is 100; Q_2 is 140. Options B and C must be incorrect—an elastic demand cannot have a coefficient of –5/6 and an inelastic demand cannot have a coefficient of –6/5. Note: Confirm your "inelastic" result using the total revenue test.

13. A 10% fall in the price of shampoo results in a 5% increase in the quantity of shampoo demanded. Demand is
    A. inelastic.
    B. elastic.
    C. unitarily elastic.
    D. perfectly elastic.

    ANSWER: A. See p. 110.

14. The price elasticity of demand can be calculated by
    A. multiplying the percentage change in quantity demanded by the percentage change in price.
    B. dividing the percentage change in quantity demanded by the percentage change in price.
    C. dividing the percentage change in price by the percentage change in quantity demanded.
    D. multiplying the percentage change in price by the percentage change in quantity demanded.

    ANSWER: B. See p. 110.

15. The supply of flapdoodles increases. There is no effect on the equilibrium quantity. Demand is
    A. perfectly inelastic.
    B. elastic.
    C. inelastic.
    D. perfectly elastic.

ANSWER: A. If demand is completely unresponsive to a price change, it is perfectly inelastic—a vertical demand curve.

16. The demand for potato chips has a downsloping straight-line demand curve. As the price of chips increases, the price elasticity of demand
    A. becomes more elastic.
    B. becomes less elastic.
    C. remains constant—the slope of a straight line is constant.
    D. remains constant—each price increase causes an equal decrease in quantity demanded.

    ANSWER: A. Slope does not give a good guide to elasticity. A general rule, though, for a straight-line demand curve is that, as price rises, demand becomes more elastic. See the "Elasticity ≠ Slope" Tip above.

17. A 10% increase in the price of video games results in a 5% decrease in the quantity of video games demanded. The elasticity of demand coefficient is ________, and demand is ________.
    A. –.5, elastic.
    B. –2.0, elastic.
    C. –.5, inelastic.
    D. –2.0, inelastic.

    ANSWER: C. Options A and D must be wrong—an "elastic" coefficient must have an absolute value of more than 1, while an "inelastic" coefficient must have an absolute value of less than 1. The relatively large price change prompts a relatively small quantity change—that's inelastic.

OTHER RELATED POINTS.

POINT 1: Predict the effect on total revenue of a price change, given the elasticity of demand coefficient. Apply the total revenue test.

Total revenue is "price x quantity." The relationship between elasticity and total revenue, as price increases, may be classified as

a.	elastic	total revenue decreases
b.	unitarily elastic	total revenue remains constant
c.	inelastic	total revenue increases

Given a good with an elastic demand (Pepsi), a small increase in price will trigger a relatively large decrease in quantity demanded, as consumers switch over to Coke and other close substitutes. Total spending on Pepsi will decrease.

Given a good with an inelastic demand (gasoline), even a large price hike will result in only a small decrease in quantity demanded, since consumers have few close substitutes for the product. Total spending on gas will increase. (page 115)

The *total revenue test* allows us to determine whether demand is elastic or inelastic when price changes. The following table gives a summary of this test.

Price	*Quantity*	*Elasticity*	*Coefficient*	*Total Revenue*
increase	decrease	perfectly elastic	$E_D = \infty$ infinite	falling to zero
increase	decrease	elastic	$E_D > 1$	falling
increase	decrease	unitarily elastic	$E_D = 1$	constant
increase	decrease	inelastic	$E_D < 1$	rising
increase	no change	perfectly inelastic	$E_D = 0$	rising

Note that usually you don't need to know the exact elasticity coefficients.

If you don't know the exact elasticity values, checking how total revenue is changing is an effective way to discover if the good has an elastic demand or not.

Practice

Know 18. The price of canned salmon increases; total spending on canned salmon remains unchanged. Canned salmon has a(n) __________ demand.

A. perfectly inelastic.
B. perfectly elastic.
C. unitarily elastic.
D. inelastic.

ANSWER: C. Total revenue will increase if salmon has an inelastic demand and will decrease if salmon has an elastic demand. This is the middle case where the price change results in no change in total spending. – Revenue stays the same

19. Total revenue will decrease if price _______ and demand is _______.

A. increases, inelastic.
B. increases, unitarily elastic.
C. decreases, inelastic.
D. decreases, elastic.

ANSWER: C. The post-secondary education tuition has an inelastic demand. Total revenue on tuition will increase if university administrators declare a price increase. By the same argument, if tuition rates are reduced, total revenue will decrease.

Know 20. An excellent harvest causes apples to fall in price by 10%. Consumers buy 5% more apples. The price decrease has caused consumers to

A. spend less on apples.
B. spend more on apples.
C. reduce the quantity of apples bought. We can't tell what has happened to spending.
D. increase the quantity of apples bought. We can't tell what has happened to spending.

ANSWER: A. The price elasticity coefficient is –.5—inelastic. A decrease in price then, we know, will reduce the number of dollars spent.

POINT 2: Explain the effects of the three determinants of price elasticity of demand.

The responsiveness of demand to changes in price is affected by the availability of substitutes, the fraction of total spending that a good absorbs, and the time factor. The elasticity of demand will *increase* if more substitutes become available, if the good commands a greater portion of the household's budget, or if the response time is longer rather than shorter. (page 118)

> **TIP:** To remember how price elasticity is influenced by its determinants (the availability of substitutes, the fraction of total spending that a good absorbs, and time), make up a few intuitive examples.

TIP, continued: Substitutes: Petro-Canada gas has an elastic demand because there are many substitutes (Esso, Shell, etc.); gasoline, in general, has few substitutes—elasticity will be lower. Pepsi has many substitutes, electricity has few.

As more substitutes become available, demand becomes more elastic. The drug that combats AIDS—AZT,—at one time had no substitutes—inelastic demand. The producer was attacked for setting price too high and reaping substantial revenues. The emergence of substitutes will make AZT's demand more elastic.

Fraction of total spending: Suppose Bazooka Joe bubblegum (or salt, or pepper) doubled in price. It's such a small portion of expenditures for most people that the price increase would pass almost unnoticed, and quantity demanded would respond only slightly—inelastic demand. In contrast, a doubling in the price of a good that is important in one's budget (gasoline, perhaps) will provoke a greater response.

Time: The longer the consumer has to "shop around" following a price increase, the more responsive he or she can be. In the late 1970s, for instance, gas prices rose rapidly. Initially, drivers planned trips more carefully. Then came car pooling. Eventually, as cars aged, newer, more fuel-efficient models were bought. Progressively, fuel consumption was reduced.

In each example, remember to apply the total revenue test. If gasoline increases in price, your gas bill will increase (inelastic demand). If Pepsi increases in price, your spending on Pepsi will decrease (elastic demand).

Practice

21. Emina is a fourth-year student at Mount Allison University in New Brunswick. Probably, she will have the most elastic demand for
    A. the tuition fee.
    B. warm clothing in December.
    C. Petro-Canada gasoline.
    D. the university yearbook.

    ANSWER: C. There should be many substitutes (other companies' gasoline), and Emina is likely to consider gas as an important part of her budget. Tuition may be important in Emina's budget, but few substitutes are likely to be available.

POINT 3: Distinguish between and calculate cross-price elasticity of demand and income elasticity of demand.

Income elasticity of demand—which measures how much a demand curve shifts position when income level changes—measures whether goods are inferior, normal, or luxuries.

a.	inferior	negative coefficient	
b.	normal	positive coefficient less than one, or	
c.	luxuries	positive coefficient greater than one.	(page 119)

Comment: No good is automatically "inferior," "normal," or a "luxury." For a poor person gaining extra income, a bus ride may be a luxury, while that same bus ride might be inferior for a millionaire. You should also realize that a "luxury" (e.g., bubblegum) need not be equated with "high-priced," nor "necessity" (dental care) with "low-priced." Clearly, there may be a link between income elasticity and price elasticity: Whether a good has many substitutes may be linked with whether it is considered a luxury or a necessity.

Cross-price elasticity of demand—which measures how the demand curve for Good A shifts when the price of Good B changes—measures whether a substitute relationship or a complement relationship exists.

a.	substitute	positive elasticity coefficient, or	
b.	complement	negative elasticity coefficient.	(page 119)

The main point here is the sign (positive or negative) of the relationship rather than the magnitude. If it's a positive relationship, the goods are substitutes; if it's negative, the goods are complements. As a secondary issue, the larger (in absolute terms) the coefficient, the more related are the two goods. For instance, a small decrease in the price of Pepsi may trigger a sizeable decrease in the demand for Coke (close substitutes) but a smaller decrease in the demand for Yop Yogurt Drink.

> **TIP:** Check these results by "plugging in" your own examples from Chapter 4.
>
> **Substitutes.** An increase in the price of Pepsi will lead to a decrease in the quantity demanded of Pepsi and an increase in the demand for Coke (positive sign).
>
> **Complements.** An increase in the price of CDs will lead to a decrease in the demand for CD players (negative sign).
>
> **Inferior Goods.** Potatoes, beans, and generic aspirin are good examples of inferior goods. As your income increases, you will probably decrease your spending on such goods (negative sign).
>
> **Normal Goods.** As your income increases, you will probably increase your spending on soft drinks, books, clothes, CDs, etc. (positive sign).
>
> **Luxury Goods.** Home ownership might be a luxury. If your income is low, you can only rent. If your income rises, you may qualify for mortgage loans and enter the house-purchasing market. Expenditure on house purchases rises more than the increase in income in such a case.

> **TIP:** Remember: put the "**number**" term (quantity) in the **numerator** and the "**dollar**" term (price or income) in the **denominator**.
>
> From this point, it's easy to alter the original midpoint formula to introduce the concepts of income elasticity (measuring how much *quantity* responds to a change in *income*), or even cross-price elasticity (measuring how much *quantity demanded of Good A* responds to a change in the *price of Good B*).

Practice

22. The cross-price elasticity coefficient between Petro-Canada gas and Mobil oil is –.7. Petro-Canada gas and Mobil oil are ________. The cross-price elasticity coefficient between Petro-Canada and Shell gas will be ________.
    A. substitutes, positive.
    B. substitutes, negative.
    C. complements, positive.
    D. complements, negative.

    ANSWER: C. A negative cross-price elasticity coefficient indicates that goods are complements. Because Petro-Canada and Shell are substitutes, the cross-price elasticity coefficient will be positive.

23. The income elasticity coefficient of Mobil oil is .6. We can conclude that Mobil oil
    A. is an inferior good.
    B. is a normal good, but not a luxury.
    C. is a luxury.
    D. has a demand that is not very sensitive to changes in its price.

    ANSWER: B. An increase in income will raise demand for Mobil. The coefficient is positive but less than one, so it is not a luxury. Option D does not refer to income elasticity.

24. Two goods are complements. Their cross-price elasticity of demand coefficient will be
    A. a negative number.
    B. a positive number.
    C. a positive number greater than one.
    D. one.

    ANSWER: A. An increase in the price of one item in the pair will reduce the quantity demanded. Because fewer are being demanded, fewer will also be demanded of the other item in the pair.

PRACTICE TEST

I. MULTIPLE CHOICE QUESTIONS. Select the option that provides the single best answer.

_____ 1. Price elasticity of demand is –.50. Price increases by 10%. We would predict a
    A. 50% increase in quantity demanded.

B. 20% decrease in quantity demanded.
C. 5% increase in quantity demanded.
D. 5% decrease in quantity demanded.

_____ 2. Sellers of Frisbees want to raise their revenues. They should ________ price by 30¢ if they believe demand to be ________ in that price range.
A. lower, elastic.
B. lower, inelastic.
C. raise, elastic.
D. Two of the above are feasible scenarios.

_____ 3. A 10% fall in the price of apples results in a 20% increase in the quantity of apples demanded. Demand is
A. inelastic.
B. elastic.
C. unitarily elastic.
D. perfectly elastic.

_____ 4. Which of the following is NOT a determinant of price elasticity of demand for gasoline?
A. the quantity of gasoline produced.
B. the amount of time given to adjust to a price change.
C. the availability of close substitutes.
D. the importance of gasoline in one's budget.

_____ 5. Price elasticity of demand is a measure of the
A. extent of competition in the market.
B. percentage change in quantity times the percentage change in price.
C. slope of the demand curve.
D. degree of consumer responsiveness to changes in price.

_____ 6. The price elasticity of demand for Esso gas will tend to be
A. less elastic, the lower the price of substitutes.
B. less elastic, the smaller the share of consumers' income spent on Esso gas.
C. less elastic, the greater the availability of close substitutes for Esso gas.
D. more elastic, the more urgently gas is needed.

_____ 7. Two goods are complements. Their cross-price elasticity of demand will be
A. a negative number.
B. a positive number.
C. a positive number greater than one.
D. one.

Use the graph below to answer the next two questions.

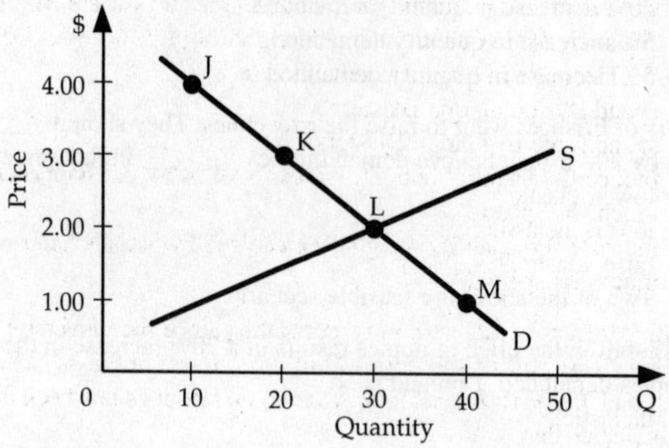

_____ 8. Which statement is false? "Demand for this product is _________ in the range ________."
A. elastic; J to K.
B. elastic; J to L.
C. inelastic; L to M.
D. elastic; K to L.

_____ 9. Suppose a price ceiling of $1.00 is set. This will cause an
A. excess supply of 50 units.
B. excess demand of 50 units.
C. excess demand of 30 units.
D. excess supply of 30 units.

_____ 10. The income elasticity coefficient of Good A is positive, and the cross-price elasticity between Good A and Good B is negative. Good A is a(n)
A. normal good and a substitute for Good B.
B. inferior good and a substitute for Good B.
C. normal good and a complement for Good B.
D. inferior good and a complement for Good B.

_____ 11. The price of a Frisbee rises from $5 to $6. Total revenue falls from $400 to $360. We can conclude that price elasticity of demand coefficient is (roughly) _________, which means that demand is ___________.
A. –.579, inelastic.
B. –1.571, elastic.
C. –.579, elastic.
D. –1.571, inelastic.

_____ 12. Good C has a *negative* income elasticity. Which of the following goods is most likely to be Good C?
A. Alfa Romeo sports car.
B. A vacation in Europe.
C. A compact disc.
D. A can of generic soda pop.

_____ 13. An increase in the labour costs of the sellers of a product, combined with a relatively inelastic demand curve, will result in
A. a relatively small reduction in output.
B. a relatively small increase in equilibrium price.
C. a rightward shift in the supply curve.
D. a leftward shift in the demand curve.

_____ 14. A leftward shift in the supply curve of Pan Galactic Gargle Blasters causes price to rise by 10%. Olivia Leung thereafter buys 20% fewer Gargle Blasters. The price rise has caused Olivia to
A. spend less on Gargle Blasters.
B. spend more on Gargle Blasters.
C. reduce the quantity bought. We can't tell what has happened to how much she spends.
D. increase the quantity bought. We can't tell what has happened to how much she spends.

_____ 15. Atlantic University radio station reports that, since the university eatery, *The Five Beans*, raised the price of hot dogs, fewer hot dogs have been bought and *The Five Beans*' total revenue on hot dogs has been halved. This indicates that
A. the demand schedule for hot dogs at *The Five Beans* is horizontal.
B. at present, prices are in the elastic section of the demand schedule.
C. hot dogs are an inferior good.
D. the price elasticity of demand for hot dogs is .5.

_____ 16. The closer substitutes two goods are, the ________ will be their cross-price elasticity.
A. more positive.
B. more negative.
C. less positive.
D. less negative.

Use the diagram below to answer the next three questions. The world price for gasoline is 35¢ per litre. The equilibrium price in the Canadian market is 55¢.

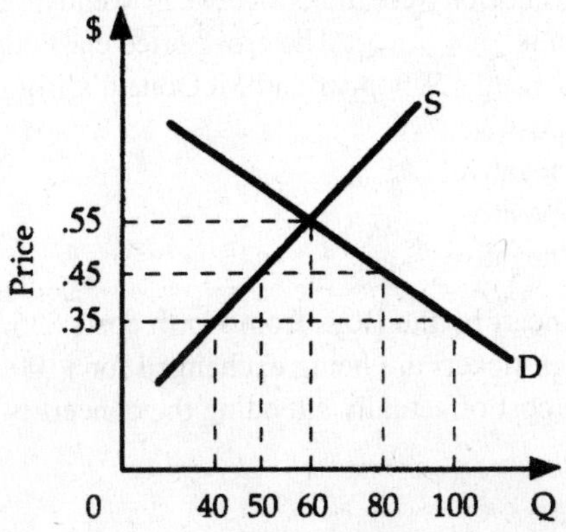

_____ 17. Assume that Canada neither imports nor exports gasoline. At the world price for gasoline, there is an ________ of gas in the Canada market of ______ units.
A. excess supply, 60.
B. excess supply, 100.
C. excess demand, 60.
D. excess demand, 100.

_____ 18. Assume that Canada imports gasoline. The government imposes an import tax that raises the price of gas to 45¢ per litre. Based on the diagram, we can infer that

A. demand is elastic.
B. demand is inelastic.
C. the market is now in equilibrium.
D. total revenue has increased to $80 million.

_____ 19. Assume that Canada imports gasoline. The government imposes an import tax that raises the price of gas to 45¢ per litre. Based on the diagram, which of the following is true?
A. Supply is price elastic between 35¢ and 45¢.
B. Government tax revenues will be 35¢ times 60 million.
C. Demand is price elastic between 45¢ and 55¢.
D. Equilibrium price is now 45¢.

_____ 20. If the proportion of income that Jasmine spends on air travel increases when her income rises, then the income elasticity of demand is
A. greater than zero but not necessarily greater than one.
B. less than zero.
C. greater than one.
D. not defined.

_____ 21. The government has decided that the free market price for baby formula is "too high." Which of the following rationing proposals will result in the **least** misallocation of baby formula resources?
A. Proposal A: establish an official price ceiling, then let sellers decide how to allocate baby formula among customers.
B. Proposal B: issue coupons for baby formula that cannot be resold.
C. Proposal C: issue coupons for baby formula that can be resold.
D. Proposal D: establish a price ceiling and require purchasers to queue.

_____ 22. The cross-price elasticity coefficient between Wendy's Biggie Fries and Wendy's Frostie is _________. The cross-price elasticity coefficient between Burger King's Whopper and McDonald's Big Mac is _________.
A. positive, positive.
B. positive, negative.
C. negative, positive.
D. negative, negative.

_____ 23. A ticket to a concert by the Boys from North costs $35. Just before the concert, however, tickets are being exchanged for $100. To a ticket holder, the opportunity cost of actually attending the concert is
A. $35.
B. $65.
C. $100.
D. $135.

_____ 24. Assume that in a free labour market, the quantity demanded equals the quantity supplied at 500 000 youth jobs and the equilibrium wage rate is equal to $5/hour. Now the government decides that the market wage is too low and imposes a wage floor (minimum wage) at $6.50. Everything else remaining equal,
A. more jobs will be created.
B. fewer people will be looking for a job.
C. the demand curve will shift to the right.
D. there will be a persistent surplus of youth workers.

_____ 25. A government-imposed ceiling on apartment rents, if set above the equilibrium rent level, would

A. have no effect on the housing market.
B. lead to a persistent shortage of apartments.
C. lead to a persistent surplus of apartments.
D. shift the supply curve for apartments to the right.

II. APPLICATION QUESTIONS.

1. You've just bought a company that publishes cookbooks. You consult your in-house economist. The conversation goes like this:
He tells you that the elasticity of demand for your cookbooks is –2.4.
Then you tell him that you want to maximize sales revenue.
Then he tells you that you should raise the price of the cookbooks.
Then you tell him that he is a useless collection of carbon-based molecules.
Explain your reaction.

2. The price of Good A and of Good B is $10, and both goods have a quantity demanded of 100 units per week. When the price of Good A falls to $9, the quantity demanded rises to 200 units per week. However, the price of Good B must fall to $8 in order to achieve sales of 200.
   a. In the price ranges given, which good has the more elastic demand?
   b. Use the total revenue test to confirm that both goods face elastic demand curves.
   c. Verify your answer by calculating the price elasticity coefficient for Good A and Good B.

3. The cross-price elasticity coefficient for Good X (to a change in Good Y's price) is –.7. The cross-price elasticity coefficient for Good X (to a change in Good Z's price) is +.7. Good X's income elasticity coefficient is –.7.
If Good X's producer wishes its demand to increase, which of the following scenarios is the most preferred?
   A. The economy experiences unexpected prosperity; the price of Good Y increases.
   B. The economy experiences an unexpected recession; the price of Good Y increases.
   C. The economy experiences unexpected prosperity; the price of Good Y decreases.
   D. The economy experiences an unexpected recession; the price of Good Z increases.
   E. The price of Good Y increases; the price of Good Z increases.
Explain your answer.

4. Consider the following diagram which shows the market for fluid milk. Quantity is in thousands of litres.

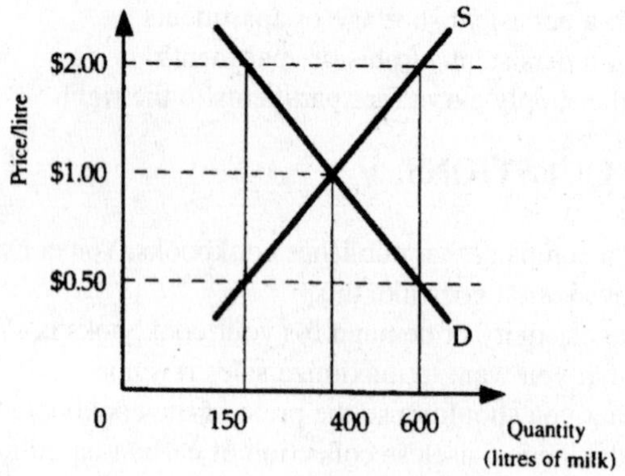

a. Calculate total income for dairy farmers.

b. Suppose that this income level is felt to be inadequate, and that a political decision is made to boost farm income to $1 200 000. Suppose the government establishes a price floor at $2.00, with the government buying the excess supply. How much milk will be supplied?

c. Who gets the milk?

d. The plan achieves the income objective, but what else has it done? There are costs involved with tampering with the price mechanism. What are they?

Now suppose the government establishes a price ceiling of 50¢ per litre.

e. How much milk would consumers actually receive?

f. Which plan is better for a milk consumer who pays no provincial tax? Why?

5. In the *Applications* section of Chapter 4, we examined the market for video cassettes where the supply and demand curves are given by Qs = 3P and Qd = 60 – 2P, respectively.

a. If the government imposes a price ceiling of $5 in this market, what will happen to the positions of the demand and supply curves?

b. Considering the demand curve in isolation, calculate the total revenue when price is $5 and when price is $10.

c. Considering the demand curve in isolation, calculate the total revenue when price is $20 and when price is $25.

d. Use the total revenue test to estimate the elasticity of demand between $5 and $10 and between $20 and $25.

e. Using the midpoint formula, calculate the price elasticity of demand between $5 and $10 and between $20 and $25.

6. In many Eastern European cities, there is a thriving market in farm produce.

a. Draw a demand and supply diagram below for the Warsaw egg market. Label the curves D_1 and S_1 respectively. Show the equilibrium price (P_1) and quantity (Q_1).

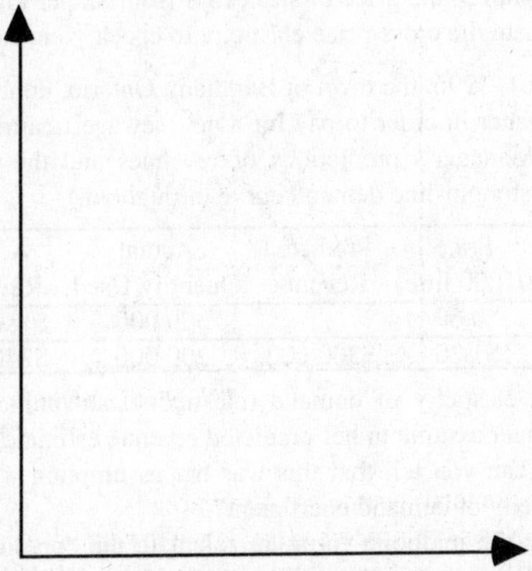

b. In August, the price of eggs tripled because of a decrease in supply caused very hot weather. Show how the market changed in August. Label the new supply curve S_2. Show the new equilibrium price (P_2) and quantity (Q_2).

c. Is the Warsaw egg market operating efficiently?

d. Suppose the government decided to maintain the initial price (P_1). Should it impose a price ceiling or a price floor? Explain whether an excess demand or an excess supply will result.

e. Is the Warsaw egg market now operating efficiently?

f. How do you think suppliers might react to the price ceiling?

g. Suggest what non-price methods might develop to circumvent the imbalance in this market.

7. Use the following demand schedule to complete the table.

Price	Quantity Demanded	Total Revenue	Elasticity (in words)	Elasticity Coefficient	As price rises, TR is:
$6	10	$60			
$5	20	$100			
$4	30	$120			
$3	40	$120			
$2	50	$100			
$1	60	$60	---	---	---

b. Work out a rule, based on your results in the last two columns, linking the change in total revenue and elasticity.

8. Use the information in the table to answer the questions below.

Month	Income per month	Quantity demand of chicken per month	Quantity demand of steak per month
1	$400	5 kgs	3 kgs
2	$800	3 kgs	5 kgs
3	$800	5 kgs	3 kgs

a. Using Months 1 and 2, is the income elasticity of chicken positive, negative, or zero? What kind of a good is chicken?

b. Using Months 1 and 2, estimate the income elasticity of steak. Is steak a normal good?

c. Intuitively, what sort of demand relationship do you think will exist between chicken and steak?

d. In Month 3, the price of steak rose from $2 per kilogram to $3 per kilogram. Estimate the cross-price elasticity to check your intuition.

9. On January 1, 1996, the town of Barkham, Ontario, doubled the rate it charged residents for water in order to pay for a new sewage-treatment plant. The table shows the Town Manager's predictions of revenues and the actual revenues collected. (Assume a straight-line demand curve throughout.)

Year	Price (/1000 litre)	Predicted Revenue	Actual Quantity Used	Actual Revenue
1995	$0.60		300 000	$180 000
1996	$1.20	$300 000	200 000	$240 000

a. What elasticity of demand (elastic/inelastic/unitarily elastic) did the Town Manager assume in her predicted revenue estimate?
b. How can you tell that this was her assumption without first calculating the elasticity of demand coefficient?
c. Using the midpoint formula, calculate the "predicted" elasticity of demand coefficient.
d. Using the midpoint formula, calculate the "actual" elasticity of demand coefficient.

Based on what happened, Alderman Mark Gupta claims that water rate hikes are an easy way to increase town funds. He proposes that the water rate be raised to $5.00 per 1000 litres.

e. What do you think will happen to the position of the demand for water curve?
f. Do you think the elasticity will be the same?
g. Explain your answer to part f.

10. Here is some information about the demand for milk in Moose Jaw College.

Price/litre	Quantity demanded
$1.50	6000
$2.00	4000

Now, suppose the price of a litre of milk rises from $1.50 to $2.00.

a. Using the midpoint formula, calculate the elasticity of demand using the prices and quantities above.
b. Calculate the change in the buyers' total expenditure.
c. On the basis of your calculations, is demand elastic or inelastic, or neither, in this price range?
d. Is your answer in part c consistent with your calculations in part a?

11. The freeze that destroyed much of the South American coffee crop in the mid-1970s increased the price of tea. Explain why, using supply and demand diagrams.

12. Illustrate the following with demand and/or supply curves.

a. A perfectly inelastic supply curve.
b. A labour supply curve along which labour supply elasticity is negative.
c. A situation of excess demand created by a price ceiling.
d. The effect of an increase in income on the price of an inferior good.
e. The effect of a sharp increase in electricity rates on the demand for and price of air-conditioners.

13. Use the following demand and supply schedule to answer the questions.

Price	Quantity Demanded	Quantity Supplied
$6	10	70
$5	20	60
$4	30	50
$3	40	40
$2	50	30
$1	60	20

a. Calculate the equilibrium price and the equilibrium quantity.

b. Now the government establishes a price ceiling of $2. Will this cause an excess supply or an excess demand? An excess of how many units?

ANSWERS AND SOLUTIONS

PRACTICE TEST

I. SOLUTIONS TO MULTIPLE CHOICE QUESTIONS

1. D. Price elasticity looks at the percentage change in quantity demanded divided by the percentage change in price. If $\%\Delta Q/\%\Delta P = -.5$ and $\%\Delta P = 10(\%)$, then $\%\Delta Q = 5(\%)$.

2. A. Check the total revenue test. If price is raised on a good with an elastic demand, many customers will stop buying it and revenue will fall. Therefore, cutting price on a good with an elastic demand will increase total revenue. See p. 124.

3. B. Price elasticity measures the percentage change in quantity demanded divided by the percentage change in price. Here, elasticity is -2.0, which is elastic.

4. A. A change in the quantity of gasoline produced is shown by a supply curve shift.

5. D. For "elasticity" read "responsiveness."

6. B. The elasticity of demand tends to be greater when an item represents a large part of our budget. An increase in its price hurts. If an item is insignificant, changes in its price are insignificant, too, and we are less sensitive to such changes. See p. 126.

7. A. Price of Good A rises, and quantity demanded falls. The other partner in the pair, Good B, experiences a decrease in demand. Cross-price elasticity measures the percentage change in quantity demanded of Good B divided by the percentage change in price of Good A—a negative divided by a positive.

8. D. Apply the total revenue test. When price is $2.00, total revenue is $60. When price is $3.00, total revenue is $60. Demand is unitarily elastic in this price range.

9. C. An effective price ceiling (set below the equilibrium price) will create an excess demand. Quantity demanded is 40, but quantity supplied is only 10.

10. C. A positive income elasticity indicates that Good A is normal. A negative cross-price elasticity indicates that Good A is a complement of Good B. See p. 128.

11. B. If price rises and total revenue falls, we have a good with an elastic demand. The elasticity coefficient must be more negative than –1. (In fact, if you work out the coefficient, it is –1.571, but this is not necessary to answer the question.)

12. D. A negative income elasticity indicates that Good C is inferior. For most people, the inferior good on the list would be the can of generic soda pop. See p. 127.

13. A. The increase in labour costs will make supply shift left. Price will rise and quantity demanded will fall. If demand is relatively inelastic, the increase in price will be relatively large and the decrease in quantity demanded relatively small.

14. A. Olivia's price elasticity coefficient is –2.0—elastic. An increase in price, then, will reduce the number of dollars she spends. See p. 123.

15. B. Price has risen and total revenue has fallen. Demand is elastic.

16. A. Substitutes have a positive cross-price elasticity. The closer they are, the more responsive buyers are to changes in price, and the higher the elasticity coefficient will be. See p. 128.

17. C. The price is below the equilibrium price, with quantity demanded being 100 and quantity supplied being only 40. An excess demand of 60 exists. See p. 107.

18. B. Apply the total revenue test. As price rises from 35¢ to 45¢, total revenue would rise from \$35 million to \$36 million. Note that total revenue is unable to rise like this because supply is restricted. See p. 123.

19. C. As price rises from 45¢ to 55¢, total spending would fall from \$36 million to \$33 million. Demand is elastic if, when price rises, total spending falls.

20. C. For luxuries, demand changes by a greater proportion than the change in income that brings it about. Since the portion of income spent on air travel has risen, air travel must be a luxury good for Jasmine.

21. C. Issuing coupons that can be resold will lead to a market for coupons with those willing and able to pay the most receiving the right to buy baby formula.

22. C. Wendy's products "go together"—a cut in the price of fries, for example, will encourage more customers to buy Frosties too. The Whopper and Big Mac are substitutes—a lower price for the Whopper will reduce demand for the Big Mac.

23. C. The opportunity cost is the value of the next best alternative given up, i.e., in monetary terms, whatever the \$100 offered price would buy.

24. D. A minimum wage, set above the equilibrium price, increases the quantity of labour supplied and at the same time, reduces the quantity demanded. This results in a surplus.

25. A. To be effective, a price ceiling must be set below the equilibrium price.

II. SOLUTIONS TO APPLICATION QUESTIONS

1. An elasticity of demand coefficient of –2.4 indicates that demand is elastic. When demand is elastic, an increase in price will cause total revenue to decrease.

2. Good A has the more elastic demand. The same "change in quantity" response is elicited with a lesser change in price.

   The total revenue test shows an elastic demand in each case. For Good A, a decrease in price, from \$10 to \$9, leads to an increase in total revenue from \$1000 to \$1800. For Good B, a decrease in price, from \$10 to \$8, leads to an increase in total revenue from \$1000 to \$1600.

More formally, the midpoint formula for Good A is:

$$\frac{(100 - 200) / [(100 + 200) / 2]}{(10 - 9) / [(10 + 9) / 2]}$$

The elasticity coefficient for Good A is –6.333.

The midpoint formula for Good B is:

$$\frac{(100 - 200) / [(100 + 200) / 2]}{(10 - 8) / [(10 + 8) / 2]}$$

The elasticity coefficient for Good B is –3.00.

3. Option D is best. Good X and Good Y are complements. Good X and Good Z are substitutes. Good X is an inferior good. A recession will increase the demand for Good X; prosperity will not. An increase in the price of Good Z will reduce the quantity demanded of Y and increase the demand for substitute Good X. An increase in the price of Y will reduce the quantity demanded of Y and reduce the demand for complementary Good X.

4. a. $400 000.
   b. 600 000 litres.
   c. 150 000 litres for the consumer, and the rest is taken by the government.
   d. Many things—milk is now more expensive and less plentiful for consumers. Taxpayers—who needn't be milk consumers—will have to pick up the subsidy tab. There will be storage and administrative costs, too. Also, there is an overallocation of resources toward milk production.
   e. Consumers will receive 150 000 litres. In this case, there will be an excess demand.
   f. The second plan is better in that the price of milk is lower.

5. a. Nothing. A change in price leads to movements along the given demand and supply curves.
   b. When the price is $5, quantity is 50 units. Total revenue is $250. When the price is $10, quantity is 40 units. Total revenue is $400.
   c. When the price is $20, quantity is 20 units. Total revenue is $400. When the price is $25, quantity is 10 units. Total revenue is $250.
   d. As price increases from $5 to $10, total revenue increases from $250 to $400. Demand is inelastic. As price increases from $20 to $25, total revenue decreases from $400 to $250. Demand is elastic.
   e. The midpoint formula when price lies between $5 and $10 is:

   $$\frac{(50 - 40) / [(50 + 40) / 2]}{(5 - 10) / [(5 + 10) / 2]}$$

   The elasticity coefficient in this price range is –.333.

   The midpoint formula when price lies between $20 and $25 is:

   $$\frac{(20 - 10) / [(20 + 10) / 2]}{(20 - 25) / [(20 + 25) / 2]}$$

   The elasticity coefficient in this price range is –3.00.

6. a. See the diagram below.

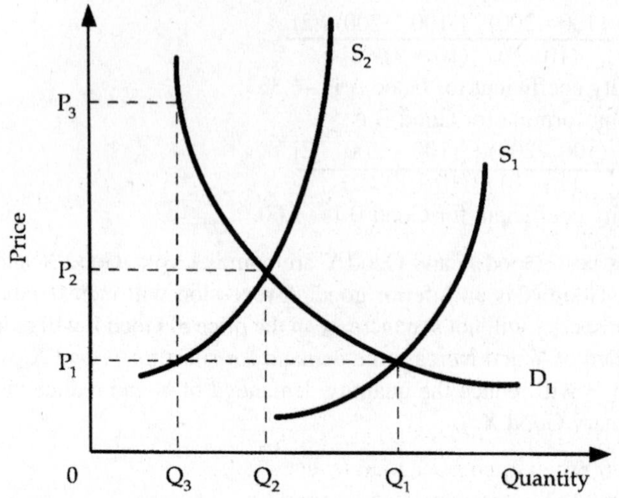

b. See the diagram above.

c. The market is efficient in that it is reflecting the change in supply and equalizing quantity demanded and quantity supplied.

d. The government should impose a price ceiling to place an upper limit on price. Quantity demanded will exceed quantity supplied—there will be an excess demand.

e. This is now a seller's market. Output is restricted to Q_3. At that output, an excess demand exists.

f. Suppliers may withdraw eggs from the controlled Warsaw market—selling them either outside Warsaw or on the black market within the city. Sub-standard (small or damaged) eggs may be offered for sale. Egg quality may be sacrificed.

g. Other rationing methods, such as queuing or preferred customers, might be used. Black markets with higher prices are likely to develop. Eggs may be sold as part of a "package" of commodities.

7. a. See the table below.

Price	*Quantity Demanded*	*Total Revenue*	*Elasticity (in words)*	*Elasticity Coefficient*	*As price rises, TR*
$6	10	$60	elastic	$E_D = 3.667$	falls
$5	20	$100	elastic	$E_D = 1.800$	falls
$4	30	$120	unit elastic	$E_D = 1.000$	is constant
$3	40	$120	inelastic	$E_D = 0.555$	rises
$2	50	$100	inelastic	$E_D = 0.273$	rises
$1	60	$60	--	--	--

b. As price rises, total revenue rises when demand is inelastic. Given a price increase, total revenue will decrease when demand is elastic.

8. a. As income rises, quantity demanded falls. Income elasticity is negative—chicken is an inferior good.

b. As income doubles, quantity demanded rises but doesn't double. Steak's income elasticity is positive but less than one—steak is a normal good.

c. They are likely to be substitutes.

d. Quantity demanded of chicken rose as the price of steak rose. Cross-elasticity is positive—chicken and steak are substitutes.

(For additional practice, calculate the elasticity coefficients that go along with your estimates.)

9. a. inelastic.
   b. An increase in price led to a (predicted) increase in total revenue.
   c. –3/11, or –2727.
   d. –3/5, or –.60.
   e. The position of the curve will remain unchanged. A change in price causes a change in quantity demanded.
   f. No, given that we have assumed a straight–line demand curve.
   g. With a straight-line demand curve, movements along the curve to higher price levels lead to less inelastic (more elastic) regions. See the Tip in Objective 4 for more on this point.

10. a. –7/5 or –1.4.
    b. A fall of $1000, from $9000 to $8000.
    c. Elastic. When price rises, total revenue falls.
    d. Both results indicate an elastic demand.

11. Higher coffee prices increased the demand for tea (a substitute). See the diagrams below.

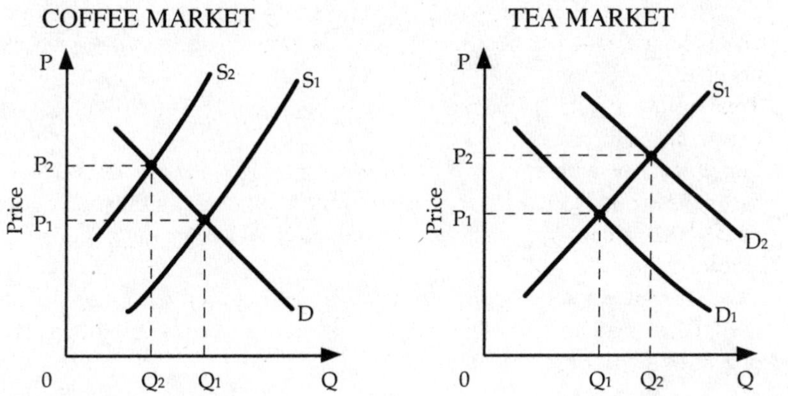

12. See the diagrams below.

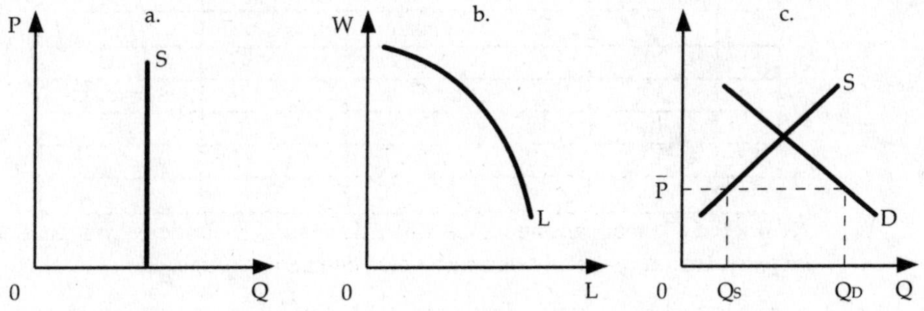

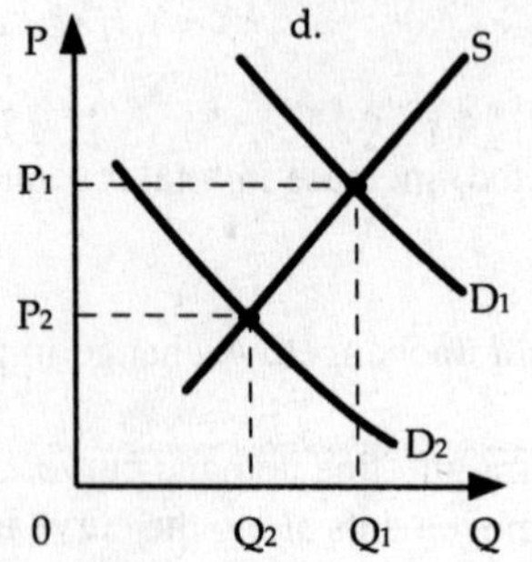

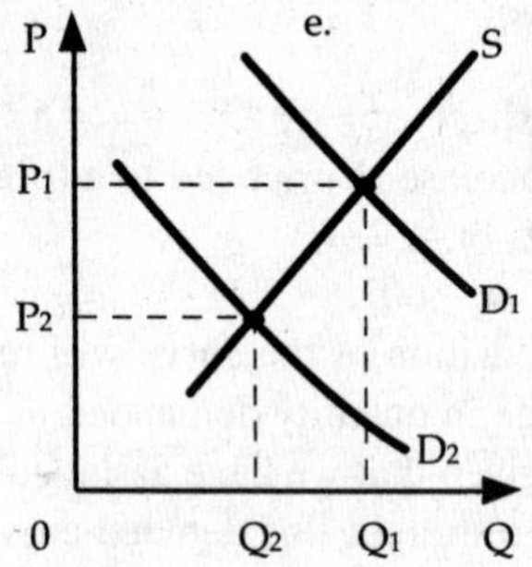

13. a. $3; 40.
    b. excess demand; 20.

6 Household Behaviour and Consumer Choice

OBJECTIVES: POINT BY POINT

After completing this chapter, you should be able to accomplish the objectives listed below.

OBJECTIVE 1: Explain the determinants of household demand.

Several factors influence the quantity of a given good or service demanded by a single household. The chief among them are the price of the product; income available to the household; the prices of other products available to the household; the household's tastes and preferences; and a measure of the household's current and expected future wealth.

(page 132)

OBJECTIVE 2: Describe the budget constraint.

Each household operates within constraints (income, wealth, and the prices of goods) and, therefore, must make choices. The textbook narrows down these choices to three:

a. which combination of goods to buy,
b. how many hours of work to provide, and
c. how much money to save rather than to spend.

To simplify the analysis, it is assumed in the analysis of household choice that there is perfect competition in all (input and output) markets, that price is governed by demand and supply, and that households are "informed"—they have perfect knowledge about the price, availability, and quality of goods, about wage rates, and (later) about interest rates.

(page 133)

Each semester, you must weigh up your own situation. How much money will the semester cost? What is essential (tuition, housing, food, textbooks, aspirin, coffee) and what is, perhaps, optional (movies, phone calls home)? How much do these items cost? How much spending power have you set aside from your summer job (wealth)? What income will you have during the semester, perhaps from a part-time job? In simplified form, the *budget constraint diagram* illustrates the limited set of opportunities available to you.

The *budget constraint* defines the maximum possible amount of goods that can be bought and is determined by the household's income, wealth, and prices. In a two-good situation, this constraint looks rather like a production possibility frontier—think of it as a "consumption" possibility frontier, if you will. The real cost of buying more of one good is the value of the other good that must be foregone. All points on and inside the constraint are combinations of goods that can be bought; they comprise the *opportunity (choice) set.* Points outside cannot be bought. The curve will shift to the right—meaning that there is an increase in possible consumption levels—if income or wealth increases or if prices fall. If the price of one good falls, the budget constraint *swivels* and the slope of the constraint changes. The slope is determined by the relative prices of the two goods. Given the constraints, decisions depend on the preferences of the household.

TIP: The "Trudee and Mark" example in the textbook is particularly effective in making the points you need to know. Be sure to cover it thoroughly.

Practice

1. The budget constraint is the limit imposed on household choices by the household's
   A. expectations about future income, wealth, and prices.
   B. wealth.
   C. income, wealth, and prices.
   D. preferences and monthly spending plan.

   ANSWER: C. See p. 133. The basic analysis provided to this point has not yet incorporated expectations about future income, wealth, or prices.

2. Gretchen's opportunity set can be increased by
   A. a decrease in prices.
   B. a decrease in income.
   C. an increase in quantity demanded.
   D. a decrease in quantity demanded.

   ANSWER: A. The opportunity set defines what is available ather than what is demanded. A decrease in prices will permit Gretchen to stretch her dollars further.

3. Jenny the Junior buys only two goods: meals and movies. This semester she has $500 in a savings account that she plans to spend, but no income. Meals cost $5 each and movies cost $10 each. Jenny's maximum spending on meals is __________ and her maximum spending on movies is __________.
   A. $500, $0.
   B. $0, $500.
   C. $250, $250.
   D. $500, $500.

   ANSWER: D. At one extreme, Jenny could spend all of her resources on meals or, at the other, all of her resources on movies.

4. Jenny the Junior buys only two goods: meals and movies. This semester she has $500 in a savings account that she plans to spend, but no income. Meals cost $5 each and movies cost $10 each. Jenny can buy a maximum of _______ meals and a maximum of _______ movies.
   A. 100, 0.
   B. 100, 100.
   C. 0, 50.
   D. 100, 50.

   ANSWER: D. With $500 and facing a meal price of $5, Jenny could buy as many as 100 meals. With $500 and facing a movie price of $10, Jenny could buy as many as 50 movies.

5. Draw Jenny's budget constraint in the space below. Place "meals" on the horizontal axis and "movies" on the vertical axis. Write in the maximum value for meals and for movies at the appropriate places.

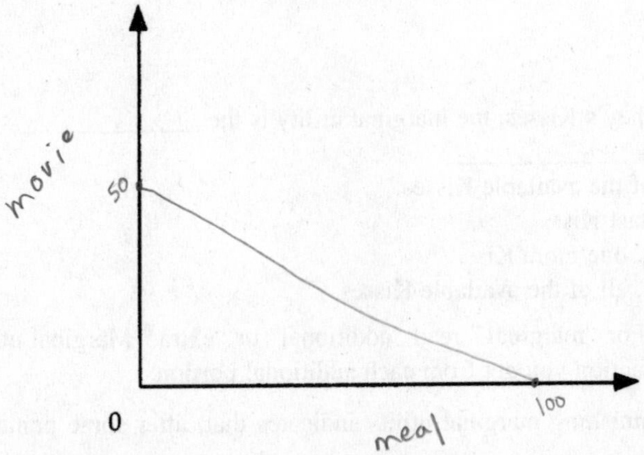

ANSWER: The budget constraint should be a downsloping straight line. The "meals" and "movies" end points should be 100 and 50, respectively.

6. The slope of Jenny's budget constraint is
   A. –2.
   B. –1/2.
   C. 1/2.
   D. 2.

   ANSWER: B. "Rise over run" is the formula for the slope of a straight line. If you are uncertain about this, check the textbook's Appendix to Chapter 1.

7. Refer to your diagram. Along the budget constraint, the opportunity cost of one movie is
   A. zero, since the goods have already been bought.
   B. 1/2 a meal.
   C. 1 meal.
   D. 2 meals.

   ANSWER: D. The $10 could have bought two meals.

8. Refer to your diagram. If ________, Jenny's new budget constraint will ________.
   A. the price of movies increases, shift out and be parallel to the initial budget constraint.
   B. her income increases, swivel inward.
   C. her income decreases, swivel inward.
   D. the price of movies decreases, swivel outward.

   ANSWER: D. Income (or wealth) changes will cause a parallel shift in the budget constraint. A lower price of movies will increase the maximum number of movies it is possible for Jenny to attend but leave unaffected the maximum number of meals she may consume.

OBJECTIVE 3: State the law of diminishing marginal utility.

Utility (satisfaction) is derived from goods and services, including leisure. The *marginal utility* you derive from a good (potato chips, for example) is the additional satisfaction you get from each additional portion. The *total utility* is the sum of these additional contributions to your level of satisfaction. The *law of diminishing marginal utility* states that extra units of a good yield less and less extra satisfaction. While the first few potato chips may provide quite significant increases in utility, subsequent chips are likely to provide progressively less utility (as your hunger decreases and your guilt increases). (page 137)

Practice

9. Regarding Hershey's Kisses, the marginal utility is the ____________ satisfaction gained by eating ____________.
   A. total, all of the available Kisses.
   B. total, the last Kiss.
   C. additional, one more Kiss.
   D. additional, all of the available Kisses.

   ANSWER: C. For "marginal," read "additional" or "extra." Marginal utility is the additional satisfaction you get from each additional portion.

10. The law of diminishing marginal utility indicates that, after some point, marginal utility
    A. decreases at a constant rate.
    B. decreases at an increasing rate.
    C. decreases at a decreasing rate.
    D. decreases.

    ANSWER: D. The rate at which marginal utility diminishes will vary from person to person and from good to good. All we can claim is that marginal utility will decrease after some point.

11. Mario plays video games. Although he is experiencing diminishing marginal utility, his marginal utility remains positive. We can say that Mario's total utility is
    A. increasing at an increasing rate.
    B. increasing at a decreasing rate.
    C. decreasing at an increasing rate.
    D. decreasing at a decreasing rate.

    ANSWER: B. Because Mario's marginal utility is positive, each new game increases his total satisfaction but at a decreasing rate of increase.

12. Candy has eaten ten Hershey's Kisses and admits that each additional Kiss has been less enjoyable than the previous one. We can deduce that, for Candy,
    A. the marginal utility of Kisses is positive but decreasing.
    B. the marginal utility of Kisses is negative.
    C. the total utility of Kisses is diminishing.
    D. the total utility of Kisses has peaked.

    ANSWER: A. This is an example of the law of diminishing marginal utility. Since Candy is still eating Kisses, she must still be deriving some (positive) marginal utility from them, so the total utility is increasing but at a decreasing rate.

Use the table below to answer the next three questions.

Susan visits the local fair and rides the Ferris wheel several times.

Number of rides	Total Utility	Marginal Utility
1	10	10
2	24	14
3	34	10
4	41	7
5	46	5

13. The marginal utility of the first ride on the Ferris wheel is
   A. 5.
   B. 10.
   C. 12.
   D. 14.

   ANSWER: B. The total utility derived from no rides must be zero. One ride added 10 units of utility.

14. The total utility of the fourth ride is
   A. 6.
   B. 7.
   C. 12.
   D. 41.

   ANSWER: D. The total utility derived from three rides is 34. The fourth ride added an additional 7 units of utility for a total utility of 41.

15. Diminishing marginal utility sets in after the ________ ride.
   A. first.
   B. second.
   C. third.
   D. fourth.

   ANSWER: B. The first ride adds 10 units of utility; the second, 14; the third, 10, so diminishing marginal utility sets in after the second ride.

OTHER RELATED POINTS: State the utility-maximizing rule in words and mathematically, and analyse how the consumer would respond to disequilibrium situations.

Assuming that households try to maximize their utility, they should select those goods that give the largest marginal utility per dollar. Utility will be maximized when the per-dollar marginal utility of the last unit of each good bought is equal. Formally it is stated:

$$MU_x / P_x = MU_y / P_y$$

All this means is that, to get the most satisfaction from one's money, the "extra benefit per dollar" must be equalized for all goods purchased.

An *imbalance* in the utility-maximizing condition, for example,

$$MU_x / P_x > MU_y / P_y$$

means that you could shuffle your income around—buying more of the good giving the greater marginal utility per dollar (X) and less of the other (Y)—and get a better deal. Buying more of X will reduce its marginal utility and buying less of Y will increase its marginal utility. So the imbalance is removed. (page 139)

> **TIP:** The idea of maximizing utility—despite the graphs and algebra—is fairly intuitive. You want to get the most satisfaction for your dollar. You should choose the good that gives you the most extra satisfaction per dollar (MU/P). In economics, remember, choices are made at the margin. (If you've forgotten this important point, review Chapter 1.) In the final analysis, with perfectly divisible goods, this becomes the utility-maximizing rule:
>
> $MU_x / P_x = MU_y / P_y$
>
> where the marginal utilities per dollar are balanced.

Practice

16. Arthur Dent is buying shirts and shoes such that the marginal utility of shirts is 12 and the marginal utility of shoes is 3. Shirts and shoes are priced at $8 and $2 respectively. It can be concluded that Arthur is
    A. spending too much on shirts and not enough on shoes.
    B. spending too much on shoes and not enough on shirts.
    C. spending his income on shirts and shoes in such a way as to maximize his satisfaction.
    D. failing to maximize his satisfaction.

    ANSWER: C. Arthur is complying with the utility-maximizing rule. The marginal utility per dollar of shirts (12/8) equals the marginal utility per dollar of shoes (3/2).

17. We discover that my $MU_{coffee} / P_{coffee} > MU_{tea} / P_{tea}$. This implies that
    A. switching some funds from coffee to tea will increase my utility.
    B. switching some funds from tea to coffee will increase my utility.
    C. coffee is more expensive than tea.
    D. tea is more expensive than coffee.

    ANSWER: B. The per dollar satisfaction from an extra cup of coffee is greater than the per dollar satisfaction from an extra cup of tea. I should spend less on tea and use the saved dollars to buy more coffee.

18. $MU_{Snickers} / MU_{Mars\ Bar} > P_{Snickers} / P_{Mars\ Bar}$. To increase my utility, I should spend
    A. more on Snickers and more on Mars Bars.
    B. more on Snickers and less on Mars Bars.
    C. less on Snickers and more on Mars Bars.
    D. less on Snickers and less on Mars Bars.

    ANSWER: B. Given my income, I cannot buy more of both goods. Because the marginal utility of Snickers is relatively high, I should spend less on Mars Bars and use the saved dollars to buy more Snickers.

OBJECTIVE 4: State the role of diminishing marginal utility in the theory of demand.

Utility analysis explains the downward slope of the demand curve. Since marginal satisfaction falls with each additional unit bought, price must fall to "encourage" additional purchases of a good. (page 140)

It is quite easy to see this "diminishing marginal utility" explanation in operation when one finds examples of "Buy the first, and get the second for half price."

Practice

19. Angela will buy additional units of a good (apples) if the value of the good's
    A. total utility exceeds the price.
    B. total utility is less than the price.
    C. marginal utility exceeds the price.
    D. marginal utility is less than the price.

    ANSWER: C. If Angela's extra benefit is greater than the cost of the apple, then the purchase will be worthwhile.

20. Consider Good X. The law of diminishing marginal utility indicates that
   A. the individual's quantity demanded for Good X will increase as the price of Good X decreases.
   B. the individual's budget constraint is downward sloping.
   C. total utility decreases as an individual consumes more of a product.
   D. Good X is an inferior good.

   ANSWER: A. Option B is true but not related to the law of diminishing marginal utility.

OBJECTIVE 5: Distinguish between the income effect and the substitution effect of a price change.

The income effect and the substitution effect provide a second explanation for the downward slope of the demand curve. Most goods are *normal* goods. As the price of a normal good (low-fat milk, for instance) rises, you become poorer because your food dollar can't stretch as far as it did before (*income effect*), and you seek cheaper substitutes such as regular milk (*substitution effect*). Both effects result in a decrease in the quantity demanded of low-fat milk as its price increases.

Although the demand curve for *inferior goods* (store-brand tuna, for example), still slopes down, the income effect is reversed. As before, a rise in price of the good (tuna) makes you seek cheaper substitutes, such as the store's brand of tuna (substitution effect). But you're poorer because of the higher price—your food dollar can't stretch as far. In the case of an inferior good, however, the income effect results in more of the good being bought. Since you're poorer after a price rise, you may no longer be able afford that salmon steak you were going to buy—tuna is the best you can manage. In general, the substitution effect (price higher—buy less) is stronger than the income effect (price higher—buy more), so, on balance, the quantity demanded falls when price rises. (page 141)

Practice

21. The substitution effect occurs when
   A. a decrease in the price of Good A makes the good relatively cheaper and encourages consumers to buy more.
   B. a decrease in the price of Good A encourages consumers to buy more of substitute Good B.
   C. a decrease in the price of Good A makes consumers better off so that they can buy more of the good.
   D. an increase in the price of Good A encourages consumers to buy less of substitute Good B.

   ANSWER: A. The substitution effect refers to the behaviour of consumers of Good A when the price of that Good A itself changes.

22. The "income effect" helps to explain why
   A. the demand curve for a normal good shifts to the right when income increases.
   B. the quantity demanded of a good increases when the price of that good decreases.
   C. the demand curve of an inferior good shifts to the left when income decreases.
   D. normal goods have higher prices than inferior goods do.

   ANSWER: B. The income effect provides part of the explanation for the slope of the demand curve as the price of the good changes.

Know 23. The "substitution effect" helps to explain why ____________ when the price of good A rises.

A. sellers switch production and increase quantity supplied of good A.
B. the demand curve for good A is sloped as it is.
C. demand for another good B rises.
D. price elasticity increases along the curve.

ANSWER: B. Together, the income effect and the substitution effect offer an alternative explanation of the negative relationship between price and quantity demanded.

24. The price of Froot Loops cereal falls. Consumers switch over from other cereals to Froot Loops because its price is relatively lower. This is the ________ in operation.

A. income effect.
B. substitution effect.
C. *ceteris paribus* effect.
D. quantity demanded effect.

ANSWER: B. The lower price is causing buyers to substitute Froot Loops for other cereals.

25. The price of Froot Loops cereal falls. Wanda finds that she has some money left over after buying her usual quantity of Froot Loops. She spends some of the extra money on more Froot Loops. This is the

A. income effect in operation.
B. substitution effect in operation.
C. normal effect in operation.
D. inferior effect in operation.

ANSWER: A. The reduced price has increased Wanda's spending power—her income, in this sense, has increased. We can see that this good is a normal good for Wanda because she buys more.

OBJECTIVE 6: Explain the meaning of consumer surplus.

For the final unit of a good purchased, the price and the value derived should be equal. Previous units should be valued more highly but the same price charged. *Consumer surplus* is the difference between the value the purchaser places on his or her purchases of a product and the price he or she pays. (page 143)

> **Graphing Pointer:** You will meet the important concept of consumer surplus several times in microeconomics. Graphically, the consumer surplus is the triangle bounded by the demand curve, the vertical axis, and the product price. Changes in the triangle's area reflect changes in consumer well-being.

Practice

26. Given your demand curve for bananas, as the price of bananas decreases, your consumer surplus will

A. increase, because the gap between the price you would pay and the price you do pay is greater than before.
B. decrease, because marginal utility diminishes as more of a good is bought.
C. remain constant, because the demand curve has not changed position.
D. remain constant, because the maximum price you would pay has not changed.

ANSWER: A. See the definition of consumer surplus on p. 144.

27. Diamonds are more expensive than water because the price of a product tends to reflect its
    A. total value.
    B. consumer surplus.
    C. marginal value.
    D. revealed preference.

ANSWER: C. The consumer assesses whether or not to buy by comparing the price with the marginal utility. If the marginal utility is low, the price will need to be low to encourage purchase.

Use the diagram below to answer the following question.

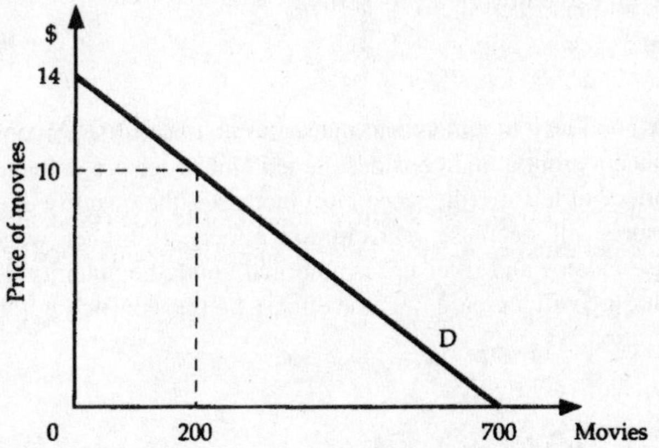

28. When the price of a movie is $10, the consumer surplus is
    A. $4.
    B. $200.
    C. $400.
    D. $800.

ANSWER: C. Consumer surplus is the area between the demand curve and the price. With a straight line demand curve it is $^1/_2(P_{max} - P)Qd$. In this case, consumer surplus is $^1/_2(14 - 10)200$, or $400.

OBJECTIVE 7: Analyze the labour-supply decision using the income and substitution effects.

A household chooses how much labour to supply (and how much leisure and unpaid work time to relinquish). The opportunity cost of paid work is leisure and unpaid work. The wage rate can be thought of as the "price" of unpaid work or leisure. If the wage rate rises, the substitution effect would encourage supplying additional labour (the opportunity cost of leisure is now higher) but the income effect would discourage additional work (higher income would make the worker want to increase consumption of normal goods, including leisure). If the income effect is stronger than the substitution effect, the labour-supply curve will bend backwards. (page 147)

TIP: Throughout the textbook, Case, Fair, Strain, and Veall stress the links between the input and output markets. For you to make sense of the remainder of the book you have to develop a good understanding of the material on household behaviour in the labour market.

There is an interesting example of a strong income effect in operation in the Algerian labour market. To attract workers, U.S. companies in Algeria in the early 1960s paid wages that were about four times the norm. To their dismay they found that, after a short time on the payroll, workers would not show up for work. The workers, who had earned a year's worth of income in a few months, simply chose to take the leisure time to enjoy their prosperity.

TIP: A good way to understand the section on labour supply is to turn the concept around and consider the amount of leisure demanded. As the "price" of leisure (the wage rate) increases, the quantity demanded of leisure will decrease (substitution effect). If higher wage rates increase income and if leisure is a normal good, the quantity demanded of leisure will increase (income effect). So two conflicting forces are in operation.

Graphing Pointer: From Chapter 4, you are used to equilibrium occurring where demand and supply curves cross. If you think about this (and you should), the competitive forces surrounding "normal" demand and supply curves drive the price toward equilibrium. Verify this. If, though, the supply curve is backward bending, will competitive forces still drive the market to equilibrium where the two curves cross? In fact, no. Check it and see.

Practice

29. In Crantown, an increase in the wage of deckhands results in an increase in the number of deckhands making themselves available for work. This indicates that the
   A. income effect is stronger than the substitution effect.
   B. substitution effect is stronger than the income effect.
   C. income effect is positive.
   D. substitution effect is negative.

   ANSWER: B. The supply of deckhands is upward sloping. This indicates that, although deckhands may wish to work less and enjoy leisure at higher wage rates (income effect), the substitution effect predominates.

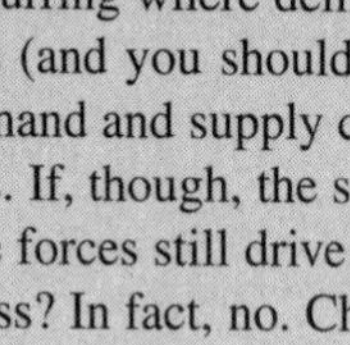

Use the diagram below, which depicts Kevin's supply of labour mowing lawns during the summer, to answer the following question.

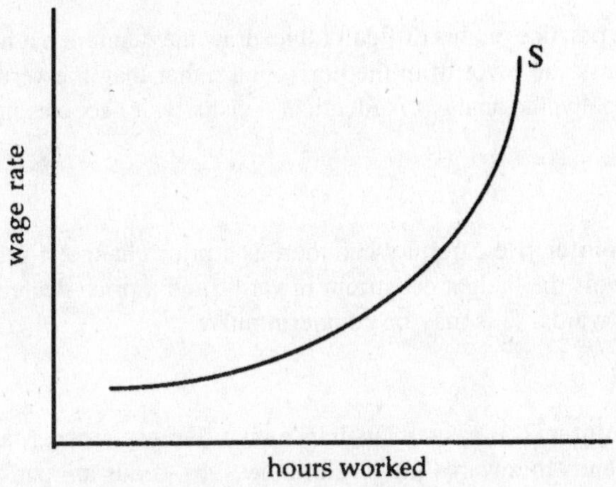

30. Along Kevin's labour supply curve,
    A. the income effect dominates the substitution effect as the wage rate increases.
    B. the substitution effect dominates the income effect as the wage rate increases.
    C. the substitution effect of a wage increase is zero.
    D. the income effect of a wage increase is zero.

    ANSWER: B. When the labour supply curve has its typical positive slope, the attractiveness of substituting labour for leisure outweighs the ability to take time off and enjoy the extra income.

OBJECTIVE 8: Analyze saving and borrowing decisions using income and substitution effects.

In addition to deciding how to allocate its present income among goods and services, a household may also decide to save or borrow. When a household saves part of its current income, it is using current income to finance future spending. When it borrows, it finances current purchases with future income.

A change in interest rates affects household behaviour in capital markets, in the same way that a change in wage rates affect them in the labour market. As interest rates change, they affect both the cost of borrowing and the return to saving. Higher interest rates mean that borrowing is more expensive. But whether higher interest rates, which mean that saving will earn a higher return, increase or decrease saving depends on the relative strength of income and substitution effects. A rise in the interest rate tends to increase saving if the substitution effect (the rising cost of spending each dollar today in terms of future consumption) is greater than the income effect (the reduced need to save as much given that more will be earned on all the savings). (page 150)

OBJECTIVE 9: Outline the basics of the indifference curve approach to household behaviour.

Indifference curves plot bundles of goods giving equal satisfaction. If there is less of one good, the individual must be compensated by having more of the other good—a negative relationship. Indifference curves cannot intersect because this would imply that the same bundle of goods could give more than one level of satisfaction. (page 155)

TIP: You'll find it easier to draw an indifference curve tangential to a given budget constraint rather than to draw the indifference curve first.

TIP: For extra practice on this difficult topic, draw the diagram but have the budget constraint pivot from the horizontal rather than the vertical axis. Theoretically, the analysis is identical—visually, it becomes more challenging.

Graphing Pointer: Be careful when there is a price change: a price increase swivels the budget constraint inwards, and a price decrease swivels it outwards. This may be counterintuitive.

Graphing Pointer: It is easy to misdraw an indifference curve. Make sure that it bends in towards the origin, unless the goods are perfect substitutes, in which case a straight line is correct. (Why?) Also, avoid curling the curve to give it a positive slope—this may not be wrong, but it is liable to lead you astray.

31. An indifference curve plots all the combinations of Good X and Good Y
    A. that may be bought with a given income level and given prices for Good X and Good Y.
    B. that give maximum satisfaction as income level changes.
    C. that give the same marginal utility.
    D. that give the same total utility.

    ANSWER: D. A movement along an indifference curve shows that the individual is gaining more of one good but losing some of the other. The gain in satisfaction from the former exactly equals the loss in satisfaction from the latter.

32. An indifference curve is downward sloping because
    A. more is preferred to less.
    B. preferences remain constant as income level increases.
    C. the marginal rate of substitution increases as one moves along the indifference curve.
    D. the marginal rate of substitution decreases as one moves along the indifference curve.

    ANSWER: A. Because more is preferred to less, an increase in the quantity of Good X consumed must be balanced by a decrease in the quantity of Good Y consumed. Option C refers to the curvature of an indifference curve, not to its slope.

OTHER RELATED POINTS: Derive a demand curve using indifference curve analysis.

The budget constraint diagram is combined with indifference curves in order to depict the utility-maximizing mix of purchases. Four assumptions are made, the main one being that the marginal rate of substitution is diminishing. An indifference curve maps all the combinations of goods that provide a particular level of utility. The curves are bent inwards because of the assumption that the rate of marginal substitution is diminishing. Higher (further right) indifference curves indicate higher levels of utility. (page 158)

The *marginal rate of substitution* is a ratio, the rate at which an individual is willing to surrender units of one good for units of the other. Put differently, it's the ratio of the marginal utility of one good to the marginal utility of the other. Formally the equation is stated:

$$MU_x / MU_y$$

In equilibrium, this ratio is equal to the price ratio, so that

$$MU_x / MU_y = P_x / P_y$$

for all pairs of goods.

> **Comment:** The analysis makes two important points. First, utility will be maximized where the budget constraint is tangent to the highest possible indifference curve—this is where the price ratio equals the marginal rate of substitution. Second, by changing the price of one good, the quantity demanded can be shown to rise—another explanation of the downward-sloping demand curve.

33. My marginal rate of substitution between a round of golf and a game of tennis is 6. This implies that
    A. a round of golf is 6 times more valuable to me than a game of tennis.
    B. a game of tennis is 6 times more valuable to me than a round of golf.
    C. tennis is 6 times as expensive as golf.
    D. golf is 6 times as expensive as tennis.

    ANSWER: A. The marginal rate of substitution represents the rate at which I am willing to substitute one good for another.

34. In a two-good world, Jason is in equilibrium when
    A. $MU_x / MU_y = P_x/P_y$.
    B. $MU_x / MU_y = P_y (P_x)$.
    C. $MU_x / MU_y = P_y/P_x$.
    D. $MU_x / MU_y = -P_y/P_x$.

    ANSWER: A. See p. 164.

PRACTICE TEST

I. MULTIPLE CHOICE QUESTIONS. Select the option that provides the single best answer.

____ 1. Good A and Good B cost \$3 and \$4, respectively. Jo, spending all of her income, buys 4 units of Good A and 3 units of Good B. The final units of each good give her 12 units of utility.
    A. Jo is maximizing her utility.
    B. Jo should buy more of Good A and less of Good B to maximize utility.
    C. Jo should buy less of Good A and more of Good B to maximize utility.
    D. Jo should buy less of both goods to maximize utility.

____ 2. P_X is \$12 and P_Y is \$6. These prices indicate that the individual can
    A. trade 12 units of Good X for 6 of Good Y.
    B. trade 1 unit of Good X for 2 of Good Y.
    C. increase his utility by buying more units of the cheaper Good Y.
    D. increase his utility by buying more of the more highly-valued Good X.

_____ 3. A given budget constraint
A. will swivel out if the price of one of the goods increases.
B. will swivel in if income falls.
C. will swivel out if income falls.
D. will swivel in if the price of one of the goods increases.

_____ 4. If prices double and income doubles, the budget constraint
A. will double.
B. will move inward.
C. will move outward by 50%.
D. will not shift position.

_____ 5. Jill's consumer surplus for Good A will
A. increase if the price of A increases.
B. increase if the price of B, a substitute for A, falls.
C. decrease if Jill's income falls and A is a normal good.
D. decrease if the price of C, a complement for A, falls.

_____ 6. The wage rate rises. If the quantity of labour supplied falls, the most likely explanation is that
A. the substitution effect and the income effect are both positive.
B. the substitution effect is negative and the income effect is positive.
C. the substitution effect and the income effect are both negative.
D. the substitution effect is positive and the income effect is negative.

_____ 7. Higher interest rates cause
A. future consumption to increase.
B. current consumption to increase.
C. current borrowing to increase.
D. current saving to decrease.

_____ 8. Laila is maximizing her utility. The price of Good A falls. Laila will
A. buy more of Good A because it is relatively cheaper—the substitution effect.
B. buy less of Good A because her marginal utility is diminishing.
C. buy more of Good A because her marginal utility is increasing.
D. buy more of Good B—the substitution effect.

_____ 9. Fred has had 4 hamburgers and 2 hot dogs this week and is now indifferent between them. Hamburgers cost $2 and hot dogs cost $1. Currently
A. Fred's marginal utility of hamburgers is double that of hot dogs.
B. Fred's total utility of hamburgers is equal to that of hot dogs.
C. Fred's total utility of hamburgers is double that of hot dogs.
D. Fred's marginal utility of hamburgers is equal to that of hot dogs.

_____ 10. In a two-good analysis, the slope of the budget constraint is determined by
A. the prices of the two goods.
B. the income and wealth of the household.
C. the income, but not the wealth, of the household.
D. the income and wealth of the household and the prices of the two goods.

_____ 11. The wage rate can be seen as a measure of the opportunity cost of
A. work.
B. saving.
C. leisure.
D. future consumption.

_____ 12. The utility-maximizing combination of two goods (cakes and ale) occurs when the MRS of cakes for ale equals
A. the MRS of ale for cakes.
B. the ratio of MU of cakes / MU of ale.
C. the ratio of the price of cakes to the price of ale.
D. the ratio of the price of ale to the price of cakes.

_____ 13. A price decrease
A. increases the choice set.
B. decreases the opportunity set.
C. makes utility maximizers worse off.
D. decreases the choice set.

_____ 14. "Utility"
A. involves the subjective weighing of the satisfaction individuals receive from goods and services.
B. is measurable.
C. can be used to compare the likes and dislikes of different individuals.
D. all of the above.

_____ 15. The diamond-water paradox is resolved recognizing that the price of a product tends to reflect its
A. use value.
B. total value.
C. consumer surplus.
D. marginal value.

_____ 16. When the price of pretzels rises, the "income effect" helps to explain why
A. opportunity cost increases along the demand curve.
B. sellers switch production and increase the quantity supplied of pretzels.
C. income rises for producers of pretzels.
D. the demand curve for pretzels is sloped as it is.

_____ 17. The market demand curve for pizza is given by Qd = 400 – 25P, where P is the price of pizza in dollars. If the price of pizza is $10, the consumer surplus is
A. $6.
B. $150.
C. $450.
D. $800.

_____ 18. Joe would pay $1.00 for his first cup of soft drink during the Canadian universities' basketball championship game. He would pay 60¢ for his second, 50¢ for his third, and 40¢ for his fourth. If the price is
A. 50¢ per cup, Joe will buy 3 cups and have a consumer surplus of $2.10.
B. 50¢ per cup, Joe will buy 3 cups and have a consumer surplus of $1.60.
C. 55¢ per cup, Joe will buy 2 cups and have a consumer surplus of 50¢.
D. 55¢ per cup, Joe will buy 2 cups and have a consumer surplus of $1.05.

Use the following information for the next two questions. Kaori's income is $100; the price of apples is $5 per unit; the price of oranges is $10 per unit. Assume a consumer choice diagram with apples on the vertical axis and oranges on the horizontal axis.

_____ 19. If Kaori's income falls to $75, but the prices of apples and oranges remain unchanged, there will be

A. a parallel shift inward of the indifference curves.
B. a parallel shift outward of the budget line.
C. a parallel shift inward of the budget line.
D. a decrease in Kaori's consumption of both apples and oranges.

_____ 20. If the price of apples increases to $10 per unit,

A. the budget line will rotate clockwise around the intersection of the budget line and the vertical axis.
B. the budget line will rotate counter-clockwise around the intersection of the budget line and the horizontal axis.
C. Kaori will be on the same indifference curve, but fewer apples will be consumed.
D. Kaori's consumption of apples will decrease.

_____ 21. An increase in the wage rate will __________ the quantity of labour supplied, according to the substitution effect, and will __________ the quantity of labour supplied, according to the income effect.

A. increase, increase.
B. increase, decrease.
C. decrease, increase.
D. decrease, decrease.

Use the following information for the next two questions. Currently, Zack is using his income to consume two goods, X and Y, in such a way that $MU_x / MU_y < P_x/P_y$.

_____ 22. To maximize his satisfaction, Zack should

A. increase consumption of Good X and increase consumption of Good Y.
B. increase consumption of Good X and decrease consumption of Good Y.
C. decrease consumption of Good X and increase consumption of Good Y.
D. decrease consumption of Good X and decrease consumption of Good Y.

_____ 23. As Zack moves towards equilibrium,

A. he will move along the same indifference curve.
B. he will move along the same budget constraint.
C. the marginal utility of Good X will decrease.
D. the marginal rate of substitution will decrease.

_____ 24. Lesley Behan can buy two goods, Good X and Good Y. Good X is represented on the horizontal axis. Which of the following will cause the budget constraint to increase its slope?

A. An increase in the price of Good X.
B. An equal increase in the price of both goods.
C. An increase in Lesley's income.
D. An increase in the price of Good Y.

II. APPLICATION QUESTIONS.

1. The indifference curve diagram below shows Jenny's utility-maximizing goods combinations (K and L) given two different prices of Good B. The vertical axis represents spending on all other goods.
   a. What is Jenny's income?

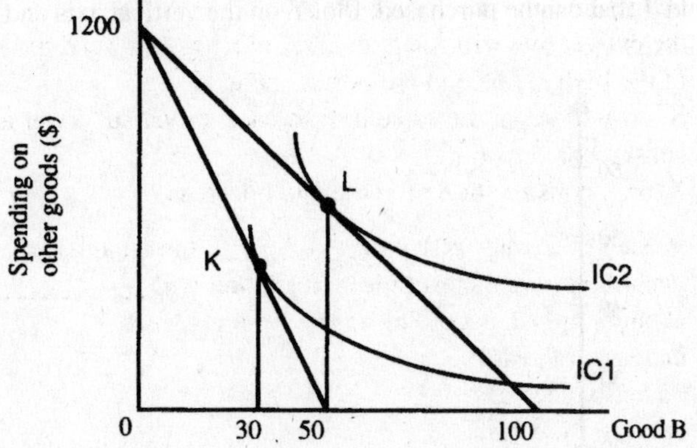

   b. What is the price of Good B at point K?
   c. What is the price of Good B at point L?
   d. When in equilibrium at point K, how much will she spend on Good B?
   e. When in equilibrium at point L, how much will she spend on Good B?
   f. If Jenny has a straight, downward sloping demand curve for Good B, plot the two points on her demand curve that you know, showing price and quantity information. Sketch in the straight-line demand curve through these points.

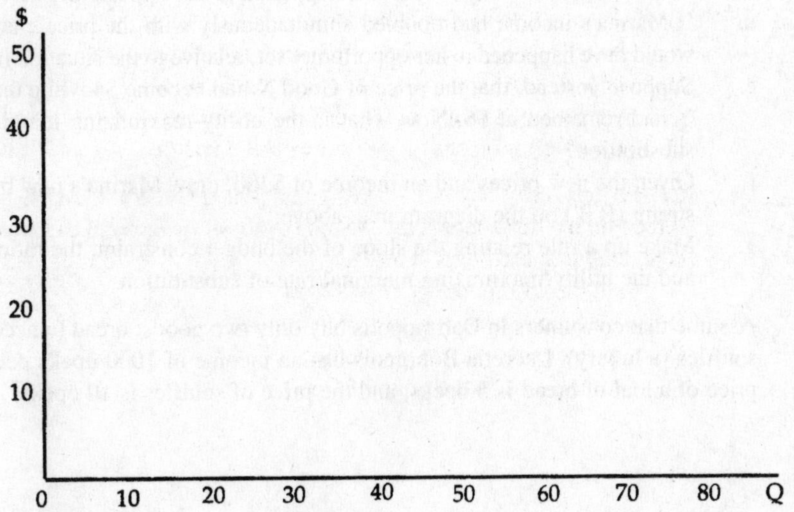

   g. Calculate her price elasticity of demand coefficient for Good B as the price changes from $12 to $24. Use the midpoint formula. (Hint: Refer to Chapter 5 if you are unsure of how to do this.)
   h. In this price range, classify Jenny's elasticity of demand for Good B as "elastic," "inelastic," or "unit elastic."
   i. Use the total revenue test to confirm your answer to part h.

j. Jenny's curve for Good B is given by Qd = 70 - (5/3)P, where P is the price of Good B in dollars. On the diagram you used in part f. above, draw in Jenny's complete demand curve to both axes. Calculate the end points.

k. Calculate Jenny's consumer surplus when the price of Good B is $12.

l. Calculate Jenny's consumer surplus when the price of Good B is $24.

2. Suppose that we are told that the price of Good X and Good Y are $1 and $6 respectively and that Marina's income is $300.

a. Draw Marina's budget constraint (BB), clearly showing the maximum values of X and Y that can be purchased. Plot Y on the vertical axis and X on the horizontal axis.

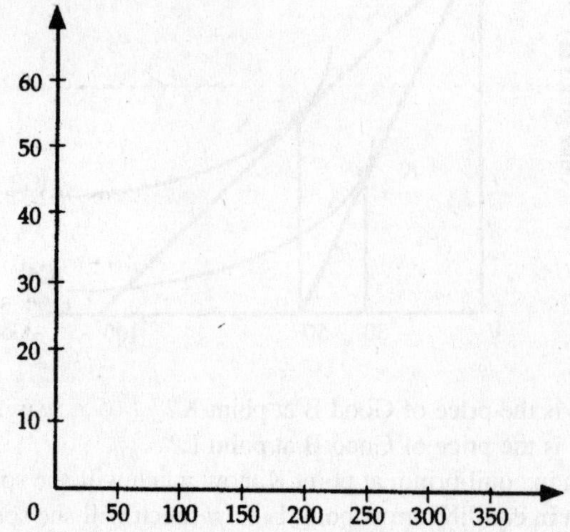

b. For Marina to maximize utility, what must be the marginal rate of substitution?

c. If the price of Good X were to rise to $3 and the price of good Y were to rise to $10, what would happen to the marginal rate of substitution when Marina is maximizing her utility? What has happened to her opportunity set?

d. If Marina's income had doubled simultaneously with the price changes, what would have happened to her opportunity set, relative to the situation in c. above?

e. Suppose, instead, that the price of Good X had become $4 while that of Good Y had remained at $6. Now what is the utility-maximizing marginal rate of substitution?

f. Given the new prices and an income of $300, draw Marina's new budget constraint (B'B') on the diagram in a. above.

g. Make up a rule relating the slope of the budget constraint, the ratio of prices, and the utility-maximizing marginal rate of substitution.

3. Assume that consumers in Dartmopolis buy only two goods: bread (a necessity) and soufflés (a luxury). Lucretia Bourgeois has an income of 1000 opeks per year. The price of a loaf of bread is 5 opeks, and the price of soufflés is 10 opeks.

a. Sketch Lucretia's budget constraint (AA).

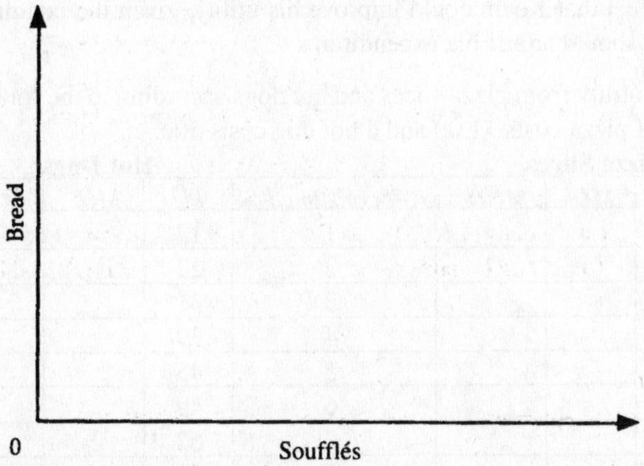

b. Shade in Lucretia's opportunity set.
c. If Lucretia were relatively poor in Dartmopolis, where on the budget constraint might you expect her choice to lie?
d. Suppose that the price of soufflés were to fall from 10 opeks to 5 opeks. Sketch Lucretia's new budget constraint (AB). What happens to the size and position of Lucretia's opportunity set on the diagram in a. above?
e. Suppose that prior to the price decrease a tax of 20% had been placed on luxury goods. Assume that the tax is paid by the consumer. Sketch the new budget constraint (AC) facing Lucretia.
f. Suppose that Lucretia's income increases from 1000 opeks to 2000 opeks. Sketch the new budget constraint (DD).

4. The following diagram depicts Bill's budget constraint. Bill has $6 to spend on candy and cigarettes. Each candy bar costs 50¢ while each pack of cigarettes costs $2.

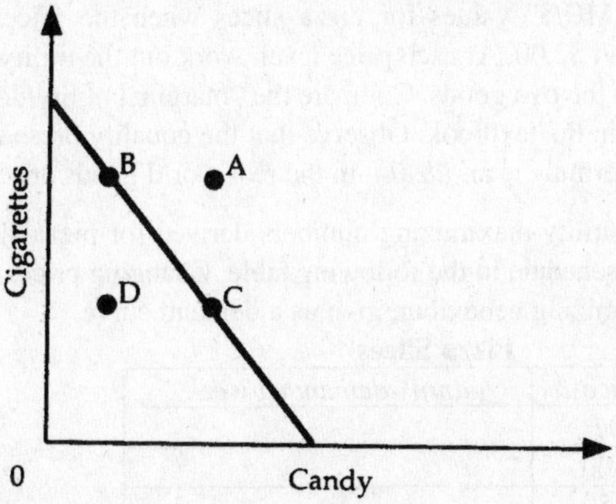

a. How many candy bars could Bill buy? How many packs of cigarettes?
b. Is the bundle of goods represented by Point A attainable? Why?
c. Is Point D attainable? What is the implication of choosing Point D?
d. Which is better—the bundle at Point B or that at Point C?
e. What would happen to the maximum levels of consumption if Bill's income rose to $10?
f. What would happen if cigarettes then increased in price to $5?

5. Kevin Koh spends all of his income on loaves of bread and two-litre bottles of Coke at prices of $1.00 and $1.50, respectively. At the moment, he is buying these two products in amounts such that the marginal utilities from the final units bought are 80 and 100 utils, respectively.

a. Is Kevin maximizing his utility? Explain your answer.

b. If you feel that Kevin could improve his utility, given the conditions, explain how he should adjust his expenditures.

6. Sally derives utility from pizza slices and hot dogs according to the following schedule. A slice of pizza costs $1.00 and a hot dog costs 50¢.

Pizza Slices				**Hot Dogs**			
TU	*MU*	*MU/$*	*<-# consumed->*	*TU*	*MU*	*MU/$*	
20	20	20 (2)	1	12	12	24	(1)
36	16	16 (5)	2	22	10	20	(3)
50	14	14 (7)	3	31	9	18	(4)
62	12	12 (9)	4	39	8	16	(6)
72	10	10 (10)	5	45	6	12	(8)
80	8	8	6	49	4	8	(11)
86	6	6	7	52	3	6	
90	4	4	8	54	2	4	
91	1	1	9	55	1	2	

a. Complete the "marginal utility" and "marginal utility per dollar" columns for each good.

b. Sally's income is $8.00. Assuming that no half units may be bought, how many slices of pizza and how many hot dogs should she consume to maximize her utility?

c. What would be Sally's total utility?

d. Sally would not maximize her utility by buying 4 slices of pizza and 5 hot dogs. Why not?

e. She wouldn't buy 5 slices of pizza and 7 hot dogs. Why not?

f. It would be possible for Sally's total utility to increase if conditions changed. Give three examples of ways in which conditions could change so that Sally's utility would be greater than before.

g. Derive "MU/$" values for pizza slices when the price/slice is 50¢, $1.00, $1.50, and $2.00. At each price level, work out the utility-maximizing combination of the two goods. Compare the "marginal utility/dollar" results with the formula in the textbook. Observe that the equality present in the utility-maximizing formula is an *ideal*—in the real world goods are "lumpy."

Use the utility-maximizing numbers derived for pizza slices to complete the demand schedule in the following table. Changing prices, combined with utility-maximizing behaviour, give us a demand curve.

Pizza Slices

Price	*Quantity demanded/week*
50¢	
$1.00	
$1.50	
$2.00	

h. Return to the original situation where the price of pizza slices and hot dogs are $1.00 and 50¢, respectively. Sally's income rises from $8.00 to $10.50. Calculate the utility-maximizing combination of goods.

i. Are pizza slices "normal" goods for Sally?

7. Soon Woo has the following indifference curve map. Her income is 60 yuan. Cotton costs 5 yuan a unit and rice costs 10 yuan a unit.

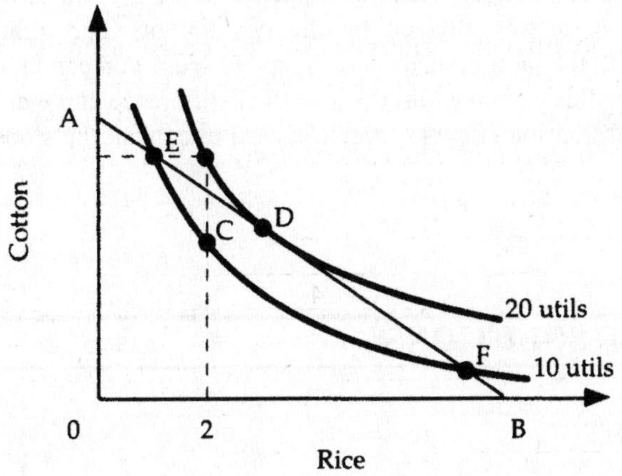

a. Calculate the maximum amount of cotton and the maximum amount of rice.
b. Soon would prefer to be at which point?
c. Suppose she buys 6 units of cotton at Point D. How many units of rice would she buy?
d. If Soon were at Point F, is she buying too much cotton or too much rice?
e. Suppose the government requires each individual to buy no more than 2 units of rice. Soon will buy ______ units of cotton and ______ units of rice. Describe where on the diagram her new combination of purchases will be. What has happened to her utility?
f. Given the government requirement, to restore her original level of utility and be in equilibrium at that level, what would have to happen? (Careful!)

8. In 1981, the U.S. Congress passed the Economic Recovery Tax Act. This legislation included, among other provisions, a major reduction in individual income tax rates. Proponents of the bill argued that the reduction in taxes would significantly increase the incentive to work, and they predicted that the result would be an increase in the labour supply. In fact, evidence suggests that for some groups labour supply actually declined. Using income and substitution effects, explain how this could be possible. (Hint: A decrease in taxes means that after-tax wages increase.) What determines whether or not labour supply will increase when tax rates are lower?

9. Suppose that two gourmet ice cream stores sell ice cream cones in your town. Tom and Jerry's cones sell for $1.25 and Johnson Howard's cones sell for $1.00. Suppose you love ice cream and have decided to budget $50 per month for ice cream cones.
a. Sketch your budget constraint and the opportunity set of combinations of Tom and Jerry's cones and Johnson Howard's cones available for $50.
b. Suppose that Tom and Jerry's cones and Johnson Howard's cones are perfect substitutes in your mind—you are indifferent between cones from either store. What point on your budget constraint will you choose?
c. Suppose that the total demand for Johnson Howard's cones is given by the equation $Qj = 50 - 2Pj$. At $Pj = \$1$, calculate consumer surplus. Now suppose that Johnson Howard raises the price to $1.25. Find the new consumer surplus. What happens to the loss in surplus?

10. First, draw Cassie's indifference map for the two goods "leisure" and "goods." Maximum leisure time is 24 hours, the wage rate is $3 per hour, and "goods" cost $6 per unit. Now draw the budget constraint. What is the end point value for "goods"? Identify the equilibrium combination of leisure and "goods" as point A. Why is this the equilibrium?

Now suppose the wage rate increases to $4/hour. Draw in Cassie's new budget constraint. Why is the combination at point A no longer the equilibrium? Identify the new equilibrium as point B. What has happened to the amount of leisure time consumed? Is your answer affected by the position of your indifference curve? Experiment with the indifference curve "map" to see if you can produce a different result. Based on this example, discuss how the indifference curve diagram—and the income and substitution effects—might be used to explain the slope of the labour-supply curve.

ANSWERS AND SOLUTIONS

PRACTICE TEST

I. SOLUTIONS TO MULTIPLE CHOICE QUESTIONS

1. B. To maximize utility the marginal utility per dollar should be equal. Currently John is receiving greater marginal utility per dollar from Good A. He should increase consumption of A and reduce consumption of B.
2. B. Good X is worth twice as much as Good Y.
3. D. The budget constraint swivels with a price change. A price increase will make the budget constraint swivel in.
4. D. The doubling in prices will not affect the slope of the budget constraint. By doubling income, too, the budget constraint will not shift.
5. C. A decrease in income will reduce the demand for a normal good and, given the market price, consumer surplus will decrease.
6. D. A higher wage rate will encourage increased labour supply through the substitution effect and discourage labour supply through the income effect. In this case, the income effect dominates.
7. A. Higher interest rates encourage more current saving and less current consumption.
8. A. Marginal utility decreases with additional consumption. More will be bought since Good A is a better buy now, relative to other products—the substitution effect.
9. A. If Fred is indifferent between the two goods, then the marginal utility per dollar must be equal. Since the price of hamburgers is twice as great as the price of hot dogs, the marginal utility of hamburgers must be twice as great as that of hot dogs.
10. A. See p. 136.
11. C. Choosing not to work means that one surrenders the wage that could have been earned.
12. C. The utility-maximizing condition is $MU_c/MU_a = P_c/P_a$.
13. A. The price decrease will cause the budget constraint to pivot outward.
14. A. Utility is subjective—comparison between individuals is not possible.

15. D. See p. 144.

16. D. The income effect and the substitution effect both help to explain the slope of the relationship between the price of pretzels and the quantity demanded of pretzels.

17. C. Given Qd = 400 – 25P, the maximum value for P is \$16 (i.e., 400/25). When P = 10, Qd = 150. Consumer surplus is $^1/_2(P_{max} - P)Qd$. See p. 143.

18. C. Consumer surplus is the difference between the price and the demand curve. Joe would buy two soft drinks because the value of the third and subsequent soft drinks is less than the price. His consumer surplus is (\$1.00 – 55¢) + (60¢ – 55¢).

19. C. Kaori can buy less of both goods—her opportunity set has been reduced.

20. B. When the price of a good increases there is a decrease in the maximum quantity that can be bought.

21. B. The substitution effect indicates that the wage rate increase will cause the opportunity cost of leisure to increase, discouraging leisure time—labour supplied increases—but the income effect indicates that the increase in the wage rate increases income, encouraging workers to consume more normal goods (including leisure).

22. C. See the diagram below. Zack is currently at point A. To maximize satisfaction, he needs to be at point B.

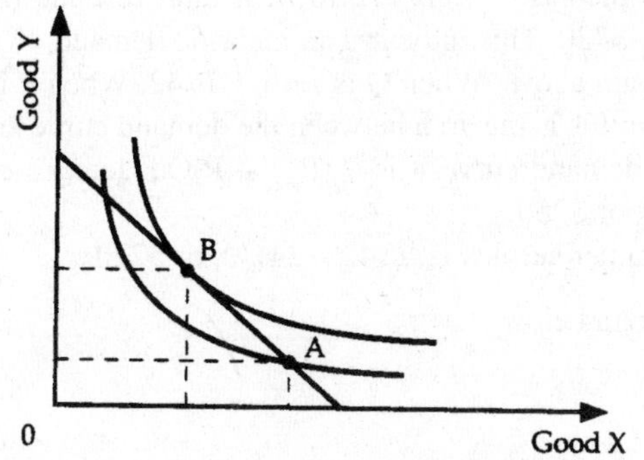

23. B. The marginal rate of substitution is less at point A (a flatter indifference curve) than at point B. It increases as we move to point B (along the budget line and to a new indifference curve).

24. A. Lesley will be able to buy less of Good A if its price increases. The end point of the budget constraint will move inwards, making the constraint steeper.

II. SOLUTIONS TO APPLICATION QUESTIONS

1. a. \$1200.
   b. \$1200/50 = \$24.
   c. \$1200/100 = \$12.
   d. Spending on Good B = price x quantity = \$24 x 30 = \$720.
   e. Spending on Good B = price x quantity = \$24 x 30 = \$600.

f. See the diagram below.

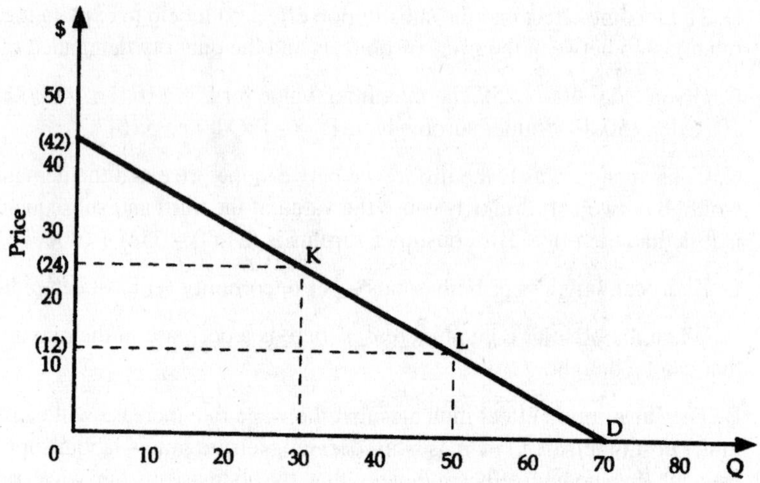

g. [(50 – 30)/[(50 + 30)/2] / [(11 – 24)/[(12 + 24)/2] = –75.

h. An elasticity value with an absolute value of less than 1.00 indicates an inelastic demand.

i. As the price increases from \$12 to \$24, total revenue (spending) increases from \$600 to \$720. This indicates an inelastic demand.

j. See the diagram above. When Q is zero, P is 42. When P is zero, Q is 70.

k. Consumer surplus is the area between the demand curve and the price. With a straight-line demand curve it is $^1/_2(P_{max} - P)Qd$. Jenny's consumer surplus is $^1/_2(42 - 2)50$, or \$750.

l. Jenny's consumer surplus is $^1/_2(42 - 24)30$, or \$270.

2. a. See the diagram below.

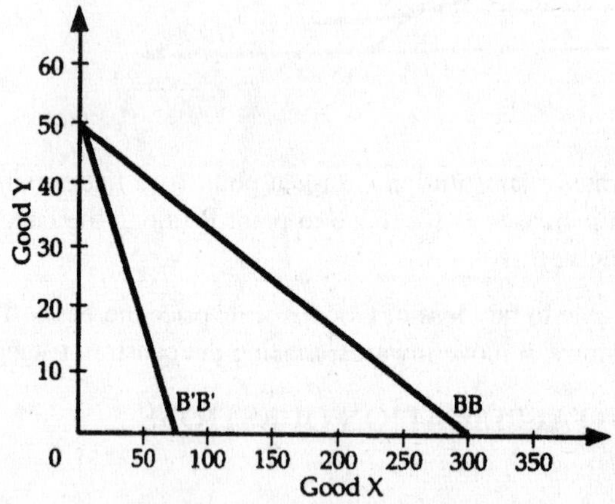

b. –1/6.

c. MRS would change to -3/10 and Marina's opportunity set would shrink.

d. Marina's opportunity set would increase, the endpoints of the budget constraint being 200 (X) and 60 (Y).

e. –2/3.

f. See the diagram above.

g. The slope of the budget constraint is determined by the ratio of the prices. When maximizing utility, the MRS will also equal this ratio.

3. a-b. See the diagram below.

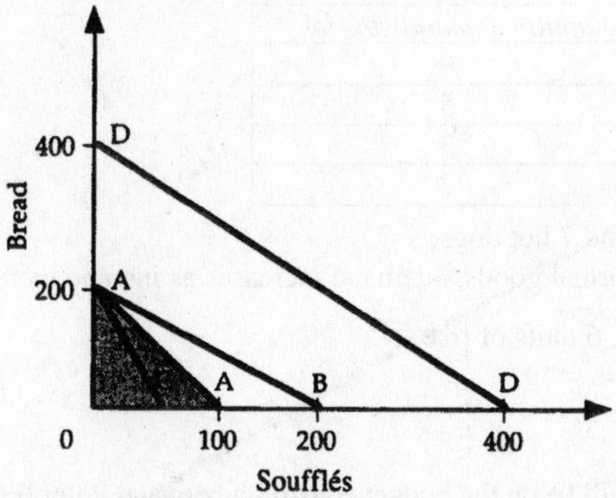

c. Presumably, Lucretia would mainly consume bread.

d-f. See the diagram above.

4. a. 12; 3.

b. The bundle at Point A is not attainable because Bill doesn't have enough money, given current prices.

c. The bundle at Point D is attainable. Choosing D would imply that Bill is not spending all of his income.

d. Without knowing Bill's preferences (smoker or sweet tooth) we can't say which bundle (B or C) is preferable.

e. Bill could buy as many as 5 packs of cigarettes or 20 candy bars.

f. Bill would be able to buy no more than 2 packs of cigarettes; he could still buy as many as 20 candy bars. His budget constraint would pivot inward.

5. a. Kevin Koh is not maximizing utility because

$$MU_{bread} / P_{bread} \neq MU_{Coke} / P_{Coke}$$

b. Since 80 utils/$1.00 > 100 utils/$1.50, he should allocate more of his income to buying bread and less to buying Coke.

6. a. See the table below.

Pizza Slices				**Hot Dogs**		
TU	*MU*	*MU/$*	*<-# consumed->*	*TU*	*MU*	*MU/$*
20	20	20	1	12	12	24
36	16	16	2	22	10	20
50	14	14	3	31	9	18
62	12	12	4	39	8	16
72	10	10	5	45	6	12
80	8	8	6	49	4	8
86	6	6	7	52	3	6
90	4	4	8	54	2	4
91	1	1	9	55	1	2

b. 5 slices of pizza and 6 hot dogs.

c. 121 utils (72 + 49).

d. The "marginal utility per dollar" values are the same but Sally would not be spending all of her income.

e. She doesn't have enough money.

f. Sally's total utility would increase if her income rose, or if the price of pizza or the price of hot dogs fell.

g. See the table below.

Pizza Slices

Price	*Quantity demanded/week*
50¢	8
$1.00	5
$1.50	3
$2.00	2

h. 7 slices of pizza and 7 hot dogs.

i. Pizza slices are normal goods—demand increases as income increases.

7. a. 12 units of cotton; 6 units of rice.

b. D.

c. 3.

d. Too much rice.

e. 8; 2. The bundle will be on the budget constraint between Point E and Point D. Her utility has been reduced.

f. Cotton would have to fall in price and rice increase in price in such a way that the budget constraint would tilt to be tangent to the indifference curve.

8. The lower tax rate increases the after-tax wage rate. The substitution effect: Leisure is more expensive relative to other goods. Each hour of leisure requires a bigger sacrifice of other goods. Thus, you would expect people to consume less leisure and to work more. The income effect: Because the after-tax wage rate has increased, people have more income—they are better off. Assuming that leisure is a normal good, you would expect people to consume more of it along with the other things that their income can buy and to work less. The two effects operate against each other.

9. a-b. You would choose 50 of Johnson Howard's cones since you are indifferent and we assume that more is better than less. See the diagram below.

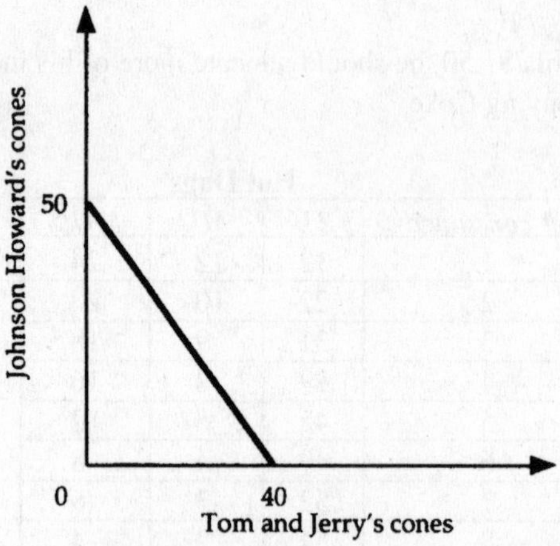

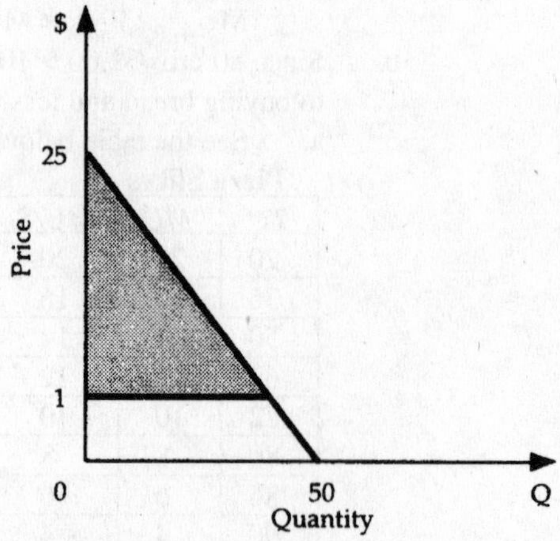

c. At P = $1, the consumer surplus will be $576; at P = $1.25, consumer surplus will be $564.06. Approximately $12 is lost. Consumers receive less utility from consuming ice cream.

10. See the diagram below. Working 24 hours will earn Cassie $72. She would be able to buy 12 goods. Point A is the equilibrium because at that point the "price" ratio is equal to the marginal rate of substitution between goods and leisure.

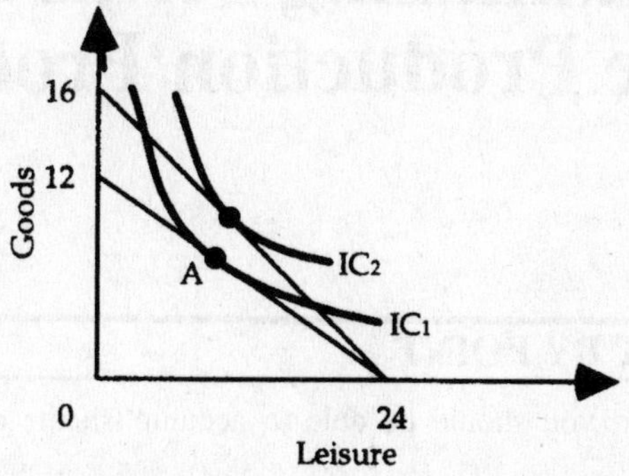

The new budget constraint pivots around with the goods end point being 16. Point A is no longer the equilibrium because the "price" ratio is no longer equal to the marginal rate of substitution between goods and leisure.

The amount of leisure time consumed may increase or decrease—it depends on the interplay between the income effect and the substitution effect. Shifting IC_2 to the left will decrease the amount of leisure and shifting it to the right will increase leisure time.

7 Behaviour of Profit-Maximizing Firms and the Production Process

OBJECTIVES: POINT BY POINT

After completing this chapter, you should be able to accomplish the objectives listed below.

General Comment

This chapter moves from the decisions of utility-maximizing households to examine the factors governing the behaviour of perfectly competitive profit-maximizing producers. It is a transition chapter that introduces many central topics, among which are productivity, costs, and economic profits. The topics introduced in this chapter will be reused in several subsequent chapters.

OBJECTIVE 1: State the characteristics of a perfectly competitive industry.

The basic assumptions used for the perfectly competitive model are: many small firms producing a homogeneous (standardized) product with easy entry into, and exit from, the market. These assumptions lead to two important implications. Each firm faces a perfectly elastic (horizontal) demand curve, and each firm is a price taker. (page 161)

A farmers' market is a reasonable example of a perfectly competitive market—tomatoes are a quite homogeneous product. No single farmer sets his/her own price independently. Any seller who prices above the going rate will make no sales.

> **TIP:** Perfect competition is the basic model of industry type in microeconomics. Later models will be developed and compared against this one. Learn the criteria that identify perfect competition.
>
> **Normal and Economic Profits:** Keep in mind that costs include an allowance for normal profits. The owner of a firm that is "breaking even" in an economic sense (total revenue equals total cost) will be quite well satisfied. Obviously, he or she would prefer even more profits, but the normal return is adequate to ensure continued production.
>
> **Examples of Perfect Competition:** The material in this chapter might put you off because of the lack of plausible examples of perfect competition—it may seem rather artificial. The traditional example is farming, while financial markets and telemarketing are others. At the school yard level, trading in baseball cards fits the criteria.

> **TIP, *continued*:** A more recent major phenomenon, with the advent of fairly cheap computer technology, is word processing. Check by going over each of the criteria. Entry and exit into these markets are easy, the supplier not even having to surrender his regular job in many cases. On university campuses, bulletin boards reveal large numbers of typists competing to produce term papers and résumés that must be executed according to established conventions, thus allowing little in the way of product differentiation.

Practice

1. In a perfectly competitive industry, the market demand curve is
   A. vertical.
   B. horizontal.
   C. downward sloping.
   D. upward sloping.

   ANSWER: C. The market demand curve is downward sloping although for each individual producer the demand curve is horizontal.

2. Elmo sells in a perfectly competitive market. A perfectly elastic demand curve implies that Elmo
   A. can attract more customers by pricing below the market price.
   B. will lose all of his customers if he prices above the market price.
   C. can increase his total revenue by pricing above the market price.
   D. can increase his total revenue by decreasing his price below the market price.

   ANSWER: B. Raising his price will lose Elmo all of his customers and all of his revenue. Elmo can attract as many customers as he wishes at the going price—he doesn't need to cut his price. Recall that a perfectly elastic demand curve is horizontal.

3. In a perfectly competitive industry which of the following is not correct?
   A. each firm faces a horizontal demand curve.
   B. there is free entry into the industry.
   C. to survive in such a competitive environment, firms must advertise.
   D. firms sell identical products.

   ANSWER: C. Advertising is unnecessary. Because firms sell identical products, no firm can advertise its good as special.

4. Elmo's firm will find it difficult to make an excess profit in its perfectly competitive industry because
   A. his firm faces a perfectly elastic demand curve.
   B. his firm, and all other firms in the industry, are price takers.
   C. his firm, and all other firms in the industry, sell identical products.
   D. firms can enter and leave this industry freely.

   ANSWER: D. The key factor that squeezes out excess profits is the assumption that firms can enter and leave the industry freely affecting market supply, price, and profits.

5. Which of the following statements about the perfectly competitive firm is true?
   A. the firm's demand curve is perfectly elastic.
   B. there is free entry into, and exit from, the market.
   C. the firm advertises in order to distinguish its product from those of its competitors.
   D. both A and B.

ANSWER: D. Firms produce homogeneous (identical) products. There is no point in advertising. Therefore C is false. Both A and B are true.

OBJECTIVE 2: Outline the three major decisions that firms must take.

All types of firms must make several basic decisions to maximize their profits, which we regard as their primary objective. These are:

(a) How much output to supply;
(b) How to produce output (technique/technology); and
(c) How much of each input to demand.

(page 163)

OBJECTIVE 3: Distinguish the short run from the long run.

The *long run* is a time period sufficiently long for the firm to alter any and all of its factors of production. The *short run* is any time period less than that—the period in which each firm has a fixed scale of production with at least one resource fixed in quantity. In the long run, new firms can enter or leave the market. In the short run, they can't. (page 167)

> **TIP:** Perhaps the best way to remember the difference between the short run and the long run is to understand the long run first. The long run is a period of time sufficiently long enough for the firm to alter all of its factors of production. Simply, the short run is any time period less than that.
>
> In the long run, firms can enter or leave the industry. In the short run, firms that want to leave the industry can reduce production to zero. (You'll find out in Chapter 8 that, since they still have some fixed resources, they still have bills to pay. In effect, the firm is still in existence.) Firms that want to get into the industry haven't had enough time to assemble all of their factors of production—maybe the machines and workers are ready but the factory hasn't been built yet.
>
> **Remember:** The short run and long run are conceptual time periods, not a specific number of days or weeks. It will be quicker to reach the long run in some industries than in others. Think of all the years of training it takes to enter the market as a dentist.

Practice

6. In the short run
   A. firms may leave the industry.
   B. firms may enter the industry.
   C. there are no fixed resources.
   D. at least one resource is fixed.

   ANSWER: D. See p. 167.

7. In the long run
   A. the majority of resources are not fixed.
   B. all firms will make positive economic profits.

C. a firm can vary all of its inputs but can't change its mix of inputs.
D. the firm can leave the industry if it so chooses.

ANSWER: D. In the long run, a firm can vary all of its inputs and its mix of inputs. It can, indeed, vary the level of its inputs all the way to zero—that is, leave the industry.

8. In the short run a firm
   A. can shut down and leave the industry.
   B. can shut down but cannot leave the industry.
   C. cannot shut down.
   D. cannot vary its output level.

   ANSWER: B. The firm can vary its output level (perhaps by laying off workers or working overtime) and can reduce output to zero but, in the short run, the firm does not have enough time to sell off all its assets and, therefore, it remains within the industry.

OBJECTIVE 4: Understand the meaning of cost and profits in economics.

Profit equals total revenue minus total (economic) cost. Note that economists distinguish between accounting costs and economic costs. *Economic cost* includes the opportunity cost of all the factors of production and a normal rate of return for the owners of the firm. In this sense, cost includes a profit component. A normal rate of return is a reward sufficient to compensate the owners for the risk and effort they have undertaken. When total revenue just covers total cost (i.e., zero economic profit), owners are receiving an adequate reward.

(page 164)

If you provided your (car repair) services to a friend "at cost," an accountant would claim that you broke even. Given that your time had some value (you might have serviced another customer, perhaps), an economist would say that you did not meet all your costs—you made a negative economic profit.

Positive economic profits (or excess profits) are a higher-than-normal reward. New firms are likely to be attracted to an industry by the presence of positive economic profits. In the long run, given negative economic profits (i.e., losses), firms will begin to leave the industry.

Nickie can earn $500 per month (after accounting costs) in Activity A. This $500 per month is the opportunity cost (the value of the next-best alternative, Activity B) for Nickie of Activity A. If, after accounting costs are paid, Nickie can clear more than $500 in Activity A, she should shift over to Activity A because she would be making positive economic profits.

Practice

Use the following information for the next three questions. Jason has a plot of land that has three alternative uses: R, S, and T. The revenue from each use is $5, $6, and $8, respectively. The accounting cost of each use is zero.

9. The opportunity cost of using the land for Use S is
   A. $5, the value in Use R.
   B. $8, the value in Use T.
   C. $1, the difference in value between Use R and Use S.
   D. $2, the difference in value between Use T and Use S.

   ANSWER: B. Opportunity cost is the value of the next-best alternative, Use T.

10. The economic profit of using the land for Use S is
   A. -$8, the value in Use T.
   B. $8, the value in Use T.
   C. -$2, the difference in value between Use T and Use S.
   D. $2, the difference in value between Use T and Use S.

   ANSWER: C. Economic profit is total revenue (which for Use S is $6) minus total costs. Accounting costs are zero but economic (opportunity) costs are $8 (the revenue from Use T).

11. To maximize profits, Jason should utilize the land for _______. If Jason is a typical producer in a perfectly competitive industry, we would expect firms to _________ this industry.
   A. use S, enter.
   B. use S, leave.
   C. use T, enter.
   D. use T, leave.

   ANSWER: C. Use T offers the highest profit ($2). In the long run, firms will be attracted to the industry by the positive economic profits.

Use the following information for the next two questions. Armen can sell as many cantaloupes as he wishes at the market price of $2.00 each. Total cost to Armen of carrying each cantaloupe to market is 50¢. He chooses to sell 10 cantaloupes.

12. His total revenue is
   A. $1.50.
   B. $2.00.
   C. $15.00.
   D. $20.00.

   ANSWER: D. Total revenue is price x quantity.

13. Armen is making
   A. a total economic profit of $15.00.
   B. a total economic profit of $20.00.
   C. a normal rate of return of 10%.
   D. a total economic profit of $1.50.

   ANSWER: A. Total economic profit is total revenue less total cost. For Armen, total revenue is $20.00 and total cost is $5.00.

14. Jocelyn Willetts starts a VCR repair service. She invests $60 000 in the business. The normal rate of return in the VCR repair trade is 12%. At the end of the first year Jocelyn's economic profit is $5000. She should
   A. leave this industry. A normal profit is $60 000 x .12, i.e., $7200 which is more than $5000.
   B. probably leave this industry. She has ignored other costs of production.
   C. stay in the industry. She is earning more than the normal rate of return.
   D. probably stay in the industry. 8.33% rate of return is below average, but it might take more time to establish customer loyalty.

   ANSWER: C. If Jocelyn has an economic profit she must be earning more than the normal rate of return, i.e., she is earning more than enough to keep her interested. Option D is wrong twice over: in perfect competition there is no customer loyalty because all sellers' products are identical.

OBJECTIVE 5: Understand how the production function relates inputs to outputs.

A *production function* is a mathematical or numerical representation of the relationship between inputs and outputs. Increasing the quantity of a variable input should cause total production to increase—marginal product is positive. *Marginal product* is the addition to total product due to the addition of a unit of an input. (page 169)

Most students are concerned with grades—Ivan Exxum certainly is. For an upcoming economics test, Ivan has some fixed resources (his textbook and lecture notes) and some variable resources (particularly study time for economics). By increasing the study time for his economics test hour by hour, Ivan seeks to increase "production" (his score on the test). In some sense, Ivan has a production function (although it isn't explicit or mathematically precise). An extra hour of study should increase his score by some number of points—this is his marginal product. Ivan may choose to adopt a relatively labour-intensive approach (himself and his notes) or a more capital-intensive approach (viewing videotapes, getting help from a study lab, hiring "human capital" in the form of a tutor).

OBJECTIVE 6: Distinguish average and marginal products.

The law of diminishing returns states that when extra units of a variable input are combined with fixed inputs, the marginal product will decline. This is a short-run concept—in the long run there are no fixed inputs. (page 169)

> **Comment:** When marginal product is increasing, the slope of the production function is positive and increasing (rising at an increasing rate). When diminishing marginal returns set in, the slope of the production function is positive but decreasing.

A frequently used illustration of the validity of the law of diminishing returns is a flowerpot. Space, in this case, is a fixed resource. If the law of diminishing returns did not hold, we could add larger and larger quantities of resources such as light and fertilizer, better hybrids and more effective insecticides, and feed everyone in the nation from the product of the one flowerpot. Clearly, the law of diminishing returns *does* apply.

The *average product* (of labour, for example) is the total product divided by the number of units (of labour) and is related to marginal product. If marginal product is more than average product, average product increases; if the marginal value is less than average value, the average value decreases. (page 170)

> **The Average-Marginal Rule:** The relationship between marginal and average values is ruled by the laws of arithmetic. If your GPA is 2.5 and you get an "A" in this course, your average will rise. If you pick up a "D," your average will fall. If the extra (marginal) value is more than the average, the average rises; if the marginal value is less than the average, the average falls. This rule, you will discover, pops up throughout your microeconomics course.

> **TIP: Diminishing Returns:** The law of diminishing returns is easier to understand if you remember the "specialization effect" and the "congestion effect." (These are just made-up names; it's the idea that's important.)

TIP, *continued*: First, imagine the inefficient use of resources if only one worker was allowed access to the (fixed) capital. Imagine adding a second worker and a third. See how production increases vigorously? Each worker is still working up to capacity, and the underemployment of machines is being reduced. The extra (marginal) product is increasing as well as the total product. What should be happening to production level per worker? It'll be rising. Call this situation where marginal product is rising the *specialization effect.*

Carry the story further. Imagine the small factory swarming with workers. What has happened? The machines are being worked up to capacity, but workers are having to wait idly to use equipment. Average product and marginal product must be falling. An extra worker will make little contribution to production. Call this the *congestion effect.*

The specialization and congestion effects coexist at all levels of factor usage. At first the benefits from the specialization effect are stronger but, as overcrowding intensifies, the congestion effect begins to prevail. Diminishing returns have set in.

Practice

Use the following table to answer the next **five** questions.

Labour (workers)	Total Product	Marginal Product	Average Product
0	0	—	—
1	15		
2	32		
3	48		
4	60		
5		10	
6			13

15. Total product, if 6 workers are employed, is
    A. 70 units of output.
    B. 73 units of output.
    C. 78 units of output.
    D. 86 units of output.

    ANSWER: C. Total product is average product times the number of workers (13 x 6).

16. Average product, if 5 workers are employed, is
    A. 10 units of output.
    B. 12 units of output.
    C. 14 units of output.
    D. 15 units of output.

    ANSWER: C. With 4 workers, total product is 60 units. The fifth worker adds 10 more units to make a total of 70. Average product is total product divided by the number of workers (70/5).

17. Diminishing returns set in with the _____ worker.
    A. first.
    B. second.

C. third.
D. fourth.

ANSWER: C. The marginal products of the first, second, and third workers respectively are 15, 17, 16. The decline begins with the third worker.

18. Average product begins to decrease with the _____ worker.
   A. first.
   B. second.
   C. third.
   D. fourth.

ANSWER: D. The average products of the first, second, third, and fourth workers respectively are 15, 16, 16, 15. The decline begins with the fourth worker.

19. The marginal product of the sixth worker is
   A. 8 units of output.
   B. 13 units of output.
   C. 14 units of output.
   D. 78 units of output.

ANSWER: A. Total product of 5 workers is 70. Total product of 6 workers is 78. The sixth worker adds 8 units of output.

20. When marginal product is decreasing, average product is
   A. decreasing.
   B. increasing.
   C. negative.
   D. none of the above.

ANSWER: D. Average product may be increasing or decreasing but, without additional information, we can't say for certain.

OBJECTIVE 7: Understand the role of input prices in the choice of technology.

Choosing the least-cost (profit-maximizing) method of production depends on the available techniques of production and the prices of the factors of production. (page 173)

For a given output level, the producer should attempt to employ the least-cost method of production. One gets the best "value for money" by hiring resources to equate the marginal product per dollar of each resource.

> **TIP:** The logic here is the same as we saw in Chapter 6 where consumers attempt to maximize utility by equating the marginal utility per dollar of each good purchased. Go back and review that discussion, if the similar point here is unclear to you.

Practice

Use the following information for the next four questions. Each technology produces the same amount of output.

Technology	Units of Capital	Units of Labour
A	2	15
B	5	8
C	9	3
D	14	1

21. The price of both labour and capital is $1 per unit. Which is the optimal production technique?
A. A.
B. B.
C. C.
D. D.

ANSWER: C. Technique C is best (least-cost). The total cost is $12.

22. If the price of labour remains at $1 per unit and the price of capital rises to $10 per unit, which is the optimal production technique?
A. A.
B. B.
C. C.
D. D.

ANSWER: A. The total cost is $35. The next best is B with a total cost of $58.

23. If the price of capital is $1 per unit and the price of labour is $5 per unit, which is the optimal production technique?
A. A.
B. B.
C. C.
D. D.

ANSWER: D. The total cost is $19. The next best is B with a total cost of $24.

24. Which production technique is the most labour intensive?
A. A.
B. B.
C. C.
D. D.

ANSWER: A. Technique A uses more units of labour than any of the other techniques.

OBJECTIVE 8: Understand the isoquant approach to production.

The appendix to Chapter 7 develops two new graphical tools: the isoquant and the isocost line. By combining these it becomes possible to work out the least costly (and profit-maximizing) combination of two inputs, given a particular output level. (page 178)

Isoquants are lines plotting all the combinations of two inputs that will produce a particular level of production. In general, they are downward sloping—the more labour we use, the less capital we need. The slope of the isoquant is the *marginal rate of technical substitution* (MRTS), the rate at which we can surrender workers and hire new machines while holding production constant. Higher levels of production are represented by isoquants that are further from the origin. (page 178)

Isocosts are lines plotting all the combinations of labour and capital that can be hired for a given amount of money. In general, isocost lines are downward sloping—the more labour we hire, the less money there is left to hire capital. The slope of the line is determined by the relative costs of labour and capital. A higher level of expenditure is represented by an isocost line that is further from the origin. (page 179)

Given the trade-off between labour and capital and the relative prices of the two inputs, the producer's goal is to find the lowest possible cost for producing a chosen level of production. This must also represent the *profit-maximizing* input mix. Equilibrium occurs when the lowest possible isocost line is just tangential to the given isoquant. Formally, the equilibrium condition is stated:

$$MP_L / P_L = MP_K / P_K$$

> **TIP:** Hopefully, you will see the relationship between the material in the appendix of this chapter and that of Chapter 6. Economists lack imagination and tend to use the same ideas over and over again. For "isoquant," read "indifference curve." For "isocost line," read "budget line." And, of course, the marginal rate of technical substitution is the production-side version of the marginal rate of substitution. If you're a little confused by the appendix of Chapter 7, review the appendix of Chapter 6.

Practice

25. A graph showing all the combinations of labour and capital that can be used to produce a given level of output is called
    A. an isocost line.
    B. an isoquant.
    C. an isotech line.
    D. a production function.

    ANSWER: B. There's no such thing as an isotech line. See p. 178 for the discussion of isoquants.

Use the following information to answer the next five questions.

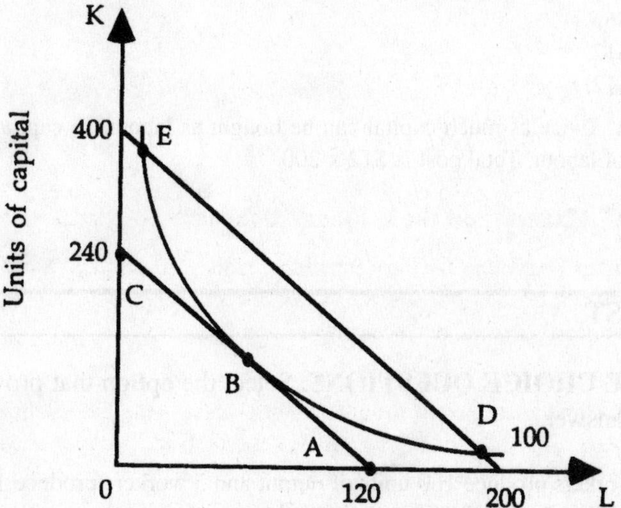

26. If the price of labour is $12 per unit, the total cost along isocost line AC
    A. is $10.
    B. is $12.
    C. is $1440.
    D. depends on the price of capital too.

    ANSWER: C. Each unit of labour costs $12, and 120 can be bought.

27. If the price of labour is $12 per unit, then the price of a unit of capital is
A. $2.
B. $6.
C. $12.
D. $1440.

ANSWER: B. Labour costs $12 per unit, and twice as many units of capital can be bought.

28. If the firm chooses to produce 100 units of output, its least-cost mix of labour and capital is represented by point
A. B.
B. D.
C. E.
D. A.

ANSWER: A. Point B is the least-cost mix because it is on the lowest possible isocost line that can achieve 100 units of output.

29. The slope of the isoquant in the diagram above is given by
A. $-TP_L/TP_K$.
B. $-TP_K/T_P$.
C. $-AP_L/AP_K$.
D. $-MP^L/MP_K$.

ANSWER: D. Slope is "rise over run." See p. 180.

30. Considering the isocost line that passes through point D: if the price of labour is still $12, the total cost must be _____ and the price of capital must be _____
A. $2400, $6.
B. $4800, $6.
C. $2400, $12.
D. $4800, $12.

ANSWER: A. Twice as much capital can be bought as labour, so capital must be half the price of labour. Total cost is $12 x 200.

PRACTICE TEST

I. MULTIPLE CHOICE QUESTIONS. Select the option that provides the single best answer.

_____ 1. Four workers produce 160 units of output and 5 workers produce 180. The marginal product of the fifth worker is
A. 32 units of output.
B. 4 units of output.
C. 20 units of output.
D. 36 units of output.

_____ 2. The return on investment that is just sufficient to satisfy the owners of a business is called
A. normal profit.
B. marginal profit.
C. economic profit.
D. excess profit.

_____ 3. The law of diminishing returns
A. applies in the short run but not in the long run.
B. requires that all factors of production must diminish in equal proportions.
C. requires that all factors of production must diminish in unequal proportions.
D. states that marginal product must always be less than average product.

_____ 4. The demand curve faced by a perfectly competitive firm is
A. always downward sloping.
B. horizontal.
C. perfectly inelastic.
D. downward sloping if the law of demand applies.

_____ 5. The short run is a period of time during which
A. all resources are fixed.
B. all resources are variable.
C. the scale of production is fixed.
D. the scale of production is variable.

_____ 6. If diminishing returns have set in, a firm that doubles the number of workers will see total production
A. decrease.
B. less than double.
C. more than double.
D. decrease by 50%.

_____ 7. Andy increases the amount of capital his workers use. The average product of labour will ________ and the marginal product of labour will ________.
A. increase, increase.
B. decrease, decrease.
C. increase, decrease.
D. decrease, increase.

_____ 8. Which of the following is most likely to reach the long run soonest? Why
A. an ice cream vendor.
B. an aircraft manufacturer.
C. a private television station.
D. a university in the province of Manitoba.

Use the following table to answer the next two questions.

Number of Workers	*Marginal Product*
1	19
2	26
3	24
4	20
5	18

_____ 9. Total product, if 4 workers are employed, is
A. 20 units of output.
B. 69 units of output.
C. 89 units of output.
D. 107 units of output.

_____ 10. Average product, if 3 workers are employed, is
A. 24 units of output.
B. 23 units of output.
C. 26 units of output.
D. 8 units of output.

_____ 11. Each of the following is a decision that must be made by a perfectly competitive firm except
A. which price level to set for its output.
B. how much of each input to demand.
C. how to produce its output.
D. how much output to supply.

_____ 12. In the short run which of the following is incorrect?
A. Existing firms cannot leave the industry.
B. New firms cannot enter the industry.
C. The firm is operating under a fixed scale of production.
D. Firms have no variable factors of production.

_____ 13. The cost-minimizing combination of labour and capital occurs when the MRTS of capital for labour equals
A. the MRTS of labour for capital.
B. the ratio of MP_L / MP_K.
C. the ratio of the price of labour to the price of capital.
D. the ratio of the price of capital to the price of labour.

_____ 14. On a given isoquant a firm is hiring too much capital (and not enough labour).
A. the firm is failing to minimize costs.
B. the marginal product of capital is greater than the marginal product of labour.
C. the price of capital will fall.
D. the marginal product of capital is less than the marginal product of labour.

Note: Try drawing this one.

Use the following diagram to answer the next four questions.

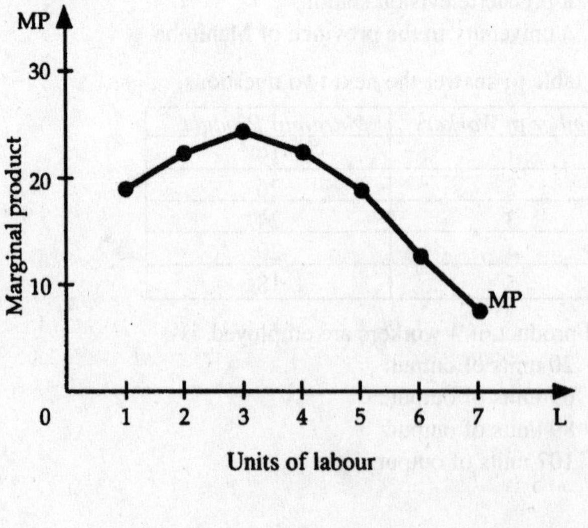

_____ 15. Based on the diagram above, the marginal product of labour for the fifth worker is
A. 22 units of output.
B. 19 units of output.
C. 13 units of output.
D. 5 units of output.

_____ 16. Based on the diagram above, the total product of labour when there are 2 workers is
A. 22 units of output.
B. 38 units of output.
C. 41 units of output.
D. 44 units of output.

_____ 17. Based on the diagram above, the average product of labour when there are 4 workers is
A. 5.5 units of output.
B. 6 units of output.
C. 21.75 units of output.
D. 87 units of output.

_____ 18. Based on the diagram above, diminishing returns set in with the
A. first worker.
B. second worker.
C. third worker.
D. fourth worker.

_____ 19. The cost-minimizing equilibrium condition is
A. $MP_L/P_L = MP_K/P_K$.
B. $-MP_L/MP_K = -P_L/P_K$.
C. $-MP_L/P_L = MP_K/P_K$.
D. $P_K/P_L = -MP_L/MP_K$.

_____ 20. When marginal product is zero, total product is ________ and average product is ________.
A. maximized, maximized.
B. maximized, decreasing.
C. decreasing, maximized.
D. decreasing, decreasing.

_____ 21. The perfectly competitive firm has no choice regarding
A. the price that may be charged.
B. how much output to produce.
C. the choice of technology.
D. how much of each input to hire.

_____ 22. Ms. Prudence Juris decides to open a law office. She quits her job as a Crown attorney (annual salary: $25 000), borrows $50 000 at 10% annual interest, hires a secretary at $20 000 per year, and rents office space at $55 000 per year. During her first year, she receives revenues of $100 000. Assuming costs and revenues as represented, what is her **economic profit** for the year?
A. $20 000.
B. zero, but she does earn a normal profit.
C. –$5000.
D. –$50 000.

_____ 23. Because of the law of diminishing returns, the general appearance of the production function graph is that it
A. increases at an increasing rate.
B. increases at a decreasing rate.
C. decreases at an increasing rate.
D. decreases at a decreasing rate.

Use the following information for the next two questions. Russell is making plans to open a car wash. His research has isolated four distinct methods of production, each of which will produce the same number of gleaming clean cars.

Technology	*Units of Capital*	*Units of Labour*
A	2	20
B	4	15
C	6	11
D	8	8

_____ 24. If the hourly price of a unit of capital is $60 and the hourly wage is $6, which production technology should Russell choose in order to minimize costs?
A. A.
B. B.
C. C.
D. D.

_____ 25. Which is the most labour-intensive method of production?
A. A.
B. B.
C. C.
D. D.

II. APPLICATION QUESTIONS.

1. Here are three different mixes of capital and labour and how they change as output level increases.

Output	*--Mix 1--*		*--Mix 2--*		*--Mix 3--*	
	K	L	K	L	K	L
11	6	1	4	4	2	7
12	7	3	6	6	3	10
13	9	5	8	8	4	14
14	12	7	10	10	5	20
15	15	9	12	12	6	26
16	21	11	14	14	7	32

a. In general, which input mix is the most desirable?
b. Which input mix will be chosen if the firm wishes to produce 11 units of output and the price of capital is $4 per unit and the price of labour is $2 per unit?
c. Will this still be cheapest if the input prices change to $3 and $3, respectively?
d. Or $2 and $4, respectively?
e. For each of the three sets of prices in b., c., and d. above, establish which input mix is cheapest at each output level. To do this you will have to calculate total costs. Note that no one technology, capital-, or labour-intensive, or intermediate is always cheapest.

2. Total cost is $200. The price of a unit of labour is $10 and the price of a unit of capital is $20. See the diagram below.

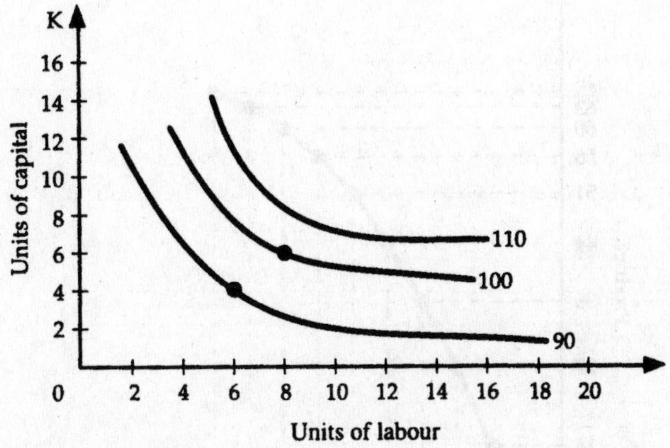

a. Draw the isocost line. Call the point of tangency Point A.
b. What is the maximum output level attainable?
c. How many units of labour and capital are used?
d. Check that this solution complies with the total cost of $200.
e. At Point A, is the marginal product of the last unit of labour greater or less than the marginal product of the last unit of capital.
f. Graph the effect of an increase in the price of labour to $20.
g. Calculate the new cost-minimizing combination of inputs.

3. Kevin Koh is a highly-paid economics professor making $15 000 per year. He thinks that there must be a better way to make a living and decides to go into hog farming. Kevin resigns his teaching job, rents some land, and hires an agricultural university graduate to help around the farm, drive the tractor, and slop the hogs.

At the end of the year, Kevin has incurred the following explicit costs:

Labour	$20 000
Rent	$40 000
Fuel, feed, seed, fertilizer, piglets	$33 000

As for revenue, Kevin sold 110 pigs during the year for an average revenue of $1000 each. How much economic profit did the farm earn? Assuming that teaching is his only option, should he continue in the hog business?

4. Below is the production function for Wilma's Wicker Baskets.

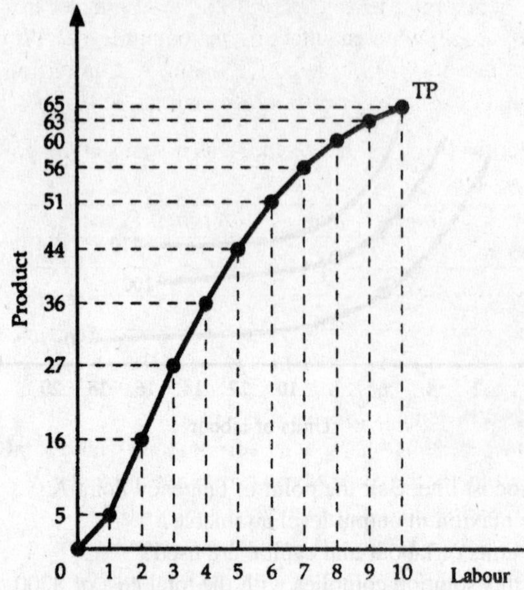

a. Compute the marginal product and average product values in the table below.

Labour	Total Product	Marginal Product	Average Product
1			
2			
3			
4			
5			
6			
7			
8			
9			
10			

b. With which worker do diminishing returns occur?

5. Consider the following diagram which shows isoquants and an isocost constraint. The price of a unit of capital is \$20 and the price of a unit of labour is \$10.

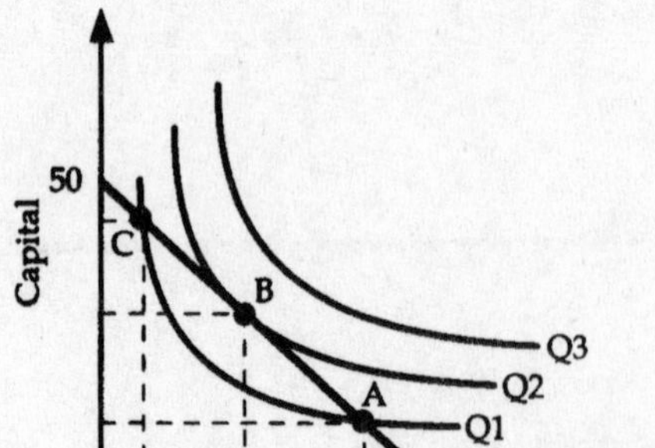

a. Calculate the total cost of producing Q2 units of output.

b. Calculate the slope of the isocost line.

c. Describe what is happening to output if output changes from Q2 to Q1.

d. At point A, compare the marginal rate of technical substitution to the input price ratio. If this information was all that the producer had, how should he adjust his input mix while maintaining the output level? Why?

e. Consider the movement from point C to point A. Can this move take place in the short run, or can it only occur in the long run?

6. A perfectly competitive firm can sell as much as it wants at the going market price. The price is $10 per unit.

Quantity	*Total Revenue*	*Marginal Revenue*
1		
2		
3		
4		
5		

a. Fill in the total revenue column.

b. If you graphed these numbers, what sort of slope would total revenue have? Marginal revenue is the extra revenue brought in by selling one more unit of production (coming up in Chapter 8).

c. Use this information to fill in the marginal revenue column.

d. If you were to graph the marginal revenue numbers, how would the graph look?

7. Use the following table for this question.

Number of Workers	*Marginal Product*	*Total Product*	*Average Product*
1	12		
2	16		
3	14		
4	13		
5	10		

a. Complete the total product and average product columns.

b. With which worker do diminishing returns occur?

c. Graph the marginal and average product curves.

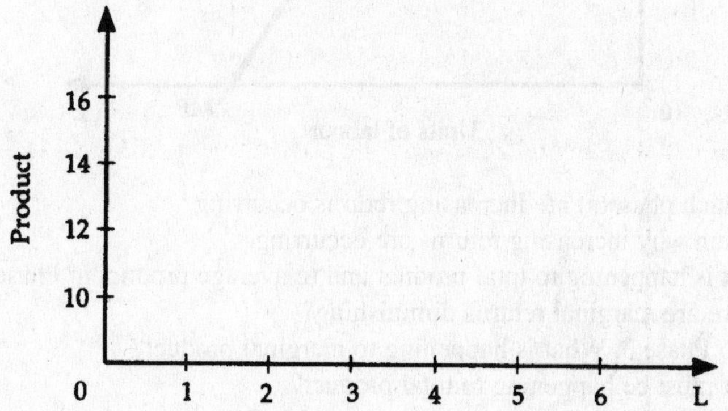

8. The diagram below is a typical short-run production function.

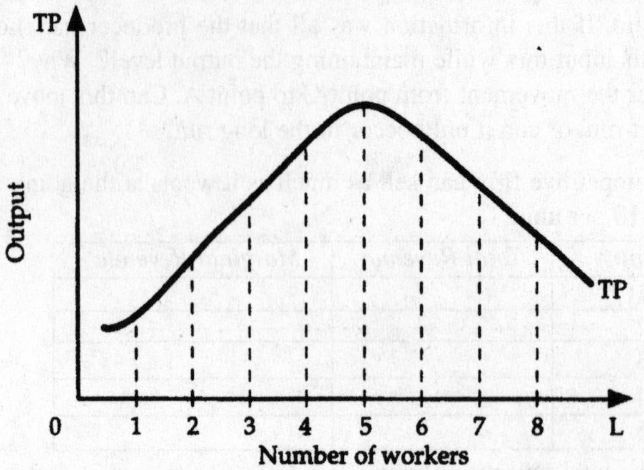

a. There exists a unique quantity of labour that no rational, profit-maximizing firm will exceed. Find and label that quantity of labour.
b. Explain why a firm would never use more than that amount.
c. What must be happening to the marginal product of labour after this point?

9. The diagram below is a marginal product of labour diagram, showing its three distinct phases, with increasing, decreasing/positive, and decreasing/negative marginal product. These are labelled Phases 1, 2, and 3, respectively.

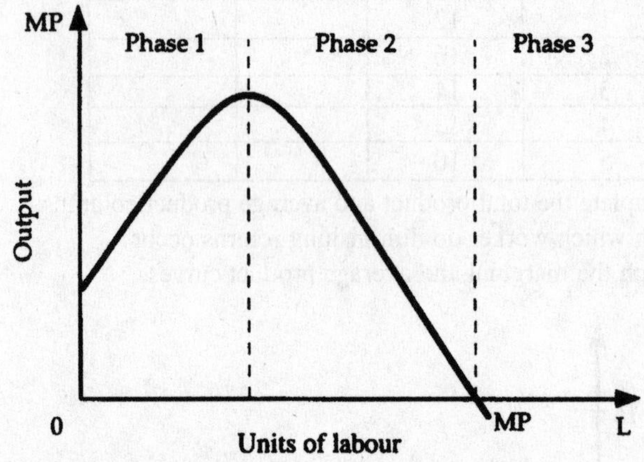

a. In which phase(s) are increasing returns occurring?
b. Explain why increasing returns are occurring.
c. What is happening to total product and to average product in Phase 1?
d. Where are marginal returns diminishing?
e. Go to Phase 3. What is happening to marginal product?
f. What must be happening to total product?
g. What must be happening to average product?
h. What is happening to marginal, average, and total product in Phase 2?
i. Why does average product show this behaviour?

10. The diagram below shows the various combinations of capital and labour that can be used to produce 100 units of output:

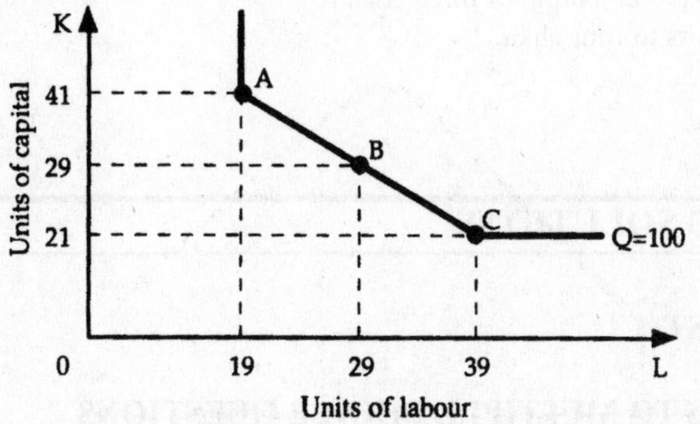

a. Consider the techniques represented by points A, B, and C. If the price of labour and capital were $2 each and the firm decided to produce 100 units of output, which technique would the firm employ?

b. If a payroll tax were imposed that pushed the price of labour up to $3 but left the price of capital at $2, which technique would the firm choose?

c. If a profits tax pushed the price of capital up to $3 but left the price of labour at $2, which technique would the firm choose?

11. Assume that wooden chairs can be produced using two different techniques, A and B. The following table provides data on the total input requirement of each at four different output levels.

	Q = 1		Q = 2		Q = 3		Q = 4	
Technique	K	L	K	L	K	L	K	L
A	5	2	8	4	11	5	15	5
B	3	3	6	5	8	7	11	10

a. If labour costs $2 per unit and capital costs $3 per unit, what is the minimum cost of producing:
1 chair?
2 chairs?
3 chairs?
4 chairs?

b. Graph total cost of production as a function of output. (Put output on the X axis and cost on the Y axis.)

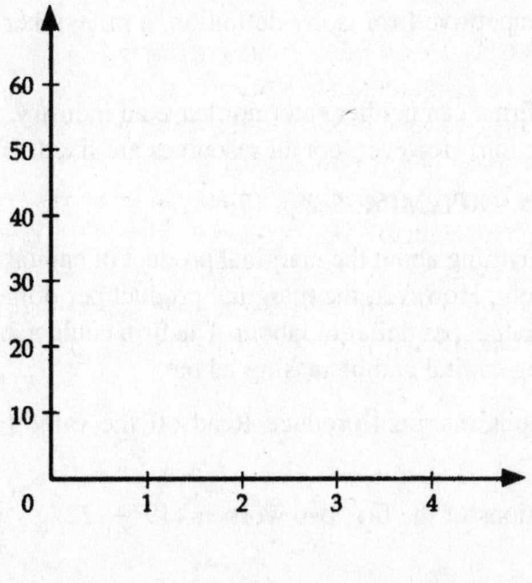

c. How much does it cost a profit-maximizing firm to go from an output of:
one chair to an output of two chairs?
two chairs to an output of three chairs?
three chairs to four chairs?

ANSWERS AND SOLUTIONS

PRACTICE TEST

I. SOLUTIONS TO MULTIPLE CHOICE QUESTIONS

1. C. Marginal product is the change in total product that occurs when an additional unit of a resource is added.
2. A. See p. 165.
3. A. This law requires that a variable resource is added to a given quantity of a fixed resource. Fixed resources can occur only in the short run.
4. B. Each firm is a price taker facing a perfectly elastic (horizontal) demand curve.
5. C. In the short run, at least one factor must be fixed thus locking the firm into a given scale of production.
6. B. Unless marginal product is negative (which is unlikely), an increase in resources will result in an increase in output. Because each new worker is producing less than previous workers, output will increase but not double.
7. A. Each worker will become more productive, causing marginal product to increase. If each worker produces more, average product will also increase.
8. A. The ice cream vendor has few resource requirements and those he or she does have can be adjusted rapidly, as opposed to, say, a university or a television station, which may have severe limitations on land and equipment availability.
9. C. Total product is the sum of the preceding marginal products—19 + 26 + 24 + 20.
10. B. Average product is total product divided by the number of workers—(19 + 26 + 24)/3 = 23.
11. A. The perfectly competitive firm is, by definition, a price taker and cannot set the price for its output.
12. D. In the short run, firms can neither enter nor leave an industry, nor can they adjust their scale of production. However, not all resources are fixed.
13. C. The MRTS equals –MPL/MPK. See p. 179.
14. A. We don't know anything about the marginal product of capital relative to the marginal product of labour. However, the marginal product per dollar for capital is less than the marginal product per dollar of labour. The firm could achieve the same level of output by reducing capital and increasing labour.
15. B. The diagram graphs marginal product. Read off the value for the fifth worker which is 19.
16. C. Add the contributions of the first two workers (19 + 22).

17. C. Total product is 87 (19 + 22 + 24 + 22). Average product is 87/4.

18. D. The third worker contributes 24 extra units of output; the fourth worker's contribution is only 22.

19. A. See p. 181.

20. B. When marginal product becomes negative, total product passes its peak and begins to fall. Given that average product has been positive, an extra (non-productive) worker will drag down the average.

21. A. The perfectly competitive firm is a price taker.

22. C. Prudence makes an economic loss of $5000. Her costs are $(25 000 + 5000 + 20 000 + 55 000).

23. B. Although initially the production function may increase at an increasing rate, because of the law of diminishing returns it increases at a decreasing rate.

24. A. The total cost is $[(2 x 60) + (20 x 6)], or 240.

25. A. See p. 180.

II. SOLUTIONS TO APPLICATION QUESTIONS

1. a. You can't tell which is the "best" (cheapest) mix without input price information and, even then, there may not be a single correct answer.
   b. Mix 3 is cheapest at $22.
   c. Mix 1 is cheapest at $21.
   d. Mix 1 is cheapest at $16.
   e. See the tables below.

Capital at $4, and labour at $2.

Output	*--Mix 1--*	*--Mix 2--*	*--Mix 3--*
11	26	24	**22**
12	34	36	**32**
13	46	48	**44**
14	62	**60**	**60**
15	78	**72**	76
16	106	**84**	92

Capital at $3, and labour at $3.

Output	*--Mix 1--*	*--Mix 2--*	*--Mix 3--*
11	**21**	24	27
12	**30**	36	39
13	**42**	48	54
14	**57**	60	75
15	**72**	**72**	96
16	96	**84**	117

Capital at $2, and labour at $4.

Output	*--Mix 1--*	*--Mix 2--*	*--Mix 3--*
11	**16**	24	32
12	**26**	36	46
13	**38**	48	64
14	**52**	60	90
15	**66**	72	116
16	86	**84**	142

2. a. See the diagram below.

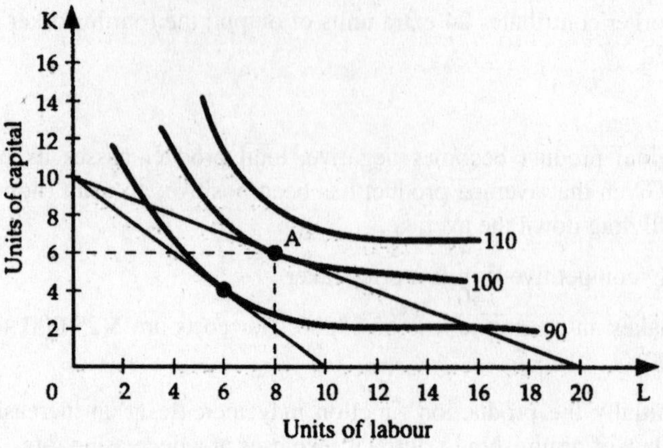

b. 100 units.
c. 8 labour; 6 capital.
d. (8 x $10) + (6 x $20) = $200.
e. greater than. MPL/PL = MPK/PK in equilibrium. Because the price of labour is less than the price of capital, the marginal product of labour exceeds the marginal product of capital.
f. See the diagram in part a. above.
g. 6 units of labour and 4 units of capital.

3. Kevin's revenue is $110 000. His accounting cost is $93 000, as indicated by the table. However, he has an opportunity cost too—the $15 000 he could have made teaching. His total (economic) cost is $108 000. Since his total revenue exceeds his total cost, he should stay in farming. He is earning an economic profit of $2000.

4. a. See the table below.

Labour	Total Product	Marginal Product	Average Product
1	5	5	5.0
2	16	11	8.0
3	27	11	9.0
4	36	9	9.0
5	44	8	8.8
6	51	7	8.5
7	56	5	8.0
8	60	4	7.5
9	63	3	7.0
10	65	2	6.5

b. Diminishing returns set in with the fourth worker.

5. a. Total cost is $1000.
b. –1/2.
c. A movement from Q2 to Q1 is a decrease in output.
d. At point A, the marginal rate of technical substitution is less than the price ratio. The firm should reduce its labour input and increase its capital input because the final dollar spent on labour provides a lower marginal product than

the final dollar spent on capital provides.

e. The movement from point C to point A requires that the quantities of both labour and capital change. In the short run, at least one input must be fixed. Only in the long run can the quantities of all inputs vary.

6. The price is $10 per unit.

Quantity	*Total Revenue*	*Marginal Revenue*
1	$10	$10
2	$20	$10
3	$30	$10
4	$40	$10
5	$50	$10

a. See the table above.
b. Total revenue would graph as a straight, upward-sloping line.
c. See the table above.
d. Marginal revenue would graph as a horizontal line, equal to price.

7. a. See the table below.

Number of Workers	*Marginal Product*	*Total Product*	*Average Product*
1	12	12	12
2	16	28	14
3	14	42	14
4	13	55	13.75
5	10	65	13

b. Diminishing returns set in with the third worker.
c. See the diagram below. [Note that marginal curves are drawn halfway between the quantity values.]

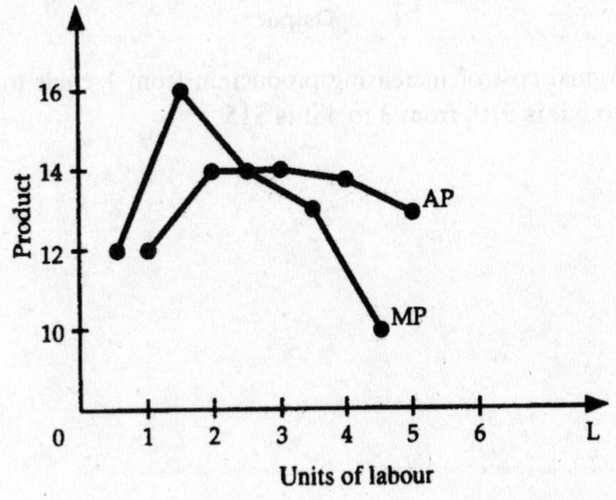

8. a. 5 workers.
b. Hiring more than 5 workers will cause total production to fall.
c. Marginal product of labour not only is diminishing, it is *negative*.

9. a. Phase 1.
b. The "specialization effect" is stronger than the "congestion effect."
c. Average product is rising but is less than marginal product. Total product is rising rapidly.
d. Over the remainder of the diagram—Phases 2 and 3.
e. Marginal product has become negative.
f. Total product must be falling.

g. Average product must be falling.
h. Marginal product is falling because the congestion effect has prevailed; total product is rising; average product is rising and then falling.
i. This is an example of the "average-marginal rule."

10. a. If the price of capital (PK) and the price of labour (PL) are both $2, Technique B is the least expensive. 100 units cost $116, while costs are $120 for both Technique A and Technique C.
b. When PL = $3, Technique A wins with a cost of $139.
c. When PK = $3, Technique C wins with a cost of $141.

11. a. In each case, Technique B is the less expensive.

Technique	Q = 1	Q = 2	Q = 3	Q = 4
A:	$19	$32	$43	$55
B:	$15	$28	$38	$53

b. See the diagram below.

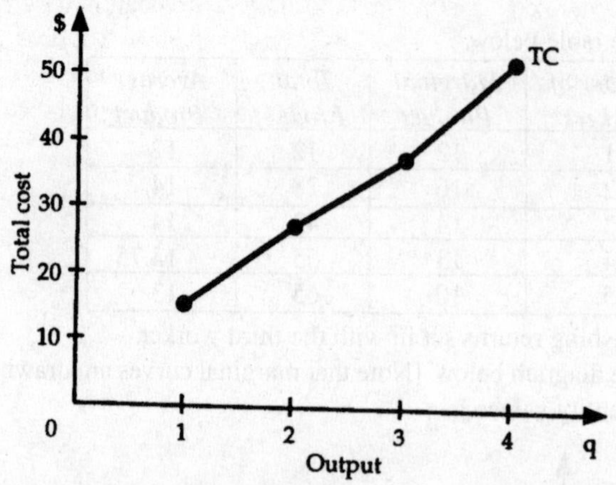

c. The marginal cost of increasing production from 1 chair to 2 chairs is $13; from 2 to 3 it is $10; from 3 to 4 it is $15.

8 Short-Run Costs and Output Decisions

OBJECTIVES: POINT BY POINT

After completing this chapter, you should be able to accomplish the objectives listed below.

General Comment

Throughout this chapter keep in mind that the authors are dealing only with the short run. Fixed resources have costs, and those costs don't change. Because fixed costs don't change, they don't enter into the decision whether or not to produce. In that sense, in the short run fixed costs don't matter—variable costs (and so, marginal costs) do.

There are a lot of definitions and a lot of graphical relationships to learn in this chapter. However, the cost relationships will be recycled through the next several chapters so your "time investment" will be worthwhile. Your ultimate goal is to master Figures 8.9 and 8.10—these are the diagrams that you will be using most. Remember that if you know the "average" values and the quantity produced then you can work back to the "total" cost values.

OBJECTIVE 1: Define, distinguish, and explain the relationships among total cost, total fixed cost, and total variable cost.

In the short run, the costs of fixed resources are called *total fixed costs*, and those of variable resources are called *total variable costs*. Added together they are *total costs*. In the short run, fixed costs are unavoidable and must be paid even if the firm has ceased production. In the long run, however, all resources and all costs are variable. Total variable cost is the cost associated with the cheapest combination of inputs at each level of production. (page 185)

Average fixed cost (TFC ÷ q) graphs as a downward-sloping line—as output increases the overheads are being spread out over more units. *Average variable cost* (TVC ÷ q) is U-shaped, and it is influenced by the marginal cost curve because of the "average-marginal" rule. *Average total cost* is TC ÷ q or AFC + AVC. (page 186)

> **TIP:** To establish the distinction between fixed and variable costs, consider your own situation in university. Your output is knowledge (measured by GPA, perhaps). Fixed costs are the costs you must pay even if nothing is produced. Tuition, dorm room rent, living expenses, and perhaps a computer are examples of fixed costs. Variable costs are those incurred while increasing knowledge. Books, pencils, notepads, library fines, some travelling expenses, and perhaps a toner cartridge, black coffee, and aspirins are examples. Because costs, to an economist, need not be financial outlays, the opportunity cost of the time spent studying and in class should be included too.

Graphing Pointer: Cost curves represent economic concepts. For instance, the AFC (= TFC/q) can never touch the horizontal axis because overhead costs will never be zero. If the numerator of a fraction is positive, then the fraction is positive. Always draw the ATC curve above the AVC curve—total cost must be larger than any single component of costs. The vertical gap between ATC and AVC represents the level of AFC. (This understanding will help you to later calculate economic profit from a graph.

Practice

1. Which of the following statements about fixed costs is true?
   A. fixed costs increase as time goes by.
   B. average fixed cost graphs as a U-shaped curve.
   C. fixed costs are zero in the long run.
   D. fixed costs are zero when the firm decides to produce no output.

   ANSWER: C. All resources (and all costs) are variable in the long run.

2. As output increases, total fixed costs
   A. increase.
   B. remain constant.
   C. decrease.
   D. decrease and then increase.

   ANSWER: B. Because fixed resources are a given quantity, the costs of those resources are a given quantity too.

3. The ____________ curve decreases continuously as output increases.
   A. average fixed cost.
   B. average variable cost.
   C. total fixed cost.
   D. total variable cost.

   ANSWER: A. Total fixed cost remains constant as output increases. AFC (TFC/q) is reduced as quantity increases.

4. Of the following, ____________ is the most likely to be a variable cost.
   A. the wage of a security guard.
   B. the firm's rent on its factory building.
   C. the firm's electricity bill.
   D. the firm's interest payment on a bank loan.

   ANSWER: C. In the other three cases, as output level changes, the cost is unlikely to change.

5. As output level increases, the difference between average total cost and average variable cost
   A. increases, because total cost includes fixed costs.
   B. decreases, because additional units of output spread fixed cost over a larger number of units and reduce its importance.
   C. remains constant, because total fixed cost (which is included in total cost) is a constant.
   D. decreases and then increases, because they are U-shaped curves.

   ANSWER: B. See the reason given. ATC = AVC + AFC. AFC decreases as output level increases.

6. If labour is a variable resource and the wage rate increases, then the total variable cost curve will _____ and the total cost curve will _____ .
 A. shift upward at all levels of output, shift upward at all levels of output.
 B. shift upward at all levels of output, pivot upward.
 C. pivot upward, shift upwards at all levels of output.
 D. pivot upward, pivot upwards.

ANSWER: D. When output is zero, variable cost is zero. Both curves will pivot upward from their point of intersection with the vertical axis.

7. Complete the following table. Total fixed cost is $10.

q	TC	TFC	TVC	ATC	AFC	AVC
0	10	10	0	0	—	0
1	18	10	8	18	10	8
2	24	10	14	12	5	7
3	30	10	20	10	$10/3$	$20/3$
4	36	10	26	9	2.5	6.5
5	40	10	30	8	2	6
6	54	10	44	9	$5/3$	$22/3$
7	70	10	60	10	$10/7$	$60/7$

ANSWER: See the Answers and Solutions section.

8. Eva and ZsaZsa own small factories producing decorative boxes. Eva uses a production process that has high fixed costs and low variable costs while ZsaZsa uses a process that has low fixed costs and high variable costs. Each factory is producing 100 boxes per week and the total costs are equal. If each firm increases output by 10 boxes per week
 A. Eva's total cost will increase more than ZsaZsa's.
 B. Eva's total cost will increase less than ZsaZsa's.
 C. Eva's total fixed cost will increase more than ZsaZsa's.
 D. Eva's total fixed cost will increase less than ZsaZsa's.

[handwritten margin notes:]
Eva ↑TFC ↓TVC
Zsa ↓TFC ↑TVC
$TC_{100} = TE_{100}$
E Z

ANSWER: B. An increase in output will increase variable costs and ZsaZsa's variable costs, which are higher, will increase more. Total fixed costs do not change as output changes.

OBJECTIVE 2: Describe marginal cost and marginal revenue.

Marginal cost is the increase in total cost—and total variable cost—of hiring resources that occurs when an extra unit of output is produced. In the short run, because of the given fixed resources that the firm has, marginal cost will eventually increase because the law of diminishing returns will apply and marginal productivity will decrease. (page 188)

Each Formula One Auto Race driver has a pit crew that services his car when he stops during a race. What an extra crew member produces, in effect, is "seconds of time saved." If Pierre Sarti has no pit crew (and has to do all servicing himself) the gain from hiring a helper would be quite significant. From Chapter 7 (diminishing returns), we know that additional crew members might exhibit increasing marginal productivity initially but that, after some point, the contribution to "time saved" by extra workers would decrease. However, crew members are all paid the same wage. The addition to total cost is the same each time an extra worker is hired, but his addition to total product is less than those who have already been hired. Because of diminishing returns, the marginal cost of additional "time saved" is increasing.

The marginal cost curve intersects the average variable cost curve and average total cost curve at the lowest point of each.

TIP: As in Chapter 7, the "average-marginal rule" applies to the relationship between the marginal (extra) value and the average value. Remember that marginal cost indicates how total cost has changed as output changes. Because total fixed cost doesn't change, it has no effect at all on marginal cost.

TIP: The cost diagram represented by AVC, ATC, and MC is important in this and subsequent chapters and it's crucial that you learn to draw it correctly. Your note taking and understanding will improve if you can draw and interpret the diagram quickly and accurately.

Graphing Pointer: Practise drawing the diagram. It's not merely a collection of randomly positioned U-shaped curves. The marginal cost curve must cut through the others at their minimum value.

The easiest way to draw the diagram correctly is to draw the MC curve first then the ATC curve. Be sure that the ATC curve bottoms out just as it meets the MC curve (because of the "average-marginal rule"). Finally, draw in the AVC curve—it also bottoms out when it reaches the MC curve. Be careful that you draw the AVC curve so that it gets closer to the ATC curve as quantity increases—the difference between

The demand curve faced by the perfectly competitive firm is perfectly elastic (horizontal) and is identical to the demand curve. Total revenue is price x quantity sold, while *marginal* revenue is how much total revenue changes as an extra unit is sold. In perfect competition, marginal revenue equals price (because each extra unit sold increases total revenue by the amount of the price). (page 197)

TIP: Mathematically, *marginal revenue* is change in total revenue (TR) divided by change in quantity. Total revenue is price times quantity, and "change in total revenue" is "change in price x change in quantity." However, in perfect competition, price remains constant as the firm's output level changes. The only way that total revenue can change, then, is through a change in quantity. The marginal revenue formula becomes

MR = Price x change in quantity / change in quantity

Because the "change in quantity" terms cancel, we can see that MR equals price (and demand) and, therefore, is constant.

Practice

9. Marginal cost can be defined as
   A. the value of total cost divided by the value of quantity produced.
   B. the change in total variable cost divided by the change in quantity produced.
   C. the change in average total cost divided by the change in quantity produced.
   D. the change in average variable cost divided by the change in quantity produced.

   ANSWER: B. Marginal cost reports how much total cost (or total variable cost) changes as output level changes.

10. When average cost is greater than marginal cost,
   A. average cost is rising.
   B. average cost is falling.
   C. marginal cost is rising.
   D. marginal cost is falling.

   ANSWER: B. This is an application of the "average-marginal rule." If the extra value is less than the average value, the average is pulled down. Option C is quite good, but MC does decrease before it increases.

11. As marginal product decreases,
   A. marginal cost increases.
   B. marginal cost decreases.
   C. average cost increases.
   D. average cost decreases.

   ANSWER: A. As productivity falls, the cost of making extra units rises.

12. Refer to the table you completed in Practice Question 7 above. The marginal cost of the fourth unit of output is
   A. \$6.
   B. \$10.
   C. \$26.
   D. \$36.

   ANSWER: A. Total (variable) cost changes by \$6 (\$36 – \$30) while quantity changes by 1.

13. Marginal revenue is defined as
   A. total revenue divided by quantity.
   B. total revenue divided by change in quantity.
   C. change in total revenue divided by quantity.
   D. change in total revenue divided by change in quantity.

   ANSWER: D. "Marginal" concepts refer to changes. See p. 197.

OTHER RELATED POINTS: State how firms determine the profit-maximizing level of output and explain why profit is maximized at that production level.

To maximize profits, the firm should produce at the level of production where price (or marginal revenue) is equal to marginal cost. The profit-maximizing condition, then, is MR = MC. (page 198)

> **TIP:** To simplify your study, you can immediately adopt the "MR = MC" profit-maximizing formula, instead of the "P = MC" formula used in Chapter 8. Either formula is correct for perfect competition, but the "MR = MC" formula applies in all the cases you will encounter (e.g., monopoly, monopolistic competition). Knowing how to find the profit-maximizing level of output is one of your most powerful tools in microeconomics.
>
> When MR exceeds MC, output should be increased—the marginal unit brings in more revenue than it costs. When MR is less than MC, output should be decreased—the marginal unit costs more than it earns in revenue.

> **TIP,** *continued:* In general, the firm first locates the profit-maximizing level of production—*quantity* is decided first. In perfect competition, the firm is a price taker. In other market structures, you will discover, the price is specified *following* the selection of the level of production.
>
> To see the profit-maximization process in a way you've seen it before, reread Application 8 (Deal B) in Chapter 1 of this Guide.

Practice

14. Complete the following table based on the information given. The price of this product is $10 per unit.

q	TC	TR	MC	MR
0	10	0	—	—
1	18	10	8	10
2	24	20	6	10
3	30	30	6	10
4	36	40	6	10
5	40	50	4	10
6	54	60	14	10
7	70	70	16	10

ANSWER: See the *Answers and Solutions* section.

15. Referring to the table above, what is the profit-maximizing output level?
    A. 3 units.
    B. 5 units.
    C. 6 units.
    D. 7 units.

ANSWER: B. Five units is the last output level at which marginal revenue exceeds marginal cost.

16. Referring to the table above, the maximum total profit is
    A. zero.
    B. $6.
    C. $10.
    D. $50.

ANSWER: C. At five units, total revenue is $50 and total cost is $40.

17. Luc and Veronique Dumais produce earthenware mugs. They can sell their mugs at $2 each. They find that the marginal cost of production for the first, second, third, fourth, and fifth mug is 50¢, $1.00, $1.50, $2.00, and $2.50 respectively. Assuming that Luc and Veronique do produce some mugs, which of the following statements is true?
    A. the profit-maximizing output level is three mugs.
    B. Luc and Veronique can make a positive profit from selling their mugs.
    C. Luc and Veronique should produce the fourth mug.
    D. because marginal cost is increasing by 50 cents per mug, there is a constant rate of increase in total cost.

ANSWER: C. The fourth mug allows them to maximize profits (assuming that profits are made). Option B is wrong because we have no information about total cost, only how it's changing. Option D is incorrect—see the information in the next question.

Use the following information about the Dumais' enterprise, Mugs-R-Us, for the next three questions. Total fixed cost is $4.00. Mugs sell for $2.50 each.

q	TC	TR	MC	MR	
0	4	0	—	—	$\frac{TVC}{q}$
1	4.5	2.5	.50	2.5	
2	5.5	5	1.00	2.5	
3	7	7.5	1.50	2.5	
4	9	10	2.00	2.5	
5	11.5	12.5	2.50	2.5	
6	14.5	15	3.00	2.5	

18. Total revenue for four mugs is _____ and total cost is _____.
 A. $2.50, $
 B. $10, $9.
 C. $2.50, $9.
 D. $10, $4.

 ANSWER: B. TR = $2.50 x 4 = $10. TC = $4 + .50 + 1.00 + 1.50 + 2.00 = $9.

19. At 3 units of output, marginal revenue _____ marginal cost. To maximize profits, Mugs-R-Us should _____ production.
 A. exceeds, increase.
 B. exceeds, decrease.
 C. is less than, increase.
 D. is less than, decrease.

 if MR > MC, should produce more

 ANSWER: A. MR = P = $2.50. MC = $1.50. They should increase production.

20. To maximize profits, Mugs-R-Us should produce _____ mugs. Luc and Veronique Dumais will make a total economic profit of _____.
 A. 4, $1.
 B. 4, -$1.
 C. 5, $1.
 D. 5, -$1.

 ANSWER: C. MR = MC at 5 units of output. TR = $12.50 and TC = $11.50.

21. If the total fixed cost of production increased to $6.00, Mugs-R-Us should produce _____ mugs. Luc and Veronique Dumais will make a total economic profit of _____.
 A. 4, $1.
 B. 4, -$1.
 C. 5, $1.
 D. 5, -$1.

 6
 6.5
 7.5
 9
 11
 13.5

 ANSWER: D. MC will not be affected by the change in fixed cost, so the profit-maximizing output level will remain at 5 units. TR will still be $12.50 but TC will now be $13.50.

 Note: See the completed table in the *Answers and Solutions* section.

OBJECTIVE 4: Derive the short run supply curve.

Marginal cost is identified with the firm's short-run supply curve. As price (and marginal revenue) increase, the firm will increase production. The determining factor is the behaviour of marginal cost.

Note that for a portion of its length—the portion where MC lies below AVC—the marginal cost curve is not the firm's short-run supply curve. In the case where the price is so low that the firm is unable to cover its variable costs, it will close down. The MC curve is therefore the short-run supply curve above the AVC curve. (page 202)

In the Mugs-R-Us example above, if the price of mugs was $1.00, Luc and Veronique would sell only 2 mugs to maximize profits (or, in this case, to minimize losses). If the price was $1.50, they would sell 3. If the price was $2.00, 4 mugs would be sold.

> **TIP:** Table 8.5 in the text offers a convenient summary of many of the points made in the chapter.
>
> **The Supply Curve and Marginal Cost:** Think back to Chapter 4 and the factors that determine the position of the supply curve—revenues and *costs*. Read pages 87-90 again, keeping the definition of marginal cost in your mind. The decision to produce is based on price (marginal revenue) and the extra cost of production (marginal cost).

Practice

Refer to the following table used for the next four questions.

q	*TC*	*MC*
0	3.00	--
1	4.50	1.50
2	5.50	1.00
3	7.00	1.50
4	9.00	2.00
5	11.50	2.50
6	14.00	3.00
7	17.50	3.50
8	21.50	4.00

22. Given the cost information in the table, if the market price is $1.00, the profit-maximizing quantity produced is ______ and the economic profit is ______.
    A. 0, -$3.00.
    B. 0, -$2.00.
    C. 2, -$3.50.
    D. 2, -$4.50.

    ANSWER: A. Producing any quantity will result in a greater economic loss than no production at all. When the firm closes down, its loss will equal its fixed costs.

23. Given the cost information in the table, if the market price is $1.50, the profit-maximizing quantity produced is ______ and the economic profit is ______.
    A. 0, -$3.00.
    B. 2, -$2.50.
    C. 3, -$2.50.
    D. 3, $-5.50.

    ANSWER: C. If the firm closes down, it will lose $3.00. Producing 3 units will generate $4.50 in total revenue which will partly offset the total cost of $7.00.

24. Given the cost information in the table, if the market price is $3.00, the profit-maximizing quantity produced is ______ and the economic profit is ______.
    A. 5, $3.50.
    B. 6, $4.00.

C. 7, $4.00.
D. 8, $2.50.

ANSWER: B. Total revenue is $3.00 x 6 = $18.00. Total cost is $14.00.

25. Based on your calculations above, fill in the following table.

Price	Output
1.00	0
1.50	3
2.00	4
2.50	5
3.00	6
3.50	7
4.00	8

Note: See the completed table in the *Answers and Solutions* section.

PRACTICE TEST

I. MULTIPLE CHOICE QUESTIONS. Select the option that provides the single best answer.

_____ 1. The TVC of 11 units is $100. The TVC of 12 units is $120. Marginal cost of the 12th unit is
A. $60.
B. $10.
C. $120.
D. $20.

_____ 2. The short-run supply curve for a perfectly competitive firm is upward sloping because, as production increases,
A. the firm must pay higher hourly wages to its workers.
B. total fixed costs increase.
C. the firm is able to assign its work force to specialized tasks.
D. the marginal productivity of additional workers decreases.

_____ 3. In the short run, which of the following is possible?
A. AFC may be greater than ATC.
B. MC may intersect ATC when ATC is decreasing.
C. AFC may be greater than AVC.
D. TFC falls as output rises.

_____ 4. ABC Corp. and XYZ Corp. have identical total variable costs. ABC's total fixed costs are $10 000 per month higher than XYZ's are. ABC's MC curve
A. is identical to that of XYZ.
B. has the same shape but is higher than that of XYZ.
C. has the same shape but is lower than that of XYZ.
D. is higher than that of XYZ and need not have the same shape.

_____ 5. The firm is at the output level where marginal cost intersects average variable cost. We can infer that
A. average variable cost is rising.
B. average variable cost is falling.

C. average total cost is falling.
D. average total cost is rising.

_____ 6. The firm's total cost curve is a straight line sloping up to the right. The marginal cost is
A. upward sloping as output increases.
B. downward sloping as output increases.
C. horizontal.
D. horizontal and equal to zero.

_____ 7. In the short run, profits will be maximized at the output level where
A. price is equal to marginal revenue.
B. marginal cost is equal to average variable cost (which is when AVC is minimized).
C. average total cost is minimized (and is equal to marginal cost).
D. marginal cost is equal to price (which is equal to marginal revenue).

_____ 8. At the current production level, ATC is increasing. Of the following situations, we should consider increasing production if
A. price is less than average total cost.
B. price is greater than average total cost.
C. price exceeds average variable cost but less than average total cost.
D. price is equal to average total cost.

_____ 9. In the short run, profits will be maximized at that output level where
A. total revenues are maximized.
B. total costs are minimized.
C. marginal costs and marginal revenues are equalized.
D. variable costs are minimized.

_____ 10. HAL Corp., a perfectly competitive firm, is currently producing 20 units. The price is \$10 per unit, total fixed costs are \$10, and average variable costs are \$3. The firm
A. is making a total profit of \$130.
B. is maximizing profit.
C. is making a loss of \$3 per unit.
D. is making a profit of \$7 per unit.

Use the following information for the next four questions.

Notebooks sell for \$4 apiece. Write On Inc. can produce 1 notebook for a total cost of \$3, 2 notebooks for a total cost of \$6, 3 for \$10, 4 for \$15, and 5 for \$21. Total fixed cost is \$1.

_____ 11. The marginal revenue of the fourth unit is
A. \$2.
B. \$3.
C. \$4.
D. \$5.

_____ 12. The marginal cost of the second unit is
A. \$2.
B. \$3.
C. \$4.
D. \$6.

_____ 13. To maximize profits, Write On will produce
A. 2 units.
B. 3 units.

C. 4 units.
D. 5 units.

_____ 14. The average variable cost of 5 units is
A. $20.
B. $4.
C. $21.
D. $6.

Use the following information for the next two questions. Total fixed cost is $20.

Output	*ATC*
2	20
3	15
4	14
5	16

_____ 15. Which of the following statements is false?
A. the total cost of producing 4 units is $56.
B. the marginal cost of the fifth unit is $2.
C. the average variable cost of the fifth unit is $12.
D. the marginal cost of the third unit is $5.

_____ 16. If the price of this product was $10, ______ units should be produced. ______ profit would be made.
A. 3, $15.
B. 3, -$15.
C. 4, $16.
D. 4, -$16.

Use the following diagram, which refers to Luc and Veronique's Mugs R Us, to answer the next six questions.

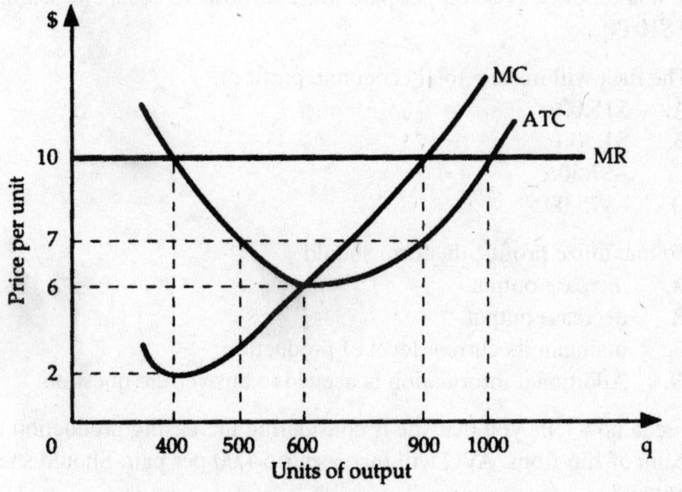

_____ 17. In the diagram above, the profit-maximizing output level is
A. 400 mugs.
B. 600 mugs.
C. 900 mugs.
D. 1000 mugs.

_____ 18. In the diagram above, if the firm produces 600 mugs, its profit will be
A. zero.
B. $2400.

C. $3600.
D. $6300.

_____ 19. In the diagram above, if the firm produces 400 mugs, its total cost will be
A. $10.
B. $400.
C. $800.
D. $4000.

_____ 20. In the diagram above, if the firm is producing 600 mugs it should __________ to maximize profits.
A. increase output to 900 mugs.
B. increase output to 1000 mugs.
C. maintain its current output level.
D. increase price to $20 and increase output to 1000 mugs.

_____ 21. In the diagram above, if the firm produces 900 mugs, total revenue is
A. $2700.
B. $5600.
C. $6300.
D. $9000.

_____ 22. In the diagram above, if the firm expands production from 600 to 900 mugs, profit will
A. increase from zero to $2700.
B. decrease from $2400 to zero.
C. decrease from $2400 to $1800.
D. increase from $2400 to $2700.

Use the following information to answer the next three questions.

Freda's Flip-Flops, a perfectly competitive firm, is producing 10 units of output (pairs of flip-flops). The market price is $6.00 per pair, average variable costs are $3.50, and total fixed costs are $10.00.

_____ 23. The firm will make a total economic profit of
A. $15.00.
B. $1.50
C. –$7.50.
D. –$75.00.

_____ 24. To maximize profits, this firm should
A. increase output.
B. decrease output.
C. maintain its current level of production.
D. Additional information is needed to answer the question.

_____ 25. Freda now tells you that she is considering increasing production to 11 pairs of flip-flops. AVC will increase to $4.00 per pair. Should she expand output?
A. yes, because Freda will make an economic profit of $22.00.
B. yes, because the marginal cost of the eleventh pair of flip-flops is less than the marginal revenue.
C. no, because the marginal cost of the eleventh pair of flip-flops exceeds the marginal revenue.
D. no, because Freda's average profit will decrease.

II. APPLICATION QUESTIONS.

1. Here is a production function for XYZ Incorporated.

# of workers	Output	TVC	TFC	TC	AVC	AFC	ATC	MC
0	0				—	—	—	—
1	12	___	___	___	___	___	___	___
2	31	___	___	___	___	___	___	___
3	41	___	___	___	___	___	___	___
4	50	___	___	___	___	___	___	___
5	58	___	___	___	___	___	___	___
6	64	___	___	___	___	___	___	___
7	67	___	___	___	___	___	___	___

The firm's overheads/day are:

Taxes	$ 15
Rent	$ 50
Machines	$ 45
Total/day	$110

The variable costs per day are the $30 wage for each worker hired.

a. The firm is operating in the short run. How can you tell?

b. What is happening to marginal product? Why? (Refer to Chapter 7 if you're uncertain.) At which output level is marginal product greatest?

c. Use the figures given to derive the cost information for the table.

d. Use the figures to sketch diagrams of the average cost curves and marginal cost. (Remember that the "average-marginal rule" guarantees that MC will intersect AVC and ATC at their minimum points.)

e. Compare the output level where MP peaks with the output level where MC bottoms out. Why are they the same?

2. You are hired as a consultant by Ken's Cuddly Critters, a manufacturer of soft toy animals. Ken has the most modern equipment and a well-motivated workforce, but he is not sure whether he is maximizing his profits. You are given the following information about Ken's costs and the market he faces. Ken informs you that production comes in "batches" of 100 animals.

Note: The "Other Costs" category includes items like rent, interest on bank loans incurred by Ken, and an allowance for capital depreciation.

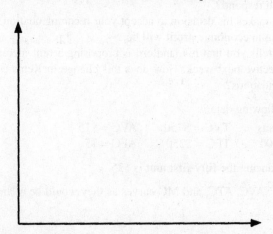

Animals Per Week	Labour Costs Per Week	Material Costs Per Week	Other Costs Per Week	Sales Revenue Per Week
0	$ 200	$ 0	$ 300	$ 0
100	$ 250	$ 150	$ 300	$ 430
200	$ 350	$ 320	$ 300	$ 860
300	$ 470	$ 510	$ 300	$ 1290
400	$ 610	$ 720	$ 300	$ 1720
500	$ 770	$ 950	$ 300	$ 2150
600	$ 950	$ 1200	$ 300	$ 2450
700	$ 1150	$ 1470	$ 300	$ 3010

a. What is the price per stuffed animal?

b. Calculate Ken's total fixed cost.

c. Calculate Ken's marginal costs per animal and complete the following table.

Animals Per Week	Marginal Costs Per Week
0 – 100	
101 – 200	
201 – 300	
301 – 400	
401 – 500	
501 – 600	
601 – 700	

d. Having compiled your information, you ask Ken for his present output level and are told that it is 200 animals per week. Ken asks if this the profit-maximizing output level and, if not, how he should adjust his production. How should you respond?

e. Before he makes his decision to accept your recommendation, Ken asks what the maximum economic profit will be.

f. Ken now tells you that his landlord is proposing a rent increase to $200 per week, effective next week. How does this change in Ken's costs affect your recommendations?

3. Examine the following data:

q = 50 units　　TVC = $750　　AVC = $15
TC = $1000　　TFC = $250　　AFC = $5

The cost of producing the fifty-first unit is $25.

Sketch the AFC, AVC, ATC, and MC curves as they would be at an output level of 50 units.

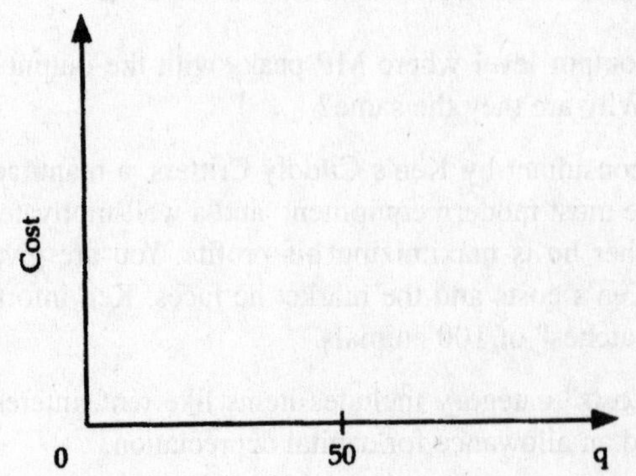

4. Average total cost is $300, total fixed cost is $2000, and total cost is $6000. Calculate the average variable cost.

5. Total fixed cost is $20, average variable cost is $10, and average total cost is $11. Calculate total variable cost, total cost, and the output level.

   TVC ________ TC ____________ q ____________

   Extra practice: In each case, sketch the cost curves and indicate the given level of production.

6. Following is the Average Total Cost schedule for the Graduation Pin Corp.

Quantity	ATC
200	$200
201	$201
202	$202

   The firm is currently maximizing profits by selling 201 pins. The president of the corporation, Theodore Christot, is approached by Yotonto University with an urgent request for an additional pin. He is offered $300.

   Assume that the additional sale will not influence present market sales.

   If his only criterion is maximizing profits, should he fill the order? Why?

7. Examine the following information about two methods of producing hockey pucks.

	Method 1		*Method 2*		*Costs*	
Output	*Capital*	*Labour*	*Capital*	*Labour*	*TVC*	*TC*
11	7	2	2	6		
12	8	4	3	9		
13	10	6	4	13		
14	12	9	7	18		
15	15	11	10	25		
16	19	14	13	31		

Overheads are $40. Machines and workers cost $4 and $2 respectively.

   a. Work out the total costs and total variable costs of production. Which method of production is cheaper?
   b. Which method is cheaper at low levels of production?
   c. When should the firm switch to the other method?

   Note that, if input prices for capital and labour were $2 and $4, respectively, different conclusions about the methods of production would be drawn.

   d. If the price of a puck is $13, how many should the firm produce to maximize profits?
   e. Given your answer in Part d, how much profit is made?

8. Suppose that the total costs of a purely competitive firm are as follows:

Output	TFC	MC	TVC	TC	TR	P (MR)	Profit
0	$20	0					
1		$10					
2		$20					
3		$30					
4		$40					
5		$50					
6		$60					

   a. Complete the TVC and TC columns.
   b. The price of the product is $30. Fill in the TR column.
   c. Compare the TC and TR columns to fill in the profit column.

d. To maximize profits, what output should the firm choose? What will be the firm's total profit?

e. Fill in the P (MR) column. Using the P = MC (profit maximization) rule, what output should the firm choose?

f. What do you predict will happen to the number of firms in this industry? In that case, what will happen to supply and to the market price?

g. Now work out the profit-maximizing output levels when price is $20 ______ $40 ______ $50 ______ $60 ______

h. Graph these points on the diagram below. It's a marginal cost curve, and—because it shows how much will be supplied at each price level, a supply curve too.

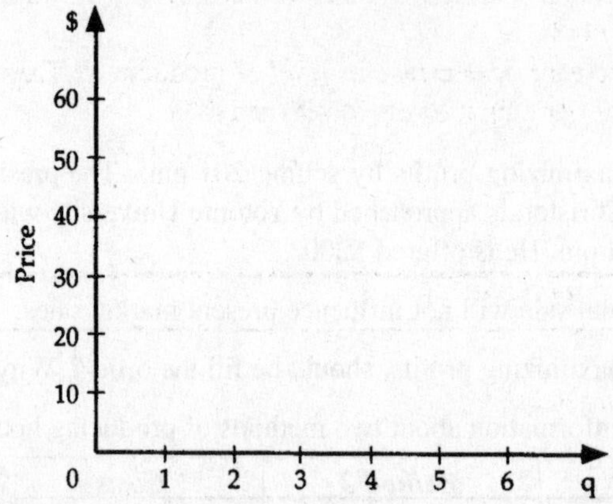

9. ABC Baseball Corp. checks its production costs. Its overheads are $200 daily, and 3 workers (the only variable resource) are hired daily, each for $25. Production is running at 500 units per day. If a fourth worker is employed, production would rise to 550 units per day.

a. Calculate the marginal product of the fourth worker and the (approximate) marginal cost of the 550th unit.

b. Sketch the MC, AVC, and ATC curves for the firm, based on your knowledge and the information given.

c. If the price of baseballs is $1 each, is this firm at its profit-maximizing output level? If not, why not? Should the firm increase or decrease its level of production? Explain. Calculate total profit at output levels of 500 and 550.

10. The table includes information about a perfectly competitive firm.

Output	*Total Cost*
0	10
1	40
2	60
3	90
4	130

Use the table to find the following values.

a. Marginal cost of the third unit.

b. Total fixed cost.

c. AVC if 4 units are produced.

d. The number of units the firm should produce if the price is $30 each.

e. The firm's maximum profit.

11. a. If average total costs are $500, total fixed costs are $4000, and total costs are $10 000, calculate the AVC.

b. If total fixed costs are $30, average variable costs are $28, and average costs are $31, calculate TVC ______ and the output level.

c. If average total costs are $300, total fixed costs are $2000, and total costs are $6000, calculate the AVC.

d. If total fixed costs are $20, average variable costs are $10, and average total costs are $11, calculate TVC and the output level.

12. ABC Baseball Corp. checks its costs of production. Total fixed costs are $100 daily, and 3 workers (the only variable resource) are hired daily, each for $20. Production is running at 400 units per day. If a fourth worker is employed, production would rise to 440 units per day.

a. Calculate the marginal product of the fourth worker.

b. Calculate the marginal cost of the 440th unit.

c. If the price of baseballs is $2 each, is this firm at its profit-maximizing output level? If not, why not?

d. Should the firm increase or decrease its level of production? Explain.

e. Calculate total profit at output levels of 400 and 440.

ANSWERS AND SOLUTIONS

Answers to Practice Questions

7.

q	TC	TFC	TVC	ATC	AFC	AVC
0	10	10	0	--	--	--
1	18	10	8	18.00	10.00	8.00
2	24	10	14	12.00	5.00	7.00
3	30	10	20	10.00	3.33	6.67
4	36	10	26	9.00	2.50	6.50
5	40	10	30	8.00	2.00	6.00
6	54	10	44	9.00	1.67	7.33
7	70	10	60	10.00	1.43	8.57

14.

q	TC	TR	MC	MR
0	10	0	—	—
1	18	10	8	10
2	24	20	6	10
3	30	30	6	10
4	36	40	6	10
5	40	50	4	10
6	54	60	14	10
7	70	70	16	10

18-21.

q	TC	TR	MC	MR
0	4.00	0	--	--
1	4.50	2.50	.50	2.50
2	5.50	5.00	1.00	2.50
3	7.00	7.50	1.50	2.50
4	9.00	10.00	2.00	2.50
5	11.50	12.50	2.50	2.50
6	14.50	15.00	3.00	2.50

25.

Price	Output
1.00	0
1.50	3
2.00	4
2.50	5
3.00	6
3.50	7
4.00	8

PRACTICE TEST

I. SOLUTIONS TO MULTIPLE CHOICE QUESTIONS

1. D. Marginal cost is the change in total cost ($20) divided by the change in quantity produced (1).

2. D. The shape of the marginal cost curve is affected by marginal productivity. The upward-sloping section of the MC curve is related to diminishing returns as additional units of variable inputs (workers) are added.

3. C. When low levels of output are produced, few variable resources are hired and fixed costs can exceed variable costs.

4. A. Fixed costs (which do not change as output level changes) have no effect on the value of marginal cost.

5. C. AVC will be at its minimum value and neither rising nor falling. Because marginal cost is lower than ATC, ATC will be decreasing.

6. C. MC is the change in total cost divided by the change in quantity produced, i.e., the slope of the TC curve. With a straight-line TC curve, MC is constant.

7. D. In perfect competition, price and marginal revenue have the same value. To maximize profits, the firm should produce at the level of output where MR = MC.

8. B. If ATC is rising, MC must be above it. In perfect competition, price equals MR. The profit-maximizing firm should increase production only if MR exceeds MC. This may be the case only if price (MR) exceeds ATC. In all other cases, MR is less than MC and output should be reduced. Draw the diagram to verify this.

9. C. The profit-maximizing condition is that MR should equal MC.

10. A. TR = P x q = $10 x 20 = $200. TVC = AVC x q = $3 x 20 = $60. TC = TFC + TVC = $10 + $60 = $70. Total economic profit = TR – TC = $200 - $70 = $130.

The following table applies to the next four questions.

q	0	1	2	3	4	5
TC	1	3	6	10	15	21
MC	—	2	3	4	5	6
MR	—	4	4	4	4	4

11. C. Marginal revenue is a change in total revenue divided by the change in quantity and is constant for all output levels.

12. B. See the table above.

13. B. Write On should produce at the level of output where MR = MC.

14. B. TVC = TC – TFC = $21 - $1 = $20. AVC = TVC/q = $20/5 = $4.

15. B. TC at 4 units of output is $56 ($14 x 4). TC at 5 units of output is $80 ($16 x 5). MC = $24/1 = $24.

16. B. At 3 units, MR = $10 and MC = $5. At 4 units, MR = $10 and MC = $11. At 3 units, TR = $30 and TC = $45.

17. C. MR = MC when the output level is 900.

18. B. TR = $10 x 600 = $6000. TC = $6 x 600 = $3600.

19. D. TC = ATC x q = $10 x 400 = $4000.

20. A. MR = MC at 900 units of output. Note: The perfectly competitive firm is a price taker and cannot increase its price.

21. D. TR = P x q = $10 x 900 = $9000.

22. D. At 600, TR - TC = $6000 – $3600 = $2400. At 900, TR – TC = $9000 - $6300 = $2700.

23. A. Total economic profit is total revenue minus total cost. Total revenue is $6.00 x 10 = $60.00. Total cost is TVC plus TFC. TVC is AVC x quantity, or $35.00 ($3.50 x 10). TFC is $10.00.

24. D. Surprisingly, in fact, none of the other options is certainly true. To maximize profits, this firm needs to know the relationship between marginal revenue, which is $6.00, and marginal cost, which is unknown. Because the firm is making an economic profit, the shutdown case (see Chapter 9) is ruled out.

25. C. Freda's average profit will decrease (Option D) but this is not relevant to her decision—total profit may increase even when average profit is decreasing. Freda must compare marginal revenue and marginal cost. Total variable cost of 10 units is $35.00; total variable cost of 11 units is $44.00. MC is $9.00. MR is $6.00. Because MR is less than MC, the eleventh unit should not be produced.

II. SOLUTIONS TO APPLICATION QUESTIONS

1. a. There are some fixed costs. That can happen only in the short run.
   b. Marginal product is decreasing as production increases. This is happening because of diminishing marginal productivity. Marginal productivity is greatest with the second worker (19 units).
   c. See the table below.

# of workers	*Output*	*TVC*	*TFC*	*TC*	*AVC*	*AFC*	*ATC*	*MC*
0	0	0	110	110	--	--	--	--
1	12	30	110	140	2.50	9.16	11.67	2.50
2	31	60	110	170	1.94	3.55	5.48	1.58
3	41	90	110	200	2.20	2.68	4.88	3.00
4	50	120	110	230	2.40	2.20	4.60	3.33
5	58	150	110	260	2.59	1.90	4.48	3.75
6	64	180	110	290	2.81	1.72	4.53	5.00
7	67	210	110	320	3.13	1.64	4.78	10.00

d. See the diagram below. Note that marginal curves are drawn halfway between the quantity values.

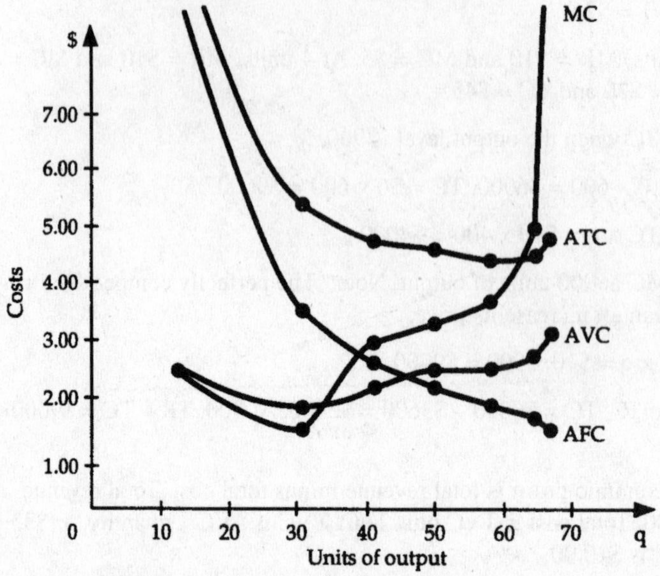

e. The two levels are the same. At that output level, the extra worker is the most productive of all, so the extra hiring cost is spread over the largest number of extra units.

2. a. $4.30.

b. Ken's total fixed cost includes any costs that are present when output is zero, therefore, total fixed cost equals $500.

c.

Animals Per Week	Marginal Costs Per Week
0 – 100	$2.00
101 – 200	$2.70
201 – 300	$3.10
301 – 400	$3.50
401 – 500	$3.90
501 – 600	$4.30
601 – 700	$4.70

d. If output if 200, marginal cost is $2.70. Because the price is $4.30, the marginal revenue is also $4.30. Because marginal cost is less than marginal revenue, Ken should increase output. In fact, the profit-maximizing output level is 600.

e. Ken's maximum profit is TR - TC = $2580 – $2450 = $560.

f. This change in Ken's costs will not affect the profit-maximizing output level. Rent is a fixed cost which, therefore, does not influence marginal cost.

3. See the diagram below.

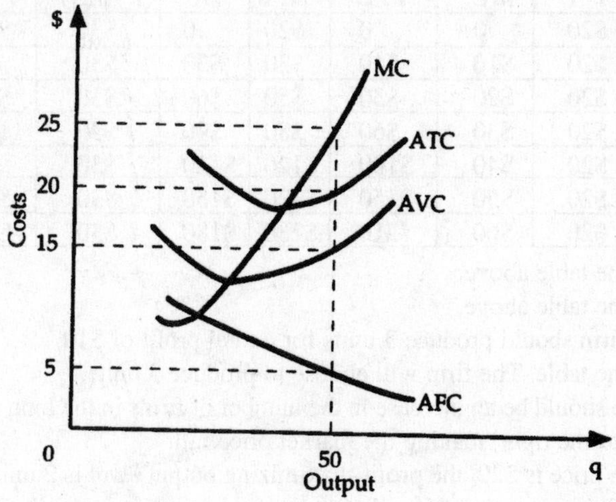

4. TVC = TC − TFC = 6000 − 2000 = 4000
q = TC / ATC = 6000 / 300 = 20
So, AVC = 4000 / 20 = 200.

5. AFC = ATC − AVC = 11 - 10 = 1
q = TFC / AFC = 20 / 1 = 20
TVC = AVC x q = 10 x 20 = 200
TC = TVC + TFC = 200 + 20 = 220.

6. Christot should not produce the extra pin. To determine this, we need to know marginal revenue and marginal cost information. The marginal revenue is $300. The marginal cost is $401.

Quantity	*ATC*	*TC*	*MC*
200	$200	$40 000	
201	$201	$40 401	$401
202	$202	$40 804	$403

Because the marginal cost of the extra unit exceeds $300, Christot's total economic profit would be reduced by filling the order.

7. a. See the table below. Neither is always cheaper.
b. Method 2 is cheaper up to and including 14 units of output.
c. After producing the 14th unit of output, Method 1 is cheaper.

	Method 1		*Method 2*		*Costs*	
Output	*Capital*	*Labour*	*Capital*	*Labour*	*TVC*	*TC*
11	7	2	2	6	20	60
12	8	4	3	9	30	70
13	10	6	4	13	42	82
14	12	9	7	18	64	104
15	15	11	10	25	82	122
16	19	14	13	31	104	144

d. Produce 13 units.
e. Total profit would be (13 x 13) − 82 = 87.

8. a. See the table below.

Output	*TFC*	*MC*	*TVC*	*TC*	*TR*	*P (MR)*	*Profit*
0	$20	0	0	$20	0	$30	–$20
1	$20	$10	$10	$30	$30	$30	0
2	$20	$20	$30	$50	$60	$30	$10
3	$20	$30	$60	$80	$90	$30	$10
4	$20	$40	$100	$120	$120	$30	0
5	$20	$50	$150	$170	$150	$30	–$20
6	$20	$60	$210	$230	$180	$30	–$50

b. See the table above.

c. See the table above.

d. The firm should produce 3 units for a total profit of $10.

e. See the table. The firm will choose to produce 3 units.

f. There should be an increase in the number of firms in the long run. Supply will shift to the right, making the market price fall.

g. When price is $20, the profit-maximizing output level is 2 units; at $40, it's 4; at $50, it's 5; and at $60, it's 6.

h. See the diagram below.

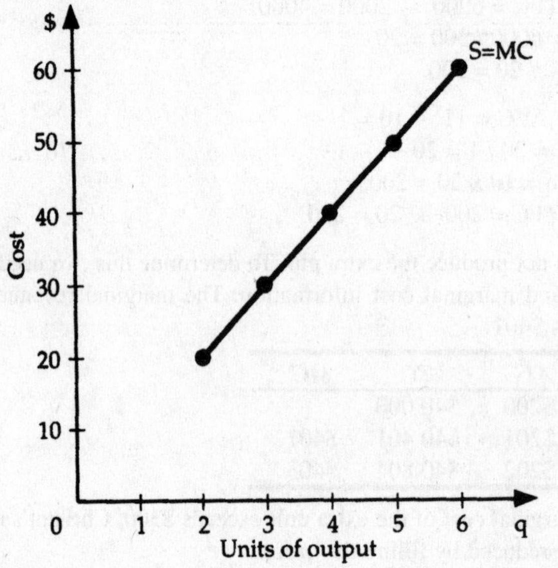

9. a. Marginal product of the fourth worker is 50 units (550 – 500). The approximate marginal cost of the 550th unit is 50¢. $25 wage ÷ 50.

b. See the diagram below. Note that this diagram shows only the parts of the curves about which we have information—some guesswork is involved. ATC is falling, from 55¢ (275/500) to 54.54¢ (300/550), indicating that MC is below ATC. AVC is rising, from 15¢ (75/500) to 18.2¢ (100/550), indicating that MC is above AVC.

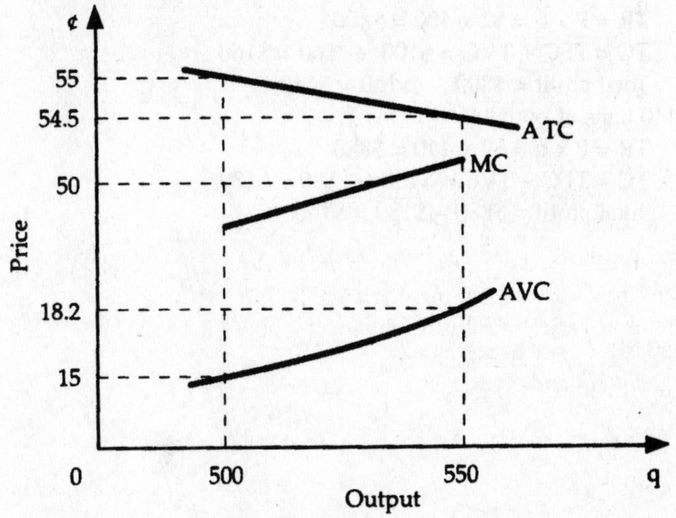

c. Price (marginal revenue) is greater than marginal cost. To maximize profit it should increase production until P = MC. At 500 units the firm's profit is $225, and at 550 units its profit is $250.

10. a. Marginal cost is change in total cost ($90 - 60) divided by change in quantity (1). MC = $30.
b. When no output is produced, no variable resources are hired and all costs are fixed. TFC = $10.
c. TVC = TC - TFC. At 4 units, TVC = 130 – 10 = $120. AVC = TVC/q = 120/4 = $30.
d. If the price is $30, then MR is also $30. The firm should produce up to the output level where MC is $30—that is, 3 units.
e. TR = P x q. At three units, TR = $30 x 3 = $90. TC = $90. The firm is earning a normal profit.

11. a. TC = ATC x q = 10 000 = 500 x q => q = 20
TVC = TC – TFC = 10 000 – 4000 = 6000
AVC = TVC/q = 6000/20 = 300.
b. AFC = ATC - AVC = 31 – 28 = 3
TFC = AFC x q => 30 = 3 x q => q = 10
TVC = AVC x q = 28 x 10 = 280.
c. TC = ATC x q = 6000 = 300 x q => q = 20
TVC = TC – TFC = 6000 – 2000 = 4000.
AVC = TVC/q = 4000/20 = 200.
d. AFC = ATC – AVC = 11 – 10 = 1
TFC = AFC x q => 20 = 1 x q => q = 20.
TVC = AVC x q = 10 x 20 = 200.

12. a. MP = change in total product (40) divided by change in quantity of input (1) = 40.
b. MC = change in total cost ($20) divided by change in quantity of output (40) = 50¢.

c. The firm is not at its profit-maximizing output level because marginal revenue ($2.00) is not equal to marginal cost (50¢).

d. The firm should increase production. The 441st baseball, for instance, will increase profits by $1.50.

e. Total profit = total revenue – total cost.

At 400 units of output:

TR = P x q = $2 x 400 = $800

TC = TFC + TVC = $100 + $60 = $160

Total profit = $800 – $160 = $640.

At 440 units of output:

TR = P x q = $2 x 440 = $880

TC = TFC + TVC = $100 + $80 = $180

Total profit = $880 – $180 = $700.

9 Costs and Output Decisions in the Long Run

OBJECTIVES: POINT BY POINT

After completing this chapter, you should be able to accomplish the objectives listed below.

OBJECTIVE 1: Grasp the relation between short-run market conditions (profits, losses, or breakeven) and long-run market adjustment.

In the short run, the firm must be

(1) making an economic profit;
(2) breaking even, i.e., making a normal profit; or
(3) making a loss. This firm will continue to produce, if it can cover its operating expenses, or shut down. (page 208)

In the long run, each of the cases above produces a different response.

(1) The firm making an economic profit will try to expand; new firms, attracted by the extra profits, will enter the industry.
(2) The firm making a normal profit will maintain its production level; no incentive exists for firms to enter or leave the industry.
(3) The firm making a loss will leave the industry. (page 214)

> **Graphing Pointer:** As a general point, the diagrams in this chapter are especially detailed. Practice is essential. Redraw each of the four short-run cases—(1) making economic profits, (2) breaking even, (3) making a loss but producing, and (4) making a loss and closing down.

> **Graphing Pointer:** Always start with the "short-run cost diagram," comprised of AVC, ATC, and MC, because this is the most difficult part to draw correctly. The trick then is to position the horizontal price (marginal revenue) line to get the particular result you want.

> **TIP:** Here is an extended graphical example giving each of the possible short-run cases covered by the textbook.
>
> Initially, you're interested only in the "average" curves. For (1), make the price line slice through the ATC curve. For (2), the price line just grazes the ATC curve at its minimum point. For (3), the price line slices through AVC but "misses" ATC. For (4), the price line "misses" AVC entirely.

TIP, *continued:*

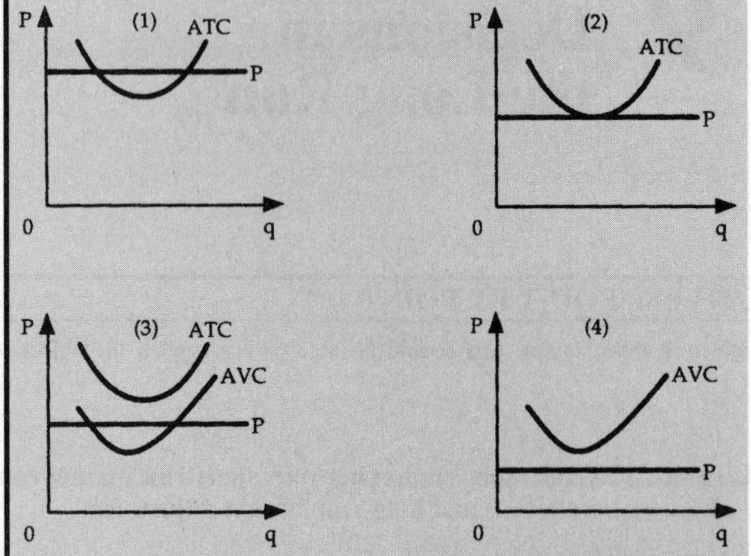

After you've drawn the price line, seek out the profit-maximizing (loss-minimizing) P = MC intersection point. Where these curves intersect, that's the profit-maximizing quantity (q*).

Next, work out the total economic profit (Case 1) or loss (Case 3). Find the difference between price and ATC at q*, then multiply by the number of units produced. That gives total profit (or loss). Case 2 gives normal profit. Case 4 gives a loss equal to total fixed costs.

Graphing Pointer: It's easy to end up with a diagram cluttered with horizontal price lines. While practising, use a ruler to represent the demand curve. Moving it up and down the cost picture avoids the profusion of lines but still lets you do the analysis.

Practice

Use the following diagram, which describes cost and revenue information for Luc and Veronique Dumais's Mugs-R-Us pitchers, for the next fifteen questions.

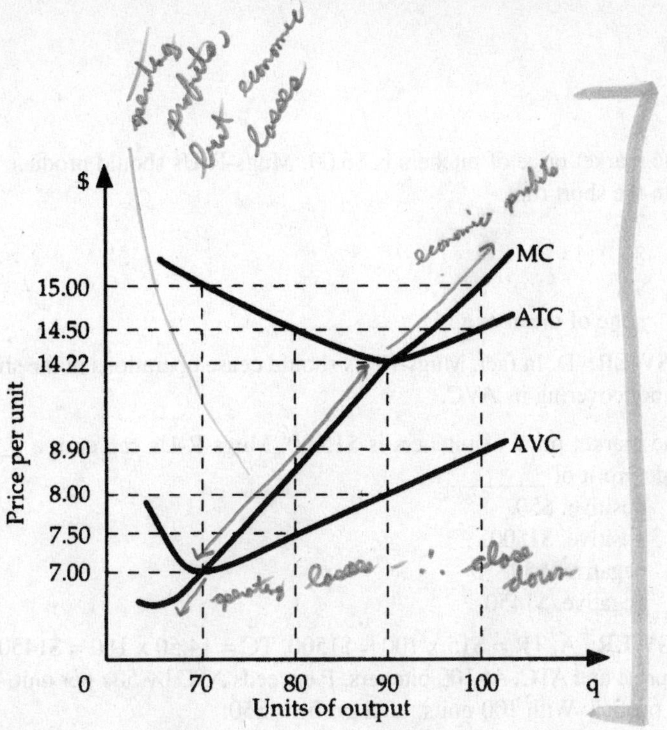

1. If the market price of pitchers is \$14.22, Mugs-R-Us should produce _______ pitchers in the short run.
   A. 70.
   B. 80.
   C. 90.
   D. 100.

   ANSWER: C. The profit-maximizing MR = MC point would be at this output level.

2. If the market price of pitchers is \$15.00, Mugs-R-Us should produce _______ pitchers in the short run.
   A. 70.
   B. 80.
   C. 90.
   D. 100.

   ANSWER: D. The profit-maximizing MR = MC point would be at this output level.

3. If the market price of pitchers is \$8.90, Mugs-R-Us should produce _______ pitchers in the short run.
   A. 70.
   B. 80.
   C. 90.
   D. 100.

   ANSWER: B. The profit-maximizing MR = MC point would be at this output level.

4. If the market price of pitchers is \$7.00, Mugs-R-Us should produce _______ pitchers in the short run.
   A. 70.
   B. 80.
   C. 90.
   D. 100.

   ANSWER: A. The profit-maximizing MR = MC point would be at this output level.

5. If the market price of pitchers is \$6.00, Mugs-R-Us should produce _______ pitchers in the short run.
   A. 70.
   B. 80.
   C. 90.
   D. none of the above.

   ANSWER: D. In fact, Mugs-R-Us should cease operations in the short run because it is not covering its AVC.

6. If the market price of pitchers is \$15.00, Mugs-R-Us can earn a _________ economic profit of ________.
   A. positive, \$50.
   B. positive, \$1500.
   C. negative, \$50.
   D. negative, \$1450.

   ANSWER: A. TR = \$15 x 100 = \$1500. TC = 14.50 x 100 = \$1450. Also, you can use price and ATC. At 100 pitchers, P exceeds ATC by 50¢ per unit. This is the "per unit profit." With 100 units, total profit is \$50.

7. If the market price of pitchers is \$14.22, Mugs-R-Us can earn an economic profit of ________.
   A. zero.
   B. –\$90.
   C. –\$560.
   D. –\$540.

   ANSWER: A. P = ATC = MC = \$14.22.

8. If the market price of pitchers is \$8.90, Mugs-R-Us can earn a _________ economic profit of ________.
   A. positive, \$478.80.
   B. positive, \$112.
   C. negative, \$448.
   D. negative, \$425.60.

   ANSWER: C. TR = \$8.90 x 80 = \$712. TC = \$14.50 x 80 = \$1160.

9. At an output level of 70 pitchers, total variable cost is ________ and total fixed cost is ________.
   A. \$490, \$560.
   B. \$490, \$1050.
   C. \$560, \$490.
   D. \$560, \$1050.

   ANSWER: A. TC = TVC + TFC = > ATC x q = AVC x q + (ATC – AVC) x q = 15 x 70 = (7 x 70) + (15 – 7)70 = 490 + 560.

10. At an output level of 70 pitchers, with a price of \$7, Mugs-R-Us makes an economic loss of _________. If it closes down, Mugs-R-Us will make an economic loss of _________.
    A. \$490, \$490.
    B. \$490, \$560.
    C. \$560, \$490.
    D. \$560, \$560.

ANSWER: D. If Mugs-R-Us chooses to produce, TR will be \$7 x 70 = \$490. TC will be \$15 x 70 = \$1050. Mugs-R-Us will lose \$560. If it closes down, TR will be zero and it will have to pay its fixed costs (\$560).

Note: At any price less than \$7, it is better off closing down.

OBJECTIVE 2: Describe conditions under which a firm will shutdown in the short run.

When revenues are insufficient to cover even variable costs, firms suffering losses find it advantageous to shutdown, even in the short run. (page 213)

OBJECTIVE 3: Identify the role of shutdown point in the derivation of the short-run supply curve.

In the short run, the border between producing at a loss and shutting down occurs where average variable cost is at its minimum (and where marginal cost intersects it). If the price per unit isn't high enough to cover even these minimum average operating expenses, the firm should shut down. Any price above the minimum AVC value will lead to "profit-maximizing" behaviour, producing where P = MC. Therefore, the portion of the MC curve above its intersection with the AVC curve is the firm's short-run supply curve. (page 213)

> **TIP:** Table 9.4 in the text is an excellent summary. Refer to it often throughout this chapter.

The industry supply curve is derived by aggregation. In the short run anything that affects marginal cost and in the long run alters the number of firms in the industry can shift the industry supply curve. (page 214)

Practice

11. Use the answers to questions 1-5 above to construct a short-run supply schedule for Mugs-R-Us pitchers.

Price	Output
\$15.00	100
\$14.22	90
\$ 8.90	80
\$ 7.00	70
\$ 6.00	0

ANSWER: See the *Answers and Solutions* section.

12. A firm makes an operating loss if
    A. price is less than average total cost.
    B. price is less than average total cost but greater than average variable cost.
    C. price is less than average variable cost.
    D. price is less than average fixed cost.

ANSWER: C. Variable costs are the ones that are actively incurred during the firm's operation.

13. If Mugs-R-Us shuts down in the short run, then
    A. total revenue will be zero, and total cost will be zero.
    B. total revenue will be zero, but total fixed costs will still have to be paid.
    C. total revenue will be zero, but total variable costs will still have to be paid.
    D. total profit will be zero, and total costs will be positive.

    ANSWER: B. In the short run there are some fixed resources (and some fixed costs).

14. If Mugs-R-Us faces a price of $8.90, it will experience an operating
    A. profit of $112.
    B. profit of $448.
    C. loss of $112.
    D. loss of $448.

    ANSWER: A. Operating profit or loss depends on price and AVC (times quantity). See p. 210.

15. In the short run, Mugs-R-Us will earn a positive economic profit as long as the price is greater than ______ and will produce as long as the price is greater than ______.
    A. $7.00, $7.00.
    B. $7.00, $14.22.
    C. $14.22, $7.00.
    D. $14.22, $14.22.

    ANSWER: C. Economic profit occurs as long as price is greater than the minimum ATC value. The firm will continue in operation as long as operating profits can be made (as long as price is greater than the minimum AVC value).

OBJECTIVE 4: Distinguish between economies and diseconomies of scale.

These are long-run phenomena. In the long run there are no fixed factors of production. Firms can choose any scale of production.

The shape of a firm's long-run average cost depends on how costs vary with scale of operation. Economies (or more correctly internal economies of scale) occur when an increase in 'a firm's' scale of production leads to lower average cost per unit produced. In the other hand, (internal) diseconomies of scale occur when an increase in 'the firm's' scale of production leads to higher average cost. Therefore, the long-run average cost curve is U-shaped not because of increasing and diminishing returns to a fixed input, but because of internal economies and diseconomies of scale.

Internal economies of scale (increasing returns to scale) are revealed when the firm's long-run average costs fall as its production increases. If a firm doubles all inputs, it will more than double output. Such cost-reducing improvements might be due to standardization or bulk buying. *Internal diseconomies of scale* (decreasing returns to scale) occur when the firm's long-run average costs increase as its production expands. Diseconomies are most frequently blamed on managerial inefficiency as a business becomes too large and unwieldy to operate effectively. Constant returns to scale are a third possibility. (page 216)

Learn the "other names" for internal economies and diseconomies of scale—increasing returns and decreasing returns, respectively. This material is intended to explain the downward- and the upward-sloping long-run average cost curve—why it is U-shaped. As with diminishing returns in the short run, you can think of economies and diseconomies fighting for dominance as the firm increases output. Initially, economies of scale represent the stronger effect and push average costs down, but as output rises, the diseconomies begin to prevail and costs start to rise. (page 215)

> **TIP:** Keep this material separate from external economies and diseconomies of scale. They're there to explain why the firm's LRAC curve might shift position (falling in the presence of external economies and rising in the presence of external diseconomies) as output rises. A quick example: As an industry expands, the skilled workers it needs will be able to command higher wages, pushing costs up for each firm. This will affect even those firms that are not expanding production. (page 228)

Practice

16. If a firm experiences constant returns to scale, its long-run average cost curve will be
    - A. horizontal.
    - B. U-shaped.
    - C. upward sloping.
    - D. downward sloping.

    ANSWER: A. See p. 218.

17. Each point on the long-run average cost curve indicates, at the given output level, the
    - A. minimum possible average cost when the scale of production can be changed.
    - B. minimum possible average cost when the scale of production is fixed.
    - C. average cost due to economies of scale.
    - D. average cost due to diseconomies of scale.

    ANSWER: A. See p. 218.

18. Vigour Vitamins discovers the following long-run information. When it produces 100 units, its total cost is $50; when it produces 200 units, its total cost is $76; and when it produces 300 units, its total cost is $99. Vigour is exhibiting ________ between 100 and 200 units of output and ________ between 200 and 300 units of output.
    - A. economies of scale, economies of scale.
    - B. economies of scale, diseconomies of scale.
    - C. diseconomies of scale, economies of scale.
    - D. diseconomies of scale, diseconomies of scale.

    ANSWER: A. At 100 units, LRAC is 50¢; at 200 units, LRAC is 38¢; at 300 units, LRAC is 33¢. LRAC is decreasing.

In the diagram below, cost and revenue information is presented for Vigour Vitamins, a typical firm in the vitamin industry. In the short run, Vigour's total fixed costs are $10. Assume that Vigour is currently producing 200 units. Use the diagram below to answer the next three questions.

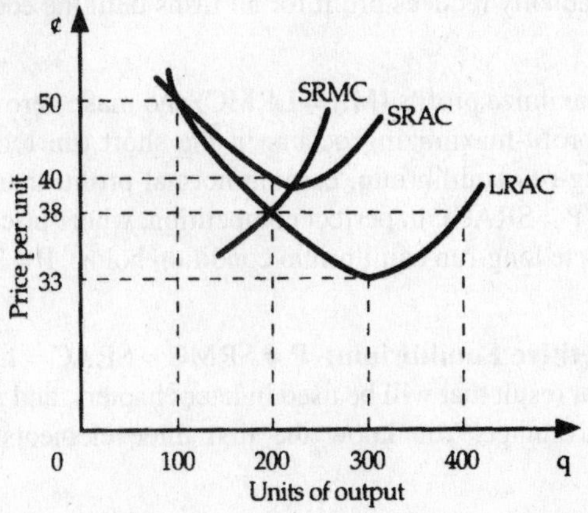

19. If the price per unit is 38¢ and the firm is producing 200 units, we can say that, in the short run, the firm
   A. is earning a normal profit.
   B. is earning a positive economic profit.
   C. is earning a negative economic profit.
   D. should close down.

   ANSWER: C. The SRAC of 40¢ is greater than 38¢ at 200 units of output. This firm is not maximizing profits in the short run because MR (38¢) does not equal SRMC.

20. In the short run, at 200 units of output, Vigour is making an operating ________; in the long run, market price will __________.
   A. profit, increase.
   B. profit, decrease.
   C. loss, increase.
   D. loss, decrease.

   ANSWER: B. Vigour's total cost is \$80 and total fixed cost is \$10. TVC is \$70, while TR is \$76. In the long run, price will be driven down to the lowest point on the LRAC.

21. In the long run, Vigour will ________ its scale of operations and price will ________.
   A. increase, increase.
   B. increase, decrease.
   C. decrease, increase.
   D. decrease, decrease.

   ANSWER: B. To survive in this industry, Vigour must become more efficient by adjusting its scale of production. As Vigour and others become more efficient, price will decrease (to 33¢).

OBJECTIVE 5: Analyze long-run market adjustment processes.

In the short run, firms can be operating at a profit or suffering economic losses. In these cases, the industry is not at an equilibrium, and firms will change their behaviour in the long run.

When firms are enjoying economic profit its total revenue exceeds its total cost. Remember that perfectly competitive firms maximize profit by producing at P=MC. The existence of economic profits will attract new entrants to the industry. And also, if the existing firms in the industry have not fully realized all the economies of scale available to them, they have an incentive to expand. Both the entrance of new firms and the possible expansion of existing firms cause the short-run supply curve to shift to the right. As this happens, price falls. This gradually reduces profit for all firms until the economic profit is wiped out. (page 220)

In the long run, firms will maximize profits (MR = LRMC) and make zero economic profit (P = LRAC). However, profit-maximizing occurs in the short run too, where MR = SRMC. If the firm is in long-run equilibrium, earning normal profit, then this condition also applies in the short run (P = SRAC). In perfect competition, where price always equals marginal revenue, the complete long-run equilibrium condition holds: P = SRMC = SRAC = LRAC. (page 221)

> **Long-Run Competitive Equilibrium:** P = SRMC = SRAC = LRAC. This is an important result that will be used in later chapters, and it may be dissected to advantage. You know the first three elements from Chapter 8.

The firm maximizes profits where P (or MR) = SRMC. MC = SRAC reveals that unit costs are minimized and that average productivity is maximized—inputs are being allocated efficiently. (Recall that the SRMC and SRAC curves intersect at the minimum point on the average cost curve.)

Competition requires that only normal profits be made in the long run, so P = LRAC. In the short run, a similar logic holds, so P = SRAC. You may question this—can't economic profits occur in the short run? Yes, but to achieve long-run equilibrium, they must have been competed away in a perfectly competitive industry. Notice that, in equilibrium, the typical firm produces at the lowest possible cost per unit in the short run and in the long run. This result occurs because of free entry into and exit from the market, forcing the firm to the most cost-efficient output level.

Why is this an equilibrium? Because there's no incentive to change. No new firms want into the industry (forcing price down); no existing firms are dissatisfied with their normal profits and seeking to leave (forcing price up).

When firms are suffering from a short-run loss, will have an incentive to get out of industry thus reducing supply - shifting the supply curve to the left. As this happens, price rises. This gradual price rise reduces losses for firms remaining until those losses are eliminated.

Practice

In the diagram below, cost and revenue information is presented for Pastry Pie Bakery, a typical firm in the pastry industry. In the short run, Pastry Pie's total fixed costs are $1000. Assume that there are no external economies or diseconomies of scale. Use the diagram to answer the next five questions.

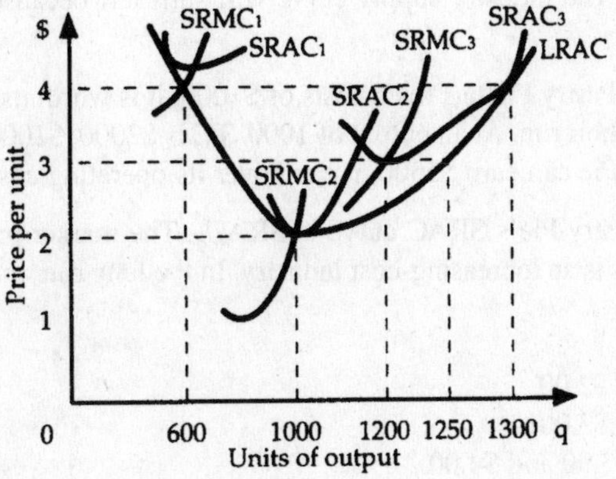

22. Diseconomies of scale set in after
    A. 600 units.
    B. 1000 units.
    C. 1250 units.
    D. 1300 units.

ANSWER: B. Diseconomies make the LRAC curve slope upward.

23. In the long run, the equilibrium price will be ________ and the equilibrium output level will be ________.
A. $2, 1200 units.
B. $2, 1000 units.
C. $3, 1200 units.
D. $3, 1000 units.

ANSWER: B. In the long run, the equilibrium price and equilibrium output level will depend on the minimum point of the LRAC curve.

24. Suppose that Pastry Pie's SRAC curve is $SRAC_3$. The market price is $4.00. In the long run,
A. firms will enter the industry and price will rise because each firm is experiencing internal diseconomies of scale.
B. Pastry Pie will increase its scale of production because it is earning excess profits.
C. Pastry Pie will decrease its scale of production to increase its economic profits.
D. Pastry Pie will reduce its output and the industry will increase output.

ANSWER: D. Pastry Pie will be forced to earn normal profits at the minimum LRAC point. Because more firms enter the industry, production will increase. Pastry Pie can't earn economic profits in the long run. The scale of production will decrease (Option C), but economic profit will be zero in the long run.

25. Suppose that Pastry Pie's SRAC curve is $SRAC_2$. Demand decreases and the market price falls to $1.50.
A. in the short run, Pastry Pie should shut down.
B. in the long run, the industry supply curve will shift left.
C. in the long run, market demand will increase because the market price has fallen.
D. in the long run, the industry supply curve will not change position.

ANSWER: B. The industry supply curve will shift left because firms are leaving the industry.

Note: Because Pastry Pie has fixed costs of $1000, it is worth its while to remain in business in the short run. At an output of 1000, TC is $2000, $1000 of which is TVC. Because Pastry Pie can earn $1500, it can cover its operating costs.

26. Suppose that Pastry Pie's SRAC curve is $SRAC_3$. The market price is $3.00. Also, suppose that this is an increasing-cost industry. In the long run, the equilibrium price will certainly be
A. $3.00.
B. more than $2.00.
C. more than $3.00.
D. between $3.00 and $4.00.

ANSWER: B. More than $2.00 is the best answer. If there were constant costs, the equilibrium price would be $2.00. Because of profits, the industry will grow, pushing up the LRAC curve. Equilibrium price will certainly be greater than $2.00.

OBJECTIVE 6: Describe the role of external economies and diseconomies in the derivation of the long-run industry supply curve.

An industry may be decreasing-cost (which means that it benefits from external economies of scale and has a downward-sloping long-run industry supply curve), increasing-cost (which means that it suffers from external diseconomies of scale and has an upward-sloping long-run industry supply curve), or constant-cost (where the long-run industry supply curve is horizontal). (page 228)

External economies of scale are caused by growth in the entire industry and result in decreases in the firm's long-run average costs. If industry growth results in increases in long-run average costs, an *external diseconomy of scale* is present. The *long-run industry supply curve*, which shows how price and total output change as an industry expands in response to an increase in demand, depends on whether external economies or external diseconomies are present. (page 229)

Practice

27. The typical firm in a perfectly competitive increasing-cost industry is making economic profits. Predict what will happen in this industry in the long run.
    A. firms will enter this industry. The industry supply curve will shift to the right, and the LRAC curve will shift down.
    B. firms will enter this industry. The industry supply curve will shift to the right, and the LRAC curve will shift up.
    C. firms will leave this industry. The industry supply curve will shift to the right, and the LRAC curve will shift down.
    D. firms will leave this industry. The industry supply curve will shift to the right, and the LRAC curve will shift up.

    ANSWER: B. Profits attract firms to the industry, and supply will increase. Extra competition for scarce resources will make long-run average costs increase.

28. At all points along the long-run industry supply curve
    A. industry price level is constant.
    B. all firms earn a normal profit.
    C. all firms earn an economic profit.
    D. industry output level is constant.

    ANSWER: B. In the long run, firms can only earn a normal profit.

29. Refer to the diagram for Vigour Vitamins above, (at question 19). Between output levels 300 and 400, the firm is experiencing
    A. internal economies of scale.
    B. internal diseconomies of scale.
    C. external economies of scale.
    D. external diseconomies of scale.

    ANSWER: B. LRAC is increasing. This indicates diseconomies of scale within the firm. See p. 216.

30. Vigour is currently producing 300 units and is in long-run equilibrium. Suddenly demand increases. In the long run, the industry's new equilibrium price stabilizes at 35¢ per unit. This indicates that the industry has experienced external _________. The long-run industry supply curve is _________.
    A. economies of scale, upward sloping.
    B. economies of scale, downward sloping.
    C. diseconomies of scale, upward sloping.
    D. diseconomies of scale, downward sloping.

    if P↑, diseconomy of scale

    ANSWER: C. The long-run equilibrium price was 33¢ (minimum LRAC). As the industry grew, price increased. This must be due to external diseconomies.

PRACTICE TEST

I. MULTIPLE CHOICE QUESTIONS. Select the option that provides the single best answer.

_____ 1. ABC Corp. cuts usage of all inputs by 50%. Production falls by more than 50%. This firm is experiencing
A. external economies of scale.
B. external diseconomies of scale.
C. increasing returns to scale.
D. decreasing returns to scale.

_____ 2. In the short run, a perfectly competitive firm incurring losses should still produce if it can cover its
A. average costs.
B. variable costs.
C. fixed costs.
D. economic costs.

_____ 3. An industry has external economies of scale. In the long run, an increase in demand will
A. decrease price.
B. increase price.
C. not change price.
D. cause an indeterminate change in price.

_____ 4. Suddenly there is an increase in the demand for Frisbees. The most likely result would be
A. higher prices in the short run, followed by an increase in production in the long run that would cause prices to decline somewhat.
B. higher prices in the short run, followed by larger long-run price increases as the stock of Frisbees is depleted.
C. higher prices in the short run because of greater sales volume, and even higher prices later on as plant sizes are increased.
D. lower prices in the short run because of higher sales, but higher prices in the long run as the stock of Frisbees is depleted.

_____ 5. In the long-run perfectly competitive equilibrium, each of the following conditions will hold, except
A. P = MR.
B. P = SRMC.
C. LRAC is minimized.
D. SRMC is minimized.

_____ 6. An increasing-cost industry experiences external __________ of scale and has a(n) __________ long-run industry supply curve.
A. economies, upward-sloping.
B. economies, downward-sloping.
C. diseconomies, upward-sloping.
D. diseconomies, downward-sloping.

Use the following table to answer the next seven questions. The data refer to a perfectly competitive firm.

Output	*Marginal Cost*	*AVC*	*ATC*
1	$6.00	$6.00	$24.00
2	$4.00	$5.00	$14.00
3	$2.00	$4.00	$10.00
4	$4.00	$4.00	$8.50
5	$6.00	$4.40	$8.00
6	$8.00	$5.00	$8.00
7	$10.00	$5.72	$8.30

_____ 7. The total fixed cost at 6 units of output is
A. $24.00.
B. $8.00.
C. $18.00.
D. $3.00.

_____ 8. The firm will shut down in the short run if the price falls below
A. $8.00.
B. $4.00.
C. $2.00.
D. $6.00.

_____ 9. The price is currently $7.70. In the short run, to maximize profits, the firm should
A. produce 6 units.
B. produce 7 units.
C. produce 5 units.
D. shut down.

_____ 10. At this price ($7.70), the firm will make a short-run
A. profit of $1.50.
B. profit of $2.00.
C. loss of $1.50.
D. loss of $2.00.

_____ 11. At this price ($7.70), the firm will make a short-run operating
A. profit of $1.50.
B. profit of $16.50.
C. loss of $1.50.
D. loss of $16.50.

_____ 12. In the long run, firms will ________ this industry, and the price will probably ________.
A. enter, increase.
B. enter, decrease.
C. leave, increase.
D. leave, decrease.

_____ 13. If this is an industry that is experiencing external diseconomies of scale, the long-run price could be
A. $7.70.
B. $8.00.
C. $8.30.
D. $9.00.

_____ 14. A perfectly competitive decreasing-cost industry in long-run equilibrium experiences a permanent decrease in market demand. When the industry reaches its new long-run equilibrium, the equilibrium price of its good will be __________ than before, and the equilibrium industry output will be __________ than before.
A. higher, higher.
B. higher, lower.
C. lower, higher.
D. lower, lower.

_____ 15. A firm will not produce where MR = MC when
A. it is earning positive economic profits.
B. it is making an operating loss.
C. it is earning negative economic profits.
D. it is making an operating profit.

_____ 16. Jenny's Gemstones is making an operating loss. It should ________ in the short run and ________ in the long run.
A. shut down, leave the industry.
B. leave the industry, shut down.
C. increase its price, leave the industry.
D. increase its price, reduce production.

_____ 17. Jenny's Gemstones is making an operating loss. The industry supply curve will shift ________ in the ________,
A. right, short run.
B. right, long run.
C. left, short run.
D. left, long run.

_____ 18. Lambert's Lamps finds that when it increases its inputs by 20%, its output increases by 25%. It can conclude
A. that it is operating in an increasing-cost industry.
B. that it is operating in a decreasing-cost industry.
C. that it is operating in a constant-cost industry.
D. none of the above.

_____ 19. A perfectly competitive firm sells its output for $40 per unit. Its current output is 1000 units. At that level, its marginal cost is $50 and increasing, average variable cost is $35, and average total cost is $60. To maximize short-run profits, the firm should
A. increase production.
B. increase price.
C. decrease production.
D. shut down.

Use the following information to answer the next three questions. A perfectly competitive firm, operating in an industry that is experiencing external diseconomies of scale, Johnny's T-shirts is in long-run equilibrium producing 500 t-shirts per week. Suddenly, the price of all variable factors of production falls. Also, market demand for t-shirts increases.

_____ 20. In the short run, Johnny's T-shirts will
A. produce more T-shirts, but the effect on profits is uncertain.
B. produce fewer T-shirts and possibly close down.
C. earn positive (economic) profits, but the effect on output is uncertain.
D. produce more T-shirts and earn positive (economic) profits.

_____ 21. In the long run, Johnny's T-shirts will
A. produce more than 500 T-shirts per week, but the effect on profits is uncertain.
B. produce fewer than 500 T-shirts per week and earn normal profits.
C. earn normal profits, but the effect on output is uncertain.
D. earn positive (economic) profits, but the effect on output is uncertain.

_____ 22. The short-run industry supply curve will have shifted to the __________, and the long-run industry supply curve is __________.
A. right, upward sloping.
B. right, downward sloping.
C. left, upward sloping.
D. left, downward sloping.

_____ 23. When P < LRAC, we would expect __________ and ______ firms in this industry.
A. investment, more.
B. investment, fewer.
C. disinvestment, more.
D. disinvestment, fewer.

Use the following diagram, which refers to Luc and Veronique's Mugs-R-Us, to answer the next two questions. LRAC is minimized at 600 units of output.

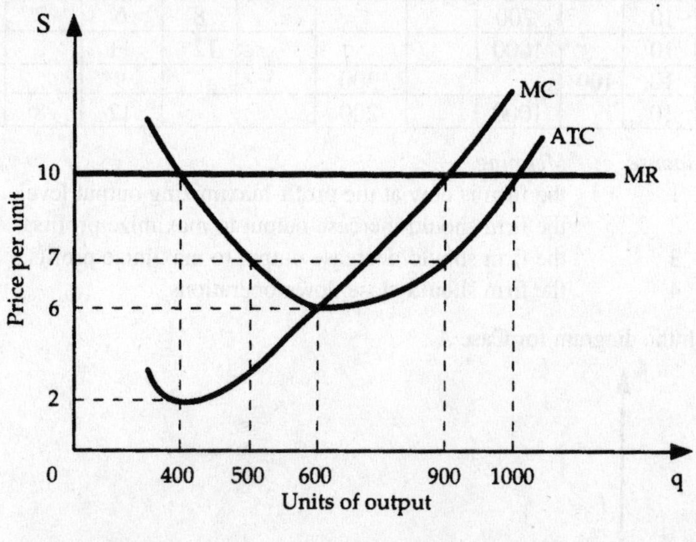

_____ 24. Assume that this firm is maximizing profit in an industry that is experiencing neither external economies nor diseconomies of scale. In the long run,
A. each existing firm will expand production, and new firms will enter the industry.
B. each existing firm will expand production, and new firms will leave the industry.
C. each existing firm will reduce production, and firms will enter this industry.
D. each existing firm will reduce production, and firms will leave this industry.

_____ 25. Assume that this firm is operating in an industry that is experiencing external economies of scale. In the long run,
A. price will be $6 per unit.
B. price will be between $10 per unit and $6 per unit.
C. price will be less than $6 per unit.
D. price will be $10 per unit.

II. APPLICATION QUESTIONS.

1. Check your understanding of the short-run relationships among costs, revenue, and the behaviour of the firm in the table below.

Treat each of the examples as a separate case.

Assume that MC is increasing as output is increasing. The asterisk (*) indicates that the value given is the *minimum* ATC or AVC.

Fill in the spaces and enter in the "response" column one of the responses provided.

	P	*q*	*TR*	*TC*	*TFC*	*TVC*	*ATC*	*AVC*	*MC*	*Response*
A.	10		500				12*	9		
B.	10	200			300			8*		
C.	10		1000		200			4	10	
D.			2000		1500	1400		7	4	
E.	10		700				8	6	7	
F.	10		1000				12*	11		
G.	10	100			300			9*		
H.	10		1000		200			12	8	

Response	*Meaning*
1	the firm is now at the profit-maximizing output level.
2	the firm should increase output to maximize profits.
3	the firm should decrease output to maximize profits.
4	the firm should close down operations.

Sketch the diagram for Case A.

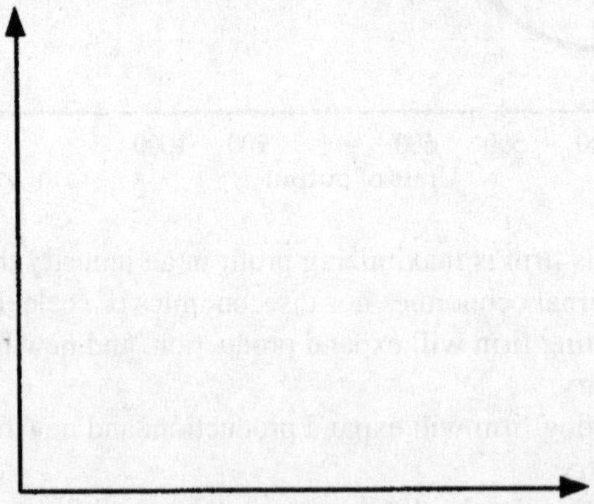

2. Suppose you are a consultant for ABC Inc., a firm in a perfectly competitive industry. Your research reveals two facts: (1) that the cost of producing the final unit of output is just equal to the market price, and (2) that the firm's total revenue is greater than its total variable cost and less than its total fixed cost. What would you recommend ABC do in the short run and in the long run?

Now XYZ, a firm in the same industry, requests your advice. Your research reveals that: (1) the cost of producing the final unit of output is just equal to the market price, and (2) the firm's total revenue is greater than its total fixed cost and less than its total variable cost. What would you recommend XYZ do in the short run and in the long run?

3. Currently your firm is losing $2000 per month. Variable costs are running at $1200 per month. Your economist advises you to shut down. Why or why not should you accept her advice? The economist adds that your firm is experiencing diminishing marginal product but increasing returns to scale. Isn't there an inconsistency here? Should you fire her?

4. You have been hired as a consultant for DEF, Inc., a firm in a perfectly competitive industry with no external economies or diseconomies of scale. You have developed the following total cost information, based on three feasible plant sizes ("small," "medium," and "large").

q	TCsmall	TCmedium	TClarge
0	$1.00	$3.40	$5.00
1	$5.00	$7.40	$12.00
2	$8.00	$10.40	$18.00
3	$9.60	$12.90	$21.00
4	$12.00	$15.00	$23.60
5	$16.00	$16.00	$25.00
6	$20.40	$16.80	$25.80
7	$28.00	$17.50	$26.67
8	$44.80	$18.00	$27.60
9	$68.40	$22.50	$28.71
10	$96.00	$30.00	$30.00
11	$127.60	$41.25	$31.35
12	$163.20	$57.00	$33.00
13	$202.80	$78.00	$36.40
14	$252.00	$112.00	$42.00

a. Calculate the average total cost information and complete the table below.

q	ATCsmall	ATCmedium	ATClarge
1	____	____	____
2	____	____	____
3	____	____	____
4	____	____	____
5	____	____	____
6	____	____	____
7	____	____	____
8	____	____	____
9	____	____	____
10	____	____	____
11	____	____	____
12	____	____	____
13	____	____	____
14	____	____	____

b. Calculate the marginal cost information and complete the table below.

q	MCsmall	MCmedium	MClarge
1			
2			
3			
4			
5			
6			
7			
8			
9			
10			
11			
12			
13			
14			

c. The market price is $2.40. Based on the information you have, and knowing that DEF is intending to produce 4 units of output, in which plant size, if any, would you advise the firm to invest?

d. The market price is $2.40. If DEF wishes to maximize profits, which is the optimal plant size, in your opinion? How many units should be produced? Calculate the firm's economic profit.

e. Draw DEF's short-run average cost curves and then the long-run average cost curve.

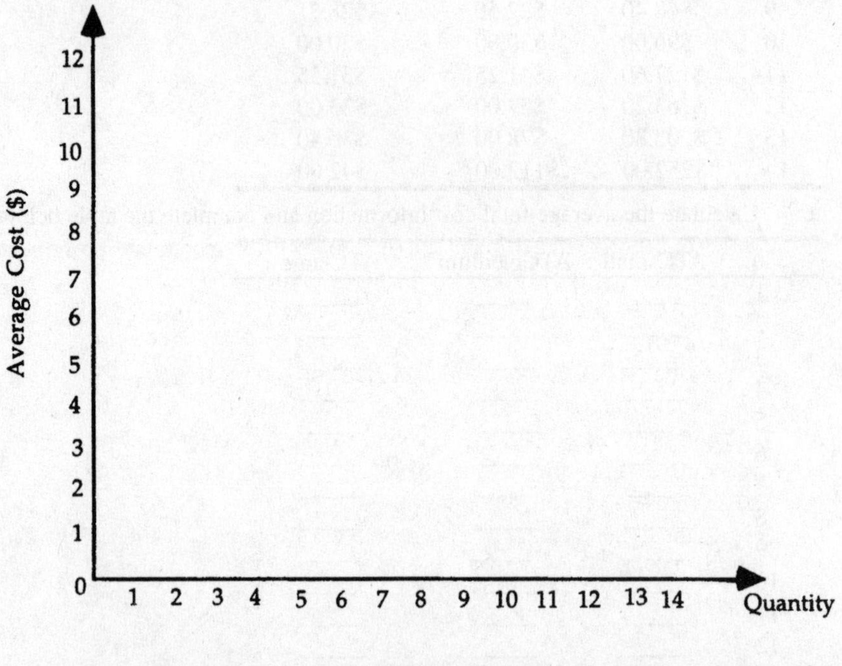

f. Over what range of output is DEF experiencing internal economies of scale? Internal diseconomies?

g. Consider your answer to part d. Is this the end of the adjustments that DEF will face? Describe any further changes that will occur in this industry. Draw a diagram with market demand and supply curves and the long-run industry supply curve.

5. In the following diagram, draw the firm's demand curve.

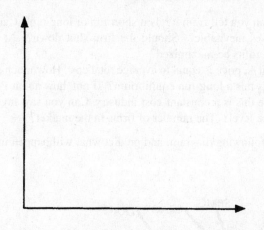

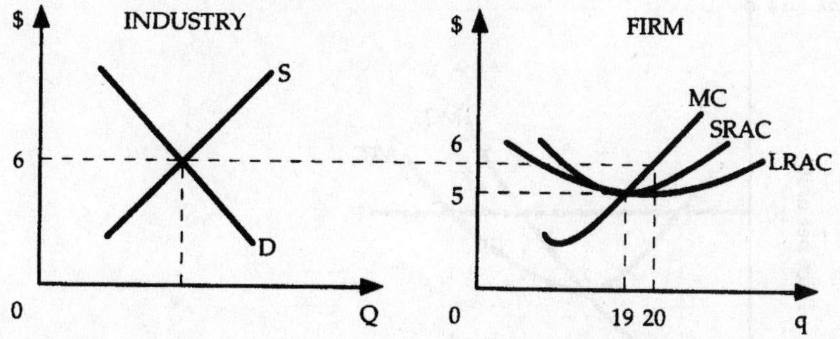

Determine the market price. The firm will make a short-run _______ (profit/loss) of $__________. Determine the short-run profit-maximizing output level. We would expect firms to _________ (enter/leave) this industry.

6. Draw the "short-run cost diagram" comprised of AVC, ATC, and MC.

a. Draw in a horizontal demand curve (D_a) such that economic profits can be earned. Pick out the profit-maximizing output level (q_a).
b. Repeat the process, drawing the demand curve (D_b) so that only normal profits occur (q_b).
c. Repeat the process, drawing the demand curve (D_c) so that a loss is made but the firm continues to produce (q_c).
d. Draw in the demand curve (D_d) which would just permit the firm to cover its operating expenses (q_d).
e. Lastly, present the "shutdown" case (D_e).
f. Highlight all the points on the MC curve where production will occur. Confirm that it's the short-run supply curve.

7. Examine the following diagram.

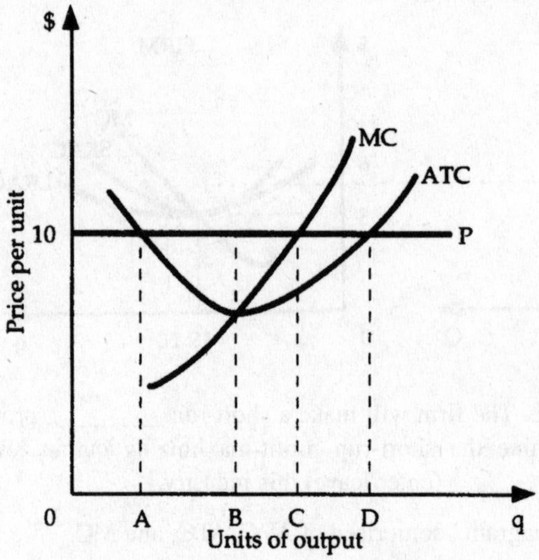

a. What can you tell from it? Is it short run or long run? Can profits be made or are losses inevitable? Should the firm shut down? At which output level would profits be maximized?

b. At Point A, price is equal to average total cost. How much profit is being made here? Is this a long-run equilibrium? If not, how about Point D?

c. Suppose this is a constant-cost industry. Can you say anything definite about the price level? The number of firms in the market?

8. Interpret the following diagram, and predict what will happen in this industry.

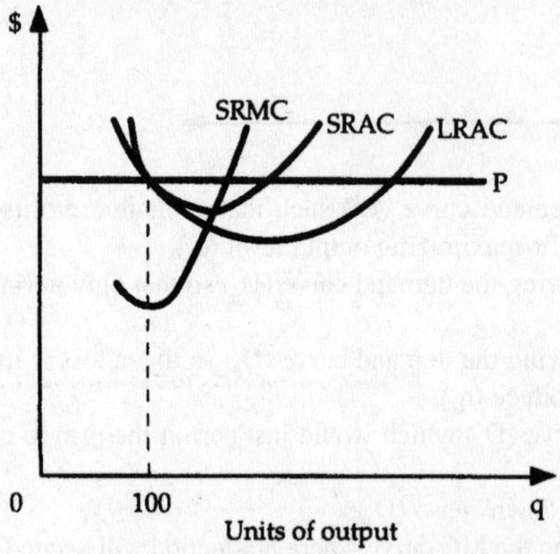

a. In the short run, at 100, are any profits being made?

b. In the long run, what will happen in this industry?

9. Study the following diagram. Assume constant costs for the industry. The firm's long-run average cost curve is $LRAC_1$.

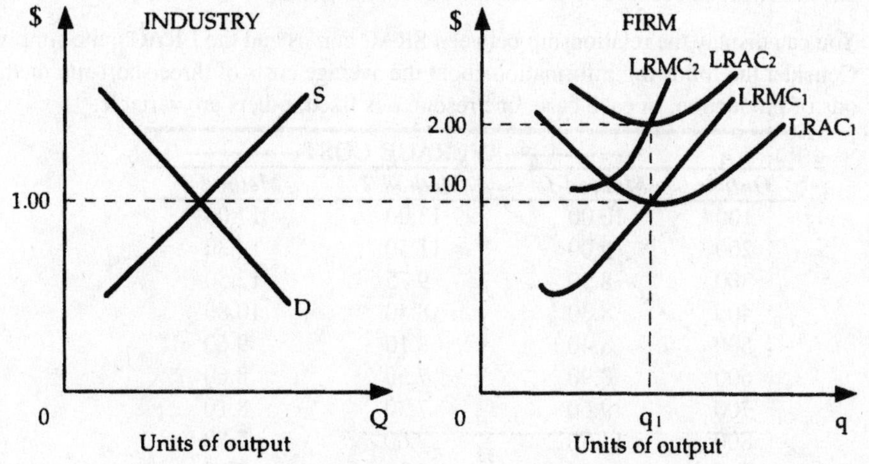

a. Verify that the firm is making normal profits and that it is in long-run equilibrium at a price of $1.
b. Suppose that there is an increase in average costs to $LRAC_2$. What will happen to the average and marginal cost curves?
c. What will happen to the short-run profits of the typical firm in this industry?
d. What will happen to output in the short run and why?
e. What will happen to industry supply in the long run and why?
f. If this had been an increasing-cost industry, would average cost be experiencing a pressure to rise or fall?

10. In the following diagram, which is for a firm operating in a constant-cost industry, use the curves having the notation "1"—e.g., demand curve D_1. The firm is at q_1.

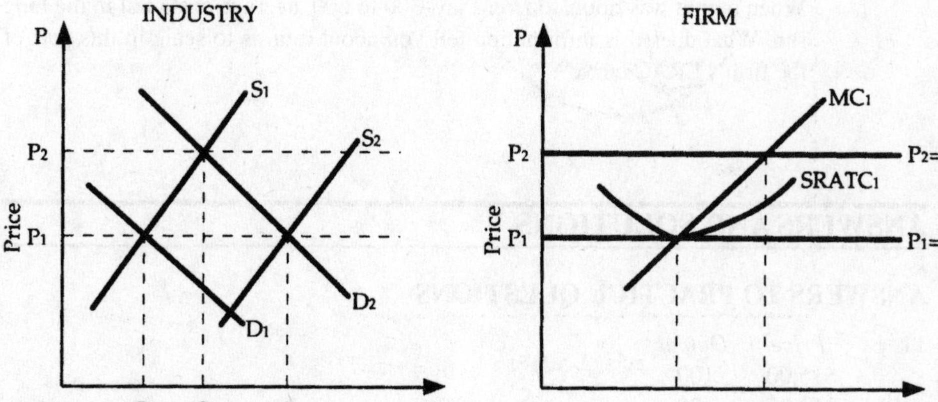

a. What will this typical firm do in the short run?
b. Now suppose demand rises to D_2. What are the immediate effects on the industry and on the firm?
c. In the short run, the firm will produce _______ units, and the industry will produce _________ units.
d. Examine the graph. Does your answer in part c. represent an equilibrium?
e. Depict the firm's short-run profits on your diagram.
f. Explain your answer to part d.

g. What will happen to this industry in the long run? How far will price fall? Note that although more is being supplied by more firms, the size of the typical firm has not changed because of the assumption of a constant-cost industry.

11. You can display the relationship between SRAC curves and the LRAC quite simply. Consider the following information about the average costs of three short-run methods of production. In each case, one resource is fixed; others are variable.

	----------------AVERAGE COST--------------		
Output	*Method 1*	*Method 2*	*Method 3*
100	10.00	13.00	17.00
200	9.00	11.50	14.30
300	8.50	9.75	12.50
400	8.30	8.40	10.80
500	8.40	8.10	9.60
600	8.90	7.50	8.60
700	9.60	7.30	8.10
800	11.70	7.60	7.80
900	14.80	8.10	8.00
1000	17.00	8.90	8.30
1100	23.00	10.20	9.00

a. Is each curve a "typical" short-run ATC curve?
b. Which method should be used if an output of 100 is desired?
c. Which method should be used if an output of 500 is desired?
d. Which method should be used if an output of 1000 is desired?
e. Plot each of the curves on a single piece of graph paper.
f. You're using Method 1. If you want to move from an output level of 100 units to 1000 units, what would happen to average cost in the short run?
g. In the long run, what would be your lowest-cost strategy?
h. What does this firm's LRAC curve look like?
i. Why is this the *long-run* AC curve?
j. When output was doubled from, say, 300 to 600, average costs fell in the long run. What does this information tell you about returns to scale in this part of the firm's LRAC curve?

ANSWERS AND SOLUTIONS

ANSWERS TO PRACTICE QUESTIONS

11.

Price	*Output*
$15.00	100
$14.22	90
$ 8.90	80
$ 7.00	70
$ 6.00	0

PRACTICE TEST

I. SOLUTIONS TO MULTIPLE CHOICE QUESTIONS

1. C. External (dis)economies of scale refer to industry-wide changes. See p. 228.
2. B. If a firm can earn an operating profit, it will minimize losses by producing.
3. A. See p. 230.
4. A. Initially, existing firms will increase production as higher prices earn them greater profits. In the long run, new firms will enter the industry, increasing supply and decreasing the price level.
5. D. In the long run, price will equal the minimum value of average cost. See Figure 9.7 on p. 221.
6. C. As the number of firms increases, costs increase. This pushes up the price charged by the industry.
7. C. At one unit of output, TC = ATC x q = $24.00 and TVC = AVC x q = $6.00. TFC = TC - TVC.
8. B. If price is less than the minimum AVC ($4.00), then the firm should shut down.
9. C. P = MR = $7.70. To maximize profits, increase production where MR is equal to or exceeds MC.
10. C. When the output is set at 5 units, TR = $7.70 x 5 = $38.50. TC = ATC x q = $8.00 x 5 = $40.00. The firm will make a negative economic profit of $1.50.
11. B. TR = $7.70 x 5 = $38.50. TVC = $4.40 x 5 = $22.00.
12. C. Because losses are being experienced, firms will leave the industry. Market supply will decrease, causing the price to increase (unless there are external economies of scale resulting in a downward-sloping industry supply curve).
13. A. At a price of $7.70, firms will leave this industry in the long run. In an industry experiencing external diseconomies of scale, this reduction in output will reduce average cost from $8.00 and reduce equilibrium price.
14. B. In a decreasing-cost industry, costs decrease as output increases, and they increase as output decreases.
15. B. A firm that is making an operating loss will close down. Note: Making a negative economic profit is not an adequate answer because the firm could still be making an operating profit.
16. A. Perfectly competitive firms can't change the price they face—they are price takers. Because Jenny can't cover her variable costs, she should shut down in the short run and leave the industry in the long run.
17. D. Firms will leave the industry in the long run.
18. D. The behaviour of costs for an individual firm (its internal economies of scale) are no guide to the behaviour of costs for the entire industry (its external economies of scale).
19. C. If price is $40, then marginal revenue is also $40. MR is less than MC—the firm's output level is too high. It should not shut down as it can cover its variable costs.
20. D. Marginal cost is affected by the behaviour of variable costs. A decrease in variable costs will decrease marginal cost. An increase in price will increase marginal

revenue. Together, these effects will increase the profit-maximizing output level. In long-run equilibrium, Johnny's T-shirts was earning a normal profit. With higher prices and lower costs, the firm will earn an economic profit.

21. C. In the long run, the competitive firm always earns normal profits. As the industry expands, external diseconomies (increasing costs) are experienced, reducing the firm's profit-maximizing output level. Without extra information, we cannot say whether the final output level will be greater than, equal to, or less than 500 T-shirts.

22. A. New firms have entered this industry, shifting the short-run supply curve to the right. The long-run industry supply curve is upward sloping because of the external diseconomies of scale.

23. D. If price is less than long-run average cost, disinvestment will occur, and firms will leave the industry in search of normal profits in other activities.

24. C. New firms will enter, attracted by the economic profits, pushing down the price. As price falls, existing firms will cut back production.

25. C. As firms enter the industry, external economies of scale will reduce costs. The minimum average cost will be less than $6. In equilibrium, price equals average cost.

II. SOLUTIONS TO APPLICATION QUESTIONS

1. See the following table.

	P	*q*	*TR*	*TC*	*TFC*	*TVC*	*ATC*	*AVC*	*MC*	*Response*
A.	10	50	500	600	150	450	12*	9	12	3
B.	10	200	2000	1900	300	1600	9.5	8*	8	2
C.	10	100	1000	600	200	400	6	4	10	1
D.	10	200	2000	2900	1500	1400	14.5	7	4	2
E.	10	70	700	560	140	420	8	6	7	2
F.	10	100	1000	1200	100	1100	12*	11	12	3 or 4
G.	10	100	1000	1200	300	900	12	9*	9	2
H.	10	100	1000	1400	200	1200	14	12	8	2 or 4

A (fairly complex) sketch that would describe the situation in Case A is presented below. (For more practice, try to do the other cases—without first peeking at the sketches that follow.)

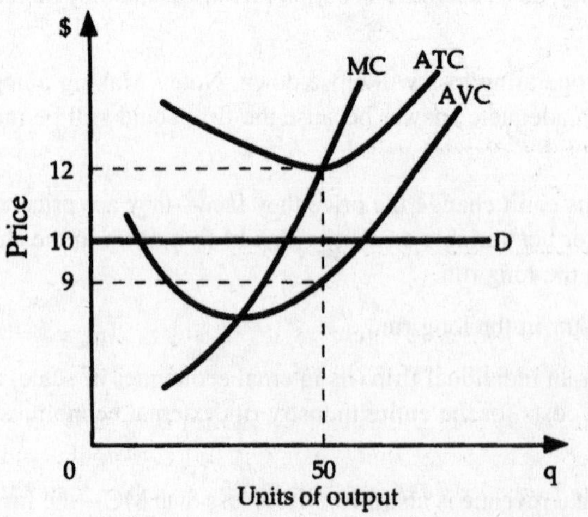

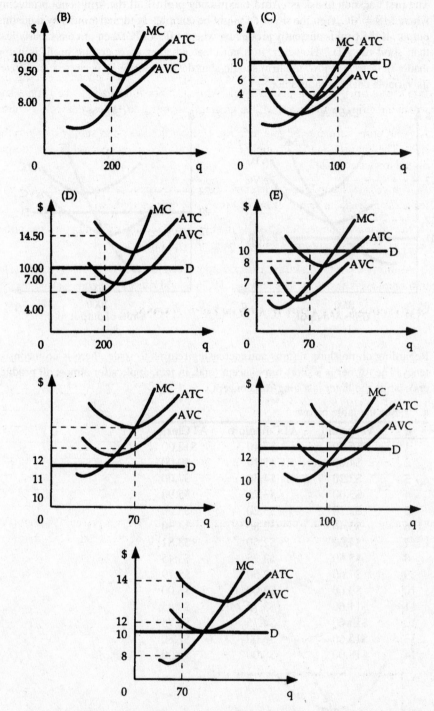

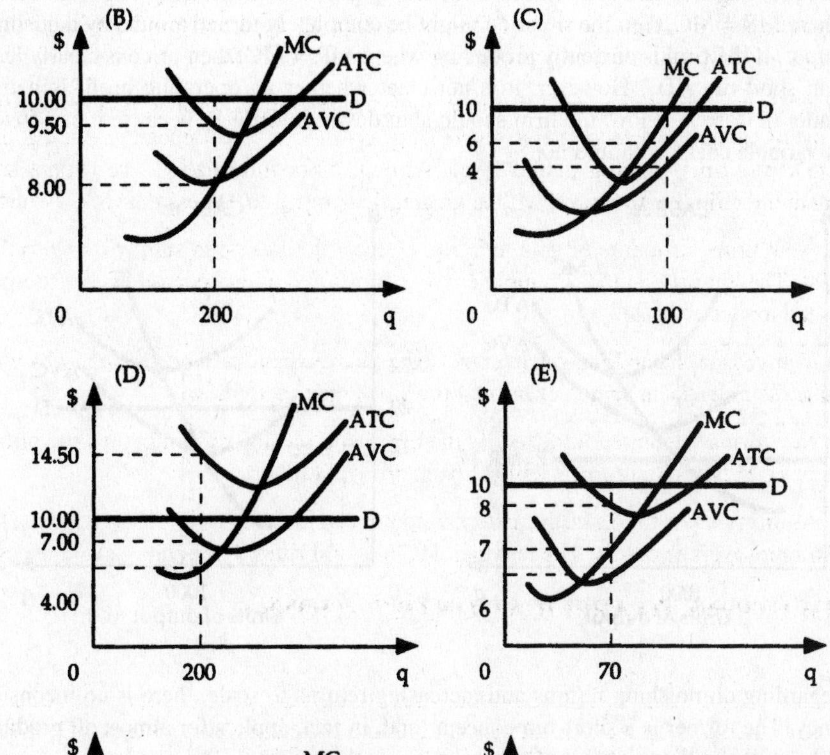

Note: Case F and Case H have two possible outcomes, depending on the behaviour of AVC. Again, try sketching these cases and try to get the different results.

2. ABC. Fact 1 means that MR = MC. Fact 2 means that the firm is making an economic loss but, because it is covering its variable (operating) costs, it should continue to produce in the short run. In the long run, the firm should leave the industry.

XYZ. Fact 1 means that MR = MC. Fact 2 means that the firm is making an economic loss and that it is not covering its variable (operating) costs—it should cease production in the short run. In the long run, the firm should leave the industry.

3. The first question to ask is: Am I maximizing profits? If the firm is not producing where MR = MC, then the situation might be completely turned around by adjusting output. If the firm is currently producing where MR = MC, then price is clearly less than short-run ATC. However, it is not clear whether an operating profit is being made. In Case A below, the firm should shut down; in Case B, because it can cover its variable costs, it should not.

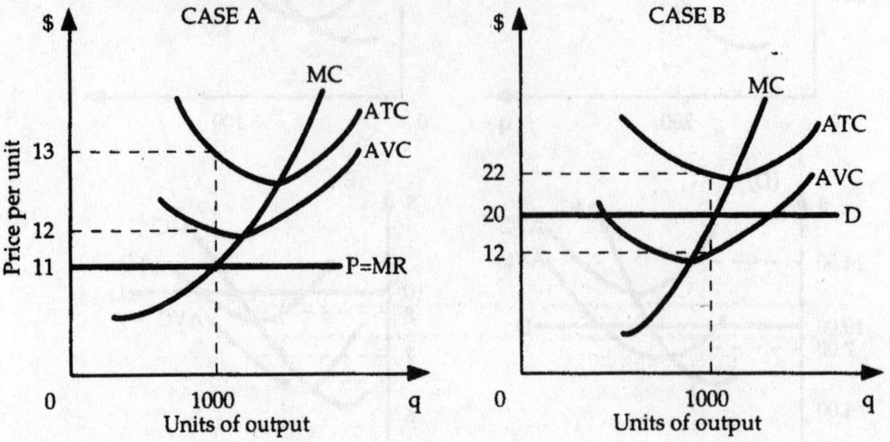

Regarding diminishing returns and increasing returns to scale, there is no inconsistency. The former is a short-run concept (and, in fact, applies for almost all producers), while the latter is a long-run concept.

4. a. See the table below.

q	ATCsmall	ATCmedium	ATClarge
1	$5.00	$7.40	$12.00
2	$4.00	$5.20	$9.00
3	$3.20	$4.30	$7.00
4	$3.00	$3.75	$5.90
5	$3.20	$3.20	$5.00
6	$3.40	$2.80	$4.30
7	$4.00	$2.50	$3.81
8	$5.60	$2.25	$3.45
9	$7.60	$2.50	$3.19
10	$9.60	$3.00	$3.00
11	$11.60	$3.75	$2.85
12	$13.60	$4.75	$2.75
13	$15.60	$6.00	$2.80
14	$18.00	$8.00	$3.00

b. See the table below.

q	MCsmall	MCmedium	MClarge
1	$4.00	$4.00	$7.00
2	$3.00	$3.00	$6.00
3	$1.60	$2.50	$3.00
4	$2.40	$2.10	$2.60
5	$4.00	$1.00	$1.40
6	$4.40	$0.80	$0.80
7	$7.60	$0.70	$0.87
8	$16.80	$0.50	$0.93
9	$23.60	$4.50	$1.11
10	$27.60	$7.50	$1.29
11	$31.60	$11.25	$1.35
12	$35.60	$15.75	$1.65
13	$39.60	$21.00	$3.40
14	$49.20	$34.00	$5.60

c. The firm should not produce. Even in the case of the small plant, the firm will incur a loss because $2.40 x 4 is less than $12. If the firm had committed to the small plant, in the short run it should shut down because it cannot cover its variable costs. Note that total fixed costs are only $1.00, with variable costs accounting for the remainder.

d. The medium plant is best, with the lowest total costs. Neither of the two other plant sizes has an average cost as low as the price. Producing up to the output where price equals (or is greater than) marginal cost, DEF should produce 8 units of output. The firm's economic profit is ($2.40 – $2.25) x 8, or $1.20.

e. See the diagram below.

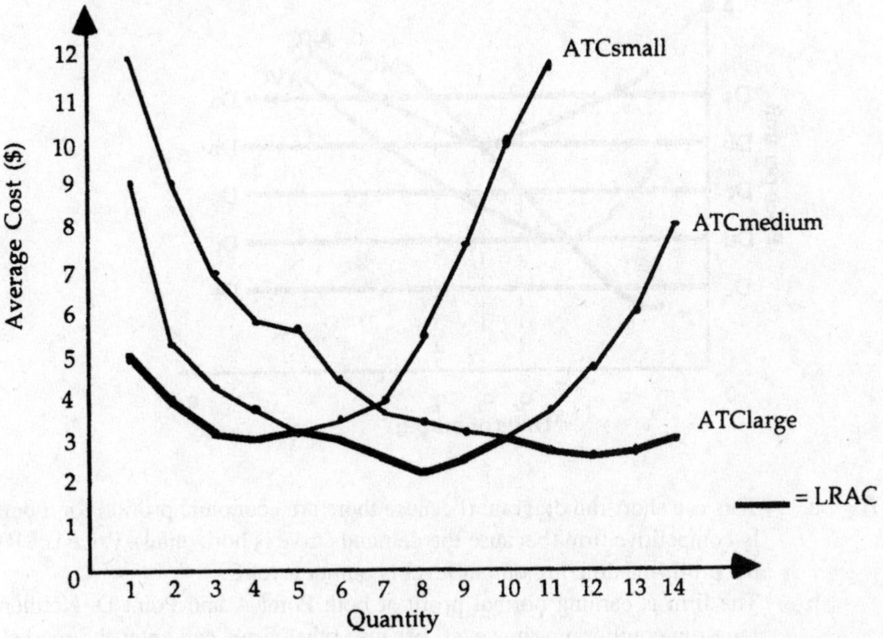

f. Internal economies of scale occur until the minimum point of the long-run average cost curve, i.e., at 8 units, after which point diseconomies take over.

g. Because DEF is earning an economic profit, new firms will enter the industry. There are no external economies or diseconomies of scale, so the firm's long-run average cost curve will not change position. For the same reason, the long-run industry supply curve is horizontal. As new firms enter, market supply increases from S1 to S2, and the market price will decrease from 2.40 to $2.25, at which point the process will cease because the market price has reached the minimum long-run average cost. Economic profits have been competed away. Given DEF's marginal cost values, the firm's output will remain at 8 units.

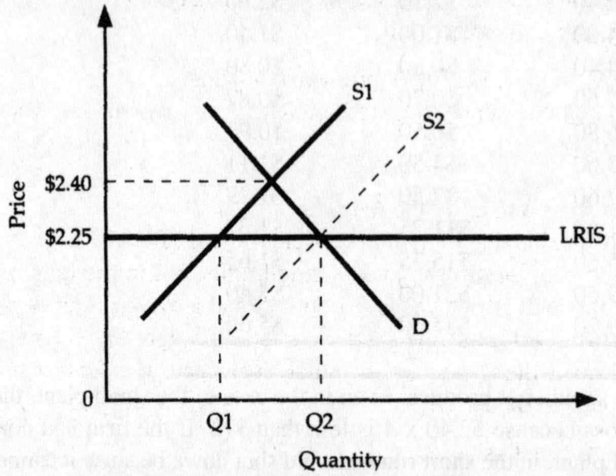

5. The firm's demand curve graphs as a horizontal line. It is set at the industry level by the forces of demand and supply at a level of $6.

   The market price is $6. The firm will make a short-run profit of $20 at an output level of 20 units. We would expect firms to enter this industry.

6. See the diagram below.

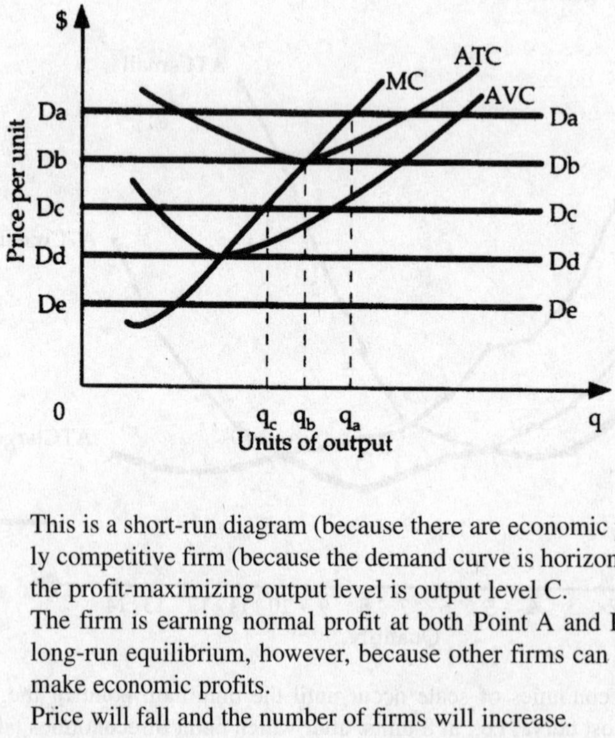

7. a. This is a short-run diagram (because there are economic profits) for a perfectly competitive firm (because the demand curve is horizontal). Price is $10 and the profit-maximizing output level is output level C.

   b. The firm is earning normal profit at both Point A and Point D. Neither is a long-run equilibrium, however, because other firms can enter the market and make economic profits.

   c. Price will fall and the number of firms will increase.

8. a. The firm is making normal profits (P = ATC), but is not maximizing profits because it is not producing where MR = MC.

   b. In the long run, since price is greater than the minimum LRAC point, firms will enter the industry, forcing price to fall.

9. a. Check that P = MR = SRMC = SRAC = LRAC.
   b. Average and marginal cost curves will rise.
   c. Short-run losses will be encountered.
   d. Some firms will shut down in the short run, and supply will fall for the industry.
   e. Supply will decrease as firms exit the industry.
   f. Fall. As output rises for an increasing-cost industry, costs rise. Here output is shrinking, and costs would fall.

10. a. Stay as it is, since it is already profit-maximizing.
    b. Price and quantity supplied increase in each case, and the number of firms is unchanged.
    c. q2; Q2.
    d. Yes in the short run; no in the long run.
    e. The profit-maximizing output level occurs where MR = MC.
    f. In the short run, the firm is maximizing profits, but in the long run the economic profits will attract new competitions and a change in price will occur.
    g. Entering firms will push the supply curve to the right (to S2), and price will decline. Price will fall back to its initial level since, at any other price, profits or losses will be made.

11. a. Yes, each ATC is U-shaped.
    b. Method 1, which is cheapest until about 425 units.
    c. Method 2 is cheapest from about 425 units until about 875.
    d. Method 3 is cheapest from about 875 units on.
    f. ATC would rise to $17.00.
    g. Maintain Method 1 until production has grown to 425 units, then switch to Method 2. Maintain Method 2 until production has grown to 875 units, then switch to Method 3. In effect, you are tracing out the LRAC for this firm.
    h. U-shaped, in this case.
    i. We release the fixed resource constraint as we move from one method of production to the next.
    j. The firm has increasing returns to scale (economies of scale).

10 Input Demand: The Labour and Land Markets

OBJECTIVES: POINT BY POINT

After completing this chapter, you should be able to accomplish the objectives listed below.

General Comments

While there is much new material in this chapter, there is also a lot of familiar material. The discussion of the input markets reuses tools that you have already developed—e.g., profit maximization, marginal product, demand curves, and elasticity. Take this as a reminder that (for better or for worse) economics is a cumulative discipline. New material doesn't supplant earlier material; it builds on it.

Keep in mind too that, although the chapter talks mostly in terms of labour demand, the conclusions apply equally to other inputs, including capital.

OBJECTIVE 1: Understand derived demand.

When the management of the Chicago Bulls signs Michael Jordan to a contract, it does so because of the "output" (points and excitement) that Jordan can produce for the team. The demand for his labour services is a demand derived from the demand for the team's output by its public. This specific conclusion is true generally for the demand for all types of input. (page 233)

> **TIP:** The main theme of this chapter is that the value of any input depends on society's valuation of the output produced by that input. Inputs will be hired as long as their contribution to the value of production is greater than their cost. Keep this point in mind as you go through the chapter.

Practice

1. Which of the following is a "derived demand"?
   A. the demand by this *Study Guide*'s author for a word processor.
   B. the demand for Cracker Jacks at the ball game.
   C. the demand for RRSP eligible mutual funds by a highly paid executive seeking to reduce his tax payments.
   D. the demand for wood to help you build a doghouse for your new puppy.

   ANSWER: A. This option is the only one involving the demand for an input by a producer. Cracker Jacks and mutual funds are not inputs. Wood, bought by a construction firm, is an input; bought by an end-user, it is not.

OTHER RELATED POINTS: Explain why inputs are simultaneously complements and substitutes.

Although fans of the Bulls might disagree (for them, the only valid product is a "W" in the win column), the product of the Chicago Bulls is "entertainment"—the Bulls compete with movies, rock concerts, and so on for the public's leisure dollars. The facilities in the Bulls' stadium add to the entire entertainment package (inputs are complements) but they may be seen as substitutes for Michael Jordan (a team without a Michael Jordan may be able to attract fans by offering other facilities instead). At the team level, one player can assist (complement) another's play and can also substitute for that player. (page 234)

Practice

2. Which of the following is true about input markets?
   A. firms demand inputs in the labour market and supply inputs in the capital market.
   B. firms supply inputs in the labour market and demand inputs in the capital market.
   C. households supply inputs in the labour market and demand inputs in the capital market.
   D. households supply inputs in the labour market and supply inputs in the capital market.

   ANSWER: D. Households supply inputs to all resource markets; firms demand in all resource markets.

3. To produce cloth, a mill owner must hire a weaver and a loom. The weaver and the loom are
   A. substitutable inputs.
   B. complementary inputs.
   C. both substitutable and complementary inputs.
   D. not inputs—they are factors of production.

   ANSWER: B. To produce cloth, both inputs are required. Note: Factors of production are inputs.

4. To mine coal, a mine owner can use a robotic drill or a team of coal miners. The drill and the coal miners are
   A. substitutable inputs.
   B. complementary inputs.
   C. both substitutable and complementary inputs.
   D. unrelated inputs.

   ANSWER: A. This is an either/or situation. The inputs are substitutes in this case.

5. To mine coal, a mine owner can use a robotic drill or a team of coal miners. Within the group, the coal miners are
   A. substitutable inputs.
   B. complementary inputs.
   C. both substitutable and complementary inputs.
   D. unrelated inputs.

   ANSWER: C. Each miner helps the others to produce coal (complements), and each can take over from another worker (substitutes). See p. 234.

OBJECTIVE 2: Define marginal revenue product.

Marginal revenue product (MRP) is the addition to total revenue attributable to the hiring of an additional input. It can be defined as the extra units of output (marginal product) times the price of the product. Marginal revenue product of labour is the addition to revenue that occurs when an additional worker is hired—it's the dollar value of the extra merchandise he produces, i.e., (MP_L.P). In the short run, as extra workers are hired, MRP falls because of diminishing marginal productivity. The MRP curve is typically downward sloping. (page 234)

Practice

Tom grows tomatoes, which he sells for 75¢ per pound. His variable resource is labour and he has recorded the productivity of his workers in the table below.

Number of Workers	Total Product	Marginal Product	Marginal Revenue Product
0	0	—	—
1	15	15	11.25
2	28	13	9.75
3	38	10	7.5
4	46	8	6
5	52	6	4.5

6. Fill in the marginal product and marginal revenue product columns.

   ANSWER: See the *Answers and Solutions* section.

7. Graph the marginal product curve for the first 5 workers on part A of the diagram.

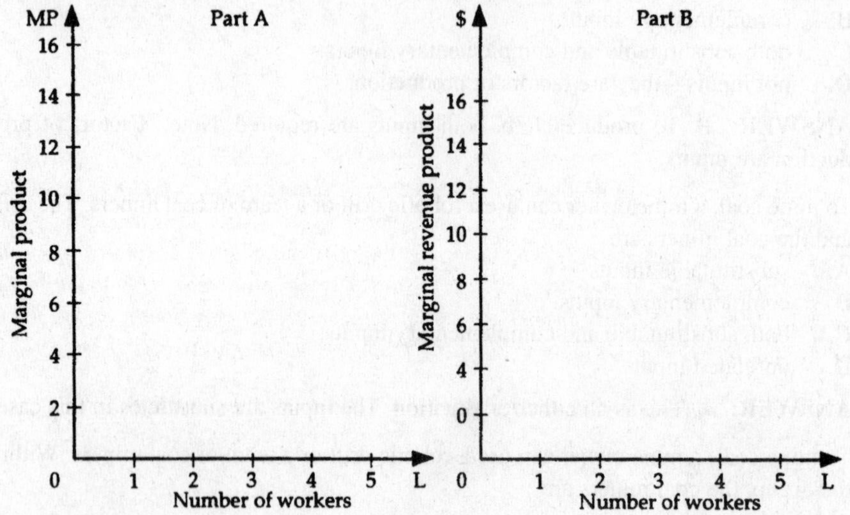

ANSWER: See the *Answers and Solutions* section.

OBJECTIVE 3: Understand the profit maximizing hiring decision.

To maximize profits, the employer should hire each input up to the point at which MRP equals the cost of hiring that input. For labour, wage will equal MRP. (page 236)

The MRP curve for a factor of production is identical with the demand curve for that factor. The demand curve for labour is the marginal revenue product of labour curve. (page 237)

Profit Maximization and the Hiring Decision: Two rules from earlier chapters crop up in the "hiring decision." The logic of profit maximization ($P = MC$) leads to Wage = MRP_L. No profit-maximizing employer will hire a worker who doesn't pay his or her way.

Recall the rule developed to describe the consumer's utility-maximizing mix of purchases: the final dollar spent on each good must provide the same utility. The same logic applies to profit maximization. It shows up as: $MP_L/P_L = MP_K/P_K = MP_A/P_A$—the final dollar spent on each input must generate the same amount of additional production.

Practice

8. If the wage is $10, Tom should hire
   A. 2 workers.
   B. 3 workers.
   C. 4 workers.
   D. 5 workers.

   ANSWER: B. To maximize profits, Tom should not hire any worker whose MRP is less than $10. The MRP of the third worker is $10.

9. The maximum wage that Tom would pay if he were to hire 4 workers is
   A. $8.00.
   B. $6.00.
   C. $10.00.
   D. $13.00.

   ANSWER: A. To maximize profits, Tom should not hire the fourth worker (whose MRP is $8.00) at any wage above $8.00.

OBJECTIVE 4: Distinguish between the output effect and the substitution effect of a factor price change.

The same profit-maximizing principles are applied with two variable factors of production as with one variable factor of production. However, when more than one factor is involved, an increase in the price of an input has a factor substitution effect and an output effect. These effects explain why as wage increases, the quantity demanded of labour decreases. As the wage rises, capital is substituted for the now relatively more expensive labour—the factor substitution effect. Also, higher wages may mean higher production costs, lower production, and less use of all inputs, including labour—the output effect. (page 241)

TIP: You can depict the factor substitution effect and the output effect on a diagram. Draw a labour demand curve. Suppose the price of robot car machines decreases and that there is job loss on the assembly line. In the labour market, which factor is stronger: the factor substitution effect or the output effect?

The lowered price of robots will increase management's desire to substitute capital for labour. The labour demand curve will decrease—this represents the factor substitution effect. Because production costs have fallen (cheaper robots), the company will wish to expand production because, with lower costs and the same selling price, the company will earn higher profits. Expanding production means that the demand for labour will increase—this is the output effect. If labour demand fell, on balance, the factor substitution effect would be stronger.

The firm's input demand curve will shift position if demand for the firm's product changes (causing its price to change); if the amount, productivity, or price of other inputs change; or if the state of technology changes. Each of these changes will affect MRP—the dollar value of the extra merchandise produced by an additional unit of an input. (page 241)

Practice

10. The tendency of firms to move away from usage of a factor whose price has increased is called the
    A. output substitution effect.
    B. factor substitution effect.
    C. complementarity effect.
    D. income effect.

    ANSWER: B. See p. 241.

11. The output effect indicates that the quantity demanded of labour
    A. will increase if the price of the final product increases.
    B. will decrease when the price of other factors increases.
    C. will increase if the price of labour increases.
    D. will increase if the price of labour decreases.

    ANSWER: D. The output effect helps explain why the quantity of labour demanded increases as the price of labour decreases.

12. Labour is a normal input. If the price of labour increases, the factor substitution effect will cause the demand for labour to ________, and the output effect will cause the demand for labour to ________.
    A. increase, increase.
    B. increase, decrease.
    C. decrease, increase.
    D. decrease, decrease.

    ANSWER: D. Other resources will be used instead of the more expensive labour (factor substitution effect). Because costs of production have risen, less will be produced and less labour will be demanded (output effect).

13. The wage of workers (a variable resource) is increased. This will cause each of the following to occur except
    A. the firm's profit-maximizing output level will decrease.
    B. the firm will substitute away from labour to capital.
    C. the output effect will lead to a decrease in the demand for capital as well as labour.
    D. the MRP of the final worker hired will decrease.

    ANSWER: D. Fewer workers are being hired. As extra workers are hired, MRP decreases; as fewer are hired, the MRP of the final worker increases.

14. The demand for labour will increase if
    A. the wage paid to labour increases.
    B. the wage paid to labour decreases.
    C. there is an increase in the amount of capital used.
    D. there is a decrease in the amount of capital used.

    ANSWER: C. Additional capital (machinery) will let workers be more productive, thus affecting MRP.

15. A technological advance increases labour productivity. This will cause
   A. an increase in the demand for labour.
   B. an increase in the supply of labour.
   C. a decrease in the demand for labour.
   D. a decrease in the supply of labour.

   ANSWER: A. MRP_L (MP_L .P) has increased.

16. Mauro uses labour and capital to produce soccer balls. He finds that as the price of capital rises, he hires more workers and cuts back on the use of capital. This behaviour is consistent with
   A. labour and capital being complementary inputs.
   B. the factor substitution effect.
   C. the increasing marginal productivity of labour.
   D. the dominance of the factor substitution effect over the output effect for capital.

   ANSWER: B. Simply, Mauro is switching from one input to the other to reduce costs.

17. The demand for soccer balls decreases. This will cause Mauro to ________ his demand for labour and ________ his demand for capital.
   A. increase, increase.
   B. increase, decrease.
   C. decrease, increase.
   D. decrease, decrease.

   ANSWER: D. Mauro will produce less because his costs have risen. He will need fewer workers and less capital.

OBJECTIVE 5: Understand the model for land markets.

The market for land is similar to the market for labour but differs in one important respect: land prices are demand-determined due to the fact that land is strictly fixed in supply. The return to any factor of production in fixed supply is called a *pure economic rent*. Any site has a variety of uses and should be allocated to the user who is willing to pay the most. (page 242–243)

> **TIP:** Pure economic rent emerges when *any* factor (not just land) is fixed in supply. Any payment greater than zero is a "bonus."
>
> Example: Suppose that Marlene has a word processor she's willing to lend out (lease, if you want) to her room-mates, Charlene, Arlene, and Darlene. Each has a term paper due tomorrow morning and is willing to pay for the use of the word processor (which is the only one available at such short notice). Marlene would take $6, but asks for bids. Charlene offers $7, Arlene, $8, and Darlene, $10. Darlene would have the use of the word processor, and Marlene would receive an economic rent of $4.

Practice

18. The supply of land of a particular quality at a given location is
    A. perfectly elastic.
    B. perfectly inelastic.
    C. unitarily elastic.
    D. dependent on demand.

    ANSWER: B. The supply of land isn't dependent on demand—the price is. The supply, however, is perfectly insensitive to changes in price.

19. A tax on landowners will ________ the quantity of land supplied and will ________ rents charged.
    A. decrease, decrease.
    B. decrease, not affect.
    C. not affect, decrease.
    D. not affect, not affect.

    ANSWER: D. The supply, however, is perfectly insensitive to changes in price or taxes. Because the rent charged is demand-driven, rents will not change. Economic rent will be reduced.

OBJECTIVE 6: Learn the profit maximizing condition in input markets.

The profit-maximizing equilibrium is to "balance the margins" according to the following rule: $MRP_L/P_L = MRP_K/P_K = MRP_A/P_A = 1$ (the marginal revenue product/dollar of the final unit of each input should be equal and have a value of one). Put differently, $MP_L/P_L = MP_K/P_K = MP_A/P_A$. (page 244)

Practice

20. Sellco finds that its workers have an average revenue product of \$20 (the final worker adding \$10), and its machines have an average revenue product of \$100 (the final machine adding \$60). Workers earn \$15 and machines cost \$50. Assuming that Sellco is at the profit-maximizing output level, it should hire ________ workers and hire ________ machines.
    A. more, more.
    B. more, fewer.
    C. fewer, more.
    D. fewer, fewer.

    ANSWER: C. Compare MRP (not average revenue product) with the price of the input. MRP_L is less than P_L and MRP_K is greater than P_K.

OBJECTIVE 7: Identify factors that shift input demand curves.

A profit-maximizing employer will hire any worker who pays his or her way. As the wage changes, the hiring level will change too, based on the MRP schedule—the demand for the input and the MRP curve are identical. Each point on the demand schedule equates input price and MRP. The equilibrium hiring condition is: W = MRP. It is equivalent to the P = MC profit-maximization rule in output markets. The input demand curve will shift right if marginal productivity increases or if the price of the product increases. (page 245)

Graphing Pointer: Initially, it is easy to become confused by input market diagrams. If you can determine whether demand (or supply) will increase or decrease, the curves shift just as they do in product market diagrams—right for an increase, left for a decrease.

Practice

21. Graph the MRP curve on part B of the previous diagram.

    ANSWER: See the *Answers and Solutions* section.

22. If tomatoes sell for 75¢ a pound, Tom's demand for labour curve will have the same *shape* as the
    A. marginal product curve.
    B. total product curve.
    C. product demand curve.
    D. marginal cost curve.

    ANSWER: A. See the diagram you've drawn above.

23. Petra's Portland Cement is a perfectly competitive firm. Cement sells at $4 per bag. Petra employs 15 workers at a wage of $12 per hour. The marginal revenue product of the fifteenth worker is $8 per hour. To increase profits, Petra should
    A. increase employment until the MRP of labour equals $12.
    B. decrease employment until the MRP of labour equals $12.
    C. increase the price of cement to at least $8 per bag.
    D. increase the price of cement to at least $12 per bag.

    ANSWER: B. In a perfectly competitive industry, the producer has no control over price. Because wage exceeds MRP, Petra should reduce her labour force.

24. The supply of labour falls in the fishing industry. Which of the following events will occur? The wage rate will ________ and firms will ________ employment until MRP equals the new wage.
    A. increase, increase.
    B. increase, decrease.
    C. decrease, increase.
    D. decrease, decrease.

    ANSWER: B. See Figure 10.3 on p. 237. A decrease in supply increases the price of labour (wage). To restore equality, MRP must increase. To accomplish this, fewer workers will be hired.

25. We saw in Chapter 8 that there is a link between marginal cost and marginal product; in fact, $MC = W / MP_L$. We now know that $MRP_L = MP_L.P$. If Mr. Pita Bread's marginal revenue product of labour is greater than the wage, it must be the case that
    A. total revenues exceed total costs.
    B. the wage is greater than the marginal cost.
    C. Mr. Pita's price exceeds its marginal cost.
    D. Mr. Pita's price is less than its marginal cost.

    ANSWER: C. We know that $MRP_L = MP_L.P$ and are told that $MRP_L > W$, so $MP_L.P > W$. We know that $MC = W / MP_L$, so $MP_L.MC = W$. If $MP_L.P > W$ and $MP_L.MC = W$, then $P > MC$.

PRACTICE TEST

I. MULTIPLE CHOICE QUESTIONS. Select the option that provides the single best answer.

_____ 1. The firm has two inputs: capital and labour. Economic theory suggests that
- A. these are complementary but not substitutable.
- B. these are substitutable but not complementary.
- C. these are both complementary and substitutable.
- D. labour is complementary, while capital is substitutable.

_____ 2. Labour demand is a "derived" demand because
- A. it is derived from the demand for capital.
- B. it depends on the demand for outputs.
- C. it is derived from firms.
- D. it is derived from marginal revenue product.

_____ 3. The firm has one variable input: labour. The demand for labour is labour's
- A. total product curve.
- B. productivity times the wage rate.
- C. marginal product curve.
- D. marginal revenue product curve.

_____ 4. The firm is hiring labour and capital such that $MRP_L = P_L$ and $MRP_K < P_K$. The firm should certainly hire
- A. more labour and more capital.
- B. less capital.
- C. less labour and less capital.
- D. less labour and more capital.

_____ 5. You are told that $MP_L/MP_L > MP_K/P_K$. Given a fixed amount of funds to produce more output, the firm should
- A. shift dollars away from labour and towards capital.
- B. shift dollars away from capital and towards labour.
- C. hire more capital to increase MP_K.
- D. hire more capital to decrease MP_K.

_____ 6. Downtown land is a normal input. If the price of downtown land decreases, then the factor substitution effect will _________ the quantity demanded, and the output effect will _________ the quantity demanded.
- A. increase, increase.
- B. increase, decrease.
- C. decrease, increase.
- D. decrease, decrease.

_____ 7. The firm has two variable inputs: labour and capital. Now the price of labour falls. The output effect indicates that
- A. output will fall.
- B. fewer of all factors will be demanded.
- C. more labour will be demanded.
- D. less labour will be demanded.

_____ 8. A firm has one variable input: labour. An increase in the price of the output will
A. increase the demand for labour.
B. decrease the demand for labour.
C. cause the factor substitution effect to outweigh the output effect.
D. cause the output effect to outweigh the factor substitution effect.

_____ 9. The total product from 3 workers is 32 units and that from 4 is 40 units. Output is selling at $2. What is the maximum the firm would be willing to pay the fourth worker?
A. $10.
B. $8.
C. $16.
D. $20.

_____ 10. The firm has two variable inputs, labour and capital. Now the price of labour rises. The factor substitution effect indicates that
A. the marginal product of labour will fall.
B. the marginal product of capital will fall.
C. more labour will be demanded.
D. less capital will be demanded.

_____ 11. Tennis players earn more than economics professors. This is best explained by noting that
A. consumers are willing to spend more to watch a tennis match than to listen to an economics professor.
B. tennis players are more athletic.
C. economics professors last longer—their income is spread out more.
D. the demand for economics professors is more inelastic.

Use the following information to answer the next two questions.

There are five apartment buildings in town. Each year, the non-land cost of Building #1 is $10 000; for Building #2, it's $20 000; for Building #3, it's $30 000; and so on.

_____ 12. If each apartment building could generate $100 000 of revenues each year, how much is the pure economic rent of Building #1?
A. $100 000.
B. $90 000.
C. $50 000.
D. $40 000.

_____ 13. If each apartment building could generate $40 000 in revenues each year, which building would earn zero pure economic rent?
A. Building #4.
B. Building #3.
C. Building #5.
D. All plots will earn pure rents.

Use the following information to answer the next five questions.

Rhonda grows peaches, which she sells for $2 per kilogram. Her variable resource is labour, and she has recorded the productivity of her workers in the table below.

Number of Workers	Total Product	Marginal Product	Marginal Revenue Product
0	0	—	—
1	15	___	___
2	40	___	___
3	60	___	___
4	75	___	___
5	85	___	___

_____ 14. The marginal product of the fifth worker is
A. 10.
B. 15.
C. 17.
D. 19.

_____ 15. The marginal revenue product of the second worker is
A. $25.
B. $30.
C. $40.
D. $50.

_____ 16. If the wage is $36, Rhonda should hire
A. 2 workers.
B. 3 workers.
C. 4 workers.
D. 5 workers.

_____ 17. The wage is $36. Currently, Rhonda is employing two workers. If she hires a third worker, her profits would
A. increase by $4.
B. increase by $6.
C. decrease by $4.
D. decrease by $6.

_____ 18. The maximum wage that Rhonda would pay if she were to hire 3 workers is
A. $20.
B. $30.
C. $35.
D. $40.

_____ 19. The price of labour decreases. The quantity demanded of labour will
A. increase, because capital will be substituted for labour.
B. increase, regardless of the relative strengths of the output effect and the factor substitution effect.
C. be indeterminate—the factor substitution effect and the output effect work in opposite directions.
D. decrease—if the output effect dominates the factor substitution effect.

Use the following diagram to answer the next four questions.

Drushka has a small firm that manufactures *matrushka* dolls. His variable resource, labour, exhibits the marginal productivity behaviour shown in the diagram below.

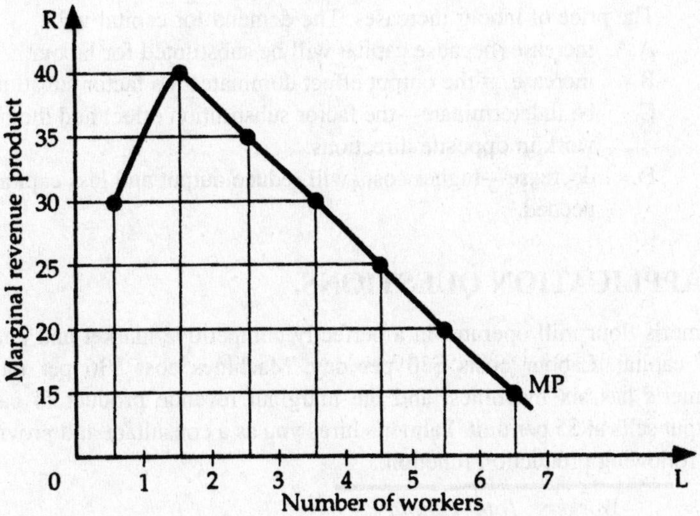

_____ 20. The marginal revenue product of the third worker is
- A. 35 rubles.
- B. 30 rubles.
- C. 60 rubles.
- D. 70 rubles.

_____ 21. If the wage is 40 rubles, Drushka should hire
- A. 3 workers.
- B. 4 workers.
- C. 5 workers.
- D. 6 workers.

_____ 22. The wage is 50 rubles. Currently, Drushka is employing 5 workers. If he hires a sixth worker, his profits would
- A. increase by 5 rubles.
- B. increase by 10 rubles.
- C. decrease by 5 rubles.
- D. decrease by 10 rubles.

_____ 23. The maximum wage that Drushka would pay if he were to hire four workers is
- A. 30 rubles.
- B. 40 rubles.
- C. 50 rubles.
- D. 60 rubles.

_____ 24. Hitoshi, the owner of a Japanese restaurant, tells you that because of an increase in the wage rate, he has sold the tables and chairs he used for outside seating and has reduced his hours of business. In economic terms, you could tell him each of the following except that
- A. he might have made a mistake. The factor substitution effect should have led him to substitute away from labour and to increase his capital.
- B. he has made a smart move. The wage hike has caused higher costs which should lead him to cut production according to the output effect.

C. he has made a smart move. The output effect of the wage hike has caused less demand for all inputs.

D. he might have made a mistake. He should have increased output and hired more of all inputs to cover the increased labour costs.

____ 25. The price of labour increases. The demand for capital will

A. increase, because capital will be substituted for labour.

B. increase, if the output effect dominates the factor substitution effect.

C. be indeterminate—the factor substitution effect and the output effect work in opposite directions.

D. decrease—higher costs will reduce output and less capital will be needed.

II. APPLICATION QUESTIONS.

1. Palmer's flour mill operates in a perfectly competitive market and employs labour and capital. Labour costs $30 per day. Machines cost $36 per day. Currently, Palmer's has six machines, and the marginal revenue product of capital is $30. Output sells at $5 per unit. Palmer's hires you as a consultant and provides you with the following production function.

Workers	*Total Output*
1	9
2	17
3	24
4	30
5	35
6	39
7	42

a. In the short run, how many workers do you recommend Palmer's should hire per day?

b. Is Palmer's maximizing profit? How can you tell?

c. In the short run, how can Palmer's improve its profitability?

d. In the long run, if Palmer's maintains its current output level, how can the firm improve its profitability?

e. Given your answer to part d., explain how the marginal revenue product values of labour and capital will change.

f. Explain to Dusty Palmer, the owner of the mill, why your answer to part d. is not the end of the analysis.

2. The number of haircuts given by Shear Delight each day is given by the equation $q = 10L - .5L^2$, where L is the number of hours of labour. MP_L is 10 - L. The haircut industry is perfectly competitive with a price of $10 per haircut.

a. What is the firm's demand for labour schedule?

b. How many hours of labour will be hired at a wage of $20 per hour? A wage of $40 per hour?

c. If the price of haircuts rose to $20, and the wage was $40 per hour, calculate the number of hours of labour hired and the number of haircuts provided.

d. Given your answer to part c., calculate Shear Delight's daily profit.

3. The city of Kings Town contains three firms, each of which operates in a perfectly competitive industry. The three firms are a fireworks factory, a poultry processing plant, and a textiles mill. Each firm employs unskilled workers who can move easily between firms.

The price of output is given in the following table.

Firm	Output Price
Fireworks Factory	$8
Poultry Plant	$1
Textiles Mill	$2

Weekly marginal productivity information is given in the following table. Assume that marginal productivity diminishes at a constant rate between each set of data points.

	-----------Marginal Product per worker-----------		
Workers	***Fireworks Factory***	***Poultry Plant***	***Textiles Mill***
0	—	—	—
100	100	1200	500
200	90	1000	450
300	80	800	400
400	70	600	350
500	60	500	300
600	50	400	250
700	40	300	200
800	30	200	150
900	20	100	100
1000	10	0	50

a. Calculate the marginal revenue product values and include them in the following table.

	------Marginal Revenue Product per Worker------		
Workers	*Fireworks Factory*	*Poultry Plant*	*Textiles Mill*
100	____	____	____
200	____	____	____
300	____	____	____
400	____	____	____
500	____	____	____
600	____	____	____
700	____	____	____
800	____	____	____
900	____	____	____
1000	____	____	____

b. Calculate the total demand for labour in Kings Town at each of the weekly wage rates in the following table.

Wage	*Fireworks Factory*	*Poultry Plant*	*Textiles Mill*	*Total Labour Demand*
$800	____	____	____	____
$700	____	____	____	____
$600	____	____	____	____
$500	____	____	____	____
$400	____	____	____	____
$300	____	____	____	____
$200	____	____	____	____

c.

Wage	*Total Supply*
$800	
$700	
$600	
$500	
$400	
$300	
$200	

As the wage level increases, the quantity of labour supplied in Kings Town increases, as shown in the equation, $Q = 1100 + 2W$, where W is the weekly wage. Complete the table above.

d. Graph the labour-demand and labour-supply curves below. Determine the equilibrium wage and level of employment.

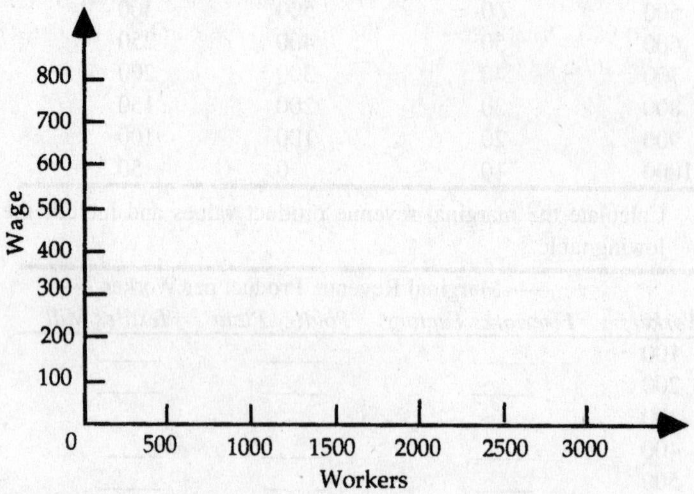

e. Calculate the level of employment in each industry.

Firm	Employment
Fireworks Factory	
Poultry Plant	
Textiles Mill	

f. Verify that the profit-maximizing equilibrium conforms to the rule: $MRP_{ff}/P_{ff} = MRP_{pp}/P_{pp} = MRP_{tm}/P_{tm} = 1$.

4. In a central area of the city of Frederic Town there are 300 vacant lots suitable for development. As the price per lot increases, the quantity demanded decreases, as indicated in the following table.

Price per Lot	*Lots Demanded*
$30 000	0
$25 000	100
$15 000	300
$10 000	400
$5 000	500

a. Graph the market for vacant lots in Frederic Town. Show the equilibrium price.

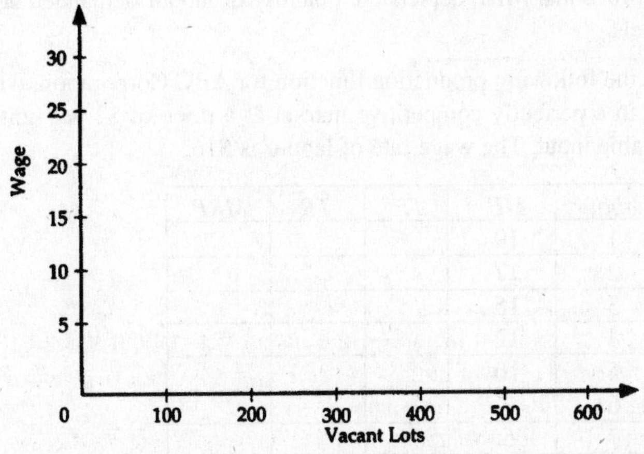

b. Suppose that the city government imposed a maximum price per lot of $10 000. What effect will this have on the number of lots available? What allocation problems will occur?

5. Suppose that ABC Corporation sells audio cassettes in a perfectly competitive market at a price of $1 per unit and that the wage rate is $15.

Labour	*MP*	*TP*	*TR*	*MRP*
1	10			
2	20			
3	25			
4	23			
5	20			
6	18			
7	15			
8	12			

a. Calculate total product, total revenue, and MRP.

b. Draw the MRP schedule below, and plot the wage too.

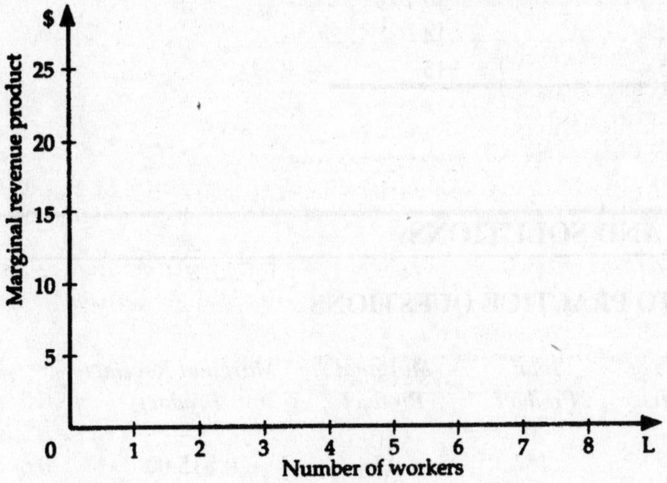

c. Note that MRP rises initially. Why?

d. Consider the first worker. Should she be hired if the wage rate is $15?

e. Which is the first worker who won't be hired?

f. Make up a "hiring rule of thumb" for the profit-maximizing employer.
g. Confirm that MRP depicts the quantity of labour demanded at different wage levels.

6. Examine the following production function for ABC Corporation, which sells audio cassettes in a perfectly competitive market at a price of $2 per unit. Labour is the only variable input. The wage rate of labour is $16.

Labour	*MP*	*TP*	*TR*	*MRP*
1	19			
2	17			
3	15			
4	12			
5	10			
6	7			
7	5			

a. Calculate total product, total revenue, and MRP.
b. How many workers should be hired?

7. Your firm is currently hiring labour and capital. The MRP of labour is $80, and that of capital is $120. Price of the final product is $2. The price of labour is $10 per unit, and the price of capital is $20 per unit.
a. Is your firm maximizing profits? Explain.
b. Given your current budget, what should you do?
c. What will happen to the marginal productivity of capital? The marginal productivity of labour?

8. Assume that shoes are produced with one variable factor of production, labour. Using the following production function, estimate the amount of labour that a competitive firm would hire, assuming that labour is available for $35 per day and that shoes sell for $10 per pair. (Hint: First determine the MRP schedule.)

Units of Labour (Days)	Total Output (Pairs of Shoes)
1	5
2	9
3	12
4	14
5	15

ANSWERS AND SOLUTIONS

ANSWERS TO PRACTICE QUESTIONS

6.

Number of Workers	*Total Product*	*Marginal Product*	*Marginal Revenue Product*
0	0	—	—
1	15	15	$15.00
2	28	13	$13.00
3	38	10	$10.00
4	46	8	$ 8.00
5	52	6	$ 6.00

7-10. See the diagrams below.

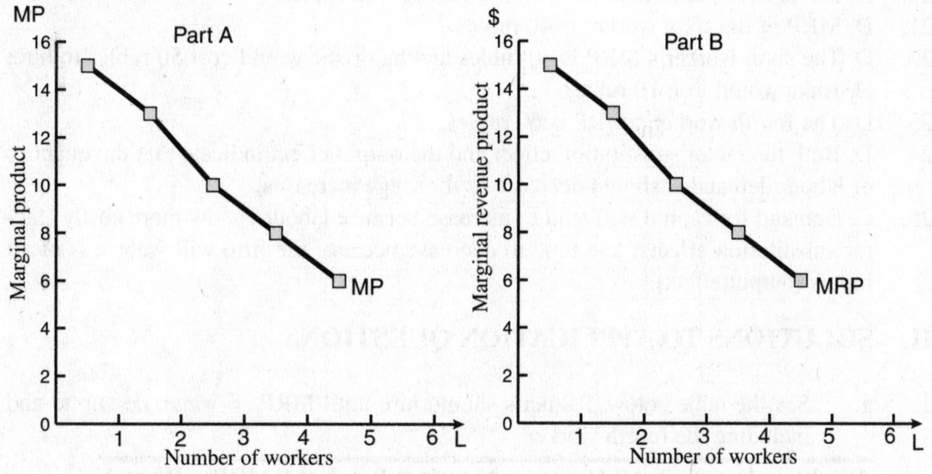

PRACTICE TEST

I. SOLUTIONS TO MULTIPLE CHOICE QUESTIONS

1. C. See p. 234.
2. B. See p. 233.
3. D. The value of production by each additional worker determines how much he or she will be paid.
4. B. The marginal revenue product of the final machine is less than the cost of hiring it. The businessperson should cut back on capital usage.
5. B. Per dollar, labour is contributing more than capital is.
6. A. When the price of a normal input decreases, the factor substitution effect and the output effect both increase the quantity demanded. See p. 241.
7. C. Total cost of production is reduced because of the factor price decrease. More output is produced and more of all factors (including labour) is hired.
8. A. An increase in the price of output will increase the input's MRP. MRP is the demand for the input.
9. C. Marginal product of the fourth worker is 8 units. MRP = MP x P = 8 x \$2 = \$16. This worker is worth as much as \$16.
10. B. As less labour is hired, the marginal productivity of labour will increase. More of the relatively cheaper capital will be hired, resulting in a decrease in marginal productivity.
11. A. Earnings depend on MRP. MRP depends on the selling price of output.
12. B. With a normal profit, Building #1 should earn \$10 000. The additional \$90 000 is economic rent.
13. A. With a normal profit, Building #4 should earn \$40 000. If revenue is \$40 000, this building earns zero economic rent.
14. A. Recall that MP is the change in total product (85 - 75) divided by the change in the number of workers (1).
15. D. MRP = MP x P. See p. 234.
16. B. To maximize profits, Rhonda should not hire any worker whose MRP is less than \$36. Point to ponder: What about the first worker?
17. A. The worker costs \$36 and contributes \$40, a gain of \$4.
18. D. The third worker's MRP is \$40. To maximize profits, Rhonda should not hire the fourth worker (whose MRP is \$30) at any wage above \$30.

19. B. Both effects work in the same direction.
20. D. MP is 35. MRP = MP x P = 35 x 2 rubles = 70 rubles.
21. D. MRP of the sixth worker is 40 rubles.
22. D. The sixth worker's MRP is 40 rubles and he or she would cost 50 rubles to hire. Drushka would lose 10 rubles.
23. D. The fourth worker's MRP is 60 rubles.
24. D. Both the factor substitution effect and the output effect indicate that the quantity of labour demanded should decrease as the wage increases.
25. C. Demand for capital will tend to increase because labour is now more costly (factor substitution effects) and tend to decrease because the firm will want less of all inputs (output effect).

II. SOLUTIONS TO APPLICATION QUESTIONS

1. a. See the table below. Palmer's should hire until MRP_L = wage, i.e., up to and including the fourth worker.

Workers (Days)	Total Output	Marginal Product	MRP	Wage
1	9	9	\$45	\$30
2	17	8	\$40	\$30
3	24	7	\$35	\$30
4	30	6	\$30	\$30
5	35	5	\$25	\$30
6	39	4	\$20	\$30
7	42	3	\$15	\$30

b. Palmer's is not maximizing profit. The profit-maximizing input combination follows the rule that the marginal revenue product/dollar of the final unit of each input should be equal. This is not so in this case because $MRP_L/P_L > MRP_K/P_K$.

c. Palmer's can't improve its profitability in the short run—it's tied to the decisions it has made.

d. Because $MRP_L/P_L > MRP_K/P_K$, Palmer's should reduce its capital. If the output level is maintained, and labour and capital as substitutes, more labour should be hired. The effect will be to reduce total cost and, therefore, to increase profit.

e. *Ceteris paribus*, as additional workers are added, marginal revenue product of labour will decrease. *Ceteris paribus*, as fewer machines are hired, marginal revenue product of capital will increase. Both movements will help correct the imbalance between the ratios of MRP per dollar.

f. In part d. you note that given the same output level, the firm should hire more workers and fewer machines and reduce total cost. Another way to look at this is to maintain the total cost and increase output. Output will increase because inputs are being allocated more efficiently than before. However, with less than 6 machines, the marginal productivity of *labour* will fall, making the rise in labour less than that predicted by the answer to part d. Similarly, with more than 4 workers, the marginal productivity of *capital* will increase, making the decrease in capital less than that predicted by the answer to part d.

2. a. MP_L is 10 – L, and P = \$10, then MRP_L = \$10 x [10 - L] = \$100 - \$10L. The demand for labour schedule is given by MRP_L = W. Substituting W for MRP_L in the equation gives us the demand for labour schedule, W = \$100 - \$10L.

b. If W = $20, then $20 = $100 - $10L, therefore L = 8.
If W = $40, then $40 = $100 - $10L, therefore L = 6.

c. MP_L is 10 – L, and P = $20, then MRP_L = $20 x [10 – L] = $200 – $20L. The demand for labour schedule is given by MRP_L = W. Substituting W for MRPL in the equation gives us the demand for labour schedule, W = $200 – $20L. If W = $40, then $40 = $200 – $20L, therefore L = 8. If L = 8, the equation q = 10L – .5L_2 gives q = 80 – 32, or 48 haircuts (i.e., 6 per hour).

d. Labour is the only input: total cost is $40 x 8, or $320. Total revenue is $20 x 48, $960. Profit is $640.

3. a.

	-------Marginal RevenueProduct per worker-------		
Workers	*Fireworks Factory*	*Poultry Plant*	*Textiles Mill*
100	$800	$1200	$1000
200	$720	$1000	$900
300	$640	$800	$800
400	$560	$600	$700
500	$480	$500	$600
600	$400	$400	$500
700	$320	$300	$400
800	$240	$200	$300
900	$160	$100	$200
1000	$80	$0	$100

b.

Wage	*Fireworks Factory*	*Poultry Plant*	*Textiles Mill*	*Total Labour Demand*
$800	100	300	300	700
$700	225	350	400	975
$600	350	400	500	1250
$500	475	500	600	1575
$400	600	600	700	1900
$300	725	700	800	2225
$200	850	800	900	2550

c.

Wage	*Total Labour Supply*
$800	2700
$700	2500
$600	2300
$500	2100
$400	1900
$300	1700
$200	1500

d. See the following diagram.

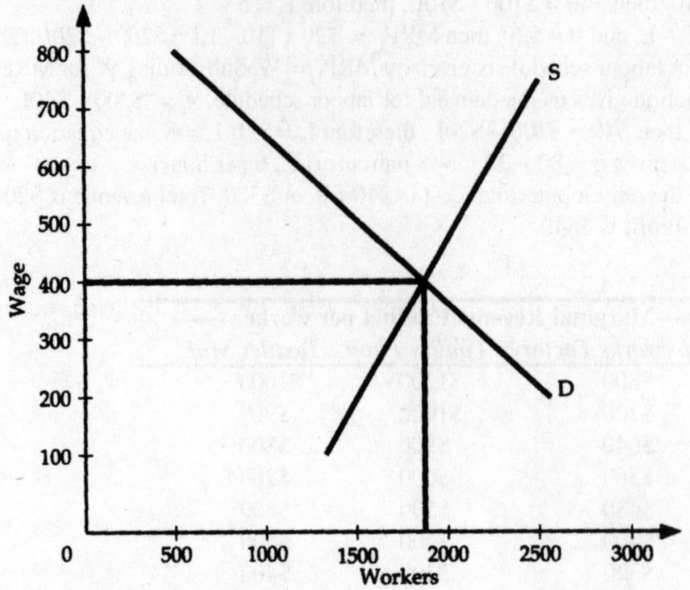

The equilibrium wage is $400 per week, and 1900 workers will be employed each week.

e.

Firm	Employment
Fireworks Factory	600
Poultry Plant	600
Textiles Mill	700

f. The profit-maximizing equilibrium rule is that the marginal product/dollar of the final unit of each input should be equal. In each case, MRP is $400 and the wage is $400.

4. a. See the diagram below. The equilibrium price is $15 000.

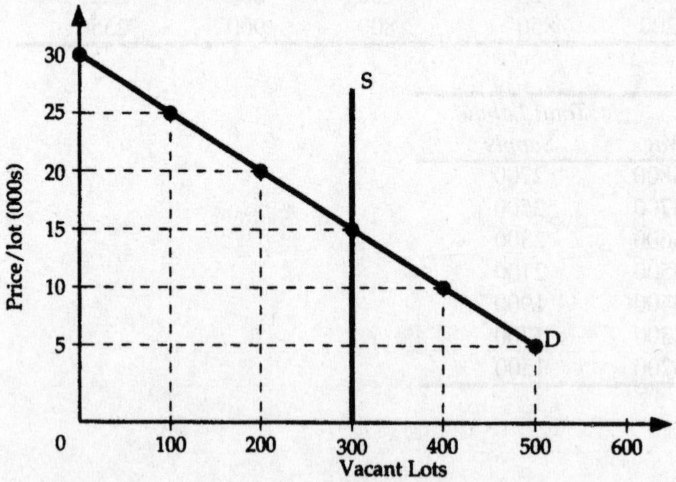

b. The number of lots available will remain at 300. However, because of the lower price, there has been an increase in quantity demanded to 400, and an excess demand exists. Because market price is no longer able to perform its rationing function, some other method of allocating lots to demanders will have to be found, e.g., first come, first served, special government permit, bribery, waiting lists, a tedious application process.

5. a. See the table below.

Labour	MP	TP	TR	MRP
1	10	10	$10	$10
2	20	30	$30	$20
3	25	55	$55	$25
4	23	78	$78	$23
5	20	98	$98	$20
6	18	116	$116	$18
7	15	131	$131	$15
8	12	143	$143	$12

b. See the diagram below. Note that marginal values are typically shown between units because they indicate change.

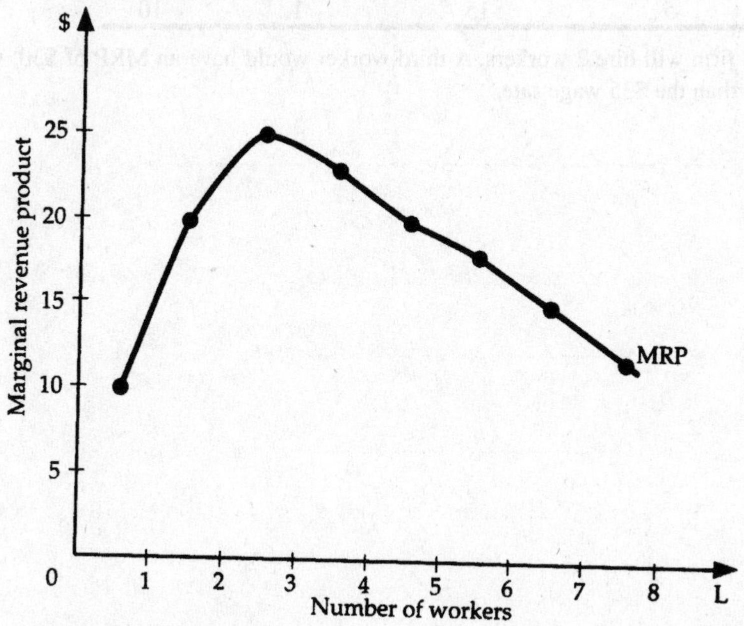

c. Increasing productivity.

d. Yes. Although ABC will take a loss because MRP is only $10, the first worker must be hired to hire subsequent, "profitable," workers.

e. The eighth worker won't be hired.

f. Hire any input that at least pays its way.

g. Yes, it does. At a wage of $15, for example, 7 workers are demanded; at $18, 6 workers are demanded.

6. a. See the table below.

b. 5 workers should be hired.

Labour	MP	TP	TR	MRP
1	19	19	$38	$38
2	17	36	$72	$34
3	15	51	$102	$30
4	12	63	$126	$24
5	10	73	$146	$20
6	7	80	$160	$14
7	5	85	$170	$10

7. a. No. The final dollar spent on each input must generate the same additional production. We should hire such that $MP_L/P_L = MP_K/P_K$.
   b. Cut back on capital and hire more workers.
   c. Rise; fall.

8. If we assume that shoes sell for $10 per pair over and above the cost of leather and materials, we can derive the following table.

Units of Labour (Days)	Total Output (Pairs of Shoes)	Marginal Product	MRP
1	5	5	50
2	9	4	40
3	12	3	30
4	14	2	20
5	15	1	10

The firm will hire 2 workers. A third worker would have an MRP of $30, which is less than the $35 wage rate.

11 The Capital Market and the Investment Decision

OBJECTIVES: POINT BY POINT

After completing this chapter, you should be able to accomplish the objectives listed below.

General Comment

In approaching this chapter, note the similarities between the conclusions reached about hiring decisions in the labour and land markets and those in the capital market. Capital may seem different because of the time dimension, but businesspeople still weigh the benefits and the costs of employing new resources. The time element makes the calculations more difficult—both revenues and costs may extend into the future. Also, note that capital accumulation is not undertaken only by the business community; households, the government, and you (human capital) make capital-investment decisions.

OBJECTIVE 1: Define capital, investment, and depreciation.

Capital goods are those goods that can be used as inputs into the production process now and in the future. Capital may be *tangible* (machines, all construction, and inventories) or *intangible* (human capital, goodwill, brand loyalty). Capital accumulation occurs not only in the business sector but also in the public sector (social capital, such as highways) and in the households sector. (page 252)

Stocks are variables that are measured at a point in time (capital stock), while *flows* are measured over a period of time (earnings per month, investment per quarter, depreciation per year). *Investment* has a specific meaning for economists—investment is the creation of capital. It is not financial purchases.

Depreciation is the decline in the economic value of an asset over time—think of it as an ageing process. A unit of capital (a machine, perhaps) might depreciate simply because of wear and tear or because new technology renders it obsolete. (page 254)

TIP: It's easy to overlook the importance of **intangible capital**. Choose a business with which you are familiar and identify all the types of intangible capital in use—goodwill, name recognition, human capital of managers and employees. If, overnight, the firm's intangible capital evaporated, production and sales would shudder to a halt. Even with an excellent product, a salesperson who fails to "connect" with a customer will be ineffectual—trust is as important as it is intangible.

Capital: Because capital is so diverse, it is measured by its dollar value. However, keep in mind at all times that capital should be thought of as a physical factor of production and not as a monetary unit.

Practice

1. The construction of a new house is investment in
   A. social capital.
   B. a consumer durable good.
   C. tangible capital.
   D. human capital.

   ANSWER: C. All construction (including residential construction) is classified as capital. Social capital is usually provided by the government.

2. HAL Corp. institutes a training program to introduce its employees to the new Orange computer. This should increase productivity. This is an investment in
   A. tangible capital.
   B. human capital.
   C. social capital.
   D. infrastructure capital.

   ANSWER: B. The quality of the labour force is being improved.

3. Which of the following is not an example of capital?
   A. an AST computer warehouse.
   B. a Macintosh computer used by an IBM employee.
   C. a car used by a Corel service representative.
   D. the revenue earned by Microsoft this year.

   ANSWER: D. Money is not capital. See p. 253.

4. Capital is a __________ , investment is a __________, and depreciation is a __________.
   A. stock, stock, stock.
   B. stock, flow, stock.
   C. flow, flow, stock.
   D. stock, flow, flow.

   ANSWER: D. The capital stock is measured at a point in time. Investment takes place over time, as does depreciation.

5. A columnist once argued that his educated brain cells were part of his __________ capital; to the extent that they were being depleted as time passed, they should be counted as __________ (for tax purposes).
   A. social, investment.
   B. depreciation, depreciation.
   C. human, investment.
   D. human, depreciation.

   ANSWER: D. The quality of human resources counts as human capital. Wear and tear (and the death of brain cells through the passage of time) is depreciation. Note: Revenue Canada is not convinced by this argument.

6. Which of the following is not an act of investment?
   A. a marketing firm buys a new automated mailing machine.
   B. Pierre Charest's university education is paid for by his parents.
   C. Purolator delivers the mail.
   D. the Cleghorns build a new vacation home.

   ANSWER: C. Mail delivery is a productive activity, but Purolator is not increasing its productive capacity in the process. Note that a new vacation home is construction of a residential structure—the use it will be put to is not considered.

OBJECTIVE 2: Explain the role of capital markets.

Ownership of capital generates *capital income* (usually profit and interest), which rewards households for postponing consumption and channeling resources instead into investment. Capital markets act as one method of channelling these funds to investment purposes. Capital income is the income flow paid to the owners of capital that induces them to supply funds. It is also the spur that provokes the process of capital allocation and accumulation. (page 254)

> **TIP:** Nature abhors a vacuum. It's the same with profit opportunities in an efficient market. The presence of economic profits in an industry will draw in resources, including capital.

Practice

7. The two most important types of capital income are
   A. investment and saving.
   B. profit and interest.
   C. dividends and rents.
   D. pure economic rent and disposable income.

   ANSWER: B. See p. 255.

8. The ultimate suppliers of financial capital are
   A. households.
   B. the private banking sector.
   C. the central bank (the Bank of Canada).
   D. businesses.

   ANSWER: A. Ultimately, all income—and therefore all funds for investment purposes—derives from households.

9. Walt asks Virginia to lend him $3000 for 12 months. Walt agrees to pay Virginia $3150 at the end of that time. The interest rate that Virginia could have earned if she had not loaned to Walt is 6%. Virginia has earned an economic profit of
   A. –$30.
   B. $30.
   C. $150.
   D. –$9.

   ANSWER: A. Virginia earned $150 in interest. She could have earned $180 ($3,000 x 1.06). The loan to Walt cost her $30.

Use the following information to answer the next three questions.

Eight-year-old Josh has discovered that the price his friends can charge while selling lemonade on the sidewalk has doubled because of the hot summer weather. Lemonade selling is a perfectly competitive industry and, previously, the reward was not quite enough to encourage Josh to participate. Now, however, he rushes home to borrow ingredients from his parents, build a lemonade stand, and write out a price list.

10. Josh's ingredients are __________ capital and his lemonade stand and price list are __________.
    A. inventories, durable equipment.
    B. inventories, non-residential construction.
    C. intangible, durable equipment.
    D. intangible, non-residential construction.

ANSWER: A. Stocks of inputs or unsold output is inventory. The lemonade stand is durable.

11. Josh promises his parents, using his candy allowance as collateral, to repay the face value of his borrowed ingredients. He is financing his investment with
    A. venture capital.
    B. economic profits.
    C. retained earnings.
    D. a zero-interest direct loan.

    ANSWER: D. If Josh repays the full value of the ingredients, he pays no interest. This is the equivalent of a direct loan. If Josh writes out the promise to pay, he has issued a bond.

12. As a result of the existence of economic profits caused by increased demand, resources allocated to the lemonade industry have ____________. Lemonade prices will ____________.
    A. increased, increase.
    B. increased, decrease.
    C. decreased, increase.
    D. decreased, decrease.

    ANSWER: B. More lemonade will be available and, consequently, prices and economic profit will decrease.

Use the following information to answer the next two questions.

The health club industry is perfectly competitive and in long-run equilibrium. As the baby boomers age and sag, the demand for health clubs increases.

13. Existing health clubs will earn ____________ economic profits. We would predict ____________ investment in the health club industry.
    A. short-run, increased.
    B. short-run, decreased.
    C. long-run, increased.
    D. long-run, decreased.

    ANSWER: A. Higher demand will lead to higher profits in the short run: recall that economic profits are zero in the long run for competitive firms. As existing firms expand and as firms enter the industry, capital accumulation will occur.

14. Firms outside the health club industry (but using similar resources) will see their costs _______ and will _______ the quantity of resources they use.
    A. increase, increase.
    B. increase, decrease.
    C. decrease, increase.
    D. decrease, decrease.

    ANSWER: B. Recall that "costs" to an economist are opportunity costs—the value of the next best alternative forgone. Cost depends on the reward that can be earned in an alternative activity, e.g., provision of health club services As those earnings rise, costs increase for non-participants, profits decrease, and resources will be reallocated to the health club industry.

OBJECTIVE 3: Describe how capital markets allocate saving.

Various, and sometimes complex, connections between households and firms facilitate the movement of saving into productive investment. A firm cannot invest unless it has the funds to do so. In most situations, the funds that firms use to buy capital goods come, directly or indirectly, from households. Either directly or indirectly through a financial intermediary (such as a bank), the household agrees to lend its savings to the firm. In exchange, the firm contracts to pay the household interest at some agreed-upon rate. If the household lends directly to the firm, the firm gives the household a bond, which is nothing more than a contract that promises to repay the loan at some specific time in the future. The bond also specifies the flow of interest to be paid in the meantime. (page 255)

OBJECTIVE 4: Analyze the investment decision.

The firm must form an expectation of the future earnings and costs of a project. The difference between expected future earnings and the costs of a project, expressed as a percentage of the project cost, is the *expected rate of return*. The investment decision turns on how this rate compares against the cost (interest) of providing capital for investment. If the expected rate of return exceeds the interest rate, then the investment project should be undertaken. As the interest rate rises, profitable projects become unprofitable, and the demand for funds is reduced.

By ranking the expected yield on projects, the investment demand schedule is developed. The shape and slope of the investment demand curve depend critically on the expectations of those making investment decisions—anything that affects expectations may affect investment. (page 262)

The profit-maximizing firm will employ capital up to the point at which its marginal revenue product is equal to its price, i.e., it will invest whenever the expected rate of return exceeds the interest rate. (page 263)

> **Graphing Pointer:** The geometric logic behind the investment demand curve is identical to the other demand curves. The interest rate is the "price" of investment, and the expected rate of return plays the role of "other factors" which influence investment. As before, if interest rates change, you move along the curve; if at a given rate of interest the expected rate of return changes, you shift the curve.

Practice

Use the following table for the next four questions.

Sellco has the following list of investment projects to consider.

	Project	Total Investment Amount	Expected Rate of Return (%)
A.	New corporate headquarters	$300 000	20
B.	Personal computers for sales force	$ 60 000	16
C.	Training for employees	$140 000	10
D.	Wellness program	$ 60 000	9
E.	Employee leisure facility	$ 80 000	5
F.	New canteen	$ 40 000	5

15. If the interest rate is 14%, Sellco would fund
    A. only Project A.
    B. Projects A and B.
    C. Projects A, B, and C.
    D. Projects D and E only.

ANSWER: B. Projects A and B have expected rates of return exceeding the interest rate—they are worthwhile.

16. If the interest rate is 21%, Sellco would fund
    A. only Project A.
    B. Projects B, D, and E only.
    C. Projects B and E only.
    D. none of the above.

ANSWER: D. No project offers a high enough expected rate of return to justify the expense.

17. At an interest rate of 14%, Sellco's total investment would amount to
    A. zero since no project has a return equal to 14%.
    B. $360 000
    C. $500 000
    D. $200 000

ANSWER: B. $300 000 (Project A) + $60 000 (Project B).

18. If the interest rate is 5%, Sellco would fund
    A. Project E only.
    B. Project F only, because it is less expensive than Project E.
    C. Projects E and F only, because their expected rate of return is equal to 5%.
    D. all the projects.

ANSWER: D. The rule is that the firm should undertake any and all projects that have an expected rate of return equal to or greater than the interest rate.

19. The expected cost of an investment
    A. depends on the interest rate.
    B. is zero if the firm uses its own funds.
    C. is zero if the investment is undertaken by the government.
    D. is inversely related to its expected income stream.

ANSWER: A. See p. 262.

20. An increase in the market interest rate will cause
    A. a rightward shift in the investment demand curve.
    B. a leftward shift in the investment demand curve.
    C. a movement up the investment demand curve.
    D. a movement down the investment demand curve.

ANSWER: C. See p. 263.

21. Firms become quite pessimistic when the federal government announces higher business taxes. This will cause the investment demand curve to shift ________ and the level of investment to ________.
    A. right, increase.
    B. right, decrease.
    C. left, increase.
    D. left, decrease.

ANSWER: D. See p. 263.

22. Sellco is a perfectly competitive profit-maximizing firm. It will invest in new capital up to the point at which
    A. the rate of return equals the expected interest rate.
    B. the expected rate of return equals the interest rate.
    C. the expected rate of return equals the expected interest rate.
    D. the rate of return equals the interest rate.

    ANSWER: B. The interest rate is incurred today, at the time of the investment; the earnings will accrue in the future and, today, they are estimates.

23. A recently released report by a task force on the issue of corporate taxes in Canada calls on the government to drastically reduce corporate taxes. Assuming that the task force's recommendations are fully implemented by the government, it will most likely cause firms to
    A. plan to increase investment because of the expectation that interest rates would be lower.
    B. plan to increase investment because of the expectation of higher after-tax income.
    C. plan to decrease investment because less effort would be needed to achieve a given level of after-tax income.
    D. plan to leave investment unchanged because business tax cuts would not affect the demand for their product and, ultimately, the demand for an input is a "derived" demand.

    ANSWER: B. Lower taxes lead to higher after-tax profits and higher expected rates of return.

OBJECTIVE 5: Distinguish the role of risk and time in the investment decision.

The most important discussion of capital is that it exists through time. While, for example, labour services are used at the time they are provided, capital exists now and into future. In building an office tower, a developer makes an investment that will be around for a long *time*.

The state of information under which a decision is made has important implications for predictability of the outcome of that decision. If there is full information, the outcome of a decision will be foreseen clearly. Under conditions of uncertainty (when there is less than full information), however, a decision-maker may foresee several potential outcomes to a decision and the exact outcome is not known in advance. In this case we may say that the individual or firm is operating under conditions of risk, where there will be a probability distribution of possible outcomes. (page 261)

OBJECTIVE 6: Calculate present values.

In order for a firm to decide whether or not to undertake an investment project, it should compare the expected returns with the expected costs of the investment. When the flow of returns (and hence the costs) is realized over time, the firm should use a method of evaluating future profit known as present (discounted) value analysis.

When considering discounting and the role of *present (discounted) value* in evaluating investment projects, remember that future dollars are worth less than dollars in hand today and should be discounted in value. Discounting puts dollars of all vintages on a common basis–present value. The discount rate is the interest rate and the formula used is:

$$PV = R \div (1 + r)^t$$

where R is the future value of payments, r is the interest rate, and t is the number of time periods. Investment should go ahead if the present value of the expected stream of earnings is greater than the cost of the project. The rate of return and present value methods of evaluation are equivalent. (page 268)

Discounting the value of future income by the market interest rate gives that income's value in today's dollars. If the expected future income of a project shows a present value that is greater than the cost of the investment, then it should be undertaken.

Note: The formula tells us that as interest rates rise, the present value of a project will fall and the project will be less likely to be undertaken. This is the same conclusion that we arrived at with the method using investment demand and the expected rate of return.

Present Value Example: What is the opportunity cost of removing, for a year, $100 from your bank account? The interest. If the interest rate is 10%, then the opportunity cost is $10.00. The $100 will be worth $110 at the end of the year if left in the bank. $100 today equals $110 in a year. Turn this the other way: $110 future dollars are worth $100 today, given the interest rate—$110 ÷ (1 + .1) = $100.

What would that $100 be worth at the end of two years if it were left in the bank? $121.00 or $100 x 1.1 x 1.1. Or, $121 in the future is worth $100 today. Formally, this relationship is:

Present Value = Future Value ÷ (1 + interest rate)t

A Present Value Table: Here is a table showing the present value of $100 payable at various dates and at various interest rates. Example: The promise of $100 two years from today has a present value of $90.00 if the interest rate is 6 per cent.

Interest rate (r)	*1 Year*	*2 Years*	*3 Years*	*10 Years*	*20 Years*
.03	97.09	94.26	91.51	74.41	55.37
.04	96.15	92.46	88.90	67.56	45.64
.05	95.24	90.70	86.38	61.39	37.69
.06	94.34	90.00	83.96	55.84	31.18
.07	93.46	87.34	81.63	50.83	25.84
.08	92.59	85.73	79.38	46.32	21.45

TIP: Remember that future dollars are worth less—we discount their value.

Practice

24. The market interest rate is 25% The present value of $500 in one year is
    A. $400.
    B. $125.
    C. $625.
    D. $2000.

    ANSWER: A. PV = $R \div (1 + r)^t = 500 \div 1.25^1 = \$400$.

25. Sellco should invest in a project if the present value of its income stream
    A. is greater than the full cost of the project.
    B. is greater than (or equal to) the full cost of the project.
    C. is greater than the interest rate.
    D. is greater than (or equal to) the interest rate.

ANSWER: B. If the value today of the project's earnings is greater than or at least equal to the cost of implementing the project, Sellco will make a profit.

PRACTICE TEST

I. MULTIPLE CHOICE QUESTIONS. Select the option that provides the single best answer.

_____ 1. In 1996 and part of 1997, the central bank (the Bank of Canada) lowered interest rates several times. Which of the following explanations best describes the Bank's view of the economy?

A. a decrease in interest rates will reduce investment, which, in turn, will reduce production, making the economy's expansion less rapid. .
B. lower interest rates will lead to lower expectations about profits, which will shift the investment demand curve to the left.
C. lower prices will lead to lower marginal revenue product of capital, which will discourage investment and will reduce GDP.
D. lower interest rates make investments more profitable and, because the demand for investment goods is part of national demand, national demand and the national income will be higher than otherwise.

_____ 2. A frequently heard argument is that government deficits cause higher interest rates. Assuming that this is so, then, *ceteris paribus*, reducing the government deficit should ___________ investment and ___________ the marginal product of capital.

A. increase, increase
B. increase, decrease
C. decrease, increase
D. decrease, decrease

_____ 3. Changes in the physical capital stock are caused by

A. investment and stock purchases.
B. investment and depreciation.
C. obsolescence and interest rate changes.
D. accumulation and discounting of value.

_____ 4. Which of the following is not an act of investment?

A. paying for courses at a technical college.
B. construction of a bridge by the provincial government.
C. the purchase of new solar technology by a business.
D. buying a government bond.

_____ 5. Which of the following is not an example of capital?

A. an office block owned by the Bank of Montreal.
B. brand loyalty of consumers to IBM.
C. a share of Bell Canada Enterprise stock.
D. an AST computer.

_____ 6. In which case will investment be greatest?

	Market Interest Rate	Inflation Rate
A.	8	7
B.	9	0
C	6	2
D.	7	3

_____ 7. A new machine will yield $500 a month in earnings for one year. The machine's maintenance is estimated to cost $2000 a year. Its scrap value will be zero. If the current market interest rate is 8%, the firm would be willing to pay __________ to get the machine.
A. $62 500.
B. $6250.
C. $50 000.
D. $75 000.

_____ 8. Kevin Koh knows that he will buy a new Jeep either this month or a year from now. The current price is $10 000, and next year he estimates that it will be $12 000. If his discount rate is 10%, he should
A. not buy either this year or next.
B. buy now.
C. buy next year.
D. be indifferent, since both options have the same present value.

_____ 9. The expected rate of return on an investment depends on all of the following except
A. the expected interest rate.
B. the amount of revenue attributable each year to the project.
C. the length of time that the project provides additional cost savings or revenue.
D. the price of the investment.

_____ 10. Investment projects will be funded up to the point where
A. the interest rate and the expected rate of return are equal.
B. the expected rate of return is zero.
C. the rate of return is maximized.
D. the expected rate of return is maximized.

_____ 11. A bond pays $1000 in one year (and nothing else before or after). The interest rate is 20%. The most one should pay for this bond is
A. $1200.
B. $800.
C. $909.09.
D. $833.33.

_____ 12. The expected cost of an investment is _____ if the funds are borrowed and is _____ if the project is self-financed.
A. positive, positive.
B. positive, zero.
C. zero, positive.
D. zero, zero.

_____ 13. Goodwill _____ a form of capital, and inventory _____ a form of capital.
A. is, is.
B. is, is not.
C. is not, is.
D. is not, is not.

_____ 14. As the interest rate increases, the cost of new investment projects becomes ________, and the number of profitable investment projects becomes ________.

A. higher, higher.
B. higher, lower.
C. lower, higher.
D. lower, lower.

_____ 15. When the interest rate increases, the expected rate of return of an investment ________, and the present value of the investment ________.

A. decreases, decreases.
B. decreases, does not change.
C. does not change, decreases.
D. does not change, does not change.

II. APPLICATION QUESTIONS.

1. Camille has an important career decision to make. She intends to retire in five years. If she stays in her present job, she expects to earn $22 000 per year for the five years. However, she has been offered the opportunity to take a two-year training program, after which she will earn $40 000 per year for the remaining three years of her work life. The training program is free, but Camille will be unable to work during the two-year period. She has sufficient savings to tide her over the two-year training period.
   a. Camille has asked her sister Clarissa which option she should take. Clarissa said that she should go for the training program because, after all, $22 000 times 5 is less than $40 000 times 3. Camille is still unconvinced and asks your opinion. What would you advise?
   b. Explain to Camille the problem with the basis of Clarissa's advice.
   c. Suppose the interest rate is 10%. Can you now offer Camille a definitive answer to her career choice?
   d. The training program is an investment in human capital as is a university education for high-school graduates. If the government wished to encourage additional investment in human capital, should it increase or decrease the interest rate?
   e. Based on your answer to part d., should the government adopt a "high-interest-rate" strategy or a "low-interest-rate" strategy if it wished to encourage long-term rather than short-term investment projects?

2. Two of your assistants, Judy and Jody, have each devised an investment project costing $750 and earning a total income of $1000. Judy's project will return a steady stream of income, $200 per year, for five years. Jody's project starts more slowly, with $100 in each of the first three years, then $300 and $400 in the last two. The interest rate is 10%. How can you explain, non-technically, to Jody why his project is unacceptable, although Judy's has been given the go-ahead? If he pressed you for proof, what would you do?

3. The U.S. lottery system of prize disbursement is different from the Canadian system in that the prize, in the former, is normally disbursed in instalments over a long period. In July 1993, excitement in the United States was very high because the Powerball lottery prize was $100 million. The prize would be disbursed to the winner at a rate of $5 million per year for 20 years. Given these numbers, did the winner really win $100 million?

4. Many alumni donate funds to their college or university.
   a. G. P. A. Crammer has just pledged $500 000 payable on his retirement, which will be in 20 years. In present value terms, if the interest rate is 7%, how much

did Crammer pledge? ____________ Use the present value table in the *Point By Point* section (Objective 4).

b. If the interest rate falls to 3%, what is the present value of Crammer's pledge?

5. The Johnson family decides to have a house built that costs $100 000. This year, the Johnsons have a disposable (after-tax) income of $40 000, of which $25 000 is spent on current consumption, and the rest is used as a down payment on the house. The additional $85 000 is borrowed from aged Aunt Agatha who earns no income and currently lives off her wealth. Assume that Aunt Agatha sells some shares of stock to acquire the cash for the loan. Jack Diamond, who earned $200 000 last year, buys the stock from Aunt Agatha for $85 000 and spends $115 000 on current consumption.

For each of the three parties, calculate:

a. The amount of saving during the period.

Johnsons	Aunt Agatha	Jack Diamond
________	________	________

b. The quantity of investment during the period.

Johnsons	Aunt Agatha	Jack Diamond
________	________	________

c. Any change in net worth.

Johnsons	Aunt Agatha	Jack Diamond
________	________	________

d. Any change in capital stock.

Johnsons	Aunt Agatha	Jack Diamond
________	________	________

6. Imagine a 10-year bond issued by ABC Corp., with a face value of $1000 and an interest rate of 12%.

a. What is the annual interest payment? ____________

b. How much would you pay for the bond if the bond had 3 years to maturity and the market interest rate is 12%? ____________

c. If the market rate was ____________, the bond would be less attractive, and its price would ____________.

d. If the market rate changed to 8%, and the bond had 3 years to maturity, the value of the bond would ____________ to ____________.

e. When the market rate is below the interest rate of the bond, the market price of the bond will be ____________ than its face value. When the market rate is above the interest rate of the bond, the market price of the bond will be ____________ than its face value.

7. Consider the investment demand schedule. Indicate if investment would increase (I) or decrease (D) in the following cases.

a. ______ an increase in interest rates
b. ______ the development of a new technology
c. ______ the expectation of new technological developments
d. ______ the expectation of a corporate tax increase
e. ______ the expectation of more generous tax write-offs for depreciation
f. ______ a new product line is introduced
g. ______ the industry is experiencing short-run economic losses
h. ______ the industry is encountering diseconomies of scale

8. Judy and Jody each devise an investment project costing $900 and earning a total income of $1200. Judy's project will return a steady stream of income, $300 per year, for 4 years. Jody's project starts more slowly, with $100 in each of the first 3 years, then $900 in the last year. The interest rate is 10%.

Use present value to decide if either project should be undertaken.

9. A dollar today and a dollar next year have different values. Discounting puts dollars of all vintages on a common basis–present value. The following case exemplifies this and highlights the importance of the market interest rate.

Here are two projects. Each has the same total cost and revenue.

	Project 1		Project 2	
Year	*Costs*	*Revenues*	*Costs*	*Revenues*
1	$700	$ 0	$300	$100
2	$100	$100	$300	$600
3	$ 0	$900	$200	$300
	$800	$900	$800	$900

a. Is the rate of return equal for both projects?
b. Intuitively, which project is the better investment?
c. Suppose the interest rate is 10%. Which project is the better investment?
d. What else is revealed?

10. Consider the investment demand schedule.

a. What economic variables does it relate?
b. What determines its slope and its position?
c. It is said that investment is volatile. Do you think that this is reflected by the shape of the curve, by its position, or by both?

Explain how investment behaviour would be affected by:

d. a cut in interest rates.
e. the development of a new technology.
f. the expectation of new technological developments.
g. the expectation of a corporate tax increase.

ANSWERS AND SOLUTIONS

PRACTICE TEST

I. SOLUTIONS TO MULTIPLE CHOICE QUESTIONS

1. D. Given the investment demand schedule, lower interest rates prompt more investment and higher demand in the economy.

2. B. Reducing the government deficit should decrease interest rates and increase investment. As investment increases, the marginal revenue product of capital will decrease because marginal productivity will decrease.

3. B. The capital stock increases through investment and decreases through wear and tear (depreciation).

4. D. Investment is the creation of new productive capacity. Option A represents an improvement in human capital. Option D is the transfer of a financial asset.

5. C. A share of Bell Canada Enterrprise stock is a financial asset. Brand loyalty is a type of "goodwill."

6. A. Investment will be greatest when the real interest rate is lowest. The real interest rate is the market interest rate minus the inflation rate.

7. C. Earnings are \$6000 per year and costs are \$2000. The expected profit is \$4000. Cost = expected profit divided by interest rate = \$4000 / .08 = \$50 000.

8. B. PV of purchase today = \$10 000. PV of purchase next year = \$12 000 / 1.1 = \$10 909.09. Because the PV today is less, he should buy today.

9. A. The current market interest rate is the key factor, not the expected interest rate.

10. A. See p. 264.

11. D. Price of bond = future value / (1 + r) = \$1000 / (1.2) = 833.33.

12. A. Even if a project is self-financed, there is an opportunity cost—the interest rate foregone. See p. 262.

13. A. Goodwill is intangible capital; inventory is tangible capital. See p. 253.

14. B. In general, the higher the interest rate, the cost of new investment projects will be higher and the number of profitable investment projects will be fewer. Note that the investment demand curve is downward sloping.

15. C. Present value is affected by interest rate changes, expected rate of return is not.

II. SOLUTIONS TO APPLICATION QUESTIONS

1. a. Clarissa's advice may be sound, but for the wrong reason. You really can't give Camille much help without knowing the interest rate.

   b. Clarissa is assuming a dollar today and a dollar five years in the future are identical in value. She is ignoring present value (or assuming that the interest rate is 0%).

   c. Camille should not accept the offer of the training program.
   The present value of \$22 000 per year for five years is:
   22 000/1.1 + 22 000 / (1.1^2) + 22 000 / (1.1^3) + 22 000 / (1.1^4) + 22 000 / (1.1^5) = \$20 000.00 + \$18 181.81 + \$16 528.93 + \$15 026.30 + \$13 660.27 = \$83 387.31.
   The present value of \$40 000 per year for the three final years is:
   40 000 / (1.1^3) + 40 000 / (1.1^4) + 40 000 / (1.1^5) = \$30 052.59 + \$27 320.54 + \$24 836.85 = \$82 209.98.
   Because the present value of the current position exceeds that of the "training plus new position," Camille is better advised to retain her present position.

   d. To encourage investment of any kind, the government should decrease the interest rate. At the extreme, using Clarissa's assumption of a 0% interest rate, the PV of the training program would exceed the PV of the 5-year position (\$120 000 exceeds \$110 000).

   e. A "low-interest rate" strategy will promote longer-term investments—the "discount" applied to future earnings is smaller. Lowering the interest rate makes the present value of all future income streams higher, but the effect is more pronounced over longer time periods.

2. Although each project earns a total income of \$1000, the present value of Jody's project is lower. This is because each dollar earned 5 years from now is worth less than each dollar earned 1 year from now. Judy's project accumulates revenue faster.

   If Jody demanded proof, set up the following table calculating present values. Judy's project has a present value of \$758.16, while Jody's trails at \$701.96.

	Judy's Project		Jody's Project	
Year	*Income*	*PV*	*Income*	*PV*
1	$200	$181.82	$100	$ 90.91
2	$200	$165.29	$100	$ 82.64
3	$200	$150.26	$100	$ 75.13
4	$200	$136.60	$300	$204.90
5	$200	$124.18	$400	$248.37
	$1000	$758.16	$1000	$701.96

3. No, the winner didn't really win $100 million in current dollars. If the interest rate is assumed to be 5% (for example), the final $5 000 000 would be worth only $1,884,447 in present value terms (5 000 000 / 1.05^{20}).

4. a. Given an interest rate of 7%, $100 would be worth $25.84. $500 000 would be worth $129 200.
   b. Given an interest rate of 3%, $100 would be worth $55.37. $500 000 would be worth $276 850.

5.

		Johnsons	*Aunt Agatha*	*Jack Diamond*
a.	Saving	$15 000	can't tell	$85 000
b.	Investment	$100 000	0	0
c.	Change in net worth	$15 000	0	$85 000
d.	Change in capital stock.	$100 000	0	0

6. a. $120.
   b. 120 / 1.12 + 120 / (1.12^2) + 120 / (1.12^3) + 1 000 / (1.12^3) = $107.14 + $95.66 + $85.14 + $711.78 = $1 000.00.
   c. higher; fall.
   d. rise; 120/1.08 + 120/(1.08^2) + 120/(1.08^3) + 1 000/(1.08^3) = $111.11 + $102.88 + $95.26 + $793.83 = $1 103.08.
   e. higher; lower.

7. a. D   b. I   c. I or D   d. D
   e. I   f. I   g. D   h. D

8. Judy's project should be undertaken. Present value is $950.96, which is greater than the $900 cost, but Jody's project would bring in only $863.40 in present value.

9. a. No.
   b. Project 2.
   c. Project 2 is clearly superior, once all the values have been converted to a common basis. Some calculation can be avoided by looking at the net cash flow (revenue - cost).

	Project 1			Project 2		
Year	*Cash Flow* +	*Conversion*	*PV*	*Cash Flow*	+ *Conversion*	*PV*
1	–$700	1.1	–$636.36	–$200	1.1	–$181.82
2	0	1.21	0.00	$300	1.21	$247.93
3	$900	1.331	$676.18	$100	1.331	$ 75.13
			$39.82			$141.24

   d. Both projects are profitable, so the rate of return exceeds 10%.

10. a. Investment demand relates the market interest rate (the cost of borrowing funds) to the quantity of new capital (investment) demanded.
    b. The investment demand curve's slope and position are critically affected by the expectations of those making investment decisions. Expectations can be influenced by political events, circumstances abroad, or changes in the domestic economy.

c. Volatility is reflected by both the shape and position of the curve. If demand is elastic, changes in the interest rate will provoke large changes in the level of investment. The curve will shift position, perhaps dramatically, as expectations change.

d. When there is a cut in interest rates, the cost of financing a new project falls. Given that the revenue from the project remains unchanged, profits will rise. More projects will become profitable and more investment will occur.

e. The development of a new technology may make the existing capital stock obsolete (or less competitive), forcing a wave of new investment.

f. If new technological developments are expected, firms may delay investment because they don't want to lock into an old technology. Investment will fall.

g. If there is an expectation that corporate taxes will increase, there is an expectation that after-tax profits will decrease. This is likely to dampen investment.

12 General Equilibrium And The Efficiency Of Perfect Competition

OBJECTIVES: POINT BY POINT

After completing this chapter, you should be able to accomplish the objectives listed below.

General Comment

This chapter plays three major roles. First, while presenting a general equilibrium model, it serves as a review chapter for all of the partial equilibrium material developed for the perfectly competitive model from Chapter 6 onward. Second, it establishes an "efficiency" benchmark against which subsequent market structures (monopoly, etc.) and related topics will be measured. Last, Chapter 12 previews the upcoming chapters, 13 through 17, in a sense providing a convenient "road map" for the remainder of your micro principles course. Chapter 12 is both a beginning and an end.

The first half of the chapter is pretty much a review of previous material. Use it as such. The wine industry example gives you a chance to check up on your understanding of changes in demand, cost curves, the role of profit and loss, and long-run adjustments.

Although a formal proof of general equilibrium is mathematically complex, you can see the big picture if you use your intuition. If you've done a little physics or chemistry, thinking of a system in equilibrium will help. When the system is shocked, all portions of it will adjust until "balance" is restored.

OBJECTIVE 1: Distinguish between partial and general equilibrium analysis.

Firms and households make simultaneous decisions in output and input markets, trying to maximize profit and utility, respectively. A *partial equilibrium* approach looks at individual markets for specific goods, but some issues require a broader view—a *general equilibrium* perspective. Changes in one market will affect other markets—products have substitutes and complements, for example. General equilibrium analysis corrects this inadequacy. (page 273)

If a hard frost damages the Florida orange crop, it is easy to go beyond partial equilibrium analysis (the price of oranges will increase) to a wider analysis (the price of orange juice will increase, as will the price of substitutes such as grapefruit juice). In real life, we do this all the time, especially when moving from input markets to product markets. It was easy to predict that the 1991 Persian Gulf War would affect the pump price of gasoline. The more closely related two markets are, the more significant the effect on one if there is a change in the other.

TIP: Trace through the implications of the textbook's extended example on the wine industry (pp. 276-279). It is, simultaneously, a good review of partial equilibrium concepts and a good example of general equilibrium analysis.

TIP: Use Application 6 below as a review of the equilibrium concepts developed in the partial equilibrium analysis of previous chapters.

Practice

1. General equilibrium analysis ignores which of the following questions?
   A. are equilibria in different markets compatible?
   B. can all markets achieve equilibrium simultaneously?
   C. how will a change in demand in Market A affect circumstances in other markets?
   D. what are the equilibrium conditions for markets other than Market A?

   ANSWER: D. General equilibrium analysis is not concerned with single markets.

2. General equilibrium exists whenever
   A. normal profits are being earned.
   B. total excess demand equals total excess supply.
   C. quantity demanded equals quantity supplied in each market.
   D. income is allocated equitably.

   ANSWER: C. See p. 273.

Use the following information for the next four questions:

Arboc has only two products: ground nuts and goat cheese. These goods are substitutes and are produced by perfectly competitive firms. Initially, both markets are in equilibrium. Now consumer preferences shift away from goat cheese and towards ground nuts.

3. Given the information above, which of the following will not occur?
   A. In the short run, goat cheese producers will incur losses.
   B. In the short run, there will be an increase in the demand for ground nut workers.
   C. In the long run, more firms will enter the ground nut industry.
   D. More capital will flow into the production of goat cheese.

   ANSWER: D. Less capital will flow into the production of goat cheese.

4. Given the information above, we would expect
   A. short-run profits in the ground nut industry.
   B. long-run losses in the goat cheese industry.
   C. long-run profits in the ground nut industry.
   D. short-run losses in the ground nut industry.

   ANSWER: A. You can't get long-run profits or losses.

5. As a goat cheese producer, your best short-run strategy is to
   A. leave the industry and enter the ground nut industry.
   B. switch over to ground nut production.
   C. set your output level to equalize marginal cost and the market price.
   D. cut your price to become more competitive and to increase your market share.

   ANSWER: C. To maximize profits, produce where P = MC. If you can't cover your operating costs, you'd be better off closing down.

6. The demand for inputs used in goat cheese production will __________, and the demand for inputs used in ground nut production will __________.
   A. increase, increase.
   B. increase, decrease.
   C. decrease, increase.
   D. decrease, decrease.

   ANSWER: C. Input demand, recall, is influenced by the price of the final product. As goat cheese producers scale back operations, they will cut their demand for inputs. Ground nut producers will increase their input demand.

OBJECTIVE 2: Analyze market adjustment while recognizing interdependencies.

A general equilibrium exists when all markets in an economy are in simultaneous equilibrium. An event that disturbs the equilibrium in one market may disturb the equilibrium in many other markets. For example, a shift in consumers preferences, as it happened in the Canadian wine industry during the 1970s, caused the demand for wine to increase, driving the price of wine up. This shift in their preferences also caused the Canadian households demand for other products to drop, driving their prices down. The wine makers immediately increased their output while the firms in other sectors cut back their production. Eventually, more firms entered the wine industry as some firms existed from other sectors (industries). Note that a general equilibrium is not reached until equilibrium is reestablished in all markets. (page 277)

OBJECTIVE 3: Define Pareto efficiency.

Efficiency is one criterion for evaluating any given economic system or market and for flagging potential problems in the perfect operation of the market system. An allocatively efficient economy produces, as cheaply as possible, the commodities that consumers want. A change is *efficient* if at least one person is made better off and no person is made worse off as a result of that change. Sometimes this is called Pareto efficiency. An efficient economy is one in which no such change is possible. Even if a change "hurts" some individuals, it is still *potentially efficient* if the gains outweigh the losses. (Gainers could bribe losers and still come out ahead.) (page 279)

> **Efficiency:** You may have some difficulty with the concept of efficiency. One way to assess an economy's performance is in terms of how well it meets the needs of its consumers. The efficiency concept captures this notion. The major point to take away from this chapter is that perfectly competitive markets result in maximum allocative efficiency—the "best" mix of outputs, produced as cheaply as possible. Movements away from the perfectly competitive ideal (externalities, for example) lead to distortions—either too much or too little of a good is produced, or the price or cost is too high.

Practice

7. Pareto optimality is present in Robinson Crusoe Land when
   A. any improvement in the welfare of Robinson reduces the welfare of Friday.
   B. the benefits from production are divided evenly.
   C. an improvement in the welfare of Robinson does not reduce the welfare of Friday.
   D. the benefits from production are divided according to effort.

ANSWER: A. Pareto optimality pertains to any situation where making one or more persons better off has an adverse impact on the welfare of another.

8. On Mindy's Milk Farm, overtime (which runs to 20 hours per week) has traditionally been awarded on the basis of seniority. Old Joshua Merriweather (who has been on the farm since he was a lad, 80 years ago) invariably does all the overtime himself. The four other farm workers (who want to work some overtime) propose a "fair shares for all" method of allocating overtime. We can conclude that
   A. the new method is certainly Pareto optimal.
   B. the traditional method is certainly Pareto optimal.
   C. both methods are certainly Pareto optimal.
   D. neither method is certainly Pareto optimal.

   ANSWER: D. An increase in the welfare of the four workers will reduce Joshua's welfare. The traditional method is not certainly optimal because the four workers' loss in welfare may exceed Joshua's increase in welfare.

9. You own a calculus book from a course you took last term. You paid $40 for it as a used textbook at the university bookstore. You value it at $15, but its sell-back value at the bookstore is only $10. Is selling the book to the bookstore Pareto efficient?
   A. yes, because $10 is better than nothing, and you could use the cash.
   B. yes, because it is a voluntary exchange—no one is twisting your arm.
   C. no, because the market price of the book is $40.
   D. no, because the $10 is less that the $15 value you place on the book.

   ANSWER: D. Selling for $10 an item that you value at $15 results in a loss. If, as in Option A, you could use the cash, this should have affected your valuation of the book.

10. You have a calculus book from a course you took last term. You paid $40 for it as a used textbook at the university bookstore. Because its sell-back value is only $10 and you value it at $15, you have decided to keep it. Now Arnold (a math major who values the book at $25) offers you $20. Is selling the book to Arnold Pareto efficient?
   A. yes, because both you and Arnold have gained from the trade.
   B. yes, because Arnold has compensated you for the loss imposed by the university bookstore sell-back policy.
   C. no, because you are still selling a book that costs $60 for $20.
   D. no, because you could have got $5 more—Arnold would have paid as much as $25.

   ANSWER: A. A voluntary exchange must make at least one of the participants better off. In this case, you dispose of a book worth $15 to you for $20 (gain), and Arnold receives a book worth $25 to him for $20 (gain). Note that, given the decision not to sell to the bookstore, that transaction becomes irrelevant.

OBJECTIVE 4: Understand the conditions needed for Pareto efficiency and how these conditions are met in a perfectly competitive economy.

The perfectly competitive model developed over the previous chapters leads to an efficient (optimal) allocation of resources. The system works because resources are allocated among firms efficiently, final products are allocated among households to maximize utility, and the system produces the goods and services (including leisure) that society wants. (page 281)

Graphing Pointer: Efficient Output Mix—P = MC: It's important to grasp that, by operating where P = MC, firms produce the most efficient combination of outputs. The logic is displayed graphically in Figure 12.4—take some time to get a good understanding of the diagram. You saw the right-hand side of the diagram in Chapter 6, and the left-hand side in Chapter 10. Now is a good time to go back and review that material.

Remember, too, that the marginal cost of Good X includes the opportunity cost of the next most preferred alternative foregone, say Good Y. If the price that consumers are willing to pay for Good X is less than that, i.e., the value of Good Y—then producing the extra unit of Good X must reduce their utility. If the marginal cost of producing Good X is lower than the price of Good X, then more of Good X should be produced.

Finally, don't forget that perfect competition extends to input markets—workers and employers are both price takers in the labour market, for instance. If the equilibrium condition—W = MRP—doesn't hold, there will be inefficiency.

Practice

11. If an economy has competitive input and output markets, and firms that maximize profits, the economy will
    - A. achieve an efficient allocation of resources.
    - B. achieve an equitable distribution of income.
    - C. minimize differences between the marginal revenue products of different types of inputs.
    - D. allow the marginal utility of consumers to be maximized.

    ANSWER: A. Barring "market failures" (discussed in the textbook on p. 284), economic conditions will result in an efficient allocation of resources.

12. The condition that ensures that consumers get the goods they want is
    - A. MR = MC.
    - B. P = MC.
    - C. MR = P.
    - D. P = ATC.

    ANSWER: B. In this case, the marginal cost of a good for society is equal to the value placed on that good by society.

13. The price of jelly beans is $1.00. The total cost of producing 24 units of jelly beans is $24.75. The total cost of producing 25 units of jelly beans is $25.25. The total cost of producing 26 units of jelly beans is $26.00. Currently, 25 units of jelly beans are being produced. Society would benefit
    - A. if the 26th unit of jelly beans is produced.
    - B. if production is kept at 25 units.
    - C. if the price of jelly beans is increased.
    - D. if production is reduced to 24 units of jelly beans.

    ANSWER: A. MC of the 26th unit is 75¢. Because price exceeds MC, the 26th unit should be produced.

14. The social value of a unit of jelly beans is
   A. the price of the unit of jelly beans.
   B. the marginal revenue of the unit of jelly beans.
   C. the marginal cost of the unit of jelly beans.
   D. the total cost of the unit of jelly beans.

   ANSWER: A. Price reflects the value society puts on a good. See p. 283.

15. Marginal cost of a unit of jelly beans is a measure of
   A. the value society places on a unit of jelly beans.
   B. society's net gain when the unit of jelly beans is produced.
   C. society's net loss when the unit of jelly beans is produced.
   D. what society gives up to produce the unit of jelly beans.

   ANSWER: D. Marginal cost measures the opportunity cost to society of the resources used in producing the jelly beans.

16. Dot and Ted Sfeir own a firm ("Dotted Spheres") that produces size 3 soccer balls in a perfectly competitive market. They produce 60 balls a week at a cost of $7 per ball, which is the lowest possible long-run average cost. The market price is $10. Which of the following is true?
   A. Dotted Spheres' current output level is efficient because average cost is minimized.
   B. society would be better off if Dotted Spheres increased its current output level because price exceeds marginal cost.
   C. society would be better off if Dotted Spheres increased its current output level because price exceeds average cost.
   D. society would be better off if Dotted Spheres decreased its current output level because this will increase the firm's profits.

   ANSWER: B. If average cost is minimized at $7, then marginal cost is also $7. (If you're uncertain on this, review Chapter 8.) Price, then, exceeds the cost of producing an extra ball, so more should be produced.

OBJECTIVE 5: Distinguish real-world markets from perfectly competitive markets.

The fact that a perfectly competitive market system produces an efficient allocation of resources, an efficient mix of output, and an efficient distribution of income rests on a set of assumptions: all firms and households are price takers in input and output markets; they have perfect information; that all firms maximize profits, etc. But these assumptions do not usually hold in real-world markets. When this is the case, the conclusion that free, unregulated market will produce an efficient outcome breaks down. (page 283)

OBJECTIVE 6: Identify potential sources of market failure.

In the real world, the stringent conditions of the perfectly competitive model might not be met. In such a situation, a *market failure* occurs and inefficiencies creep into the system of unregulated markets. The result is waste or lost value. Four sources of market failure are: imperfect market structure; public goods; externalities; and imperfect information. (page 284)

OBJECTIVE 7: Explain the meaning of imperfect competition, public good, externalities, and imperfect information.

a. *Imperfect competition*, such as monopoly, arises when firms have some measure of control over price and/or competition. Economic profits may be maintained indefinitely if competition can be barred from entry. The consequences are more restricted production and higher prices than would occur in a competitive environment—consumers lose.

b. *Public goods* provide benefits to more than one consumer at a time. Because one can consume without having to pay, there is a powerful incentive to be a free rider. Although private firms might produce most public goods, the problem is that they will not produce enough of them because they cannot compel consumers to pay their fair share. By using tax dollars, the government can produce public goods and improve efficiency.

c. *Externalities*, which are costs or benefits encountered by a party outside a transaction, do not enter into the calculations of profit- and utility-maximizing firms and consumers. If externalities are a factor, the allocation of resources is likely to be suboptimal.

d. *Misinformation or poor information* affects the market participant's ability to make an informed choice. The less informed he or she is, the more likely a suboptimal outcome is.

Inefficient Output Mix—$P \neq MC$: Although in different ways, the efficient $P = MC$ condition is infringed in each of the four cases.

Practice

17. In the market for apples, there is a consumer surplus, and a short-run economic profit is being made. This is conclusive evidence of
    A. externalities.
    B. market failure.
    C. apples being a public good.
    D. none of the above.

    ANSWER: D. Consumer surplus and short-run economic profits are possible in a perfectly competitive industry. See p. 143 in the textbook to review the concept of consumer surplus.

18. The firms in a perfectly competitive industry merge into one big firm and impose barriers to entry into the industry. We can say that
    A. we can expect that externalities will begin to appear.
    B. the product of this industry is a public good.
    C. the price of the product will be higher, and the output lower, than the values under perfect competition.
    D. this firm will be unable to maximize profits.

    ANSWER: C. Imperfect markets are a source of inefficiency. See p. 284.

19. The production of Good Z involves positive externalities. A perfectly competitive industry will ____________ this good; a monopoly will _________ this good.
    A. overproduce, overproduce.
    B. overproduce, underproduce.
    C. underproduce, overproduce.
    D. underproduce, underproduce.

    ANSWER: D. The presence of a positive externality means that the market does not capture the full benefits to society flowing from this good.

20. Public goods are a source of market failure because
    A. they permit economic profits to occur in the long run.
    B. they are provided by government agencies.
    C. their benefits cannot be limited to those who purchase them.
    D. they can be produced more cheaply by private firms.

ANSWER: C. Because benefits cannot be limited to those who purchase them, the demand for public goods does not reflect their social value.

21. The production of Good Y imposes a cost on the purchaser. Good Y
    A. has negative externalities.
    B. has positive externalities.
    C. is a public good.
    D. is a typical good.

    ANSWER: D. All goods involve costs (and benefits). Only those goods that pass costs (or benefits) on to third parties exhibit externalities.

22. The licensing of cosmetologists is an attempt to
    A. control provision of a public good.
    B. improve the imperfect information for buyers of this service.
    C. impose externalities on potential competitors.
    D. correct an imperfectly competitive market structure.

    ANSWER: B. Licensing offers buyers the benefit of knowing that practitioners have achieved a given quality of performance. It may also operate as a barrier to entry (not an externality).

23. Ground nuts are sold by a monopoly, and goat cheese is sold by perfectly competitive firms. When both markets are in equilibrium,
    A. P > MC for both goods.
    B. P = MC for both goods.
    C. P = MC for ground nuts and P > MC for goat cheese.
    D. P > MC for ground nuts and P = MC for goat cheese.

    ANSWER: D. In perfect competition, MR = P = MC. In monopoly, P > MR = MC.

24. Which of the following is not a public good?
    A. National defence.
    B. Clean air.
    C. A toll bridge.
    D. A lighthouse.

    ANSWER: C.

25. A museum in Britain once mounted a display of Roman coins. After some time, a small boy approached the curator and pointed out that one of the "coins" was, in fact, a dirty plastic bottle top. An economist would say that
    A. society lost because the value of the exhibit was reduced.
    B. society lost because, although the exhibit might never be sold, society now knew that the coin was a fake.
    C. society gained, because better information about the exhibit was now available.
    D. society gained because now the remaining coins were even more rare.

    ANSWER: C. See p. 287.

A Look Ahead

The previous chapters have set up the perfectly competitive framework—the economist's version of the best of all possible worlds. If perfect competition cannot be attained in the market, though, neither can allocative efficiency. Imperfections—externalities, public goods, inadequate information, monopoly power—occur in the real world and mess things up. The conclusions reached in this and the preceding chapters will be used to assess the performance of markets where imperfections exist.

PRACTICE TEST

I. MULTIPLE CHOICE QUESTIONS. Select the option that provides the single best answer.

_____ 1. Which of the following indicates that we have an efficient output market?
- A. Wage equals marginal revenue product of labour.
- B. Price of the output equals the marginal cost of the output.
- C. Price of the output equals the marginal revenue product.
- D. Marginal utility is greater than the price of the output.

Use the following information to answer the next five questions.

Chicken and beef are the only goods produced in the economy. Each is a constant-cost industry, and each is currently in equilibrium. Suddenly there is a permanent shift in the preferences of consumers in favour of chicken and away from beef.

_____ 2. We would expect
- A. short-run losses in the beef industry.
- B. long-run losses in the beef industry.
- C. short-run losses in the chicken industry.
- D. long-run losses in the chicken industry.

_____ 3. Relative to the current price, the price of chicken would ____________ in the short run and ____________ in the long run.
- A. rise, remain unchanged.
- B. fall, remain unchanged.
- C. rise, fall.
- D. fall, rise.

_____ 4. As a beef producer, in the short run, your best strategy is to
- A. shut down immediately.
- B. keep operating as long as you can cover your fixed costs.
- C. keep operating as long as you can cover your variable costs.
- D. cut the price of your beef to win your customers back.

_____ 5. As a chicken producer, in the short run, your best strategy is to
- A. increase your beef-producing facilities.
- B. cut price to increase market share.
- C. expand production until marginal cost is again equal to price.
- D. buy more of every input to expand production.

_____ 6. As the economy moves from the initial long-run equilibrium to the final long-run equilibrium we would expect that, with respect to inputs,
- A. each industry will continue to use the same amounts of inputs because these are constant-cost industries.
- B. all input markets will be affected.
- C. the labour market will not be affected.
- D. only the labour and capital markets will be affected because land is fixed in supply.

_____ 7. Sellco introduces a new policy that reduces the cost of joining the company club but limits how frequently club members can use the facilities. As a result, some employees will lose and some will gain. On balance, the new plan bestows benefits of $1000 at a cost of $300. The company's previous policy was ____________. The new policy is ____________.

A. inefficient, potentially efficient.
B. Pareto optimal, potentially efficient.
C. efficient, Pareto optimal.
D. inefficient, Pareto optimal.

_____ 8. Barriers to entry are most closely linked with
A. externalities.
B. public goods.
C. monopolies.
D. perfect competition.

_____ 9. Pollution is an example of
A. a public good.
B. an externality.
C. imperfect competition.
D. imperfect information.

_____ 10. Dana, a potato farmer in the PEI perfectly competitive potato farming industry, is facing a marginal cost of $0.30 per kg. The industry's price is $0.40/kg. In order to maximize profit, Dana should
A. raise her price.
B. lower her price.
C. lower her marginal cost.
D. increase her production until P = MC.

_____ 11. Mike's Milkery is able to exclude other firms from entering its market. This is an example of
A. externalities.
B. external competition.
C. a monopoly.
D. a public good.

_____ 12. All of the following are sources of market inefficiency except
A. public goods.
B. externalities.
C. monopolistically competitive firms.
D. lack of control by individual firms over price.

_____ 13. Relative to perfect competition, imperfect competition will produce
A. lower prices and more output.
B. lower prices and less output.
C. higher prices and more output.
D. higher prices and less output.

_____ 14. A market is efficient if
A. any change that improves the welfare of one individual reduces the welfare of another.
B. income is equally distributed.
C. output is equally distributed.
D. it produces any mix of output at the lowest cost.

_____ 15. Which of the following activities is least likely to generate an externality?
A. wearing perfume.
B. smoking a cigarette.
C. reading a comic book.
D. plowing snow from a road.

_____ 16. Ruth tithes (i.e., gives one tenth of her income) to her church. Which of the following is true?
A. this exchange is Pareto optimal, because Ruth can use this charitable contribution as a tax deduction.
B. this exchange is Pareto optimal, otherwise the two parties would not voluntarily agree to the exchange.
C. this exchange is not Pareto optimal because, as the church has no option but to
accept the money, it is not a voluntary exchange.
D. this exchange is not Pareto optimal because Ruth does not necessarily receive any good or service in exchange.

_____ 17. The hog industry, a highly competitive and a booming industry in the southeastern part of the United States. Opponents, however, point out the presence of negative externalities that firms ignore. When deciding how much to produce, the typical firm will
A. produce more than the efficient output level.
B. produce less than the efficient output level.
C. produce the efficient output level because the firm is competitive.
D. produce the efficient output level because the industry is competitive.

_____ 18. Suppose that you own a soy bean farm, but your land can also be used for the production of tobacco. You are operating in an industry that consists of hundreds of small farmers like yourself. Recent evidence, however, suggests that cigarette smoking shortens a smoker's life. Assuming that this leads to a shift in preferences away from tobacco products and towards soy bean consumption and that the producers adjust their production accordingly,
A. all farms producing tobacco will experience short-run losses.
B. more farmers will move their capital input into tobacco production to make up for the loss of land resources.
C. the labour market will not be affected because unskilled workers are employed in both types of farming activities.
D. the market for land will be affected because jobs in soy beans farms require different skills.

_____ 19. Using the information in question18, your best profit-maximizing strategy is to
A. cut your prices to increase your market share of the expanding industry.
B. plant tobacco because, as fewer farmers plant tobacco, its price will rise.
C. increase soy bean production to earn short-run economic profits.
D. decrease soy bean production to force the price higher.

II. APPLICATION QUESTIONS.

1. Two refugees, Alex (who likes candy) and Branko (who likes to smoke), have found their way to a Red Cross camp in Eastern Europe. They each receive a Red Cross parcel containing 20 cigarettes and 20 pieces of candy.

	Alex		Branko	
	Cigarettes	Candy	Cigarettes	Candy
Red Cross	20	20	20	20
Experiment	12	30	24	10
Trade I	____	____	____	____
Trade II (Pavel)	____	____	____	____

Suppose you (an entrepreneur) are also in the refugee camp and that you know the preferences of your two colleagues. As an "experiment," you ask Alex how many cigarettes he would trade in order to receive 10 more units of candy. Alex replies eight. You ask Branko how many cigarettes he would need to be induced to trade 10 units of candy. He replies four.

a. Suppose you act as a middleman and reallocate the candy and cigarettes between Alex and Branko according to the numbers provided by the experiment. Who gains? Does anyone lose? Is this a Pareto optimal action?
b. Can you see any way of profiting from the present situation? If so, how? Write the results of the trade in the table above. You have provided a service. Assuming no half cigarettes or half pieces of candy, derive the maximum possible profit. Call this "Trade I." Who gains? Does anyone lose? Is this a Pareto optimal action?
c. Suppose a rival trader (Pavel) observes the economic profits that you are earning and decides to undercut you when the next Red Cross parcels are distributed to Alex and Branko. Assuming no half cigarettes or half pieces of candy, derive the maximum possible profit for Pavel. Call this "Trade II."
d. When will this process end, and who are the major winners?

2. There is certainly a demand for, and supply of, aerosol sprays. Suppose they are produced by a perfectly competitive industry. Evidence suggests that aerosols may be responsible in part for destroying the ozone layer in the upper atmosphere. Does the presence of this side effect pose any problems for our analysis?

3. Consider the market for personal computers that began booming in the early 1980s. In what ways did that boom affect the labour market? What new skills were demanded? How were those skills produced? Suppose Andrea Hacker just bought a PC for $2000. If PCs didn't exist, how might Andrea have spent the same $2000? What happens to employment in the sectors where these items are produced?

4. If I buy a good—for example, a new CD—and share it with my friend, allowing her to tape from it, does my action improve or diminish the allocative efficiency of the economic system? Why?

   Suppose, instead, I resell the CD to my friend. Does this affect your answer?

5. We have an economy which produces only two goods—military and civilian goods. Each industry is perfectly competitive and there are constant returns to scale. You have been appointed as assistant to the Assistant Deputy Mininister of Industry. Because of a reduction in geo-political tensions, the demand for military goods is expected to decrease quite substantially in the near future while, because of the peaceful climate, the demand for civilian goods will increase. The Assistant Deputy has asked you to prepare a report on the full effects of this change.

   What will be the effect on:

   a. the price and quantity of military goods?
   b. the price and quantity of civilian goods?

6. Given the profit-maximizing output level, a firm will seek to minimize costs—you can't earn maximum profits if you allow a more costly than necessary method of production. The connection between utility maximization and profit maximization is less evident. The following example lets you work through the link between the maximizing behaviour of households and of firms.

   a. What, in words, is the utility-maximizing rule? (Check back to Chapter 6 for the "household equilibrium condition" if you're not too sure.)

b. With only two goods, A and B, what is the utility-maximizing formula?

The ratio $MU_A/MU_A = P_A/P_B$ must be true for every pair of goods. If you want, put in numbers to confirm the ratios.

c. What, in words, is the profit-maximization rule?

d. Write down an interpretation of the meaning of MC.

e. Now write down the profit-maximizing formula. Does it hold for all profit maximizers?

f. Let's generalize by noting that $P_A = MC_A$ and $P_B = MC_B$.
Observe that the two results combined give:

$$MU_A/MU_B = MC_A/MC_B.$$

The perfectly competitive model results in the production of exactly those quantities of each of the goods requested by consumers, given their opportunity costs—i.e. the optimal output mix.
Now let's violate the equalities in this formula to check understanding. Suppose, for example, that Good A is apples and Good B is butter and the following is true:

$$MU_A = 50,\ MC_A = 40 \text{ and } MU_B = 60,\ MC_B = 30$$

Substitute these values into the formula. What does the inequality tell you?

g. What should be the response?

h. What will happen to each of the 4 values?
Here is evidence that profit maximizers will respond to consumer demands to produce the desired product mix.

7. Match up the "market failure" with the infringed "perfectly competitive" assumption and the correct example.

	Market Failure	*Assumption*	*Example*
a.	Externality	______	______
b.	Imperfect competition	______	______
c.	Public goods	______	______
d.	Partial information	______	______

Assumptions

A. all participants will be price takers

B. all costs and benefits will be borne by producers and consumers

C. perfect knowledge

D. to benefit from consumption, one must pay the supplier

Examples

National defence

Monopoly

"Lemons" in the car market

Noise pollution

ANSWERS AND SOLUTIONS

PRACTICE TEST

I. SOLUTIONS TO MULTIPLE CHOICE QUESTIONS

1. B. See p. 282.
2. A. A reduction in demand will reduce profits in the beef industry.
3. A. The demand for chicken has increased. In the short run, this will result in higher prices and higher profits. In the long run, new firms will enter the industry, increasing supply and reducing price. Because the industry is constant-cost, price will return to the original level.
4. C. In the short run you, have fixed costs to consider. If you can cover your variable (operating) costs, you should produce.
5. C. The profit-maximizing rule is to set production at the level where P (MR) = MC.
6. B. One industry has expanded and the other has contracted, so they would not maintain the same usage of inputs. We should see all input markets being impacted by the change in demand for outputs.
7. A. The previous plan was inefficient because the benefits of the new plan outstrip the costs. We can't say that the new plan is Pareto optimal because further changes might improve the welfare of employees still more.
8. C. See p. 284.
9. B. See p. 285.
10. D. Dana is a perfectly competitive (price taking) producer. She would maximize her profit by setting production at the level where P = MC. Since her MC is currently below the market price, she should increase her production and exploit the existing profit opportunity.
11. C. If Mike can exclude others from his market, he has established a monopoly through the use of barriers to entry.
12. D. Lack of control over price is a hallmark of perfect competition.
13. D. Typically, imperfectly competitive producers will restrict output and charge higher prices.
14. A. See p. 280.
15. C. See p. 286.
16. B. Because the exchange takes place and is voluntary, neither party is hurt, and at least one of the two parties must gain.
17. A. Even if an industry is perfectly competitive, when the social cost of a negative externality is ignored by the producer, production will be too high.
18. A. There should be a general decline in the quantity of all resources used in tobacco production.
19. C. As consumption of soy beans increases, so does its price. Therefore, you should increase production as long as your MC is below the new market price and maximize your profit.

II. SOLUTIONS TO APPLICATION QUESTIONS

1. a. If you merely replicate the experiment, no one gains. Alex and Branko get different, but no more satisfying, allocations. The experiment, recall, asked what an equivalent allocation would be. Because you have taken some trouble to effect the exchange, but have received no reward for your enterprise, you have lost. This exchange is not a Pareto optimal action.

	Alex		*Branko*	
	Cigarettes	***Candy***	***Cigarettes***	***Candy***
Red Cross	20	20	20	20
Experiment	12	30	24	10
Trade I	12	30	24	10
Trade II (Pavel)	13	30	24	10

b. In general, given identical initial parcels of goods, different preferences, and zero transactions costs, trade will always be beneficial. It's easy to forget that you, as facilitator, need a reward.
Trade I: "Borrow" 10 pieces of candy from Branko, promising him cigarettes in return. Give Alex the 10 pieces of candy and take 8 cigarettes in return—Alex has not lost. "Pay" Branko 4 cigarettes for the borrowed candy—Branko has not lost. You have gained 4 cigarettes. Because no one has lost and you have gained, this is a Pareto optimal action.

c. Trade II: Pavel "borrows" 10 pieces of candy from Branko, promising him cigarettes in return. Pavel gives Alex the 10 pieces of candy and generously takes 7, not 8, cigarettes in return—Alex has gained. "Pay" Branko 4 cigarettes for the borrowed candy—Branko has not lost. Pavel has gained 3 cigarettes. No one has lost and Pavel and Branko have gained—this is a Pareto optimal action. Note: You have not lost because you were not a participant in this round of trading.

d. The process ends when profits are pushed so low that they can be pushed no lower, i.e., normal profits are being earned. As the entrepreneurs take less of a cut, the consumers, Alex and Branko, keep more and, therefore, gain.

Note: Alex and Branko gain because of competition. You and Pavel have an incentive to collude and/or impose barriers to entry to reduce competition and keep profits high. Such action reduces market efficiency.

2. The basic conclusion in this chapter is that perfect competition will provide the "best" allocation of resources. However, we should recall that the presence of externalities undermines this conclusion. Aerosols may, indeed, produce externalities that our perfectly competitive producers choose to ignore.

3. Demand for technically trained labour increased. Programmers, designers, systems analysts of all kinds, and skilled assembly workers experienced an increase in demand. Technical schools and major universities began training programs. Firms did on-the-job training. Andrea might have done any number of things, like buying a (used) car or some new clothes or travelling. Employment falls in those sectors.

4. Home taping of CDs reduces economic efficiency. It represents an externality. The market demand for CDs does not accurately represent the true demand for CDs. Because the market for new CDs is affected by the market for used CDs, resale does not reduce efficiency.

5. a. The demand for military goods will shift to the left—the price and quantity traded will decrease in the short run. Firms will leave the industry because short-run economic losses are being made. This exodus of firms will make the market supply curve shift to the left. This movement will continue until normal profits are achieved. Given constant returns to scale, the long-run industry supply curve will be horizontal, and the initial price level will be restored. The quantity of resources allocated to this industry will be reduced.
   b. The demand for civilian goods will shift to the right—the price and quantity traded will increase in the short run. Firms will enter the industry because short-run economic profits are being made. The additional firms will make the market supply curve shift to the right. This movement will continue until normal profits are achieved. Given constant returns to scale, the long-run industry supply curve will be horizontal, and the initial price level will be restored. The quantity of resources allocated to this industry will be increased.

6. a. The last dollar spent on each good should purchase an equal amount of marginal utility.
   b. $MU_A/P_A = MU_B/P_B$.
   c. Produce until the quantity is reached where marginal revenue is inadequate to cover marginal cost.
   d. Marginal cost is the opportunity cost of the resources used to produce the final unit of output—the value of the other goods that we could have produced instead.
   e. P = MR = MC. This is true for all profit maximizers in perfect competition.
   f. The per dollar cost of the last units of satisfaction from apples is relatively too high (50 / 40 < 60 / 30).
   g. Spend less on apples and reallocate funds to butter.
   h. Diminishing marginal utility will drive MU_A up and MU_B down, while decreasing marginal productivity will make MC_A fall and MC_B rise until a balance is struck.

7. a. B Noise pollution
   b. A Monopoly
   c. D National defence
   d. C "Lemons" in the car market

13 Monopoly

OBJECTIVES: POINT BY POINT

After completing this chapter, you should be able to accomplish the objectives listed below.

OBJECTIVE 1: Describe the types of imperfectly competitive markets.

A market in which individual firms have some control over price is imperfectly competitive. Such firms exercise market power. The three forms of imperfect competition are monopoly, oligopoly and monopolistic competition. A monopoly is an industry with a single firm that produces a product that can control its price and its volume of production. An oligopoly is a small number of firms, each of which is large enough to have an impact on the market price and its output. Finally, monopolistic competition exists when an industry has a large number of firms, each producing a slightly different product. (page 296)

> **Graphing Pointer:** You have already derived the cost curves for a perfectly competitive firm and industry. The cost curves used in this and subsequent chapters are the same as those that you've seen before. The only differences occur in the revenue parts of the diagram.

Practice

1. A pure monopoly is an industry with a single firm that produces a product that has _________ close substitutes and in which there are _________ barriers to entry.
   - A. many, significant.
   - B. many, no.
   - C. no, significant.
   - D. no, no.

   ANSWER: C. See p. 296.

2. Peter's Pan Pizzeria operates in an imperfectly competitive market. Which of the following statements does not apply to this firm?
   - A. Peter's Pan Pizzeria has some control over the price it charges.
   - B. Peter's Pan Pizzeria has a downward-sloping demand curve.
   - C. Peter's Pan Pizzeria does not compete with the other pizzerias in town.
   - D. Peter's Pan Pizzeria has some market power.

   ANSWER: C. If other pizzerias produce substitutes for Peter's pizza, Peter's is a monopolistically competitive firm and does compete.

OBJECTIVE 2: Outline the factors that define industry boundaries.

An industry can be defined as broadly or narrowly as desired. The more broadly we define the industry, the fewer substitutes there are, and the less elastic demand for that industry's product there is likely to be. For example, the grain industry is a broadly defined industry for which there are no substitutes. Clearly, the market structure characterizing the food industry is one of monopoly. On the other hand, a firm that produces a specific brand of bread or cereal would belong to a narrowly defined industry characterized by several substitutes and very little market power. (page 296)

Practice

3. The _________ broadly we define an industry, the _________ substitutes it has, and the _________ elastic the demand for its products.
   A. more, more, more.
   B. more, fewer, less.
   C. less, more, less.
   D. less, fewer, less.

   ANSWER: B. The broader the definition of an industry, the more difficult it is to find a substitute, and the less elastic the demand. See p. 296

OBJECTIVE 3: Describe the potential barriers to entry.

The University residence for the first-year students is close to being a monopoly. The student may be required to reside in a residence. A pure monopoly, for example, occurs when there is a single firm in an industry producing a product with no close substitutes (campus accommodation). *Barriers to entry* are the reason that this situation can arise and endure. A barrier to entry is something that prevents new firms from entering and competing in imperfectly competitive industries. Different forms of barriers to entry are: legal (franchises, patents), economies of scale, and exclusive ownership of a necessary input. (page 297)

Practice

4. Your local electric company maintains its monopoly because of
   A. a patent.
   B. product differentiation.
   C. ownership of a scarce resource.
   D. a government franchise.

   ANSWER: D. Cable TV and local telephone companies are other examples. See p. 295.

OBJECTIVE 4: Analyze the profit maximizing price/output decision of a monopolist in the short run and the long run.

Monopolists (and other types of imperfectly competitive firms) must decide how much output to produce, how to produce it, and how much of each input to hire, just as a perfectly competitive firm must do. However, monopolists must also decide which price to set. This is determined by the "MR = MC" rule. The "demand side," then, limits the monopolist. The firm can't charge any price because they are limited by the demand for their product. (page 307)

> **Marginal Revenue and the Profit-Maximizing Rule: MR = MC:** Marginal revenue—the amount by which total revenue changes as output increases by one unit—is a key concept that you've seen before. Perfect competition is a special case, where P = MR. For any firm with a downward-sloping demand curve, price is greater than marginal revenue. The profit-maximizing output level can *always* be found by equating marginal revenue and marginal cost (MR = MC). The monopolist, therefore, doesn't charge the highest price to get the most profit—he or she takes both cost and revenue (demand) information into account.

> **Graphing Pointer:** The monopolist charges the highest price possible without reducing profit. Graphically, identify the profit-maximizing output level (where MR = MC) and move vertically to the demand curve. At that point, you have found the profit-maximizing price.

> **Graphing Pointer:** Having found where MR = MC, it is a common error to move immediately to the vertical axis and identify that value as the price—e.g., OF in the diagram in the Practice questions below.

> **Graphing Pointer:** See Application 6 below.

In imperfect competition, *marginal revenue is less than price* because, to sell an extra unit, the firm must cut price, and the price cut applies to all units bought. The addition to revenue from selling the extra unit is less than the price charged. When few items are affected by the price cut, the increase in sales increases total revenue, and marginal revenue is positive. However, as progressively more items suffer a lower price, the increase in revenue from the new sales is offset by the decrease in revenue from existing sales and total revenue decreases—marginal revenue becomes negative. (page 301)

> **Tip:** In order to understand what is happening to revenue as price and quantity change, examine the following diagram.

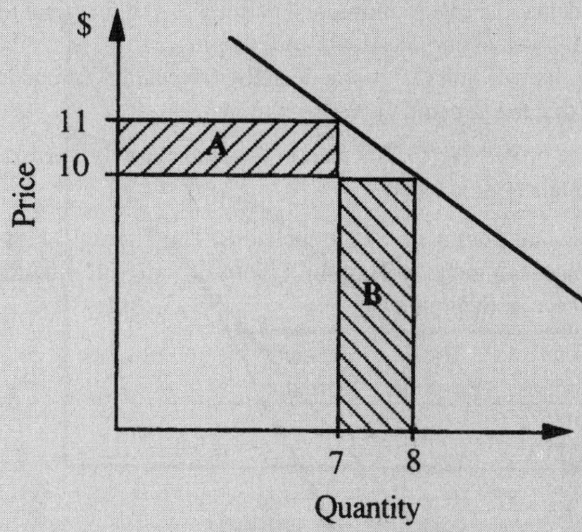

> When price is \$11 and \$10, respectively, total revenue is \$77 and \$80, respectively. Marginal revenue is \$3. Now consider area A and area B. Verify that they are \$7 and \$10 respectively. Area A represents the revenue lost because of the price change, while area B represents the revenue gained. Comparing the two lets us calculate MR visually. As price falls and output expands, the one-unit revenue increase dwindles in importance beside the multi-unit revenue decrease—imagine the difference in areas if, rather than 7 and 8 units, the diagram showed 1007 and 1008 units.

TIP: Review Chapter 5's section on price elasticity and the total revenue test. Note that as price decreases, total revenue increases when demand is elastic (MR is positive), and that total revenue decreases when demand is inelastic (MR is negative).

Graphing Pointer: In terms of graphing, the only difference between a regular monopoly and a natural monopoly is in the positioning of the demand curve. To draw a regular monopoly, make demand slice through the average cost curve when ATC is rising—to the right of the intersection of ATC and MC. To draw a natural monopoly, have demand slice through ATC while ATC is still falling. The economics behind this is as follows—with a natural monopoly, economies of scale endure for so long that demand becomes low relative to costs, falling short of ATC's minimum point.

Graphing Pointer: Most people find it easier to draw the "cost diagram" first and then put in the demand and marginal revenue curves afterwards.

Practice

5. In a monopoly,
   A. the market demand curve is above, and parallel to, the marginal revenue curve.
   B. the marginal revenue curve is downward sloping.
   C. increasing price will not result in a decrease in quantity demanded.
   D. we assume that the demand curve is unknown.

   ANSWER: B. See p. 302. Note: The market demand curve is above, but is not parallel to, the marginal revenue curve.

Use the following table to answer the next four questions. The Thornhill Jays hockey team is the only live sports entertainment in Thornhill. Here is some information about their ticket prices and attendance at their games.

Ticket Price	Total Attendance	Total Revenue	Marginal Revenue
$14	100	1400	_____
$12	200	_____	_____
$10	300	_____	_____
$8	400	_____	_____
$6	500	_____	_____
$4	600	_____	_____

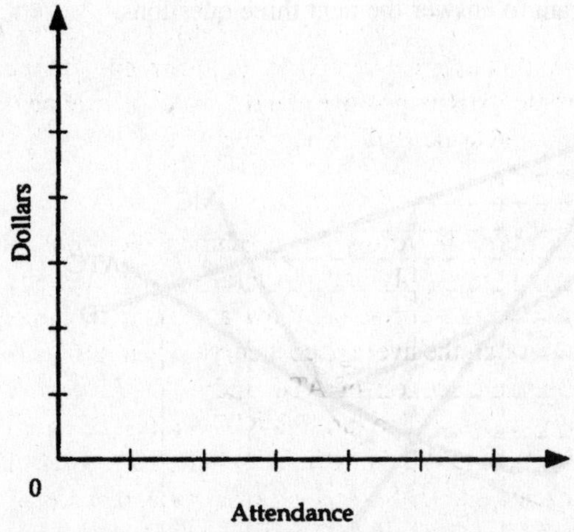

6. Fill in the total revenue and marginal revenue columns in the table above, then graph the demand and marginal revenue curves above.

ANSWER: See the *Answers and Solutions* section.

7. At a price of $12 per ticket, the Jays attract 200 spectators. For the Jays to attract 300 spectators, they would have to ________ price. Total revenue would ________.
   A. increase, increase.
   B. increase, decrease.
   C. decrease, increase.
   D. decrease, decrease.

ANSWER: C. See the table above.

8. When the Jays decrease price from $12 to $10 to attract 300 spectators, total revenue increases, indicating that demand is ____________ and that marginal revenue is ____________.
   A. elastic, positive.
   B. elastic, negative.
   C. inelastic, positive.
   D. inelastic, negative.

ANSWER: A. See p. 303 and Figure 13.4.

9. If the Jays cut price from $12 to $10 per ticket, each new customer will ______________ and each regular customer will ______________.
   A. increase total revenue by $10, increase total revenue by $2.
   B. increase total revenue by $10, decrease total revenue by $2.
   C. decrease total revenue by $10, increase total revenue by $2.
   D. decrease total revenue by $10, decrease total revenue by $2.

ANSWER: B. MR = 600. TR increases by 100 x $10 (new customers) and decreases by 200 x $2 (regular customers).

10. A monopoly produces where marginal revenue exceeds marginal cost.
   A. the firm could increase profits by increasing output.
   B. the firm could increase profits by decreasing output.
   C. the firm is making an economic profit.
   D. the firm is earning a negative economic profit (loss).

ANSWER: A. The firm should produce at the output level where MR = MC. Because we don't know anything about the relationship between price and ATC, we can't say whether or not a profit is being made (Option C).

Use the following diagram to answer the next three questions.

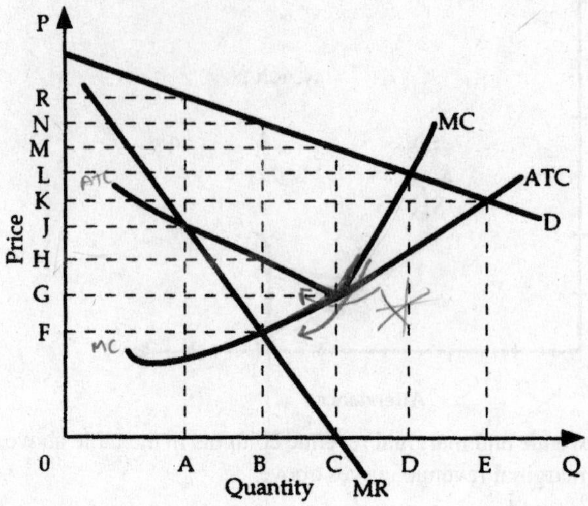

11. The profit-maximizing output level is
    A. OA.
    B. OB.
    C. OD.
    D. OE.

    ANSWER: B. This is the output level where MR = MC.

12. The profit-maximizing price is
    A. OF.
    B. OG.
    C. OH.
    D. ON.

    ANSWER: D. At output level OF, the demand curve shows that the price can be as high as ON.

13. The firm's maximum profit is
    A. OB x HN.
    B. OC x GM.
    C. OB x FN.
    D. OC x HN.

    ANSWER: A. Total profit is (price – ATC) x Q.

OBJECTIVE 5: Identify the social costs of monopoly.

In terms of welfare and efficiency, monopoly compares poorly with perfect competition. Assuming similar costs, the monopolist will overprice and underproduce. The monopolist is not efficient because output is not set where P = MC, the firm does not use the lowest-cost production method, and the distribution of income is altered (through the appropriation of excess profits, which is like a private tax).

If a competitive industry were to become a monopoly, price would increase and quantity would decrease. Consumers would lose through the higher prices and reduced level of production—in general, society loses when a monopoly replaces perfect competition. We can therefore conclude that monopoly leads to an inefficient mix of output. (page 308)

Graphing Pointer: It is often convenient to use letters to assist in interpreting diagrams. In the diagram below, note that price, for example, is the vertical line from the origin to the point R, and is reported as 0R, (or alternatively, TS, which is the same length). The profit-maximizing quantity is 0T, (or alternatively, RS, which is the same length). Finally, note that 0Y and YZ are equal lengths—the marginal revenue curve intersects the horizontal axis at half the quantity of the demand curve. See p. 308.

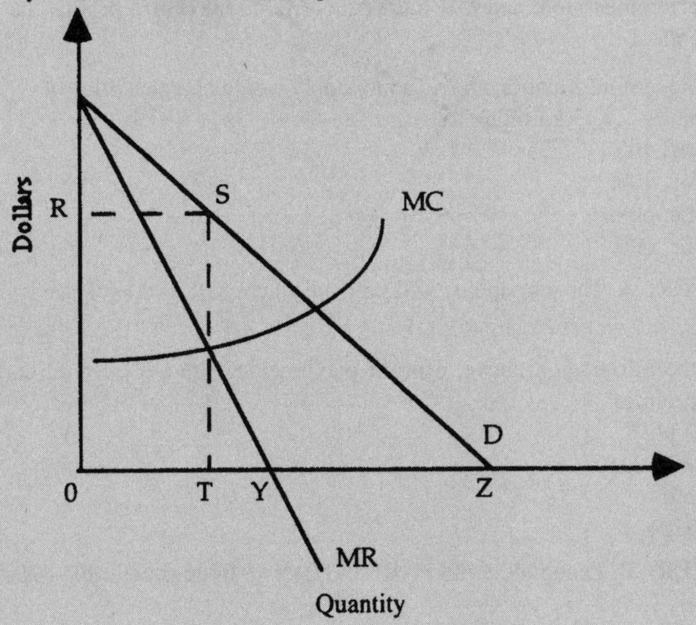

See multiple choice questions 8–13 in the *Practice Test* for some more examples.

Monopoly: Remember the long-run perfectly competitive equilibrium result: P = MC = LRAC (minimum) = SRAC (minimum). First, in monopoly, the firm will not minimize average costs. Second, the monopolist will not produce the output society considers to be optimal (where P = MC).

Natural monopoly can avoid these criticisms because of the benefits derived from economies of scale. Demand just isn't sufficient to warrant producing where costs are minimized.

Practice

Use the following table, which provides long-run information about the market for apples, to answer the next four questions. Price is price per kilogram of apples.

Quantity (kg)	*Price per kg*	*Marginal Revenue*	*Marginal Cost*	*Average Total Cost*
100	\$1.40	—	—	\$2.00
200	\$1.07	\$ .74	\$ .50	\$1.50
300	\$ .92	\$ .62	\$ .46	\$ .75
400	\$ .80	\$ .44	\$ .44	\$ .70
500	\$ .66	\$ .10	\$ .43	\$ .65
600	\$ .50	–\$ .30	\$ .50	\$ .50
700	\$ .30	–\$ .80	\$ .59	\$1.00

14. Given the cost information above, a perfectly competitive industry would charge a price of _____ per kg and produce _____ kg of apples.
A. 80¢, 400.
B. 44¢, 400.
C. 50¢, 600.
D. 30¢, 600.

ANSWER: C. The perfectly competitive industry will produce at the lowest point on its long-run average cost curve. Because price and marginal revenue are identical in perfect competition, and MR must equal MC to maximize profits, the price will also be 50¢.

15. Given the cost information above, a monopoly would charge a price of _____ per kg and produce _____ kg of apples.
A. 80¢, 400.
B. 44¢, 400.
C. 50¢, 600.
D. 30¢, 600.

ANSWER: A. The monopolist will produce where MR = MC. Price is then determined.

16. Given the information above, a profit-maximizing monopoly would earn an economic profit of
A. $144.
B. $40.
C. zero.
D. -$104.

ANSWER: B. Economic profit is (P - ATC) x Q. In this case, (80¢ –70¢) x 400 = $40.

17. From the previous questions, we can formulate the following long-run rule: The monopolist will produce ________ and charge ________ than the perfectly competitive industry.
A. more, more.
B. more, less.
C. less, more.
D. less, less.

ANSWER: C. If this is still unclear, review the answers to the three previous questions and read pp. 308–310 in the textbook.

Use the following diagram, which shows the revenue and cost curves for coffee, to answer the next two questions. Initially, this is a perfectly competitive industry.

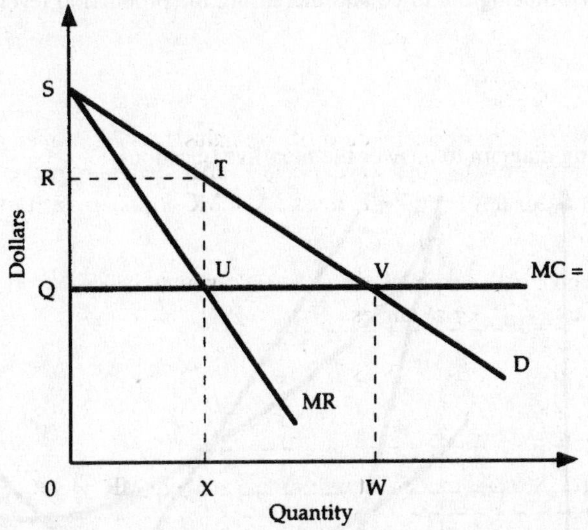

18. If the coffee industry becomes a monopoly, the loss in social welfare is equal to _______. The monopolist will be willing to spend an area equal to _______ to preserve the monopoly.
    A. TUV, QRTV.
    B. TUV, QRTU.
    C. QRTU, TUV.
    D. QRTV, TUV.

    ANSWER: B. The perfectly competitive firm would produce W units at a price of Q dollars. The monopolist will reduce output to X units and charge the higher price of R dollars. The welfare loss due to the decrease in output and the increase in price is TUV. The monopolist's profit [(price – average cost) x quantity], i.e., QRTU, is the amount he or she is willing to spend to maintain the monopoly.

19. If the coffee industry becomes a monopoly, the loss in consumer surplus will be
    A. TUV.
    B. RST.
    C. QRTU.
    D. QRTV.

    ANSWER: D. With perfect competition, the consumer surplus would be QSV. With monopoly, the consumer surplus shrinks to RST. QRTV represents the difference in consumer surplus. See the textbook's p. 143 to review this concept.

OBJECTIVE 6: Describe the natural monopoly.

A *natural monopoly* occurs where average costs continue to decrease as output levels rise. In such circumstances, a single-firm industry can be the most efficient way to organize production. Here it would be undesirable to break up the monopoly because having one producer is the "best" way to organize the market. Such an industry is usually regulated—often with average cost pricing to allow normal profits. (page 312)

National defence is, perhaps, an example of a natural monopoly. The defence of another million Canadians could be done with little additional expense (ATC is still decreasing). It would make little sense to break up defence of Canada into individual provincial-level defence units. (In Chapter 16, national defence is given as an example of a public good.)

The *socially optimal output level* is where price equals marginal cost; this solution would result in losses for the firm, however. The average cost output level lets the firm earn a normal profit while reducing the price and increasing the production level for the benefit of society.

Practice

Use the following diagram to answer the next five questions.

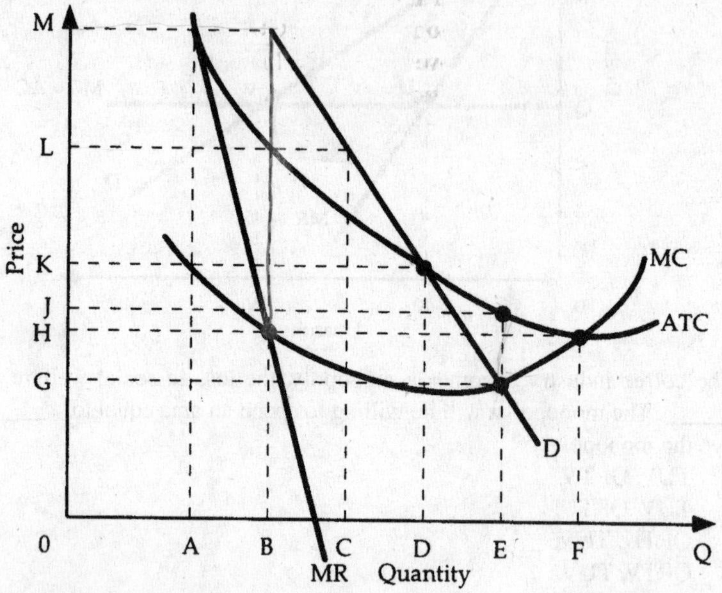

20. The type of industry depicted in the diagram above is best described as
    A. a pure monopoly.
    B. a natural monopoly. —Why?
    C. imperfectly competitive.
    D. an artificial monopoly.

    ANSWER: B. For all relevant levels of demand, ATC slopes downward.

21. At the most efficient output level, this firm would earn an economic
    A. profit of OB x HM.
    B. profit of OE x GJ.
    C. loss of OB x HM.
    D. loss of OE x GJ.

    ANSWER: D. The most efficient output level is where P = MC. At that level (OE), price is less than average cost—the firm will make a loss.

22. If Max, the owner of this firm, could choose his own output and price levels, he would choose an output of ______ and a price of ______.
    A. OB, OM.
    B. OD, OK.
    C. OE, OG.
    D. OF, OH.

    ANSWER: A. Max will produce where MR = MC.

23. If a price ceiling were imposed at OG, Max would
   A. still produce OB units because this is where MR = MC.
   B. have to receive a subsidy of HM dollars per unit.
   C. have to receive a subsidy of GJ dollars per unit.
   D. earn an economic profit of OE x GJ.

ANSWER: C. The price ceiling establishes a price that is less than the average cost of production. See p. 314.

24. If a price ceiling were imposed at OK,
   A. Max would earn an economic profit of OD x GJ.
   B. the government would have to subsidize Max to the tune of KG dollars per unit.
   C. Max would produce OB units because this is where MR = MC.
   D. Max would make a normal profit and remain in the industry.

ANSWER: D. See p. 314.

25. If a natural monopoly is split into a number of smaller competing firms, price will
   A. increase, because smaller firms will have higher average costs.
   B. increase, because each firm will experience diseconomies of scale.
   C. decrease, because additional competition is taking place.
   D. increase in the short run because of the disruption, but decrease in the long run because of the additional competition.

ANSWER: A. Each firm is driven up along the average cost curve as output level falls. The firms don't experience diseconomies of scale—they aren't large enough.

26. For the typical natural monopolist, in the short run, fixed costs are relatively _______ and marginal costs are relatively _______.
   A. high, high.
   B. high, low.
   C. low, high.
   D. low, low.

ANSWER: B. See p. 313.

OBJECTIVE 7: Analyze monopsony: market power in the input markets.

Monopsony is the situation in which there is only one buyer in the input market. The employer faces an upward-sloping input supply curve—he is not an input price taker. To attract extra workers, for example, the wage must be increased. Since the wage increase applies to all workers, the extra cost of hiring a worker is greater than the wage that worker receives. Marginal factor cost (of labour) measures the extra cost of hiring one extra worker and is also upward sloping. As in perfect competition, the monopsonist will hire workers until the marginal revenue product equals the marginal factor cost. (page 315)

> **Monopsony:** There are parallels between downward-sloping output demand curves and marginal revenue curves, and upward-sloping input supply curves and marginal factor cost curves. If you can understand why MR is less than demand, extend your insight to explain why MFC is more than supply.

> **Graphing Pointer:** Just as P > MR translates into a graph where the demand curve is above the MR curve, MFC > W is graphed with the MFC curve above the labour supply curve.

Practice

Use the following table about labour supply to answer the next five questions. Maxine is a monopsonistic employer in Thornhill.

Wage	Total Workers	~~Marginal~~ Total Factor Cost	Marginal Factor Cost
$14	7	98	26
$12	6	72	22
$10	5	50	18
$8	4	32	14
$6	3	18	10
%4	2	8	–

27. Complete the table.

ANSWER: See the *Answers and Solutions* section.

28. At a wage of $10, Maxine the Monopsonist can hire 5 workers. For Maxine to hire 6 workers, she would have to ________ wage. The total wage bill (factor cost) would ________.

A. increase, increase.
B. increase, decrease.
C. decrease, increase.
D. decrease, decrease.

ANSWER: A. See the table above.

29. If Maxine increases the wage from $10 to $12, the new worker will increase total factor cost by _____, and each previous worker will increase total factor cost by _____.

A. $12, $12.
B. $12, $2.
C. $2, $12.
D. $2, $2.

ANSWER: B. MFC = 22 = $12 (the new worker) + $2 x 5 (other workers).

30. At the profit-maximizing hiring level for labour for a monopsonist,

A. the marginal factor cost is equal to the marginal revenue product and is less than the wage.
B. the marginal factor cost is greater than the marginal revenue product and is equal to the wage.
C. the marginal factor cost is less than the marginal revenue product and is greater than the wage.
D. the marginal factor cost is equal to the marginal revenue product and is greater than the wage.

ANSWER: D. See p. 316.

31. We know that marginal revenue product decreases as additional workers are hired. See Chapter 10 if you're unsure about this point. In this question, however, assume that MRP is constant at $14. Maxine will hire ________ workers and pay a wage of ________.

A. 4, $8.
B. 4, $14.
C. 7, $12.
D. 7, $14.

ANSWER: A. Maxine will hire until MFC is equal to MRP. She will not hire the fifth worker. The labour supply curve indicates that she can hire 4 workers for $8 each.

PRACTICE TEST

I. MULTIPLE CHOICE QUESTIONS. Select the option that provides the single best answer.

_____ 1. A pure monopoly is best defined as a firm
- A. selling a product for which there are no close substitutes.
- B. making short-run economic profits.
- C. with a degree of market power.
- D. with a downward-sloping demand curve.

_____ 2. Which of the following is not a barrier to entry?
- A. patent rights.
- B. ownership of private property.
- C. the possession of a government franchise.
- D. substantial economies of scale.

_____ 3. A monopolist who is producing where MR is less than MC, should
- A. increase production.
- B. reduce price.
- C. reduce production.
- D. produce where price is equal to marginal cost.

_____ 4. The profit-maximizing monopolist must decide all of the following except
- A. output level.
- B. price level.
- C. the wage level.
- D. the combination of inputs.

_____ 5. A monopolist is currently maximizing profits. We can conclude that
- A. he is maximizing total revenue and minimizing total cost.
- B. he has reduced the difference between marginal revenue and marginal cost to zero.
- C. he is maximizing total revenue and marginal revenue.
- D. he is producing where marginal revenue equals average cost.

_____ 6. A natural monopoly is usually regulated to produce an output level such that
- A. P = MC.
- B. MR = MC.
- C. P = ATC.
- D. MR = ATC.

_____ 7. Mandy the Monopolist operates a firm that is not a natural monopoly. Relative to a perfectly competitive industry, we would expect Mandy to have
- A. lower prices and lower output.
- B. lower prices and higher output.
- C. higher prices and higher output.
- D. higher prices and lower output.

Use the diagram below to answer the next six questions.

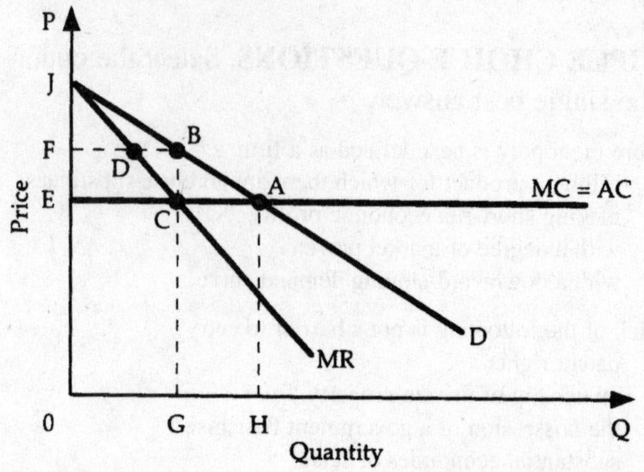

_____ 8. This perfectly competitive industry becomes a monopoly. Price will __________, quantity will __________.
A. fall to E, fall to G.
B. fall to E, rise to H.
C. rise to F, rise to H.
D. rise to F, fall to G.

_____ 9. With a profit-maximizing monopolist, the net loss of social welfare is shown by area
A. FBCE.
B. BAC.
C. EABF.
D. BCD.

_____ 10. To preserve the monopoly, this firm would be willing to spend up to
A. FBCE.
B. BAC.
C. EABF.
D. ABDC.

_____ 11. If this industry were initially perfectly competitive and then became a monopoly, the amount of consumer surplus transferred to the monopolist is shown by the area
A. DBC.
B. ABC.
C. FBCE.
D. FBAE.

_____ 12. If this industry were perfectly competitive, consumer surplus would be shown by the area
A. ABC.
B. JEA.
C. FBCE.
D. FBAE.

_____ 13. If this industry were a monopoly, consumer surplus would be shown by the area
- A. ABC.
- B. HEA.
- C. JFB.
- D. ECBH.

_____ 14. The average total cost curve of a natural monopoly is
- A. upward sloping where it crosses the market demand curve for the good.
- B. upward sloping at all points.
- C. downward sloping at all points.
- D. downward sloping where it crosses the market demand curve for the good.

ATC

_____ 15. Refer to the following diagram. To have a normal rate of profit, this firm's price should be set
- A. at P1.
- B. at P2.
- C. at P3.
- D. where MR = MC.

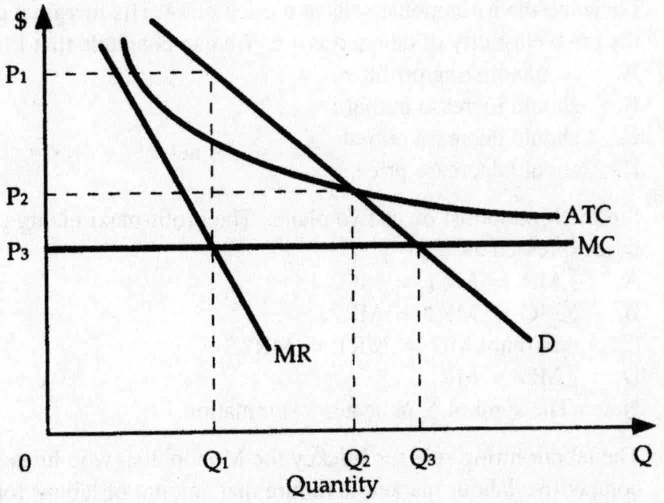

_____ 16. Mike the Monopolist produces where marginal revenue equals marginal cost equals average total cost. His economic profits will be
- A. positive.
- B. negative.
- C. zero.
- D. indeterminate—it depends on demand conditions too. (Try sketching this one.)

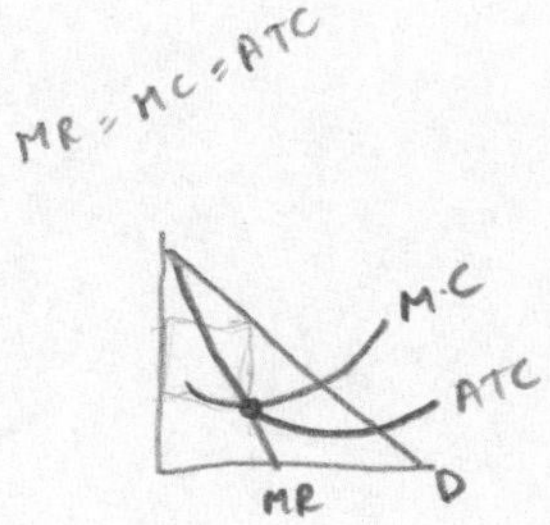

_____ 17. A monopsonist will hire _________ workers and pay them _________ wages than would a price-taking employer.
- A. more, more.
- B. fewer, less.
- C. more, less.
- D. fewer, more.

_____ 18. Use the following information for Firm A. Total revenue = $1200. Total cost = $400. Price = $12. MR = $10. Total variable cost = $300. MC = $6. This is a ____________ firm currently in a ________ situation.

A. perfectly competitive, short-run.
B. monopolistic, short-run.
C. monopolistic, long-run.
D. perfectly competitive, long-run.

_____ 19. Molly the Monopolist faces an elastic demand curve. If she decreases price, marginal revenue will be ________ and total revenue will ________.

A. positive, rise.
B. positive, fall.
C. negative, rise.
D. negative, fall.

_____ 20. The additional cost of using an additional unit of an input is

A. marginal cost.
B. marginal revenue.
C. marginal revenue product.
D. marginal factor cost.

_____ 21. Lucienne the Monopolist sells at a price of $4. His marginal cost is $3 and the price elasticity of demand is –.6. We can conclude that Lucienne

A. is maximizing profit.
B. should increase output.
C. should decrease output.
D. should decrease price.

_____ 22. Siu the Monopolist owns two plants. The profit-maximizing condition is best expressed as

A. $\Sigma MR = MC1 = MC2$.
B. $\Sigma MC = MR1 = MR2$.
C. minimum $MC = MR1 = MR2$.
D. $\Sigma MC = MR$.

Note: The symbol Σ indicates a summation.

_____ 23. The labour hiring rule for Mickey the Monopolist, who hires in a perfectly competitive labour market, is to hire that amount of labour for which the wage equals

A. marginal revenue.
B. marginal revenue product.
C. marginal product.
D. marginal factor cost.

_____ 24. South Manitoba Cablevision is a natural monopoly earning economic profits. It is split up into a number of smaller competing firms. The price of cable television will

A. increase because the smaller firms will experience higher average costs than did LSMC.
B. increase because rent-seeking behaviour will intensify.
C. decrease because competition has increased.
D. decrease because, in perfect competition, prices are driven to the point where economic profits are zero.

_____ 25. The Snow White Mining Corporation, a monopsonist, hires 6 dwarfs for a total factor cost of $98. If a seventh dwarf, Dopey, is hired, the total factor cost rises to $140. When 7 dwarfs are hired, the wage per worker is ______, and the marginal factor cost of the seventh dwarf is ______.

A. $140, $20.
B. $20, $42.
C. $20, $20.
D. $140, $42.

II. APPLICATION QUESTIONS.

1. In 1998, the Canadian airline industry is radically transformed. Following a vicious price war and a series of mergers, one company (United Canada Airlines) has emerged as the sole survivor. United adopts a new slogan (Fly United—or Walk) and hires you as a consultant on pricing policy. United offers a one-way trip from Toronto to Edmonton. The marginal cost for each passenger is $40. Fixed cost is $500 000. Demand information is shown below. Note: The demand and marginal revenue curves are linear.

Price of One-Way Trip Tickets	*One-Way Trips Demanded Per Year (Thousands)*	*Marginal Revenue*
______	______	______
______	______	______
______	______	______
$140	6	______
$130	8	______
$120	10	______
$110	12	______
$100	14	______
$90	16	______
$80	18	______
$70	20	______

a. Complete the table.
b. Give the demand equation in the form P = X + YQd, where X and Y are numbers and Qd is the quantity demanded.
c. Calculate the quantity demanded when the price is zero.
d. Give the marginal revenue equation in the form MR = X - Qd, where X and Y are numbers and P is the price of a one-way ticket.
e. Calculate the quantity demanded when the marginal revenue is zero. Careful!

Suppose that United's corporate chiefs wish to charge a single, profit-maximizing ticket price for all their Toronto-Edmonton customers.

f. Which price will maximize profits?
g. Calculate United's total cost at the profit-maximizing output level.
h. Calculate United's economic profits.
i. Draw a diagram showing the demand, marginal revenue and marginal cost curves.
j. Calculate the consumer surplus and interpret your finding for United's top brass.
k. Determine the efficient output level and price.
l. A noted economist, Dr. Michael Frank, who is opposed to United's monopoly position, has claimed that the loss in social welfare caused by United has a monetary value of $300 000. How would you advise United to reply?
m. Is it coincidental that the welfare loss and the consumer surplus values are identical?

n. A campaign is being waged to split up United into smaller independent units. The management wants to know the maximum amount they should allocate to a "war chest" to lobby and to buy political favours.
o. Calculate Untied's economic profits at the efficient output level.
p. If the government required that United price tickets at the efficient price, what would be Untied's long-run response?
q. Suppose the government requires that the price be set at the efficient level, but will offer United a subsidy to maintain the flight. How great a subsidy per passenger would the government have to offer United to induce them to keep the flight open?

2. Veterinary services can be provided at any level for an opportunity cost of $60 000 per vet. Yearly demand for veterinary services is given by P = $300 000 – 4Qd. (P is the dollar price per vet.)
   a. Calculate the marginal revenue equation.
   b. In the space below, graph the demand, MR, MC, and AC curves for veterinary services. Put in numerical values where possible.

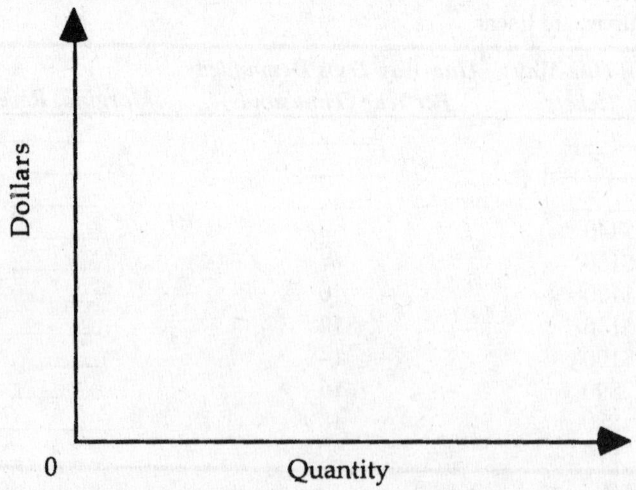

   c. Canadian Veterinary Association operates as a profit-maximizing monopoly. Calculate the price and output level in this industry.
   d. Calculate the total economic profit per vet.
   e. If entry into this industry was unrestricted, state the price and output level that would emerge.

3. You are a profit-maximization consultant specializing in monopolies. Three firms seek your advice but, in each case, the information the firm can provide is incomplete. You will be able, however, to recommend one of the following short-run actions and write a justification of your proposal. To verify your answer and for some additional graphing practice, try sketching the diagram in each case.

Recommended actions
1. Remain at current output level.
2. Increase output.
3. Decrease output.
4. Shut down.
5. Uncertain—the figures provided cannot possibly be correct.

Firm	Price	MR	TR	Q	TC	MC	ATC	AVC
A	6.40	3.10	______	1000	6400	3.00	______	3.24

Recommendation: ________
Justification:

Firm	Price	MR	TR	Q	TC	MC	ATC	AVC
B	12.80	_____	_____	2000	_____	12.80	12.00	9.24

Recommendation: ________
Justification:

Firm	Price	MR	TR	Q	TC	MC	ATC	AVC
C	5.00	4.00	30 000	_____	_____	4.00	5.10	5.05

Recommendation: ________
Justification:

4. a. Fill in the blanks in the table which refers to a monopolist.

Price	*Quantity*	*TR*	*MR*
$8	2		---
$7		$21	
$6	4		
$5			$1
$4	6		
$3		$21	

b. Why, when price falls from $6 to $5, does total revenue increase by only $1?

5. The food service at your university is run by a single firm (Food Service). The table below shows the monthly demand for meals and total costs.

a. Complete the table.

Sales (units)	*Price (per meal)*	*Total Cost*	*MR*	*MC*
4 000	$1.50	$6 100		
5 000	$1.40	$6 400		
6 000	$1.30	$6 800		
7 000	$1.20	$7 300		
8 000	$1.10	$8 000		
9 000	$1.00	$9 000		
10 000	$0.90	$10 200		

b. If Food Service tries to maximize profits, it will set the price per meal at ________ (of the choices given here).

c. Students form a committee to regulate the food service. They want to maximize consumers' welfare, given that total costs are covered. The price they set should be ________.

d. Between which two price levels is the market demand curve unitarily elastic?

6.

Graphing Pointer: This diagram is meant to depict a monopoly in long-run equilibrium. P* and Q* are equilibrium quantity and price, respectively. However, if this is the situation that is meant to be shown, there are several errors in the graph. Indicate as many errors as possible and explain, based on your economic understanding, *why* they are errors.

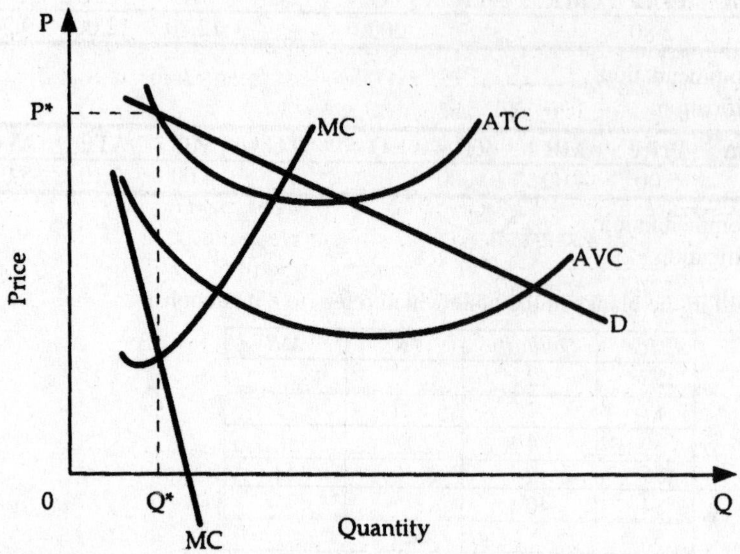

7. The following example lets you use your intuition to construct a diagram for a monopoly.

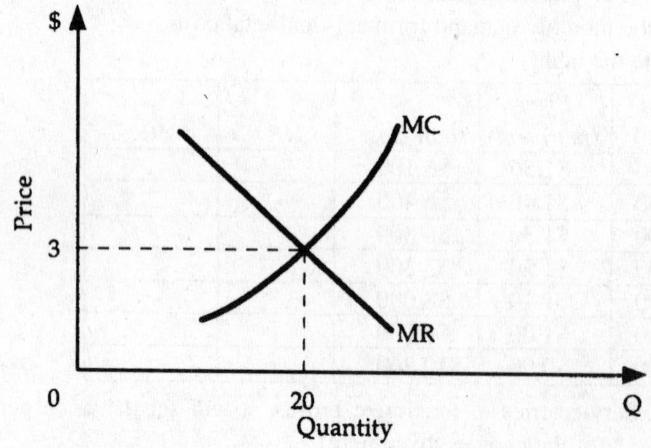

a. Where on the diagram will the firm maximize profits (or minimize losses)?
b. What is the price?
c. Draw your own demand curve on the diagram. Now work out price.
d. Finally, sketch in an average cost curve. Is this firm making a profit or a loss?
e. Are losses feasible in the long run?

Note: The distinction between the typical monopoly and a natural monopoly can be shown with this diagram. Because cost and revenue profiles are determined independently, the demand curve can intersect AC at any point. If it intersects AC where AC is rising, it's your common or garden monopoly; if it intersects where AC is falling, it's a natural monopoly.

8. In this industry the minimum average cost value is $1. It is reached when a firm produces 1000 units of output per month. The monthly demand schedule for the product produced by this industry is given in the following table.

Price	*Quantity Demanded*
$3.00	1 000
$2.00	8 000
$1.00	12 000
$0.50	20 000

Is this industry a natural monopoly? Why?

9. A mind-bender: Suppose the monopolist's demand curve is not a straight line but a rectangular hyperbola—i.e., a line with the same area underneath it at all points.
   a. What does this tell you about total revenue?
   b. What do you think the marginal revenue values will be? What will the MR curve look like?
   c. What will be the elasticity along this demand curve?
   d. Use the following table to confirm your predictions.

Price	*Quantity*	*TR*	*MR*
$24	1		—
$12	2		
$8	3		
$6	4		
$4	6		
$3	8		
$2	12		

   e. Now graph demand and marginal revenue.

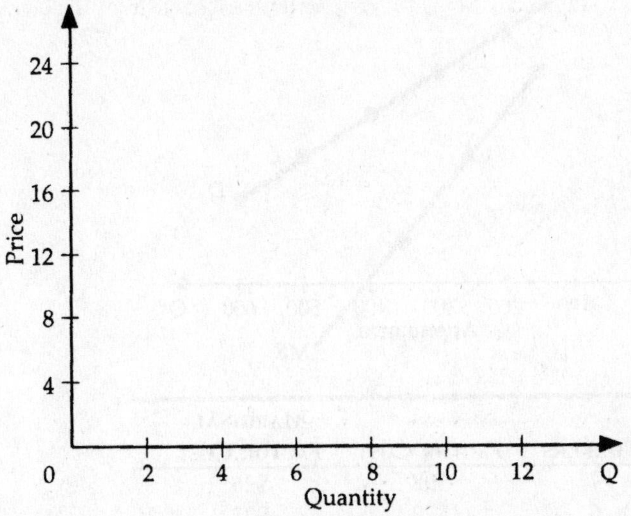

   f. Define "marginal cost." Can MC ever be zero?
   g. Now, on your diagram, draw a "typical" marginal cost curve. Where will the profit-maximizing output level be?

ANSWERS AND SOLUTIONS

ANSWERS TO PRACTICE QUESTIONS

6.

Ticket Price	Total Attendance	Total Revenue	Marginal Revenue
$14	100	$1400	
$12	200	$2400	$10
$10	300	$3000	$6
$8	400	$3200	$2
$6	500	$3000	–$2
$4	600	$2400	–$6

Note: Recall that marginal revenue is found by dividing the change in total revenue by the change in quantity.

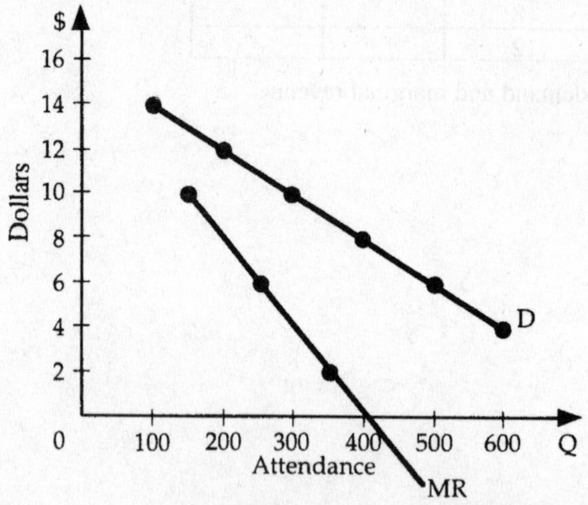

27.

TOTAL WAGE	WORKERS	FACTOR COST	MARGINAL FACTOR COST
$14	7	$98	$26
$12	6	$72	$22
$10	5	$50	$18
$ 8	4	$32	$14
$ 6	3	$18	$10
$ 4	2	$ 8	

PRACTICE TEST

I. SOLUTIONS TO MULTIPLE CHOICE QUESTIONS

1. A. Monopoly means "single seller." See p. 296.
2. B. There are no barriers to entry into a perfectly competitive industry, although the means of production may be privately owned.
3. C. To maximize profits, the firm should produce where MR = MC. When MR is less than MC, too much is being produced.
4. C. The labour market determines the wage level, and this market may be perfectly competitive. The monopolist would be a wage taker with no control.

5. B. To maximize profits, the firm must be producing where MR = MC.

6. C. This strategy permits the monopolist to make a normal profit. See p. 314.

7. D. See Figure 13.9 on p. 309. Note: The natural monopolist is an exception to this rule.

8. D. In the perfectly competitive industry, output is established where P = MC. In the monopoly, output is where MR = MC. Given the demand curve, price will rise.

9. B. See Figure 13.9 on p. 309.

10. A. The monopolist's economic profit is (P – AC) x Q. He or she would be willing to sacrifice all of this in order to maintain the monopoly.

11. C. See p. 309.

12. B. See p. 309.

13. C. See p. 309.

14. D. Typically, for a natural monopolist, the demand curve intersects the ATC curve where the ATC is downward sloping. Note: The ATC curve *may* be horizontal. For a "regular" monopolist, the demand curve intersects the ATC curve where the ATC is upward sloping.

15. B. A normal rate of profit is achieved at the output level where P = ATC.

16. A. For the monopolist, the demand curve is above the MR curve. If MR = ATC, the price exceeds ATC, and Mike is earning an economic profit.

17. B. All firms will hire until marginal factor cost equals MRP. For the monopsonist, MFC is upward sloping; for the perfectly competitive employer, MFC is horizontal.

18. B. Price is not equal to MR—Firm A is not perfectly competitive. Because total costs are greater than variable costs, there must be fixed costs—a short-run phenomenon.

19. A. A decrease in price represents a movement down Molly's demand curve. When demand is elastic, marginal revenue (addition to total revenue) is positive and, given a decrease in price, total revenue will increase.

20. D. See p. 316.

21. C. If MR is –.6, demand is inelastic and MR is negative. If so, MC must exceed MR, and Lucienne should reduce output.

22. D. To maximize profits, the monopolist follows the MR = MC rule. In a multiplant situation, the relevant marginal cost is the sum of the marginal costs of the individual plants. See p. 306.

23. B. If Mickey were a monopsonist as well as a monopolist, the wage would equal marginal factor cost. In this case (perfect competition in the labour market), the wage will equal the marginal revenue product of labour.

24. A. The distinguishing feature of a natural monopoly is that it reaps cost-reducing economies of scale not available to a smaller firm.

25. B. The wage per worker is the total factor cost divided by the number of workers. The marginal factor cost is the change in the total factor cost as an additional worker is hired.

II. SOLUTIONS TO APPLICATION QUESTIONS

1. a. See the table below.

Price of One-Way Trip Tickets	*One-Way Trips Demanded Per Year (Thousands)*	*Marginal Revenue*
$170	0	—
$160	2	$160
$150	4	$140
$140	6	$120
$130	8	$100
$120	10	$80
$110	12	$60
$100	14	$40
$90	16	$20
$80	18	$0
$70	20	–$20

b. P = 170 – 5Qd. The slope is rise over run. As price falls by $10, quantity rises by 2—the slope is –5. The vertical intercept, i.e., when Qd is zero, occurs when price is 170. We get the equation P = 170 – 5Qd.

c. Given P = 170 – 5Qd, when P = 0, 170 = 5Qd, therefore Qd = 34.

d. MR = 170 – 10Qd. Recall that the marginal revenue curve has the same vertical intercept as the demand curve, i.e., $170. The slope is twice as steep as that of the demand curve, i.e., –10.

e. Given MR = 170 – 10Qd, when MR = 0, 170 = 10Qd, therefore Qd = 17. Comment: Note that the table seems to give the value as 18. This apparent discrepancy is because the table reports the marginal revenue in the range from 16 to 18. The table reports discrete values, while the formula is a continuous function.

f. Set MR = MC, i.e., 170 - 10Qd = 40. Qd = 13. When Qd = 13, P = $105.

g. TC = TFC + TVC. TFC is given as $500 000. To get TVC, recall that MC is the addition to total cost as extra units are produced, i.e., variable cost. TVC =$40 x 13 000 = $520 000. TC = $500 000 + $520 000 = $1 020 000

h. Economic profits = TR – TC. TR = P x Q = $105 x 13 000 = $1 365 000. TC = $1 020 000. Economic profits = $345 000.

i. See the diagram below.

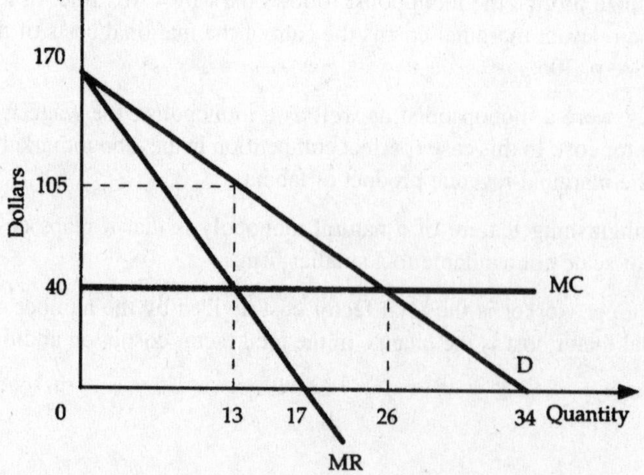

j. Consumer surplus is the area between price and the demand curve, i.e., .5(170 –105) x 13 000 = $422 500. Consumer surplus refers to the difference between the value of the extra benefits derived by customers and the price they paid.

k. The efficient output level is where P = MC. Because MC is constant at $40, P must equal $40. Substituting that price into the demand equation, we get output to be 26.

l. The social loss is .5($105 – $40) x (26 000 – 13 000), or $422 500. This, in fact, is greater than the value given by Dr. Michael Frank. It's probably best, therefore, to make no comment. If comment is required, either United should not dispute Frank's claim or, in an attempt to confuse the issue, mention the consumer surplus value which exceeds $300 000. This is, of course, a complete red herring.

m. Given straight-line curves, it's not a coincidence. Because the MR curve is twice the slope of the demand curve, it bisects MC. From that point, geometry requires identical triangles for the two concepts. Other examples, and the real world, are not so clear cut.

n. Rent-seeking behaviour tells us that the firm can allocate all of their economic profits ($345 000) to defeat the campaign.

o. Economic profits = TR – TC. TR = P x Q = $40 x 26 000 = $1 040 000.
TC = TFC + TVC. TFC = $500 000. TVC = $40 x 26 000 = $1 040 000.
TC = $500 000 + $1 040 000 = $1 540 000. Economic profits = -$500 000.

p. United would stop offering this flight—no firm will make an economic loss indefinitely.

q. The economic loss is -$500 000 to fly 26 000 passengers. The subsidy would be $19.23 (approximately).

2. a. a. MR = $300 000 – 8Qd. Recall that the marginal revenue curve has the same vertical intercept as the demand curve, i.e., $300 000. The slope is twice as steep as that of the demand curve, i.e., –8.

b. See the diagram below.

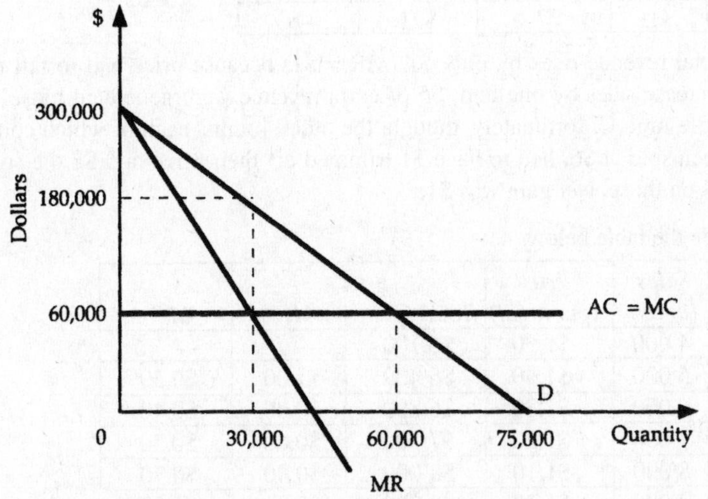

c. The profit maximizing output level is where MR = MC, i.e., where Q = 30 000. When Q is 30 000, P is $180 000.

d. Total economic profit = TR –TC. TR = P x Q = $180 000 x 30 000 = $5 400 000 000. TC = ATC x Q = $60 000 x 30 000 = $1 800 000 000. Total economic profit equals $3 600 000 000.

e. In perfect competition, economic profits would be driven to zero. The price would be \$60 000 (i.e., equal to marginal cost). When P = \$60 000, quantity is \$60 000.

3. See each of the cases below.

Firm	Price	MR	TR	Q	TC	MC	ATC	AVC
A	6.40	3.10	6400	1000	6400	3.00	6.40	3.24

Recommendation: 2
Justification: Firm A is earning a normal profit, even when not maximizing profit. Because MR > MC, the firm should expand production.

Firm	Price	MR	TR	Q	TC	MC	ATC	AVC
B	12.80	<12.80	25 600	2000	24 000	12.80	12.00	9.24

Recommendation: 3
Justification: MR is less than price and, therefore, less than 12.80. MR < MC. The firm should reduce output. It should not close down, however, because an economic profit can be earned.

Firm	Price	MR	TR	Q	TC	MC	ATC	AVC
C	5.00	4.00	30 000	6,000	30 600	4.00	5.10	5.05

Recommendation: 4
Justification: MR = MC. The firm should shut down because it is unable to cover its variable costs of production.

4. a. See the table below.

Price	*Quantity*	*TR*	*MR*
\$8	2	\$16	—
\$7	3	\$21	\$5
\$6	4	\$24	\$3
\$5	5	\$25	\$1
\$4	6	\$24	–\$1
\$3	7	\$21	–\$3

b. Total revenue rises by only \$1 (MR = \$1) because price had to fall to \$5 to increase sales by one unit. \$5 of extra revenue were generated by selling the extra unit. Unfortunately, though, the other 4 units, each of which could have been sold at \$6, had to have \$1 trimmed off their price tag. So the seller lost \$4 on those. Net gain was \$1.

5. a. See the table below.

Sales (units)	*Price (per meal)*	*Total Cost*	*MR*	*MC*
4 000	\$1.50	\$6 100	—	—
5 000	\$1.40	\$6 400	\$1.00	\$0.30
6 000	\$1.30	\$6 800	\$0.80	\$0.40
7 000	\$1.20	\$7 300	\$0.60	\$0.50
8 000	\$1.10	\$8 000	\$0.40	\$0.70
9 000	\$1.00	\$9 000	\$0.20	\$1.00
10 000	\$0.90	\$10 200	\$0.00	\$1.20

b. \$1.20, where MR < MC for the next step of 1000 units.
c. \$1.00, where P = MC.
d. Between 90¢ and \$1.00. The demand curve is unitarily elastic where MR is zero. Confirm this with the total revenue test—as price increases, total revenue remains constant in this price range.

6. The cost diagram: MC doesn't intersect AVC or ATC at their minimum points. The diagram shows a short-run situation, since ATC – AVC = AFC. Fixed costs can show up only in the short run.
The revenue diagram: The down-sloping MC curve should be labelled MR. MR = MC tells us that this firm is maximizing profits—as we'd expect. At that output level (Q*), price equals average cost. Normal profits are being earned. However, a section of the demand curve lies above ATC, which must mean that economic profits are possible. Therefore, the demand and the marginal revenue curves don't agree.

7. a. Where MR = MC.
   b. It is unknown because there is no demand curve shown.
   c. The demand curve is downward sloping and above the MR curve. (Note for perfectionists: With a straight-line demand curve, the slope of MR is twice as steep as that of the demand curve.) Remember that the quantity variable is *already determined*: only that knife-edge vertical line rising from the "20 units" output level is of any significance. Read off the price when output is 20 units.
   d. The final diagram may reveal normal *or* economic profits or losses being made—it depends on where you've positioned the demand curve and the ATC curve.
   e. No! The monopolist would leave the industry. Only two cases are possible, the one with economic profits being the typical representation of a monopolist.

8. This industry is not a natural monopoly. To see why not, sketch an average cost curve, with its minimum value of $1 occurring at 1000 units of output per month. Now draw in the demand curve. At 1000 units of output, the price would be $3. Also, the demand curve slices through the cost curve when the cost curve is rising—a sure sign that this is not a natural monopoly.

9. a. Total revenue is the same at all price levels.
   b. Marginal revenue will be constant at zero. This would be shown as a horizontal line drawn on the quantity axis.
   c. Because, as price rises, TR neither rises (inelastic demand) nor falls (elastic demand), demand is unitarily elastic at all points.
   d. See the table below.

Price	*Quantity*	*TR*	*MR*
$24	1	24	—
$12	2	24	0
$8	3	24	0
$6	4	24	0
$4	6	24	0
$3	8	24	0
$2	12	24	0

e. See the diagram below.

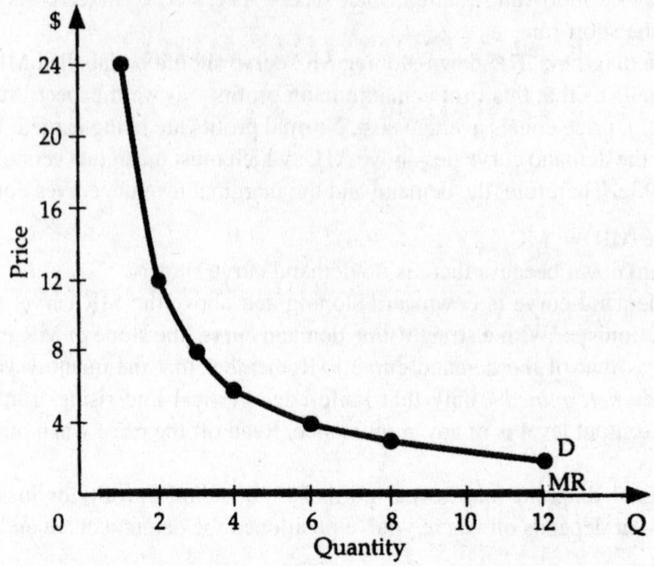

Demand has a regular shape (downward sloping), although it is a curving line instead of a straight line. Marginal revenue, though, is unusual—it graphs along the horizontal axis because it is always zero.

f. Marginal cost is the additional cost caused by increasing output by one unit. It can't be zero (if, as is usually assumed, inputs are infinitely divisible).

g. Do you see a problem? In this unusual case, MR doesn't seem to equal MC at any level of output. The solution? The firm gets the same total revenue at each output level so, to maximize profits, it will produce one unit—enough to get the revenue but where total costs are minimized. Think about it: MR for the first unit is $24, since TR must be zero when none are sold. (Notice we've broken the "rectangular hyperbola" assumption.) Rest assured that your "MR = MC" profit-maximization rule will work for all cases you'll have to analyse. This example is merely to challenge your understanding.

14 Monopolistic Competition and Oligopoly

OBJECTIVES: POINT BY POINT

After completing this chapter, you should be able to accomplish the objectives listed below.

General Comment

As you read through this chapter, you will find it helpful to keep in mind the classifications made by **industrial organization** economists. They classify their investigations into an industry under three broad categories:

a. Market structure: How many firms are there? Are there economies of scale? How big are the four, or eight, largest firms?
b. Conduct: How do firms behave? How are prices set? Do firms advertise?
c. Performance: Is the industry efficient? Does it promote growth?

Pose questions like these as you examine monopolistic competition and oligopoly (and monopoly).

OBJECTIVE 1: Describe monopolistically competitive market structure.

Monopolistic competition is characterized by a large number of firms, none of which can control market price, but which produce differentiated products. There are no barriers to entry in monopolistic competition. Restaurants are an excellent example.

Product differentiation (making one's product appear unique) is important in monopolistic competition, and advertising can be an important aid in making the firm's or industry's demand curve less elastic. Supporters of advertising argue that the firm must make consumers aware of their products and differentiate its product from those of its competitors; opponents claim that advertising contains little information, distorts consumer preferences, and is wasteful. There is no clear answer one way or the other. (page 321)

> **Right Answers in Economics:** Harry Truman, the U.S. president, once wished for a "one-handed economist." On all issues his economic experts invariably told him "on the one hand, this and, on the other hand, that." Economics often gives "maybe" answers—in the current chapter, for example, advertising has benefits *and* costs.
>
> **Product Differentiation:** Keep in mind that advertising and expectations play a powerful role in product differentiation, as the following (true) story shows. Regulars in a bar were firm supporters of one or the other of the two brands of cheap Scotch offered. Sometimes, the bar would run out of the favourite brand of one faction, and its patrons would unwillingly have to consume the other. Invariably, expressing dissatisfaction, they swore that they could tell the difference. The point is that they drank with their eyes: both bottles contained the *same* brand of Scotch. The barman topped them up before opening time—using a third, even cheaper, brand.

Local radio is another example of monopolistic competition-the air waves are abuzz with radio stations. However, in major metropolitan areas, despite the fact that there is a wider range of choices , a large number of radio stations tend to bunch up at the lower end with playlists that make them virtually undistinguishable from those of their competitors. In order to move to the city's premium group, radio stations must initiate a change in their format: a "new" product (music). However, because barriers to switching formats in this monopolistically competitive industry are low, other stations tend to follow suit with their own similar actions.

> **TIP:** Monopoly has *one* firm, oligopoly a *few*, perfect competition and monopolistic competition *many*. The distinguishing characteristic of monopolistic competition is product differentiation. Except for the downward-sloping demand and marginal revenue curves, the perfectly and monopolistically competitive short-run and long-run stories are very similar. Monopolistic competition differs from monopoly and oligopoly in that firms in these industries can't affect the market price by virtue of their size. The oligopolist may or may not differentiate its product—as with most things in oligopoly, it depends.

> **TIP:** Keep in mind clear examples of each market structure:
>
> a. Perfect competition: the stock market (unless there is insider trading), word processing.
>
> b. Monopolistic competition: your local restaurant scene.
>
> c. Oligopoly: De Beers, the diamond cartel that functions almost like a monopoly; OPEC, the cartel with a fairly homogeneous product (oil); the domestic airline industry, which tries to differentiate.
>
> d. Pure monopoly: Burroughs-Wellcome, the developers of the anti-AIDS drug, AZT.

Practice

1. Each of the following is a characteristic of monopolistic competition except
   A. many firms.
   B. product differentiation.
   C. no barriers to entry.
   D. mutual interdependence.

   ANSWER: D. See p. 321. Mutual interdependence characterizes oligopoly.

2. In monopolistic competition, firms achieve some market power
   A. by growing larger.
   B. by merging with other firms into a cartel.
   C. by establishing barriers to exit from the industry.
   D. through product differentiation.

   ANSWER: D. See p. 322.

3. Monopolistic competition differs from perfect competition because in monopolistic competition
   A. there are few firms.
   B. there are no barriers to entry.

C. there are many firms.
D. firms can differentiate their products.

ANSWER: D. See the list of characteristics on p. 321.

OBJECTIVE 2: Outline the basic issues in the debate over the impact of product differentiation and advertising on social welfare.

The advocates of free and open competition believe that differentiated products and advertising give the market system its vitality and are the basis of its power. They are the only ways to begin to satisfy the enormous range of tastes and preferences in a modern economy. Product differentiation also helps to ensure high quality and efficient production, while advertising provides consumers with valuable information on product availability, quality and price.

The critics argue product differentiation and advertising result in waste and inefficiency. Advertising raises the cost of products and contains very little information. (page 324)

OBJECTIVE 3: Explain the formal model of profit maximization under monopolistic competition.

Graphically, monopolistic competition is similar to Chapter 13's monopoly picture. Demand is downward sloping, as in monopoly, but more elastic because of the many close substitutes for the monopolistic competitor's product. Profit maximization occurs at the production level where marginal revenue is equal to marginal cost. Short-run profits or losses are possible. In the long run, normal profits must prevail due to easy entry into, and exit from, the industry. Economic profits attract new firms which, in turn, lessen the demand for each firm's product, driving the demand curve leftward towards the average cost curve and normal profits. (page 325)

> **TIP:** The "cost diagram" for monopolistic competition and oligopoly is the same as that for perfect competition and monopoly—it's the demand side that's different. Draw the cost curves first, then fit in the demand and marginal revenue curves to suit your needs.

> **Graphing Pointer:** In monopolistic competition, the long-run picture must have the demand curve just touching the average cost curve—MR = MC at that same output level!

> **Graphing Pointer:** See Application 9 below.

Practice

4. Monopolistic competition differs from perfect competition because, unlike the perfect competitor, the monopolistically competitive firm
   A. faces a perfectly inelastic demand curve.
   B. can earn positive economic profit in the short run and in the long run.
   C. cannot earn positive economic profit even in the short run.
   D. does not have the same marginal revenue at every output level.

   ANSWER: D. Because demand is downward sloping for the monopolistically competitive firm, marginal revenue will lie below it.

5. Unlike a monopolist, a monopolistically competitive firm
   A. can earn positive economic profit in the short run but not in the long run.
   B. has a downward sloping marginal revenue curve.
   C. can never cover its minimum average cost in the long run.
   D. may sell to many buyers.

   ANSWER: A. Easy entry into the market will compete away any short-run economic profits.

6. In monopolistic competition, when profits are being maximized, the price
   A. equals marginal revenue.
   B. exceeds marginal cost.
   C. is less than marginal revenue.
   D. equals marginal cost.

   ANSWER: B. To maximize profits, MR = MC. Because price exceeds MR, price exceeds MC.

7. The monopolistically competitive firm's demand curve will be ________ elastic than that of the perfectly competitive firm. The monopolistically competitive market demand curve will be downward sloping, ________ the market demand curve in perfect competition.
   A. more, like.
   B. more, unlike.
   C. less, like.
   D. less, unlike.

   ANSWER: C. Given product differentiation, the degree of substitutability will be less than it is in perfect competition. The market demand curve is downward sloping in both market structures. The *firm*'s demand curve is horizontal in perfect competition.

Use the following diagram to answer the next eight questions. This diagram depicts a monopolistically competitive firm.

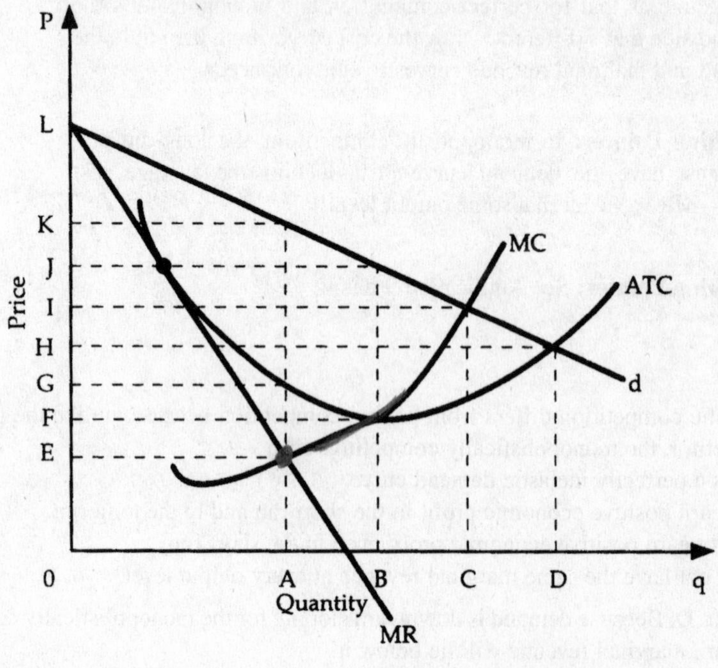

8. The profit-maximizing output level is
   A. OA.
   B. OB.
   C. OC.
   D. OD.

   ANSWER: A. This is the output level where MR = MC.

9. The profit-maximizing price is
   A. OE.
   B. OF.
   C. OG.
   D. OK.

   ANSWER: D. Use the demand curve to determine price.

10. This firm will earn a total economic profit of
    A. OA x OG.
    B. OA x OK.
    C. OA x GK.
    D. OA x EK.

    ANSWER: C. Total economic profit equals (P – ATC) x q.

11. This diagram depicts a monopolistic competitor in the
    A. short run, because marginal cost is less than average total cost at the profit-maximizing output level.
    B. short run, because economic profits are being earned.
    C. long run, because no fixed costs are shown.
    D. long run, because the firm is maximizing its profits.

    ANSWER: B. As shown in question 10, this firm is earning an economic profit. Because of easy entry into the industry, such a circumstance cannot be maintained in the long run.

12. In the long run, firms will __________ this industry and, for the typical firm, demand will equal __________.
    A. enter, marginal cost.
    B. enter, average total cost.
    C. exit, marginal cost.
    D. exit, average total cost.

    ANSWER: B. Firms enter, attracted by short-run economic profits. See p. 328.

13. In the long run, this firm's demand curve will shift to the __________ and become more __________.
    A. right, inelastic.
    B. right, elastic.
    C. left, inelastic.
    D. left, elastic.

    ANSWER: D. Each firm will lose some of its market share as firms enter the industry. Demand will become more elastic because of the larger number of substitutes.

14. In the long run, this firm's marginal revenue curve will shift to the __________ and become more __________.
    A. right, inelastic.
    B. right, elastic.
    C. left, inelastic.
    D. left, elastic.

ANSWER: D. See the answer to question 13 above. Demand and marginal revenue are linked. If you can't see why, review pp. 300–303.

15. Assuming that the cost curves of this typical firm remain unchanged, in the long run, there will be ________ firms in this industry, each producing _______ output.
    A. more, more.
    B. more, less.
    C. fewer, more.
    D. fewer, less.

    ANSWER: B. Given short-run profits, more firms will enter the industry. If MR shifts left and MC remains unchanged, the profit-maximizing output level will decrease.

OTHER RELATED POINTS: Identify and analyze the factors in monopolistic competition that cause inefficiency and resource misallocation.

The presence of monopolistic competition has some welfare consequences. Because the firm produces where MR = MC and, because price is greater than MR, price is greater than marginal cost at the profit-maximizing output level. This is inefficient because society wants production to occur up to the point where P = MC. In the long run, because demand is downward sloping, average cost is not minimized—or, to put it another way, resources are not used to their maximum efficiency—there is excess plant capacity. Note, though, that despite the inefficiencies generated by this market structure, there are benefits springing from an extensive menu of choices. (page 328)

Practice

16. Peter's Pan Pizzeria is a monopolistically competitive firm. In the short run, Peter is producing at the output that minimizes his average total cost. In the long run, Peter will ________ production, and average total cost will ________ (assuming constant returns to scale in the pizza industry).
    A. increase, increase.
    B. increase, remain unchanged.
    C. decrease, increase.
    D. decrease, remain unchanged.

    ANSWER: C. Try drawing this one. Peter must be earning economic profits. Where ATC is minimized, ATC = MC. To maximize profits, MC = MR. MR, though, must be less than price; therefore, ATC must be less than price. Firms will enter the industry. Peter's market share will contract and his average costs will increase.

17. Monopolistic competition
    A. is efficient because entry is unrestricted and only normal profits can be earned in the long run.
    B. is efficient because society receives as much of the good as is demanded.
    C. is not efficient because too little output is produced at too high a cost.
    D. is not efficient because there are too many small firms, each involved with a small share of the entire market.

    ANSWER: C. In long-run equilibrium, the typical firm does not operate where its costs per unit are minimized. Also, the profit-maximizing output level results in too little of the good being produced. Options A and D also describe perfect competition.

OBJECTIVE 4: Define oligopoly.

Oligopoly is the market structure with a "few" interdependent firms, each having market power and exerting strong barriers to entry. The behaviour of one firm in an oligopolistic industry depends on the reactions of the others. Because the actions of each firm depend on the expected reactions of its rivals, this market structure is notoriously complex.

OBJECTIVE 5: Analyze price and output decisions using a variety of oligopoly models. (page 329)

Models, such as the kinked demand-curve model, have been devised to display the interdependence. Collusion and price leadership are attractive strategies. The concept of a "perfectly contestable market" suggests that if there is free entry into and exit from the industry and that capital is very mobile, the oligopolists will behave like perfectly competitive firms. (page 329)

TIP: The best way to see why the MR curve must have a gap in the kinked demand-curve model is by extending the two demand curves back to the "price" axis and then drawing the associated MR curves from there. Remember that the MR curve is twice as steep as the demand curve, so the demand curve will, in each case, hit the horizontal axis at a quantity twice as great as that for marginal revenue. The existence of the gap is then a matter of geometry.

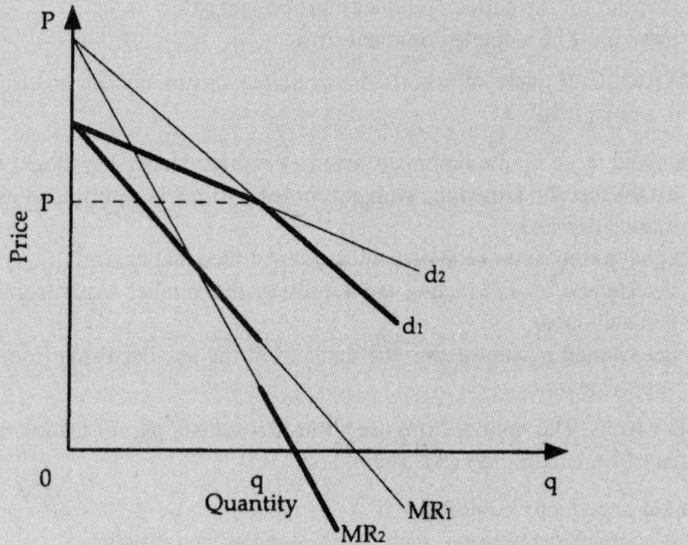

Practice

18. Monopolistically competitive firms differ from oligopolists in that each monopolistically competitive firm
    A. faces a downward-sloping demand curve, but an oligopolist does not.
    B. tries to differentiate its products from those of its rivals, but an oligopolist does not.
    C. may compete with others on price, but an oligopolist never does.
    D. is small relative to the size of its industry; an oligopolist frequently is large relative to the size of its industry.

ANSWER: D. There are many firms in monopolistic competition, few in oligopoly.

19. Olga, an oligopolist, faces a kinked demand curve for her goods. She believes that her competitors will ________ their prices if she lowers her price and will ________ their prices if she raises her price.
    A. lower, raise.
    B. lower, not raise.
    C. not lower, raise.
    D. not lower, not raise.

    ANSWER: B. If Olga lowers her price, her rivals may lower price too—she gains a few extra customers. If Olga raises her price, her rivals may not—she loses many customers.

20. If profit-maximizing oligopolists collude, the result is the same as if the industry were
    A. monopolistically competitive.
    B. perfectly competitive.
    C. a monopoly.
    D. using price leadership.

    ANSWER: C. Several profit-maximizing oligopolists operating together are the equivalent of a monopolist. See p. 330.

21. For a cartel to operate,
    A. the members must be producing a homogeneous (standard) product.
    B. demand for the cartel's product must be elastic.
    C. demand for the cartel's product must be inelastic.
    D. there must be a single dominant firm.

    ANSWER: C. If many substitutes are available, customers can go elsewhere when there is a price hike.

22. The demand faced by the dominant firm in the price-leadership model is
    A. established first, then the demand for other firms is determined based on total market demand.
    B. equal to the sum of the demand curves of the smaller firms.
    C. determined by subtracting the supply of the smaller firms from the market-demand curve.
    D. determined by subtracting the demand of the smaller firms from the market-supply curve.

    ANSWER: C. The smaller firms are allowed to satisfy part of market demand—the dominant firm handles the rest. See p. 332.

23. A market is perfectly contestable if
    A. it contains many firms, each with a standardized product.
    B. entry to and exit from the industry are costless.
    C. each firm has a small share of the market, and only normal profits are earned in the long run.
    D. only normal profits are earned in the short run and in the long run.

    ANSWER: B. The main point about contestable markets is that it is easy to get into them and to get out of them.

24. Of the following, ________ is most likely to have contestable markets?
    A. nuclear power generation.
    B. trucking.
    C. dentistry.
    D. automobile manufacturing.

ANSWER: B. It is fairly cheap to enter and leave the trucking industry.

Use the following information and pay off matrix to answer the two questions. Lewis and Clark each run a cement business. Demand is not strong enough to justify raising price, so each is limited to maintaining the current price or reducing it. The following table gives the pay off matrix.

Clark's Action

		Cut price	*Maintain price*
Lewis's Action	*Cut price*	Lewis's profit $80 000	Lewis's profit $40 000
		Clark's profit $80 000	Clark's profit $60 000
	Maintain price	Lewis's profit $60 000	Lewis's profit $20 000
		Clark's profit $40 000	Clark's profit $20 000

25. Lewis's dominant strategy
    A. is to wait and see what Clark does.
    B. is to maintain her price.
    C. is to cut her price.
    D. is unknown, because it depends on her risk preference.

    ANSWER: C. If Lewis maintains her price, her profit may be as low as $20 000. If she cuts her price, the lowest profit she should get is $40 000. Clark's position is identical. We are looking at a potential price war.

26. If Lewis and Clark agree to collude to improve each firm's pay off, the best short-run profit-maximizing strategy for Lewis is to agree that
    A. neither firm will cut price and then to honour the agreement.
    B. neither firm will cut price and then cut price anyway.
    C. both firms will cut price and to honour the agreement.
    D. both firms will cut price and then cut price anyway.

    ANSWER: B. If Clark maintains his price and Lewis cheats, Lewis gains. If Clark cheats (and cuts price), then Lewis's lowering of her price is still the optimal choice for her. (Note: In the long run, Lewis and Clark would be better advised to honour their collusive agreement.)

OTHER RELATED POINTS: Describe ways in which an oligopolistic industry may be inefficient.

There is some debate regarding the efficiency of oligopolists. Oligopoly tends to be inefficient because output is restricted to less than that which society would prefer (P > MC). Firms may end up in wasteful deadlocks. Product differentiation and advertising may also be wasteful. Although they may reap economies of scale and foster technological improvements, the balance of opinion is that oligopolies allocate resources inefficiently.

(page 338)

Practice

27. In oligopoly, an inefficient output level will occur except in the
    A. cartel model.
    B. perfectly contestable market model.
    C. Cournot model.
    D. kinked demand-curve model.

ANSWER: B. Because it is easy to enter and leave the industry, the threat of competition forces oligopolists to behave efficiently. See p. 336.

28. In the kinked demand curve model, the oligopolist is
    A. efficient, because he or she can maintain a stable price even if average cost increases.
    B. efficient, because he or hse can maintain a stable price even if marginal cost increases.
    C. inefficient, because he or she fails to produce the output level at which society's welfare is maximized.
    D. inefficient, because changes in demand are not reflected by changes in price and output level.

ANSWER: C. The oligopolist will produce where MR = MC. This is not where P = MC.

PRACTICE TEST

I. MULTIPLE CHOICE QUESTIONS. Select the option that provides the single best answer.

_____ 1. In the long run, economic profits earned in a monopolistically competitive industry will cause _________ the industry and a ___________ shift of the typical firm's demand curve.
   A. entry into, rightward.
   B. entry into, leftward.
   C. exit from, rightward.
   D. exit from, leftward.

_____ 2. Industrial organization economists analyse industries by considering three broad categories. Which of the following is not one of those categories?
   A. behaviour.
   B. market structure.
   C. performance.
   D. efficiency.

_____ 3. Each of the following is a characteristic of monopolistic competition except
   A. products are differentiated.
   B. there is a large number of sellers.
   C. firms will charge the same price.
   D. each firm has some degree of market power.

_____ 4. Each of the following is an example of product differentiation except
   A. advertising.
   B. after-sales service.
   C. development of "new and improved" products.
   D. producing where marginal revenue equals marginal cost.

Bonnie and Clyde are caught robbing a store. They may be charged with armed robbery—a more serious crime. The police can't prove armed robbery unless one of the pair confesses to it. The following table gives the "punishment matrix."

		Clyde's Action	
		Don't Confess	*Confess*
Bonnie's Action	*Don't Confess*	Both get 2 years in jail	Clyde gets 6 months Bonnie gets 10 years
	Confess	Clyde gets 10 years Bonnie gets 6 months	Both get 6 years in jail

_____ 5. If both Bonnie and Clyde adopt the strategies that minimize the damage that the other can do, then
A. neither will confess.
B. both will confess.
C. only Clyde will confess.
D. only Bonnie will confess.

_____ 6. Price leadership
A. makes tacit collusion difficult to detect.
B. is a strategy used in monopolistic competition.
C. is possible only when homogeneous goods are marketed.
D. is possible only when differentiated goods are marketed.

_____ 7. A kinked demand curve
A. discourages non-price competition.
B. should make prices more stable.
C. should make prices less stable.
D. is present only in the case of two firms—a duopoly.

_____ 8. All oligopolistic industries
A. have significant barriers to entry.
B. practise product differentiation.
C. have fewer than 16 firms.
D. have firms large enough to exercise some control over the market price.

_____ 9. A group of firms that get together to set price and output jointly is called
A. an oligopoly.
B. a duopoly.
C. a cartel.
D. a price-leadership industry.

_____ 10. An oligopoly in which entry or exit is costless fits which theory best?
A. the kinked demand-curve model.
B. the perfectly contestable market.
C. game theory.
D. collusion.

_____ 11. For a cartel to operate, which of the following conditions need not be present?
A. the members must comply with the cartel's rules.
B. the members must be firms of similar size.
C. demand must be inelastic.
D. there must be few substitutes for the cartel's product.

_____ 12. The Cournot model assumes all of the following except that
A. each firm anticipates the price movements of the other.
B. there are only two firms in the industry.
C. both firms maximize profits.
D. each firm takes the output of the other as given.

The following diagram is for a typical firm in a monopolistically competitive industry. Use it to answer the next six questions.

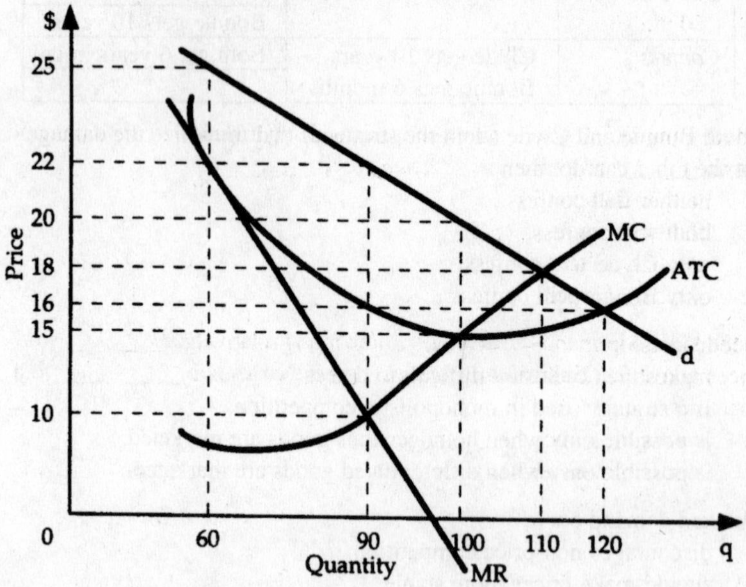

_____ 13. The profit-maximizing price is
A. $10.
B. $15.
C. $18.
D. $22.

_____ 14. The equilibrium output for this firm is
A. 60.
B. 90.
C. 100.
D. 110.

_____ 15. This firm is making an economic profit of
A. $540.
B. $1040.
C. $420.
D. $630.

_____ 16. In the long run, we would expect to see the
A. demand curve shift to the right and the average total cost curve shift down.
B. demand curve shift to the left and the marginal cost curve shift up.
C. marginal revenue curve shift to the left and the average total cost curve shift up.
D. marginal revenue curve shift to the left and the demand curve shift to the left.

_____ 17. The efficient output level (the one that would maximize consumer welfare) is
A. 60 units.
B. 90 units.
C. 100 units.
D. 110 units.

_____ 18. In long-run equilibrium, the firm produces an output of 70 units. Assuming no change in the position of the cost curves, the firm's excess capacity is
A. 10 units.
B. 20 units.
C. 30 units.
D. 40 units.

_____ 19. Advertising should make the monopolistically competitive firm's demand curve _______ and marginal revenue curve _______.
A. flatter, flatter.
B. flatter, steeper.
C. steeper, flatter.
D. steeper, steeper.

_____ 20. In the kinked demand-curve model, demand is relatively _________ at prices above the kink because competitors are expected _________ to a price increase.
A. elastic, to respond.
B. elastic, not to respond.
C. inelastic, respond.
D. inelastic, not to respond.

Use the following information to answer the next two questions.

The Upper Crust Bakery Company, a monopolistically competitive firm, produces 10 000 loaves per day at a price of $2.00 per loaf. Marginal revenue and marginal cost are each $1.70. At that production level, total cost is $30 000, and total fixed cost is $7500.

_____ 21. Upper Crust should
A. maintain the current output level, making short-run economic profits.
B. maintain the current output level, despite making short-run economic losses.
C. increase output level to the point where price equals marginal cost.
D. shut down.

_____ 22. Relative to the individual firm's demand curve in the short run, we would predict that the surviving bakeries will face demand curves that are
A. further to the right and more elastic.
B. further to the right and less elastic.
C. further to the left and more elastic.
D. further to the left and less elastic.

_____ 23. The only oligopoly model in which price equals marginal cost in the long run is
A. the Cournot model.
B. the contestable markets model.
C. the price-leadership model
D. the kinked demand-curve model.

_____ 24. A firm that makes decisions according to the maximin criterion chooses the strategy that gives the
A. highest possible maximum loss to the firm.
B. highest possible minimum pay off to the firm.
C. lowest possible maximum loss to the firm.
D. lowest possible minimum pay off to the firm.

_____ 25. You are the manager of a monopolistically competitive office-cleaning firm. The firm is in long-run equilibrium. In an effort to boost sales and to distinguish your firm from its rivals, you launch an advertising campaign. What will be the effects of the advertising campaign (assuming that it is successful) as the firm moves to a new long-run equilibrium?

A. average cost will increase; demand and marginal revenue curves will shift right and become more elastic; price will increase.
B. average cost will increase; demand and marginal revenue curves will shift right and become less elastic; price will increase.
C. marginal cost will shift to the right; demand and marginal revenue curves will shift right and become more elastic; price will increase.
D. marginal cost will shift to the right; demand and marginal revenue curves will shift right and become less elastic; price will increase.

II. APPLICATION QUESTIONS.

1. Often, economists don't have complete demand schedules and cost curves—they must make do with a few numbers. Suppose that you have the following numbers for a Rose's Tea Shop, a firm in a monopolistically competitive industry.

Total Revenue = \$1200	Total Cost = \$700	Price = \$12
Marginal Revenue = \$10	Total Variable Cost = \$300	MC = \$6

Explain how you know that:

a. This firm is imperfectly competitive.
b. This firm is not maximizing profit.
c. This firm is operating in the short run.
d. The demand curve is further right than it will be in the long run.
e. There is excess capacity.
f. Sketch the diagram for this firm based on your information and your economic knowledge of cost and revenue curves. Put in numerical values where you can.

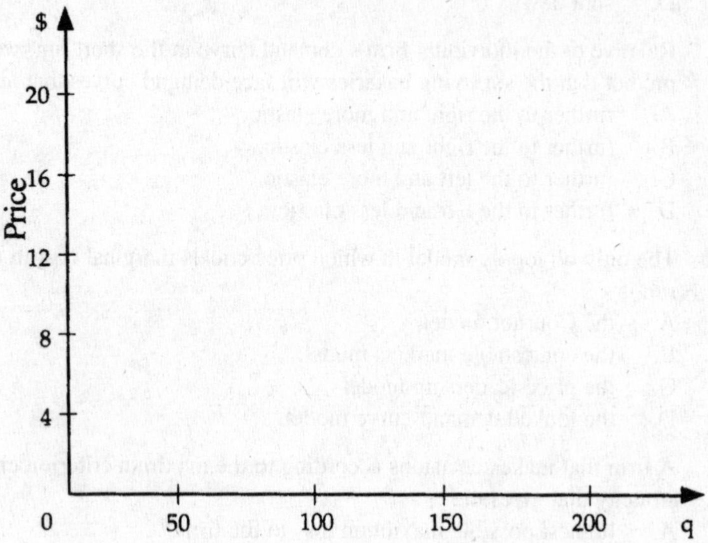

2. Suppose that you have the following table of numbers for a firm. You know that the firm is operating in a monopolistically competitive industry.

Output	Cost	Total Cost	Marginal Demanded	Quantity Price	Marginal Revenue
0	$28	____	0	$30	____
1	40	____	1	28	____
2	50	____	2	26	____
3	58	____	3	24	____
4	68	____	4	22	____
5	80	____	5	20	____
6	94	____	6	18	____
7	110	____	7	16	____
8	130	____	8	14	____
9	160	____	9	12	____

a. Calculate the marginal cost and marginal revenue values at each output level and enter them in the table.

b. Determine the profit-maximizing price and output level.

c. Calculate total economic profit.

d. Describe what will happen to the number of firms in this industry in the long run, and explain why.

e. Describe what will happen to this firm's demand curve in the long run, and explain why.

3. Watch 10 ads on TV; listen to 10 on the radio; read 10 in a weekly magazine and another 10 in the daily newspaper. Does the amount of information in each differ? Which medium seems to contain the most information? Which the least? Do the different media attract a similar mix of monopolistically competitive and oligopolistic firms? In which medium is oligopoly most prominent? In which are monopolistically competitive firms most important? Why do you think these differences occur?

4. Suppose you obtain a licence to sell ice cream on the beach. There is only one other licensed seller of ice cream on the beach. How would you respond to his or her presence? Where would you locate? How would you make your pricing decisions? Would you compete?

5. Lou and Howard own a small monopolistically competitive pizza parlour—The Nice Slice. Because of declining sales they have hired you as a consultant to examine their pricing and advertising strategy. You are provided with some information regarding The Nice Slice's daily demand under three conditions—when there is no advertising; when only The Nice Slice advertises; when all pizzerias advertise. You are also told that, when The Nice Slice advertises, it costs a flat fee of $20 per day.

	No Advertising		The Nice Slice Advertises		All Pizzerias Advertise	
Pizza Price	Quantity Demanded	Marginal Revenue	Quantity Demanded	Marginal Revenue	Quantity Demanded	Marginal Revenue
$16	3		7		5	
$15	4	____	8	____	6	____
$14	5	____	9	____	7	____
$13	6	____	10	____	8	____
$12	7	____	11	____	9	____
$11	8	____	12	____	10	____
$10	9	____	13	____	11	____

a. Complete the table.

Now that you have the revenue information, you ask Lou and Howard about their costs. Howard tells you that each pizza costs a constant $4 to make. Advertising costs are not included.

b. Determine the profit-maximizing daily output level and price for The Nice Slice under each of the three advertising conditions.

Condition	Price	Output
No advertising	____	____
The Nice Slice advertises	____	____
All pizzerias advertise	____	____

c. Calculate The Nice Slice's economic profit under each of the three conditions.

Condition	TR	TC	Profit
No advertising	____	____	____
The Nice Slice advertises	____	____	____
All pizzerias advertise	____	____	____

d. Complete your assignment by writing a brief report to Lou and Howard advising them on the best advertising strategy to adopt.

6. You have been called in to analyse the pricing strategy of Chewsday Gum, a brand of bubblegum operating in an oligopolistic non-collusive industry. You are given the following information regarding the firm's demand schedule. The firm's price is currently $1.40 per pack of gum. If the firm assumes that a price change will provoke no matching price change from rivals, the demand schedule is d1. If, however, any price change prompts a retaliatory price change from rivals, the relevant demand schedule is d2.

Price	(d1) Quantity Demanded	Marginal Revenue	(d2) Quantity Demanded	Marginal Revenue
$2.20	0		0	
$2.10	25	____	0	____
$2.00	50	____	0	____
$1.80	100	____	0	____
$1.60	150	____	0	____
$1.50	175	____	100	____
$1.40	200	____	200	____
$1.30	225	____	300	____
$1.20	250	____	400	____
$1.00	300	____	600	____

a. Complete the table.

b. Draw the kinked demand-curve diagram below.

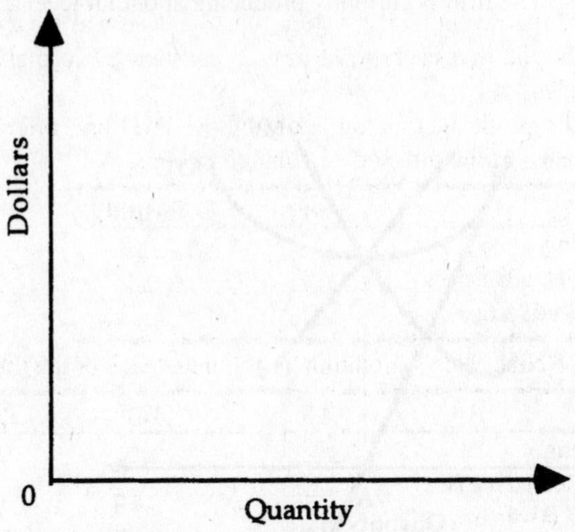

Jack and Ruby, the owners of Chewsday, tell you that their marginal cost is constant at $1.20. Total fixed costs are an additional $50.

c. Are Jack and Ruby making an economic profit?
d. Are Jack and Ruby maximizing profit?
e. Jack and Ruby ask for your recommendations. What would you suggest?
   i. Should they close down in the short run? Why?
   ii. What might happen if they raise their price by 10¢?

7. Examine the following graph which depicts a monopolistically competitive firm.

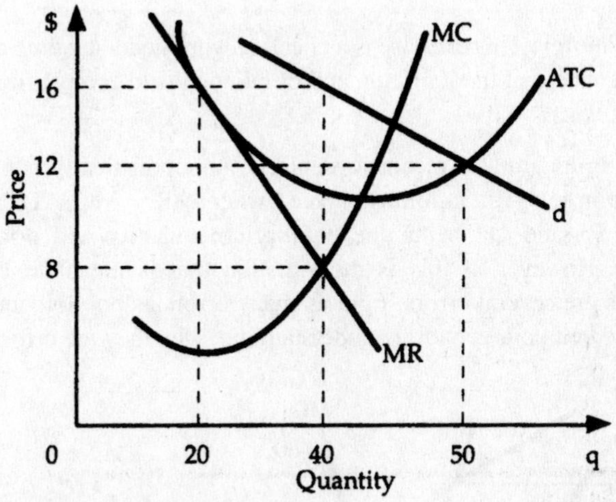

The profit-maximizing output level is ________. The price is $_______. Marginal revenue is $______. Total revenue is $______. Total cost is $_______. Total profit is $_______.

8. The firm represented by the following diagram is either monopolistically competitive or a monopoly. The firm is currently producing at output level A.

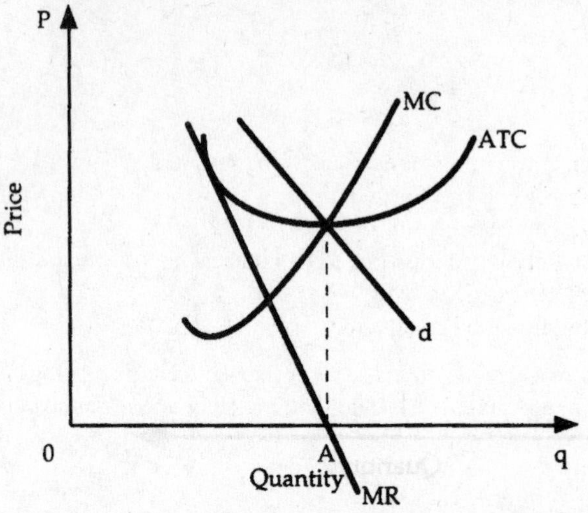

a. At output level A, is the firm maximizing profits?
b. What price is this firm charging currently? (Sketch your answer on the graph and label the price P_1.)
c. If different from P_1, sketch in the profit-maximizing price as P_2.
d. Is this a short-run or long-run situation, or can't you tell?
e. This is an *imperfectly* competitive firm. How do you know?
f. If this is the long run, what kind of imperfectly competitive industry is this, or can't you tell?
g. If the firm raises production past level A, what will happen to total revenue?

9.

Graphing Pointer: This exercise is a check on your understanding of graphs, the concept of the long run, and of monopolistic competition.

The following diagram is meant to depict a monopolistically competitive firm in long-run equilibrium (i.e., when MR = MC, ATC = Price) with P* and Q* being the equilibrium quantity and price respectively. However, if this is the situation that is meant to be shown, there are several errors. Find as many errors as possible and explain, based on your economic understanding, why they are errors.

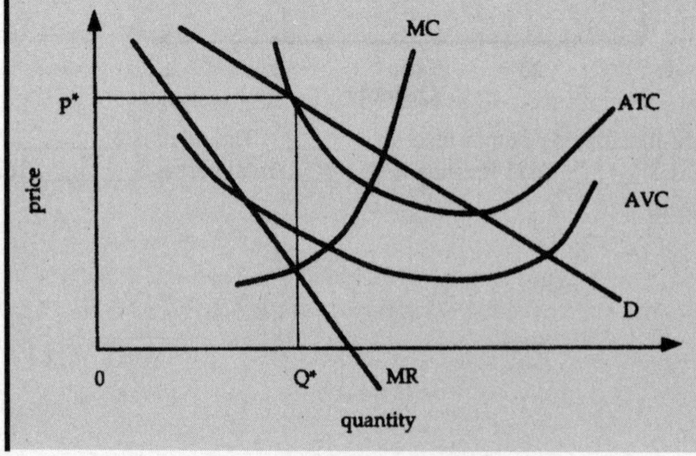

10. Here is a list of the major companies in the fast-food industry:
    a. McDonald's
    b. Burger King
    c. Taco Bell
    d. KFC
    e. Second Cup

    Here is a list of characteristics for each fast-food restaurant chain:
    U. The place to get good coffee and muffins.
    W. The place to get chicken.
    X. The fast-food place that kids love. The number-one fast-food restaurant.
    Y. The place to get Mexican food.
    Z. The other big fast-food restaurant.

    Note that the list of characteristics does not include advertising slogans, names of products, or corporate symbols. Despite that, match up the restaurant chain with its description.

ANSWERS AND SOLUTIONS

PRACTICE TEST

I. SOLUTIONS TO MULTIPLE CHOICE QUESTIONS

1. B. Economic profits attract new firms. Each firm will have a smaller market share, depicted by a leftward shift of the demand curve.

2. D. Efficiency is a yardstick of performance, rather than an organizational classification.

3. C. Typically, monopolistic firms, e.g., restaurants, do not charge the same price.

4. D. Producing where MR = MC is a guide to maximizing profits. It has nothing to do with product differentiation.

5. B. If Bonnie confesses, Clyde would minimize the damage by having confessed too. Six years is better than 10. Bonnie would argue similarly.

6. A. See p. 330.

7. B. The profit-maximizing oligopolist will produce where MR = MC. Because the MR curve has a gap at the existing output level, MC can increase or decrease and the same profit-maximizing output level and price will be sustained.

8. D. Influence over market price is a common feature. Many oligopolistic models assume high barriers to entry—the perfectly contestable markets model does not.

9. C. See p. 330. See OPEC.

10. B. In this theory, firms must have mobile and transferable resources that can be switched from one use, and one industry, to another. See p. 336.

11. B. In OPEC (a very successful and long-lasting cartel), some member countries, such as Saudi Arabia, are very large oil producers while others, such as Gabon and Ecuador, are comparatively small.

12. A. In the Cournot model, output is given. The two firms in the duopoly do not guess each other's price movements.

13. D. Profits are maximized where MR = MC. Given the output level, the equilibrium price, based on the position of the demand curve, will be $22.

14. B. Profits are maximized at the output level where MR = MC.

15. A. Economic profit = (P − ATC) x q = ($22 − $16)90 = $540.

16. D. The typical firm is earning an economic profit in the short run. The presence of economic profits will attract new firms, resulting in a reduction in each firm's market share. This change will affect demand and marginal revenue. See p. 327.

17. D. Consumer welfare is maximized at the output level where P = MC.

18. C. Average costs are minimized at an output level of 100 units. If, in the long run, the firm produces only 70 units, it has an excess capacity of 30.

19. D. Advertising is intended to make consumers more interested in purchasing a product and in making other rivals appear less attractive. At a given output level, demand should become less elastic (steeper curve), and this will have a similar effect on marginal revenue.

20. B. If the firm increases price, the assumption is made that rivals will not increase price. This would lead consumers to leave the firm that has raised its price in search of relatively low price alternatives.

21. D. TVC = TC – TFC = $30 000 – $7500 = $22 500.
AVC = TVC / q = $22 500 / 10 000 = $2.25. Because P is less than AVC, the firm should shut down.

22. B. As firms, such as Upper Crust, leave the industry, the market will be divided among a smaller number of firms, each with fewer substitutes.

23. B. See p. 336.

24. B. See p. 336.

25. B. Average cost will increase; demand and marginal revenue curves will shift right and become less elastic as the firm becomes more "different" from its rivals; price will increase (because costs have risen).

II. SOLUTIONS TO APPLICATION QUESTIONS

1.

Total Revenue = $1200	Total Cost = $700	Price = $12
Marginal Revenue = $10	Total Variable Cost = $300	MC = $6

a. This firm is imperfectly competitive because the demand curve is downward sloping. (P > MR)

b. This firm is not maximizing profit because MR ≠ MC. (Because MR is greater than MC, the firm should expand production.)

c. We know that this firm is operating in the short run for two reasons. First, there are fixed costs (which can occur only in the short run) because TC > TVC. Second, this monopolistically competitive firm is making economic profits, which can only happen in the short run.

d. The demand curve is further right than it will be in the long run because as new firms enter attracted by the economic profits, the firm's market share will erode.

e. There is excess capacity because the firm is not producing where average cost is minimized. If P = \$12 and TR = \$1200, the firm must be selling 100 units. If TC = \$700, average total cost must be \$7, which is higher than MC. If the extra cost is less than the average cost, then the average cost must be falling and, therefore, not being minimized.

f. See the diagram below.

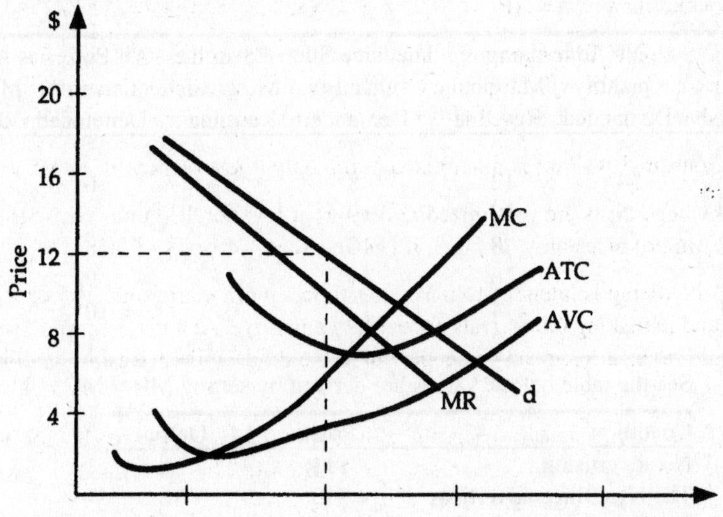

2. a. See the table below.

Output	Cost	Total Cost	Marginal Demanded	Quantity Price	Marginal Revenue
0	$28	12	0	$30	28
1	40	10	1	28	24
2	50	8	2	26	20
3	58	10	3	24	16
4	68	12	4	22	12
5	80	14	5	20	8
6	94	16	6	18	4
7	110	20	7	16	0
8	130	30	8	14	-4
9	160		9	12	

b. 5; 20.

c. \$20 (\$100 – \$80).

d. In the long run, firms will enter this industry, attracted by the higher-than-normal profits.

e. The demand curve will shift over to the left and become less inelastic because of the presence of more (and closer) substitutes. This move will continue until the demand curve is just tangential to the average total cost curve, and the firm is earning normal profits.

3. You should find that different companies and different types of companies use different media. National oligopolies (Coke, Petro-Canada, Air Canada, CIBC) use TV and magazines, for instance. Radio and newspapers tend to attract more local and more monopolistically competitive advertisers. Advertising represents a barrier to entry; by advertising lavishly, perhaps oligopolies prevent the entrance of credible rivals.

4. If you believe your ice cream to be as good as, or better than, that of your competitor, you should locate in the middle of the beach. This should be the most convenient spot for your customers and should not give your rival an overall advantage. You should get a 50% share of the customers. Any other location will bring you fewer customers. If you fear that you might lose in a price war with your rival, a quiet piece of negotiation might produce a cartel from which both sellers would gain.

5. a.

	No Advertising		The Nice Slice Advertises		All Pizzerias Advertise	
Pizza Price	Quantity Demanded	Marginal Revenue	Quantity Demanded	Marginal Revenue	Quantity Demanded	Marginal Revenue
$16	3		7		5	
$15	4	12	8	8	6	10
$14	5	10	9	6	7	8
$13	6	8	10	4	8	6
$12	7	6	11	2	9	4
$11	8	4	12	0	10	2
$10	9	2	13	–2	11	0

b. See the table below. Values are derived by setting MR = MC = 4.

Condition	Price	Output
No advertising	$11	8
The Nice Slice advertises	$13	10
All pizzerias advertise	$12	9

c.

Condition	TR	TC	Profit
No advertising	$88	$32	$56
The Nice Slice advertises	$130	$40 + $20	$70
All pizzerias advertise	$108	$36 + $20	$52

d. If The Nice Slice chooses to advertise, its short-run profits will be $70 per day, up from the current level of $56 per day. However, this is based on the assumption that the rival pizzerias do not retaliate by advertising too. If they do retaliate, The Nice Slice will end up with an economic profit of $52 per day, less than the current level of $56 per day. Because the downside loss is slight ($4 per day) and the gain substantial ($14 per day), advertising is a good strategy. The less probable it is that rivals will retaliate, the more advisable it is to advertise.

6. a.

	(d1)		(d2)	
Price	*Quantity Demanded*	*Marginal Revenue*	*Quantity Demanded*	*Marginal Revenue*
$2.20	0	—	0	—
$2.10	25	2.10	0	—
$2.00	50	1.90	0	—
$1.80	100	1.60	0	—
$1.60	150	1.20	0	—
$1.50	175	0.90	100	1.50
$1.40	200	0.70	200	1.30
$1.30	225	0.50	300	1.10
$1.20	250	0.30	400	0.90
$1.00	300	0.00	600	0.60

b. See the diagram below.

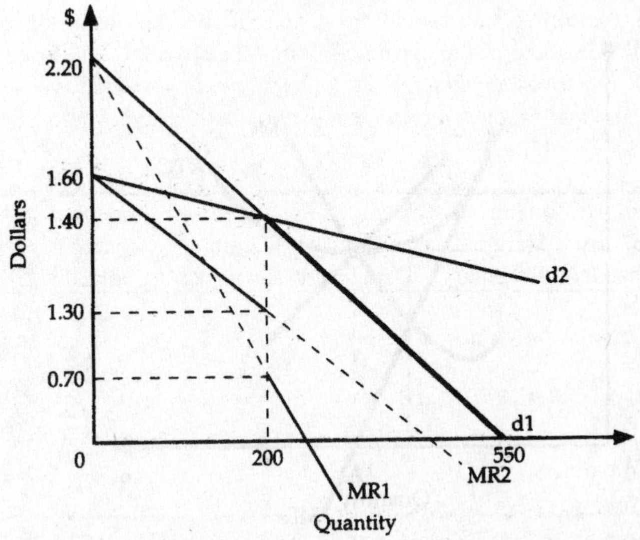

c. TC = TFC + TVC. TFC = \$50. TVC = \$1.20 x 200 = \$240. TC = \$290. TR = P x q = \$1.40 x 200 = \$280. Chewsday is making an economic loss of \$10.

d. Yes. MR is in the range between \$0.70 and \$1.30, as is MC (\$1.20).

e. i. They should not close down in the short run—their price is high enough to cover their variable costs.

ii. If they raise their price by 10¢, it is difficult to predict what will happen. It depends on the reaction of their rivals.
If their rivals do not react, they will operate along demand curve d1, with quantity demanded of 175, and marginal revenue of 90¢.

TC = TFC + TVC. TFC = \$50. TVC = \$1.20 x 170 = \$210. TC = \$260. TR = P x q = \$1.50 x 175 = \$262.50.

Chewsday, which is not maximizing at this point (MR < MC), would make an economic loss of \$2.50.
If their rivals do react, they will operate along demand curve d2, with quantity demanded of 100 and marginal revenue of \$1.50.
TC = TFC + TVC. TFC = \$50. TVC = \$1.20 x 100 = \$120. TC = \$170. TR = P x q = \$1.50 x 100 = \$150.

Chewsday, which is not maximizing at this point (MR > MC), would make an economic loss of \$20.00.
Raising price by 10¢ will still result in losses. How great those losses will be depends on the reaction of Chewsday's rivals.

7. a. q* = 40. p* = \$16. MR = \$8. TR = P x q = \$16 x 40 = \$640.
TC = ATC x q = \$12 x 40 = \$480.
Economic profit = TR - TC = \$640 - \$480 = \$160.

8. a. No. (MR < MC).

b. See the diagram below.
c. See the diagram below.

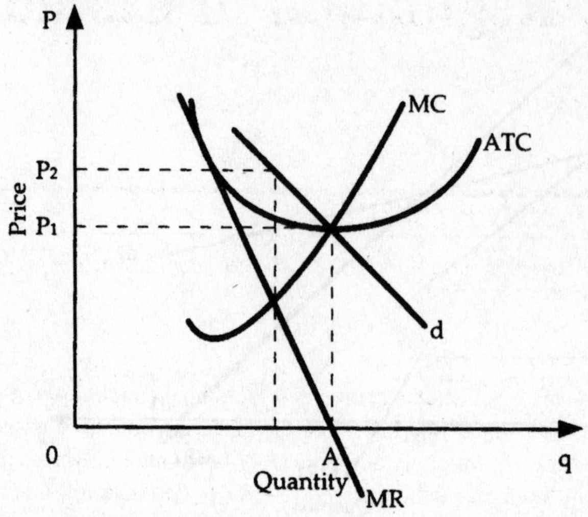

d. We can't tell yet if it's a long-run or short-run situation. See answer f. below.
e. The demand curve is downward sloping, so it can't be perfectly competitive.
f. It must be a monopoly. Monopolistically competitive firms make only normal profits in the long run.
g. Total revenue will fall because marginal revenue is negative.

9. Error 1: The MC curve should intersect both the ATC and the AVC curves at their minimum points. The "average-marginal" rule determines this.

   Error 2: The profit-maximizing output level (q*, not Q*) occurs, as shown, where MR = MC, but the demand and ATC intersection is inconsistent. At higher output levels, demand exceeds ATC, indicating economic profits, whereas at "Q*," only normal profits occur.

   Error 3: The existence of economic profits indicates that this is not a long-run situation. The existence of fixed costs (ATC - AVC) also reveals this to be a short-run diagram.

   Note: If you had trouble with this problem, review Application 5 in Chapter 13.

10. Here is my list, based on my perceptions.
   a. X.
   b. Z.
   c. Y.
   d. W.
   e. U.
   Even if your selections differ from those given here, it is of interest that you could distinguish among restaurant chains. What differences do you perceive and where do you think these differing perceptions have come from? They have probably been guided by effective advertising campaigns. Burger King's apparent lack of image poses a problem to the company.

15 Competition Policy And Regulation in Canada

OBJECTIVES: POINT BY POINT

After completing this chapter, you should be able to accomplish the objectives listed below.

General Comment

There's a lot of history and detail in this chapter—avoid being caught up in it. Make a time line of the main pieces of competition law; note the practices they tried to outlaw, and tie these into your knowledge of monopoly and oligopoly behaviour. Government bodies and subsequent acts to plug loopholes can be added to your potted history. This will help you to detect the evolution in competition law. On the whole, competition policy was not applied effectively prior to 1986. In addition, early approach to competition policy was legalistic. The current Competition Act focuses primarily on promoting competition and economic efficiency.

OBJECTIVE 1: Describe the goals of competition policy.

There are two possible goals of competition policy, one economic, the other political. The economic goal of competition is to ensure an efficient and equitable allocation of scarce resources. The political goal is to discourage the concentration of economic and political power in the hands of a few. (page 347)

Practice

1. Competition policy in Canada is designed to:
   A. deregulate natural monopolies.
   B. discourage competitive behaviour.
   C. promote rent seeking.
   D. promote competition.

   ANSWER: D. Competition law's main objective of ensuring efficient allocation of resources is pursued through promotion of competition.

OBJECTIVE 2: Identify the anti-competitive practices addressed in Canadian competition law.

The anti-competitive practices are business practices that reduce economic welfare. The following list identifies some of these practices: mergers, cartels; predatory pricing; resale price maintenance; price discrimination; misleading advertising; refusal to supply; abuse of dominant position, etc. (page 347)

Practice

2. Canadian competition policy is designed to stop:
   A. predatory pricing.
   B. misleading advertising.
   C. exclusive dealing.
   D. both A and B.

   ANSWER: D. Predatory pricing and misleading advertising are among the anti-competitive practices that Canadian competition policy aims to stop.

OTHER RELATED POINTS:

POINT 1: List and explain the contribution of various pieces of competition law passed since Confederation. State the goals of competition policy.

Competition policy in Canada was first introduced in a piece of legislation titled An Act for the Preservation and Suppression of Combinations in Restraint of Trade, passed through Parliament in 1889 and enacted into the Criminal Code of Canada in 1892. Successive amendments to competition policy expanded the coverage of competition law into several areas. The 1986 Act, however, introduced radical changes to competition law. (page 346)

Two pieces of legislation, the Competition Act and the Competition Tribunal, now govern Canadian competition policy. (page 351)

> **TIP:** The chapter discusses the issue of the enforcement as well as the weakness (ineffectivenss) of the competition law of 1889. Make lists of the main points here.

Practice

3. The 1889 legislation failed to consider explicitly any of the following as an offence except
   A. predatory pricing.
   B. monopoly.
   C. conspiracy.
   D. resale price maintenance.

   ANSWER: C. See p. 349.

4. The only case of merger before the Crown prior to 1945 involved
   A. Safeway and Woodward stores.
   B. Hoffmann and Laroche.
   C. Western Fruits and Vegetables.
   D. Sherman and Clayton.

   ANSWER: C. The case of merger between Safeway and Woodward dates back only to 1986. The other cases are fictitious.

5. Judgements of the Competition Tribunal are based on
   A. criminal law.
   B. civil law.
   C. verdicts given by the Ministry of Attorney General.
   D. earlier recommendations by Industry Canada.

   ANSWER: B. See p. 351.

6. In 1997 and 1998, announcements of a series of bank merger proposals dominated the news. Which of the following can potentially prevent these proposed mergers from happening?
   A. The Bank of Canada because the mergers would violate the course of monetary policy.
   B. Attorney General of Canada because the mergers would be in violation of the Criminal Code.
   C. The Bureau of Competition Policy.
   D. A Senate Act.

   ANSWER: C. The Competition Act of 1986 charges the Bureau of Competition Policy with operations and investigations called for under the Act. Mergers fall under the activities of the Bureau. However, the Federal Minister of Finance has the ultimate say in this matter.

7. Competition laws are based on the premise that
   A. regulation is the most efficient form of market control.
   B. competition is the best way to achieve efficiency.
   C. public ownership of the private means of production gives superior results than ownership by self-interested profit maximizers.
   D. as a firm increases its market share, it is able to reap the benefits of economies of scale.

   ANSWER: B. See p. 348.

8. The most important implication of the 1986 Act which places mergers under civil law and thereby the Competition Tribunal rather than the courts in charge of cases is that
   A the criminal cases become secondary to laws of land.
   B the Tribunal becomes an appointed chamber rather than an elected one.
   C for the first time in Canada, economic criteria can be used as the basis for making decisions.
   D the courts are found less strict than the Tribunal.

   ANSWER: C. See p. 352.

POINT 2: Identify the two major policy positions adopted by the government with respect to promoting/restricting competition within an industry exhibiting monopoly characteristics.

When imperfect competition fails to produce the efficient level of output, the government may choose to intervene to improve the allocation of society's resources. There are two apparently conflicting government stances—first, promotion of competition and restriction of market power through *competition law*, and second, restriction of competition by *regulation* of industries. (page 345)

9. The policy positions taken by the government with respect to imperfectly competitive industries are to __________ competition through competition law and to __________ competition through regulation.
   A. promote, promote.
   B. promote, restrict.
   C. restrict, promote.
   D. restrict, restrict.

   ANSWER: B. Broadly, competition law breaks up large companies into smaller units or prevents mergers, while regulation establishes a single supplier of a product and then controls the firm's behaviour.

OBJECTIVE 3: Outline the debate over competition policy.

Canadian competition policy is not without critics. The basic argument against competition policy is that it uses resources unnecessarily. International competition and efficient capital markets will ensure that monopoly profits do not last for long. Others argue that competition policy should focus more on political goals. Concentrations of power can undermine democracy, and competition policy should protect democratic institutions even if it does so with loss in economic welfare. (page 352)

OBJECTIVE 4: Identify the approaches to natural monopoly regulation.

Given large economies of scale, efficiency would require having only one firm—a natural monopoly—and then regulating it to prevent abuse of its monopoly power. With a natural monopoly, the government has three options:

a. set the efficient price (P = MC) and provide a subsidy, or
b. set price equal to average cost, or
c. impose a two-part tariff on each user of the monopoly's good or service.

(page 353)

OBJECTIVE 5: List the problems of regulation.

There are problems, however—trucking, airlines, and telecommunications (among others) have all been regulated although none, in fact, is a natural monopoly. Lack of information, lack of incentives to be efficient, and a surfeit of non-price competition dog the regulated industries. The Averch-Johnson effect refers to the tendency of a monopoly to accumulate excessive amounts of capital. Regulation has fallen from favour and gone into a decline in recent years. (page 354)

> **Effectiveness:** Don't assume that government intervention always has the desired effect—the Averch-Johnson effect should warn you that it may not.
>
> The critics of regulation have argued that deregulation and increased competition would better serve the public. Technological and institutional changes in the economy have put additional pressure on government to deregulate industries. Although, in the past, regulatory agencies were broadly regarded as critical to the health of the economy, many have ceased to exist or have been rendered practically irrelevant. Today, even the electric utility, which is the classic example of a natural monopoly, with large fixed costs, no close substitute, and producer of an essential product, is going through rapid deregulation.

Practice

10. The exception to the rule that competitive markets are the most efficient markets is that of the
    A. contestable market.
    B. natural monopoly.
    C. monopolistically competitive firm that does not practise price discrimination.
    D. cross-subsidizing oligopolist.

    ANSWER B. Natural monopolies gain benefits from economies of scale that, with competition, would be lost.

11. The ___________ involves setting price equal to marginal cost and providing a subsidy out of general government revenues.
  A. average-cost-pricing strategy.
  B. efficient-price strategy.
  C. price-discrimination strategy.
  D. fixed-cost service charge.

  ANSWER B. See p. 354.

12. The Averch-Johnson effect occurs in the presence of
  A. privatization, as stockholders attempt to maximize dividends.
  B. horizontal mergers, as firms accumulate additional productive capacity.
  C. the threat of anticombine action, as firms scale back profits.
  D. regulation, as the firm builds more capital than is necessary.

  ANSWER D. The Averch-Johnson effect refers to the tendency of regulated monopolies to accumulate more capital than is needed.

13. The Averch-Johnson effect typically occurs if
  A. profits are high enough in a regulated industry to justify additional capital accumulation.
  B. profits are so low in a regulated industry that additional capital accumulation is necessary.
  C. the regulated industry's rate of return is based on a percentage of fixed costs.
  D. the regulated industry's rate of return is based on a percentage of variable costs.

  ANSWER: C. See p. 354.

OBJECTIVE 6: State the case for and against deregulation.

The defenders of deregulation argue that regulation encourages rent seeking. They also argue that the public would be better served by deregulation and increased competition. Furthermore, technological changes introduce new substitutes that significantly reduce the market power of natural monopolies and make it increasingly difficult to keep competition at bay.

The critics argue that government involvement, whether in the form of regulation of competition, competition policy or Crown corporations, in the economy is essential. Unchecked monopoly power, collusion, and price fixing can be enormously expensive to society. Recent evidence suggests that deregulation in the hydro industry in Alberta and California is nothing short of a disaster. (page 357)

Practice

14. Which of the following Crown corporations has survived the recent wave of privatization?
  A. Canadian National Railway (CNR).
  B. Air Canada.
  C. Petro-Canada.
  D. CBC.

  ANSWER: D. CBC is the only crown corporation that has not been privatized.

A Look Ahead: Government Intervention

Enforcement of competition law and regulation are only two roles that the government plays in the economy. The next three chapters explore other areas of government involvement: externalities and public goods (Chapter 16), income distribution (Chapter 17), and taxation (Chapter 18).

PRACTICE TEST

I. MULTIPLE CHOICE QUESTIONS. Select the option that provides the single best answer.

_____ 1. In addition to regulating industries, governments, in Canada, have been able to restrict competition by
   - A. encouraging privatization.
   - B. cross-subsidization.
   - C. becoming directly involved in business via crown corporations.
   - D. enforcement of competition law.

_____ 2. In Canada, Crown corporations are normally created by
   - A. the federal government.
   - B. the provincial governments.
   - C. both levels of government.
   - D. replacing public enterprises.

_____ 3. In reference to the 1986 Competition Act, which of the following may be legal in Canada?
   - A. price fixing and predatory pricing.
   - B. price discrimination.
   - C. tied selling.
   - D. mergers within industries with substantial economies of scale.

_____ 4. One argument against competition is that it
   - A. prevents firms from maximizing profit and growing to become efficient.
   - B. cannot be sustained as the affected firms may take legal action against regulatory agencies.
   - C. is simply unnecessary in today's global economy as international competition ensures low prices and economic efficiency.
   - D. may result in the creation of a natural monopoly.

_____ 5. Regulation is made more difficult by
   - A. lack of information about the industry.
   - B. lack of incentives to be efficient.
   - C. excessive price competition.
   - D. both A and B.

_____ 6. Supporters of competition policy suggest
A. competition laws operate as a deterrent to actions against the public interest.
B. price discrimination intended to lessen competition is illegal.
C. the tendency to accumulate more capital than needed is outlawed.
D. both A and B.

_____ 7. Opponents of enforcement of anticombines legislation have suggested that it does all of the following except
A. penalize success.
B. reduce the ability to compete against domestic companies.
C. reduce the ability to compete against foreign companies.
D. limit the ability or willingness to undertake research and development.

_____ 8. Most natural monopolies have ______ fixed costs and ______ marginal costs.
A. high, high.
B. high, low.
C. low, high.
D. low, low.

_____ 9. Jack Swindell of Swindell and Chita (attorneys) charges $500 to attend to some probate matters for Olaf Olson. He charges Olga Oppenheimer $100 for the same services. This is an example of
A. price fixing.
B. competitive pricing.
C. price discrimination.
D. sex discrimination.

Use the following diagram, of a natural monopoly, to answer the next three questions.

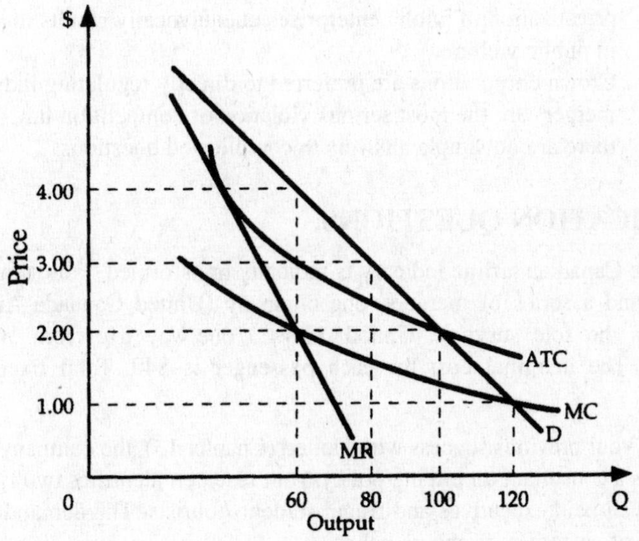

_____ 10. The profit-maximizing output level is ______ units, with a price of
A. 60, $4.
B. 80, $3.
C. 100, $2.
D. 120, $1.

_____ 11. At the most efficient output level, ATC is $1.75. To produce at this level, the company would require a subsidy of at least
A. $75.00
B. $90.00.
C. $150.00
D. $350.00.

_____ 12. At the output level where the company just receives a normal return on invested capital, the price would be $_____, and _____ units would be produced.
A. 4, 60.
B. 3, 80.
C. 2, 100.
D. 1, 120.

_____ 13. The cable television industry has been regulated according to the principle of average-cost pricing. A firm in this industry
A. will earn economic profits, although less than the amount it would have received without regulation.
B. will produce at the efficient output level.
C. will require a subsidy to continue in operation.
D. will earn a rate of return equal to normal profits.

_____ 14. A firm that uses excess profits from one part of its operation to cover losses in another part of its operation is engaged in
A. an activity known as cream skimming.
B. an activity known as cross subsidization.
C. creating the Averch-Johnson effect.
D. unfair marketing practices.

_____ 15. One important lesson that we should take from this chapter is that
A. privatization of public enterprises unequivocally results in an increase in public welfare.
B. Crown corporations are preferred to directly regulating industries.
C. mergers are the most serious violation of competition law.
D. there are no simple answers to complicated questions.

II. APPLICATION QUESTIONS.

1. In 1998, the Canadian airline industry is radically transformed. Following a vicious price war and a series of mergers, one company (United Canaada Airlines) has emerged as the sole survivor. United offers a one-way trip from Winnipeg to Edmonton. The marginal cost for each passenger is $40. Total fixed costs are $500 000.

Because of your previous success with United (Chapter 13), the company once more hires you as a consultant on pricing policy. Your research identifies two types of passengers—well-paid executives and frugal students/tourists. The demand by each of these types of customers is shown below.

Price of One-Way-Trip Tickets	One-Way-Trips Demanded Per Year Executives	Students/Tourists	Total Demand	"Total" Demand's Marginal Revenue
$140	7 000	0	____	____
$130	8 000	0	____	____
$120	9 000	1 000	____	____
$110	10 000	2 000	____	____
$100	11 000	3 000	____	____
$90	12 000	4 000	____	____
$80	13 000	5 000	____	____
$70	14 000	6 000	____	____
$60	15 000	7 000	____	____

Note: In each case, the demand curve is a straight line and can extend beyond this price range.

a. Complete the table by calculating total demand by both types of passengers and the associated marginal revenue values.
b. Determine the profit-maximizing output level and price.
c. Calculate the number of executives who will fly at this price.
d. Calculate the monetary value of the executives' consumer surplus.
e. Calculate the number of students/tourists who will fly at this price.
f. Calculate the monetary value of the students/tourists' consumer surplus.
g. Calculate the total monetary value of the passengers' consumer surplus.
h. Determine the level of economic profits.

United wishes to change its "one price for all" pricing policy in order to increase profits.

i. State, in words, a feasible policy to maximize United's profits. (Hint: Think of United as two firms: one servicing executives, the other servicing students and tourists.)
j. Complete the following table.

Price of One-Way-Trip Tickets	One-Way-Trips Demanded Per Year Executives	Student/Tourists	Executive Marginal Revenue	Student/Tourist Marginal Revenue
$140	7 000	0	____	____
$130	8 000	0	____	____
$120	9 000	1 000	____	____
$110	10 000	2 000	____	____
$100	11 000	3 000	____	____
$90	12 000	4 000	____	____
$80	13 000	5 000	____	____
$70	14 000	6 000	____	____
$60	15 000	7 000	____	____

k. Determine the profit-maximizing output level and price for executives.
l. Calculate the monetary value of the executives' consumer surplus.
m. Determine the profit-maximizing output level and price for students/tourists.
n. Calculate the monetary value of the students/tourists' consumer surplus.
o. Calculate the total monetary value of the passengers' consumer surplus.
p. Determine the level of economic profits derived from executives.
q. Determine the level of economic profits derived from students/tourists.
r. Determine the overall level of economic profit and compare this with the results before price discrimination.

Suppose that United's Board of Directors rejects the price discrimination scheme for fear of attracting adverse public scrutiny. Nonetheless, the government decides to regulate United.

s. If the regulators require that United produces at the efficient output level, what price will be established?

t. At the efficient output level, how many passengers will United carry? (Hint: Remember that the demand curve for each class of passengers is a straight line.)

u. How can you tell that demand is inelastic at this price level?

v. Calculate United's economic profit under this regulatory requirement.

w. What will be United's short-run and long-run responses under this regulatory requirement?

x. If the regulators require that United produces at an output level that will provide a normal rate of return on invested capital, how great an economic profit (or loss) will United make?

2. The Arbezani Construction Group, a monopoly, manufactures prefabricated storage buildings and sells them in the domestic market for $700 each. The company is maximizing its profits. The marginal cost of each building is $300.

The neighboring nation of Arboc has traditionally kept the price of storage buildings low but excluded imports. The present maximum price, which is $400, has resulted in an excess demand for storage buildings in Arboc of 100 units.

As a consequence of trade talks, the two countries have formed AAFTA (Arboc-Arbez Free Trade Association), and Arboc has agreed to the importation of Arbezani storage buildings. Assume that Arbocali builders have been denied access to the Arbezani market—Arbezanis are notoriously hard bargainers, and the Arbezani Construction Group is a powerful political force.

a. Should the Arbezani Construction Group export storage buildings to Arboc and, if so, how many? Ignore transportation costs.

b. Comment on the efficiency consequences of this action.

3. A telephone system is to be established in Dartmopolis (a new city in Nova Scotia). The initial capital investment of $80 million will be financed by issuing 7% bonds. Fixed costs would be $5.6 million ($80 million x .07). The variable costs are calculated to be 10¢ per call.

a. Fill in the cost table.

Total Quantity	*Total Fixed Cost*	*Total Variable Cost*	*Total Cost*	*Marginal Cost*	*Average Total Cost*
0				—	—
20 mill.					
40 mill.					
60 mill.					
80 mill.					
100 mill.					
120 mill.					

b. Graph your information about average total cost and marginal cost.

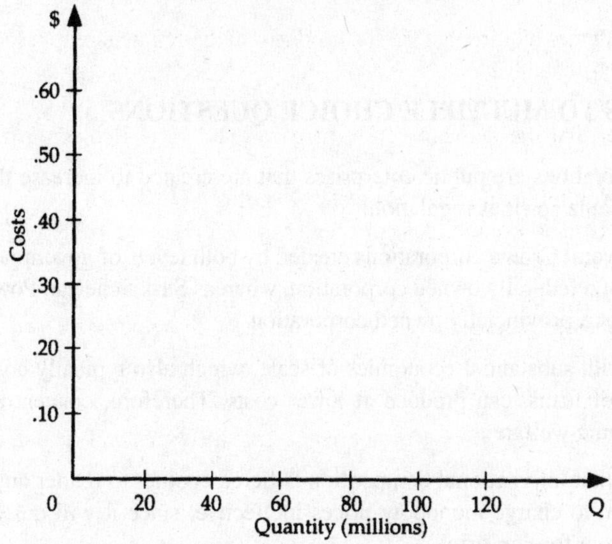

c. Suppose the price per call is set by the regulators at 10¢. What will happen if the residents of Dartmopolis make 40 million calls?

d. What would happen if 100 million calls were made at a price per call of 10¢?

e. Now sketch in a demand curve, starting at 60¢ on the vertical axis and ending at 120 million on the horizontal axis. Draw in the associated marginal revenue curve—remember that MR's slope is twice that of the demand curve.

f. What is the profit-maximizing price and output level?

g. What is the "average cost" price and output level?

h. What is the efficient price and output level (approximately)?

4. Suppose water in the town of St. Agatha, PEI, is provided by a private company, Water King, which is a monopoly. Water rates are regulated by the PEI local authorities, whose chairman is Jack Finney. Rates are currently established at $.0055 per cubic metre. Water King supplies water to 8000 customers, each of whom uses an average of 61 200 cubic metres of water per year. Variable costs are $.00258 per cubic metre and fixed costs total $799 632 per year. Capital invested by the stockholders of Water King amounts to $6 million. Water King has applied to Jack for permission to increase the water rate. Jack's department is committed to a normal profits policy, where a fair return on capital is 12%.

a. What is Water King's total variable cost?

b. What is Water King's total cost?

c. What is Water King's total revenue?

d. Calculate Water King's total return.

e. Calculate Water King's rate of return.

f. Should Jack recommend a rate increase? If so, what should the price per cubic metre of water be in order to give a 12% rate of return?

ANSWERS AND SOLUTIONS

PRACTICE TEST

I. SOLUTIONS TO MULTIPLE CHOICE QUESTIONS

1. C. Crown corporations are public enterprises that are created to increase the public welfare in the same spirit as regulation.
2. C. There are several Crown corporations created by both levels of government. CBC is an example of a federally owned corporation, whereas Saskatchewan Power Corp. is an example of a provincially owned corporation.
3. D. Industries with substantial economies of scale, which also typically consist of a small number of firms, can produce at lower costs. Therefore, concentration can improve economic welfare.
4. C. It is argued that international competition is fierce enough to render any attempt by a single firm to charge monopoly prices ineffective, since it will quickly force consumption from foreign firms.
5. D. See discussion on p. 354.
6. D. Competition law does not outlaw capital accumulation. Both A and B are illegal and deemed harmful. See p. 347.
7. B. See the discussion on p. 354.
8. B. The extra cost of generating an extra unit of electricity at a nuclear power station is low; the sunk cost (fixed) of establishing the generating capacity are very high.
9. C. Swindell might be practising sex discrimination (we don't know), but he is certainly discriminating in terms of price. See p. 348.
10. A. Profit maximizing occurs where MR = MC, at 60 units. Given that output level and the demand curve, the price will be $4.
11. B. The most efficient output level is where P = MC, at 120 units. Price is $1.00. If ATC is $1.75, a subsidy of (1.75 – 1.00) x 120 is required.
12. C. Normal return on invested capital occurs where P = ATC, at 100 units. P = $2.00.
13. D. Economic profit = (price-average cost) quantity. With average cost pricing, P = ATC; therefore, economic profit is zero, i.e., the firm earns a normal profit.
14. B. For example, when regulatory agencies attempt to ensure that telephone rates faced by customers in urban and rural areas are approximately the same, they would force telephone companies to absorb a loss. In order to compensate, however, the private firm would be allowed to make excess profits on some other part of its operation.
15. D. Although there are strong arguments for government involvement in the economy through competition policy, regulation, and Crown corporations, it is clear that government policy can and does impose costs on society.

II. SOLUTIONS TO APPLICATION QUESTIONS

1. a. See the following table.

Price of One-Way-Trip Tickets	One-Way-Trips Demanded Per Year Executives	Students/Tourists	Total Demand	"Total" Demand's Marginal Revenue
$140	7 000	0	7 000	$80
$130	8 000	0	8 000	$60
$120	9 000	1 000	10 000	$80
$110	10 000	2 000	12 000	$60
$100	11 000	3 000	14 000	$40
$90	12 000	4 000	16 000	$20
$80	13 000	5 000	18 000	0
$70	14 000	6 000	20 000	–$20
$60	15 000	7 000	22 000	–$40

b. Profit-maximization occurs where MR = MC. MC is $40; MR is $40 when 14 000 passengers fly and the price is $100.

c. 11 000 executives.

d. .5($210 – $100) x 11 000 = $605 000.

e. 3000 students/tourists.

f. .5($130 – $100) x 3000 = $45 000.

g. $650 000.

h. When 14 000 passengers fly, total revenue is $100 x 14 000, or $1 400 000. Total cost includes total fixed cost and total variable cost. TFC = $500 000. TVC = $40 x 14 000 = $560 000. TC = $1 060 000. Economic profit = TR – TC = $340 000.

i. United should determine the marginal revenue values for each type of passenger separately and set price according to the MR = MC rule in each case.

j. See the following table.

Price of One-Way-Trip Tickets	One-Way-Trips Demanded Per Year Executives	Student/Tourists	Executive Marginal Revenue	Student/Tourist Marginal Revenue
$140	7 000	0	$80	0
$130	8 000	0	$60	0
$120	9 000	1 000	$40	$120
$110	10 000	2 000	$20	$100
$100	11 000	3 000	0	$80
$90	12 000	4 000	-$20	$60
$80	13 000	5 000	-$40	$40
$70	14 000	6 000	-$60	$20
$60	15 000	7 000	-$80	0

k. Following the MR = MC rule, and recalling that MC = $40, 9000 executives will fly at a price of $120.

l. .5($210 – $120) x 9000 = $405 000.

m. Following the MR = MC rule, and recalling that MC = $40, 5000 students/tourists will fly at a price of $80.

n. .5($130 – $80) x 5000 = $125 000.

o. $530 000. Note that, by price discrimination, a portion of the consumer surplus has been appropriated by United.

p. Economic profit = TR – TC. TR = $120 x 9000 = $1 080 000. TC = TFC + TVC. TVC = $40 x 9000 = $360 000. TFC is a bit trickier because the $500 000 shouldn't be applied in total to executives. The total number of passengers is 14 000, of which 9/14 are executives. 9/14 of $500 000 is $321 428.57.
TC = $681 428.57. Economic profit = $398 571.43.

q. Economic profit = TR – TC. TR = $80 x 5000 = $400 000. TC = TFC + TVC. TVC = $40 x 5000 = $200 000. 5/14 of $500 000 is $178 571.43.
1. TC = $378 571.43. Economic profit = $21 428.57.

r. $398 571.43 + $21 428.57 = $420 000. Using price discrimination, United can increase its profits by $80 000.

s The efficient output level is where P = MC and, because MC = $40, P = $40.

t. The demand schedule table can be extended.

Price of One-Way-Trip Tickets	One-Way-Trips Demanded Per Year Executives	Students/Tourists	Total Demand	"Total" Demand's Marginal Revenue
$70	14 000	6 000	20 000	–$40
$60	15 000	7 000	22 000	–$80
$50	16 000	8 000	24 000	–$120
$40	17 000	9 000	26 000	–$160

u. When marginal revenue is negative (when P = $40, MR = –$160), demand is inelastic. See Chapter 13.

v. United will make an economic loss of $500 000. TR = $1 040 000 and TC = $500 000 + ($40 x 26 000).

w. In the short run, United will continue to provide service because its revenue can (just) meet its variable costs. In the long run, United will stop providing the service. If a subsidy equal to the loss were offered, United would continue to offer the service.

x. If United is receiving a normal rate of return on invested capital, it is earning a normal profit.

2. a. The Arbezani Construction Group should "fill the gap" in the market and export 100 units. Profits will be increased because the Arbocali price ($400) exceeds the Group's marginal cost ($300). Note that as each of the units can be sold for $400, marginal revenue is also $400. There is, in fact, additional scope for the Arbezani Construction Group to penetrate this market to a greater extent—we just don't have enough information.

b. Efficiency is unaffected in Arbez but is improved for Arbocali consumers. The situation is not Pareto optimal because trade is restricted between the two economies and is restricted within Arboc (because of the price ceiling). Complete liberalization of the market forces would improve efficiency.

3. a. See the table below.

Total Quantity	*Total Fixed Cost*	*Total Variable Cost*	*Total Cost*	*Marginal Cost*	*Average Total Cost*
0	$5.6 mill.	0	$5.6 mill	—	—
20 mill.	$5.6 mill.	$2 mill.	$7.6 mill.	10¢	38.0¢
40 mill.	$5.6 mill.	$4 mill.	$9.6 mill.	10¢	24.0¢
60 mill.	$5.6 mill.	$6 mill.	$11.6 mill.	10¢	19.3¢
80 mill.	$5.6 mill.	$8 mill.	$13.6 mill.	10¢	17.0¢
100 mill.	$5.6 mill.	$10 mill.	$15.6 mill.	10¢	15.6¢
120 mill.	$5.6 mill.	$12 mill.	$17.6 mill.	10¢	14.7¢

b. See the diagram below.

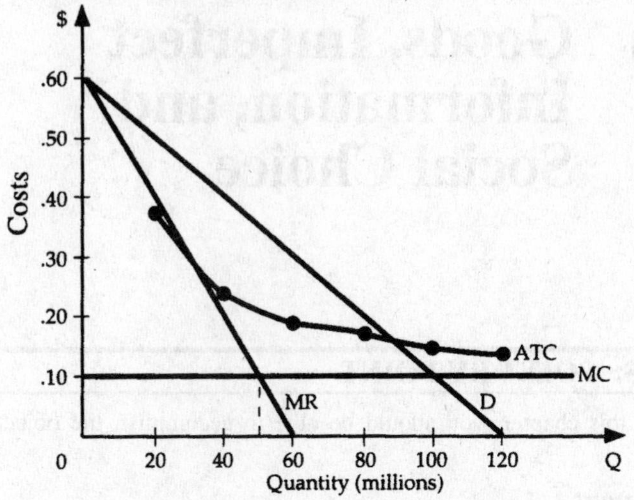

c. The phone company will lose 14¢ per call, or $5.6 million. The company would be wise to shut down.

d. The phone company will lose 5.6¢ per call, or $5.6 million. The company will lose its fixed costs whatever the number of calls is if price is made to equal marginal cost. (Think about the link between marginal cost and variable cost for a moment to verify this.)

e. See the diagram above.

f. 35¢ per call and 50 million calls.

g. About 16.65¢ and 85 million calls.

h. 10¢ and 100 million calls—the $5.6 million loss would be made in this case.

4. a. TVC = AVC x Q = $.00258 x 61 200 x 8000 = $1 263 168.

b. TC = TVC + TFC = $1 263 168 + $799 632 = $2 062 800.

c. TR = $.0055 x 61 200 x 8 000 = $2 692 800.

d. TR – TC = $2 692 800 – $2 062 800 = $630 000.

e. $630 000 ($6 000 000 = .105 = 10.5%.

f. 10.5% is less than the desired rate of 12%, so a rate increase is justified. Return should be .12 x $6 000 000 = $720 000. Given total cost ($2 062 800), TR should be $2 062 800 + $720 000 = $2 782 800. Price per cubic metre should be $2 782 800 (61 200 x 8000) = .005684.

16 Externalities, Public Goods, Imperfect Information, and Social Choice

OBJECTIVES: POINT BY POINT

After completing this chapter, you should be able to accomplish the objectives listed below.

General Comment

Keep in mind that this chapter examines examples of market failure. The past three chapters have looked at only one aspect—imperfect competition. The cases in the present chapter can occur even in perfectly competitive industries. Go back and review Chapters 13, 14, and 15. In Chapter 12, review Figure 12.5—note how externalities upset the scales in this diagram.

OBJECTIVE 1: Define externality and describe the goal of environmental economics.

Externalities, public goods, and imperfect information are major sources of *market failure*—that is, a situation when the perfectly competitive market is unable to reach an allocatively efficient competitive equilibrium. (page 361)

Externalities occur when the actions or decisions of one person or group impose a cost or bestow a benefit on some second or third parties. There is no incentive to figure these costs (or benefits) into the decision to act. Inefficient decisions are the outcome of this failure to consider the third party effect (social costs or benefits).

Practice

1. In perfect competition, a market failure occurs when, in the long run, the industry
   A. produces so much that average costs are minimized.
   B. produces so much that total profits are maximized.
   C. produces so much that the marginal benefit of the last unit produced exceeds its marginal cost.
   D. increases production past the output level where price is first equal to marginal revenue.

   ANSWER: C. The industry should produce until marginal benefit equals marginal cost. If marginal benefit does not equal marginal cost, a market failure has occurred. All other options refer to long-run equilibrium conditions in perfect competition.

2. Papyrus Paper Mill is producing where marginal revenue equals marginal cost. Marginal cost exceeds average total cost. Papyrus is an example of
   A. an externality.
   B. a market failure.
   C. a public good.
   D. imperfect information.

   ANSWER: B. Papyrus may be generating externalities—we don't know. We do know, however, that Papyrus is producing at an average cost that is greater than the minimum, because MC > AC.

OBJECTIVE 2: Distinguish marginal private costs from marginal social costs.

With a negative externality, a wedge is driven between marginal cost, as faced by producers or consumers, and price. Producers look only at *marginal private cost.* A broader view would encompass all extra costs of production—*marginal social costs.* The difference between the two is *marginal damage cost.* When we fail to consider these additional costs (or benefits) to society, inefficient outcomes emerge. When external costs are present, more production occurs than society would prefer. When external benefits are present, the market, on its own, will produce less than society would like. Pollution is the "classic" example of an external cost. (page 362)

> **TIP:** Keep in mind an example of a good having an external cost (a paper mill producing effluent), and an example of a good having an external benefit (the CD you borrow from a friend and tape).

> **TIP:** Calling externalities "spillover costs" and "spillover benefits" will help you. Remember that an externality exists any time marginal social benefit differs from marginal private benefit or marginal social cost differs from marginal private cost. Externalities may occur during the production of a good or during its consumption.
>
> The concept of externalities is easy to grasp—pollution is all around us. Think of some topical and local examples of your own. Don't forget externalities providing benefits. Many goods provide both external costs and benefits. The classic example is the bee-keeper and his neighbour, the apple grower—the bees sting the workers, yet pollinate the apple trees, and the bee-keeper receives "free" honey.
>
> What is less obvious is that the quantification of externalities (and so, claims for compensation) is extremely difficult—almost any position can be plausibly defended. Take the local examples you've thought of, and look for the counter-argument (the "silver lining" to a negative externality).

Practice

3. Assume there are no externalities. If price exceeds marginal cost, the benefits to consumers are __________ than the cost of resources needed to produce the good. __________ should be produced.
   A. greater, More.
   B. greater, Less.
   C. less, More.
   D. less, Less.

   ANSWER: A. If the price exceeds the cost of the final unit produced, society is deriving extra benefits. Production should increase until P = MC.

4. __________ is the sum of the marginal costs of producing a good and the correctly measured damage costs involved in the process of production.
   A. marginal damage cost.
   B. marginal social cost.
   C. marginal private cost.
   D. marginal external cost.

   ANSWER: B. MSC (marginal social cost) includes both the internal and external costs of production. See p. 363.

5. When marginal social cost exceeds the firm's marginal private cost, the industry's supply curve is too far to the _______ and ________ is being produced.
   A. right, too much.
   B. right, too little.
   C. left, too much.
   D. left, too little.

   ANSWER: A. Marginal cost is underestimating the true cost to society. Recall that the firm's (and the industry's) supply curve is based on MC.

6. As production increases, marginal damage costs are likely to
   A. remain constant.
   B. increase.
   C. decrease.
   D. become negative.

   ANSWER: B. See p. 364 and Figure 16.3 in the textbook.

7. An individual will continue an activity until
   A. marginal benefit equals marginal social cost.
   B. marginal benefit equals marginal damage cost.
   C. marginal social cost equals marginal private cost.
   D. marginal benefit equals marginal private cost.

   ANSWER: D. The individual will compare the marginal benefit with the extra privately borne cost.

OTHER RELATED POINTS: Draw a graph depicting a negative externality. Explain why the presence of a negative (positive) externality will lead to an overproduction (underproduction) of the good.

Practice

Use the following diagram, which depicts information for the chemical producer, Tox Inc., for the next five questions.

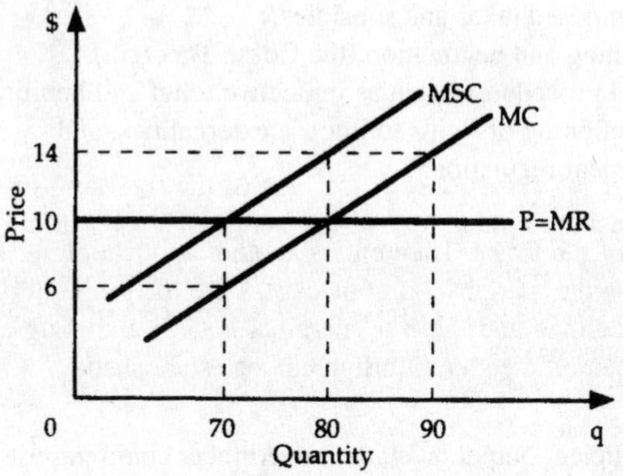

8. The firm depicted in the diagram is operating in a(n) _______________ competitive industry. External __________ are present.
   A. perfectly, benefits.
   B. perfectly, costs.
   C. imperfectly, benefits.
   D. imperfectly, costs.

   ANSWER: B. Demand is horizontal—perfect competition. MSC is higher than MC—marginal damage costs are present.

9. The profit-maximizing firm will produce
   A. 60 units of output.
   B. 70 units of output.
   C. 80 units of output.
   D. 90 units of output.

   ANSWER: C. The firm will produce where P (MR) = MC.

10. The efficient output level is
    A. 60 units of output.
    B. 70 units of output.
    C. 80 units of output.
    D. 90 units of output.

    ANSWER: B. The efficient output level is where MSC = MB (as represented by price).

11. The marginal damage cost imposed by this firm is
    A. $4 per unit of output.
    B. $6 per unit of output.
    C. $10 per unit of output.
    D. $14 per unit of output.

    ANSWER: A. Marginal damage cost is the difference between the marginal social cost and the marginal cost. In the diagram, at 80 units of output, MSC is $14 and MC is $10.

OBJECTIVE 3: Identify ways to potentially internalize an externality.

Externalities may be controlled in a variety of ways, although no one way works in all circumstances. Five remedies for the problem of externalities are possible. These are:

a. government-imposed taxes and subsidies,
b. private bargaining and negotiation (the Coase Theorem),
c. legal rules and procedures (such as injunctive relief and liability rules),
d. the sale or auctioning of rights to impose externalities, and
e. direct government regulation. (page 369)

> **TIP:** Think of the Coase Theorem as another application of the idea of "balancing the margins." In this case, once the property rights to a good are defined and the true marginal benefit and marginal cost determined, an efficient equilibrium can be established.

12. To achieve an efficient output level, the government could impose a tax of
 A. $4 per unit.
 B. $6 per unit.
 C. $10 per unit.
 D. $14 per unit.

 ANSWER: A. This tax will increase the (private) production costs and make them the same as the marginal social costs.

OBJECTIVE 4: Define public good.

Public goods are goods whose benefits are received collectively by all members of society (non-rival) and/or whose benefits can be denied to no one (non-excludable), even if they refuse to pay. Because of these characteristics, public goods will either be underproduced or not produced at all if the private sector is made responsible for their provision. Two problems of public goods are the free-rider problem and the drop-in-the-bucket problem. (page 375)

The legal system is a classic example of a public good. What would society be like without known and enforced laws? Much of the framework of the market economy would collapse. Property rights and possessions would be endangered. There would be an unwillingness to trade by mail, to accept cheques, or to offer trade credit. We derive benefits from law enforcement, but what choices do we have as individuals? We could each hire our own law enforcer in the "law market," but that wouldn't entirely solve the problem because enforcement would be neither uniform nor just. In addition, there would still be no mechanism for establishing laws, except by precedent and tradition.

The only effective solution is for society to act as a unit, levying taxes to pay for a system of justice. This publicly provided good does not erode the free-market system; rather, it *enhances* it. The justice system is non-excludable and non-rival in consumption (unless there is a sudden crime wave). Also, note that the "drop-in-the-bucket" and "free-rider" problems are present. A town that is crime-free when a new resident moves into it doesn't experience extra costs from his relocation. His tax dollars will make no great difference in the fight against crime, and if he avoids payment, he will still receive protection.

> **TIP:** Keep in mind a clear example of a public good (a lighthouse or, better still, national defence). Confirm that, for a good to be a public good, consumption is non-rival and that consumers can't be excluded from the benefits provided.

> **TIP,** *continued:* Not all goods provided by the government are public goods, as far as economists are concerned. The heart of the public goods issue is that the market fails to provide an adequate amount of such goods because there is neither an incentive to buy nor to sell privately. Consumers can "free ride," and the provision of a unit of the good, given non-rivalry in consumption, will service purchasers and free riders alike.

Practice

13. Public goods are ________ in consumption and non-purchasers ________ be excluded from their benefits.
    A. rival, can.
    B. rival, cannot.
    C. non-rival, can.
    D. non-rival, cannot.

    ANSWER: D. These are the two characteristics of public goods. Plug in an example (national defence) to see how they relate. See p. 376.

14. Because public goods are non-excludable, individuals are usually unwilling to pay for them. This characteristic is known as the
    A. drop-in-the-bucket problem.
    B. impossibility theorem.
    C. Coase Theorem.
    D. free-rider problem.

    ANSWER: D. See p. 376.

15. As the number of recipients of a public good increases, the number of free riders will tend to
    A. increase because, as the size of the group increases, it is more difficult to detect free riders.
    B. increase because, as the size of the group increases, individuals become rivals for the benefits of the good.
    C. decrease because, as the size of the group increases, the per person payment will decrease.
    D. decrease because, as the size of the group increases, it is easier to exclude non-contributors.

    ANSWER: A. See p. 376.

OBJECTIVE 5: Analyze the optimal provision of a public good.

To determine the optimal (most efficient) level of provision, Samuelson devised the demand curve for public goods. The price each consumer is willing to pay is summed at each output level. An efficient provision of public goods will still leave many consumers dissatisfied, however, because some will prefer more and others less. To ensure an efficient level of provision, the preferences of each consumer would have to be revealed, which is possible only in theory because of the incentive not to reveal one's preferences. In practice, imperfect social choice mechanisms, such as majority rule, are used.

The Tiebout hypothesis offers the possibility that an efficient mix of public goods may be produced if consumers make their preferences known by changing location in response to government-offered goods. (page 379)

Practice

16. The optimal level of provision of a public good occurs when society's ____________ is equal to the ____________ of the good.
    A. total willingness to pay, total cost.
    B. total willingness to pay, marginal cost.
    C. marginal willingness to pay, total cost.
    D. marginal willingness to pay, marginal cost.

    ANSWER: B. The demand curve totals the willingness to pay and this is equated with the marginal (social) cost to determine the optimal output level.

Use the following table for the three questions. Society consists of two persons—Robinson and Friday. The table shows the quantity demanded by each of units of a public good—defence. Assume that each person's demand curve is a straight line.

Price	Robinson's Quantity Demanded	Friday's Quantity Demanded
$3.00	3	1
$2.00	5	2
$1.00	7	3

17. Each of the following is a point on society's demand curve for defence except
    A. 1 unit at a price of $7.00.
    B. 3 units at a price of $4.00.
    C. 5 units at a price of $2.00.
    D. 7 units at a price of $2.00.

    ANSWER: D. The demand curve must be summed vertically, i.e., at each output level. Example: Friday will pay $3.00 to receive 1 unit and Robinson will pay $4.00 to receive 1 unit (Robinson's demand curve is a straight line). One unit, not 2, is produced to be shared.

18. Complete the following demand schedule.

Society's Quantity Demanded	Price
7	_____
6	_____
5	_____
4	_____
3	_____
2	_____
1	_____

ANSWER: See the *Answers and Solutions* section.

19. The marginal cost of each unit of defence is $4.00. What is the optimal number of units of defence that should be provided?
    A. 2 units.
    B. 3 units.
    C. 4 units.
    D. 5 units.

    ANSWER: B. Society should produce until P = MC.

OBJECTIVE 6: Describe adverse selection and moral hazard.

These two issues arise because of imperfect information. The absence of full information can cause households and firms to make mistakes. Firms as well as consumers can be the victims of incomplete or inaccurate information. Adverse selection can occur when a buyer or seller enters into an exchange with another party who has more information, the outcome of which will be more low quality goods and less high quality goods exchanged than desired. (page 381)

Moral hazard arises when one party to a contract passes the cost of his or her behaviour on to the other party to the contract. This is a problem that arises frequently in insurance markets. This problem that can lead to inefficient behaviour is very much like the externality problem in which firms and households have no incentive to consider the full costs of their behaviour. (page 382)

Society attempts to reduce the threat of imperfect information. The buyer is protected by "truth in lending" and "truth in advertising" legislation, for instance, and consumer organizations may pressure corporations to improve information. Risks remain and they reduce the willingness of individuals to trade.

There is a joke about an economics professor who accepted a marriage proposal by saying that the decision was based on the belief that the marginal benefit of a continued search had become less than its marginal cost.

Practice

20. Consumers should continue to search out information until the ________ benefit from the search equals the ________ cost of the search.
    A. total, total.
    B. total, marginal.
    C. marginal, total.
    D. marginal, marginal.

    ANSWER: D. This is entirely a marginal decision.

21. In the used-car market, there are lemons and cherries and, although buyers cannot distinguish between them, sellers can. We would expect ________ lemons to enter the market and ________ cherries to enter the market.
    A. too many, too many.
    B. too many, too few.
    C. too few, too many.
    D. too few, too few.

    ANSWER: B. See p. 382 for a discussion of this example.

OBJECTIVE 7: Outline potential remedies for imperfect information.

There are two sets of remedies (solutions) for imperfect information: market solutions, and government solutions. Since information is valuable, often information is produced by consumers and producers themselves. This type of information-gathering process is called market search. Consumers and firms gather information as long as the marginal benefits from continued search are greater than the marginal costs of engaging in it. Despite the fact that the market handles many information problems efficiently, some information problems are not handled well by the market.

Information being essentially a public good is non-rival in consumption. When it is very costly for individuals to collect and dispose, it may be cheaper for government to produce it once for everyone. (page 383)

OBJECTIVE 8: Define social choice.

Arrow's impossibility theorem illustrates the difficulty of establishing a consistent consensus given a lack of unanimity. The impossibility theorem proves that it can't be done. The voting paradox is an example of this theorem. Due to a lack of incentives and avoidance of tough choices, government may be inefficient. However, the ultimate question remains *how much* government involvement is required, not *whether* it is required. (page 384)

Practice

22. The demonstration that majority-rule voting can produce contradictory and inconsistent results is known as
    A. the impossibility theorem.
    B. the voting paradox.
    C. adverse selection.
    D. moral hazard.

    ANSWER: B. The voting paradox exemplifies the impossibility theorem.

    Use the following information to answer the next two questions. Axl, Brigitta, and Carl have to choose one of four options (A, B, C, D). Individual preferences, from highest to lowest, are shown below. Majority voting will be used by pairing options, the loser being excluded from further consideration.

Axl	*Brigitta*	*Carl*
A	B	C
B	C	A
C	A	D
D	D	B

23. If A is first paired against B, the option finally selected will be
    A. A.
    B. B.
    C. C.
    D. D.

    ANSWER: C. Carl will vote for A over B. Pairing A and C, Brigitta will cast the swing vote for C. Everyone prefers C over D.

24. If B is first paired against C, the option finally selected will be
    A. A.
    B. B.
    C. C.
    D. D.

    ANSWER: A. Axl will vote for B over C. Pairing A and B, Carl will cast the swing vote for A. Everyone prefers A over D.

OBJECTIVE 9: Outline potential sources of government inefficiency.

Be aware that during the last several chapters, a battle has been raging between those who believe that the free market works efficiently and those who believe that more structured control is required. You might pigeon-hole the two camps as the "Small Government" and "Big Government" schools of public policy.

In this chapter, "Big Government" is drawing attention to ways in which the free market fails if left uncorrected. For externalities, "Small Government" retaliates with the Coase Theorem and the private sale or auction of externality rights. For public goods, the debate tends to centre on the question of which goods are clearly public goods. The "Small Government" school also retaliates with such concepts as "the voting paradox" and "the impossibility theorem"—hoping to undermine the belief that the government allocates efficiently.

Recent work has held the view that government officials are assumed to maximize their own utility, not the social good. Furthermore, whereas, an inefficient firm that is producing at a higher than necessary cost will be driven out of business, that is not necessarily the case for the public sector. (page 386, 387)

The battle continues in Chapter 17…

PRACTICE TEST

I. MULTIPLE CHOICE QUESTIONS. Select the option that provides the single best answer.

_____ 1. Which of the following is a good example of an externality?
A. a hamburger.
B. noise pollution.
C. Jack's cigarette smoke for Jane, who doesn't smoke.
D. both B and C.

_____ 2. For the Coase theorem to work, all of the following must be true except
A. the basic rights at issue must be understood.
B. the majority of concerned individuals participate.
C. there must be no impediments to bargaining.
D. only a few people can be involved.

_____ 3. Which one of the following is not advanced as a method of remedying an externality?
A. government subsidies.
B. private taxation.
C. private bargaining.
D. direct government regulation.

_____ 4. Firm A is producing at an output level where the marginal benefits to consumers are less than the marginal cost. Assuming no externalities, the price
A. equals marginal cost.
B. is less than marginal cost.
C. is greater than marginal cost.
D. is less than marginal damage cost.

_____ 5. When the marginal social cost of a good exceeds its marginal private cost,
A. too many units will be produced by the market.
B. the market price will be too high.
C. it is an example of a beneficial externality.
D. too few resources will be allocated to its production.

_____ 6. The production of a good imposes external costs on society. If these costs are not internalized, then, from society's point of view, the firm is likely to
A. underproduce.
B. allocate too many resources to the production of the good.
C. charge too high a price.
D. make economic profits in the long run.

_____ 7. Your campus radio station is best described as an example of
A. an external cost.
B. a good that is non-rival in consumption but that generates benefits which are excludable.
C. a good that is non-rival in consumption and that generates benefits which are non-excludable.
D. a public good plagued by the easy-rider problem.

_____ 8. Which of the following is the best example of a public good?
A. a hamburger.
B. a high school.
C. police protection.
D. a toll bridge.

_____ 9. All of the following are true about the voting paradox except that
A. it is an example of the impossibility theorem.
B. it demonstrates the power wielded by the one who sets the voting agenda.
C. it shows that, when preferences for public goods differ, any attempt to add the preferences can lead to inconsistencies.
D. with majority rule, logrolling is necessary to get things done.

Use the following information to answer the next two questions.

Arboc is an economy comprised of three individuals: Ed, Ted, and Ned. The table shows the maximum price that each will pay for various quantities of a good.

Quantity	*Ed*	*Ted*	*Ned*
1	$7	$10	$17
2	$5	$9	$15
3	$4	$7	$11
4	$3	$4	$10

_____ 10. The maximum price that the private market would pay for the third unit is
A. $4.
B. $7.
C. $11.
D. $22.

_____ 11. Now suppose that the good is a public good. The maximum price that society would pay for the third unit is
A. $7.
B. $7.33 (approximately).
C. $11.
D. $22.

_____ 12. If there are external costs, and these are not considered by perfectly competitive firms, then, at the equilibrium output level,
A. P = MC and P = MSC.
B. P = MC and P < MSC.
C. P < MC and P = MSC.
D. P < MC and P < MSC.

_____ 13. The two problems in the provision of public goods are
A. non-rivalry in consumption and the drop-in-the-bucket problem.
B. externalities and non-excludability.
C. non-excludability and moral hazard.
D. free riders and the drop-in-the-bucket problem.

_____ 14. To derive the market demand for a public good, we sum the
A. quantity demanded by each consumer at each possible price level.
B. demand curve of each consumer horizontally.
C. amounts that each consumer is willing to pay at each level of output.
D. marginal social cost curve of each producer vertically.

_____ 15. There are external costs, and these are not considered by perfectly competitive firms. The government imposes a tax so that the market is producing at the efficient output level. We can say that
A. P = MSC and MDC = 0.
B. P = MSC and MDC > 0.
C. P < MSC and MDC = 0.
D. P < MSC and MDC > 0.

_____ 16. Your local public television station is having a fund drive. Public TV is the only TV station you watch. You rationalize your failure to contribute by telling yourself that your pledge would make no difference one way or the other. This is an example of the _______________ problem. Because you will still be able to tune in whether you pledge or not, you are a(n)
A. free-rider, free rider.
B. free-rider, externality.
C. drop-in-the-bucket, free rider.
D. drop-in-the-bucket, externality.

_____ 17. Hugo is selling his Yugo in the used car market, a market with imperfect information. The going price for a Yugo is $1000, and this is Hugo's asking price. Sadly, Hugo's Yugo is a "lemon." If price is used by buyers as an indication of quality in this market, Hugo should
A. keep his asking price at $1000.
B. raise his asking price above $1000.
C. lower his asking price below $1000.
D. withdraw his car from the market.

Use the following information to answer the next three questions.

Research has shown that Hayley Mills Incorp., a firm in the perfectly competitive paper industry, also produces pollution in the nearby Chicken River. The following table has been compiled showing the marginal cost (MC) and marginal social cost (MSC) of paper production. The market price of paper is $600 per tonne.

Tonnes of paper	MC	MSC
1	$400	$500
2	$500	$600
3	$600	$800
4	$700	$1100

_____ 18. The marginal damage cost borne by society from the production of 4 tonnes of paper is
A. $1100 per tonne.
B. $275 per tonne.
C. $400 per tonne.
D. $100 per tonne.

_____ 19. Hayley is able to ignore the damage costs. The firm will produce _______ tonnes of paper; the efficient output level is _______ tonnes.
A. 2, 2.
B. 3, 2.
C. 3, 3.
D. 4, 3.

_____ 20. To force this firm to produce at the efficient level, the government should
A. impose a tax of $100 per tonne.
B. impose a tax of $200 per tonne.
C. grant a subsidy of $100 per tonne.
D. grant a subsidy of $200 per tonne.

II. APPLICATION QUESTIONS.

1. From the rubble of disowned economic dogmas and disenchanted citizens, a new state has been built in Eastern Europe—Freedonia. The newly elected Freedonian government is, naturally, keen to avoid the pitfalls of its predecessors, but it does realize that some (public) goods and services should be provided by the state. Jan Lipska, the Minister for Public Goods, has devised the following matrix, using the characteristics of public goods that she has read about in an economics textbook by Case, Fair, Strain, and Veall.

PUBLIC/PRIVATE GOOD MATRIX

	RIVAL	NON-RIVAL
Excludable	I	II
Non-excludable	III	IV

The minister now calls in a top western economic adviser (you) to interpret the matrix.

a. Ms. Lipska asks you what sort of good would be included in Category I, asks for examples, and asks how the government should treat these goods.
b. Ms. Lipska now asks about the kind of good that should be included in Category IV, asks for examples, and asks how the government should treat these goods.
c. Ms. Lipska now asks about the kind of good that should be included in Categories II and III, asks for examples, and asks how the government should treat these goods.
d. The Minister considers Category I (pure private goods) and focuses on a particular industry—steel. She points out that steel is traditionally a polluter of the environment. Assuming that the government should do "something" about this issue on behalf of injured citizens, what might that "something" be?
e. Some goods, the Minister muses, can generate undesirable side effects at the consumption stage—a car, for example, can pollute. You see the way the Minister's mind is working. You set up a matrix for externalities.

EXTERNALITY MATRIX	PRODUCTION	CONSUMPTION
Negative externality	I	II
Positive externality	III	IV

Interpret the matrix for the Minister.

f. Ms. Lipska asks what actions the government might take in each of these categories. How would you reply?

2. The inhabitants of the city of Ruppert Town, B.C., have for years been coping with a transportation problem. The city is on an isthmus, and to connect it to the rest of civilization, there is one rocky, treacherous road that, almost invariably, is closed during the winter months. The proposed solution is to build a bridge to link Ruppert Town to the "mainland" more directly. Elija Woodward, the City Manager, has hired you to conduct an analysis of the costs and benefits of this project. He points out that the project is all or nothing—you can't build half a bridge. Having taken an introductory economics course in university, he agrees with you when you suggest that the community's consumer surplus of the bridge should be figured into the calculations.

After some work, you have estimated the demand schedule below.

Toll Fee	Usage Per Year	Annual Revenues	Consumer Surplus	Total Annual Benefits
$1.00	0	______	______	______
$0.80	20 000	______	______	______
$0.60	40 000	______	______	______
$0.40	60 000	______	______	______
$0.20	80 000	______	______	______
$0.10	90 000	______	______	______
$0.00	100 000	______	______	______

a. Complete the table.

The City Manager now tells you that the building and maintenance of the bridge can be financed through a loan that will cost $40 000 per year, regardless of the amount of traffic. (Ignore present value considerations.)

b. Left to a free market and the demand curve above, would the bridge be built? Why?

c. Comparing the total annual benefit and the total annual cost, do you recommend that Ruppert Town goes ahead with the project?

d. If Woodward's objective is to maximize social welfare, should he impose a toll fee? If so, how much? Why?

e. If Woodward wishes to offset as much of the cost as possible through toll revenues, which toll level should he set?

f. The strategies developed in part d. and part e. still leave Ruppert Town with an unpaid bill for the bridge. Recommend a method of deriving funds.

g. Woodward, who is familiar with Freedonian politics (see Application Question 1 above), asks where the Ruppert Town bridge would fit into the "public/private goods matrix." How would you reply?

There remains an unresolved issue. The bay, and the land surrounding it over which the bridge is to be built, is owned by five families. The right to build the bridge must be bought from them. The bridge will certainly reduce the amenity of the exceptionally fine shoreline. $10 000 per year has been budgeted as compensation for the five families to be divided equally.

Each family places a monetary value on the amenity of the bay. Four different possible sets of values (A–D) are given in the following table. The higher the monetary value, the greater the amenity and the greater the loss of amenity if the bridge is built.

The amenity of the bay is a public good for the five families (none can be excluded, and the scenery is non-rival), so the compensation should be accepted only if the value of the compensation exceeds the value of the bay.

	Distributions			
Family	**A**	**B**	**C**	**D**
Singh	$1500	$3000	$5000	$2500
Howe	$1500	$3000	$3000	$2500
Archard	$1500	$3000	$1000	$2500
Yamato	$1500	$3000	$1000	$500
Viccars	$1500	$1000	$1000	$500

h. In which of the four cases should the compensation be accepted by the five families, allowing Ruppert Town's bridge project to go forward?

The families get together and, in true Ruppert Town fashion, decide to abide by majority rule.

i. Using majority rule, in which of the four cases will the compensation be accepted by the five families?

j. In which cases will the compensation be accepted even though its benefits do not adequately compensate the five families?

k. Majority rule may result in inefficient choices. In some sense, an enforced decision that affects one adversely is like a negative externality—the actions of others adversely affect the individual. Referring to your answer to part i. and to the Coase Theorem, how might the families negotiate among themselves, and with what result regarding the offered compensation?

3. We can move from the textbook discussion of externalities to a graphical presentation. Recall the concepts of marginal social cost and marginal (private) cost—MSC and MPC, respectively. Similarly, define marginal social benefit and marginal private benefit—MSB and MPB, respectively. MPC and MPB are the same as the supply and demand curves with which you're familiar.

In the graph below, without externalities, MSC = MPC and MSB = MPB. P1 and Q1 indicate the price and quantity of widgets traded in a free market. Because all costs and benefits are internalized, there is no market failure.

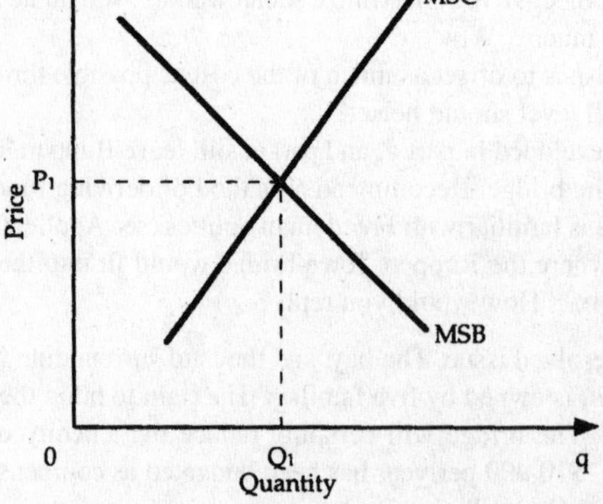

a. Negative externalities in production: What will happen if some of the costs are passed on to a third party? Draw the MPC curve. What effect have the spillover costs had? Can you think of an example of this situation?

b. Negative externalities in consumption: Return to the original diagram. Suppose that the consumption of widgets reduces the well-being of others. Why might this occur? Where will the MPB curve be, in relation to MSB, and what is the effect on resource allocation?

c. Positive externalities in consumption: Return to the original diagram. Suppose that the benefits from widgets accrue to persons other than the purchasers. What will happen to the diagram? What will be the effect on price and resource allocation? Can you think of any examples?

d. Positive externalities in production: Return to the original diagram. Suppose that the firm pays the cost of resources from which it derives no use. Can you think of an example? What will be the relationship between MSC and MPC?

4. We have a society with three individuals—Ted, Ned, and Fred. The following table lists the maximum price each will pay for various quantities of a public good.

Quantity	*Ted's Price*	*Ned's Price*	*Fred's Price*
1	$9	$12	$16
2	$7	$10	$12
3	$5	$6	$9
4	$3	$4	$6
5	$1	$2	$3

a. How much will society pay for the second unit of the good?

b. Graph society's demand curve for this public good.

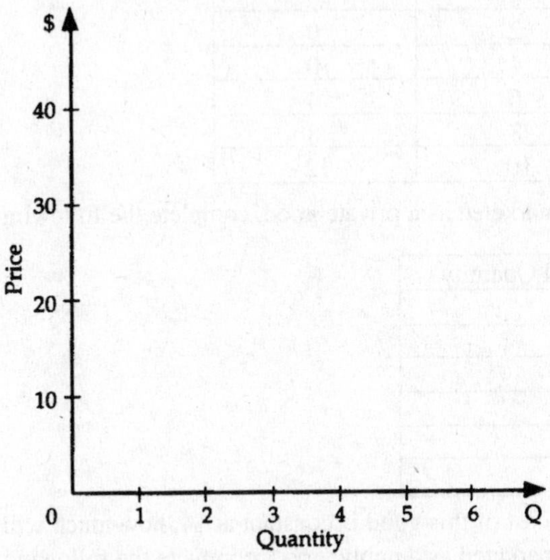

c. Suppose that the marginal cost of producing this good is $14 for each additional unit of output. What is the efficient level of provision?

d. Graph marginal cost to confirm your result.

e. If each person is charged an equal amount to cover the cost of provision, will any of them be happy with the situation?

5. What do you think is the best way to deal with the following situations? Choose one of the following options.

Situations

a. a smoky factory
b. noise pollution from a recently built airport
c. pornographic magazines
d. noise from car exhaust systems
e. unsightly billboards
f. noise pollution from a building site
g. your room-mate always parties on the night before your exams

Options

A. tax or subsidy
B. bargaining and negotiation
C. legal rules
D. direct regulation

6. Jilly, Lilly, and Billie are room-mates. Each likes a different kind of music. Jilly loves jazz, tolerates loud rock, and hates classical. Lilly loves loud rock, is impartial to classical, but loathes jazz. Billie adores classical, can live with jazz, and despises loud rock. Their apartment has one (communally owned) radio. Billie asks your advice—how can she guarantee that only classical will be played?

7. We have a society with two consumers—Liz and Boris. The following table lists how much each will demand of a good at various prices.

Price	Liz's Quantity	Boris' Quantity
$10	0	0
$8	2	0
$6	4	0
$4	6	4
$2	8	8
$0	10	12

a. If this good is marketed as a private good, complete the following table.

Price	Total Quantity
$10	
$8	
$6	
$4	
$2	
$0	

b. If the marginal cost of this good is constant at $4, how much will be traded?
c. If this good is marketed as a public good, complete the following table.

Price	Quantity
$16	
$13	
$10	
$7	
$4	
$1	
$0	

d. If the marginal cost of this good is constant at $4, how much will be traded?

ANSWERS AND SOLUTIONS

ANSWERS TO PRACTICE QUESTIONS

20. See the following demand schedule.

Society's Quantity Demanded	Price	Robinson	Friday
7	$1.00	$1.00	—
6	$1.50	$1.50	—
5	$2.00	$2.00	—
4	$2.50	$2.50	—
3	$4.00	$3.00	$1.00
2	$5.50	$3.50	$2.00
1	$7.00	$4.00	$3.00

PRACTICE TEST

I. SOLUTIONS TO MULTIPLE CHOICE QUESTIONS

1. A. There is no external cost or external benefit attached to the production and/or consumption of a hamburger.
2. B. See p. 371 for a discussion of the three requirements.
3. B. See p. 369 for a summary of the methods of remedying an externality.
4. B. See p. 364.
5. A. The additional (external) costs reduce society's welfare, indicating that too much is being produced. See p. 366.
6. B. See p. 366.
7. C. Your consumption of the radio station does not reduce its availability for others, nor can the radio station exclude any listeners.
8. C. Public goods are non-rival and non-excludable. Police protection is a community-wide service that is available to all.
9. D. In the voting paradox example, things get done, but outcomes needn't be consistent.
10. C. In the private market, sum the demands vertically at each output level. Ned would be willing to pay $11 to buy the third unit.
11. D. Sum the demand information vertically at each output level for a publicly provided good. Price will be $22 ($4 + $7 + $11).
12. B. In perfect competition, the firm will set P (MR) = MC to maximize profits. If there are external costs, MC will be less than MSC, therefore P < MSC.
13. D. See p. 376.
14. C. See p. 378.
15. B. If there are externalities, MDC is positive. The profit-maximizing firm produces where P = MC which, with the tax, is equal to MSC.
16. C. See p. 376.

17. B. If Hugo raises his asking price, he is signalling to gullible buyers that his car is not a "lemon."

18. C. Marginal damage cost is MSC - MC. See p. 368.

19. B. The firm will produce where P = MC while the efficient output level is where P = MSC.

20. A. At the efficient output level of 2 tonnes, the government must increase the firm's private cost from $500 to $600.

II. SOLUTIONS TO APPLICATION QUESTIONS

1. a. Category I includes pure private goods—goods that are rival in consumption and excludable. Freedonian sausage, clothing, and private cars would be examples. The government should leave well enough alone and let market forces provide this type of good.

   b. Category IV includes pure public goods—goods that are non-rival in consumption and non-excludable. Clean air, national defence, police protection, the legal system, public health, and fire protection would be examples. The government should provide this type of good.

   c. Categories II and III are where the government needs to be careful because they include goods possessing one or other of the characteristics of public goods. The private sector can produce those goods in Category II because free riders can be excluded, but the private sector might underproduce, i.e., exclude those who are unwilling to pay even though their inclusion is virtually costless. Examples include the post office, public transport, and cable television. The private sector is unable to produce goods in Category III because free riders cannot be excluded. There is rivalry, so public provision might best have a user fee included. National parks during peak season or highways at rush hour are examples.

   d. Given a negative externality in production, the offending firm will tend to overproduce. The government could impose a quota on production, or set a tax that would equate the marginal (private) cost and the marginal social cost.

   e. Category I includes firms that impose spillover costs, such as the polluting steel industry.

      Category II includes those goods that impose spillover costs when used by consumers—Ms. Lipska's car, or noise pollution from a loud radio.

      Category III includes firms that provide spillover benefits: a bee-keeper's bees provide pollination services; a new tourist attraction will draw visitors who spend money at restaurants and other local businesses; the training of entry-level employees who might be "pirated" by other firms/industries/regions.

      Category IV includes consumption that provides beneficial side effects. Examples may be less obvious for this case. Higher education, which might make students more responsible citizens, is an example. The purchase of medical injections for an infectious disease, careful tending of the weeds in your garden, or allowing someone to listen to or tape your CDs are other examples.

   f. In the presence of negative externalities, the typical government policy is to tax to the extent of the marginal damage cost. Example: a high sales tax might be imposed on noisy boom boxes. In the presence of beneficial externalities, the government might provide a subsidy to stimulate production. Example: grants, or low-interest loans, for higher education.

2. a.

Toll Fee	Usage Per Year	Annual Revenues	Consumer Surplus	Total Annual Benefits
$1.00	0	—	—	—
$0.80	20 000	$16 000	$2 000	$18 000
$0.60	40 000	$24 000	$8 000	$32 000
$0.40	60 000	$24 000	$18 000	$42 000
$0.20	80 000	$16 000	$32 000	$48 000
$0.10	90 000	$9 000	$40 500	$49 500
$0.00	100 000	—	$50 000	$50 000

Example of consumer surplus calculation. When the fee is \$.40, the consumer surplus is .5(1.00 – .40) x 60 000, or \$18 000. See p. 152.

b. The bridge would not be built. The maximum possible revenue that can be obtained is \$25 000, with a toll of 50¢. Because the cost is \$40 000, a private firm would make an economic loss of at least \$15 000.

c. Ruppert Town should proceed because the total benefit exceeds the total cost.

d. The City Manager should not impose a toll fee. Any fee will reduce the total benefits from its maximum of \$50 000. Suppose the toll were \$1.00—no revenue would be raised. No benefits would accrue to Ruppert Town. By paying the bridge bill, the City would simply have lost \$40 000. If, however, the toll were \$0.00—no revenue would be raised, but \$50 000 in consumer surplus would accrue. By paying the bridge bill, the City would gain \$10 000.

e. If a fee were to be charged, a toll of 50¢ would be preferred because revenues would be maximized at \$25 000.

f. Using the answer to part d., where no toll is charged, Ruppert Town will need to raise \$40 000. Increasing taxes by \$40 000 within the community would achieve the result. Note: issuing bonds within the community is preferred because individuals can choose whether or not to buy the bonds.

g. A bridge is a "mixed" good and should be located in Category II. It is mixed because, although it is nonrival (public), it is excludable (private)—Ruppert Town can charge a toll and exclude free riders, for example.

h. Compensation will be accepted with Distribution A and, if negotiation and trade between families is allowed, Distribution D. See the table below. The total value of the bay's amenity is less than \$10 000 in each of these cases.

	Distributions			
Family	**A**	**B**	**C**	**D**
Singh	$1500	$3000	$5000	$2500
Howe	$1500	$3000	$3000	$2500
Archard	$1500	$3000	$1000	$2500
Yamato	$1500	$3000	$1000	$500
Viccars	$1500	$1000	$1000	$500
Total Value of Amenity	$7500	$13 000	$11 000	$8500
Voting to Accept	Yes 5/No 0	Yes 1/No 4	Yes 3/No 2	Yes 2/No 3
Decision	Accept	Reject	Accept	Reject
Efficient Choice	Efficient	Efficient	Inefficient	Inefficient

i. The compensation will be accepted with Distributions A and C. See the table above.

j. Distribution C. See the table above.

k. With Distribution C, the families would accept compensation of $10 000, although the loss of amenity is valued at $11 000—a bad choice, especially for Singh and Howe. Coase's Theorem suggests that these two families could bribe one other (e.g., Archard) to vote with them. If Archard were given $1000, his would become the swing vote. Even if Yamato and Viccars retaliated, the higher values placed on amenity by Singh and Howe would reverse the decision. The bridge project would not go through.

3. a. The MSC curve will no longer represent all the costs borne by the firm. MPC will be lower.
Lower price, more resources allocated to widget production.
Pollution.

b. Noise pollution from a loud radio, air pollution from cars.
MSB will be lower than MPB.
Price will be higher, and more resources than the optimal amount will be allocated to widgets.

c. MSB will be higher than MPB.
Prices will be lower, and less than is socially optimal will be allocated.
Purchase of medical injections for an infectious disease, careful tending of the weeds in your garden, or allowing someone to listen to or tape your CDs.

d. Training entry-level employees who are subsequently "attracted away" by other firms/industries/regions.
MPC will be higher, and production will be less than the socially optimal level.

4. a. $29. Add Ted, Ned, and Fred's price together for the second unit of the good.

b. See the diagram below.

c. 3 units.

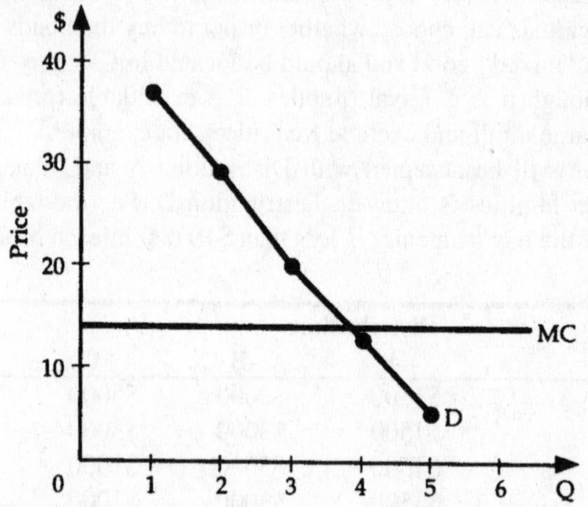

d. See the diagram above.

e. No one will be really happy. Each consumer would prefer to have more of the good produced, given its current price and their revealed preferences.

5. a. D or A (regulation or taxation).

b. D (regulation of flight patterns and jet engines and damages).

c. D (regulation).

d. D (regulation about mufflers).

e. A (licence fee—i.e., a tax).

f. C (injunction).

g. B (bargaining).

Most of these have several possible remedies. If your answers differ from these, reassess the pros and cons of each option.

6. First off, it's unlikely that Billie will prevent the others from having some say in what's played. She might, however, offer to buy them off, essentially renting the radio for her own use. The cost will depend on the preferences of her room-mates.

   Perhaps you could suggest a cheaper alternative. Billie could request a round-table discussion and vote on the single kind of music acceptable to all. She should rig the voting sequence so that the first vote is jazz vs. loud rock. Jazz would win—Jilly and Billie vs. Lilly. The second vote should be between jazz and classical. Classical will win. Billie should then promptly adjourn the meeting before the others have time to think about the guile of their manipulative room-mate.

7. a. See the table below.

Price	Total Quantity
$10	0
$8	2
$6	4
$4	10
$2	16
$0	22

   b. 10 units.

   c. See the table below.

Price	Quantity
$16	0
$13 (8 + 5)	2
$10 (6 + 4)	4
$7 (4 + 3)	6
$4 (2 + 2)	8
$1 (0 + 1)	10
$0	12

   d. 8 units.

17 Income Distribution And Poverty

OBJECTIVES: POINT BY POINT

After completing this chapter, you should be able to accomplish the objectives listed below.

General Comment

Much of the material in this chapter is descriptive rather than theoretical. Aim to have a general idea about the sources of income in the economy, the trend in poverty, the major income-redistribution programs, and the arguments for and against them.

> **TIP:** The entire chapter deals with the question of equity, rather than with the efficiency criterion which has dominated the previous chapters. The introductory section distinguishes between the equity (or fairness) criterion and the efficiency criterion for income distribution, and draws attention to three questions:
>
> a. What causes inequality?
> b. How can it be measured?
> c. What is the appropriate role for the government?
>
> Use this three-part scheme to make sense of the material being presented.

> **TIP:** Do not equate equity or fairness with equality. It may be very equal if your professor gives everyone the same grade on your next exam, but it's unlikely to be fair or equitable.

OBJECTIVE 1: Identify the various sources of income.

Households derive their income from three basic sources: (1) from wages or salaries received in exchange for labour; (2) from property (capital, land, etc.); and (3) from government. About 64% of personal income in Canada (1995) was received in the form of wages and salaries. Income from property takes the form of profits, interest dividends, and rents (20%). Income from the government is also referred to as transfer payments, (15%). Transfer payments are payments by government to people who do not supply goods and services in exchange. These payments are generally designed to provide income to those in need.
(page 394)

OTHER RELATED POINTS: Outline the factors that cause differences in household income.

Several factors may produce inequalities in income distribution. Wage and salary differences may arise because of the nature (quality) of the workers—skills, level of education or training, physical ability—or from the nature of the job—degree of risk, difficulty, or glamour. The distribution of unemployment and the number of wage earners in the family will also have an effect. Property income and transfer payments are also unevenly distributed, with wealthier families tending to have more income-earning property than do poorer families. The concept of human capital is important—we can "invest" in job skills and education. (page 399)

Certainly, accidents of birth may affect income distribution because property (and property income) can be passed on from one generation to the next. Socialist or Marxist economies, in particular, levy high "death duties" or estate taxes to reduce this source of inequality. An interesting example of this issue emerged in Britain in 1993 when Queen Elizabeth (reputedly the world's richest woman) "volunteered" to pay income taxes.

Practice

1. Branka earns a degree in electrical engineering. This is an example of
   A. investment in human capital.
   B. wealth accumulation.
   C. income redistribution.
   D. a compensating differential.

   ANSWER: A. The degree improves Branka's knowledge and skills.

2. The major source of household income is
   A. wages and salaries.
   B. government payments.
   C. property income.
   D. inheritances and bequests.

   ANSWER: A. See p. 399.

3. In some jobs, workers earn "danger money." Danger money is an example of
   A. payment for human capital.
   B. a compensating differential.
   C. an equity differential.
   D. a bonus.

   ANSWER: B. Compensating differentials are paid to reward workers who undertake dangerous or unpleasant jobs.

4. Compensating differentials are best described as
   A. government transfer payments to poor families to increase their standard of living.
   B. wage differences caused by differences in human capital.
   C. wage differences caused by differences in working conditions.
   D. wage differences caused by differences in worker productivity.

   ANSWER: C. See p. 395.

5. ____________ comprise property income.
   A. economic profits and economic rents.
   B. profits, rents, interest earnings, and dividends.
   C. profits and dividends.
   D. unearned interest payments and dividends.

   ANSWER: B. See p. 398.

6. Which of the following statements is false?
   A. transfer payments reduce income inequality.
   B. transfer payments are payments to individuals or households who provide no good or service in exchange.
   C. transfer payments are used by the government to alleviate poverty.
   D. eligibility for transfer payment is restricted to those in poverty.

   ANSWER: D. Almost all workers are eligible for social security.

7. In 1998, the government offered a relief package for parts of Quebec and Ontario that were hit by a severe ice storm. This is
   A. a compensating differential.
   B. a transfer payment.
   C. property income (rent).
   D. sweat equity.

   ANSWER: B. No good or service is required in return for the benefits received.

OBJECTIVE 2: Outline how income and wealth in Canada is distributed.

There are two possible definitions of income: (1) Economic income, which includes wages, salaries, dividends, interest received, income of unincorporated business, transfers from the government, rent, etc. In addition, the capital gain arising from appreciation of, say, shares of stocks, is part of the economic income (whether these assets are sold to realize the gain or not. (2) Money income, excludes non-cash transfer payments, capital gains income, gifts, inheritances, etc. Therefore, money income is less inclusive than economic income and hence distributed more equally due to the concentration of capital gains, inheritances, etc. Due to the immense difficulty in measuring economic income, income distribution data produced by Statistics Canada involve money income only. Definitions are extremely important. (page 399)

OBJECTIVE 3: Describe how inequality and poverty are measured.

The distribution of income in Canada has remained quite stable for several decades. The *Lorenz curve* is a graphical device for describing the distribution of income in an economy. The *Gini coefficient* is a numerical measure of income inequality. A Gini coefficient of zero indicates a perfectly equal income distribution, while the maximum score (one) indicates perfect inequality. If income were distributed equally, the Lorenz curve would be a 45° line. The more unequal distribution is, the more the curve bends below the 45° line, and the greater the Gini coefficient will be. Canada income distribution is affected by regional differences, education, and family type. (page 400)

Practice

8. The amount of money a household can spend without changing its net assets is called its
   A. money income.
   B. net property income.
   C. economic income.
   D. after-tax (disposable) income.

   ANSWER: C. See the definition on p. 399.

9. According to the textbook, the top 20% of households earned more than ______ times as much as the bottom 20%.
   A. two.
   B. three.
   C. six.
   D. five.

   ANSWER: C. See p. 400 and Table 17.1.

10. A Gini coefficient of one means that
   A. income is distributed equally.
   B. all income is earned by one individual.
   C. 50% of income is earned by the poorest 50% of the population.
   D. 20% of income is earned by the richest 20% (quintile) of the population.

   ANSWER: B. If the Gini coefficient is one, one individual earns all the income. The Lorenz curve would lie along the horizontal axis until 100%.

11. The bottom 40% received almost__________ of transfer payments paid to all households, as opposed to _________ of total income.
   A. 22%, 18.4%.
   B. 50.7%, 18.4%.
   C. 15.2%, 6.4%.
   D. 12.4%, 35.8%.

   ANSWER: B. See p. 400.

12. The Gini coefficient indicates
   A. the percentage of households below the poverty line.
   B. the extent of income inequality in the economy.
   C. the proportion of households with below-average earnings.
   D. the proportion of money income that is in the form of transfer payments.

   ANSWER: B. The Gini coefficient is a measure of income inequality.

OTHER RELATED POINTS: Give the official definition of poverty. Describe the trend in poverty in Canada over the past few decades, and discuss the problems of definition of poverty.

Poverty is a very complicated word to define. Some argue that it is culturally defined and is therefore a relative concept. Others argue that poverty should be measured by determining how much it costs to buy the "basic necessities of life"—minimum standard of living. There is no official poverty line in Canada and Statistics Canada does not produce statistics on poverty. However, Statistics Canada produces a set of low income cut offs that are commonly quoted in reference to poverty in Canada. These low income cut offs are selected on the basis that families below these limits normally spend about 55% or more of their income on food, shelter, and clothing. The poverty rate is higher among families headed by an individual under 24 years of age and also among lone parent families, especially headed by women. (page 402)

> **Poverty:** As you read through the statistics and assess the income-redistribution programs outlined in this chapter, bear in mind the following: the poor are most often the children of the poor, and the rich are most often the children of the rich. Poverty is strongly linked to family background. Additionally, those with high school or less education are over-represented in the lowest quintile and under-represented in the highest quintile. What should this tell you about the importance of *human capital*?

Keep in mind the *underclass*, that group which even the statistics fail to measure, or the programs to help, simply because they have dropped out of the system. Do our poverty and income distribution figures record people such as teenage runaways, the rural unemployed, deinstitutionalized mental patients, or drug addicts? Are these groups part of the poverty problem?

Practice

13. Of the following groups, the one more likely to have low income is
    A. the university educated.
    B. women living in households with their husbands.
    C. children under 16.
    D. the top quintile.

    ANSWER: C. See p. 403.

14. Based on the criteria set by Statistics Canada in regard to low income cut offs, _______of lone parent families headed by women can be considered below poverty line.
    A. 65.5%.
    B. 43.5%.
    C. 56.0%.
    D. 17.7%.

    ANSWER: C. See p. 404.

OBJECTIVE 4: State the arguments for and against redistribution of income.

The main argument *against income redistribution* is that one should be allowed to retain one's earnings—for Angela to receive extra income, for example, Bill must lose some of his. A disincentive to work may exist both for the individual who loses income *and* for the transfer's recipient. It is argued that the Canadian economic system is based on private property ownership and freedom of contract. Redistribution might undermine the system and reduce incentives to improve oneself. (page 405)

The main argument *in support of income distribution* is a moral appeal—the rich should help those less fortunate than themselves to enjoy the necessities of life. The utilitarians, Rawls, and Marx have all constructed quite sophisticated philosophical formulations in support of this view. (page 406)

In practice, most countries undertake some redistribution of income and wealth. Usually, this is done through a progressive income tax system—where progressively higher tax rates are applied to the incomes of individuals with higher incomes—and through government payments (transfers). In Canada, while some progressivity is present in the overall tax system, it is very slight. However, some programs are designed to redistribute income or aid to the poor in the form of cash or non-cash benefits. These include Child Tax Benefits, Employment Insurance, Guaranteed Income Supplement, and Housing Subsidies.

Practice

15. "A dollar is worth less to a rich person than to a poor person." This is a basic belief of
   A. utilitarian justice.
   B. Rawlsian justice.
   C. Marxian justice.
   D. social justice.

   ANSWER: A. Utilitarians would argue that redistribution from rich to poor increases society's total utility. See p. 406.

16. ____________ is a theory of income distribution that claims that the social contract emerging from the original position would maximize the well-being of the ____________.
   A. utilitarian justice, most typical member of society.
   B. utilitarian justice, worst-off member of society.
   C. Rawlsian justice, most typical member of society.
   D. Rawlsian justice, worst-off member of society.

   ANSWER: D. In the original position, each member of society, according to Rawls, will be concerned about the position of the least fortunate.

17. Which of the following is an assumption in Rawls's theory?
   A. individuals are risk averse.
   B. individuals may become rich.
   C. individuals may become poor.
   D. all of the above.

   ANSWER: D. They all are. See p. 406.

18. Marx argued that ______ value derives from labour and that profits were
   A. all, a necessary return for ownership of resources and risk taking.
   B. all, an expropriation of surplus value.
   C. some, a necessary return for ownership of resources and risk taking.
   D. some, an expropriation of surplus value.

   ANSWER: B. According to Marx, the value of production depends solely on the amount of labour required to produce it.

OBJECTIVE 5: Outline the main features of Canadian redistribution programs.

The government has used two broad sets of programs to affect the distribution of income, taxes, and expenditure programs. (page 407)

a. *The tax system.* The progressivity of the income tax system is set against evidence that the Canadian tax system overall is almost proportional—each taxpayer, regardless of income, pays pretty much the same percentage of her or his income to the government. Conclusion: There's little income distribution being caused by the tax system.

b. It is important to recognize that Canadian expenditures on income support, as a percentage of GDP, are only marginally higher than those by governments in the United States and significantly lower than expenditures by most European governments. The data suggest that distribution of income has changed little despite the growth of redistribution programs. Poverty among children is growing. Only the elderly have experienced significant improvements over time.

Practice

19. ___________ is the transfer program given the credit for significantly reducing poverty among senior citizens.
    A. transfers to the elderly, e.g. The Guaranteed Income Supplement.
    B. employment Insurance.
    C. food Stamps.
    D. aid to Families with Dependent Children.

    ANSWER: A. See p. 409.

20. The government transfer programs include all of the following programs except
    A. Employment Insurance.
    B. The Child Tax Benefit.
    C. health insurance program.
    D. RRSPs.

    ANSWER: D. See p. 409. An RRSP is a registered saving plan to which individuals contribute in order to reduce their annual taxable income.

> **TIP:** This is the last chapter in the sequence examining the advantages and disadvantages of the market system. Chapter 18 begins a sequence of "topics" chapters. It's a good time to review your notes and summarize what has been covered. You may find it useful to re-read Chapters 1 and 2.

Conclusion

The chapter ends by pulling together some of the themes developed during earlier chapters. A market system, operating with complete efficiency, may still not be considered fair because some people—through handicap or inborn talent, luck, lack of education, or unemployment—will have more or less than others. In theory, efforts at redistribution should be aimed at redistributing well-being or *utility*, which (unfortunately) is neither observable nor measurable. Income and wealth are substitute measures of utility. The government's income-redistribution program itself is an imperfect instrument, and the debate continues as to the appropriate extent of government intervention in the economy.

PRACTICE TEST

I. MULTIPLE CHOICE QUESTIONS. Select the option that provides the single best answer.

_____ 1. Inefficiency is shown in a utility possibility frontier diagram by
  A. a point inside the curve.
  B. a point outside the curve.
  C. the point where the curve reaches the vertical axis.
  D. any point not on the curve.

_____ 2. If the Gini coefficient is equal to zero, all of the following certainly are true except
A. the Lorenz curve graphs as a straight line.
B. income is equally distributed.
C. the lowest quintile of the population will receive as many dollars as the highest quintile.
D. we have an efficient distribution of income.

_____ 3. Society consists of two individuals: Richie Rich, (a millionaire who is so obsessed with money that his marginal utility of income increases with each extra dollar he gets) and Kermit the Hermit (a recluse who has rejected money and other earthly goods and finds that his marginal utility of income decreases with each extra dollar he gets). If income is transferred from the rich to the poor, we can say that society's
A. total utility will increase.
B. total utility will decrease.
C. total utility will remain unchanged.
D. total utility will change, but the net effect is uncertain.

_____ 4. Government retraining programs can be viewed as
A. an inefficient method of income redistribution.
B. an investment in human capital.
C. a movement away from the utility possibility frontier.
D. regressive programs.

_____ 5. A key feature of a negative income tax is that it
A. treats the poor harsher than alternative policies.
B. focuses on efficiency rather than equity.
C. lowers investment income and pushes low-income cut-offs further down.
D. links transfers to one's income.

_____ 6. A politician promising to support greater equality of property income on the one hand, and a more efficient allocation of resources on the other, may well be committed to
A. two conflicting objectives. Equality and efficiency are not the same.
B. two conflicting objectives. To achieve efficiency, it may be necessary to let investors earn large rewards from their investment.
C. two complementary objectives. Efficiency and equality must go hand in hand in a growing market economy.
D. two complementary objectives. The more efficient and rewarding the property market is, the more participants there will be.

_____ 7. If the resource markets work correctly, then rewards are based on productivity. Therefore,
A. because capital adds to the productivity of labour, owners of capital should earn a higher return.
B. because labour is essential to all production processes, labour should be paid a higher rate of return.
C. wages and salaries should be paid in accordance with the marginal productivity of workers.
D. because there are more workers than machines, labour should be cheaper to hire and so earn less.

_____ 8. Income redistribution is considered to be a public good. Which of the following is a problem for implementing income redistribution as it relates to public goods?
   A. people see no point in contributing voluntarily because their contribution will be insignificant.
   B. people deserve to retain the fruits of their labours.
   C. giving people handouts may reduce their incentives to work and save.
   D. the poor are often "free riders" living on welfare.

_____ 9. The income tax system is "progressive." This means that
   A. progressively more persons are taxed each year.
   B. those with higher income pay a higher percentage of it in taxes.
   C. if a person earning \$10 000 pays \$3000 in taxes, a person earning \$20 000 would pay twice as much (\$6000) in taxes.
   D. the more you earn, the more you pay.

_____ 10. Which of the following is an argument against income redistribution?
   A. everyone is entitled to keep the fruits of his or her own efforts.
   B. freedom of contract.
   C. redistribution reduces incentives to work, save, and invest.
   D. all of the above.

_____ 11. In successive decades, Country A records a Gini coefficient of .3 (1960s), .7 (1970s), and 1.0 (1980s). Population has remained stable throughout the time period. We can state that
   A. Country A's income distribution has become more equal as time has passed.
   B. Country A had fewer poor people in the 1980s than in the 1960s.
   C. the top 20% of income was earned by a smaller number of families in the 1980s than in the 1960s.
   D. the gap between Country A's Lorenz curve and the 45° line has decreased as time has passed.

_____ 12. Jackie Blue is a police officer who patrols a dangerous high-crime neighbourhood. Jackie earns more than officers who work in low-crime neighbourhoods. This is an example of
   A. a return on human capital.
   B. a compensating differential.
   C. a productivity differential.
   D. a compensating productivity differential.

_____ 13. If we plot a Lorenz curve for Canadian income and another for Canadian wealth, the Lorenz curve for income will be ________ bowed; its Gini coefficient will be ________.
   A. more, larger.
   B. more, smaller.
   C. less, larger.
   D. less, smaller.

_____ 14. The Canadian government could probably reduce the Gini coefficient by
   A. reducing government spending on welfare programs.
   B. eliminating student-loan programs.
   C. increasing taxes on inherited wealth.
   D. cutting the capital gains tax rates.

_____ 15. If the area between the Lorenz curve and the line of perfect equality became larger, we could conclude that the distribution of income had become

A. more unequal.
B. less unequal.
C. more inefficient.
D. less inefficient.

_____ 16. According to Marx, the major source of inequality in the distribution of income is

A. property income.
B. labour income.
C. human capitalism.
D. social contracts.

_____ 17. Alice and Betty have trained as nurses in Regina. Alice moves to New York to work in a private hospital and earns $50 000. Betty stays in Regina to work as a community health nurse and earns $15 000. The cost of living is about 100% higher in New York than in Regina. Which of the following is true?

A. Alice is better off than Betty because she earns $35 000 more.
B. Betty must be better off because she did not need to take the job for $50 000.
C. Alice must be better off because her earnings are more than three times those of Betty but the cost of living in New York is less than double that in Regina.
D. we cannot determine who is better off because income is an imperfect measure of utility.

Use the following utility possibilities frontier to answer the next question.

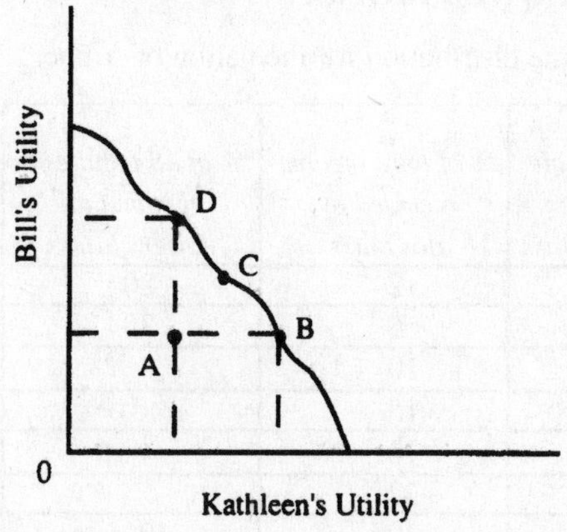

_____ 18. Which of the following moves is (are) efficient?

A. A to B.
B. A to C.
C. A to D.
D. All of the above moves are efficient.

Use the following Lorenz curve for the nation of Arboc to answer the next two questions.

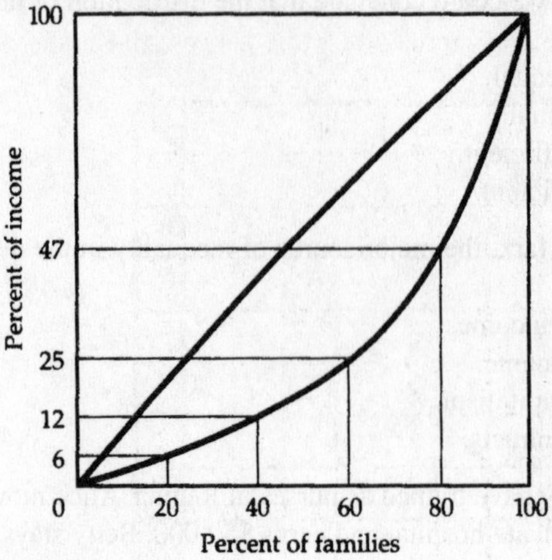

_____ 19. The top fifth of Arbocali families earn _____ % of income.

A. 20.
B. 47.
C. 53.
D. 80.

_____ 20. The third fifth of families earn _____ % of income.

A. 6.
B. 12.
C. 13.
D. 25.

II. APPLICATION QUESTIONS.

1. Use the following income distribution for the nation of Arboc.

Personal income class	*% of all families in this class*	*% of total income received by this class*	*% of all families in this and all lower classes*	*% of total income received by this and all lower classes*
Under $5000	20	2	20	2
5000–9999	10	5	30	7
10 000–14 999	12	10		
15 000–19 999	15	15		
20 000–24 999	20	16		
25 000–49 999	13	22		
50 000 and over	10	30	100	100

a. Complete the table above.

b. Households earning less than $10 000 make up the lowest ____% of the population and receive ____% of the income, while those earning $25 000 or more make up ____% of the population and receive ____% of the income.

c. Use the information in the table to plot a Lorenz curve in the space below. Remember to plot the zero-zero point and to draw as smooth a curve as possible. Shade in the area on the graph that indicates inequality in income.

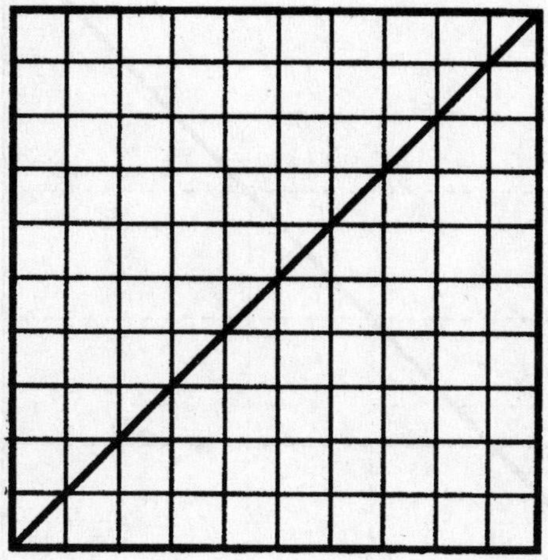

2. A tax is progressive (p. 439) if those with higher incomes pay a higher percentage of their income in tax. The opposite is called a regressive tax, i.e., those with higher incomes pay a lower percentage of their income in tax.

a. A progressive tax will make income distribution ________ (more/less) equal.

Three sales tax proposals have come before your provincial government. In each case, identify whether the tax will be progressive or regressive and, therefore, the effect on the distribution of income.

b. A 20% sales tax on fur coats.

c. A 12% sales tax on groceries.

d. A general sales tax of 6% on all goods.

3. Statistics Canada provides the following information for four-person families. There are 1 455 600 four person families in Canada.

Income	Percentage of Families	Percentage of Income (Cumulative)
$75 000 and over	15.3	100.0
$50 000 – $74 999	22.5	37.5
$35 000 – $49 999	22.9	25.0
$25 000 – $34 999	14.9	17.5
$15 000 – $24 999	12.4	12.5
$10 000 – $14 999	4.8	7.5
$5000 – $9999	4.6	5.0
Under $5000	2.7	2.5

a. Using the data points you have, plot a Lorenz curve for four-person families.

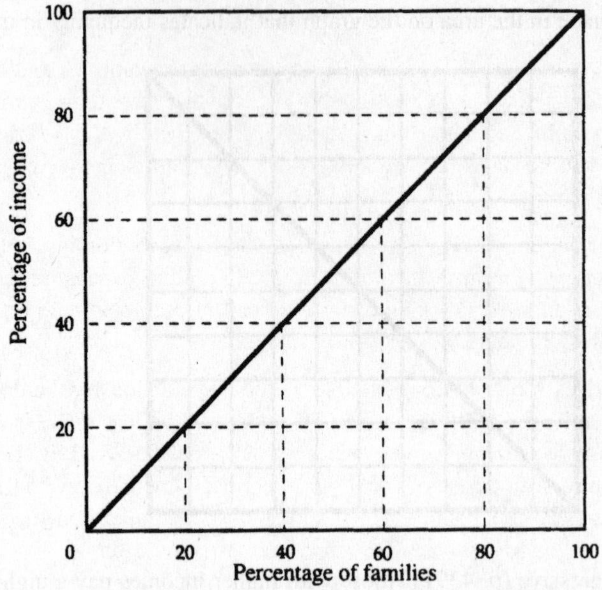

b. Draw line (AB) perpendicular to the 45° line to the lower right-hand corner of the Lorenz curve diagram. The portion of this line between the Lorenz curve and the 45° line (AC), when divided by AB, gives an approximate estimate of the Gini coefficient. Estimate the Gini coefficient for this economy.

Mona Gregson is a 25-five year old unmarried mother with three children: Rachel, 8, Peter, 7, and Michael, 2. Mona dropped out of high school when she became pregnant with Rachel and never graduated. She has no marketable job skills and has never had a job. Each month, Mona receives $800 in social assistance and $300 in the housing subsidy. She has applied for a housing subsidy but has been rejected. Assume that she pays no taxes.

c. What is the Gregsons' money income? In the income distribution above, where does Mona's family fit?

d What is Mona's annual economic income?

e. Mona's social assistance allowance is increased to $900 per month. How does this affect her economic income? Her money income? Her position in the income distribution?

The provincial government has instituted a 15-week vocational training program. The participant's welfare benefits are maintained and she receives a modest travel allowance. Day care facilities are available during the program and for the first year after the trainee begins to work.

On completion of the program, the graduate will receive a $7.25 per hour clerical job with the provincial government. Monthly income is $1200. However, 9% will go to the payroll tax. Annual income tax payments will be $660. Commuting/parking fees amount to $25 per month.

f. If Mona completes the program and gets the promised clerical job, will the Gregsons be better off or worse off than before?

g. Calculate the "tax" imposed on Mona as she moves from welfare to work.

h. If Mona wishes to maximize her net income, should she stay on welfare or enter the training program?

The provincial government implements a 15% tax on food items.

i. How will this new tax affect the distribution of income in Mona's province? How will the Gini coefficient change?

You decide to contribute $100 to help alleviate poverty. Family A and Family B are identical in all respects except that Family A is much poorer than Family B.

j Would you be happier seeing your $100 go to Family A or to Family B?

k. Would you be happy if you kept your money and someone else contributed $100 to Family A?

Case, Fair, Strain, and Veall suggest that income redistribution is a public good (p. 438). My happiness because income inequality is reduced does not interfere with your happiness—non-rivalry. If income distribution becomes more equal, I cannot be excluded from the benefits—non-excludability.

Two points arise: Contributions provide (some) satisfaction for the donor but, acting independently, probably the donor's benefits will be less than his costs. As the income level of the recipient rises, the marginal benefit derived by the donor from extra contributions decreases. The MB (marginal benefit) curve in the diagram below reflects these conclusions. The marginal cost of a dollar donated is a dollar for the contributor. The MC private curve reflects this conclusion.

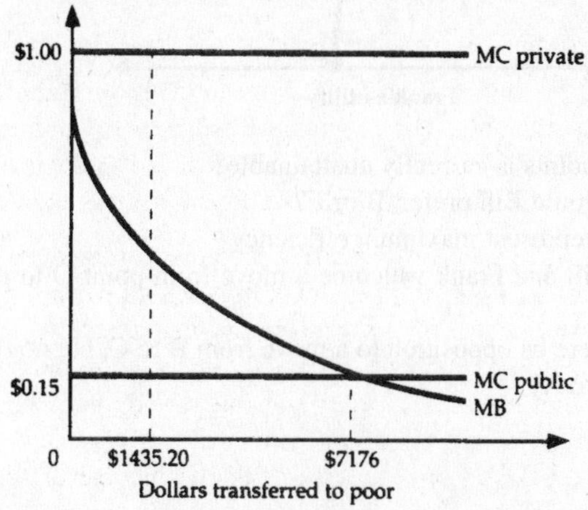

Suppose the poverty line is drawn at $14 352 and about 12% of families are "poor." Suppose that the average income of "poor" households is $14 352 ÷ 2, or $7176. The distribution above shows that 60% of families (the "well-off") earn $35 000 or more.

l. Each poor family requires how much, on average, to reach the poverty line? Ignore taxes and so on.

m. If each "well-off" family contributes an equal amount, how much would they have to contribute to alleviate poverty?

n. Explain why each well-off family, acting independently, will not contribute the amount you determined in part m. Use the diagram above.

o. The well-off families get together and sign a binding contract to contribute $1435.20 each to help alleviate poverty. Explain why each well-off family will find it worthwhile to contribute.

p. Explain why such a contract is unlikely to be enacted.

4. Suppose that you lose your job (either real or imagined). Although you still have whatever savings and other assets you previously had, you have no other immediate source of income, including welfare cheques or parents. You still have any financial commitments previously contracted. How would you react to this financial crisis? As the days pass, you may begin to see the real distress concealed behind unemployment and poverty statistics and the genuine relief offered by government programs.

5. To get a feel for poverty, volunteer at a local soup kitchen.

6. Suppose that, in a two-person economy, there exists the following utility possibility frontier.

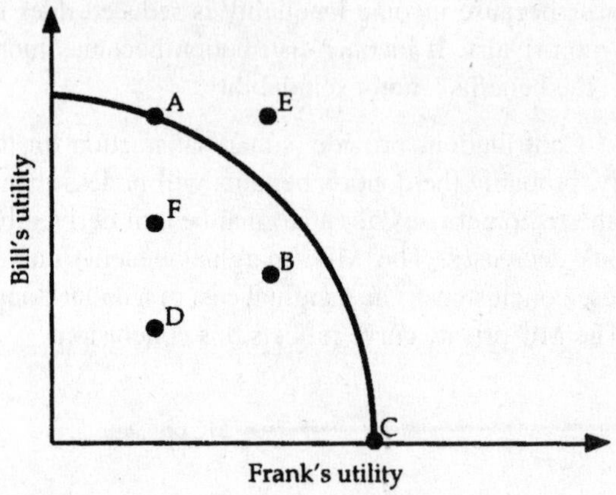

a. Which of the points is currently unattainable?
b. Which point would Bill prefer, B or F?
c. Which points represent maximum efficiency?
d. Why would Bill and Frank welcome a move from point D to point B on the curve?
e. Why would there be opposition to a move from D to C, but no opposition to a move from D to A?

ANSWERS AND SOLUTIONS

PRACTICE TEST

I. SOLUTIONS TO MULTIPLE CHOICE QUESTIONS

1. A. A point inside the curve indicates that individual I or J, or both, could increase satisfaction without the other individual losing anything.

2. D. The income distribution is certainly equal, but it doesn't follow that it is efficient.

3. B. This is the opposite case to the one suggested by the utilitarians. See p. 406.

4. B. Training or retraining programs develop the talents and improve the skills of the labour force—i.e., they are an investment in human capital.

5. D. See p. 408.

6. B. The politician is dealing with the arguments for and against redistribution (p. 376). One argument against redistribution is that it reduces incentives to work and, therefore, reduces efficiency.

7. C. Note, though, that this is not the Marxian view.

8. A. This is the drop-in-the-bucket problem. See p. 376.

9. B. With a progressive tax system, extra earnings are taxed at higher rates. Option D is true whenever the marginal tax rate is positive, even if the tax system is not progressive.

10. D. They all are used by those who do not favour income redistribution.

11. C. As the Gini coefficient increases, income inequality increases.

12. B. Because Jackie has a more dangerous, less attractive beat, the extra payment she receives is a compensating differential. See p. 395.

13. D. Canadian income is more evenly distributed than Canadian wealth is, so the Lorenz curve for income will be less bowed. The gap between the 45 line and the Lorenz curve (the Gini coefficient) will be smaller.

14. C. Taxing inheritances would reduce property income for subsequent generations.

15. A. The greater the gap, the greater the inequality.

16. A. See p. 406.

17. D. It is important that you remember throughout this chapter…that income and wealth are imperfect measures of well-being. See p. 394.

18. D. A move is efficient if the utility of one individual increases without a decrease in the utility of the other.

19. C. 80% of families earn 47% of the income; the remaining 53% of income is earned by the top 20%.

20. C. The lowest 40% earn 12% of income. The lowest 60% earn 25%. By subtraction, the third fifth of families earn 13%.

II. SOLUTIONS TO APPLICATION QUESTIONS

1. a. See the table below.

Personal income class	*% of all families in this class*	*% of total income received by this class*	*% of all families in this and all lower classes*	*% of total income received by this and all lower classes*
Under $5000	20	2	20	2
5000–9999	10	5	30	7
10 000–14 999	12	10	42	17
15 000–19 999	15	15	57	32
20 000–24 999	20	16	77	48
25 000–49 999	13	22	90	70
50 000 and over	10	30	100	100

b. 30; 7; 23; 52.

c. See the diagram below.

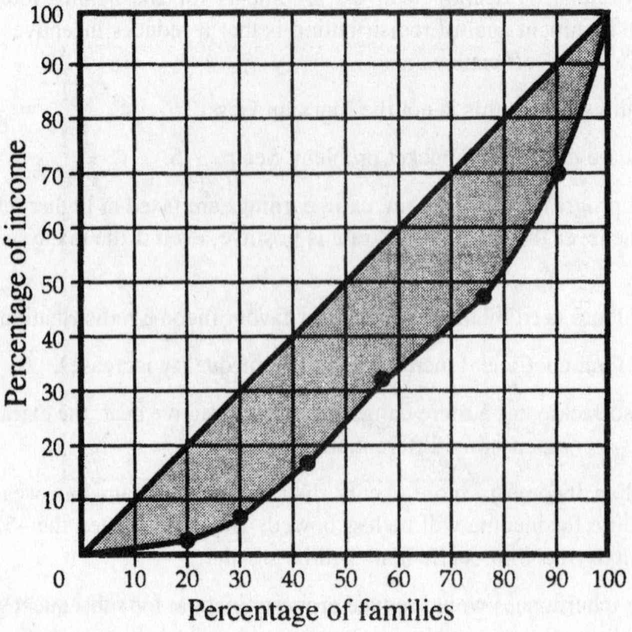

2. a. more.
   b. Progressive. Fur coats are bought predominantly by rich individuals so poor families will be unaffected, while rich purchasers will pay the tax.
   c. Regressive. A 12% sales tax on groceries must be paid by all households, but the poor spend a relatively larger proportion of their income on groceries so, relatively, their tax payment will be greater.
   d. Regressive. A general sales tax is more broadly based than a food tax but, because poor households spend most or all of their income while rich households do not, the relative tax payment of the poor will be greater.

3. a. See the diagram below.

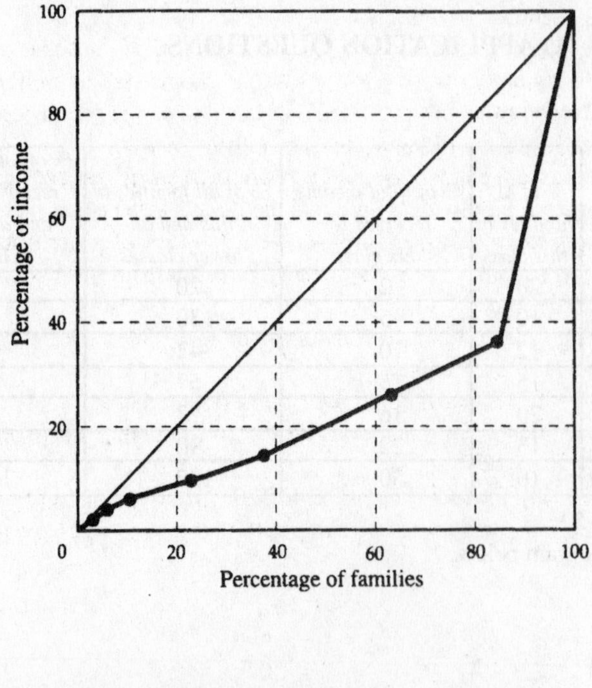

b. The Gini coefficient = AC/AB = 11 / 28 = .39. See the diagram below.

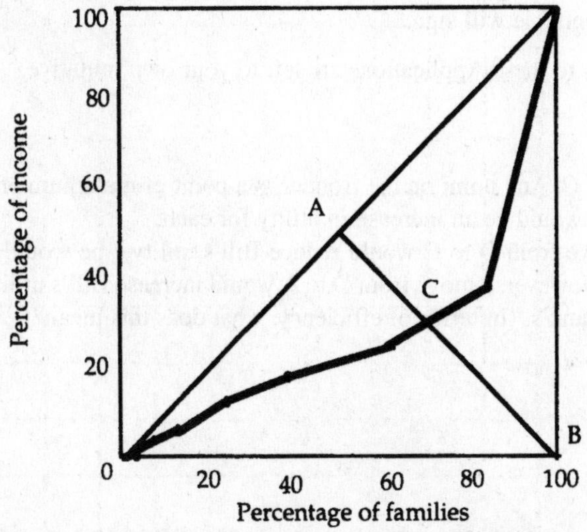

c. The Gregsons' yearly income is $800 x 12, or $9600. The housing subsidy, which is in-kind transfers, is not figured in. In the table above, the Gregsons would be in the third lowest category.

d. Economic income would include both the cash and in-kind payments. The Gregsons' annual economic income would be ($800 + $300) x 12 = $13 200.

e. Mona's economic income will rise by $100 per month. Annual economic income is $14 400 and so is her money income. Therefore, her position in the income distribution is higher.

f. Mona's gross annual income will be $1200 x 12 = $14 400, which, after the deductions and expenses, will leave her $12 144. This is less than her economic income from welfare ($14 400).

g. Taxes while on welfare = $0. Taxes while working = $1956. Change = $1956. Welfare income = $14 400. Work income: $14 400. Change = $0.
Mona's income didn't change, but her tax liability increased by $1956. This is a clear disincentive to work.

h. Unless she wishes to feel self-supporting, or she believes that the starting-level job will lead to higher-wage positions, Mona should stay on welfare.

i. The distribution of income will become less equal. See the answer to part b. The Gini coefficient will move closer to a value of 1.00.

j. Most persons would agree that the $100 would be worth more to Family A and that helping that family would provide the greater satisfaction.

k. Most persons derive satisfaction from the alleviation of poverty, especially if they don't have to pay for it. We cannot be excluded from this benefit if we refuse to contribute.

l. If the average income of "poor" households is $7176, each family needs an additional $7176 on average.

m. (12%/60%) x $7176 = $1435.20 per "well-off" household.

n. The marginal benefit of transferring $1435.20 is less than the private marginal cost.

o. The families will find contributing $1435.20 worthwhile because, by acting as a group, the marginal cost of transferring $7176 dollars has been reduced for each family.

p. Poverty alleviation is a public good. If every other well-off family contributes and I don't, I get the benefits without the cost. If each family follows the same logic, no one will sign.

4-5. The answers to these Applications are left to your own initiative.

6. a. E.
   b. F.
   c. A and C. Any point on the frontier is a point of maximum efficiency.
   d. There would be an increase in utility for each.
   e. A move from D to C would reduce Bill's utility—he would certainly oppose this. However, a move from D to A would increase Bill's utility without reducing Frank's. (In terms of efficiency, what does this mean?)

18 Public Finance: The Economics Of Taxation

OBJECTIVES: POINT BY POINT

After completing this chapter, you should be able to accomplish the objectives listed below.

General Comment

There are many previously developed concepts at work in this chapter—demand and supply, consumer surplus, elasticity, income and substitution effects, marginal thinking, opportunity costs, etc. For example, with respect to increasing the incentive to save: By cutting the marginal tax rate, the opportunity cost of a dollar spent is increased, so fewer dollars will be spent and more will be saved.

OBJECTIVE 1: Define basic tax concepts.

Ultimately all taxes are paid by households. Each tax has two components: a *base*—the value on which the tax is levied—and a *rate structure*. The tax base of an income tax is income. Tax bases may be either stock measures or flow measures. The local property tax is a tax on the value of residential, commercial or industry property. Other taxes are levied on flows, e.g., income tax. Three candidates for "best" tax base are consumption, income, and wealth. A given tax may be progressive, proportional, or regressive. A *progressive (regressive)* tax takes a larger (smaller) fraction of income from a high-income person than from a low-income person. A *proportional* tax takes the same fraction of income from everyone, regardless of income. With progressive taxes, the marginal tax rate is higher than the average tax rate. With regressive taxes, the marginal tax rate is lower than the average tax rate. (page 450)

> **TIP:** Perhaps the single most important paragraph in Chapter 18 occurs on page 452, where marginal and average tax rates are distinguished. Keep in mind that it's the *marginal* tax rate that influences an individual's behaviour—his or her outlook on working, saving, and investing.

Practice

1. The measure or value on which a tax is levied is called the
   A. tax burden.
   B. tax structure.
   C. tax base.
   D. tax incidence.

   ANSWER: C. See p. 419.

2. A regressive income tax has a(n) __________ marginal tax rate and a(n) __________ average tax rate.
   A. increasing, increasing.
   B. increasing, decreasing.
   C. decreasing, increasing.
   D. decreasing, decreasing.

   ANSWER: D. As income increases, more taxes must be paid, but a relatively smaller fraction of income is taxed away.

3. We have a progressive income tax system. Jack earns $20 000 and pays $6000 in taxes. Jill earns $40 000. She could pay __________ in taxes.
   A. $6000.
   B. $9000.
   C. $12 000.
   D. $14 000.

   ANSWER: D. Jill's income is double Jack's. In a progressive tax system, her tax liability will be more than double that of Jack.

Use the following table to answer the next four questions.

Income	Total Taxes
$10 000	$1 000
$20 000	$4 000
$30 000	$7 000
$40 000	$12 000

4. As income increases from $20 000 to $30 000, the marginal tax rate is
   A. 10%.
   B. 20%.
   C. 25%.
   D. 30%.

   ANSWER: D. Marginal tax rate is change in total tax/change in income. (7000 – 4000) / (30 000 – 20 000) = 30%.

5. As income increases from $20 000 to $40 000, the marginal tax rate is
   A. 20%.
   B. 25%.
   C. 30%.
   D. 40%.

   ANSWER: D. Marginal tax rate is change in total tax/change in income. (12 000 – 4000) / (40 000 –20 000) = 40%.

6. When the income level is $20 000, the average tax rate is
   A. 10%.
   B. 20%.
   C. 25%.
   D. 30%.

   ANSWER: B. Average tax rate is total tax/income. 4000/20 000 = 20%.

7. The tax structure in this example is
   A. progressive.
   B. proportional.
   C. regressive.
   D. progressive at first, then regressive.

   ANSWER: A. Average tax rates increase as income level increases.

OTHER RELATED POINTS: Distinguish between the benefits-received principle and the ability-to-pay principle of taxation.

Two principles are used to judge whether a tax is "fair":

a. the *ability-to-pay principle* suggests that those who are more able to pay should pay more.

b. the *benefits-received principle* suggests that those who receive the benefits of the expenditures financed by a tax should be the ones to pay. (page 422)

> **TIP:** Make up a list of taxes and try to determine which principle is present. You should find that the ability-to-pay principle is favoured in Canada.
>
> Note the disincentives that can occur with the ability-to-pay principle—the harder you work, the more you earn, and the more you pay. On the other hand, the "benefits-received" option implies that the poor and/or unemployed should be the ones to pay for their own income-support programs.

Practice

8. A _______________ is the tax most likely to ensure vertical equity.
   A. progressive income tax.
   B. regressive income tax.
   C. sales tax on alcohol.
   D. head tax of $100 per citizen.

   ANSWER: A. Vertical equity is related to the ability-to-pay principle.

9. Which of the following taxes is based on the benefits-received principle?
   A. a progressive property tax if the revenue is used to finance public education.
   B. a regressive property tax if the revenue is used to finance public education.
   C. a progressive property tax if the revenue is used to finance national defence.
   D. a flat-rate tax on car owners used to maintain and improve roads.

   ANSWER: D. Those who pay the tax are the ones who derive the benefit in terms of improved driving conditions.

OBJECTIVE 2: Give arguments for and against alternative tax bases.

Three candidates for the most appropriate tax base are consumption, economic income, and wealth. The arguments for and against each are presented in the textbook. (page 422)

Note that the effect of a tax on savings is important in this discussion. A consumption tax, such as a national sales tax, would tax savings once, while an income tax affects savings twice. (page 425)

> **TIP:** Avoid the temptation to declare all taxes to be bad. Read through this section in the textbook critically. Which tax system would be least burdensome for you, personally, at the present time? Which would be least burdensome after you graduate? How does each affect you as a senior citizen? Last, are your needs and society's needs the same in each case?

Practice

10. A tax on consumption may be preferable to a tax on income for all of the following reasons except that
    A. one's standard of living depends on consumption, not income.
    B. a consumption tax can raise more revenue than an income tax.
    C. a consumption tax can reduce the double taxation of savings.
    D. a consumption tax can raise the level of economic growth.

    ANSWER: B. A consumption tax may or may not raise more revenue—it depends on the tax structure. See p. 423 for a full discussion of this debate.

Use the following information to answer the next two questions.

Brenda, an unmarried banker, rents her apartment and earned $40 000 last year. Her firm paid her dental care worth $5000 and contributed $4 000 to her retirement plan. Brenda's rich uncle sent a cheque for $5000 for her birthday. Brenda's hobbies include gardening—last year she grew $100 of produce. She has no time to do anything with her stock market portfolio, and its value fell from $8000 to $6000 last year.

11. Which of the following items would not be included in Brenda's economic income?
    A. The $8000 in her stock market portfolio.
    B. The unearned gift of $5000 from her uncle.
    C. The $100 of produce that never reached a market.
    D. The decrease of $2000 in the value of Brenda's stock portfolio.

    ANSWER: A. This is wealth, not income.

12. The best estimate of Brenda's economic income is
    A. $46 100.
    B. $52 100.
    C. $54 100
    D. $60 100.

    ANSWER: B. Each item above should be included. The change in the value of the stock portfolio must be subtracted.

OBJECTIVE 3: Distinguish legal from economic tax incidence.

When a government levies a tax, it writes a law assigning responsibility for payment to specific people or specific organizations. Remember that (a) the burden of a tax is ultimately borne by individuals and households, and (b) the burden of a tax is not always borne by those initially responsible for paying it - tax shift. Tax incidence is the ultimate distribution of its burden. (page 425)

However, it is important to distinguish between who is legally responsible for writing a cheque to the government and who actually pays the tax by experiencing a loss in general well being. This distinction in economics is known as the distinction between legal and economic incidence of a tax. (page 60)

Practice

13. The incidence of a tax refers to
    A. the structure of the tax.
    B. how frequently the tax is collected.
    C. who bears the economic burden of the tax.
    D. the impact of the tax on prices or wages.

    ANSWER: C. See p. 425 for the definition.

14. The government imposes a tax on oranges. Most households reduce their purchases of oranges and buy other fruits instead. Their behaviour is an example of
    A. tax incidence.
    B. tax shifting.
    C. tax restructuring.
    D. tax evasion.

    ANSWER: B. Tax shifting occurs when a taxpayer changes her/his behaviour to avoid a tax.

15. Of the following, ____________ would be the easiest to shift.
    A. a $100 tax per citizen.
    B. a 10% excise tax on oranges.
    C. a proportional income tax.
    D. a 5% consumption tax.

    ANSWER: B. It would be fairly easy to avoid the tax by not purchasing oranges.

OBJECTIVE 4: Analyze economic tax incidence of payroll and corporate income taxes.

Taxes can distort economic decisions and change behaviour. Demand and supply can both be affected by the presence of a tax, as can prices. Payroll taxes are largely shifted to workers, and are regressive. Corporate tax seems to be borne by the owners of companies, with only slight impact on workers—tax shifting is less successful in this case. Provincial and local taxes are mildly regressive, but federal taxes are mildly progressive. The Canadian tax system is mildly progressive. (page 464)

The notion that households ultimately bear the burden of all taxes may seem difficult to grasp. The burden from sales taxes, property taxes, and personal income taxes is fairly easy to see. Capital gains taxes or corporate profit taxes, though, are also borne by households—households, in the final analysis, own the firms.

> **TIP:** Check your own list of taxes to see in which cases tax shifting is possible. Remember that taxes change behaviour and that, eventually, the tax burden is borne by households.

Practice

Use the following diagram to answer the next three questions. The diagram shows the demand (D) and supply (S) curves in the labour market. A payroll tax of $1.00 is imposed.

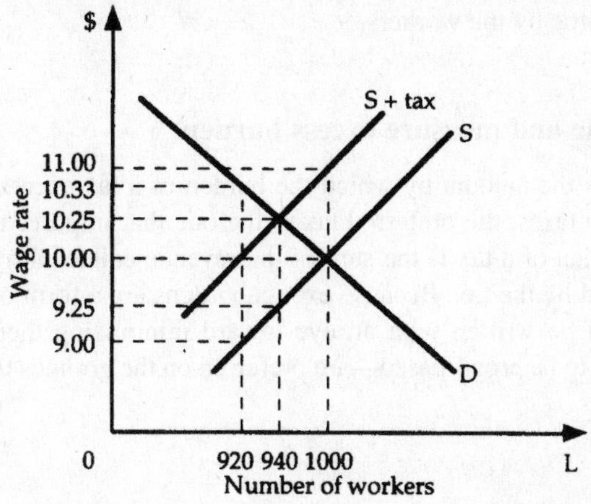

16. Before the imposition of the payroll tax, the equilibrium wage rate was ________ and the equilibrium level of employment was ______.
   A. $10.00, 1000.
   B. $10.00, 940.
   C. $10.25, 1000.
   D. $10.25, 940.

   ANSWER: A. This is where the labour demand curve and the original labour supply curve intersect.

17. After the tax is imposed, _____ workers will each take home _______.
   A. 1000, $10.00.
   B. 1000, $11.00.
   C. 940, $10.25.
   D. 940, $9.25.

   ANSWER: D. Equilibrium hiring level is 940. At this level, firms will pay no more than $9.25 per worker.

18. The workers' share of the tax burden is ________; the employer's share is _______.
   A. $235, $235.
   B. $235, $705.
   C. $705, $235.
   D. $705, $705.

   ANSWER: C. Tax revenues are $940. Each worker lost 75¢ in wages; each employer has to pay 25¢.

19. The imposition of a corporate income tax will _________ profits in the corporate sector and ________ profits in the non-corporate sector.
   A. increase, increase.
   B. increase, decrease.
   C. decrease, increase.
   D. decrease, decrease.

   ANSWER: D. Competitive forces will equalize profits throughout the economy. Higher taxes will reduce profits in all sectors.

20. The ____________ labour supply is, the ___________ the proportion of a payroll tax will be borne by employees.
   A. more elastic, greater.
   B. less elastic, less.
   C. more inelastic, greater.
   D. more inelastic, less.

   ANSWER: C. In the extreme case, when labour supply is perfectly inelastic, all of a payroll tax will be borne by the workers.

OBJECTIVE 5: Define and measure excess burden.

The *excess burden* of a tax is the amount by which the burden of a tax exceeds the total revenue collected. Given two taxes, the preferred tax is the one that imposes the smaller excess burden. The total burden of a tax is the sum of the revenue collected from the tax and the excess burden created by the tax. Because excess burdens are a form of waste, or lost value, tax policy should be written with an eye toward minimizing them. *Neutral taxes*—which are most likely to be broad-based—are preferred on the grounds that they do not hurt efficiency. (page 431)

TIP: Note also that, when Case, Fair, Strain, and Veall look at the size of excess burdens, the logic they use is the same as that you encountered in Chapter 13 when looking at the welfare loss from monopoly.

Practice

Use the following information to answer the next three questions.

In the production of sweatbands, the current lowest-cost mix of labour and capital costs \$6.00 per 10 sweatbands. A 50¢ tax is imposed per unit of labour. Producers react by switching to a different input mix, using only 5 units of labour to produce 10 sweatbands. The new input mix increases the cost of producing 10 sweatbands to \$9.00.

21. If 1000 sweatbands are sold, the total tax revenue collected is
    A. \$30.00.
    B. \$25.00.
    C. \$250.00.
    D. \$300.00.

    ANSWER: C. Total tax on 10 sweatbands = 5 x 50¢ = \$2.50. Total tax on 1000 sweatbands = \$2.50 x 100 = \$250.

22. If 1000 sweatbands are sold, the total tax burden is
    A. \$30.00.
    B. \$45.00.
    C. \$300.00.
    D. \$450.00.

    ANSWER: C. Total tax burden = (\$9.00 – \$6.00) x100 = \$300.

23. If 1000 sweatbands are sold, the excess burden of the tax is
    A. \$30.00.
    B. \$50.00.
    C. \$250.00.
    D. \$300.00.

    ANSWER: B. The excess burden = the total tax burden – tax revenue = \$300 – \$250.

OBJECTIVE 6: Describe the principle of the second best.

The principle of second best refers to the fact that a tax that distorts an economic decision does not always imply that such a tax imposes an excess burden. If previously existing distortions exist, such a tax may actually improve efficiency. (page 433)

Practice

24. We would most likely wish to impose a non-neutral tax if ________ are present.
    A. externalities and public goods.
    B. inelastic demand and other distortionary taxes.
    C. externalities and other distortionary taxes.
    D. inelastic demand and public goods.

    ANSWER: C. The adverse effects of both externalities and other distortionary taxes can be offset by non-neutral taxes.

25. The principle of the second best states that
    A. taxes should be neutral.
    B. excess burdens will be minimized if demand is perfectly inelastic.
    C. a distortionary tax can improve economic efficiency if imposed in a situation where previous distortions were present.
    D. a broad-based tax is preferable to a tax on a specific product.

    ANSWER: C. The principle of the second best is based on the argument that distortion may be corrected by the imposition of offsetting distortions.

OTHER RELATED POINTS: Demonstrate, using graphs, the presence of the excess burden following the imposition of a tax, linking the resulting distortion to the relative elasticity of demand.

The shifting of taxation can impose an *excess burden* (over and above the revenues collected) on society. The size of the burden depends on the responsiveness of buyers and sellers, as measured by price or income elasticity. (page 437)

> **TIP:** You'll get more out of the section on tax neutrality if you reread Chapter 12 first. Many of the concepts developed there are reused in this section.

Practice

26. A broad-based tax, such as a general energy tax, tends to distort choices ______ and impose ________ excess burdens than a specific tax, (i.e., a gasoline tax) does.
    A. more, higher.
    B. more, lower.
    C. fewer, higher.
    D. fewer, lower.

    ANSWER: D. The specific tax is more shiftable, leading to more distortions and greater excess burdens.

27. The total burden of a tax can be described as
    A. the tax revenue minus the after-tax consumer surplus.
    B. the before-tax consumer surplus minus the after-tax consumer surplus.
    C. the tax revenue minus the excess burden.
    D. the excess burden minus the tax revenue.

    ANSWER: B. The total burden is measured by how much consumer welfare has been reduced.

28. In two communities, Balado and Clathy, the level of demand for gasoline is identical, but it is more elastic in Balado. Marginal cost is assumed to be constant. The imposition of a gasoline tax will cause a greater decrease in consumption in _________ and a greater excess burden in _________.
    A. Balado, Balado.
    B. Balado, Clathy.
    C. Clathy, Balado.
    D. Clathy, Clathy.

    ANSWER: A. As demand is more elastic in Balado, the tax-induced price hike will result in a larger decrease in consumption.

PRACTICE TEST

I. MULTIPLE CHOICE QUESTIONS. Select the option that provides the single best answer.

____ 1. The government imposes a new tax on insurance companies. Economic theory suggests that, ultimately, the tax will be paid by
A. the owners of the insurance companies.
B. the employees of the insurance companies.
C. the banking sector.
D. households, some of whom may not even have any form of insurance.

____ 2. Assuming "normally shaped" labour demand and supply curves, which of the following is not true of a payroll tax?
A. the greater the elasticity of the supply of labour, the greater will be the proportion of the tax borne by firms.
B. the tax will cause workers' wages to rise.
C. some job loss is likely.
D. the greater the substitutability of capital for labour, the greater the fall in wages.

Use the following information to answer the next three questions.

An economy has two sectors—agricultural and manufacturing—made up of farms and firms, respectively. In each sector, capital earns a normal rate of return equal to 10%. The government imposes a 50% surtax on accounting profits in the manufacturing sector.

____ 3. After the economy has fully adjusted to the new tax, who is the least likely to bear any of the tax burden?
A. owners of firms.
B. owners of farms.
C. consumers who buy mainly agricultural goods.
D. consumers who buy mainly manufactured goods.

____ 4. After the economy has fully adjusted, we would expect
A. after-tax return to capital to be greater for firms than for farms.
B. after-tax return to capital to be greater for farms than for firms.
C. after-tax return to capital to be the same for both firms and farms.
D. before-tax return to capital to be greater for farms than for firms.

____ 5. If the demand for manufactured goods is very inelastic, the increase in tax rate will be paid
A. equally by firms and their customers.
B. equally by farms and firms.
C. mainly by firms.
D. mainly by buyers of manufactured goods.

____ 6. The "excess burden" of a tax
A. is equal to the tax revenues collected by it.
B. occurs whenever the imposition of a tax distorts economic behaviour.
C. is equal to the consumer surplus.
D. is equal to the increase in price caused by the tax increase.

_____ 7. In Canada, most of the payroll tax is borne by workers because
A. the elasticity of labour demand is close to zero.
B. the elasticity of labour demand is close to one.
C. the elasticity of labour supply is close to zero.
D. the elasticity of labour supply is close to one.

_____ 8. The retail sales tax is regressive because
A. a rich person pays more tax than a poor person does.
B. a rich person pays less tax than a poor person does.
C. a rich person pays a lower proportion of her/his income in tax than a poor person does.
D. a rich person pays a higher proportion of her/his income in tax than a poor person does.

_____ 9. The cardinal principle of tax analysis is that
A. the burden of a tax is borne by individuals or households.
B. institutions are the final payers of taxes.
C. wage earners are the final source of taxes.
D. the incidence of a tax cannot be shifted.

_____ 10. A new labour tax is levied on employers—the tax is \$1 per unit of labour. The wage rate falls by 30¢. We can conclude that
A. the income effect is stronger than the substitution effect.
B. employees pay the bulk of the tax.
C. the amount of labour used by firms has increased.
D. the result would have been the same if the tax had been imposed on the workers, not the employers.

_____ 11. Which of the following statements is false?
A. the marginal tax rate has a greater influence on behaviour than the average tax rate has.
B. tax shifting occurs when the government moves taxes towards those who have the ability to pay more.
C. the retail sales tax is more difficult to avoid than the excise tax.
D. with relatively elastic demand, an excise tax causes a high degree of distortion.

Use the following diagram to answer the next four questions.

The diagram shows the demand (D) and supply (S1) curves for ball-bearings which are produced in a perfectly competitive industry.

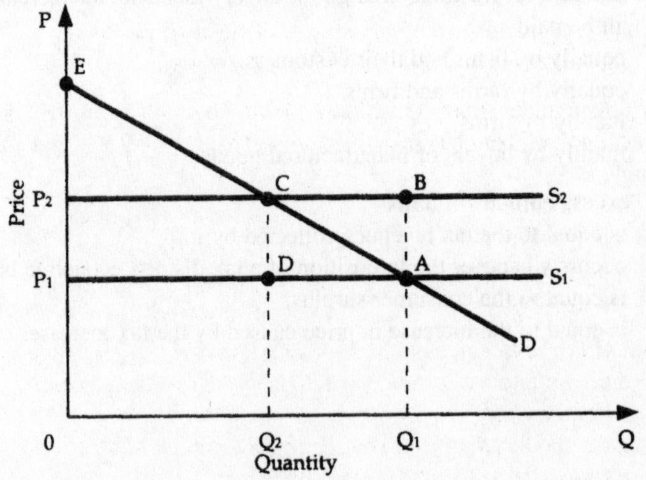

_____ 12. Their price is P_1. Which area represents the consumer surplus?
A. P_1AE.
B. ACD.
C. P_1P_2CD.
D. P_2EC.

_____ 13. Now a tax of $T is imposed that raises the price to P_2. Which area represents the tax revenue?
A. $0P_1DQ_2$.
B. P_1P_2CD.
C. Q_1Q_2AC.
D. ABCD.

_____ 14. Which area represents the excess burden of the tax to the consumer?
A. ABC.
B. CDA.
C. Q_1Q_2AC.
D. Q_1Q_2AD.

_____ 15. The total burden of the tax is
A. Q_2CAQ_1.
B. Q_2CBQ_1.
C. P_2CAP_1.
D. P_1ABP_2.

_____ 16. An income tax that "double taxes" saving tends to _________ the proportion of income consumed and _________ the proportion saved.
A. increase, increase.
B. increase, decrease.
C. decrease, increase.
D. decrease, decrease.

_____ 17. Most of a payroll tax is borne by _________ because labour supply is quite _________.
A. employers, elastic.
B. employers, inelastic.
C. employees, elastic.
D. employees, inelastic.

_____ 18. Which of the following statements about income taxation is false?
A. income tax discourages saving.
B. income tax results in double taxation.
C. income tax taxes the individual on her/his ability to pay.
D. income taxes in Canada are mildly regressive.

_____ 19. Your boss explains that she will have to cut your wages by 10% because the local government has hiked her property taxes by 20%. This is an example of
A. tax shifting.
B. a regressive tax.
C. a progressive tax.
D. tax evasion.

_____ 20. Which of the following is a tax levied on a flow?
A. a tax on interest earned on savings in your bank account.
B. a property tax.
C. a tax on the savings in your bank account.
D. a tax on the value of the stocks you own.

Use the following information to answer the next four questions.

A basketball, which is produced in a perfectly competitive industry, can be produced using either of two processes as summarized in the table. Currently, the price of a unit of labour is $2, and the price of a unit of capital is $2. Demand is perfectly inelastic at a quantity of 100 basketballs. Assume that costs are constant.

	Units of Capital	Units of Labour
Process A	5	4
Process B	2	8

_____ 21. The long-run market price of a basketball is
A. $12.
B. $18.
C. $22.
D. $24.

_____ 22. Now the government imposes a $1 per unit tax on each unit of capital used. The long-run market price of a basketball will be
A. $16.
B. $22.
C. $23.
D. $24.

_____ 23. The government imposes a $1 per unit tax on each unit of capital used. The government's tax revenue is
A. $4.
B. $100.
C. $200.
D. $400.

_____ 24. The government imposes a $1 per unit tax on each unit of capital used. The excess burden of the tax is
A. $100.
B. $200.
C. $300.
D. $400.

II. APPLICATION QUESTIONS.

1. Jack and Jill are twins. They have identical salaries and, at birth, each was given a $100 000 bond (which would pay $10 000 each year) by Dame Dobb. Jack lives in a condominium with a rent of $10 000 each year. He uses the interest from the bond to pay his rent. Jill lives in an identical condo next door but she sold the bond, bought the condo, and pays no rent. In terms of income taxes, which twin is the better off?

2. The phenomenon of "bracket creep" has become less important, in terms of personal income tax, because of the reduction in the number of tax brackets. It is still present for other tax bases, however, the effect being to increase the fraction of the tax base claimed by the government as inflation occurs.

   A numerical example will quickly clarify this issue. Suppose that the marginal tax rate (MTR) is 30% on all income up to $30 000, and 50% on all income above that. Initially, Fred Fiscal earns $30 000.

   a. How much does he pay in taxes?

   Now suppose that there is a sudden doubling of all values denominated in dollars.

   b. Will there be any distributional effects?
   c. Calculate Fred's new tax liability.

Note that prices have doubled, but that Fred's take-home pay has failed to keep pace: Spending power has been redistributed from Fred to Ottawa.

3. A successful computer consultant, Mike Macintosh, charges a fee of $50 per hour. The personal income tax system has very progressive marginal tax rates: The rate that he faces is 50%.

   a. How much does he earn per hour after tax?

   Mike's house needs some work. In addition to the materials, the painter, Peter, will charge for labour at a rate of $30 per hour.

   b. Should Mike hire Peter or should he paint the house himself?

   c. Mike discovers that Peter's marginal tax rate is 25%. How might Mike and Peter attempt to circumvent the tax system?

   d. What other possibilities exist in this situation?

   e. Mike and Peter agree to barter services. Painting the house takes 4 hours, while the computer services take 2 hours. How is this beneficial for both?

4. A hearing aid can be produced in one of two ways, as shown in the table. Assume that the marginal cost of additional hearing aids is constant.

	Units of Capital	*Units of Labour*
Process A	6	3
Process B	4	6

   The price of capital is $1 and the price of labour is $1. Demand is perfectly inelastic at a level of 100 units.

   a. The long-run price in this unregulated competitive industry will be $_______, and Process _____ will be chosen.

   b. Now the government imposes a $1 tax per unit of capital used. Price now would be $________ using the original process, and $________ using Process ______. The preferred process will be Process ______.

   c. Tax revenue will be $_______. The excess burden of the tax will be $_______. The total burden of the tax is $_______.

5. The graph below gives the labour demand and supply curves before and after the imposition of a $1.00 payroll tax.

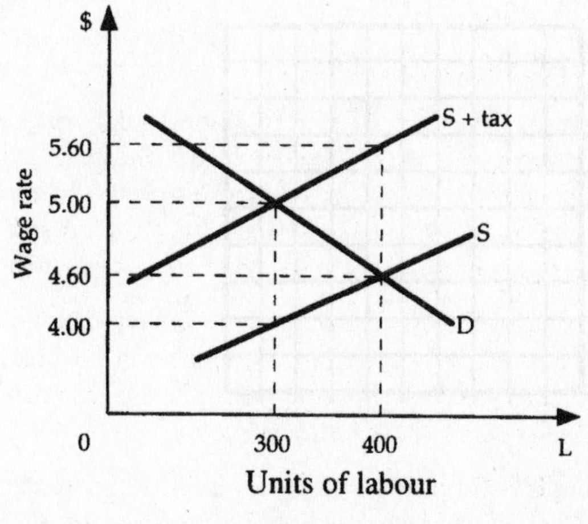

What was the original equilibrium wage rate and employment level? After the tax is imposed, the equilibrium wage and hiring level are $_______ and ______ jobs. Total tax revenue is $_______. The share of the tax paid by employees is $________ and that paid by employers is $________.

6. Sketch a Lorenz curve, showing some income inequality, in each of the three diagrams below. (If necessary, check back to Chapter 17 to review the Lorenz curve.)

a. In the diagram below, show how the curve would change if the government introduced a more progressive tax system.

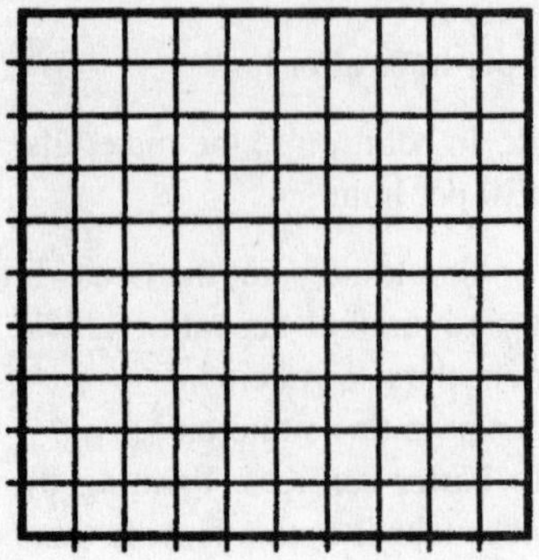

0

b. In the diagram below, show how the curve would change if the government introduced a more regressive tax system.

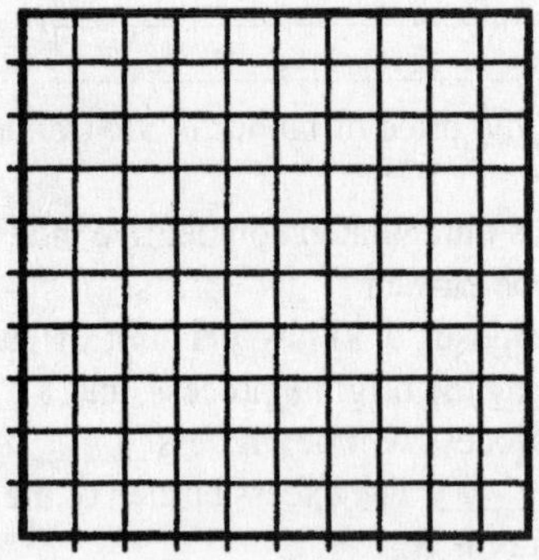

0

c. In the diagram below, show how the curve would change if the government introduced a proportional tax system.

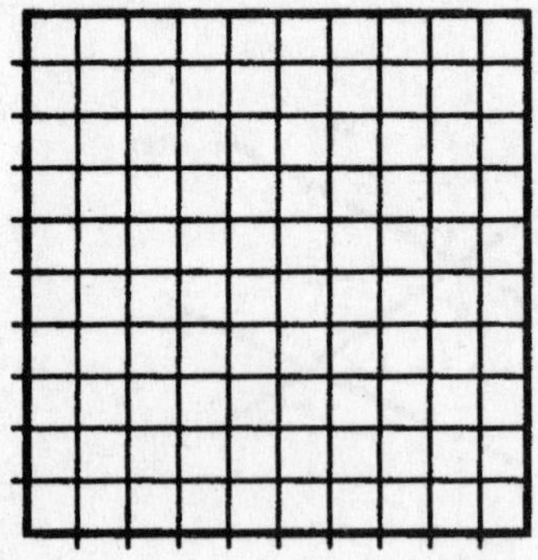

0

7. Following is a tax table, showing average and marginal tax rates. However, there are some blanks.

a. Use your economic knowledge to complete the table.

Total Income	Total Taxes	Average Tax Rate	Marginal Tax Rate
$5 000	$750	_____	_____
$10 000	_____	_____	.090
$15 000	_____	.100	_____
$20 000	$1600	_____	_____
$25 000	_____	_____	.130
$30 000	_____	.110	_____

b. Is this system progressive, regressive, or proportional?

ANSWERS AND SOLUTIONS

PRACTICE TEST

I. SOLUTIONS TO MULTIPLE CHOICE QUESTIONS

1. D. Ultimately, all taxes are paid by households. See p. 429.
2. B. Workers will receive lower wages. Higher taxes increase costs of labour for firms, leading them to cut back hiring. The resultant surplus of workers will drive down the wage rate. See p. 429.
3. C. Certainly firms and their customers will lose. Farms will lose because manufactured goods are part of their inputs. Farm customers will be most insulated from the new tax. Note that the less elastic the demand for farm products, the more of the tax will be borne by farm customers.
4. C. Competitive forces will equalize the after-tax returns in the two sectors.
5. D. Because the purchase of manufactured goods is difficult to avoid, manufacturers will be able to pass on the tax to their customers with little decrease in sales.
6. B. See p. 432.
7. C. The elasticity of labour supply is close to zero, meaning that the labour is fairly insensitive to decreases in wage caused by the imposition of the payroll tax.
8. C. The mark of a regressive tax is that the average tax rate decreases as income level increases.
9. A. Ultimately, all taxes are paid by households. See p. 429.
10. D. See p. 428 for a discussion of this issue.
11. B. Tax shifting occurs when taxpayers adjust their behaviour to avoid a tax.
12. A. Consumer surplus is the (triangular) area between the price and the demand curve.
13. B. Tax revenue depends on the tax rate (the distance P_1P_2) and the quantity sold.
14. B. Total revenue collected is P_1P_2CB. The loss in consumer surplus is P_1P_2CA. The difference is the excess burden of the tax.

15. C. The total burden is the tax burden (P_1P_2CD) plus the excess burden (CDA), or, looked at another way, the decrease in consumer surplus.

16. B. Because the benefits from saving are reduced, taxpayers will tend to consume more and save less of their income.

17. D. When labour supply is inelastic, employers are more able to pass on the burden of the payroll tax to employees. See p. 429.

18. D. Income taxes in Canada are mildly progressive. See p. 431.

19. A. Tax shifting occurs when a tax is avoided, perhaps (as in this case), by passing on the burden to another party.

20. A. Interest is earned during a period of time, i.e., it is a flow variable. Each of the other tax bases is a stock measured at a point in time.

21. B. The lower-cost input mix (A) will be chosen. The cost of production is ($2 x 5) + ($2 x 4) = $18.

22. B. Process A now costs $23 per ball while Process B costs only $22 per ball.

23. B. Total tax = 100 (basketballs) x 2 (units of capital) x $1 = $200.

24. B. Excess burden = total burden - tax revenues collected. Total burden = tax-induced increase in price x quantity sold = ($22 — $18) x 100 = $400. Taxes collected = $200.

II. SOLUTIONS TO APPLICATION QUESTIONS

1. Jill has made the wiser move, at least in terms of income taxes. Jack earns $10 000 more income than Jill and he will be taxed on this. If, however, property taxes are present, the situation changes, and Jack may be relatively better off than Jill.

2. a. $9000.
   b. Yes. See the table below.

Pre-tax Income	*MTR*	*Tax liability*	*After-tax income*
$30 000	30%	$ 9 000	$21 000
$60 000	50%	$24 000	$36 000

   c. $24 000 = $9000 + ($30 000 x .5).

3. a. $25.00.
   b. Mike should paint his house himself—this is an example of a tax distortion. His after-tax income is $25.00 per hour; he is better employed in an activity that saves him $30 per hour. (The price system is signalling that Mike's efforts are worth $50 per hour, yet he is rational in allocating time to an activity saving him $30 per hour.)
   c. Mike could offer Peter a "cash basis" transaction. If Peter's marginal tax rate is 25%, the $30 pre-tax income is the equivalent of $22.50 after tax. Peter gains if he negotiates an "off-the-books" price of $24, and Mike's bill is lower.
   d. One possibility is that Mike and Peter can barter services, although this is unlikely given Mike's occupation, which is not easy to barter. Perhaps Mike can computerize Peter's billing and accounting system in exchange for the painting services.
   e. Painting the house takes 4 hours and the computer services take 2 hours. Mike has saved 4 hours ($25.00 x 4 = $100) at the cost of 2 hours (worth $50.00). Similarly, Peter has worked 4 hours for a reward of $30 x 4 x .75 = $90 but received services that would have cost him $100 on the open market. Mike can gain, as can Peter, who can also avoid tax payments. The "underground economy" is created, in part, by a desire to avoid taxes.

4. a. \$9. Average cost and marginal cost will both be \$9. In perfect competition, P = MR, and, to maximize profits, MR = MC. Therefore, P = MC = \$9. Process A is cheaper, given the price of labour and capital.
   b. \$15, because 6 units of capital are used. The entire tax hike will be passed on to the consumer because demand is perfectly inelastic. \$14, (\$10 + \$4), will be the price using Process B. Process B is cheaper.
   c. Tax revenue = \$4 x 100 units = \$400. The excess burden of the tax = tax burden - revenues = \$500 – \$400 = \$100. The total burden of the tax = (new price – initial price) x 100 = (\$14 – \$9) x 100 = \$500.

5. Original equilibrium wage is \$4.60 with 400 jobs. The new equilibrium wage is \$4.00 with 300 jobs. Total tax revenue is \$300. The share of the tax paid by employees is \$180, and that paid by employers is \$120.

6. See the diagrams below.

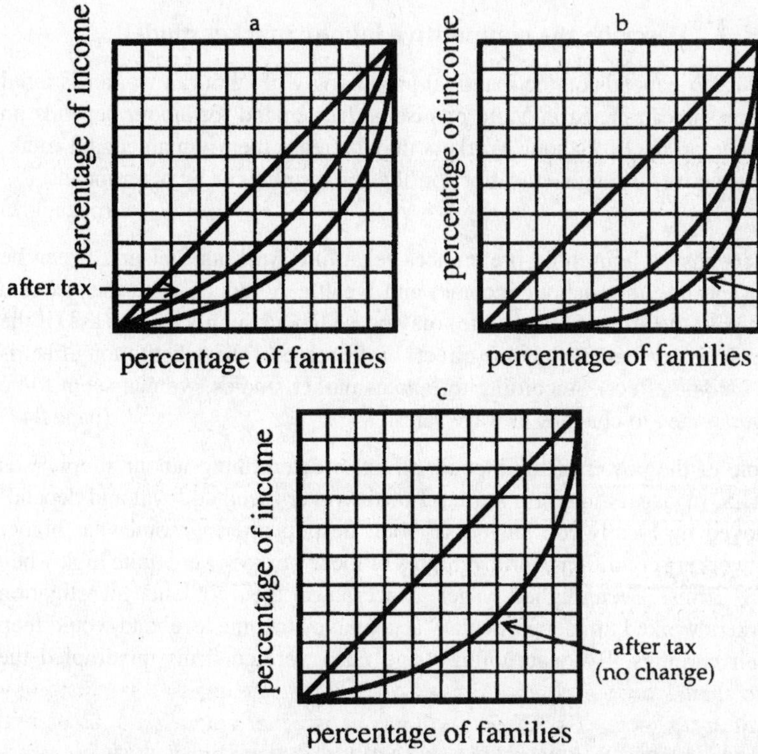

7. a.

Total Income	Total Taxes	Average Tax Rate	Marginal Tax Rate
\$5 000	\$750	150	.150
\$10 000	\$1200	.120	.090
\$15 000	\$1500	.100	.060
\$20 000	\$1600	.080	.020
\$25 000	\$2250	.090	.130
\$30 000	\$3300	.110	.210

   b. This system is regressive until one's income reaches \$20 000, after which it becomes progressive.

19 The Economics Of Labour Markets And Labour Unions

OBJECTIVES: POINT BY POINT

After completing this chapter, you should be able to accomplish the objectives listed below.

OBJECTIVE 1: Describe the competitive labour market model.

The *demand for labour* depends on the marginal productivity of labour; a worker is hired only for what he or she can produce. More precisely, the demand for labour depends on the marginal revenue product of labour. Workers may increase their human capital (making them more productive) through education, on-the-job training, or by other means. (page 442)

Labour supply depends on household preferences regarding work and leisure. It can be affected by the wage rate, non-labour income, and wealth. A reduction in the tax rate (which would increase the after-tax wage rate) may cause labour supply to increase (if the substitution effect is larger than the income effect) or decrease (if the substitution effect is smaller than the income effect). According to labour-market studies, women seem to be more responsive than men to changes in wage rates. (page 443)

A curious example of the power of the income effect in determining labour supply was encountered by U.S. managers in North Africa. Local workers seemed loyal and dependable when employed by locally run businesses, but, despite offering somewhat higher wages and better working conditions, turnover rates of local workers were quite high when working for U.S. firms. Even higher wages exacerbated the problem. Investigation revealed that workers worked up to a particular "acceptable" income level and would then quit to enjoy their earnings. By quadrupling wage rates, foreign firms quadrupled the turnover rate.

> **TIP:** The first part of this chapter is purely a review and a great chance to check on what you've learned during your microeconomics course. Make up a list of topics that are reused in this chapter. Go back and read over Chapter 10 and, for the income and substitution effects that influence labour supply, Chapter 6.

> **TIP:** The examples given in this chapter (Carrie, McDonald's, and David) feature the sort of questions labour economists address. More important for you, they use "economic thinking." Try making analyses like these for yourself, applying economic concepts and logic, perhaps based on your own labour market experiences.

Labour Supply: The study of labour supply is made complicated because supplying labour involves two decisions: whether to work or not and (once the decision to work is made) how many hours to work. Keep in mind that the decision to increase the number of hours worked means a decision to reduce the amount of leisure. When tracing through the effects of wage increases or reductions in tax rates, it can be easier to think of the decision in terms of leisure.

Practice

1. For the perfectly competitive firm, the marginal revenue product of labour is equal to the
   A. marginal physical product times the price of labour.
   B. marginal physical product times the price of output.
   C. change in the wage bill divided by the number of workers.
   D. change in the wage bill divided by change in the number of workers.

   ANSWER: B. See p. 442.

2. Marginal revenue product of labour will increase if
   A. labour productivity improves.
   B. the wage rate decreases.
   C. the demand for output decreases.
   D. the supply of labour increases.

   ANSWER: A. MRP is dependent upon marginal physical product and the price of final output.

Use the following labour market diagram to answer questions 3–6.

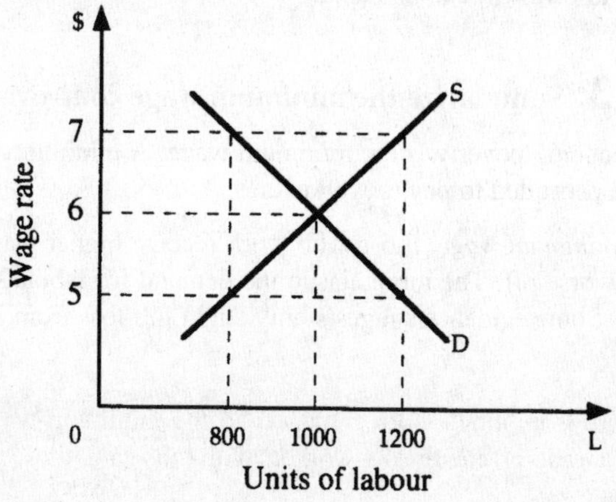

3. Refer to the diagram above. If the wage rate is currently $5, there is an excess ____________ labour equal to ______ units of labour.
   A. demand for, 400.
   B. demand for, 1200.
   C. supply of, 400.
   D. supply of, 800.

   ANSWER: A. The wage rate is below the equilibrium wage rate, causing quantity demanded to exceed quantity supplied by 1200 – 800.

4. The labour market is in equilibrium. If labour productivity increased, we would expect the wage rate to ____________ and employment to ____________ 1000.
   A. rise above $6, exceed.
   B. rise above $6, be less than.
   C. fall below $6, exceed.
   D. fall below $6, be less than.

   ANSWER: A. The current equilibrium situation is a wage rate of $6 and a hiring level of 1000. The improved productivity will increase the demand for labour.

OBJECTIVE 2: Define human capital.

The stock of knowledge, skills and talents that people possess by nature or through education and training is called human capital. Households, firms and governments invest in human capital. The principal form of human capital investment financed primarily by households is education. The principal form of human capital investment financed primarily by firms is on-the-job training. Government's contribution in this regard is in the form of subsidized or sponsored training as well as subsidized public education.

(page 443)

When you decide to go to university (invest in human capital), you are making a decision regarding benefits and costs. The explicit costs (tuition, books, and so on) are fairly obvious. Loss of earnings over four years is a less obvious factor. The benefits from a degree have been much more difficult to pin down. According to 1995 data from Statistics Canada, a university degree is worth $22 391 (before tax) per year in extra pay.

> **TIP:** Review Application Question 1 in Chapter 11 for more on the decision to invest in human capital.

OBJECTIVE 3: Summarize the minimum wage controversy.

One strategy for reducing poverty is the minimum wage. A minimum wage is the lowest wage that firms are permitted to pay to workers.

As a result of the *minimum wage*, those who work receive higher wages, but those who lose their jobs are worse off. The more elastic the demand for labour, the greater will be the unemployment. Some evidence suggests only slight job-loss from increasing the minimum wage.

(page 448)

> **TIP:** There is no single correct answer to the minimum-wage issue. There is a trade-off involved—workers with jobs gain, those who lose their jobs lose.

Practice

5. Refer to the diagram above. If a minimum wage of $7 were imposed, there would be an ____________ workers and the wage rate would ____________
   A. excess demand for, increase.
   B. excess demand for, decrease.
   C. excess supply of, increase.
   D. excess supply of, decrease.

   ANSWER: C. The equilibrium wage is $6. The minimum-wage imposition sets up a disequilibrium, forcing the wage rate higher and creating an excess supply of 400 workers.

6. Refer to the diagram above. If the minimum wage is set below the equilibrium wage, at $5,
   A. there will be an excess demand for labour of 400.
   B. there will be an excess supply of labour of 400.
   C. the equilibrium wage rate will move from $6.
   D. there will be no effect on the labour market.

   ANSWER: D. A minimum wage places a lower limit on the wage rate. In this market, given demand and supply conditions, the lowest the wage will go is $6.

OBJECTIVE 4: Analyze the impact of redistribution policy on labour market outcomes.

The government influences the operation of the market in a variety of ways. Here, four policies are discussed: the minimum wage policy; tax policy; income maintenance programs; and employment insurance.

Cutting the marginal tax rate has a substitution effect (which raises labour supply) and an income effect (which reduces labour supply). (page 484)

There seems to be a gender difference with respect to the elasticity of labour supply. Males are somewhat unresponsive to changes in wage rates, while female workers respond positively. Although conventional wisdom and theory maintain that income maintenance programs (welfare) create a disincentive to work, recent evidence shows that most workers prefer to lose benefits and work if they can. (page 449)

Practice

7. Wage elasticity of labour supply is (+).10. Assume labour demand is perfectly inelastic and that the labour market is in equilibrium with 100 000 workers employed. If a minimum wage is imposed that is 10% higher than the equilibrium wage, unemployment will
   A. increase by 1000.
   B. decrease by 1000.
   C. increase by 10 000.
   D. decrease by 10 000.

   ANSWER: A. A 10% wage increase will increase labour supply by 1%. 100 000 x .01 = 1000.

8. As the wage increases, the __________ effect will encourage workers to supply _______ labour, and the __________ effect will encourage workers to supply less labour.
   A. income, more, substitution.
   B. income, less, substitution.
   C. substitution, more, income.
   D. substitution, less, income.

   ANSWER: C. As the wage rises, the opportunity cost of leisure increases, and the substitution effect will encourage workers to supply more labour. The income effect makes leisure more attractive and reduces labour supply.

9. Empirical studies show that when there is a wage increase, the _________ dominates for males, and the _________ dominates for females.
   A. income effect, income effect.
   B. income effect, substitution effect.
   C. substitution effect, income effect.
   D. substitution effect, substitution effect.

   ANSWER: B. The income effect operates to reduce labour supply when there is a wage increase. See p. 450.

10. The wage elasticity of women is .94. This means that a 10% increase in wage will result in a _________ increase in the supply of female labour.
   A. .094%.
   B. .6%.
   C. .94%.
   D. 9.4%.

   ANSWER: D. The wage elasticity formula is "change in labour supply/change in wage."

11. The benefits from income maintenance programs are increased. We would expect the income effect to _________ labour supply, and the substitution effect to _________ labour supply.
   A. increase, increase.
   B. increase, decrease.
   C. decrease, increase.
   D. decrease, decrease.

   ANSWER: D. Both effects operate in the same direction. See p. 450.

12. An increase in Employment Insurance payments will _________ job search time by _________.
   A. increase, increasing expected benefits.
   B. increase, reducing search costs.
   C. decrease, increasing expected benefits.
   D. decrease, reducing search costs.

   ANSWER: B. See p. 455.

13. As the wage increases, the _________ effect indicates that leisure becomes _________ expensive.
   A. income, more.
   B. income, less.
   C. substitution, more.
   D. substitution, less.

   ANSWER: C. See p. 450.

14. An increase in the marginal tax rate will _________ labour supply according to the income effect and will _________ labour supply according to the substitution effect.
   A. increase, increase.
   B. increase, decrease.
   C. decrease, increase.
   D. decrease, decrease.

   ANSWER: B. A tax rate increase reduces earnings per hour and, therefore, reduces the opportunity cost of leisure. Workers substitute leisure for work. As earnings have fallen, though, poorer workers will wish to work more.

15. Jane is unemployed. She should continue to search for a job as long as the expected gains from continuing to search
   A. are positive.
   B. are greater than zero.
   C. are greater than the additional costs of searching.
   D. are greater than the total costs of searching.

   ANSWER: C. As in much of economics, search decisions are based on marginal considerations. See p. 454.

OBJECTIVE 5: Outline sources of wage and income differential.

Reasons for the diversity in wages include compensating differentials, occupational segregation, and discrimination. Discrimination occurs when an identifiable group of workers receives inferior treatment because of some characteristic irrelevant to job performance. Such treatment might include being barred from particular occupations, receiving lower wages, or having fewer promotion prospects. (page 455)

An interesting example of segregation showed up in the former Soviet Union—70% of all Soviet medical doctors were female. By comparison, less than 20% of Canadian doctors are female, and less than a third of medical school graduates in Canada are women.

> **TIP:** The material on occupations and wages is completely descriptive. When you reach "comparable worth," review the box on this topic in Chapter 17 (p. 396).

Practice

16. Labour market discrimination, which restricts access to immigrant workers but not to the native born, reduces the economy's welfare because the marginal product of immigrants is reduced
   A. more than the marginal product of natives is increased.
   B. more than the marginal product of natives is reduced.
   C. less than the marginal product of natives is increased.
   D. less than the marginal product of natives is reduced.

   ANSWER: A. See p. 456.

OBJECTIVE 6: Describe the roles and functions of unions.

Unions, in this country, have represented workers in bargaining over wages, have provided a social support system, and have taken political actions. (page 458)

OBJECTIVE 7: Analyze the impact of unions on labour market outcomes.

Unions may try to restrict the supply of labour or to increase the demand for labour in order to force up wages. Working conditions and numbers of jobs are other areas of union concern. However, there is a conflict of interest—higher wages reduce the quantity of labour demanded, and union members might lose their jobs. (page 461)

Feather-bedding is a tactic intended to reduce job loss. It may be disguised as a concern for customer safety—e.g., the required use of a third pilot or navigator in a two-pilot plane.

Traditionally, it has been argued that unions may represent a labour market imperfection hiking wages and reducing Canadian competitiveness. On the other hand, when there is one hirer of labour (a monopsonist), unions may exert countervailing power, thus resulting in a *more* efficient wage rate and hiring level than would otherwise have arisen. Alongside the common gloomy view of the impact of unions, there is some recent evidence that suggests that unions may boost productivity and increase the communication between workers and management. (page 463)

Point to Ponder: Are the benefits of a union a public good? Better conditions and higher wages are non-excludable and non-rival, so a non-union worker can be a free rider. She is also subject to the drop-in-the-bucket argument.Does one additional union member make any difference?

Practice

Use the following diagram to answer the next four questions.

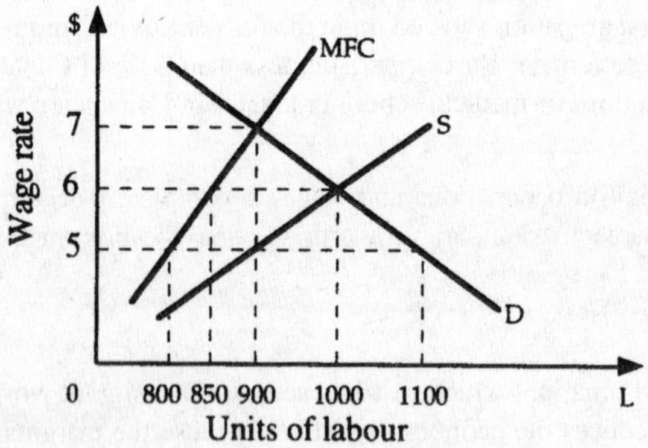

17. In the diagram above, the competitive wage rate is
    A. $5.
    B. $6.
    C. $7.
    D. indeterminate.

    ANSWER: B. In perfect competition, demand and supply will determine the wage.

18. A monopsonist will pay a wage of
    A. $5.
    B. $6.
    C. $7.
    D. between $5 and $7.

    ANSWER: A. The monopsonist will hire where marginal factor cost equals marginal revenue product. The wage is then determined by the labour supply curve.

19. If this labour market ceases to be perfectly competitive and becomes monopsonistic, the employment level will
    A. increase from 900 to 1000.
    B. increase from 900 to 1100.
    C. decrease from 1000 to 900.
    D. decrease from 1000 to 850.

    ANSWER: C. In perfect competition, demand and supply will determine employment level. The monopsonist will hire until marginal factor cost equals marginal revenue product.

20. If a union enters the monopsonistic market, the wage rate will be
  A. between $5 and $6.
  B. between $5 and $7.
  C. between $6 and $7.
  D. $7.

ANSWER: B. The result will be indeterminate, depending on the relative negotiating strengths of the two sides.

PRACTICE TEST

I. MULTIPLE CHOICE QUESTIONS. Select the option that provides the single best answer.

_____ 1. Which of the following does not affect the quantity of labour supplied?
  A. The wage rate.
  B. The marginal tax rate.
  C. Workers' preferences for leisure.
  D. The marginal physical product of labour.

_____ 2. The price of leisure may be measured by
  A. the marginal physical product of labour.
  B. the wage rate.
  C. the slope of the supply curve.
  D. the average product of labour.

_____ 3. If welfare benefits are increased, the income effect will operate to _________ labour supply, and the substitution effect will operate to _______ labour supply.
  A. increase, increase.
  B. decrease, increase.
  C. increase, decrease.
  D. decrease, decrease.

_____ 4. While male workers have access to either Occupation A or B, female workers are forced into Occupation B. Labour market discrimination
  A. has no effect on efficiency if workers are paid according to their marginal revenue product.
  B. will distort wage levels. Wages in Occupation A will be higher than otherwise.
  C. is inefficient. The high wages in Occupation A will cause unemployment.
  D. has no effect on efficiency. All workers will be able to find a job.

_____ 5. Employment Insurance benefits tend to _________ the cost of the job search and ___________ job-search time.
  A. decrease, decrease.
  B. decrease, increase.
  C. increase, decrease.
  D. increase, increase.

_____ 6. Which of the following is least likely to be a union strategy for raising wages?
  A. Encouraging capital investment to boost labour productivity.
  B. Restricting the supply of labour through pressure on legislators.
  C. Imposing a union wage through threat of striking.
  D. Advertising the product produced by union members.

_____ 7. Which of the following is incorrect?
  A. The Canadian Labour Congress is the largest national federation of labour
  organization in Canada.
  B. "Feather-bedding" is the imposition of racial and/or gender barriers to restrict union membership.
  C. Collective bargaining is the process by which union leaders bargain with management as the representatives of all union employees.
  D. It is widely believed that unions have succeeded in raising wages.

_____ 8. According to a study by Freeman and Medoff, union members display all of the following characteristics except that they
  A. have lower quit rates than non-union workers.
  B. remain more loyal to the firm than non-union workers.
  C. maintain a higher morale than non-union workers.
  D. are less cooperative on the job than non-union workers.

_____ 9. A key aspect of the economic philosophy known as "Reagonomics" or "Supply Side Economics" in the 1980s in the United States was that marginal tax rates should be__________ so that labour __________ would increase.
  A. lowered, supply.
  B. lowered, demand.
  C. raised, demand.
  D. raised, supply.

_____ 10. Bill is considering investing in additional education. A cut in Bill's marginal tax rate would ___________ the cost and _________ the net benefits from the extra education.
  A. decrease, decrease.
  B. decrease, increase.
  C. increase, decrease.
  D. increase, increase.

_____ 11. Empirical reports suggest that a net increase in the wage would
  A. unambiguously increase the quantity supplied by both male and female.
  B. unambiguously decrease the quantity supplied by both male and female.
  C. have a relatively small impact on labour supply by all genders.
  D. have opposite effects on women.

_____ 12. Compensating differentials refer to
  A. Employment Insurance benefits.
  B. wage differences between desirable and less risky jobs and those that are less desirable and more risky.
  C. the payments made to workers in case of injuries.
  D. the union dues which tend to equalize the cost of membership to all members.

_____ 13. The marginal revenue product of labour is the additional
A. product generated by hiring an additional worker.
B. factor product cost of hiring an additional worker.
C. average product cost of hiring an additional worker.
D. revenue generated by hiring an additional worker.

_____ 14. Which of the following statements is false?
A. A monopsonist is the sole purchaser of labour services in the labour market.
B. "Feather-bedding" is a way of cushioning the fall in the supply of workers.
C. Income maintenance programs produce income and substitution effects that operate in the same direction.
D. The costs of a continued job search include foregone earnings and time.

_____ 15. Over the past 30 years, the male labour-force participation rate has _________, and the female labour-force participation rate has _________.
A. increased, increased.
B. increased, decreased.
C. decreased, increased.
D. decreased, decreased.

_____ 16. There is an increase in benefits from income maintenance programs. The income effect would predict a(n) __________ in work effort; the substitution effect would predict a(n) _________ in work effort.
A. increase, increase.
B. increase, decrease.
C. decrease, increase.
D. decrease, decrease.

_____ 17. Suppose that in the labour market for professional hockey players, team owners operate as a monopsony. If players form a union, we would expect to see wages __________ and the market becoming _________ efficient.
A. increasing, more.
B. increasing, less.
C. decreasing, more.
D. decreasing, less.

_____ 18. Recent studies indicate that the existing income maintenance programs impose a very high implicit tax. If this is in fact the case, then a drop in marginal tax rates will cause labour supply to__________ and the opportunity cost of leisure relative to work to __________.
A. increase, increase.
B. increase, decrease.
C. decrease, increase.
D. decrease, decrease.

_____ 19. Unions often seek to increase the demand for goods made by union members. This is intended to ___________ employment and __________ wages.
A. increase, increase.
B. increase, decrease.
C. decrease, increase.
D. decrease, decrease.

_____ 20. In a monopsonistic labour market, the entrance of a labour union may result in _________ wages, _________ employment, and _________ efficiency.
A. higher, more, greater.
B. higher, less, greater.
C. higher, less, less.
D. lower, more, less.

_____ 21. Wage elasticity of labour demand is (-).05. Wage elasticity of labour supply is (+).15. The labour market is in equilibrium with 1 000 000 workers employed. If a minimum wage is imposed that is 10% higher than the equilibrium wage, lay-offs will be ________, and there will be __________ unemployed new entrants.
A. 5000, 15 000.
B. 5000, 150 000.
C. 50 000, 15 000.
D. 50 000, 150 000.

_____ 22. Modern cross-sectional studies have found that unions have succeeded in increasing wages of their members by between
A. 10% and 25%.
B. 15% and 20%.
C. 0% and 15%.
D. 50% and 100%.

_____ 23. While male workers have access to either Occupation A or B, female workers are forced into Occupation B. Labour market discrimination should lead to relatively
A. greater use of capital in Occupation A and in Occupation B.
B. greater use of capital in Occupation A and less use in Occupation B.
C. less use of capital in Occupation A and greater use in Occupation B.
D. less use of capital in Occupation A and in Occupation B.

_____ 24. Marginal tax rates are reduced and the tax base is expanded simultaneously. Leisure should
A. increase, because these actions result in only a substitution effect.
B. increase, because the income effect will dominate the substitution effect.
C. decrease, because these actions result in only a substitution effect.
D. decrease, because the substitution effect always exceeds the income effect.

_____ 25. The Dog Catchers Union has successfully negotiated a wage increase and an increase in employment for its members. The union has
A. increased the demand for union labour.
B. decreased the demand for union labour.
C. increased the supply of union labour.
D. decreased the supply of union labour.

II. APPLICATION QUESTIONS.

1. The nation of Arbez has 600 native Arbezani workers and 2400 immigrant Arbocali workers. The wage elasticity of labour demand in Occupation A is –.40, while the wage elasticity of labour demand in Occupation B is –.20. Assume that labour supply is perfectly inelastic. In equilibrium, 1000 workers are employed in Occupation A and 2000 are employed in Occupation B; the equilibrium wages are equal at 10 opeks per worker.

   a. Draw diagrams of the initial situation in Occupation A and Occupation B. Designate the supply of labour curves as S_A1 and S_B1, respectively.

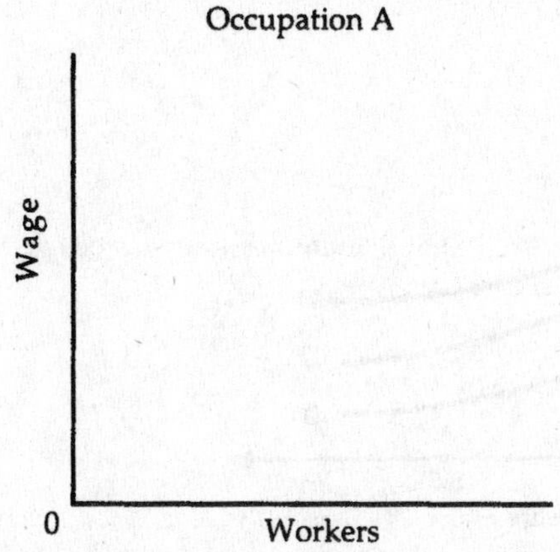

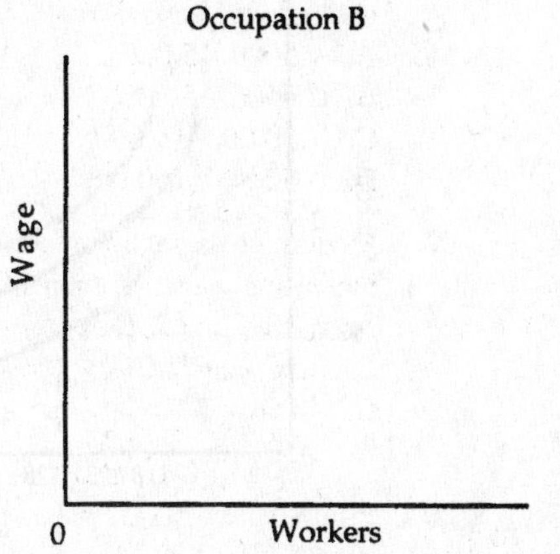

Now, native Arbezani workers are able to limit entry into Occupation A exclusively to native Arbezanis, of which there are 600.

   b. Describe what will happen to wages in Occupation A and Occupation B.
   c. Calculate (approximately) the new wage and employment levels in Occupation A and Occupation B.
   d. Draw the new situation in Occupation A and Occupation B on the previous diagram. Designate the supply of labour curves as S_A2 and S_B2, respectively.
   e. We know that MRP (marginal revenue product) represents the change in production caused by a change in the number of workers. (If you're unsure, check out Chapter 10.) Using the diagram above, can you show the production loss caused by Arbezani discrimination.

2. Below is a labour demand schedule for lifeguards.

Wage per Hour	Hours Demanded per Week	Number of 50-Hour Workers Demanded	Total Weekly Income of Lifeguards	Weekly Income per Lifeguard
\$5	100 000	_______	_______	_______
\$6	80 000	_______	_______	_______

The lifeguards' union has established wage and work conditions in negotiation with employers. The contracted wage is \$5 per hour with a required work week of 50 hours.

   a. Fill in the blanks in the table.

The union now wishes to renegotiate to get a wage of \$6 and hires you as an advisor.

   b. From the calculations you made to complete the table, you should be able to estimate whether the wage elasticity of demand for lifeguards is elastic or inelastic.

The union leadership has reviewed your information and is dismayed at the probable job losses.

c. Suggest a proposal that will increase the wage to $6, but not result in job loss.

3. The following application uses indifference curve analysis. If this has become unfamiliar to you, review the Appendix to Chapter 6 in the textbook.

The diagram below shows the indifference curve map for Cosmo Kramer. Hours of leisure are plotted on the horizontal axis. Income is plotted on the vertical axis.

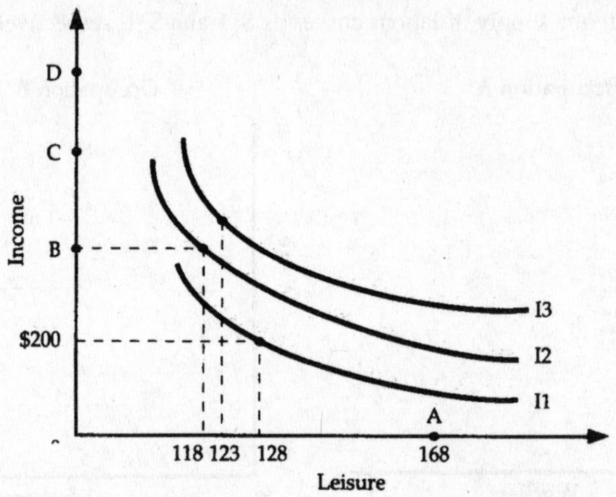

a. Calculate the maximum number of hours of leisure per week for Kramer.
b. If Kramer is offered $5 per hour, calculate his maximum income per week.
c. Kramer works 40 hours per week, at $5 per hour. Calculate his income per week. Draw in Kramer's budget constraint and label it AB.
d. If Kramer is offered $6 per hour, calculate his maximum income per week.
e. Kramer works 50 hours per week, at $6 per hour. Calculate his income per week. Draw in Kramer's budget constraint and label it AC.
f. An increase in wage has increased Kramer's number of hours worked. Which is stronger: the income effect or the substitution effect? How do you know?
g. If Kramer is offered $7 per hour, calculate his maximum income per week.
h. Kramer works 45 hours per week, at $7 per hour. Calculate his income per week. Draw in Kramer's budget constraint and label it AD.
i. Interpret the effect of the wage increase from $6 to $7 on the number of hours Kramer will work. Which is stronger: the income effect or the substitution effect? How do you know?
j. Graph Kramer's labour supply curve on the graph below.

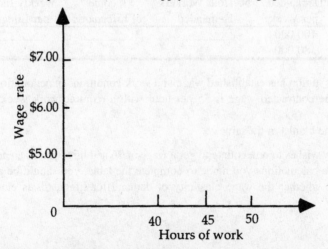

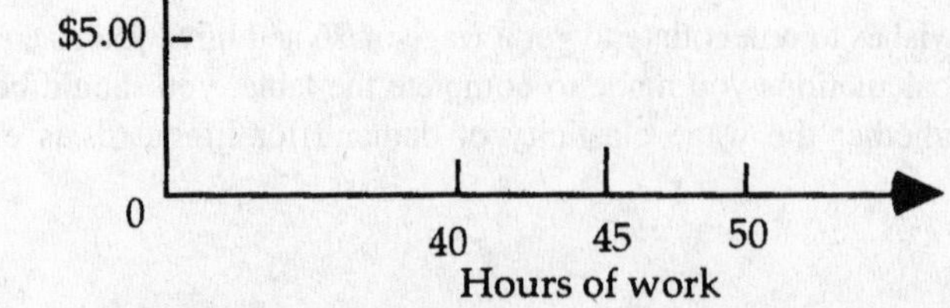

Note that the results you have found are the equivalent of a sequence of flat-tax rate changes. If the pre-tax wage rate is $8 but the marginal tax rate is 37.5%, after-tax wage is $5. If the tax rate is reduced to 25%, after-tax wage is $6. If the tax rate is reduced to 12.5%, after-tax wage is $7. Changing the marginal tax rate may increase or decrease the quantity of labour supplied, as determined by the income and substitution effects.

4. Suppose that Jack and Jill are "typical" male and female workers. Jill earns $14 000 and Jack $20 000, ignoring taxes. (Note: In the real world, full-time female pay is about 73% of full-time male pay. You might wish to ponder on the reasons for the persistence of this differential.)
   a. A new job, offering a 10% wage increase, would translate into $_______ for Jill and $_______ for Jack. (Note: The expected gains are greater for the man.)
   b. Which of the two would be more aggressive in the job search?
   c. Why?
   d. Now suppose that Jack and Jill are equally well qualified and both are laid off. The explicit costs of retraining/education are equivalent. Under prevailing labour market conditions, who will gain the higher expected reward from human capital investment?

5. Use the information in the table to answer questions about a profit-maximizing firm.

# of Workers	*Total Product*	*Product Price ($)*	*MPP*	*Total Revenue Product ($)*	*MRP ($)*	*Wage ($)*	*MFC*
0	0	2.10	—	0	—	—	—
1	15	2.00				$2.00	
2	28	1.90				$3.00	
3	39	1.80				$4.00	
4	48	1.70				$5.00	
5	55	1.60				$6.00	
6	60	1.50				$7.00	

   a. Complete the table above. Calculate total revenue product to get the marginal revenue product. Similarly, calculate total resource cost to get the values for marginal factor cost.
   b. How many workers will this firm choose to employ? (Assume that the firm can hire only "whole" workers.) How many units of output will the firm produce?
   c. Explain how you arrived at your answers.
   d. What is the equilibrium wage? What is the selling price of the product?
   e. The resource market is (perfectly/imperfectly) competitive, and the product market is (perfectly/imperfectly) competitive.
   f. Explain how you arrived at your answer.
   g. Draw a sketch of the labour market diagram for this firm. Include MRP and

MFC curves, the equilibrium wage, and quantity of workers hired.

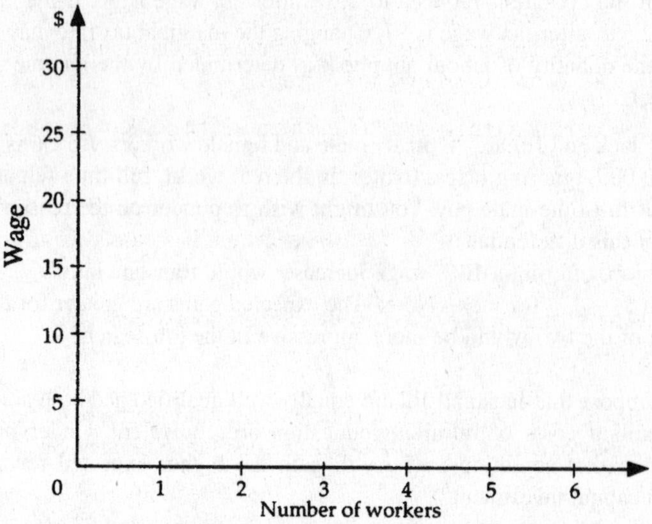

6. Let's try to analyse the issue of countervailing power in the labour market. First, sketch demand and supply of labour curves. Keep it simple—assume that the supply curve is not backward bending. Suppose that perfect competition is present in the output market and in the input market. What does this mean, though?
   a. There is perfect competition in the output market for the goods produced by the workers. If more workers are hired by a company, what will happen to the price of output?
   b. What, then, is the relationship between the demand for labour curve and the marginal revenue product curve?
   c. Turning to supply, in perfect competition, what is the relationship between the supply curve and the marginal factor cost curve?

   The perfectly competitive wage rate is where demand and supply intersect. Call the wage W_1 and number of workers hired Q_1.
   d. How does your diagram change if you now assume that the employer is a monopsonist?
   e. The employer will hire up to the point where ________ equals ________. The new wage will be ________ (higher/lower) than W1 and the hiring level will be ________ (higher/lower) than Q_1.
   f. Explain why the monopsonist's MFC lies above the supply curve.
   g. A union may be able to ________ (increase/decrease) wages while potentially achieving a ________ (more/less) efficient use of resource.

ANSWERS AND SOLUTIONS

PRACTICE TEST

I. SOLUTIONS TO MULTIPLE CHOICE QUESTIONS

1. D. Marginal physical product affects the demand for labour. See p. 442.
2. B. The wage rate is the opportunity cost of not working.

3. D. Both effects will operate to reduce work effort and, at any given wage rate, the labour supply. See p. 450.

4. B. This model is known as the "dual market model." Supply is restricted in Occupation A, forcing the wage higher. Workers suffering discrimination crowd into Occupation B, with a correspondingly lower wage.

5. B. Employment benefits increase search time because the costs of remaining out of a job are reduced. See p. 455.

6. A. Although unions have favoured strategies designed to increase the demand for labour, the threat of redundancy due to mechanization has caused Option A to be viewed with caution.

7. B. Feather-bedding is the preservation of unnecessary jobs. See p. 462.

8. D. See p. 463.

9. A. Reducing the marginal tax rate, it was believed, would increase the opportunity cost of leisure and encourage higher labour-force participation rates. See p. 449.

10. D. A cut in the marginal tax rate would increase the opportunity cost of not working (studying) and would raise Bill's after-tax income following graduation.

11. C. Hum and Simpson show that the estimates of wage elasticities for both males and females in Canada are close to zero indicating that tax changes have small impact on labour supply. See p. 450.

12. B. Some jobs, like those in coal mining, involve higher risks than others. Some jobs are more desirable than others. Therefore, wages paid to different types of jobs are different. See p. 455.

13. D. See the definition on p. 442.

14. B. "Feather-bedding" is a way of cushioning the fall in the demand for workers.

15. D. See the table on p. 456.

16. D. Both effects operate in the same direction—to reduce work effort. See p. 451.

17. A. This is an example of countervailing power. See p. 464.

18. A. Cutting the marginal tax rate increases the opportunity of not working. Labour supply, then, should increase.

19. A. Given the supply of labour, an increase in demand will boost hiring levels and the wage. Recall that MRP is affected by the price of the final output.

20. A. The labour union exerts countervailing power and, while increasing wages and employment, moves the industry towards a more efficient position.

21. A. A 10% wage increase will decrease the quantity of labour demanded by 0.5% (i.e., 1 000 000 x .005 = 5000) and will increase the quantity of labour supplied by 1.5% (i.e., 1 000 000 x .015 = 15 000).

22. A. See p. 463.

23. B. As labour becomes more expensive in Occupation A, capital will be substituted. The opposite is true in Occupation B.

24. C. Lower tax rates make leisure more expensive without providing extra income.

25. A. An increase in demand will boost the wage and employment levels.

II. SOLUTIONS TO APPLICATION QUESTIONS

1. a. See the diagrams below.

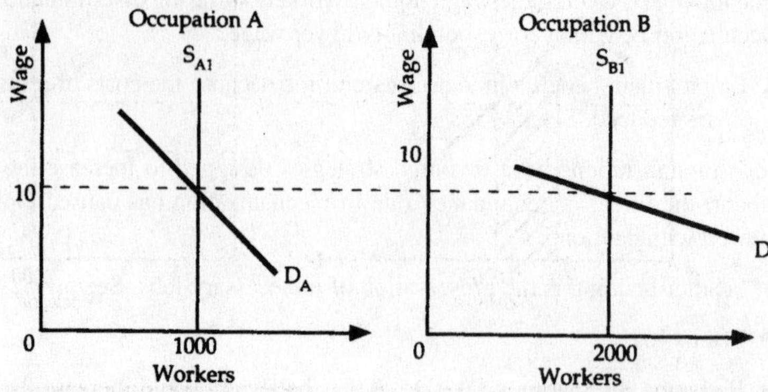

b. Wages will increase in Occupation A and decrease in Occupation B.

c. Employment in Occupation A will decrease by 40% to 600 and that in Occupation B will rise by 20% to 2400. Using the wage elasticity values, a decrease in the quantity of labour available in Occupation A will increase the wage by 100% to 20 opeks, while an increase in the quantity of labour available in Occupation B will decrease the wage by 100% to 5 opeks.

d. See the diagrams below.

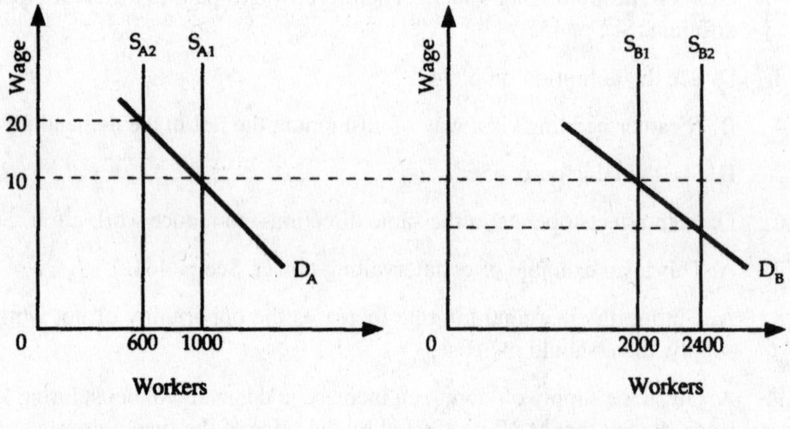

e. See the diagrams on the next page. The shaded area in the left-hand diagram represents the value of production lost by removing 400 workers from Occupation A. The shaded area in the right-hand diagram represents the value of production gained by adding 400 workers from Occupation B. The latter area is smaller than the former—production has fallen as a result of discrimination.

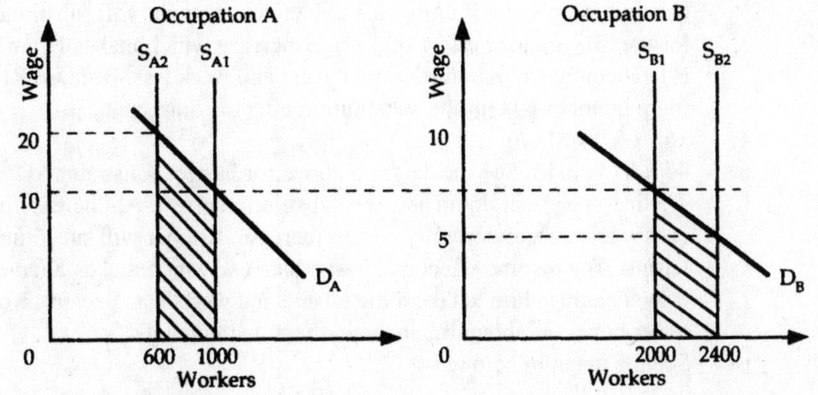

2. a. See the table below.

Wage per Hour	Hours Demanded per Week	Number of 50-Hour Workers Demanded	Total Weekly Income of Lifeguards	Weekly Income per Lifeguard
$5	100 000	2000	$500 000	$250
$6	80 000	1600	$480 000	$300

b. Elastic. As wage increases, total income (total revenue) decreases. In fact, elasticity is –1.22. If necessary, see Chapter 5 to review this material.

c. The union could ask for the wage increase and a decrease in the working week to 40 hours. The need for improved quality of vigilance could be used as a reason for the reduced hours. This proposal will maintain the number of lifeguards at 2000.

3. a. 24 x 7 = 168 hours per week.

b. 168 x $5 = 840.

c. 40 x $5 = $200. See the diagram below for the budget constraint AB. Note: This diagram is not drawn to scale.

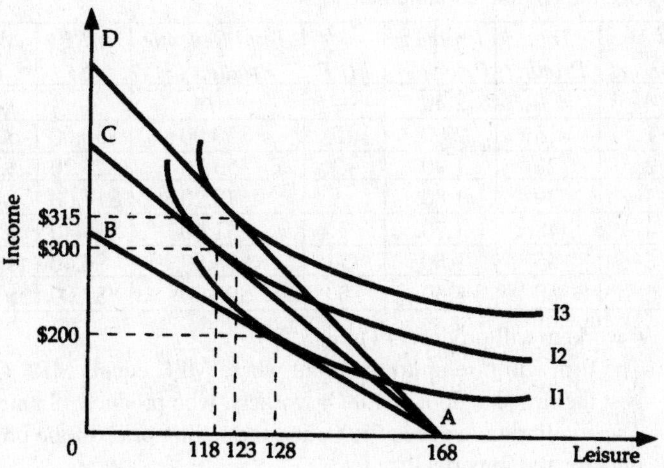

d. 168 x $6 = $1008.

e. 50 x $6 = $300. See the diagram above for budget constraint AC.

f. The substitution effect dominates the income effect. An increase in wage rate causes leisure's opportunity cost to increase. Kramer will substitute labour for leisure. The income effect of a wage increase which makes Kramer better off is to encourage him to take more leisure and work less. Because Kramer offers more hours of labour, the substitution effect is dominant.

g. 168 x $7 = $1176.

h. 45 x $7 = $315. See the diagram above for budget constraint AD.

i. The income effect dominates the substitution effect. An increase in wage rate causes leisure's opportunity cost to increase. Kramer will substitute labour for leisure. The income effect of a wage increase which makes Kramer better off is to encourage him to take more leisure and work less. Because Kramer offers fewer hours of labour, the income effect is dominant.

j. See the diagram below.

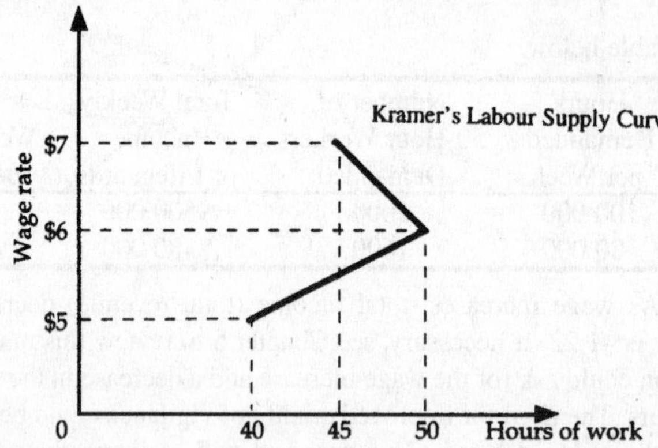

4. a. $1400; $2000.

b. Jack.

c. Because the expected gains are higher (assuming the costs are equal).

d. Jack.

5. a. See the completed table below.

# of Workers	*Total Product*	*Product Price ($)*	*MPP*	*Total Revenue Product ($)*	*MRP ($)*	*Wage ($)*	*MFC*
0	0	2.10	—	0	—	—	—
1	15	2.00	15	$30.00	$30.00	$2.00	$2.00
2	28	1.90	13	$53.20	$23.20	$3.00	$4.00
3	39	1.80	11	$70.20	$17.00	$4.00	$6.00
4	48	1.70	9	$81.60	$11.40	$5.00	$8.00
5	55	1.60	7	$88.00	$6.40	$6.00	$10.00
6	60	1.50	5	$90.00	$2.00	$7.00	$12.00

b. 4 workers will produce 48 units.

c. The firm will hire up to the point where MFC equals MRP (in our case, the best the firm can do is to hire 4 workers, who produce 48 units of output).

d. The equilibrium wage is $5.00, and the selling price of the product is $1.70.

e. imperfectly; imperfectly.

f. Imperfectly competitive product market: To sell more, the firm must reduce price—i.e., a downward-sloping demand curve.

Imperfectly competitive resource market: To hire more workers, the firm must raise the wage—i.e., an upward-sloping labour supply curve. Marginal factor cost is not equal to wage, as it would be in perfect competition.

g. See the diagram below. Ideally, the firm would hire the fifth worker for part of a day in order to match MRP and MFC; in our example, discrete units are assumed.

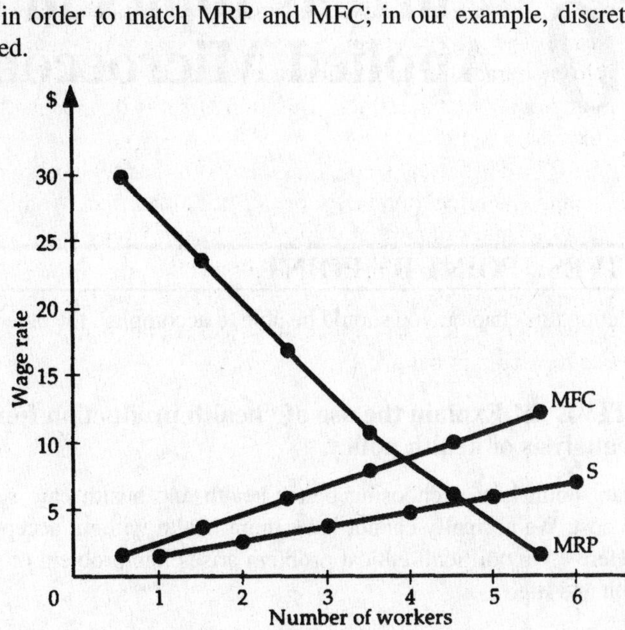

6. a. Price won't change. In perfect competition, the firm can sell as much output as it wants at the going market price.
   b. They're identical.
   c. They're identical.
   d. A marginal factor cost curve would need to be included above the supply curve. Your diagram should now look like Figure 19.6 in the textbook.
   e. MRP; MFC; lower; lower. If you decided that the wage would be higher, it's a fair bet that you went over from the intersection of MRP and MFC to determine the wage. Careful—it's a tempting mistake to make.
   f. MFC lies above the supply curve because, in order to attract an extra worker, the firm must pay him more than the going wage and must pay all other employees at the higher rate too. So the cost of the extra worker is higher than the wage he receives.
   g. increase; more.

20 Current Topics in Applied Microeconomics

OBJECTIVES: POINT BY POINT

After completing this chapter, you should be able to accomplish the objectives listed below.

OBJECTIVE 1: Explain the use of "health production functions" and the ppf in the analysis of health policy.

The important point is that choosing better health and health care service involves an opportunity cost. We normally cannot have more health without accepting less of something else. Here a very difficult ethical problem arises: the problem of putting a value on human health and life. (page 468)

The ppf is a useful analytical device that can be applied to the health policy. The ppf in this case shows all combinations of health and other goods that can be produced if resources were fully employed. Furthermore, the health production function (a function in which factors of production interact to produce health) along with the ppf can be used to organize an analysis of health issues.

One key issue here is whether resources in health care are used efficiently or not. If resources are used inefficiently, cases of waste for instance, then it is possible to obtain better health and more goods by efficiently organizing the system. Another important issue is, that assuming efficient use of resources, how is it possible and at what cost to have more health.

Practice

1. The choice between health care and others, as illustrated by a movement along a production possibility frontier, is indicative of all of the following except
   A. scarcity.
   B. opportunity cost.
   C. unlimited wants.
   D. inefficiency.

   ANSWER: D. Inefficiency would suggest that the economy is operating at a point inside ppf. Once we are on the frontier, we cannot have more of one without sacrificing some of the other one.

2. The moral hazard issue in health insurance refers to the
   A. possibility that those with pre-existing conditions will lie about them.
   B. likelihood that if patients do not bear the costs of health care they will overdemand services.
   C. likelihood that insurers will deny unnecessary procedures in order to increase profit margins.
   D. physicians risk law suits if there is malpractice.

   ANSWER: B. See p. 473.

3. Adverse selection is indicated by
   A. physicians ordering unnecessary tests as a defence against law suits.
   B. physicians selecting which information to tell the patient.
   C. insurance clients knowing more about their health than insurers know.
   D. the increasing "knowledge gap" between patients and doctors.

   ANSWER: C. See p. 472.

OBJECTIVE 2: Apply the competitive market model in the analysis of health policy.

The competitive market models which tend to generate efficient mix of output are based on certain assumptions. When these assumptions hold true, the competitive market model will generate production at minimum cost and the society can then reach the production possibility frontier and an efficient mix and distribution of output, without government action. (page 470)

OBJECTIVE 3: Identify market failures that can arise in markets for health.

The competitive model outlined above is not the real world, and its assumptions and conditions do not hold in real markets for health care. Observations indicate serious inequities as well as inefficiencies in a market health care system. This failure can be attributed to: asymmetric information, fee-for-service reimbursement, externalities, imperfect market structure, and high transaction costs. (page 471)

OBJECTIVE 4: Discuss the evolution of the Canadian health care system.

Prior to World War II, health care in Canada was entirely provided and financed by the private sector. Those needing health care were responsible for covering their own costs. By 1955, five provinces had public hospital insurance programs in place. In 1966, the federal government introduced the Medical Care Act, offering to cover one-half of the costs of provincial medical insurance programs. The new system was founded on five principles set earlier: (1) comprehensiveness; (2) accessibility; (3) universal coverage; (4) public administration; and (5) portability of benefits. (page 475)

Practice

4. The principle of block grant refers to
   A. the provinces sharing the cost of medicare with the federal government on a fifty- fifty basis.
   B. the provinces covering the cost of hospitals and the federal government covering other costs.
   C. the federal government providing each province with a lump sum, partly in cash and partly by tax room.
   D. the federal government offering provinces a gift to cover health care costs.

   ANSWER: C. See p. 476.

5. Unlike the system of public health care in Canada that covers all Canadians, in the U.S. system, there are at least ________ without health insurance, and as many as ________ with inadequate insurance.
   A. 10 million, 29 million.
   B. 29 million, 10 million.
   C. 15 million, 15 million.
   D. 35 million, 50 million.

   ANSWER: D. See p. 479.

6. Universality of the public health insurance system in Canada virtually eliminates all of the following problems except
   A. adverse selection.
   B. potential externalities.
   C. transaction costs.
   D. moral hazard.

   ANSWER: D. The moral hazard problem is potentially more serious under the Canadian public insurance plan than in a private insurance system. See p. 473.

OBJECTIVE 5: Describe the main features of immigration policy in Canada.

The current immigration policy is a variation of a system that dates back to 1967. In that year the change in the official immigration policy employed a formula known as the "point system." Under the point system, applicants were awarded points based on education, language skills, and occupation. Today, a greater emphasis is placed on skilled workers applicants. The pro-European biases in the immigration policy were eliminated in the 1967 law. (page 481)

OBJECTIVE 6: State the economic arguments for and against free immigration.

The argument for immigration hinges on the benefits derived from letting labour move from regions of low wages and low productivity to regions where higher wages can be earned because productivity is increased.

The main argument against immigration is that immigrants take jobs away from low-income Canadians. Another argument is that immigrants end up on welfare rolls and become a burden to taxpayers. (page 482)

Most evidence, however, suggests that this is a minor effect. A recent study, focusing on the impacts of immigrants on government spending and taxes, suggests that, as of 1990, immigrants continue to add more in revenue than they receive in government expenditures. Another study finds that whereas immigrants in British Columbia made up 22% of the province's population in 1989, only 2.7% of social assistance recipients were foreign born. (page 483)

Practice

7. Low-wage Arbocalis emigrate to Arbez. In Arbez, the return on capital will __________. Wages will ____________ in Arboc.
   A. increase, increase.
   B. increase, decrease.
   C. decrease, increase.
   D. decrease, decrease.

   ANSWER: A. Higher production in Arbez will increase the productivity of the existing capital stock. With fewer workers, wages in Arboc will increase.

OBJECTIVE 7: Assess evidence on the net costs of immigration. In order to make such an assessment, we must determine (a) the impact of immigration on domestic wages and (b) on unemployment. The Canadian evidence suggests that immigration to Canada has not caused unemployment to rise. In terms of costs and revenues, the evidence suggests that immigrants have a positive effect. **(page 483)**

PRACTICE TEST

I. MULTIPLE CHOICE QUESTIONS. Select the option that provides the single best answer.

_____ 1. Which of the following does not belong to the five major principles of the current Canadian health care system?
   A. portability of benefits.
   B. fee for services received by patients.
   C. universal coverage.
   D. comprehensiveness.

_____ 2. Which of the following is not a characteristic of the Canadian health care system?
   A. high transactions costs.
   B. universality
   C. adverse selection.
   D. inequities.

_____ 3. The moral hazard problem is likely to occur in a public health care system such as in Canada because
   A. it cannot easily be caught.
   B. physicians have the right to deny patients medical services.
   C. of asymmetric information.
   D. all of the above.

_____ 4. Evidence suggests that recent immigrants have been net ____________ the public purse and that they ____________ the cause of job displacement for the economy as a whole.
   A. contributors to, have been.
   B. recipients from, have been.
   C. contributors to, have not been.
   D. recipients to, have not been.

II. APPLICATION QUESTION

1. Immigration is an important and complex issue.
   a. Are you in favour of a freer immigration policy or a stricter one?
   b. How would you propose to resolve the problem of slowing population growth in Canada?

ANSWERS AND SOLUTIONS

PRACTICE TEST

I. SOLUTIONS TO MULTIPLE CHOICE QUESTIONS

1. B. Patients do not pay a fee for the services they receive. Doctors, however, receive a fee for the services they offer.

2. A. Transactions costs are reduced in a public health care system such as that of Canada.

3. D. Very few people would overvisit a doctor, especially if they had to pay for it.

4. C. See p. 483.

II. SOLUTIONS TO APPLICATION QUESTIONS

1. a. The answer to this question is entirely up to you.
   b. The Canadian population is ageing rapidly, and the domestic fertility rate is not high enough to prevent this from happening. One solution would be a freer immigration policy based on a more careful system of selection. Another, though temporary, would be to increase the retirement age.

21 International Trade, Comparative Advantage, and Protectionism

OBJECTIVES: POINT BY POINT

After completing this chapter, you should be able to accomplish the objectives listed below.

OBJECTIVE 1: Define trade surplus and trade deficit.

In open economies such as Canada's, aggregate expenditures are affected by the presence of exports and imports. We have seen international trade steadily increase in importance throughout the last several decades. If exports exceed imports, the country runs a *trade surplus*. If imports exceed exports, the country runs a *trade deficit*. (page 492)

> **Tip:** Learn the difference between exports and imports. Imports are foreign-produced goods consumed here. Exports are domestically-produced goods sold to customers overseas. Imports and exports are not opposites; they are determined by different factors.

Comment: The two terms, "balance of payments" and "balance of trade," are not synonymous. The balance of trade refers only to exports and imports of goods and services, while the balance of payments (discussed in Chapter 21 of *Principles of Macroeconomics*) includes all international transactions.

Practice

1. Canada's balance of trade for goods is typically a _________ while its balance of trade for services is typically a __________.
   A. surplus, peak.
   B. surplus, minimum.
   C. surplus, deficit.
   D. deficit, surplus.

   ANSWER: C. See page 493 or Table 20.2 on p. 493 (where it is clear that the balance of trade on goods and services is usually less than the balance of trade on goods alone).

OBJECTIVE 2: Distinguish between absolute advantage and comparative advantage.

The *theory of comparative advantage* provides the rationale for free trade. Given a two-country, two-good world, and assuming that the countries have advantages in the production of different goods, Ricardo showed that both trading partners could benefit from specialization in the production of the good in which they have the comparative advantage.

Each country should specialize in the production of that good in which it has a comparative advantage and trade its surplus. Production and welfare will be maximized. Country A is said to have an *absolute advantage* if it can produce a unit of output with fewer resources than Country B. Comparative advantage, though, is a relative concept. Country A will have a *comparative advantage* in whichever good it can produce comparatively cheaper. Specialization and trade allow a country to consume more than it can produce of a good. (page 493)

> **Tip:** If you're like most individuals, you'll need several numerical examples to strengthen your grasp of pure trade theory. The Applications below take you through all the steps included in the text. Review Application questions 2, 7, and 10 in Chapter 2 of this manual. They will lead you through the opportunity cost concept that underlies the theory of comparative advantage.

> **Tip:** Comparative advantage hinges on the concept of opportunity cost. (Take a little time to go back and review the material you learned in Chapters 1 and 2.) The producer (person, firm, or country) with the lowest *opportunity cost* will hold the comparative advantage in that product.

> **Graphing Pointer:** Using the production possibility frontier (ppf) diagram, trade will be advantageous if the ppf's have differing slopes. Differing slopes mean that a comparative advantage exists—i.e., that the relative costs of production differ. Even though Country A may be more efficient in producing both goods—an absolute advantage—it is the *comparative* advantage of Country A that will establish the preferred pattern of specialization and trade. The country with the flatter curve has an advantage in the good on the horizontal axis.

OBJECTIVE 3: Explain how both countries in a trading relationship can gain from trade with appropriate terms of trade. Explain how with fixed money prices, exchange rates affect the terms of trade.

Given that specialization occurs, *the terms of trade* (the "price" of the traded commodities) must be negotiated. For trade to be beneficial, the "price" of the exported good (in terms of the imported good) must be greater than its cost of production. A range of terms of trade will exist. The deal cut within this range will depend on the relative negotiating strengths of the two partners. (page 498)

Many trade examples are discussed without reference to currency (e.g., one country trades wheat directly for cloth) but in real life, most international trade involves currencies. Trade flows are affected by prices in each country and by the exchange rate (the "price" of the domestic currency in terms of a foreign currency). There will be a range of exchange rates that will permit mutually beneficial specialization and trade. (page 499)

To buy foreign goods, there must be a purchase of foreign currency, which is bought and sold in the foreign exchange market. If the value of the dollar changes, the relative attractiveness of the foreign goods will be affected. The strengthening yen will increase the price tag of a Toyota for a Canadian buyer, but the price tag of the domestically-produced Chrysler will not change—the relative attractiveness of the Toyota will decline. Tourists watch exchange rates keenly—a stronger dollar is good news because each dollar will buy more foreign currency and, therefore, more foreign goods and services (which have, in that sense, become cheaper). Note that when we discuss the effects of exchange rate changes, we are assuming that domestic prices do not change. This seems reasonable as exchange rates can change every minute, but many goods prices change less frequently.

> **Tip:** Remember that an increase in the value of the dollar means that foreign goods cost Canadians less (imports increase), but Canadian goods cost foreigners more (exports fall).

Practice

Refer to the following table to answer the next four questions. The table shows the possible output levels from one day of labour input.

	Arbez	Arboc
Wheat	12 cubic metres	6 cubic metres
Cloth	12 metres	12 metres

2. Arbez
   A. has an absolute advantage in the production of cloth.
   B. has an absolute advantage in the production of wheat.
   C. has a comparative advantage in the production of cloth.
   D. should export cloth to Arboc.

   ANSWER: B. Arbez can produce absolutely more wheat per worker than Arboc can.

3. The opportunity cost of one cubic metre of wheat in Arboc is
   A. 1/2 metre of cloth.
   B. 2 metres of cloth.
   C. 6 metres of cloth.
   D. 12 metres of cloth.

   ANSWER: B. 6 cubic metres would cost 12 metres of cloth; therefore 1 cubic metre costs 2 metres of cloth.

4. Which of the following statements is false?
   A. Arboc has an absolute advantage in the production of wheat.
   B. Arbez should export wheat to Arboc and import cloth from Arboc.
   C. the opportunity cost of wheat is twice as high in Arboc as in Arbez.
   D. the opportunity cost of a metre of cloth in Arbez is one cubic metre of wheat.

   ANSWER: A. Arboc is half as productive per worker as Arbez in wheat production.

5. Arboc and Arbez decide to specialize according to the law of comparative advantage and trade with one another. We would expect that
   A. the trade agreement will be somewhere between 1 cubic metre of wheat for 1 metre of cloth and 1 cubic metre of wheat for 2 metres of cloth.
   B. the trade agreement will be somewhere between 1/2 cubic metre of wheat for 1 metre of cloth and 2 cubic metres of wheat for 1 metre of cloth.
   C. Arboc will benefit from trading with Arbez, but Arbez will not benefit from trading with Arboc.
   D. Arboc will specialize in the production of wheat and Arbez will specialize in the production of cloth.

   ANSWER: A. The Arbezani opportunity cost of 1 cubic metre of wheat is 1 metre of cloth. Arboc's opportunity cost of 1 cubic metre of wheat is 2 metres of cloth.

6. The ratio at which exports are traded for imports is known as
   A. the exchange rate.
   B. the trade balance.
   C. the balance of exchange.
   D. the terms of trade.

   ANSWER: D. See p. 498.

Use the following diagrams, which show hypothetical production possibility frontiers (ppf's) for Malaysia and Sri Lanka, to answer the next nine questions.

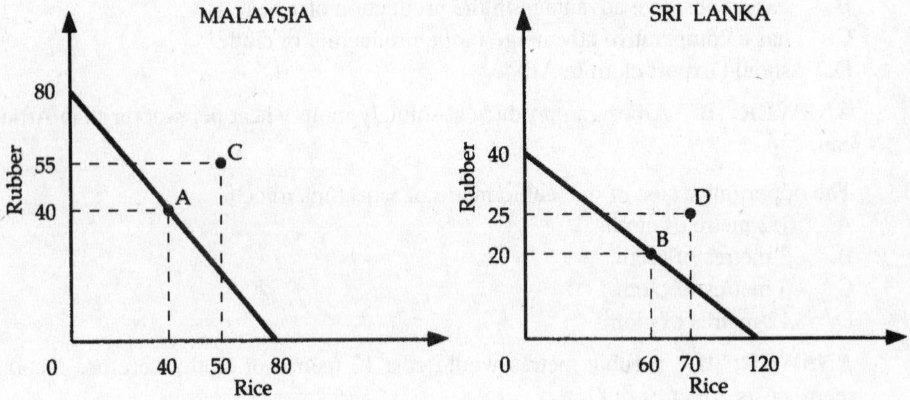

7. Which of the following statements is true?
   A. Malaysia has an absolute advantage in the production of rubber; Sri Lanka has an absolute advantage in the production of rice.
   B. Sri Lanka has an absolute advantage in the production of rubber; Malaysia has an absolute advantage in the production of rice.
   C. Malaysia has an absolute advantage in the production of both goods.
   D. Sri Lanka has an absolute advantage in the production of both goods.

   ANSWER: A. See p. 497.

8. Which statement is false?
   A. in Malaysia, the opportunity cost of one unit of rubber is one unit of rice.
   B. in Malaysia, the opportunity cost of one unit of rice is one unit of rubber.
   C. in Sri Lanka, the opportunity cost of one unit of rubber is three units of rice.
   D. in Sri Lanka, the opportunity cost of one unit of rice is three units of rubber.

   ANSWER: D. The Sri Lankan opportunity cost of one unit of rice is a third of a unit of rubber.

9. Which of the following statements is true?
   A. Malaysia has a comparative advantage in the production of rubber; Sri Lanka has a comparative advantage in the production of rice.
   B. Sri Lanka has a comparative advantage in the production of rubber; Malaysia has a comparative advantage in the production of rice.
   C. Malaysia has a comparative advantage in both goods.
   D. Sri Lanka has a comparative advantage in both goods.

   ANSWER: A. See p. 497.

10. Given that Malaysia and Sri Lanka decide to trade,
   A. Malaysia should specialize in the production of rubber; Sri Lanka should specialize in the production of rice.
   B. Malaysia should specialize in the production of rice; Sri Lanka should specialize in the production of rubber.
   C. Malaysia and Sri Lanka should each devote half their resources to the production of each commodity.
   D. Malaysia should specialize in the production of rubber; Sri Lanka should produce some rice but continue to produce some rubber.

   ANSWER: A. Malaysia's comparative advantage lies in rubber production; Sri Lanka's lies in rice.

11. Before trade, Malaysia produced at Point A on its ppf and Sri Lanka produced at Point B. Given complete specialization based on comparative advantage, total rubber production has risen by __________ and total rice production has risen by __________.
   A. 80, 120.
   B. 120, 80.
   C. 40, 60.
   D. 20, 20.

   ANSWER: D. Total rubber production was 60 (40 + 20); now it is 80. Total rice production was 100 (40 + 60); now it is 120.

12. After trade, suppose Malaysia is consuming at Point C and Sri Lanka is consuming at Point D. Malaysia is exporting __________ units of rubber and Sri Lanka is exporting __________ units of rice.
   A. 80, 100.
   B. 55, 70.
   C. 25, 50.
   D. 15, 10.

   ANSWER: C. Malaysian rubber production is 80, and domestic consumption is 55, leaving 25 for export. Sri Lankan rice production is 120, and domestic consumption is 70, leaving 50 for export.

13. After trade, suppose Malaysia is consuming at Point C and Sri Lanka is consuming at Point D. Malaysia is importing __________ units of rice and Sri Lanka is importing __________ units of rubber.
   A. 80, 100.
   B. 50, 25.
   C. 25, 50.
   D. 15, 10.

   ANSWER: B. See the answer to the previous question. In a two-country world, Country A's exports are Country B's imports.

14. Which statement is true?
   A. only Sri Lanka will benefit if the terms of trade are set at 1 : 2, rubber to rice.
   B. only Malaysia will benefit if the terms of trade are set at 1 : 2, rubber to rice.
   C. both countries will gain if the terms of trade lie between 3 : 1 and 1 : 1, rubber to rice.
   D. both countries will gain if the terms of trade lie between 1 : 1 and 1 : 3, rubber to rice.

   ANSWER: D. Check these values against the opportunity cost values you calculated in question 8. Also note the assumed value of the rubber : Rice ratio in question 12 is between 1 : 1 and 1 : 3.

15. Which statement is false? If the terms of trade are set at
   A. 1 : 1, rubber to rice, only Sri Lanka will gain.
   B. 1 : 2, rubber to rice, both countries will gain.
   C. 1 : 3, rubber to rice, only Malaysia will gain.
   D. 1 : 4, rubber to rice, both countries will wish to produce rice.

   ANSWER: D. If the terms of trade are set at 1 : 4, rubber to rice, rubber is relatively valuable and can cover its opportunity cost in both countries. Both will wish to produce rubber.

16. Suppose the exchange rate is one British pound equals $1.75. If the exchange rate changes to one British pound equals $1.50 (with constant prices), we can conclude that, for a British buyer, Canadian lumber has become ________ expensive and, for a Canadian buyer, a British cashmere sweater has become ________ expensive.
   A. more, more.
   B. more, less.
   C. less, more.
   D. less, less.

   ANSWER: B. Each pound is worth less Canadian currency—British buyers are becoming poorer. The opposite is true for Canadian buyers of British goods.

17. Given constant prices, if the exchange rate changes from one British pound equals $1.50 to one British pound equals $2.00, British traders will gain ________ from trade with Canada, and Canadian traders will gain ________ from trade with the United Kingdom.
   A. more, more.
   B. more, less.
   C. less, more.
   D. less, less.

   ANSWER: B. Each pound is worth more Canadian currency. British producers, selling the same amount of exports, will be able to claim more Canadian goods than before.

Use the following table, which shows hypothetical domestic prices per unit of steel and corn in Slovakia and Slovenia, to answer the next three questions.

18. If the exchange rate is 1 koruna = 1 tolar, then

	Slovakia	**Slovenia**
Steel	20 koruna	48 tolars
Corn	30 koruna	87 tolars

A. Slovakia will import both steel and corn.
B. Slovenia will import both steel and corn.
C. Slovakia will import steel and Slovenia will import corn.
D. Slovakia will import corn and Slovenia will import steel.

ANSWER: B. In Slovenia, the domestic prices of steel and corn are 48 tolars and 87 tolars, respectively. The imported prices are 20 tolars and 30 tolars, respectively.

19. If the exchange rate is 1 koruna = 3 tolars, then
A. Slovakia will import both steel and corn.
B. Slovenia will import both steel and corn.
C. Slovakia will import steel and Slovenia will import corn.
D. Slovakia will import corn and Slovenia will import steel.

ANSWER: A. In Slovakia, the domestic prices of steel and corn are 20 koruna and 30 koruna, respectively. The imported prices are 16 koruna and 29 koruna, respectively.

20. Two-way trade will occur only if the price of the koruna is between
A. 1.0 tolars and 3.0 tolars.
B. 1.5 tolars and 2.4 tolars.
C. 2.4 tolars and 2.9 tolars.
D. 1.5 tolars and 3.0 tolars.

ANSWER: C. If the exchange rate is 1 koruna = 2.4 tolars, no trade in steel will occur. If the exchange rate is 1 koruna = 2.9 tolars, no trade in corn will occur. Between these rates, Slovakia will import steel and Slovenia will import corn.

OBJECTIVE 4: Outline the Heckscher-Ohlin theorem.

The *Heckscher-Ohlin theorem* builds on the theory of comparative advantage by focusing on the different factor endowments of countries. Some countries seem more labour-abundant (India, China), while others are more capital-abundant (United States, Canada, Japan). The Heckscher-Ohlin theorem states that a country will specialize in and export that good whose production calls for a relatively intensive use of the input that the country has in abundance; India should export labour-intensive goods and import capital-intensive goods, for example. (page 502)

The assembly of audiocassettes requires a large stock of semi-skilled cheap labour with little capital. This favours Mexico. The production of timber requires an abundant stock of forest land—a requirement that Canada meets.

Practice

21. We observe that Arbez produces wooden ornaments (a labour-intensive activity), and that Arboc produces plastic containers (a capital-intensive activity). Which of the following statements is true?
A. Arbez has more labour than Arboc; Arboc has more capital than Arbez.
B. Arboc has more labour than Arbez; Arbez has more capital than Arboc.
C. labour is relatively abundant in Arbez.
D. labour is relatively abundant in Arboc.

ANSWER: C. Assuming that the two countries are being rational, Arbez is producing the good in which it has a comparative advantage.

OBJECTIVE 5: Describe how economies of scale in production can lead to international trade.

Another possible explanation for trade is that countries specialize in certain goods because of economies of scale. For example, perhaps a plant that just served the Canadian television market would be inefficiently small so instead Canadians buy televisions made in the United States or Japan. However, Canada might have an efficiently-sized fibre optics plant, much too big for the Canadian market alone, which thrives by exporting to markets in other countries. (page 503)

Practice

22. Switzerland is famous for watches, which it exports. This specialization is best explained by
    A. the large population of Switzerland, which provides many potential watchmakers.
    B. Swiss steel refineries which produce steel used in watch parts.
    C. Swiss diamond mines, as diamonds are used in watch mechanisms.
    D. economies of scale in the watch industry.

    ANSWER: D. As the watch industry became established, an input supply network developed within Switzerland. Also, existing watchmakers could teach their techniques to new workers. Both developments lowered the cost of firm expansion or the cost to new firms.

OBJECTIVE 6: Define tariff, export subsidy, and quota. Show how a tariff reduces the gains from trade and how the loss can be measured.

Tariffs, export subsidies, and quotas are examples of trade barriers. *Tariffs* are taxes on imports, designed to force up their price; *export subsidies* are government payments to domestic exporters, intended to make them more competitive overseas; *quotas* are limits on the quantity of imports. *Dumping* is meant to price competitors out of the market; having achieved market domination, the firm can then raise prices. (page 503)

Practice

23. A tariff imposed on imported French wine will cause the Canadian price of French wine to __________ and Canadian production of wine to __________.
    A. increase, increase.
    B. increase, decrease.
    C. decrease, increase.
    D. decrease, decrease.

    ANSWER: A. The tax will push up the price of the import. This will increase the demand for substitutes.

Use the following diagram to answer the next three questions. The diagram shows the hypothetical Canadian demand for and supply of T-shirts. The world price is $4 per shirt.

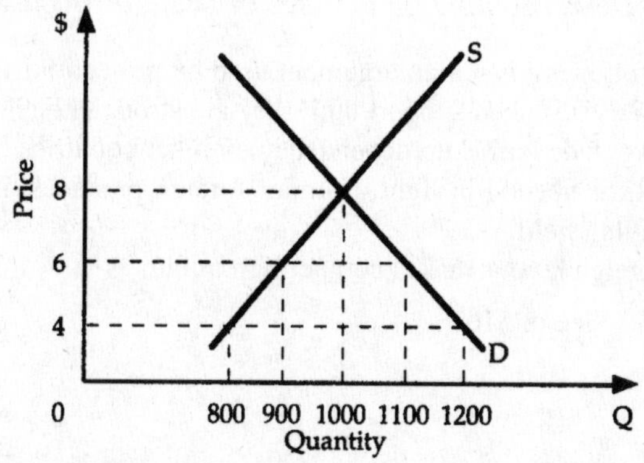

24. In an unrestricted open market, Canada will
    A. export 400 T-shirts.
    B. export 200 T-shirts.
    C. import 400 T-shirts.
    D. import 200 T-shirts.

    ANSWER: C. At a price of $4, there is an excess Canadian demand of 400.

25. The garment industry successfully lobbies the federal government to impose a $2 per shirt tax on imports. Now Canada will
    A. export 400 T-shirts.
    B. export 200 T-shirts.
    C. import 400 T-shirts.
    D. import 200 T-shirts.

    ANSWER: D. An excess demand remains that must be met from overseas.

26. The government will collect __________ in tariff revenues.
    A. $100.
    B. $200.
    C. $400.
    D. $800.

    ANSWER: C. The government collects $2 per shirt on each of the 200 imported shirts.

OBJECTIVE 7: List the pros and cons of trade protection.

Free trade may improve competition within an economy, forestall retaliatory trade restrictions by other countries, and help domestic industries that depend on foreign inputs. The case for free trade is also based on the theory of comparative advantage. Trade benefits the participants. Welfare increases if trade flows are allowed to follow their "natural" pattern; obstacles, such as tariffs and quotas, reduce that welfare. Trade restrictions increase consumer prices. (page 505)

The argument in favour of protection is based on the observation that efficient foreign competition will result in job loss for domestic workers and lost production. (The counterargument is that inefficient industries should be closed so that workers and capital move to more competitive sectors, painful as that process can be.) Individual arguments for protection from foreign competition may include claims that cheap foreign labour is "unfair," that national security must be protected, that trade encourages dependency on foreigners, and that we need to let infant industries develop. (page 508)

Practice

27. Which of the following is not an argument used by protectionists?
    A. infant industries need support until they are strong enough to complete.
    B. restricting trade builds up dependency on other countries.
    C. protection is needed in light of unfair foreign practices, in order to ensure a level playing field.
    D. cheap foreign labour makes competition unfair.

    ANSWER: B. See p. 510.

PRACTICE TEST

I. MULTIPLE CHOICE QUESTIONS. Select the option that provides the single best answer.

_____ 1. According to the textbook, which of the following is not a major export of Canada?
A. automobiles, trucks, and motor vehicle parts.
B. cocoa, coffee, and tea.
C. forest products.
D natural gas.

_____ 2. A country imports less than it exports. It has
A. an export subsidy.
B. a tariff quota.
C. a trade surplus.
D. a trade deficit.

_____ 3. Relative to Arboc, Arbez has a comparative advantage in the production of goat milk. We can say that Arbez
A. uses fewer resources to produce goat milk than does Arboc.
B. must also have an absolute advantage in the production of goat milk.
C. is the producer with the lower opportunity cost of producing goat milk.
D. should diversify into other products rather than trade with the high-cost, inefficient Arbocalis.

_____ 4. In Arbez/Arboc trade, an increase in the value of the Arbezani currency (the bandu) relative to that of the Arbocali currency (the opek) means that
A. Arbezani goods will appear to be relatively cheaper to the Arbocalis.
B. Arbocali goods will appear to be relatively cheaper to the Arbezanis.
C. Arbez will lose any comparative advantage that it had.
D. Arbez will experience a decreasing trade deficit.

_____ 5. The Heckscher-Ohlin theorem states that Arbez will have a(n) _________ advantage in the production of a good that uses its relatively _________.
A. absolute, scarce input intensively.
B. absolute, abundant input intensively.
C. comparative, abundant input intensively.
D. comparative, scarce input intensively.

_____ 6. Two goods are produced, pins and needles. Jill has a comparative advantage in the production of pins. Relative to Jack,
A. Jill is better at producing pins than at producing needles.
B. Jill is better at producing both pins and needles.
C. Jill can produce more pins per hour.
D. Jill can produce more needles per hour.

_____ 7. Jill chooses to trade pins for needles with Jack. It is likely that
A. Jill's gains equal Jack's losses.
B. pins are more expensive than needles.
C. each trader receives goods that he or she values more highly than those he or she gives up.
D. neither trader can gain more than the other.

For questions 8–10, assume that Arbez and Arboc have the same amount of resources and similar preferences for both goat milk and bananas. The table shows the number of labour hours needed to produce 1 litre of goat milk and 1 kilo of bananas.

	Arbez	**Arboc**
Goat milk	.3	.6
Bananas	.5	.2

_____ 8. According to the table above,
A. Arbez has a comparative advantage in the production of both goods.
B. Arbez has a comparative advantage in the production of bananas, and Arboc has a comparative advantage in the production of goat milk.
C. Arbez has a comparative advantage in the production of goat milk, and Arboc has a comparative advantage in the production of bananas.
D. Arboc has a comparative advantage in the production of both goods.

_____ 9. According to the table, one hour of labour produces
A. 3 litres of goat milk in Arbez and 6 litres in Arboc.
B. 5 kilos of bananas in Arbez and 2 kilos in Arboc.
C. 2 kilos of bananas in Arbez and 5 kilos in Arboc.
D. 6 litres of goat milk in Arboc and 2 kilos of bananas in Arboc.

_____ 10. For trade to occur, the terms of trade might be
A. 2 litres of goat milk for 1 kilo of bananas.
B. 1 litre of goat milk for 4 kilos of bananas.
C. 1 litre of goat milk for .7 kilo of bananas.
D. 3 litres of goat milk for 1 kilo of bananas.

_____ 11. Tariffs and quotas are economically inefficient because
A. the government does not collect any revenues under a tariff.
B. imports rise and this reduces the welfare of consumers.
C. producers are saved from the pressure of foreign competition.
D. domestic prices must be reduced.

_____ 12. Which of the following is a common argument in favour of increased protection?
A. Canadian consumers have become too dependent on foreign countries for their luxury goods.
B. political independence can be jeopardized if too many strategic supplies are produced by foreigners.
C. protection promotes competition in domestic markets.
D. higher tariffs increase the welfare of consumers.

_____ 13. Each of the following can be a trade barrier except a(n)
A. flexible exchange rate.
B. quota.
C. export subsidy.
D. tariff.

_____ 14. Statement 1: A country with an absolute advantage in the production of a good must also have a comparative advantage.
Statement 2: A country with a comparative advantage in the production of a good must also have an absolute advantage.
Statement 1 is ___________; Statement 2 is ___________.
A. true, true.
B. true, false.
C. false, true.
D. false, false.

_____ 15. A tariff ___________ increase the government's tax receipts; a quota ___________ increase the government's tax receipt.
A. does, does.
B. does, does not.
C. does not, does.
D. does not, does not.

_____ 16. In Tokyo, suppose a Big Mac sells for 500 yen. The dollar : yen exchange rate is one dollar per 125 yen. The price of the Big Mac in dollars is
A. 500.
B. .25.
C. 4.
D. 5.

_____ 17. In Tokyo, suppose a Big Mac sells for 500 yen. The exchange rate changes from one dollar for 125 yen, to one dollar for 250 yen. The price of the Big Mac in dollars
A. has increased.
B. has decreased.
C. has not changed.
D. has doubled.

_____ 18. The Heckscher-Ohlin theorem explains the pattern of trade by focusing on
A. comparative advantage.
B. absolute advantage.
C. relative factor endowments.
D. exchange rate variations.

_____ 19. As the exchange rate changes from one British pound equals $2.50 to one British pound equals $2.00, the terms of trade shift ___________ Canada. Canadian traders will gain ___________ from trade with the United Kingdom.
A. in favour of, more.
B. in favour of, less.
C. against, more.
D. against, less.

_____ 20. We would expect a tariff imposed on an import to __________ the price of the import and to __________ the price of domestic substitutes for the import.

A. increase, increase.
B. increase, not affect.
C. decrease, decrease.
D. decrease, not affect.

II. APPLICATION QUESTIONS

1. The Arbezani Minister of Trade asks your advice regarding some recent changes within the Arbezani economy. Arbez has established a free-trade region with its sole trading partner, Arboc. Previously it did not trade at all. What will be the impact of the following changes on the flow of trade, assuming the Heckscher-Ohlin theorem?
   a. Arbezani unions in a substantial number of industries lobby successfully for increased restrictions on movement between industries, e.g., longer apprenticeships, work permits, drug testing of new entrants into an industry.
   b. It has been discovered that Arbez and its trading partner, Arboc, have identical endowments of all resources.
   c. Nationalistic Arbezani politicians, concerned about the loss of sovereignty caused by a free-trade area, have successfully passed restrictions on the flow of labour and other inputs between Arbez and Arboc.

2. The nations of Noil and Regit produce loaves and fishes. The labour supply is 12 000 labour units per year in Noil while, in Regit, the labour supply is 72 000 labour units per year. Assume that labour is the only input and that costs are constant within each economy. The costs of producing loaves and fishes, in labour units, are given in the following table.

Units of Labour Supply Needed to Produce 1 Unit of:	**Noil**	**Regit**
Loaves	2	3
Fishes	1	3

   a. Calculate the maximum output levels of loaves and fishes for each economy and enter your results in the following table.

Maximum Units Produced	**Noil**	**Regit**
Loaves		
Fishes		

   b. Draw the production possibility frontiers for each nation.

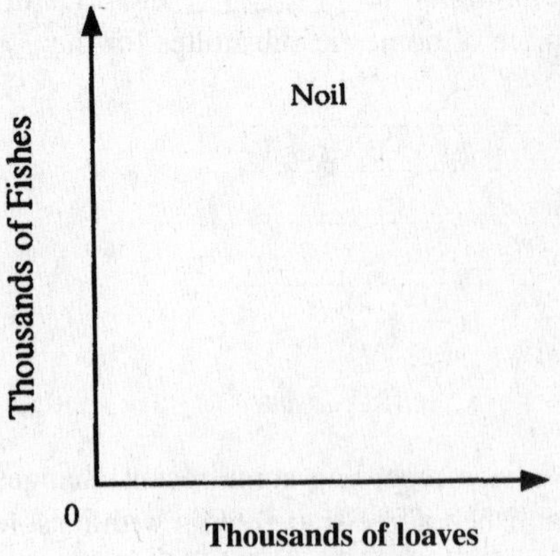

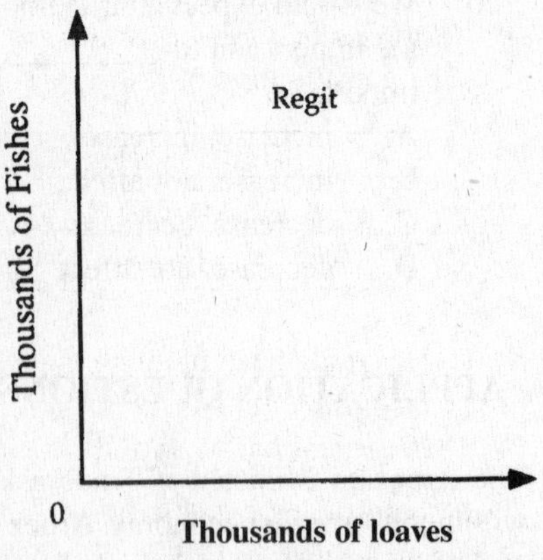

c. When questioned about the possibility of establishing trade between the two nations, the Regitani Minister of Trade states his government's official line—trade cannot benefit Regit because Regit has an advantage in the production of each good. Is the Regitani view correct?

In both nations, the custom is to consume two loaves with each fish.

d. Assume that no trade takes place. Calculate the annual production of loaves and fishes that will most satisfactorily meet demand in each country separately. Also determine the total production of loaves and fishes for the two countries without trade.

Maximum Units Produced	Noil	Regit	Total
Loaves	_____	_____	_____
Fishes	_____	_____	_____

e. Yielding to pressure, the Regitani government opens its borders to trade with Noil. Based on comparative advantage, which good should Noil specialize in producing? Explain.

f. Assuming that specialization and trade flows are dictated by comparative advantage, determine the quantity of loaves and fishes that can be produced.

g. Suppose that the terms of trade are established at 3 fishes = 2 loaves. Determine the consumption of loaves and fishes in each country.

Units Consumed	Noil	Regit
Loaves	_____	_____
Fishes	_____	_____

h. Has trade been mutually beneficial in this case?

i. Suppose that the terms of trade are established at 1 fish = 1 loaf. Determine the consumption of loaves and fishes in each country.

Units Consumed	Noil	Regit
Loaves	_____	_____
Fishes	_____	_____

j. Has trade been mutually beneficial in this case?

k. Suppose that the terms of trade are established at 2 fishes = 1 loaf. Determine the consumption of loaves and fishes in each country.

Units Consumed	Noil	Regit
Loaves	_____	_____
Fishes	_____	_____

l. Has trade been mutually beneficial in this case?

m. Determine the "price" of a loaf (in terms of fish) necessary to have mutually beneficial two-way trade.

3. The domestic price of Arbocali cloth is 4 opeks a yard. The domestic price of Arbezani leather is 12 bandu per hide. Arboc sells cloth to Arbez and Arbez sells hides to Arboc. The opek : bandu exchange rate is 2 opeks per bandu.

Ignoring transportation and other such costs, calculate the price in Arbez of a yard of imported Arbocali cloth and the price in Arboc of an imported Arbezani hide.

4. Use the diagrams below to answer this question.

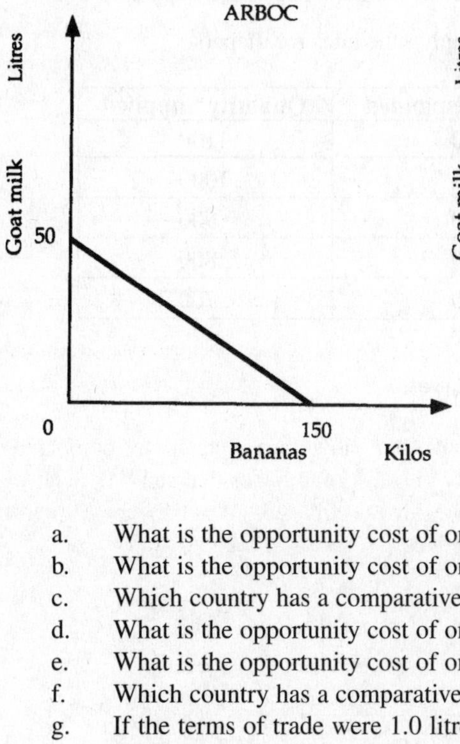

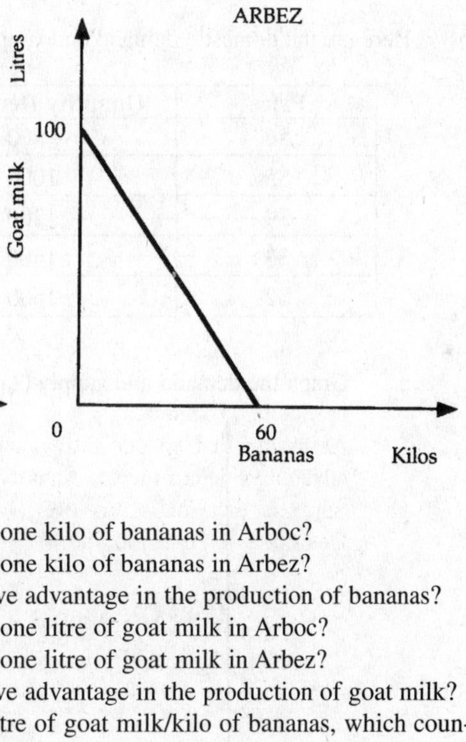

a. What is the opportunity cost of one kilo of bananas in Arboc?

b. What is the opportunity cost of one kilo of bananas in Arbez?

c. Which country has a comparative advantage in the production of bananas?

d. What is the opportunity cost of one litre of goat milk in Arboc?

e. What is the opportunity cost of one litre of goat milk in Arbez?

f. Which country has a comparative advantage in the production of goat milk?

g. If the terms of trade were 1.0 litre of goat milk/kilo of bananas, which country would want to export goat milk?

h. If the terms of trade were 3 litres of goat milk/kilo of bananas, Arboc should produce __________ and Arbez should produce __________.

i. Suppose that the terms of trade were 1 kilo of bananas/1.5 litres of goat milk. __________ would export bananas and __________ would export goat milk.

5. Arboc and Arbez produce wine and cheese, and each has constant costs of production. The domestic prices for units of the two goods are given in the table. At the moment 1 Arbocali opek is traded for 1 Arbezani bandu.

	Arboc	Arbez
Wine	40 opeks	120 bandu
Cheese	20 opeks	30 bandu

a. Which country has a comparative advantage in cheese production?
b. Which country has a comparative advantage in wine production?
c. At the present exchange rate (1 opek = 1 bandu), will two-way trade occur? Explain.
d. Which country will have a balance of trade deficit?
e. What should happen to the value of the opek, relative to the bandu?
f. If the exchange rate is 1 opek = 2 bandu, what would happen to trade?
g. Cheese making is capital-intensive, and wine making is labour-intensive. Which country should have the relatively abundant supplies of labour, if the Heckscher-Ohlin theory is correct?
h. If the exchange rate were 1 opek = 4 bandu, what would happen to trade?

6. Here are the domestic demand and supply schedules for diapers.

Price	Quantity Demanded	Quantity Supplied
$6	800	1100
$5	1000	1000
$4	1200	900
$3	1400	800
$2	1600	700

a. Graph the demand and supply curves.

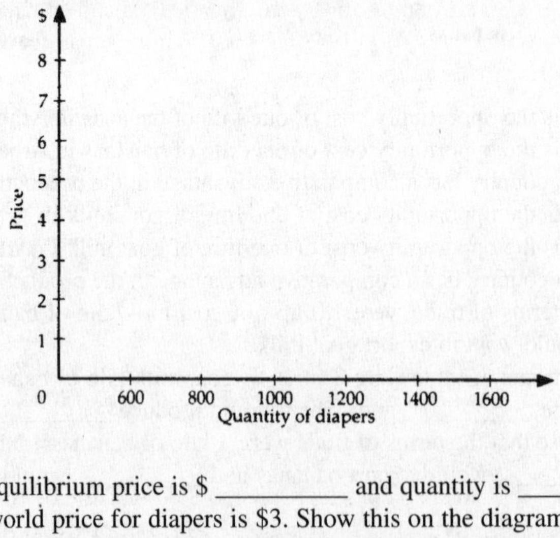

b. The equilibrium price is $ __________ and quantity is __________.
c. The world price for diapers is $3. Show this on the diagram as Pw. What will be the levels of domestic consumption and domestic production?

In order to preserve employment, diaper manufacturers contend successfully that theirs is an "infant industry" and should be protected.

d. A tariff is imposed that raises the price of imported diapers to $4. Show this on the diagram as Pt.

e. The tariff causes an increase in price and an increase in domestic production of __________ units. Consumption will fall to __________ units.

f. Imports will be __________ units. The tariff will yield $__________ in tax revenues.

g. Shade in the areas representing the net welfare loss caused by the tariff.

h. The loss in welfare is $__________.

ANSWERS AND SOLUTIONS

PRACTICE TEST

I. SOLUTIONS TO MULTIPLE CHOICE QUESTIONS

1. B. See p. 492.
2. C. See p. 492.
3. C. Arbez might be relatively inefficient in producing both goods but relatively less inefficient in producing goat milk. Because Arbez has a comparative advantage in producing goat milk, its opportunity cost of producing goat milk must be less.
4. B. As the Arbezani currency increases in value, Arbocali goods will become cheaper when calculated in terms of the Arbezani currency.
5. C. See p. 502.
6. A. Remember that comparative advantage is a relative concept. It requires that we compare two producers and two goods.
7. C. In voluntary trade, we expect each trader to gain something more than she or he traded.
8. C. Goat milk is relatively cheap to produce in Arbez and bananas require relatively few resources in Arboc. In a two-good, two-country situation, one party can never have a comparative advantage in both goods.
9. C. .5 labour hour gives 1 kilo of bananas in Arbez—1 hour gives 2 kilos. .2 labour hour gives 1 litre of milk in Arboc—1 hour gives 5 litres.
10. C. The terms of trade must lie in the range from 1 litre of goat milk : 3/5 kilo of bananas to 1 litre of goat milk : 3 kilos of bananas. If Arbez has 6 hours of labour, it could produce 20 litres of goat milk or 12 kilos of bananas—a ratio of 1 : 3/5. If Arboc has 6 hours of labour, it could produce 10 litres of goat milk or 30 kilos of bananas—a ratio of 1 : 3.
11. C. Tariffs impose welfare losses in two ways. Consumers pay a higher price and, as mentioned in this question, marginal producers are allowed to survive. Option B is incorrect—imports don't increase, they decrease. See p. 508.
12. B. See p. 510.
13. A. See p. 503 for a discussion of trade barriers.
14. D. A country with an absolute advantage in the production of Good A and Good B may have a comparative advantage in the production of Good A and, therefore, a comparative disadvantage in Good B. Similarly, a country with a comparative advantage in the production of Good A might have an absolute disadvantage relative to its partner in producing either good.

15. B. A tariff is a tax that provides revenues; a quota merely restricts the number of units that may be imported.
16. C. 125 yen equal $1. 500 yen equal $4.
17. B. 125 yen equal $1. 500 yen equal $4. 250 yen equal $1. 500 yen equal $2.
18. C. See p. 502.
19. A. Dollars are becoming relatively more valuable.
20. A. A tariff will drive up the price of the import, increasing demand for domestic substitutes whose price will then increase.

II. SOLUTIONS TO APPLICATION QUESTIONS

1. a. Heckscher-Ohlin assumes that inputs are mobile within an economy. Such restrictions will work against trade flows because, as an economy begins to specialize and trade, it will wish to reallocate inputs.
   b. According to Heckscher-Ohlin, comparative advantage is dependent upon differences in factor endowments. No differences in factor endowments, no comparative advantage: no comparative advantage, no trade. Arbez and Arboc should have no basis for trade.
   c. The new restrictions should not affect the pattern of trade. The Heckscher-Ohlin theorem assumes that inputs are not mobile between countries. (In real economies restrictions on factor movements may increase trade as goods move instead of the workers who produce the goods.)

2. a.

Maximum Units Produced	Noil	Regit
Loaves	6 000	24 000
Fishes	12 000	24 000

   b. See the following diagrams.

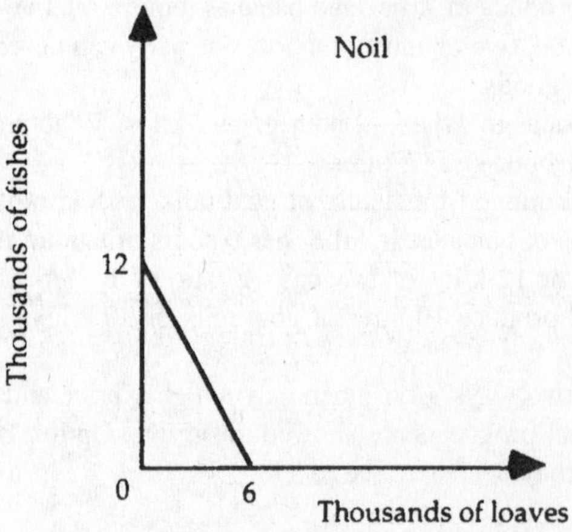

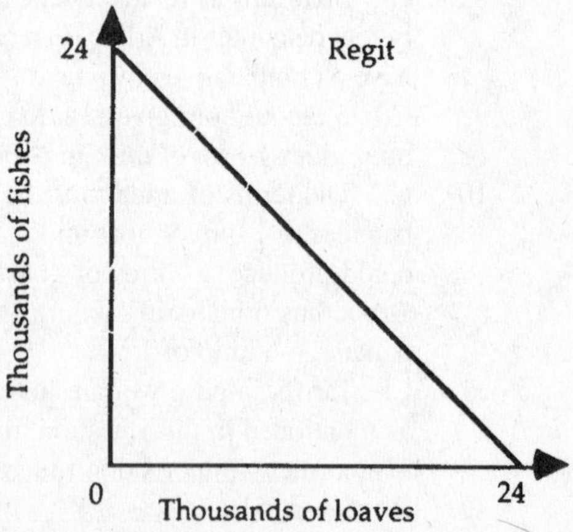

   c. The Regitani view is mainly incorrect. Regit does have an absolute advantage in the production of both loaves and fishes, but it does not have a comparative advantage in both, and it is comparative advantage that determines whether or not trade is advantageous.

d.

Maximum Units Produced	Noil	Regit	Total
Loaves	4800	16 000	20 800
Fishes	2400	8 000	10 400

One way to obtain these numbers for each country is to find where the production possibility frontier intersects with the line from the origin with slope 1/2 (corresponding to one fish for every two loaves).

e. Noil should produce fishes. In Noil, the cost of producing 1 loaf is 2 fishes while the cost of producing 1 loaf in Regit is 1 fish. Loaves are less costly in Regit. Regit has a comparative advantage in loaves; Noil has a comparative advantage in fishes.

f. Noil can produce 12 000 fishes and Regit can produce 24 000 loaves.

g.

Units Consumed	Noil	Regit
Loaves	6000	18 000
Fishes	3000	9 000

Noil can produce 12 000 fishes and export 9000, earning 6000 loaves in return. Regit can produce 24 000 loaves and export 6000, earning 9000 fishes in return. Noil can produce 12 000 fishes. It could keep them all, or it could export them all in return for 8000 loaves, or it could choose anywhere in between on its "consumption possibility frontier" which is the straight line that joins the point (0 loaves, 12 000 fishes) to the point (8000 loaves, 0 fishes). Because of the custom of consuming two loaves per fish, it will choose the point along that line in which there are two loaves per fish (i.e., the point where the consumption possibility frontier intersects the line from the origin with slope 1/2). By graphical methods or calculation you can show this point to be 6000 loaves, 3000 fishes: That is Noil will export 9000 of the 12 000 fishes it produces and earn 6000 loaves in return. Regit will give up 6000 of the 24 000 loaves it produces to leave 18 000 loaves to consume with the 9000 fishes it imports from Noil.

h. Yes.

i.

Units Consumed	Noil	Regit
Loaves	8000	16 000
Fishes	4000	8 000

Noil can produce 12 000 fishes and export 8000, earning 8000 loaves in return. Regit can produce 24 000 loaves and export 8000, earning 8000 fishes in return.

j. Trade has benefited Noil, but Regit's standard of living is unchanged.

k.

Units Consumed	Noil	Regit
Loaves	4800	19 200
Fishes	2400	9 600

Noil can produce 12 000 fishes and export 9600, earning 4800 loaves in return. Regit can produce 24 000 loaves and export 4800, earning 9600 fishes in return.

l. Trade has benefited Regit, but Noil's standard of living is unchanged.

m. The terms of trade need to be between 1 loaf = 1 fish and 1 loaf = 2 fish.

3. A yard of imported Arbocali cloth will cost 2 bandu in Arbez. An imported Arbezani hide will cost 24 opeks in Arboc.

4. a. 1/3 litre of goat milk.
   b. 1-2/3 litres of goat milk.
   c. Arboc.
   d. 3 kilos of bananas.
   e. 6/10 kilo of bananas.
   f. Arbez.
   g. Arbez, because it can produce a litre of goat milk at a cost of less than one kilo of bananas and, therefore, can gain through this specialization.
   h. bananas, bananas. One kilo of bananas can be sold for 3 litres of goat milk. Both Arboc and Arbez can produce bananas more cheaply than this (1/3 litre of goat milk and 1-2/3 litres of goat milk, respectively).
   i. Arboc, Arbez. One kilo of bananas can be sold for 1.5 litres of goat milk. Arboc can produce bananas more cheaply than this (1/3 litre of goat milk) and so will produce bananas. One litre of goat milk can be sold for 2/3 kilo of bananas. Arbez can produce goat milk more cheaply than this (6/10 kilo of bananas) and so will produce goat milk.

5. a. Arbez. Wine is four times as expensive as cheese in Arbez, but only twice as expensive in Arboc.
   b. Arboc. No country can have a comparative advantage in both goods.
   c. No. Because Arboc can produce both goods more cheaply, the Arbezanis will import both. The Arbocalis will not wish to buy either Arbezani product.
   d. Arbez, because it has some imports and zero exports.
   e. The Arbocali currency (the opek) should be heavily demanded (by Arbezanis seeking to buy Arbocali goods). The demand for the bandu will be low. The opek will rise in value; the bandu will fall in value.
   f. At a price of 30 bandu (15 opeks), Arbezani cheese will now be cheaper than Arbocali cheese (at a price of 20 opeks). Arboc will import cheese. Arbez will continue to import Arbocali wine. At a price of 40 opeks (80 bandu), Arbocali wine is still cheaper than that produced in Arbez (at a price of 120 bandu).
   g. Arboc.
   h. At a price of 30 bandu (7.50 opeks), Arbezani cheese will be cheaper than Arbocali cheese (at a price of 20 opeks). Arboc will import cheese. At a price of 40 opeks (160 bandu), Arbocali wine will be more expensive than that produced in Arbez (at a price of 120 bandu). Arboc will import wine. Arboc will have a trade deficit and Arbez a surplus.

6. a. See the diagram below.

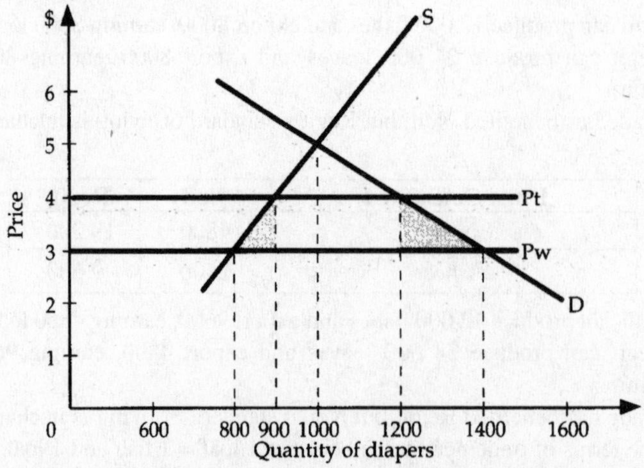

b. $5, 1000.
c. See the diagram above. 1400, 800.
d. See the diagram above.
e. 100, 1200.
f. 300, $300.
g. See the diagram above. The left triangle corresponds to the extra cost of the 100 extra diapers (between 800 and 900) that could have been purchased at the world price, but instead have cost more to produce by firms protected by the tariff. The right triangle corresponds to the loss to those consumers who would have purchased 200 extra diapers if they could have purchased at the world price but did not purchase because of the higher tariff-protected price.
h. $(50 + 100) (the areas of the two shaded triangles).

22 Economic Growth in Developing Countries

OBJECTIVES: POINT BY POINT

After completing this chapter, you should be able to accomplish the objectives listed below.

General Comment

The focus of this chapter is the ways in which developing countries might become developed and the problems that they might encounter along the way. If you study by making lists, be careful in this chapter, because three separate topics are covered—a description of the Third World, how development might be promoted, and some Third World problems. Make up lists using each of these headings.

OBJECTIVE 1: Distinguish between economic growth and economic development.

Economic growth is the increase in total output (real GDP) or output per capita (real GDP per capita). Economic development is a much broader concept and it includes improvement in average material well-being (measured perhaps by real GDP per capita) but also by health, education, the degree of poverty and perhaps less tangible but important considerations such as political and economic freedom.

In the past, the nations of the world have been roughly divided into three groups: the First World (western, industrialized), the Second World (ex-Socialist, whose future is now uncertain), and the Third World (poor, largely agricultural). There is some mobility—Taiwan, Korea, and Brazil, for instance, are breaking away from others in the Third World category, while a number of nations are lagging so far behind that they have been called the "Fourth World" group. The main characteristic of a Third World country is that the great majority of its inhabitants are poor. Other dimensions that distinguish the "haves" from the "have nots" are: health care, educational facilities, and the percentage of the population engaged in agriculture. (page 516)

> **Comment:** There's no single, unambiguous term that distinguishes the "developing nations" as the textbook deals with them. After all, in one sense, Canada is a developing economy, too. "Third World" tends to have some political undertones. Remember that these nations are a pretty varied group, including countries as diverse as Mexico and Mali, Taiwan and Togo.

Practice

1. The poorest of the developing nations are sometimes known as the
   A. First World.
   B. Second World.
   C. Third World.
   D. Fourth World.

   ANSWER: D. See p. 516.

2. Most of the Fourth World nations are to be found in
   A. Central America.
   B. sub-Saharan Africa.
   C. South America.
   D. the former republics of the Soviet Union and its satellites.

   ANSWER: B. Most of the very poorest nations are found to the south of the Sahara desert in Africa. See p. 516.

3. The developing nations of the world contain 75% of the world's population. They are estimated to receive __________ of the world's income.
   A. 5%.
   B. 20%.
   C. 25%.
   D. 33%.

   ANSWER: C. See p. 518.

4. Per capita GDP is __________ in developed countries, and infant mortality is __________.
   A. higher, higher.
   B. higher, lower.
   C. lower, higher.
   D. lower, lower.

   ANSWER: B. See Table 22.1 on p. 517 of the textbook.

OBJECTIVE 2: Describe the role of capital, human capital, and social overhead capital in economic growth and development.

No single theory has emerged to explain the development process, but various factors have been identified as potential constraints on development. These include a low rate of accumulation of physical capital, a lack of human capital, and a lack of social overhead capital (infrastructure). All of these problems constrain productivity and economic growth. Moreover, a lack of basic infrastructure (e.g., access to water, electricity and health and education facilities) can reduce the quality of life more generally. (page 519)

> **Tip:** Pay attention to what is happening in your own locality. Many of the sources and strategies discussed in this chapter are not limited to poor foreign regions. Debates on economic development are frequent at all levels of government.

Comment: As the textbook notes, economic growth and economic development are not the same phenomenon. Simply because a nation is growing economically doesn't mean that it is also developing. However, you may find it helpful to refer to Chapter 19 in *Principles of Macroeconomics* and locate the factors that promote growth.

Practice

5. The vicious-circle-of-poverty hypothesis suggests that development is stunted by the dependence of
   A. a potentially fast-growing industrial sector on a slow-growing agricultural sector.
   B. growth on the limited savings possible in a poor country.
   C. a developing nation on developed countries as markets for its output.
   D. a fast-growing agricultural sector on an undermechanized manufacturing sector.

   ANSWER: B. See p. 519.

6. The brain drain refers to
   A. the movement of talented personnel from a developing country to a developed country.
   B. the absence of skilled entrepreneurs in the developing countries.
   C. declining literacy rates.
   D. the loss of human capital through the ravages of malnutrition.

   ANSWER: A. See p. 520.

7. Each of the following has been advanced as a plausible constraint on development except
   A. the quantity of available capital.
   B. the quantity of available labour.
   C. the quantity of infrastructure.
   D. the quantity of entrepreneurial ability.

   ANSWER: B. The typical developing country has adequate numbers of workers, although specific skills may be limited.

8. Capital shortages are a typical problem for developing countries. Each of the following is a plausible cause of capital shortages except
   A. lack of incentives leading to low saving rates.
   B. the inherent riskiness of investment in a developing nation.
   C. government policies, such as price ceilings and appropriation of private property.
   D. widespread poverty resulting in little surplus after consumption needs are met.

   ANSWER: D. The vicious-circle-of-poverty hypothesis fails to account for the success of previously poor nations like Japan. See p. 519.

OBJECTIVE 3: Describe three tradeoffs affecting strategies for economic development.

At least three types of planning decisions must be made:

1. Agriculture or industry? Development used to be equated with industrialization; many Third World nations sought to move away from agriculture and toward industrial production. However, merely trying to replicate the structure of the developed nations does not guarantee development. Opinion now favours a balanced growth in both agricultural and industrial sectors—"walking on two legs."
2. Exports or import substitution? *Import substitution* calls for the encouragement of home-grown substitutes for imported goods. This strategy has failed in almost every case; it results in high-cost production protected by trade barriers. *Export promotion* calls for producing goods for the export market and

has seen some measure of success (e.g., Japan), although it depends on the willingness of the developed nations to import Third World production.

3. Central planning or the market? Finally, the economy must choose the appropriate balance between free enterprise and central planning. Planning permits coordination of economic activities that private actors in the economy might not undertake (e.g., disease and pest control, literacy training) and the channelling of funds into investment, but is difficult to administer.

(page 521)

Throughout the developing world it appears to be increasingly recognized that market forces can be valuable in allocating scarce resources.

Practice

9. Experience suggests that, of the following, the development approach most likely to succeed is
   A. rapid industrial mechanization coupled with labour migration to the industrial centres.
   B. intensive training of human capital to occupy technologically advanced positions in import-substitution industries.
   C. a balanced promotion of both the agricultural sector and the manufacturing sector.
   D. slow, careful industrial growth combined with rapid expansion in food provision to improve human capital.

   ANSWER: C. This is the "walking on two legs" strategy. See p. 523.

10. Suppose Noil is a small sub-Saharan nation with few sophisticated resources. However, it constructs an airport and hotel with lavish Western facilities and offers safari trips into its beautiful mountain ranges to groups from the developed countries. Noil is best described as having opted for a(n) __________ development strategy.
    A. import substitution.
    B. export promotion.
    C. rural exploitation.
    D. balanced growth.

    ANSWER: B. Tourism is an export.

11. Generally, import substitution policies have
    A. failed in almost every case.
    B. succeeded, but only while the cost of imported oil was held down.
    C. not been an unqualified success, but have had a better track record than export promotion policies.
    D. succeeded in Latin America, but failed in Africa and had mixed results in Asia.

    ANSWER: A. Import substitution policies reduce exports and foster inefficient, inappropriate (i.e., capital-intensive) production methods.

12. The small hypothetical Asian nation of Regit chooses to follow an import substitution strategy, and builds a fertilizer plant to serve its rice farmers. Based on similar experiments elsewhere, we would expect to see all of the following except
    A. high fertilizer production costs.
    B. the imposition of tariffs to protect domestic fertilizer production.
    C. capital-intensive fertilizer production techniques.
    D. a rise in the international competitiveness of the nation's rice farmers.

    ANSWER: D. High-cost fertilizer will reduce the ability of the rice farmers to compete with foreign rice.

13. Which would not be an export promotion strategy?
    A. reducing the value of the domestic currency relative to other currencies.
    B. increasing the nation's ability to compete domestically with the exports of other nations.
    C. the provision of subsidies to exporters.
    D. the provision of preferential investment tax breaks to exporting firms.

    ANSWER: B. This is typical of import substitution. See p. 523.

OBJECTIVE 4: Outline how rapid population growth affects economic development.

The Third World death rate has tumbled sharply because of better medical treatment, but the birth rate has declined much more slowly. Although large families may provide a cheap labour pool today and support in old age tomorrow, rapid expansion in the population places burdens on public services and may be undesirable from the viewpoint of society. In some nations, economic incentives (particularly those that expanded labour market alternatives for women) have been applied successfully to encourage smaller families. (page 524)

Practice

14. Birth rate minus death rate equals the
    A. fertility rate.
    B. mortality rate.
    C. natural rate of population increase.
    D. development rate.

    ANSWER: C. See p. 526.

15. Malthus predicted that the world population would grow at a(n) _______ growth rate while the production of food would increase more _______.
    A. increasing, rapidly.
    B. increasing, slowly.
    C. constant, rapidly.
    D. constant, slowly.

    ANSWER: D. See p. 525.

16. High fertility rates may cause all of the following except
    A. falling saving rates.
    B. reduced availability of social programs for each individual.
    C. labour shortages.
    D. food shortages.

    ANSWER: C. As the population expands, there should be no labour constraint.

OBJECTIVE 5: Outline the main agricultural policy issues in less-developed economies.

The key issue is whether food shortages are inevitable or due to policy mistakes. A nation that chooses to hold down prices for the benefit of consumers may see its farmers cutting back production, making it more vulnerable to famine. However, policies such as those associated with the so-called "Green Revolution"—the use of high-yield, resilient plants—increase productivity and food supply. (page 528)

Practice

17. Government establishment of low food prices is usually meant to
    A. discourage farming.
    B. make domestic farm production competitive with imports.
    C. please the small, but politically powerful, urban population.
    D. make domestic farm production more efficient.

    ANSWER: C. Urban dwellers may be more educated and organized—a bigger threat to the longevity of the government in power. See p. 528.

18. Policies that may alleviate Third World food shortages include all but
    A. introducing Green Revolution techniques.
    B. land reform.
    C. imposing price ceilings for farm outputs.
    D. removing price ceilings for farm outputs.

    ANSWER: C. See p. 529.

OBJECTIVE 6: Explain why the Third World debt is of global concern.

Between 1970 and 1984, capital-starved developing countries' combined debt increased by 1000% to almost US$700 billion. In the late 1970s, the world economy faltered and Third World export revenues shrank. Interest on the loans became (and remains) hard to pay. Some nations threatened to default. Many sought to reschedule their debt repayment in exchange for promises of economic austerity designed to cut back on imports and to increase exports. (page 529)

Practice

19. Under a debt rescheduling agreement, the borrowing country is expected to increase incentives to __________ and to reduce __________.
    A. consumers, export spending.
    B. consumers, imports.
    C. exporters, the federal government deficit.
    D. exporters, imports.

    ANSWER: D. A debt rescheduling agreement will require the country to increase exports and reduce imports. Only by increasing its foreign earnings can a nation hope to reduce its debt burden.

OBJECTIVE 7 (APPENDIX 22A): List six basic terms in Marxian economics. Define tragedy of the commons and explain its implications for an economy with collective ownership.

Six terms in Marxian economics (all defined in the glossary in the appendix) are *alienation, capitalist economy, communism, means of production, socialist economy*, and *surplus*.

Capitalist economies and socialist economies are at the two ends of the economic spectrum; democracy and communism are at the two ends of the political spectrum. Economic systems are classified on the basis of where the ownership of the means of production resides—in capitalism, it's with the private individual; in socialism, it's with the government. (page 533)

No economic system adheres to pure socialism or to pure capitalism—each economy is a blend of the two extremes. China is "socialist" but has (increasing) private ownership; the United States and Japan are "capitalist" but each contains a public sector.

Marx argued that economies generated a surplus, that is the amount of output in excess of what was required to maintain workers at a subsistence level and to replace capital used up in the production process. In Marx's view, this surplus was entirely attributable to the efforts of labour, but nonetheless capitalists unjustly capture most of it. Capitalists are more powerful than workers because they own the means of production and can consume their wealth if need be; workers cannot make a living if they cannot sell their labour to capitalists, who use the threat of unemployment to keep wages down. Workers suffer alienation in that they lose their sense of purpose because their main life activity, work, is under the control of their employer. Marx predicted that eventually workers would rise up and overthrow an ever more repressive capitalist system.

> **Tip:** For Marx, production becomes less labour-intensive as capitalists substitute capital for labour; with relatively less labour to exploit, the rate of profit will fall. To compensate, capitalists increase the rate of exploitation and wages are driven to the subsistence level. Eventually the system becomes unbearable, is overthrown, and is replaced by socialism and, ultimately, communism.

> **Tip:** You may have noted the adjective "Marxian." Marxian, rather than Marxist, is the correct term to use when referring to Marx's economic ideas.

Marxian theory is much different than theory elsewhere in the book, which has assumed the capitalist mixed economy as a given. Instead Marx viewed capitalism as a stage in a path from feudalism to communism. Remember, when Marx was writing in the mid-nineteenth century, almost all workers in the world were at a near-subsistence state. Now, in modern economies such as Canada's, most workers are well above subsistence, although modern Marxists would argue that this is not a stable situation.

The *tragedy of the commons* is an important idea in economics. If grazing land is held in common, individual farmers have the incentive to overgraze because the costs of the overgrazing are borne collectively, not individually as they would be if the farmer owned the land herself/himself. (When the land is owned collectively, each farmer knows that even if she or he tries to save some grass for future grazing, another farmer will likely graze it first.) Similarly the bison of Western Canada were a common resource that individuals did not own; there was no incentive for an individual to decide not to kill a bison to conserve the resource, because most likely that would simply give an opportunity for another to kill the animal and obtain its meat and hide. (It is sometimes remarked that the native peoples of Canada managed the resource of the bison for many centuries, and near-extinction did not occur until a few decades after the arrival of Europeans.)

What does this all have to do with centrally-planned economies? Every economy faces "tragedy of the commons" problems ranging from fishing rights to air pollution, but the effect is still more forceful in an economy of collective ownership. Collectively-owned farms may pay little attention to their profits and hence do not have to worry what they pay for inputs, which may be allocated by quota rather than by a market. Managers may try to get as much as possible of any available input (capital, materials, skilled labour), an effect very much like overgrazing. More generally, managers and workers have little incentive either to economize on inputs or to maximize output, because they will receive little direct reward. Under private ownership, the owners of the firm have a strong incentive to monitor managers to insure that inputs are used efficiently to produce as much output as possible, because this will maximize the financial return.

Practice

20. In a __________ economy, most capital is privately owned.
    A. democratic.
    B. communist.
    C. capitalist.
    D. socialist.

    ANSWER: C. Note that "democracy" refers to a political system, not an economic one.

21. In a true __________ economy, the people would own the means of production directly and plan as a collective, without state intervention.
    A. feudal.
    B. communist.
    C. capitalist.
    D. socialist.

    ANSWER: B. In a true communist economy, it was argued, the state would wither away. In fact, the communist economies of the world have really been socialist—e.g., the former Union of Soviet *Socialist* Republics.

22. For Marx, the "means of production" include
    A. only capital.
    B. only capital and labour.
    C. only capital and land.
    D. capital, land, and labour.

    ANSWER: C. The means of production are not equivalent to the "factors of production" you met in Chapter 3.

23. Which statement does not represent Marx's views?
    A. unemployment is used by capitalists to keep wages down.
    B. human beings should be thought of primarily as consumers, not workers.
    C. the internal conflicts in capitalism will eventually lead to its demise.
    D. capital embodies the past efforts of labour; owners of capital have no moral claim to a share of the surplus.

    ANSWER: B. See p. 534.

24. In Marxian analysis, which of the following statements is true?
    A. the rate of profit tends to fall over time.
    B. additional capital accumulation increases the rate of profit.
    C. additional capital accumulation increases surplus value.
    D. as wages fall, production will become more labour-intensive.

    ANSWER: A. Capital must be paid for but can't be exploited. Profits derive from the ability of the capitalist to exploit workers and hence fall as, over time, capital replaces labour in production.

25. The notion that collective ownership of resources may be inefficient because individuals do not bear the full cost of their own decisions is called
   A. exploitation.
   B. the tragedy of the commons.
   C. surplus value.
   D. the externality effect.

   ANSWER: B. See p. 535.

26. Each of the following is an example of the tragedy of the commons except
   A. pollution in the Great Lakes.
   B. overgrazing of shared tribal land.
   C. the decimation of the bison by nineteenth-century settlers.
   D. the slaughtering of an entire herd by a rancher.

   ANSWER: D. The herd is private property.

PRACTICE TEST

I. MULTIPLE CHOICE QUESTIONS. Select the option that provides the single best answer.

_____ 1. Which of the following are characteristics of the average developing country?
   A. large populations and high savings rates.
   B. low levels of human capital and low per capita GDP.
   C. high infant mortality but high life expectancy.
   D. low health standards and high literacy rates.

_____ 2. Import substitution occurs when a country
   A. becomes developed.
   B. erects trade barriers.
   C. no longer has sufficient foreign exchange to buy imports.
   D. strives to produce goods that were previously imported.

_____ 3. Economic development occurs when there is an increase in the
   A. per capita nominal GDP.
   B. per capita real GDP.
   C. material well-being of the nation's citizens.
   D. labour force.

_____ 4. Lack of economic development might be caused by
   A. a low marginal propensity to consume.
   B. an excess supply of private overhead capital.
   C. a high literacy rate.
   D. inadequate amounts of social overhead capital.

_____ 5. Which of the following is an example of an improvement in social overhead capital?
   A. a multinational corporation opens a new plant.
   B. a worker builds a house for his family.
   C. there is an increase in the rate of growth of per capita real GDP.
   D. a national adult literacy program is established by the government.

_____ 6. Labour is relatively abundant in Arboc. Arboc might best be able to develop by
- A. using production techniques that are capital-intensive.
- B. using production techniques that employ labour and capital in fixed and equal proportions.
- C. specializing in the production of labour-intensive commodities which should therefore be relatively cheaper to produce.
- D. specializing in the production of capital-intensive commodities, which should therefore be marketable at relatively higher prices.

_____ 7. Local firms in developing countries are unlikely to drain malarial swamps because
- A. the government provides sufficient pest control.
- B. labour shortages are typical.
- C. the "free-rider" problem will result in a low (or zero) rate of return.
- D. international agencies such as the World Bank and the IMF prefer short-term projects.

_____ 8. Adopting the strategy of "walking on two legs" means that
- A. men and women should be treated equally in the workplace.
- B. import substitution and export promotion should be attempted simultaneously.
- C. attention must be paid to developing both the industrial sector and the agricultural sector.
- D. the dependent links with old colonial nations should be severed.

_____ 9. Import substitution might fail to promote economic development if
- A. producers use domestic inputs that are lower in cost than imported inputs.
- B. firms make use of capital-intensive production methods that fail to reduce unemployment.
- C. such goods require labour-intensive methods of production.
- D. after establishment, these industries are subsidized by the state.

_____ 10. The "export promotion" strategy calls for
- A. the running of a balance of trade deficit.
- B. the production of goods that are demanded by consumers in the developed countries.
- C. the production of export goods for domestic consumers.
- D. the domestic production of goods that previously had been imported.

_____ 11. Sending savings from the imaginary Third World nation of Arboc to the developed countries __________ to growth in Arboc's physical capital. New Arbocali import controls will tend to __________ investment in Arboc.
- A. leads, increase.
- B. leads, decrease.
- C. does not lead, increase.
- D. does not lead, decrease.

_____ 12. Between 1970 and 1984, developing countries' combined debt increased
- A. 1000%.
- B. 100%.
- C. 10%.
- D. 1%.

_____ 13. IMF stabilization policies might call for
A. cutbacks in government spending and a currency devaluation.
B. nationalization of foreign investment.
C. higher subsidies to importers of capital goods.
D. tax cuts and a currency devaluation.

_____ 14. The poorest 20% of the world's population is estimated to receive __________ of the world's income.
A. .5%.
B. 2.0%.
C. 2.5%.
D. 5.0%.

_____ 15. Which of the following variables tends to be high in the developing countries?
A. life expectancy.
B. literacy rates.
C. infant mortality.
D. proportion of the population in urban areas.

_____ 16. Under a debt rescheduling agreement, the borrowing country may be expected to __________ the value of its currency in order to __________ exports.
A. increase, increase.
B. increase, decrease.
C. decrease, increase.
D. decrease, decrease.

_____ 17. All of the following discourage Third World development except
A. the lack of skilled entrepreneurs.
B. insufficient social overhead capital.
C. insufficient labour-saving technological innovation.
D. inadequate amounts of human capital.

_____ 18. __________ is a development strategy that is designed to encourage sales abroad.
A. import substitution.
B. export promotion.
C. "walking on two legs."
D. dependency.

_____ 19. Permanently higher birth rates may cause all of the following except
A. an eventual increase in the proportion of working-age adults in the population.
B. an increase in the number of dependents.
C. decreases in the rate of capital formation.
D. decreases in savings rates.

_____ 20. Governments may set food prices low in order to
A. encourage greater food production.
B. make domestic producers competitive with foreign producers.
C. stimulate a willingness to adopt more efficient farming methods.
D. maintain the political support of urban consumers.

_____ 21. According to Marx, the rate of profit has a tendency to __________, causing capitalists to __________ the rate of exploitation.
A. rise, increase.
B. rise, decrease.
C. fall, increase.
D. fall, decrease.

_____ 22. For Marx, the conflicts in capitalism include all of the following except
A. inflation and an increasing government deficit.
B. alienation and increasing exploitation.
C. progressively more violent business cycles.
D. the emiserization of the workers.

_____ 23. Capitalism and socialism are distinguished primarily by
A. the ownership of labour.
B. the number of political parties.
C. the ownership of capital.
D. the distribution of income throughout society.

_____ 24. According to Marx, the wage is largely determined by
A. the surplus value of labour.
B. the cost of the bare essentials of subsistence.
C. the marginal revenue product of labour.
D. the marginal physical product.

_____ 25. To Marx, the profit earned by the owner of a machine was
A. an illegitimate return to an exploiter of labour.
B. a legitimate return to "the means of production."
C. compensation for alienation.
D. the price of the final good produced by the machine.

_____ 26. The "tragedy of the commons" exemplifies the problem of __________ that can occur in the case of resources that are owned __________.
A. inefficiency, privately.
B. inequity, privately.
C. inefficiency, collectively.
D. inequity, collectively.

_____ 27. Surplus, in the Marxian sense, is
A. equal to the wage rate paid to the worker.
B. the difference between the subsistence wage and the actual wage received.
C. the rate of emiserization.
D. the difference between the value of production and what is needed for subsistence consumption by workers and to replace capital used in the production process.

II. APPLICATION QUESTIONS

1. Suppose that 10 units of food are required per person per year in the imaginary developing nation of Arboc. Due to improved crops and farming techniques, food production will increase by a fixed amount every 10 years—suppose this amount is 1000 units of food so that, in 2000, food production will be 11 000 units. Arboc currently exports its surplus food production. Because of high birth rates and decreasing death rates, Arboc's population increases by 50% every 10 years.

a. Given the conditions specified, complete the table below.

Year	Food Production	Population	Food Requirements	Food Surplus/Deficit
1990	10 000	400	4000	+6000
2000	11 000			
2010				
2020				
2030				

b. What happens in or about the year 2020?
c. Other things unchanged, what will happen to Arboc's balance of trade?
d. Given the situation in 2030, what do you think will happen to Arboc?

2. Some Marxian scholars focus on what is called the *labour theory of value*. Commodities are thought of as the physical embodiment of the labour that produced them; a capital good (e.g., a machine) is the physical embodiment of past labour that was used to produce it. Capitalists hire "labour power" to make products and make a profit by selling the products for more than *the value of labour power* (that is, the wages) used to produce them. The question below provides numerical illustrations of calculations empirical Marxian economists could use to analyze an economic system.

In the Marxian economy of Arboc, 500 units of value are produced. Production requires current labour and machinery, which embodies 100 units of past labour.
a. Calculate the value of current labour used in units of value.
b. If workers are paid 300 units of value, how many units of profit will capitalists derive?
c. Calculate the rate of exploitation (surplus value/value of current labour).
d. Calculate the rate of profit (surplus value/value of production).

Now suppose that output doubles with labour and capital inputs are unchanged.
e. Output is __________ units of value.
f. Calculate the value of current labour used in units of value.
g. If the wage rate is unchanged, how many units of value will the workers receive?
h. Surplus value is __________.
i. Calculate the rate of exploitation (surplus value/value of current labour).
j. Calculate the rate of profit (surplus value/value of production).

Now suppose that relative to the initial situation, output has doubled but, to achieve this, the production technique has become more capital-intensive. Machinery is worth 400 units of past labour.
k. Calculate the value of current labour used in units of value.
l. If the wage rate is unchanged, how many units of value will the workers receive?
m. Surplus value is __________.
n. Calculate the rate of exploitation (surplus value/value of current labour).
o. Calculate the rate of profit (surplus value/value of production).

Suppose that the subsistence wage is 200 units of value, given the current level of output. Machinery is worth 400 units of past labour.
p. Calculate how many units of surplus value capitalists can expropriate.
q. Calculate the rate of exploitation (surplus value/value of current labour).
r. Calculate the rate of profit (surplus value/value of production).

ANSWERS AND SOLUTIONS

PRACTICE TEST

I. SOLUTIONS TO MULTIPLE CHOICE QUESTIONS

1. B. See p. 517 for a full discussion of the characteristics of developing nations.
2. D. Import substitution is a strategy that attempts to establish a domestic industry that can provide goods to replace imports. See p. 522.
3. C. Improvements in per capita GDP do not guarantee development. See p. 516.
4. D. To grow, an economy needs an adequate quantity and quality of resources, including socially provided resources.
5. D. Social overhead capital includes projects that cannot be undertaken privately.
6. C. Incidentally, this is an application of the Heckscher-Ohlin theorem from Chapter 20.
7. C. See p. 521.
8. C. The Chinese phrase "walking on two legs" describes the need to have both agricultural and industrial sectors developing together. See p. 522.
9. B. To be effective, the strategy must play to the strengths of its own economy—typically labour-intensive production. See p. 522.
10. B. See p. 522.
11. D. See p. 519.
12. A. See p. 530.
13. A. See p. 530.
14. A. See p. 518.
15. C. See p. 517.
16. C. If the borrowing country reduces the value of its currency, its exports will be cheaper for foreigners to buy.
17. C. The quantity of labour is not a significant constraint in the Third World. Labour-saving technology, then, is not critical to successful development.
18. B. See p, 523.
19. A. As more children are born, even as the population ages, the proportion of adults will decrease.
20. D. See p. 528.
21. C. As additional capital is accumulated the rate of profit falls. This decline prompts capitalists to increase exploitation of workers. See p. 534.
22. A. Marx did not focus on inflation and the government deficit in his writings.
23. C. In a capitalist system, ownership of the means of production (capital and land) is in the hands of capitalists and in the hands of the state under a communist system.
24. B. Capitalists, in search of profits, will try to drive down the wage to the minimum (subsistence) level. See p. 534.
25. A. See p. 534.
26. C. Commons (commonly-owned land) are often treated inefficiently. See p. 535.
27. D. See p. 534.

II. SOLUTIONS TO APPLICATION QUESTIONS

1. a. See the table below.

Year	Food Production	Population	Food Requirements	Food Surplus/Deficit
1990	10 000	400	4000	+6000
2000	11 000	600	6000	+5000
2010	12 000	900	9000	+3000
2020	13 000	1350	13 500	–500
2030	14 000	2025	20 250	–6250

b. Food requirements outstrip food production.

c. As the food surplus decreases, less will be available for export and the balance of trade will become less favourable. Sometime just before 2020, the trade surplus in food will become a deficit if it is able to import the required food.

d. This is an open question. Arboc will be heavily in debt, and will need to import food to feed its population. Imports of industrial goods would slacken. Reduced health care (per person) might cause famine and disease, reducing the population. Arboc might borrow to finance its overseas spending and might have to receive ongoing foreign aid. Population control policies would have to be considered.

2 a. 500 – 100 units of past labour value = 400 units of labour value.
b. 400 units of labour value – 300 = 100 units of profit.
c. Rate of exploitation = surplus value/value of current labour = 100/400 = .25.
d. The rate of profit = surplus value/value of production = 100/500 = .2.
e. 500 × 2 = 1000.
f. 1000 – 100 units of past labour value = 900 units of labour value.
g. Still 300.
h. Surplus value = 900 – 300 = 600.
i. Rate of exploitation = surplus value/value of current labour = 600/900 = .67.
j. Rate of profit = surplus value/value of production = 600/1000 = .6.
k. 1000 – 400 units of past labour value = 600 units of labour value.
l. Still 300.
m. Surplus value = 600 – 300 = 300.
n. Rate of exploitation = surplus value/value of current labour = 300/600 = .5.
o. Rate of profit = surplus value/value of production = 300/1000 = .3.
p. Surplus value = 600 – 200 = 400.
q. Rate of exploitation = surplus value/value of current labour = 400/600 = .67.
r. Rate of profit = surplus value/value of production = 400/1000 = .4.